THE POLITICAL ECONOMY OF DEVELOPMENT AND UNDERDEVELOPMENT

W9-CNY-782

For Bob, who has spent
his life "fighting the good
fight."

Chuck

THE POLITICAL ECONOMY OF DEVELOPMENT AND UNDERDEVELOPMENT

SIXTH EDITION

Kenneth P. Jameson
Economics Department
University of Utah

Charles K. Wilber
Economics Department
University of Notre Dame

McGRAW-HILL, INC.

New York   St. Louis   San Francisco   Auckland   Bogotá   Caracas
Lisbon   London   Madrid   Mexico City   Milan   Montreal   New Delhi
San Juan   Singapore   Sydney   Tokyo   Toronto

This book was set in Times Roman by The Clarinda Company.
The editor was Lucille H. Sutton;
the production supervisor was Annette Mayeski.
The cover was designed by Rafael Hernandez.
Project supervision was done by Hockett Editorial Service.
R. R. Donnelley & Sons Company was printer and binder.

THE POLITICAL ECONOMY OF DEVELOPMENT
AND UNDERDEVELOPMENT

Copyright © 1996, 1992, 1988, 1984, 1979, 1973 by McGraw-Hill, Inc. All rights reserved. Printed in the United States of America. Except as permitted under the United States Copyright Act of 1976, no part of this publication may be reproduced or distributed in any form or by any means, or stored in a data base or retrieval system, without the prior written permission of the publisher.

This book is printed on acid-free paper.

1 2 3 4 5 6 7 8 9 0 DOC DOC 9 0 9 8 7 6 5

ISBN   0-07-070189-X

Library of Congress Cataloging-in-Publication Data

The political economy of development and underdevelopment / [edited
    by] Kenneth P. Jameson, Charles K. Wilber.—6th ed.
        p.   cm.
    Includes bibliographical references (p.   ).
    ISBN 0-07-070189-X
    1. Economic development.   2. Developing countries—Economic
conditions.   I. Jameson, Kenneth P.   II. Wilber, Charles K.
HD82.P546   1996
338.9—dc20   95-8588

ABOUT
THE AUTHORS

KENNETH P. JAMESON received his B.A. from Stanford University and his M.S. and Ph.D. from the University of Wisconsin-Madison. He has taught at the University of Notre Dame (1970–1989); Universidad Nacional San Augustin, Arequipa, Peru; the Catholic University of Peru in Lima; the Development Studies Program in Washington D.C. He is currently on the faculty of the University of Utah, since 1989, where he has also chaired the Department of Economics and has served as Associate Vice President for Academic Affairs. He began his work in development in a Peruvian village in 1964 as a member of the Peace Corps. Since that time he has researched and traveled extensively in Latin America and the Caribbean and has consulted in Peru, Bolivia, Panama, Guyana, the Dominican Republic, Jamaica, and Paraguay. His major research areas are economic development, economic methodology, and macroeconomics. He has published over 50 articles in a variety of development journals and several books, primarily on issues of agriculture and development and on the macro-financial elements in development.

CHARLES K. WILBER received his B.A. and M.S. from the University of Portland and his Ph.D. from the University of Maryland. He has taught at Multnomah College, Portland, Oregon (1958–1960); Catholic University, Ponce, Puerto Rico (1960–1961); Trinity College, Washington, D.C. (1961–1964); The American University, Washington D.C. (1964–1975); and since 1975, at the University of Notre Dame. He was Chair of the Economics Department from 1975 to 1984. He has been a consultant to the Peace Corps, Interamerican Development Bank, George Meany Center for Labor Studies, and the United States Bishop's Committee on Catholic Social Thought and the U.S. Economy. His major research areas are economic development, economic ethics, and the economic methodology. He has published over 50 articles in economics journals and a number of books including: *The Soviet Model and Underdeveloped Countries* (University of North Carolina Press, 1969); and with Kenneth Jameson, *An Inquiry into the Poverty of Economics* (University of Notre Dame Press, 1983) and *Beyond Reaganomics: A Further Inquiry into the Poverty of Economics* (University of Notre Dame Press, 1990).

Given its fatal incorrigibility, humanity will probably have to go through many more Rwandas and Chernobyls before it understands how unbelievably short-sighted a human being can be who has forgotten that he is not God.

Vaclav Havel
President Czech Republic
Speech at Stanford University
September 29, 1994

Our hope as editors, and for those who use this book, is that a sense of our common humanity, along with a bias for hope, can make the Rwandas and Bosnias artifacts of the past, as we strive for development that is truly centered on the liberation of human beings.

CONTENTS

ix

PREFACE TO THE SIXTH EDITION

The decade of the 1960s was marked by an optimism that world poverty could be conquered by economic growth. The 1970s saw that hope dashed by growing unemployment and inequality and the intractability of absolute poverty in less developed countries. The first edition of this book charted that disillusionment.

The 1970s witnessed the birth of a new optimism to replace the old. The pursuit of "growth with equity" or a strategy of targeting "basic human needs" would succeed where economic growth had failed in the developing countries. The second edition of this book captured the beginnings of this movement.

The 1980s ushered in a period of greater caution. World poverty will not be eliminated with simple economic panaceas. Resource shortages (particularly of energy), rising protectionism in the industrial world, militarism in the Third World, the international arms race, the structure of the world economy all made the design of development strategies a complex problem in political economy rather than a simple economic issue.

The fourth edition updated the continuing debate among the contending schools of thought, highlighted the international debt crisis along with the attendant stabilization and readjustment programs, and charted the resurgence of free market economics with its attack upon "development" economics. It critiqued the view that the "less developed countries" simply needed to make the adjustments required by the markets to become developed countries.

The fifth edition was published at the beginning of the last decade of the twentieth century when the old verities were collapsing. The cold war was ending, the Eastern European countries were moving from centrally planned economics of the Second World to market-oriented underdeveloped countries of the Third World. Regional conflicts were moving to center stage in the international political arena, e.g., the Persian Gulf War of 1991 and the subsequent chaos in the area. The narrow concentration by developmentalists during the 1980s on technical issues was certainly inadequate to the task of understanding the new world, and the fifth edition pointed to the many old and new challenges to development thinking and suggested how they might be met.

This sixth edition has the luxury of several years of hindsight on the disappearance of the Second World, on the continuing difficulties of the new Eastern European entrants into the ranks of the "South," and on the often devastating return to ethnic and tribal definitions of human relations. The outline of the course of events was antici-pated quite well in the previous edition.

This edition continues the focus on the complex problems and even more complex solutions of human development within this changing international political context. There are no easy answers, but if progress is to be made against the poverty that afflicts the majority of the world's people the "bias for hope" must be rekindled and combined with serious analysis of problems and solutions. We hope this book is a con-tribution to that rekindling and analysis. The perspective of the mid-1990s and the return to some international stability provide an opportunity to focus on four of the central elements of development in the 1990s: reshaping the world's economic and political relations, democracy in the countries of the South, the pivotal role of women in human development efforts, and the elements of an environmentally sustainable development process. The articles new to this edition focus primarily on these ele-ments.

Once again, we are indebted to many people for the valuable help they have given us in preparing this sixth edition. They provided critiques of the previous edition, sug-gested new readings, and encouraged us to go ahead. Most of all they remained com-mitted to understanding and encouraging development, embodying the bias towards hope that is the hallmark of developmentalists. They helped us maintain that stance as well. We especially acknowledge Terry Karl at Stanford University and Jim Weaver at American University.

Tom Bates contributed in the initial stages of article selection, while Maryam Ghadessi was instrumental in getting the manuscript ready by the deadline.

Our thanks to Scott Stratford, Lucille Sutton, Victoria Richardson, and Annette Mayeski of McGraw-Hill whose good-humored professionalism helped surmount the many barriers to getting the book out in a timely and competent manner.

Kenneth P. Jameson
Charles K. Wilber

PREFACE TO THE FIRST EDITION

Economists assume that the problem of a more human society is solved by expertise, by know-how. Since they assume that the question of the nature of a good society is already answered, the issue becomes one of solving certain practical problems. The good society is simply assumed to be an idealized version of the United States economy, that is, a consumer society. The key to a consumer society is growth of per capita income. Thus the vast bulk of the development literature has focused on growth rates as the *deus ex machina* to solve all problems. Even much of the socialist writing on development argues that the superiority of socialism over capitalism lies in faster growth rates.

There is much to be said for this approach because some minimum level of food, clothing, shelter, recreation, etc., is necessary before a person can be free to be human. However, the emphasis on consumption and growth of per capita income has not led to a decrease of poverty in the underdeveloped world. If anything it has increased. A thin layer has prospered while the vast majority of the population sinks ever deeper into the backwater of underdevelopment. Therefore, during the past several years a new look has been taken at the meaning of development. Dudley Seers, Mahbub ul Haq, Ivan Illich, and others have questioned the emphasis on chasing the consumption standards of the developed countries via economic growth. Instead they argue for a direct attack on poverty through employment and income redistribution policies. Denis Goulet and Paulo Freire argue that development must include "liberation" from oppression, cultural as well as political and economic.

Both of these positions have merit, and they are not necessarily mutually exclusive. That is, the study of political economy should lead one to ask whether stressing the importance of rapid economic growth has to mean that the growth will consist of movies, bikinis, deodorants, key clubs, and pollution. An analysis of political economic systems should lead one to see why growth has meant luxuries being produced for some while others go hungry.

This book is about economic development and underdevelopment, and is designed to be used with a standard textbook in advanced undergraduate and beginning graduate courses. The readings emphasize the *political economy* rather than the narrowly *economic* approach and issues.

Many of the readings are excellent examples of radical political economy. Political economy recognizes that man is a social being whose arrangements for the production and distribution of economic goods must be, if society is to be livable, consistent with congruent institutions of family, political, and cultural life. As a result, a political economy analysis must incorporate such noneconomic influences as social structures, political systems, and cultural values as well as such factors as technological change and the distribution of income and wealth. The readings are radical in the sense that they are willing to question and evaluate the most basic institutions and values of society.

While I hope that the work presented here is objective, there is no artificial stance of neutrality. I am committed to certain values that undoubtedly influence the choice of questions asked and the range of variables considered for selection. In general, my system of values posits material progress (at least up to some minimum level), equality, cooperation, democratic control of economic as well as political institutions, and individual freedom as positive goods. It should be noted that there may be contradictions among these criteria, and thus society is faced with choices. With these values in mind the reader can judge the degree of objectivity attained.

It is a pleasure to acknowledge my indebtedness to those who have helped me shape my ideas on economic development and underdevelopment. First of all I want to thank Professors W. Michael Bailey, James H. Weaver, Celso Furtado, Branko Horvat, E. J. Mishan, Ronald Müller, Brady Tyson, Albert Waterston, and Irving Louis Horowitz—critics, colleagues, and friends. Some of my greatest debts are to those whom I know only through their writings—Karl Polyanyi and R. H. Tawney. Their example of scholarship and social commitment has been a guide and inspiration. I want to thank Sandy Kelly for her invaluable help in editing. Barbara Conover and Nancy Perry, editors at Random House, have been invaluable in seeing the book through to publication.

My greatest debt, however, in this as in all my endeavors, is to my wife, Mary Ellen, and our children: Kenneth, Teresa, Matthew, Alice, Mary, Angela, and Louie. I owe all to their love and encouragement.

Charles K. Wilber

THE POLITICAL ECONOMY OF DEVELOPMENT AND UNDERDEVELOPMENT

PART ONE

THEORY AND METHOD IN ECONOMIC DEVELOPMENT

In *The Rise of the West* (1963, p. 591), William McNeill suggests that the history of "the West" (Europe) has exhibited marked instability since the classical Greeks. This contrasts with "civilized Asia," primarily India and China, whose complex social, economic, and cultural structures maintained themselves and never retreated for any length of time from any major geographical area. The expansion of Western Europe in the fifteenth and sixteenth centuries brought a process of change and instability to the rest of the world—which continues today. Although it might seem more appropriate to describe the current process as the "rise of the East" or the "fall of the Socialist bloc," no description can ignore the fact that political, economic, and social change pervades our contemporary world. Improvements in transportation and communication have increased the pace of social change and have extended it to all corners of the world.

But instability and change are never easy. One response is to resist, to react against changes and reject any effort to accommodate. Wiarda (1983) examines social efforts to resist change and finds many positive elements in tribalism, Islamic fundamentalism, and Latin American corporatism. Experiences such as the tribal genocide in Rwanda show the other side of the coin, that reactionary movements during a process of rapid change can cause catastrophes. On the other hand, he is certainly correct in insisting that efforts to resist change must be respected and incorporated into any development process. However, it is likely that none of these movements will be successful in resisting change, in reacting successfully against the outside influences that will become increasingly prevalent.

McNeill locates the impetus for change during the past century in the growth of human control of the environment, particularly over inanimate forms of energy, and in the readiness to "tinker" with social institutions and customs in the hope of attaining

1

desired goals (p. 794). The result has been wide acceptance of the inevitability and the desirability of change. Today some countries that long resisted external influences have acceded to the inevitability of change. For example, Albania has moved rapidly away from its fierce postwar independence. North Korea is engaged in much broader dialogue with the world community.

Development economics was spawned during the 1940s and 1950s by the acceptance of the inevitability of political, social, and economic change and the need to skew that change in a positive direction. The problem of the lagging countries of Eastern Europe stimulated much initial development thinking; the success in rebuilding Europe and Japan emboldened development economists to extend their horizon to the rest of the world. Development economics incorporated an optimism that change could be for the better and that conscious reflection on, and control over, change, often through national governments and international organizations, could harness change and encourage development. The accomplishments over the period in improving key measures of human development are undeniable.

Growth of GNP throughout the world accelerated, infant mortality decreased dramatically, and life expectancy increased rapidly; access to education was extended far beyond what would have been imaginable in 1945. Data from the *World Development Report, 1990* (Table 3.1) give a more precise sense of the changes in developing countries over a mere twenty years:

	1965	1975	1985
Consumption per capita (1985 PPP dollars)	590	780	985
Life expectancy (years)	51	57	62
Primary net enrollment rate (%)	73	74	84

The article in this part by Amartya Sen makes a strong case that the factors which development economics concentrated on, and the policies advocated by development economists, had an important and positive contribution to these improvements. Albert Hirschman (1983) noted that the optimism of development economics often gave policymakers and others the courage to confront social change, to support it, and to ensure its most positive outcomes. He describes himself and other developmentalists as having a "bias for hope."

The optimism of early development thinkers has certainly been tempered by time and experience, and the naive belief that the problems of poverty and stagnation could be solved completely and almost mechanically has long since disappeared. Human beings and societies are far too complex for any simple solution. In the words of Paul Streeten (1985), "every solution creates another problem." The articles in this section reflect an acute awareness of the complexity of development, and of the need for a political economy of development that moves beyond development economics.

For example, Sen notes that fast economic growth will often outrun the required social change, an experience that often shows that defining development correctly is quite difficult and requires an evolution in our thinking. Development economists have had to learn that "all good things do not go together," that rapid growth and economic development may be accompanied by severe political problems, such as the emergence of authoritarian governments or the brutal reaction of those whose power is threatened. In addition, sustaining rapid growth is not easy. For example, the 1980s was a lost decade for Latin America and Africa in terms of growth. Income per person in Latin America actually fell from an average of $2,512 in 1980 to $2,336 in 1988. So the challenge of a "political economy of development and underdevelopment" is to represent this complexity while at the same time maintaining a "bias for hope" that there can be positive outcomes to this continuing period of instability and change.

The difficulties of the 1970s and 1980s resulted in the loss of momentum and hope in development, and diminished the courage to proceed along a conscious development path. This stimulated free-market or laissez-faire economists to attack development economics, attributing slackening development to the interference of government in the economy, and particularly to government-induced distortions of the resource allocation role of prices. The article in this part by Deepak Lal, published by the World Bank, is a clear statement of this position and a resounding attack on what he terms the "dirigiste dogma."

Lal's stance has gained wide acceptance among economists. In part, this is a reflection of the World Bank's growing role in research on economic development. One indicator of the weight of the World Bank in development thinking comes from the affiliation of authors of articles that appeared in the five major journals of economic development between 1984 and 1986. World Bank authors were the most published in the development field, accounting for 1.6 times as many article pages in these journals as authors of the most productive independent research organization, the Institute of Development Studies at Sussex University in Great Britain. Adding the International Monetary Fund raises their joint production to 2.25 times that of Sussex. The importance of the World Bank and its corps of economists has given a major impulse to Lal's critique of development economics. Few development economists today would advocate massive government planning and control nor dismiss the price system as a mechanism for resource allocation. To this degree the World Bank approach has been accepted. That said, as Helleiner notes, "there is room for considerable political and professional disagreement on [many development questions]."

G. K. Helleiner's article examines the World Bank's approach to the macroeconomics of contemporary development, characterizing it as "conventional foolishness." He notes a series of discrepancies and inconsistencies, and suggests that such a simplification will surely be unable to deal with the complexities of contemporary development. His alternative draws on the mixed economy (government plus the private sector) strategy undertaken by the two unquestioned development success stories, Korea and Taiwan. He could also have noted that the postwar decade with the poorest development performance, the 1980s, was the decade during which the Bank's program was implemented most widely.

Both he and Sen conclude by setting out an agenda for development studies in the coming years. They agree that there is much work still to be done, that we can still understand and encourage development, although not with the ease and success that development economists had naively assumed in the early years. They implicitly suggest the need for a careful "political economy of development" and both point to several problems which have not been adequately addressed by development theory. The first of these is the environment and the imperative of sustainable development.

Development economists have not paid adequate attention to environmental limits and to the environmental costs of economic growth. True development must be "sustainable," it must take into account the viability of the natural environment that serves as a source of resources and as a sink for the by-products of economic activity. This is a truism the repetition of which is important; but what are its fundamental implications? The article by Paul Ekins addresses this question, and places it in the context of the environmental debates of the past twenty years, which began with concern about "the limits to growth." He concludes that the issue can only be addressed on a global scale, by both developed and developing countries together. The key problems require that both North (developed) and South (developing) be involved in sustainable development and adopt policies appropriate to their particular circumstances. It is likely that the decisions made in the North will have greater impact on the sustainability of world development than those made in the South.

The second problem area is the measurement of development: development is often hindered by ignoring issues of gender. In Sen's terms, the capabilities and entitlements created in the process of development often differ according to gender. If policy formulators consciously consider this element, the benefits of development efforts can be increased. Diane Elson's article examines how gender is absent from much development thinking, be it neoclassical (such as Lal's) or structural (such as Helleiner's). She then shows the implications, both for understanding and for policy development, of incorporating gender into development. Such an effort can help deal with gender inequality as well as contributing to a true "development."

The political economy of development in the post-World War II period has come full circle in a sense. After fifty years of seeming success, the development of Eastern Europe, one of its first concerns, is again an important question. And we are again confronted with problems that have been created by our solutions, most important among which is the sustainability of the development process. Nonetheless, there are important success stories to build on, most notably Korea and Taiwan. And we continue to learn about development policies and approaches. Awareness of the importance of gender in development was reflected in the United Nations Cairo Conference on Population and Development in September 1994.

One major difference from the 1940s is that we now know that the naive belief in a simple and automatic process of development is untenable. Solutions do bring problems, reactions to change do occur, and development cannot be reduced to a simple formula; it must be studied as the political economy of development and underdevelopment. The variety and challenge of the development process must attract us. The crucial question is whether the acceptance of social change and the belief that it can be positive can energize development efforts, rather than lead to reaction or disillusion. Can we maintain a "bias toward hope"? Only our own openness to the drama that is human development will answer that question.

REFERENCES

Hirschman, Albert. "The Rise and Decline of Development Economics." In his *Essays in Trespassing: Economics to Politics and Beyond.* Cambridge: Cambridge University Press, 1981.

McNeill, William. *The Rise of the West.* New York: The New American Library, 1963.

Streeten, Paul. "A Problem to Every Solution: Development Economics Has Not Failed." *Finance and Development,* 22, 2 (June 1985): 1–16.

Wiarda, Howard. "Toward a Nonethnocentric Theory of Development: Alternative Conceptions from the Third World." *Journal of Developing Areas* (July, 1983): 433–452.

World Bank. *World Development Report, 1990.* Oxford: Oxford University Press, 1990.

CHAPTER 1

DEVELOPMENT: WHICH WAY NOW?

Amartya Sen

Harvard University

I. THE PROMISE AND THE DEFAULT

"Development economics is a comparatively young area of inquiry. It was born just about a generation ago, as a subdiscipline of economics, with a number of other social sciences looking on both skeptically and jealously from a distance."[1] So writes Albert Hirschman, but the essay that begins so cheerfully turns out to be really an obituary of development economics—no longer the envy of the other social sciences. In this illuminating essay, aptly called "The Rise and Decline of Development Economics," Hirschman puts his main thesis thus:

> our subdiscipline had achieved its considerable lustre and excitement through the implicit idea that it could slay the dragon of backwardness virtually by itself or, at least, that its contribution to this task was central. We now know that this is not so.[2]

The would-be dragon-slayer seems to have stumbled on his sword.

There is some plausibility in this diagnosis, but is it really true that development economics has no central role to play in the conquest of underdevelopment and economic backwardness? More specifically, were the original themes in terms of which the subject was launched really so far from being true or useful? I shall argue that the obituary may be premature, the original themes—while severely incomplete in coverage—did not point entirely in the wrong direction, and the discipline of development economics does have a central role to play in the field of economic growth in developing countries. But I shall also argue that the problematique underlying the approach of

Published in *Economic Journal,* 93 (December 1983), pp. 745–62. Copyright © 1983 by The Royal Economic Society. Reprinted by permission of Cambridge University Press.

traditional development economics is, in some important ways, quite limited, and has not—and could not have—brought us to an adequate understanding of economic development. Later on, I shall take up the question as to the direction in which we may try to go instead.

There is a methodological problem in identifying a subject—or a subdiscipline as Hirschman calls it—with a given body of beliefs and themes rather than with a collection of subject matters and problems to be tackled. But Hirschman is certainly right in pointing towards the thematic similarities of the overwhelming majority of contributions in development economics. While some development economists such as Peter Bauer and Theodore Schultz have not been party to this thematic congruence, they have also stood outside the mainstream of what may be called standard development economics, as indeed the title of Peter Bauer's justly famous book, *Dissent on Development*,[3] indicates. The subdiscipline began with a set of favourite themes and the main approaches to the subject have been much moulded by these motifs. Clearly, the subject cannot live or die depending just on the success or failure of these themes, but the main approaches would need radical reformulation if these themes were shown to be fundamentally erroneous or misguided.

Hirschman identifies two major ideas with which development economics came into being, namely "rural underemployment" (including so-called disguised unemployment") and "late industrialisation." The former idea led naturally to a focus on utilisation of underemployed manpower and to acceleration of capital accumulation. The latter called for an activist state and for planning to overcome the disadvantages of lateness through what Hirschman calls "a deliberate, intensive, guided effort." The subject expended a lot of time in developing "new rationales . . . for protection, planning, and industrialisation itself."[4]

While there have been differences in assertion and emphasis *within* the mainstream of the subdiscipline, it is fair to say that in terms of policy the following have been among the major strategic themes pursued ever since the beginning of the subject: (1) industrialisation, (2) rapid capital accumulation, (3) mobilisation of underemployed manpower, and (4) planning and an economically active state.[5] There are, of course, many other common themes, e.g., emphasis on skill formation, but they have not typically been as much subjected to criticism as these other themes, and there is thus much to be said for concentrating on these four.

These themes (especially the need for planning, but also the deliberate fostering of industrialisation and capital accumulation and the acceptance of the possibility of surplus labour) are closely linked to criticisms of the traditional neoclassical models as applied to developing countries. Hirschman calls this eschewal of "universal" use of neoclassical economics the rejection of "monoeconomics." Monoeconomics sounds perhaps a little like a disease that one could catch if not careful. I shall avoid the term, though some would no doubt have thought it quite appropriate to characterise universal neoclassical economics as a contagious affliction.

It was argued by development economists that neoclassical economics did not apply terribly well to underdeveloped countries. This need not have caused great astonishment, since neoclassical economics did not apply terribly well anywhere else.

However, the role of the state and the need for planning and deliberate public action seemed stronger in underdeveloped countries, and the departure from traditional neo-classical models was, in many ways, more radical.

The discrediting of traditional development economics that has lately taken place, and to which Hirschman made reference, is undoubtedly partly due to the resurgence of neoclassical economics in recent years. As Hirschman (1981) rightly notes, "the claim of development economics to stand as a separate body of economic analysis and policy derived intellectual legitimacy and nurture from the prior success and parallel features of the Keynesian Revolution" (p. 7). The neoclassical resurgence against Keynesian economics was to some extent paralleled by the neoclassical recovery in the field of economic development. The market, it was argued, has the many virtues that standard neoclassical analysis has done so much to analyse, and state intervention could be harmful in just the way suggested by that perspective.

The neoclassical resurgence has drawn much sustenance from the success of some countries and the failure of others. The high performance of economies like South Korea, Taiwan, Hong Kong, and Singapore—based on markets and profits and trade—has been seen as bringing Adam Smith back to life. On the other hand, the low performance of a great many countries in Asia, Africa, and Latin America has been cited as proof that it does not pay the government to mess about much with the market mechanism. Recently, doubts raised about the record of China, and the vocal desire of the Chinese leadership to make greater use of material incentives, have been interpreted as proof that even a powerful socialist regime cannot break the basic principles on which the market mechanism is founded.

The attack on state activism and planning has been combined with criticism of some of the other features of traditional development economics. It has been argued that enterprise is the real bottleneck, not capital, so that to emphasise capital accumulation and the creation of surplus—as was done for example by Maurice Dobb (1951; 1960) and Paul Baran (1957)—was to climb the wrong tree. The charge of misallocation of resources has been levelled also against industrialisation, especially for the domestic market. Hirschman (1981) notes: "By itself this critique was highly predictable and might not have carried more weight than warnings against industrialisation emanating from essentially the same camp ten, or twenty, or fifty years earlier." But—as he goes on to say—the effectiveness of this critique was now greater for various reasons, including that fact that "some of the early advocates of industrialisation had now themselves become its sharpest critics" (p. 18). Hirschman refers in this context to some "neo-Marxist" writings and the views of some members of the so-called dependency school. Certainly, the particular pattern of industrial expansion in Latin America provides many examples of exploitative relations with the metropolitan countries, particularly the United States of America, and the internal effects were often quite terrible in terms of fostering economic inequality and social distortion. But to move from there to a rejection of industrialisation as such is indeed a long jump.

I should explain that Hirschman, from whom I have been quoting extensively, does not in many cases endorse these attacks on the policy strategies of traditional development economics. But he provides excellent analyses of the arguments figuring in the attacks. I believe Hirschman is more hesitant in his defence of traditional development economics than he need have been, but his own reasons for rejecting that tradition—to which he himself has of course contributed much[6]—rests primarily on the argument that development economics has tended to be contemptuous of underdeveloped countries, albeit this contempt has taken a "sophisticated form." These countries have been "expected to perform like wind-up toys and 'lumber through' the various stages of development single-mindedly." As Hirschman (1981) puts it, "these countries were perceived to have only *interests* and *no passions*" (p. 24).[7]

I believe this diagnosis has much truth in it. But I also believe that, contemptuous and simplistic though development economics might have been in this respect, the main themes that were associated with the origin of development economics, and have given it its distinctive character, are not rejectable for that reason. I shall argue that they address common problems, which survive despite the particular passions.

II. TRADITIONAL THEMES IN THE LIGHT OF RECENT EXPERIENCES

Growth is not the same thing as development and the difference between the two has been brought out by a number of recent contributions to development economics.[8] I shall take up the complex question of the content of economic development presently (in Sections III–V below). But it can scarcely be denied that economic growth is one aspect of the process of economic development. And it happens to be the aspect on which traditional development economics—rightly or wrongly—has concentrated. In this section I do not assess the merits of that concentration (on which more later), but examine the appropriateness of the traditional themes, given that concentration. Dealing specifically with economic growth as it is commonly defined, the strategic relevance of these themes is examined in the light of recent experiences. How do these theories—formulated and presented mainly in the forties and fifties—fare in the light of the experiences of the sixties and the seventies?

The World Development Report 1982 (henceforth *WDR*) presents comparative growth data for the period 1960–80 for "low-income economies" and "middle-income economies," with a dividing line at US$410 in 1980. Leaving out small countries (using a cut-off line of 10 million people) and excluding the OPEC countries which have had rather special economic circumstances during the seventies, we have fourteen countries in the low-income category for which data on economic growth (GNP or GDP) are given in *WDR*. Correspondingly, there are eighteen such countries in the middle-income category. Table 1-1 presents these data. For three of the low-income countries, namely China, Bangladesh and Afghanistan, the GNP growth figures are not given in *WDR* and they have been approximately identified with GDP growth. In interpreting the results, this has to be borne in mind, and only those conclusions can be safely drawn which would be unaffected by variations of these estimates within a wide range.

The fourteen low-income economies vary in terms of growth rate of GNP per capita during 1960–80 from *minus* 0.7% in Uganda to 3.7% in China. The top three countries in terms of economic growth are China (3.7%), Pakistan (2.8%), and Sri Lanka

(2.4%). (Note that China's preeminent position would be unaffected even if the approximated growth figure is substantially cut.) In the middle-income group, the growth performance again varies a great deal, ranging from *minus* 10% for Ghana to 8.6% for Romania. The top three countries in terms of economic growth are Romania (8.6%), South Korea (7.0%), and Yugoslavia (5.4%).

TABLE 1-1

Country	GNP per head		1980 Gross domestic investment (% of GDP)	1980 Share of industry in GDP (%)
	1980 Value ($)	1960–80 Growth (%)		
Low-income				
Bangladesh	130	1.3*	17	13
Ethiopia	140	1.4	10	16
Nepal	140	0.2	14	13
Burma	170	1.2	24	13
Afghanistan		0.9*	14	—
Zaire	220	0.2	11	23
Mozambique	230	−0.1	10	16
India	240	1.4	23	26
Sri Lanka	270	2.4	36	30
Tanzania	280	1.9	22	13
China	290	3.7*	31	47
Pakistan	300	2.8	18	25
Uganda	300	−0.7	3	6
Sudan	410	−0.2	12	14
Middle-income				
Ghana	420	−1.0	5	21
Kenya	420	2.7	22	21
Egypt	580	3.4	31	35
Thailand	670	4.7	27	29
Philippines	690	2.8	30	37
Morocco	900	2.5	21	32
Peru	930	1.1	16	45
Colombia	1,180	3.0	25	30
Turkey	1,470	3.6	27	30
S. Korea	1,520	7.0	31	41
Malaysia	1,620	4.3	29	37
Brazil	2,050	5.1	22	37
Mexico	2,090	2.6	28	38
Chile	2,150	1.6	18	37
South Africa	2,300	2.3	29	53
Romania	2,340	8.6	34	64
Argentina	2,390	2.2	—	—
Yugoslavia	2,620	5.4	35	43

*Based on GDP growth figures per head (*World Development Report 1982*, tables 2 and 17).
Source: World Development Report 1982, tables 1–5. The countries included are all the ones within the 'Low-income' and 'Middle-income' categories, other than those with less than 10 million population, members of OPEC, and countries without GNP or GDP growth figures.

How do these high-performance countries compare with others in the respective groups in terms of the parameters associated with the main theses of traditional development economics? Take capital accumulation first. Of the three top growth-performers, two also have the highest share of gross domestic investment in GDP, namely Sri Lanka with 36% and China with 31%. Pakistan comes lower, though it does fall in the top half of the class of fourteen countries.

Turning now to the middle-income countries, the top three countries in terms of growth are also the top three countries in terms of capital accumulation, namely Yugoslavia with 35%, Romania with 34%, and South Korea with 31%. Thus, if there is anything to be learned from the experience of these successful growers regarding the importance of capital accumulation, it is certainly not a lesson that runs counter to the traditional wisdom of development economics.

It might, however, be argued that to get a more convincing picture one should look also at failures and not merely at successes. I don't think the cases are quite symmetrical, since a failure can be due to some special "bottleneck" even when all other factors are favorable. Nevertheless, it is not useless to examine the cases of failure as well, especially with respect to capital accumulation, since it has been seen in traditional development economics to be such a *general* force towards economic growth.

The three worst performers in the low-income category in terms of growth rate are, respectively, Uganda with *minus* 0.7%, Sudan with *minus* 0.2%, and Mozambique with *minus* 0.1%. In terms of capital accumulation, Uganda's rank is also the worst there, with only 3% of GDP invested. Mozambique is the second lowest investor, and Sudan the fifth lowest.

What about growth failures in the middle-income countries? The worst performers in terms of growth rate are Ghana with *minus* 1%, Peru with 1.1%, and Chile with 1.6%. As it happens these countries are also respectively the lowest, the second lowest, and the third lowest accumulators of capital in the category of the middle-income countries.

So both in terms of cases of success and those of failure, the traditional wisdom of development economics is scarcely contradicted by these international comparisons. Quite the contrary.

Hans Singer (1952) in his paper entitled "The Mechanics of Economic Development," published thirty years ago, seems to be almost talking about today's worst case of growth failure in the combined category of low-income and middle-income countries, namely Ghana. Using the Harrod-Domar model with an assumed capital-output ratio, Singer argues that a country with 6% savings and a population growth rate of 1.25% will be a "stationary economy." While Ghana has managed an investment and savings ratio of just below 6% (5% to be exact) it has had a population growth between 2.4 and 3.0% during these decades as opposed to Singer's assumption of 1.25%. Rather than being stationary, Ghana has accordingly slipped back, going down at about 1% a year. The Harrod-Domar model is an oversimplification, of course, but the insight obtained from such reasoning is not altogether without merit.

I turn now to the theme of industrialisation. In the category of low-income countries, the top performers—China, Pakistan, and Sri Lanka—happen to be among the four countries with the highest share of industries in GDP. In the middle-income group, the top growers—Romania, South Korea, and Yugoslavia—are among the top five countries in terms of the share of industries in GDP.[9]

The picture at the other end, i.e., for countries with growth failures, is certainly less neat than at the top end in this case, or at either end in the case of capital accumulation. It is, however, certainly true that Uganda, which occupies the bottom position in the low-income category in terms of growth rate, also has the bottom position in terms of the share of industries, and similarly Ghana, with the lowest record of growth in the middle-income group, also has the lowest share of industries in that group. But the positions of second and third lowest are not quite so telling. In the low-income category, low-performing Sudan and Mozambique have middling industrial ratios. In the middle-income group, the second-lowest growth performer, Peru, has the third *highest* ratio of industries in that group, though the third-lowest growth performer, Chile, has a middling industrial ratio. The picture is, thus, a bit more muddled at the lower end of growth performance.[10]

Altogether, so far as growth is concerned, it is not easy to deny the importance of capital accumulation or of industrialisation in a poor preindustrial country. Turning to the thesis of underemployment and the role of labour mobilisation, there have been several powerful attempts at disestablishing the thesis of "disguised unemployment," e.g., by Theodore Schultz (1964), but they have not been altogether successful.[11] Furthermore, what is really at issue is the crucial role of labour mobilisation and use, and not whether the opportunity cost of labour is exactly zero.[12] It is worth noting, in this context, that the high-growth performers in both groups have distinguished records of labour-using economic growth, and some (e.g., China and South Korea) have quite outstanding achievements in this area. While they have very different political systems, their respective successes in labour mobilisation have been specially studied and praised.[13]

The question of planning and state activism is a field in which comparative quantitative data are particularly difficult to find. But some qualitative information is of relevance. Of the three top growing economies in the low-income group, one—China—is obviously not without an active state. While Pakistan is in no way a paradigmatic example of determined state planning, it has been frequently cited as a good example of what harm government meddling can do.[14] The third—Sri Lanka—has been recently studied a great deal precisely because of its active government intervention in a number of different fields, including health, education, and food consumption.

In the middle-income group, of the three top performers, Romania and Yugoslavia clearly do have a good deal of planning. The third—South Korea—has had an economic system in which the market mechanism has been driven hard by an active government in a planned way. Trying to interpret the South Korean economic experience as a triumph of unguided market mechanism, as is sometimes done, is not easy to sustain. I have discussed this question elsewhere,[15] and I shall not spend any time on it here. I should only add that, aside from having a powerful influence over the direction of investment through control of financial institutions (including nationalised banks), the government of South Korea fostered an export-oriented growth on the secure foundations of more than a decade of intensive import substitution, based on trade restrictions, to build up an industrial base. Imports of a great many items are still prohibited or restricted. The pattern of South Korean economic expansion has been carefully planned by a powerful government. If this is a free market, when Walras's auctioneer can surely be seen as going around with a government white paper in one hand and a whip in the other.

The point is not so much that the government is powerful in the high-growth developing countries. It is powerful in nearly *every* developing country. The issue concerns the systematic involvement of the state in the *economic* sphere, and the pursuit of *planned* economic development. The carefully planned government action in, say, China or Sri Lanka or South Korea or Romania, contrast—on the whole strongly—with the economic role of the government in such countries as Uganda or Sudan or Chile or Argentina or Ghana.

This examination of the main theses of traditional development economics has been too brief and tentative, and certainly there is no question of claiming anything like definitiveness in the findings. But, in so far as anything has emerged, it has not gone in the direction of debunking traditional development economics; just the contrary.

EDITORS' APPENDIX TO TABLE 1-1

The data used by Sen in his Table 1-1 as the empirical context for his argument were published in 1982 for the period 1960–1980. In this update we provide roughly comparable data published in 1994 and covering the period 1980–1992. We included as many of the same countries as possible. Yugoslavia disappeared and no data were available on Afghanistan. The World Bank does report data on a number of additional countries in these categories, mainly recently independent countries or those formed from the breakup of the Soviet Union. That experience would color the results, so we chose to remain with the original countries used by Sen.

Recall that Sen highlighted the fastest growing countries and the slowest in each of the groups. He then examined their relative performance on the two indicators of capital formation (share of gross investment in GDP) and industrialization (share of industry in GDP). In general he found that the fastest growing countries exhibited a higher share of gross investment and a larger industrial share. The pattern was not as clear with the slow growing countries, but the opposite was true in the main.

The general pattern found by Sen appears in these new data, though perhaps not quite so neatly. It is also apparent that one other factor, war or civil unrest, must be added as a determinant of poor performance. Let us examine the data more closely.

China, Pakistan, and Sri Lanka were the fastest growing countries in Sen's low-income group. China remains first and Pakistan second, but Sri Lanka falls to fourth, behind India. The Tamil rebellion and its disruption would account for the slippage of Sri Lanka. The four countries all rank very high on gross investment and industry's share. The data for the gross investment share in Mozambique and Tanzania are surprising and may be faulty, e.g., 1993 data have Tanzania's share at 22 percent compared with 42 percent in 1994, an unlikely occurrence. If so, only Nepal would match the investment performance of the four fastest-growing countries. And only Egypt is comparable in the share of industry.

UPDATED DATA FOR TABLE 1-1

Country	GNP per head		1992 Gross domestic investment (% of GDP)	1992 Share of industry in GDP (%)
	1992 Value ($)	1980–92 Growth (%)		
Low-income				
Mozambique	60	−3.6	47	15
Ethiopia	110	−1.9	9	13
Tanzania	110	0.0	42	12
Nepal	170	2.0	22	18
Uganda	170	—	14	11
Bangladesh	220	1.8	12	17
India	310	3.1	23	27
Kenya	310	0.2	17	19
Pakistan	420	3.1	21	27
Ghana	450	−0.1	13	16
China	470	7.6	—	34
Sri Lanka	540	2.6	23	25
Sudan	—	—	—	17
Egypt	640	1.8	18	30
Middle-income				
Philippines	770	−1.0	23	33
Peru	950	−2.8	16	—
Morocco	1030	1.4	23	33
Romania	1130	−1.1	31	49
Colombia	1330	1.4	18	35
Thailand	1840	6.0	40	39
Turkey	1980	2.9	23	30
Chile	2730	3.7	24	—
South Africa	2670	0.1	15	42
Brazil	2770	0.4	17	37
Malaysia	2790	3.2	34	—
Mexico	3470	−0.2	24	28
Argentina	6050	−0.9	17	31
Korea, Rep.	6790	8.5	—	45

Source: World Development Report 1994, *Tables 1–9. The countries included are those in Sen's Table 1-1, to the extent possible. A more inclusive list shows the same patterns.*

Mozambique, Sudan, and Uganda were the slowest growing countries in Sen's data. We have data only for Mozambique, whose growth is the lowest and whose industry share is among the lowest, while the investment share's magnitude is unlikely. We do not have growth rates for Sudan and Uganda, though the other two indicators are again at the low end of the range. Ethiopia is the next slowest growing country, and it reinforces the pattern, with both indicators at the low end of the range. All these countries have suffered from civil wars and disruption in the time period considered. Perhaps the peace which exists in all but Sudan may give different results in the future.

Turning to the middle-income economies, events have made the pattern more complex. Yugoslavia and Romania were two of the high-growth countries. The former exists no more, the latter has undergone a dramatic revolution and restructuring that has slowed growth despite the continued high gross investment and industrial share. Industry's share will fall as industries are reorganized or dismantled. Korea was the second fastest growing country. It is the fastest in the recent period and the share of industry is surpassed only by Romania's. The other two rapidly growing countries in the new period are Thailand and Chile, with Malaysia the fourth. Malaysia and Thailand correspond to the expected pattern, and Chile's gross investment is surpassed only by Romania's and Malaysia's.

The slow-growing countries were Ghana, which moved from middle to low income and whose indicators of capital formation and industrialization continue low, and Chile and Peru. Chile's performance improved dramatically, in part because of the peace of the 1980s and a return to democracy in 1989. Peru's growth is the slowest—its decline the greatest—and its investment rate is at the low end. Civil war has also affected its growth. The Philippines is the other slow growth country, although the two indicators are not at the low end. It is an exception to the pattern, such as those found by Sen in the earlier period.

In summary, the relation among growth, capital formation (investment) and industrialization that Sen noted is also present in data for a more recent period. These perennial themes of development economics will continue to play a role in our thinking about development.

Before I move on to develop some criticisms of my own, I should make one last defensive remark about traditional development economics. The general policy prescriptions and strategies in this tradition have to be judged in terms of the climate of opinion and the overall factual situation prevailing at the time these theories were formulated. Development economics was born at a time when government involvement in deliberately fostering economic growth in general, and industrialisation in particular, was very rare, and when the typical rates of capital accumulation were quite low. That situation has changed in many respects, and, while that may suggest the need to emphasise different issues, it does not in any way invalidate the wisdom of the strategies then suggested.

The point can be brought out with an example. In the 1952 paper of Hans Singer from which I have already quoted, one of the conclusions that Singer emphasised is the need to raise the then existing rate of saving. He argued, with some assumptions about production conditions, that to achieve even a 2% rate of per capita growth, with a population growing at 1.25% per year, "a rate of net savings of 16.25% is necessary," and that "this rate of saving is about three times the rate actually observed in underdeveloped countries" (Singer, 1952, pp. 397–8). The current average rate of saving is no longer a third of that figure, but substantially *higher* than the figure. The weighted average ratio of gross domestic saving for low-income developing countries is estimated to be about 22%, and that for middle-income developing countries about 25%; and, even after deducting for depreciation, Singer's target has certainly been exceeded. And, even with a faster growth of population than Singer anticipated, the weighted average of GDP growth rates per capita has been about 2.5% per year for low-income countries and more than 3% per year for middle-income countries over the seventies.[16]

The point of policy interest now is that, despite these *average* achievements, the performances of different countries are highly divergent. There is still much relevance in the broad policy themes which traditional development economics has emphasised. The strategies have to be adapted to the particular conditions and to national and international circumstances, but the time to bury traditional development economics has not yet arrived.

III. FAST GROWTH AND SLOW SOCIAL CHANGE

I believe the real limitations of traditional development economics arose not from the choice of means to the end of economic growth, but in the insufficient recognition that economic growth was no more than a means to some other objectives. The point is not the same as saying that growth does not matter. It may matter a great deal, but, if it does, this is because of some associated benefits that are realised in the process of economic growth.

It is important to note in this context that the same level of achievement in life expectancy, literacy, health, higher education, etc., can be seen in countries with widely varying income per capita. To take just one example, consider Brazil, Mexico, South Korea, China, and Sri Lanka.[17]

China and Sri Lanka, with less than a seventh of GNP per head in Brazil or Mexico, have similar life expectancy figures to the two richer countries (see Table 1-2). South Korea, with its magnificent and much-eulogised growth record, has not yet overtaken China or Sri Lanka in the field of longevity, despite being now more than five times richer in terms of per capita GNP. If the government of a poor developing country is keen to raise the level of health and the expectation of life, then it would be pretty daft to try to achieve this through raising its income per head, rather than going directly for these objectives through public policy and social change, as China and Sri Lanka have both done.

Not merely is it the case that economic growth is a means rather than an end, it is also the case that for some important ends it is not a very efficient means either. In an earlier paper (Sen, 1981b) it was shown that had Sri Lanka been a typical developing country, trying to achieve its high level of life expectancy not through direct public action, but

TABLE 1-2

Country	Life expectancy at birth 1980 (years)	GNP per head, 1980 (US dollars)
Brazil	63	2,050
China	64	290
Mexico	65	2,090
South Korea	65	1,520
Sri Lanka	66	270

primarily through growth (in the same way as typical developing countries do), then it would have taken Sri Lanka—depending on assumptions—somewhere between 58 years and 152 years to get where it already now happens to be.[18] It might well be the case that "money answereth all things," but the answer certainly comes slowly.

IV. ENTITLEMENTS AND CAPABILITIES

Perhaps the most important thematic deficiency of traditional development economics is its concentration on national product, aggregate income, and total supply of particular goods rather than on "entitlements" of people and the "capabilities" these entitlements generate. Ultimately, the process of economic development has to be concerned with what people can or cannot do, e.g., whether they can live long, escape avoidable morbidity, be well nourished, be able to read and write and communicate, take part in literary and scientific pursuits, and so forth. It has to do, in Marx's words, with "replacing the domination of circumstances and chance over individuals by the domination of individuals over chance and circumstances."[19]

Entitlement refers to the set of alternative commodity bundles that a person can command in a society using the totality of rights and opportunities that he or she faces. Entitlements are relatively simple to characterise in a pure market economy. If a person can, say, earn $200 by selling his labour power and other saleable objects he has or can produce, then his entitlements refer to the set of all commodity bundles costing no more than $200. He can buy any such bundle, but no more than that, and the limit is set by his ownership ("endowment") and his exchange possibilities ("exchange entitlement"), the two together determining his overall entitlement.[20] On the basis of this entitlement, a person can acquire some capabilities, i.e., the ability to do this or that (e.g., be well nourished), and fail to acquire some other capabilities. The process of economic development can be seen as a process of expanding the capabilities of people. Given the functional relation between entitlements of persons over goods and their capabilities, a useful—though derivative—characterisation of economic development is in terms of expansion of entitlements.[21]

For most of humanity, about the only commodity a person has to sell is labour power, so that the person's entitlements depend crucially on his or her ability to find a job, the wage rate for that job, and the prices of commodities that he or she wishes to buy. The problems of starvation, hunger, and famines in the world could be better analysed through the concept of entitlement than through the use of the traditional variables of food supply and population size. The intention here is not, of course, to argue that the supply of goods—food in this case—is irrelevant to hunger and starvation, which would be absurd, but that the supply is just one influence among many; and, in so far as supply is important, it is so precisely because it affects the entitlements of the people involved, typically through prices. Ultimately, we are concerned with what people can or cannot do, and this links directly with their "entitlements" rather than with overall supplies and outputs in the economy.[22]

The failure to see the importance of entitlements has been responsible for millions of people dying in famines. Famines may not be at all anticipated in situations of good or moderate overall levels of supply, but, notwithstanding that supply situation, acute starvation can hit suddenly and widely because of failures of the entitlement systems, operating through ownership and exchange. For example, in the Bangladesh famine of 1974, a very large number died in a year when food availability per head was at a peak—higher than in any other year between 1971 and 1975. The floods that affected agriculture did ultimately—much later than the famine—reduce the food output, but its first and immediate impact was on the rural labourers who lost jobs in planting and transplanting rice, and started starving long before the main crop that was affected was to be harvested. The problem was made worse by forces of inflation in the economy, reducing the purchasing power especially of rural labourers, who did not have the economic muscle to raise their money wages correspondingly.[23]

Entitlements may not operate only through market processes. In a socialist economy entitlements will depend on what the families can get from the state through the established system of command. Even in a nonsocialist economy, the existence of social security—when present—makes the entitlements go substantially beyond the operation of market forces.

A major failing of traditional development economics has been its tendency to concentrate on supply of goods rather than on ownership and entitlement. The focus on growth is only one reflection of this. Extreme concentration on the ratio of food supply to population is another example of the same defective vision.[24] Recently the focus has shifted somewhat from growth of *total incomes* to the *distribution of incomes*. This may look like a move in the right direction, and indeed it is. But I would argue that "income" itself provides an inadequate basis for analysing a person's entitlements. Income gives the means of buying things. It expresses buying power in terms of some scalar magnitude—given by one real number. Even if there are no schools in the village and no hospitals nearby, the income of the villager can still be increased by adding to his purchasing power over the goods that are available in the market. But this rise in income may not be able to deal at all adequately with his entitlement to education or medical treatment, since the rise in income as such guarantees no such thing.

In general, one real number reflecting some aggregate measure of market power can scarcely represent so complex a notion as entitlement. The power of the market force depends on relative prices and, as the price of some good rises, the hold of income on the corresponding entitlement weakens. With nonmarketability, it slips altogether. In the extreme case, the entitlement to live, say, in a malaria-free environment is not a matter of purchase with income in any significant way.

In dealing with starvation and hunger, the focus on incomes—though defective—is not entirely disastrous. And of course it is a good deal better than the focus on total food output and population size. The weighting system of real income and cost-of-living pays sufficient attention to food in a poor community to make real income a moderately good "proxy" for entitlement to food in most cases.[25] But when it comes to health, or education, or social equality, or self-respect, or freedom from social harassment, income is miles off the target.

V. POLITICAL COMPLEXITIES

To move from concentrating on growth to supplementing that with an account of income distribution is basically an inadequate response to what is at issue. It is also, in effect, an attempt to refuse to come to terms with the complexity of entitlement relations. The metric of income, as already discussed, is much too crude. Indeed, entitlements related even to purely economic matters, e.g., that to food, may actually require us to go beyond the narrow limits of economics altogether.

Take the case of famine relief. A hungry, destitute person will be *entitled* to some free food *if* there is a relief system offering that. Whether, in fact, a starving person will have such an entitlement will depend on whether such a public relief operation will actually be launched. The provision of public relief is partly a matter of political and social pressure. Food is, as it were, "purchased" in this context not with income but with political pressure. The Irish in the 1840s did not have the necessary political power. Nor did the Bengalis in the Great Bengal Famine of 1943. Nor the Ethiopians in Wollo in the famine of 1973. On the other hand, there are plenty of examples in the world in which timely public policy has averted an oncoming famine completely.

The operation of political forces affecting entitlements is far from simple. For example, with the present political system in India, it is almost impossible for a famine to take place. The pressure of newspapers and diverse political parties makes it imperative for the government in power to organise swift relief. It has to act to retain credibility. No matter how and where famine threatens—whether with a flood or a drought, whether in Bihar in 1967–8, in Maharashtra in 1971–3, or in West Bengal in 1978—an obligatory policy response prevents the famine from actually occurring.

On the other hand, there is no such relief for the third of the Indian rural population who go to bed hungry every night and who lead a life ravaged by regular deprivation. The quiet presence of nonacute, endemic hunger leads to no newspaper turmoil, no political agitation, no riots in the Indian parliament. The system takes it in its stride.[26]

The position in China is almost exactly the opposite of this. On the one hand, the political commitment of the system ensures a general concern with eradicating regular malnutrition and hunger through more equal access to means of livelihood, and through entitlements vis-à-vis the state; and China's achievements in this respect have been quite remarkable. In a normal year, the Chinese poor are much better fed than the Indian poor. The expectation of life in China is between 66 and 69 years in comparison with India's miserable 52 years. On the other hand, if there is a political and economic crisis that confuses the regime and makes it pursue disastrous policies with confident dogmatism, then it cannot be forced to change its policies by crusading newspapers or by effective pressure from opposing political groups.

It is, in fact, now quite clear that in China during 1959–61 there were deaths on a very large scale due to famine conditions. The extent of the disaster has only recently become evident, even though there are still many uncertainties regarding the exact estimation of extra mortality.[27] Important mortality data were released in 1980 by Professor Zhu Zhengzhi of Beijing University,[28] indicating that the death rate rose from about 10.8 per thousand in 1957 to an average of 16.58 per thousand per year during 1958–61. This yields a figure of extra mortality of 14–16 million in China in the famine-affected years—a very large figure indeed. It is, in fact, very much larger than the extra mortality (calculated in the same way) even in the Great Bengal Famine of 1943 (namely about 3 million[29]), the largest famine in India in this century.

In 1981 the noted economist Sun Yefang released some further mortality data,[30] referring to "the high price in blood" of the economic policy pursued at that time. He reported that the death rate per thousand had risen to as high as 25.4 in 1960, indicating an extra mortality of 9 million in that year alone. His figures for the four years also yield a total of around 15 million extra deaths during the Chinese famine of 1959–61.[31] Others have suggested even higher mortality.[32]

These are truly staggering figures. Even if we take a level quite a bit below the lower limit of the estimates, the sudden extra mortality caused by the famine[33] would still be on a scale that is difficult to match even in preindependent India (and there has of course been no famine in India since independence).

Is it purely accidental that a famine—indeed one on an enormous scale—could take place in China while none has occurred in postindependent India? The contrast is particularly odd when viewed in the context of the undoubted fact that China has been very much more successful than India in eliminating regular malnutrition. There may well be an accidental element in the comparative records on famines, but as already noted, on a number of occasions potentially large famines have been prevented in India through quick, extensive, and decisive government intervention. Reports on deaths from hunger reach the government and the public quickly and dramatically through active newspapers, and are taken up vigorously by parties not in power. Faced with a threatening famine, any government wishing to stay in office in India is forced to abandon or modify its ongoing economic policy, and meet the situation with swift public action, e.g., redistribution of food within the country, imports from abroad, and widespread relief arrangements (including food for work programs).

Policy failures in China during the famine years (and the Great Leap Forward period), which have been much discussed in China only recently, relate not merely to factors that dramatically reduced output, but also to distributional issues, e.g., interregional balances, and the draconian procurement policy that was apparently pursued relentlessly despite lower agricultural output.[34] Whatever the particular policy errors, the government in power was not forced to reexamine them, nor required to face harrowing newspaper reports and troublesome opposition parties. The contrast may not, therefore, be purely accidental.

In an interesting and important speech given in 1962—just after the famine—Chairman Mao made the following remarks to a conference of 7,000 cadres from different levels: "If there is no democracy, if ideas are not coming from the masses, it is impossible to establish a good line, good general and specific policies and methods. . . . Without democracy, you have no understanding of what is happening down below; the situation will be unclear; you will be unable to collect sufficient opinions from all sides; there can be no communication between top and bottom; top-level organs of leadership will depend on one-sided and incorrect material to decide issues, thus you will find it difficult to avoid being subjectivist; it will be impossible to achieve unity of understanding and unity of action, and impossible to achieve true centralism."[35] Ralph Miliband (1977), who has provided an illuminating and far-reaching analysis of the issue of democracy in capitalist and socialist societies from a Marxist perspective, points out that Mao's "argument for 'democracy' is primarily a 'functional' one" (pp. 149–50), and argues that this is an inadequate basis for understanding the need for "socialist democracy."[36] That more general question certainly does remain, but it is worth emphasising that even the purely "functional" role of democracy can be very crucial to matters of life and death, as the Chinese experiences of the famine of 1959–61 bring out.[37]

Finally, it is important to note that the protection that the Indian poor get from the active news distribution system and powerful opposition parties has very severe limits. The deprivation has to be dramatic to be "newsworthy" and politically exploitable (see Sen, 1982c). The Indian political system may prevent famines but, unlike the Chinese system, it seems unable to deal effectively with endemic malnutrition. In a normal year when things are running smoothly both in India and China, the Indian poor is in a much more deprived general state than his or her Chinese counterpart.[38]

VI. CONCLUDING REMARKS

I shall not try to summarise the main points of the paper, but I will make a few concluding remarks to put the discussion in perspective.

First, traditional development economics has not been particularly unsuccessful in identifying the factors that lead to economic growth in developing countries. In the field of causation of growth, there is much life left in traditional analyses (Section II).

Secondly, traditional development economics has been less successful in characterising economic development, which involves expansion of people's capabilities. For this, economic growth is only a means and often not a very efficient means either (Section III).

Thirdly, because of close links between entitlements and capabilities, focusing on entitlements—what commodity bundles a person can command—provides a helpful format for characterising economic development. Supplementing data on GNP per capita by income distributional information is quite inadequate to meet the challenge of development analysis (Section IV).

Fourthly, famines and starvation can be more sensibly analysed in terms of entitlement failures than in terms of the usual approach focusing on food output per unit of population. A famine can easily occur even in a good food supply situation, through the collapse of entitlements of particular classes or occupation groups (Section IV).

Fifthly, a study of entitlements has to go beyond purely economic factors and take into account political arrangements (including pressure groups and news distribution systems) that affect people's actual ability to command commodities, including food. These influences may be very complex and may also involve apparently perplexing contrasts, e.g., between (1) India's better record than China's in avoiding famines, and (2) India's total failure to deal with endemic malnutrition and morbidity in the way China has been able to do (Section V). Whether the disparate advantages of the contrasting systems can be effectively combined is a challenging issue of political economy that requires attention. Much is at stake.

NOTES

1 Essay 1 in Hirschman (1981).
2 Hirschman (1981), p. 23.
3 Bauer (1971). See also Schultz (1964) and Bauer (1981). For a forceful critical account without breaking from traditional development economics, see Little (1982).

4 Hirschman (1981), pp. 10–11.

5 See Rosenstein-Rodan (1943), Mandelbaum (1945), Dobb (1951), Datta (1952), Singer (1952), Nurkse (1953), and Lewis (1954, 1955).

6 See particularly Hirschman (1958, 1970).

7 For the conceptual framework underlying the distinction, see Hirschman (1977).

8 See, for example, Streeten (1981). See also Grant (1978), Morris (1979), and Streeten et al. (1981).

9 An additional one in this case is South Africa, and its industrial share is high mainly because mining is included in that figure. In fact, if we look only at manufacturing, South Africa falls below the others.

10 The rank correlation coefficient between per capita growth and the share of gross domestic investment in GDP is 0.72 for middle-income countries, 0.75 for low-income countries, and 0.82 for the two groups put together. On the other hand, the rank correlation coefficient between per capita growth and the share of industries is only 0.22 for middle-income countries, even though it is 0.59 for the low-income countries and 0.68 for the two groups put together.

11 My own views on this are presented in Sen (1975). See also Sen (1967), and the exchange with Schultz following that in the same number of [Economic Journal].

12 See Marglin (1976), chapter 2. Also Sen (1975), chapters 4 and 6. See also Fei and Ranis (1964).

13 See Little (1982). See also the important study of Ishikawa (1981), which discusses the empirical role of labour absorption in different Asian economies.

14 For example, Little et al. (1971).

15 Sen (1981b), and the literature cited there, especially Datta-Chaudhuri (1979).

16 See tables 2, 5, and 17 of the *World Development Report 1982*.

17 Taken from *World Development Report 1982*, table 1. The 1982 Chinese census indicates a higher expectation of life—around 69 years. The Sri Lankan figure of 66 years relates to 1971, and the current life expectancy is probably significantly higher.

18 See Sen (1981b), pp. 303–6. See also Jayawardena (1974), Marga Institute (1974), Isenman (1978), Alailima (1982), Gwatkin (1979).

19 Marx and Engels (1846); English translation taken from McLellan (1977), p. 190.

20 The notion of "entitlements" is explored in Sen (1981a). It is worth emphasizing here, to avoid misunderstandings that seem to have occurred in some discussions of the concept, that (1) "exchange entitlement" is only a *part* of the entitlement picture and is incomplete without an account of ownership or endowment, and (2) "exchange entitlement" includes not merely trade and market exchange but also the use of production possibilities (i.e., "exchange with nature").

21 Capabilities, entitlements, and utilities differ from each other. I have tried to argue elsewhere that "capabilities" provide the right basis for judging the advantages of a person in many problems of evaluation—a role that cannot be taken over either by utility or by an index of commodities (Sen, 1982a, pp. 29–38, 353–69). When we are concerned with such notions as the well-being of a person, or standard of living, or freedom in the positive sense, we need the concept of capabilities. We have to be concerned with what a person can do, and this is not the same thing as how much pleasure or desire fulfilment he gets from these activities ("utility"), nor what commodity bundles he can command ("entitlements"). Ultimately, therefore, we have to go not merely beyond the calculus of national product and aggregate real income, but also that of entitlements over commodity bundles viewed on their own. The focus on capabilities differs also from concentration on the mental metric of utilities, and this contrast is similar to the general one between pleasure, on the one hand, and positive freedom, on the other. The particular role of entitlements is *through* its effects on capabilities. It is a role that has substantial and far-reaching importance, but it remains derivative on capabilities. On these general issues, see Sen (1982a, d, 1983) and Kynch and Sen (1983).

22 See Sen (1981a, b), Arrow (1982), Desai (1983).

23 See Sen (1981a), chapter 9. Other examples of famines due to entitlement failure without a significant—indeed any— reduction of overall food availability can be found in chapter 6 (the Great Bengal Famine of 1943) and chapter 7 (the Ethiopian famine of 1973–4); see also chapter 7 (the Sahelian famines of the 1970s). On related matters, see also Sen (1976, 1977), Ghose (1979), Alamgir (1978, 1980), Chattopadhyay (1981), Oughton (1982), Ravallion (1983). See also Parikh and Rabar (1981) and Srinivasan (1982). Also the special number of *Development*, Aziz (1982).

24 On this and related issues, see Aziz (1975), Taylor (1975), Griffin (1978), Sinha and Drabek (1978), Spitz (1978), Lappé and Collins (1979), George and Paige (1982), Rao (1982).

25 However, the index of real income will continue to differ from the index of food entitlement since the price deflators will not be the same, though the two will often move together. A problem of a different sort arises from *intra*-family differences in food consumption (e.g., through 'sex bias'), as a result of which both the real income and the food entitlement of the family may be rather deceptive indicators of nutritional situations of particular members of the family. On this issue, see Bardhan (1974), Sen (1981c), Kynch and Sen (1983), and Sen and Sengupta (1983).

26 See Sen (1982b, c).

27 See Aird (1982), pp. 277–8.

28 Zhu Zhengzhi (1980), pp. 54–5. These data have been analysed by Coale (1981). See also Bernstein (1983b).

29 See Sen (1981a), appendix D. In both cases the death rate immediately preceding the famine-affected year is taken as the bench mark in comparison with which the "extra" mortality in famine-affected years are calculated.

30 Sun Yefang (1981) and People's Republic of China (1981).

31 See Bernstein (1983a, b).

32 See Bernstein's (1983b) account of the literature. See also Aird (1980). For a description of the intensity of the famine in a particular commune (the Liyuan Commune in Anhui province), see Research Group of the Fen Yang County Communist Party Committee (1983). "The commune's population of 5,730 people in 1957 had dropped to 2,870 people in 1961. More than half died of starvation *[e si]* or fled the area. . . . In 1955, the Houwang production team was a model elementary cooperative. The village had twenty-eight families, a total of 154 people. . . . fifty-nine people starved to death *[e si]*, and the survivors fled the area" (p. 36).

33 The number of deaths due to a famine must not be confused with the number actually dying of starvation, since most people who die in a famine tend to die from other causes (particularly from diseases endemic in the region) to which they become more susceptible due to undernutrition, and also due to breakdown of sanitary arrangements, exposure due to wandering, eating noneatables, and other developments associated with famines. See Sen (1981a), pp. 203–16.

34 See Bernstein (1983b), who also argues that the harsh procurement policies in China did not have the ideologically "anti-peasant" character that similar policies in the USSR did during 1932–3, but reflected "erroneous" reading of the level of output and of the economic situation.

35 Mao Zedong (1974), p. 164.

36 Miliband goes on to argue: "Much may be claimed for the Chinese experience. But what cannot be claimed for it, on the evidence, is that it has really begun to create the institutional basis for the kind of socialist democracy that would effectively reduce the distance between those who determine policy and those on whose behalf it is determined" (p. 151).

37 The Soviet famines of the 1930s and the Kampuchean famine of more recent years provide further evidence of penalties of this lacuna.

38 The crude death rate in China in 1980 was reported to be 8 per thousand in contrast with India's 14 (*World Development Report 1982,* table 18, p. 144). Only in famine situations did the reported death rate in China (e.g., 25.4 reported in 1960) exceed that in India.

REFERENCES

Aird, J. "Reconstruction of an Official Data Model of the Population of China." U.S. Department of Commerce, Bureau of Census, May 15, 1980.

———. "Population Studies and Population Policy in China." *Population and Development Review,* 8 (1982): 267–297.

Alailima, P. J. "National Policies and Programmes of Social Development in Sri Lanka." Mimeographed, Colombo.

Alamgir, M. *Bangladesh: A Case of Below Poverty Level Equilibrium Trap.* Dhaka: Bangladesh Institute of Development Studies, 1978.

———. *Famine in South Asia—Political Economy of Mass Starvation in Bangladesh.* Cambridge, Mass.: Oelgeschlager, Gunn and Hain, 1980.

Arrow, K. J. "Why People Go Hungry." *New York Review of Books,* 299 (July 15, 1982): 24–26.

Aziz, S. (ed.). *Hunger, Politics and Markets: The Real Issues in the Food Crisis.* New York: NYU Press, 1975.

———. (ed.). "The Fight against World Hunger." Special number of *Development,* 1982, p. 4.

Baran, P. A. *Political Economy of Growth.* New York: Monthly Review Press, 1957.

Bardhan, P. "On Life and Death Questions." *Economic and Political Weekly,* 9 (1974): 1293–1304.

Bauer, P. *Dissent on Development.* London: Weidenfeld and Nicolson, 1971.

———. *Equality, the Third World, and Economic Delusion.* Cambridge, Mass: Harvard University Press, 1981.

Bernstein, T. P. "Starving to Death in China." *New York Review of Books,* 30 (June 6, 1983a): 36–38.

———. "Hunger and the State: Grain Procurements During the Great Leap Forward; with a Soviet Perspective." Mimeographed, East Asia Center, Columbia University.

Chattopadhyay, B. "Notes towards an Understanding of the Bengal Famine of 1943." *Cressida,* 1 (1981).

Coale, A. J. "Population Trends, Population Policy, and Population Studies in China." *Population and Development Review,* 7 (1981): 85–97.

Datta, B. *Economics of Industrialization.* Calcutta: World Press, 1952.

Datta-Chaudhuri, M. K. "Industrialization and Foreign Trade: An Analysis Based on the Development Experience of the Republic of Korea and the Philippines." ILO Working Paper WP II-4, ARTEP, ILO, Bangkok, 1979.

Desai, M. J. "A General Theory of Poverty." Mimeographed, London School of Economics, 1983. To be published in *Indian Economic Review.*

Dobb, M. H. *Some Aspects of Economic Development.* Delhi: Delhi School of Economics, 1951.

———. *An Essay on Economic Growth and Planning.* London: Routledge, 1960.

Fei, J. C. H., and Ranis, G. *Development of the Labour Surplus Economy: Theory and Practice.* Homewood, Ill.: Irwin, 1964.

George, S. and Paige, N. *Food for Beginners.* London: Writers and Readers Publishing Cooperative, 1982.

Ghose, A. "Short Term Changes in Income Distribution in Poor Agrarian Economies." ILO Working Paper WEP 10-6/WP 28, Geneva, 1979.

Grant, J. *Disparity Reduction Rates in Social Indicators.* Washington, D.C.: Overseas Development Council, 1978.

Griffin, K. *International Inequality and National Poverty.* London: Macmillan, 1978.

Gwatkin, D. R. "Food Policy, Nutrition Planning and Survival: The Cases of Kerala and Sri Lanka." *Food Policy,* November 1979.

Hirschman, A. O. *The Strategy of Economic Development.* New Haven, Conn.: Yale University Press, 1958.

———. *Exit, Voice, and Loyalty.* Cambridge, Mass.: Harvard University Press, 1970.

———. *The Passions and the Interests.* Princeton: Princeton University Press, 1977.

———. *Essays in Trespassing: Economics to Politics and Beyond.* New York and Cambridge, England: Cambridge University Press, 1981.

Isenman, P. "The Relationship of Basic Needs to Growth, Income Distribution and Employment—The Case of Sri Lanka." Mimeographed, World Bank, 1978.

Ishikawa, T. *Essays on Technology, Employment and Institutions in Economic Development.* Tokyo: Kinokuniya, 1981.

Jayawardena, L. "Sri Lanka." In *Redistribution with Growth,* H. Chenery et al. (eds.). London: Oxford University Press, 1974.

Kynch, J., and Sen, A. K. "Indian Women: Survival and Well-Being." In *Cambridge Journal of Economics,* 7 (1983): pp. 363–380.

Lappé, F. M., and Collins, J. *Food First: Beyond the Myth of Scarcity.* New York: Ballantine Books, 1979.

Lewis, W. A. "Economic Development with Unlimited Supplies of Labour." *Manchester School* (1954): 139–191.

———. *The Theory of Economic Growth.* Homewood, Ill.: Irwin, 1955.

Little, I. M. D. *Economic Development: Theory, Policy and International Relations.* New York: Basic Books, 1982.

———. T. Scitovsky, and Scott, M. *Industry and Trade in Some Developing Countries.* London: Oxford University Press, 1971.

McLellan, D. (ed.). *Karl Marx: Selected Writings.* Oxford: Oxford University Press, 1977.

Mandelbaum (Martin), K. *The Industrialization of Backward Areas.* Oxford: Blackwell, 1945.

Mao Tse-tung (Zedong). *Mao Tse-tung Unrehearsed, Talks and Letters: 1956–71,* S. R. Schram (ed.). London: Penguin Books, 1974.

Marga Institute. *Welfare and Growth in Sri Lanka.* Colombo: Marga Institute, 1974.

Marglin, S. A. *Value and Price in the Labour Surplus Economy.* Oxford: Clarendon Press, 1976.

Marx, K., and Engels, F. *The German Ideology.* New York: International Publishers, (1846). 1947.

Miliband, R. *Marxism and Politics.* London: Oxford University Press, 1977.

Morris, M. D. *Measuring the Condition of the World's Poor: The Physical Quality of Life Index.* Oxford: Pergamon Press, 1979.

Nurkse, R. *Problems of Capital Formation in Underdeveloped Countries.* Oxford: Blackwell, 1953.

Oughton, E. "The Maharashtra Drought of 1970–73: An Analysis of Scarcity." *Oxford Bulletin of Economics and Statistics,* (1982): 169–197.

Parikh, K., and Rabar, F. (eds.). *Food for All in a Sustainable World.* Laxenburg: IIASA, 1981.

People's Republic of China. *Foreign Broadcast Information Service,* no. 58, March 26, 1981.

Rao, V. K. R. V. *Food, Nutrition and Poverty in India.* Brighton: Wheatsheaf Books, 1982.

Ravallion, M. *The Performance of Rice Markets in Bangladesh During the 1974 Famine.* Mimeographed, University of Oxford, 1983.

Research Group of the Feng Yang County Communist Party Committee. "An Investigation into the Household Production Contract System in Liyuan Commune." *New York Review of Books,* 30, 16 (June 1982): 36–38. Translated from *Nongye Jingji Congkan* (Collected Material on Agricultural Economics), November 25, 1980.

Rosenstein-Rodan, P. "Problems of Industrialization in Eastern and Southeastern Europe." *Economic Journal,* 53 (1943): 202–211.

Schultz, T. W. *Transforming Traditional Agriculture.* New Haven, Conn.: Yale University Press, 1964.

Sen, A. K. "Surplus Labour in India: A Critique of Schultz's Statistical Test." *Economic Journal,* 77 (1967): 154–161.

———. *Employment, Technology and Development.* Oxford: Clarendon Press, 1975.

———. "Famines as Failures of Exchange Entitlement." *Economic and Political Weekly,* 11 (1976): 1273–1280.

———. "Starvation and Exchange Entitlement: A General Approach and Its Application to the Great Bengal Famine." *Cambridge Journal of Economics,* 1 (1977): 33–59.

———. *Poverty and Famines: An Essay on Entitlement and Deprivation.* Oxford: Clarendon Press, 1981a.

———. "Public Action and the Quality of Life in Developing Countries." *Oxford Bulletin of Economics and Statistics,* 43 (1981b): 287–319.

———. "Family and Food: Sex Bias in Poverty." (1981c). In *Rural Poverty in South Asia,* P. Bardhan and T. N. Srinivasan (eds.) New York: Columbia University Press, 1988.

———. *Choice, Welfare and Measurement.* Oxford: Blackwell; and Cambridge, Mass.: MIT Press, 1982a.

———. "Food Battles: Conflict in the Access to Food." Coromandel Lecture, December 13, 1982. Reprinted in *Mainstream,* January 8, 1983.

———. "How Is India Doing?" *New York Review of Books,* 29 (Christmas Number, (1982c): 41–45.

———. *Commodities and Capabilities.* Hennipman Lecture, April 1982. Amsterdam and New York: North-Holland, 1985.

———. "Poor, Relatively Speaking." *Oxford Economic Papers,* 35 (1983) 153–169.

———, and S. Sengupta. "Malnutrition of Rural Children and the Sex-Bias." *Economic and Political Weekly,* 18 (1983).

Singer, H. W. "The Mechanics of Economic Development." *Indian Economic Review,*

1952. Reprinted in *The Economics of Underdevelopment,* A. N. Agarwala and A. P. Singh (eds.), London: Oxford University Press, 1958.

Sinha, R., and Drabek, A. G. (eds.). *The World Food Problem: Consensus and Conflict.* Oxford: Pergamon Press, 1978.

Spitz, P. "Silent Violence: Famine and Inequality." *International Social Science Journal,* 30 (1978).

Srinivasan, T. N. "Hunger: Defining It, Estimating Its Global Incidence and Alleviating It." Mimeographed, 1982. In *The Role of Markets in the World Food Economy,* D. Gale Johnson and E. Schuh (eds.). Boulder, Colo: Westview Press, 1983.

Streeten, P. *Development Perspectives.* London: Macmillan, 1981.

———, with S. J. Burki, Mahbub ul Haq, N. Hicks, and F. Stewart. *First Things First: Meeting Basic Needs in Developing Countries.* New York: Oxford University Press, 1981.

Sun Yefang. Article in *Jingji Guanli* (Economic Management), no. 2 (February 15, 1981). English translation in People's Republic of China, 1981.

Taylor, L. "The Misconstrued Crisis: Lester Brown and World Food." *World Development,* 3 (1975): 827–837.

Zhu Zhengzhi. Article in *Jingji Kexue,* no. 3, 1980.

CHAPTER 2

THE MISCONCEPTIONS
OF "DEVELOPMENT
ECONOMICS"

Deepak Lal

University College, London

Ideas have consequences. The body of thought that has evolved since World War II and is called "development economics" (to be distinguished from the orthodox "economics of developing countries") has, for good or ill, shaped policies for, as well as beliefs about, economic development in the Third World. Viewing the interwar experience of the world economy as evidence of the intellectual deficiencies of conventional economics (embodied, for instance, in the tradition of Marshall, Pigou, and Robertson) and seeking to emulate Keynes' iconoclasm (and hopefully renown), numerous economists set to work in the 1950s to devise a new unorthodox economics particularly suited to developing countries (most prominently, Nurkse, Myrdal, Rosenstein-Rodan, Balogh, Prebisch, and Singer). In the subsequent decades numerous specific theories and panaceas for solving the economic problems of the Third World have come to form the corpus of a "development economics." These include: the dual economy, labor surplus, low level equilibrium trap, unbalanced growth, vicious circles of poverty, big push industrialization, foreign exchange bottlenecks, unequal exchange, "dependencia," redistribution with growth, and a basic needs strategy—to name just the most influential in various times and climes.

Those who sought a new economics claimed that orthodox economics was (1) unrealistic because of its behavioral, technological, and institutional assumptions and (2) irrelevant because it was concerned primarily with the efficient allocation of given resources, and hence could deal neither with so-called dynamic aspects of growth nor with various ethical aspects of the alleviation of poverty or the distribution of income. The twists and turns that the unorthodox theories have subsequently taken may be

From *Finance and Development*, 22 (June 1985), pp. 10–13.

traced in four major areas: (1) the role of foreign trade and official or private capital flows in promoting economic development; (2) the role and appropriate form of industrialization in developing countries; (3) the relationship between the reduction of inequality, the alleviation of poverty, and the so-called different "strategies of development"; and (4) the role of the price mechanism in promoting development.

The last is, in fact, the major debate that in a sense subsumes most of the rest, and it is the main concern of this article; for the major thrust of much of "development economics" has been to justify massive government intervention through forms of direct control usually intended to supplant rather than to improve the functioning of, or supplement, the price mechanism. This is what I label the *dirigiste dogma,* which supports forms and areas of *dirigisme* well beyond those justifiable on orthodox economic grounds.

The empirical assumptions on which this unwarranted *dirigisme* was based have been repudiated by the experience of numerous countries in the postwar period. This article briefly reviews these central misconceptions of "development economics." References to the evidence as well as an elucidation of the arguments underlying the analysis (together with various qualifications) can be found in A. O. Hirschman's *Essays in Trespassing* (Cambridge, 1981).

DENIAL OF "ECONOMIC PRINCIPLE"

The most basic misconception underlying much of development economics has been a rejection (to varying extents) of the behavioral assumption that, either as producers or consumers, people, as Hicks said, "would act *economically;* when the opportunity of an advantage was presented to them, they would take it." Against these supposedly myopic and ignorant private agents (that is, individuals or groups of people), development economists have set some official entity (such as government, planners, or policymakers) which is both knowledgeable and compassionate. It can overcome the defects of private agents and compel them to raise their living standards through various *dirigiste* means.

Numerous empirical studies from different cultures and climates, however, show that uneducated private agents—be they peasants, rural-urban migrants, urban workers, private entrepreneurs, or housewives—act economically as producers and consumers. They respond to changes in relative prices much as neoclassical theory would predict. The "economic principle" is not unrealistic in the Third World; poor people may, in fact, be pushed even harder to seek their advantage than rich people.

Nor are the preferences of Third World workers peculiar in that for them too (no matter how poor), the cost of "sweat" rises the harder and longer they work. They do not have such peculiar preferences that when they become richer they will not also seek to increase their "leisure"—an assumption that underlies the view that there are large pools of surplus labor in developing countries that can be employed at a low or zero social opportunity cost. They are unlikely to be in "surplus" in any meaningful sense any more than their Western counterparts.

Nor are the institutional features of the Third World, such as their strange social and agrarian structures or their seemingly usurious informal credit systems, necessarily a handicap to growth. Recent applications of neoclassical theory show how, instead of inhibiting efficiency, these institutions—being second best adaptations to the risks and uncertainties inherent in the relevant economic environment—are likely to enhance efficiency.

Finally, the neoclassical assumption about the possibilities of substituting different inputs in production has not been found unrealistic. The degree to which inputs of different factors and commodities can be substituted in the national product is not much different in developed or developing countries. Changes in relative factor prices do influence the choice of technology at the micro level and the overall labor intensity of production in Third World economies.

MARKET VS. BUREAUCRATIC FAILURE

A second and major strand of the unwarranted *dirigisme* of much of development economics has been based on the intellectually valid arguments against laissez-faire. As is well known, laissez-faire will only provide optimal outcomes if perfect competition prevails; if there are universal markets for trading all commodities (including future "contingent" commodities, that is, commodities defined by future conditions, such as the impact of weather on energy prices); and if the distribution of income generated by the laissez-faire economy is considered equitable or, if not, could be made so through lump-sum taxes and subsidies. As elementary economics shows, the existence of externalities in production and consumption and increasing returns to scale in production, or either of them, will rule out the existence of a perfectly competitive utopia. While, clearly, universal markets for *all* (including contingent) commodities do not exist in the real world, to that extent market failure must be ubiquitous in the real world. This, even ignoring distributional considerations, provides a prima facie case for government intervention. But this in itself does not imply that any or most forms of government intervention will improve the outcomes of a necessarily imperfect market economy.

For the basic cause of market failure is the difficulty in establishing markets in commodities because of the costs of making transactions. These transaction costs are present in any market, or indeed any mode of resource allocation, and include the costs of excluding nonbuyers as well as those of acquiring and transmitting the relevant information about the demand and supply of a particular commodity to market participants. They drive a wedge, in effect, between the buyer's and the seller's price. The market for a particular good will cease to exist if the wedge is so large as to push the lowest price at which anyone is willing to sell above the highest price anyone is willing to pay. These transaction costs, however, are also involved in acquiring, processing, and transmitting the relevant information to design public policies, as well as in enforcing compliance. There may, consequently, be as many instances of bureaucratic as of market failure, making it impossible to attain a full welfare optimum. Hence, the best that can be expected in the real world of imperfect markets and imperfect bureaucrats is a second best. But judging between alternative second best outcomes involves a subtle application of second-best welfare economics, which provides no general rule to permit the deduction that, in a necessarily imperfect market economy, particular *dirigiste* policies will increase economic welfare. They may not; and they may even be worse than laissez-faire.

FORETELLING THE FUTURE

Behind most arguments for *dirigisme,* particularly those based on directly controlling quantities of goods demanded and supplied, is the implicit premise of an omniscient central authority. The authority must also be omnipotent (to prevent people from taking actions that controvert its diktat) and benevolent (to ensure it serves the common weal rather than its own), if it is to necessarily improve on the working of an imperfect market economy. While most people are willing to question the omnipotence or benevolence of governments, there is a considerable temptation to believe the latter have an omniscience that private agents know they themselves lack. This temptation is particularly large when it comes to foretelling the future.

Productive investment is the mainspring of growth. Nearly all investment involves giving hostages to fortune. Most investments yield their fruits over time and the expectations of investors at the time of investment may not be fulfilled. Planners attempting to direct investments and outputs have to take a view about future changes in prices, tastes, resources, and technology, much like private individuals. Even if the planners can acquire the necessary information about current tastes, technology, and resources in designing an investment program, they must also take a view about likely changes in the future demand and supply of myriad goods. Because in an uncertain world there can be no agreed or objective way of deciding whether a particular investment gamble is sounder than another, the planned outcomes will be better than those of a market system (in the sense of lower excess demand for or supply of different goods and services) only if the planners' forecasts are more accurate than the decentralized forecasts made by individual decision makers in a market economy. There is no reason to believe that planners, lacking perfect foresight, will be more successful at foretelling the future than individual investors.

Outcomes based on centralized forecasts may, indeed, turn out to be worse than those based on the decentralized forecasts of a large number of participants in a market economy, because imposing a single centralized forecast on the economy in an uncertain world is like putting all eggs in one basket. By contrast, the multitude of small bets, based on different forecasts, placed by a large number of decision makers in a market economy *may* be a sounder strategy. Also, bureaucrats, as opposed to private agents, are likely to take less care in placing their bets, as they do not stand to lose financially when they are wrong. This assumes, of course, that the government does not have better information about the future than private agents. If it does, it should obviously disseminate it, together with any of its own forecasts. On the whole, however, it may be best to leave private decision makers to take risks according to their own judgments.

This conclusion is strengthened by the fact, emphasized by Hayek, that most relevant information is likely to be held at the level of the individual firm and the household. A major role of the price mechanism in a market economy is to transmit this information to all interested parties. The "planning without prices" favored in practice by some planners attempts to supersede and suppress the price mechanism. It thereby throws sand into one of the most useful and relatively low-cost social mechanisms for transmitting information, as well as for coordinating the actions of large numbers of interdependent market participants. The strongest argument against centralized planning, therefore, is that, even though omniscient planners might forecast the future more accurately than myopic private agents, there is no reason to believe that ordinary government officials can do any better—and some reason to believe they may do much worse.

It has nevertheless been maintained that planners in the Third World can and should directly control the pattern of industrialization. Some have put their faith in mathematical programming models based on the use of input-output tables developed by Leontief. But, partly for the reasons just discussed, little reliance can be placed upon either the realism or the usefulness of these models for deciding which industries will be losers and which will be winners in the future. There are many important and essential tasks for governments to perform (see below), and this irrational *dirigisme* detracts from their main effort.

REDRESSING INEQUALITY AND POVERTY

Finally, egalitarianism is never far from the surface in most arguments supporting the *dirigiste dogma.* This is not surprising since there may be good theoretical reasons for government intervention, even in a perfectly functioning market economy, in order to promote a distribution of income desired on ethical grounds. Since the distribution resulting from market processes will depend upon the initial distribution of assets (land, capital, skills, and labor) of individuals and households, the desired distribution could, in principle, be attained either by redistributing the assets or by introducing lump-sum taxes and subsidies to achieve the desired result. If, however, lump-sum taxes and subsidies cannot be used in practice, the costs of distortion from using other fiscal devices (such as the income tax, which distorts the individual's choice between income and leisure) will have to be set against the benefits from any gain in equity. This is as much as theory can tell us, and it is fairly uncontroversial.

Problems arise because we lack a consensus about the ethical system for judging the desirability of a particular distribution of income. Even within Western ethical beliefs, the shallow utilitarianism that underlies many economists' views about the "just" distribution of income and assets is not universally accepted. The possibility that all the variegated peoples of the world are utilitarians is fairly remote. Yet the moral fervor underlying many economic prescriptions assumes there is already a world society with a common set of ethical beliefs that technical economists can take for granted and use to make judgments encompassing both the efficiency and equity components of economic welfare. But casual empiricism is enough to show that there is no such world society; nor is there a common view, shared by mankind, about the content of social justice.

There is, therefore, likely to be little agreement about either the content of distributive justice or whether we should seek to achieve it through some form of coercive redistribution of incomes and assets when this would infringe other moral ends, which are equally valued. By contrast, most moral codes accept the view that, to the extent feasible, it is desirable to alleviate abject, absolute poverty or destitution. That alleviating poverty is not synonymous with reducing the inequality of income, as some seem still to believe, can be seen by considering a country with the following two options. The first option leads to a rise in the incomes of all groups, including the poor, but to larger relative increases for the rich, and hence a worsening of the distribution of income. The second leads to no income growth for the poor but to a reduction in the income of the rich; thus the distribution of income improves but the extent of poverty remains unchanged. Those concerned with inequality would favor the second option; those with poverty the first. Thus, while the pursuit of efficient growth may worsen some inequality index, there is no evidence that it will increase poverty.

SURPLUS LABOR AND "TRICKLE DOWN"

As the major asset of the poor in most developing (as well as developed) countries is their labor time, increasing the demand for unskilled labor relative to its supply could be expected to be the major means of reducing poverty in the Third World. However, the shadows of Malthus and Marx have haunted development economics, particularly in its discussion of equity and the alleviation of poverty. One of the major assertions of development economics, preoccupied with "vicious circles" of poverty, was that the fruits of capitalist growth, with its reliance on the price mechanism, would not trickle down or spread to the poor. Various *dirigiste* arguments were then advocated to bring the poor into a growth process that would otherwise bypass them. The most influential, as well as the most famous, of the models of development advanced in the 1950s to chart the likely course of outputs and incomes in an overpopulated country or region was that of Sir Arthur Lewis. It made an assumption of surplus labor that, in a capitalist growth process, entailed no increase in the income of laborers until the surplus had been absorbed.

It has been shown that the assumptions required for even underemployed rural laborers to be "surplus," in Lewis' sense of their being available to industry at a constant wage, are very stringent, and implausible. It was necessary to assume that, with the departure to the towns of their relatives, those rural workers who remained would work harder for an unchanged wage. This implied that the preferences of rural workers between leisure and income are perverse, for workers will not usually work harder without being offered a higher wage. Recent empirical research into the shape of the supply curve of rural labor at different wages has found that—at least for India, the country supposedly containing vast pools of surplus labor—the curve is upward-sloping (and not flat, as the surplus labor theory presupposes). Thus, for a given labor supply, increases in the demand for labor time, in both the industrial and the rural sectors, can be satisfied only by paying higher wages.

The fruits of growth, even in India, will therefore trickle down, in the sense either of raising labor incomes, whenever the demand for labor time increases by more than its supply, or of preventing the fall in real wages and thus labor incomes, which would otherwise occur if the supply of labor time outstripped the increase in demand for it. More direct evidence about movements in the rural and industrial real wages of unskilled labor in developing countries for which data are available has shown that the standard economic presumption that real wages will rise as the demand for labor grows, relative to its supply, is as valid for the Third World as for the First.

ADMINISTRATIVE CAPACITIES

It is in the political and administrative aspects of *dirigisme* that powerful practical arguments can be advanced against the *dirigiste dogma.* The political and administrative assumptions underlying the feasibility of various forms of *dirigisme* derive from those of modern welfare states in the West. These, in turn, reflect the values of the eighteenth-century Enlightenment. It has taken nearly two centuries of political evolution for those values to be internalized and reflected (however imperfectly) in the political and administrative institutions of Western societies. In the Third World, an acceptance of the same values is at best confined to a small class of Westernized intellectuals. Despite their trappings of modernity, many developing countries are closer in their official workings to the inefficient nation states of seventeenth- or eighteenth-century Europe. It is instructive to recall that Keynes, whom so many *dirigistes* invoke as a founding father of their faith, noted in *The End of Laissez-Faire:*

> But above all, the ineptitude of public administrators strongly prejudiced the practical man in favor of *laissez-faire*—a sentiment which has by no means disappeared. Almost everything which the State did in the 18th century in excess of its minimum functions was, or seemed, injurious or unsuccessful.

It is in this context that anyone familiar with the actual administration and implementation of policies in many Third World countries, and not blinkered by the *dirigiste dogma,* should find the oft-neglected work, *The Wealth of Nations,* both so relevant and so modern.

For in most of our modern-day equivalents of the inefficient eighteenth-century state, not even the minimum governmental functions required for economic progress are always fulfilled. These include above all providing public goods of which law and order and a sound money remain paramount, and an economic environment where individual thrift, productivity, and enterprise is cherished and not thwarted. There are numerous essential tasks for *all* governments to perform. One of the most important is to establish and maintain the country's infrastructure, much of which requires large, indivisible lumps of capital before any output can be produced. Since the services provided also frequently have the characteristics of public goods, natural monopolies would emerge if they were privately produced. Some form of government regulation would be required to ensure that services were provided in adequate quantities at prices that reflected their real resource costs. Government intervention is therefore necessary. And, given the costs of regulation in terms of acquiring the relevant information, it may be second best to supply the infrastructure services publicly.

These factors justify one of the most important roles for government in the development process. It can be argued that the very large increase in infrastructure investment, coupled with higher savings rates, provides the major explanation of the marked expansion in the economic growth rates of most Third World countries during the postwar period, compared with both their own previous performance and that of today's developed countries during their emergence from underdevelopment.

Yet the *dirigistes* have been urging many additional tasks on Third World governments that go well beyond what Keynes, in the work quoted above, considered to be a sensible agenda for *mid-twentieth-century* Western polities:

> the most important *Agenda* of the State relate not to those activities which private individuals are already fulfilling, but to those functions which fall outside the sphere of the individual, to those decisions which are made by no one if the State does not make them. The important thing for governments is not to do things which individuals are doing already, and to do them a little better or a little worse; but to do those things which at present are not done at all.

From the experience of a large number of developing countries in the postwar period, it would be a fair professional judgment that most of the more serious distortions are due not to the inherent imperfections of the market mechanism but to irrational government interventions, of which foreign trade controls, industrial licensing, various forms of price controls, and means of inflationary financing of fiscal deficits are the most important. In seeking to improve upon the outcomes of an imperfect market economy, the *dirigisme* to which numerous development economists have lent intellectual support has led to policy-induced distortions that are more serious than, and indeed compound, the supposed distortions of the market economy they were designed to cure. It is these lessons from accumulated experience over the last three decades that have undermined development economics, so that its demise may now be conducive to the health of both the economics and economies of developing countries.

CHAPTER 3

CONVENTIONAL FOOLISHNESS AND OVERALL IGNORANCE: CURRENT APPROACHES TO GLOBAL TRANSFORMATION AND DEVELOPMENT

G. K. Helleiner

University of Toronto

INTRODUCTION

As I sat down to prepare some notes for this occasion, I began to realize that it is a far easier matter to give the summary paper at the end of a conference than it is to give a so-called keynote address at its beginning. At the end of a meeting, one is invariably stimulated by new ideas, newly aware of interconnections between old ones, and there are always lots of fresh papers and outrageous discussants' remarks from which one can draw quotations. A keynote speaker has particular problems when he is not altogether clear as to the precise meaning of the prescribed conference theme; and they become even greater if, upon running through the conference program, he discovers only limited overlap between the topics of the papers and the announced overall theme. I am therefore going to take what some of you will probably see as excessive liberties with my assignment.

Although some think we have come quite a long way, I believe that historians are likely to be impressed more by our continuing foolishness and ignorance than by our progress during the Post-Second-War period. Foolishness and ignorance are no doubt quite evenly spread among our various disciplines; but I have a comparative advantage in those of economics. Moreover, most influential, if not necessarily most helpful, in recent policymaking and writing on development in recent decades, most people think, have been those in my own profession of economics. I therefore shall concentrate my fire upon economics. I hope that colleagues in other disciplines may be encouraged to undertake parallel curmudgeonly activities in their own areas of comparative expertise.

From *Canadian Journal of Development Studies*, 10, 1 (1990), pp. 107–120.

I want to speak, then, of some currently conventional approaches in development economics and policymaking, and the frequent foolishness or ignorance that underlies them. I am not sure whether what I am about to say truly constitutes a keynote address, as billed in the program. Let me, in any case, tell you what I intend to do. That way, those who are unhappy with all or parts of my program can more effectively plan their departure. In the first half of my remarks, I intend to deliver myself of some general blasts about some current problems of "structural adjustment." These may be seen as very unconventional to some, but are, by now, fairly conventional for me and, I know, for some of my friends here. I shall include in this section a plea for greater terminological clarity concerning the major subject of our deliberations here. These comments probably amount, more or less, to what was expected of me. The second half of my time will be devoted to personal ruminations about some longer-term development issues which are newer to me. They include a reconsideration of our most fundamental measuring-sticks in development studies, and the relevance of recent experiences and new perceptions to some very old measurement and development debates. On these matters, again, I shall be appealing primarily to the economists and statisticians among us; but I hope that others who are often much affected by what economists are thinking or doing in developing countries may also find these reflections interesting, if only as further evidence of the limitations of the economics profession.

I. IMMEDIATE ISSUES: STRUCTURAL ADJUSTMENT

The announced theme for this conference is "*Global* Transformation and Development." The program's list of papers, however, suggests that, to the extent that the papers relate to the theme at all, authors are primarily concerned with *national* "restructuring" or "structural adjustment"—which certainly sounds a lot less ambitious.

International aid and financial communities are also abuzz with discussions of developing countries' "adjustment" at the national level. That is reason enough for independent academics to try to shed light on these issues. Evidently, the "restructuring" and "structural adjustment" now being discussed is *not* the same as the "structural change" that development analysts of my generation spoke so much of in the 1950s and 1960s. What we had in mind in discussion of this sometimes somewhat fuzzy concept related to the production structure, institutions, and other prerequisites of sustained economic growth. Industrialization and/or the deployment of more productive technology were seen as central to structural change and what Kuznets called "modern economic growth" (1966).

Is there today an agreed meaning of "structural adjustment" in the developing countries? I know what I mean by it. My meaning relates purely to external balance of payments problems and the necessity of restructuring production toward exports and import substitutes in response to a worsening prospect of external imbalance. Is that what the U.S. government or the World Bank typically mean? I am afraid not. When they use the term they have in mind across-the-board economic "liberalization" in the sense of an increased role for markets and a reduced role for the state, and increased external "openness," both to trade and to capital flows and other inputs. They thereby introduce further highly controversial and political elements to policy debates that originated purely in short- to medium-term balance of payments crisis. The developing countries originated the logic of "growth-oriented adjustment" to solve balance of payments and debt difficulties, long before U.S. Treasury Secretary James Baker, and thereafter everyone else, began to speak of it in late 1985. But when they spoke of the need for growth, they, unlike Baker and the World Bank, attached no controversial excess "liberalization" baggage to it. No doubt some of the authors of the national restructuring or adjustment papers for this conference use these terms in ways that accord neither with my balance of payments-oriented version nor with the Washington market-oriented version.

Still more would view conflict on conceptions of the "*global* transformation" of our conference title. Does it relate to the distribution of global assets, income, and power? to Brundtland style environmental and sustainability objectives? to UNIDO objectives for the relocation of global industrial activity? to the implications of the massive technical innovations in bioengineering, electronics, transport, and information systems, among others? to the sexual revolution, still hardly started at the global level? Each of these have been by themselves subject enough for many conferences.

I cannot refrain from the comment that, at the level of global transformation, I can see no greater current foolishness than that of conventional governmental approaches to the Third World's debt crisis. Human suffering is prolonged and the restoration of normal growth processes delayed by continuing official resistance to forgiving a penny of Paris Club debt (official debt incurred primarily in connection with our export promotion) or assisting in the conversion to more appropriate levels and terms of the Third World's commercial debt. It is not true that writing down the debt will do appreciable harm to the international financial system *or* that it will put an end to future financial flows to developing countries *or* that everything will turn out for the best if governments simply stand aside and wait for matters to resolve themselves. On the contrary, resolute intergovernmental action to deal with the terribly damaging "overhang" of Third World debt would do *far* more for human welfare—both in rich countries and in poor—than the bilateral trade agreements that currently so preoccupy our leaders. If all goes according to plan, according to the best estimates of the Economic Council of Canada, the U.S.-Canadian free trade agreement will raise Canadian GNP by 2 1/2% by 1998 (Economic Council, 1988). What a devastating reflection on our provincialism and myopia is this figure, and the intensity of governmental efforts and public debate about the agreement, when set beside the enormity of the Third World's debt crisis, and its implications, not least for Canada itself.

Most of the papers at this conference, as I have said, however, appear to relate to *national* "adjustment" or "restructuring" issues. Let us seek terminological clarity at least at that level. If we cannot agree as to a common usage of the "structural adjustment" terminology in our analyses—and, frankly, I think we ought to try hard, at least in scientific discourse, to do so—let us all agree, in our discussions here, to begin by defining our terms. Only then can we be sure, in what has become a very confused and heated debate, what it is we are agreeing or disagreeing about.

Conventional Washington advice notwithstanding, there is room for considerable political and professional disagreement on such matters as:

1 The basic objectives of development including such "political" and "ideological" matters as the role of the state and income distribution
2 The efficacy of alternative strategies and policy instruments in securing overall growth and development
3 The appropriate pace and sequencing of policy reforms, and, in particular, their technical and political sustainability

Needless to say, there is also room for argument concerning the appropriate degree of external intrusion into matters of domestic policy.

The World Bank, the principal repository of today's conventional wisdom in development strategy, states its primary emphasis as follows:

1 Mobilization of domestic resources through fiscal, monetary, and credit policies (including interest rates)
2 Improving efficiency of allocation and resource use in the public sector (including rationalization and divestiture of public enterprises)
3 Trade regime reforms
4 Other pricing reforms
5 "Institutional reforms supportive of adjustment with growth" (Michalopolous, 1987, p. 39)

In the short run, this translates into monetary and fiscal orthodoxy, appropriate real exchange rates, positive real interest rates, and liberal approaches on external account. As far as longer-term development strategy is concerned, the Bank urges: export expansion and eventual overall outward orientation, in the capital as well as current account; the liberalization of import barriers and an approach toward unified import incentives; and maximum reliance upon markets rather than government ownership or direction in the domestic economy. The prime emphasis is on price incentives and "getting the prices right," and the underlying presumption is that, even in a world of pervasive imperfections, markets can normally be trusted to achieve that objective better than governments. Even in the world of the second-best, its approach is consistently to liberalize that which can be liberalized.

My own foremost instinct is to resist generalizations as to the nature of desirable change at the national, regional, community, or even family level. In a policy environment such as that which today pervades the capitals of the Western world, this is not nearly as trite a proposition as it may sound. Nor, in a world of intensified donor conditionality and financially desperate Third World governments is it as innocuous in its implications as it may appear. A struggle is necessary today to allow a variety of developmental approaches and aspirations. The only weapon with which we can fight effectively is hard evidence that challenges the simplistic nostrums of the fundamentalists of economic, political, and other doctrines.

I thus see foolishness in overideological approaches to the resolution of the growth difficulties of Latin American and African countries, suggesting that reduction of the role of government and raising that of the magical marketplace will achieve what decades of previous effort have not. Mercifully, the peaks of that kind of foolishness have now probably been passed, with the retreat perhaps sped by its new association not only, as before, with "voodoo economics" but also with astrology.

Those who have dominated recent decision making in Washington also argue that the credibility and therefore the sustainability of policy reform, especially in other people's countries, is enhanced by strong action at the outset. Smaller, more gradual, changes are likely, in this view, to be easily rolled back and indicate a lack of governmental commitment. This is *still* the conventional Washington wisdom of developing country adjustment.

It can obviously equally be argued that targets and policy changes that are modest, but firm and realistic, are likely to be more credible and sustainable than large changes that are, to a degree, "leaps into the unknown." Attempts at "forced marches" toward large-scale policy change surely strain governmental capacity and strengthen the impression, dangerous in local politics, that the policy program is externally imposed rather than internally generated.

Washington ambitions for the Bank in respect of the *breadth* of coverage of their recommended policy package are no less controversial. It is difficult to disagree with the assessment by Feinberg (1986), recently quoted with approval by Mahmadou Touré of Senegal: "A long list of requirements either holds an entire programme hostage to a secondary issue or is open to highly subjective assessment" (Touré, 1987; p. 505). Moreover, when one Bank mission after another descends with detailed piecemeal recommendations upon a country (Ghana has been receiving over forty such missions per year recently), there is bound to be a certain amount of confusion, inconsistency, and, of course, recipient annoyance. The borrowing government's absorptive capacity for external advice is limited, maintenance of a domestic consensus on policy change is difficult, and it is almost certainly counterproductive to "overload the political circuits" (Sachs, 1987, p. 294).

Let me address some of the specifics of the issues in dispute.

A.   Distribution and Poverty Objectives

In the new emphasis on improved policies for overall efficiency, purveyors of the conventional wisdom have noticeably downgraded their previous concern for equity and the alleviation of poverty. The high social costs of global slowdown and the availability of alternative policies for overcoming some of them have now been demonstrated (Cornia et al., 1987). Only recently, however, has more than lip service been paid in Washington to the social impact of adjustment programs, and even now serious policy attention to these issues is limited to a relatively few countries. Difficulties in agreeing upon appropriate approaches and finding reliable data can explain some of the failures in this area; but, if there had been more will, more progress would undoubtedly have been made. At a minimum, the distributional implications of agreed programs should be understood. It has even been persuasively argued that at least one of the reasons why Korea, Taiwan, and Japan could be so effective in the efficiency-oriented restructuring that led them into their successful industrial export experience was that they had *previously* achieved reasonable equity in income distribution through major land reforms and other measures (Sachs, 1987, pp. 299–302 and 321–2).

B.   Prices, Markets, and Government

The World Bank and IMF are committed by their articles of agreement to liberal, market-oriented approaches to international economic affairs. Direct controls over foreign exchange earnings and expenditures are explicitly forbidden by the IMF except in stipulated circumstances (which include authorization for capital controls), and the World Bank is mandated to encourage and rely upon private capital flows to the maximum degree possible. Appropriate pricing—particularly in respect of the exchange rate—and incentives for individual and corporate enterprise are important elements in development policy. But there are other important elements as well. Both the IMF and the Bank were created to overcome "market failures," and their very existence is testimony to the postwar founding states' recognition of the important role to be played by government in pursuit of universally agreed social goals. It is therefore somewhat surprising to find these institutions emphasizing the universal virtues of the market in the developing countries to the degree to which they have recently done. The role of the state in development processes *has* at times been oversold and governments *have* frequently been overambitious and/or incompetent. But the "market fundamentalism" of much of Washington's recent advice cannot have been based upon a sophisticated understanding of political and economic requirements for development, or experience in varieties of "successful" countries.

There can certainly be wide agreement that governments should be selective in their activities and, where possible, more efficient. Divestment of public enterprises is undoubtedly appropriate in many cases; as a universal prescription, however, it is of dubious merit. Market imperfections and failures, distributional and "noneconomic" objectives, and political pressures of various kinds will continue to generate significant government interventions in developing countries' economies. The political and economic efficacy of markets and governments varies across countries and in individual countries over time. The complexities in this realm are dramatically illustrated by the fact that two articles were recently published, within months of one another, in leading U.S. journals, presenting econometric findings that were diametrically opposed: one showed that the size of government in GNP was associated with more rapid growth (Ram, 1986), the other that it was associated with slower growth (Landau, 1986). Policy generalizations based on ideologically rooted "priors" can only be viewed with skepticism.

The very meaning of the term "liberalization" can be ambiguous. It may refer either to "getting prices right" or to reduction in the degree of governmental intervention; the two are not synonymous, since the former may be achieved, as to some degree in Korea, with an activist state no less than via greater laissez-faire. "Liberalization" of either kind is possible, and may be appropriate in a variety of different spheres.

C.   Import Liberalization

The debate over the appropriate nature, degree, and timing of *trade* liberalization is probably the most active. World Bank missions typically recommend the earliest and fullest possible import liberalization, beginning with the replacement of quantitative import restrictions by tariffs, thereby creating both government revenue and greater transparency of incentives, and thereafter reduction in the levels and dispersion of tariffs. Gradualist approaches have generally been favoured by the more pragmatically oriented in the liberal camp and many have noted the importance of favourable macro-economic conditions (capital inflow, terms of trade, weather, etc.) in the timing of successful major policy changes. The World Bank itself has recently argued:

> The more ambitious and long-lasting liberalizations—in Portugal, Greece, Spain, Israel, Chile and Turkey—all started with macroeconomic stabilization. The countries which have tried to liberalize trade in the midst of macroeconomic crisis have failed . . . (World Bank, *WDR*, 1987, p. 109).

The link between export expansion and import liberalization is also important, and one that remains controversial. Advocates of "shock" treatment for the trade regime—as well as other reforms—are at present in the ascendancy in Washington. A leading World Bank economist recently put the case:

> Experience . . . suggests that future reforms ensure that export expansion programs be accompanied by import liberalization. . . . Experience . . . does *not* in our view suggest that import liberalization should be undertaken only after export reforms have increased the supply of foreign exchange (Michalopoulos, 1987, p. 45).

But this is a difficult case to make in terms of empirical evidence. The "lessons" from East Asian experience in respect of the transition from stabilization to liberalization, if they are transferable at all, are, to the contrary, the following:

1 There is likely to be a long time interval between stabilization and successful exporting or liberalization effort

2 Substantial external financial assistance is likely to be an essential element in successful transition

3 Import liberalization is likely to follow successful exporting with a fairly long time lag, and is *not* an essential or typical part of successful export promotion efforts

4 The public sector is likely to play an important role in the shift into successful industrial exporting (Sachs, 1987, pp. 303–10)

Beyond eventual—not necessarily immediate—"tarification" of quantitative restrictions, on which most can agree, further efforts toward "liberalization" and laissez-faire are considerably more controversial. There exist respectable orthodox arguments for nonuniform incentive structures as "second-best" policies for a "second-best" world. Modern trade theory has knocked the struts from under the conventional arguments for the uniformity of treatment that free trade achieves. Krugman has recently put a new and more theoretically sophisticated case for liberal (or free) trade. Abandoning the traditional comparative advantage arguments based upon the assumption of efficient markets, he posits instead a world in which the sophisticated trade (and other) interventions, for which "the new trade theories" call, are likely to be extremely informationally demanding, difficult to implement, low in their returns, and subject to hijacking by special interests. *Simple* policy rules, he argues, are best "in a world whose politics are as imperfect as its markets" (1987, p. 143). This stands previously conventional approaches on their head. Whereas political influences used to be blamed for the inability of governments to pursue "rational" free trade policies, now political factors are deployed to defend free trade policies against the new, economic arguments for sophisticated intervention. But his advocacy of simple policy rules would permit lots of alternatives short of overall free trade, including, say, across-the-board industrial protection, a strictly limited number of further infant industry subsidies, and across-the-board incentives for nontraditional exports.

D. Export Expansion

No one quarrels with the aspiration of expanding exports from foreign exchange constrained economies. The prospect of all of the developing countries simultaneously expanding export volume in similar products, whether primary or manufactured, however, must raise some concerns. Primary product prices are likely to suffer and protectionist barriers to manufactures to increase in consequence of concerted efforts at export growth. Even Bhagwati, among the most enthusiastic and influential of trade liberalizers, although he believes modern "export pessimism" to be unjustified, acknowledges that the international economic environment may be an important determinant of the efficacy of outward-oriented policies (1987, pp. 260 and 269–83).

The keys to successful expansion of exports are realistic exchange rates and sustained governmental support, not import liberalization and laissez-faire. It is noteworthy that the export promotion policies of Korea were successfully undertaken by a thoroughly *dirigiste* government simultaneously employing tight import controls and a tightly regulated capital market. "The Asian experience . . . suggest(s) . . . that successful development might be helped as much by raising the quality of public sector management as by privatizing public enterprises or liberalizing markets" (Sachs, 1987, p. 294).

The efficacy of export subsidies as an important weapon of trade policy also emerges as an important area for debate. Granting the greater administrative ease of currency devaluation for the purpose of rectifying antiexport bias, there may nonetheless be an important case for targeted/selective export subsidies for infant industry export promotion. Such selective export promotion was an important element in Korean penetration of overseas markets for its manufactured exports (Westphal, 1981). WIDER research on alternative stabilization programs has also noted the efficacy of targeted export subsidies as an important short-term stabilization policy instrument (Taylor, 1987).

E. Openness to External Private Capital

Controls over external private portfolio capital flows—whether inward or outward—are fairly universally seen as desirable in low-income countries. Experimentation with financial openness in the Southern Cone of Latin America had generally unhappy consequences. Policies toward direct foreign investment remain, however, a matter of some controversy. Increased incentives and receptivity to foreign investors (including the much-touted "debt-equity swaps") may simply generate quasi-rent for them if, as much of the recent evidence suggests, their investment decisions are based primarily on more fundamental and long-run factors (Moran, 1986). In recent years direct investment in developing countries, which was always highly concentrated in the same countries that attracted commercial bank lending, dropped just as far and as fast as that lending; and it is unlikely to resume until the overall economic outlook in these countries improves. Quite apart from the sensitivities of many countries regarding foreign ownership and control of domestic industries, and however desirable increased equity or equity-like finance might be, the elasticity of response by direct foreign investors to improved investment incentives in developing countries is, for the present, likely to be low.

F.   Financial Liberalization and Interest Rates

The role of interest rates in developing countries remains controversial. Increased real rates may improve the allocative efficiency of investment, reduce capital flight, and even attract savings from abroad in economies with relatively developed financial markets. The IMF's own research department concludes, however, that "despite the amount of research expended on the interest responsiveness of savings in general, and in developing countries in particular, it is still uncertain whether an increase in interest rates will, on balance, raise the savings rate" (Khan and Knight, 1985, p. 14).

Differences in behavioural responses in this sphere appear to be linked in a predictable fashion to the stage of financial development of different areas or countries. Because of capital market imperfections (severe constraints on liquidity and borrowing by private firms and individuals), private consumption and savings do not respond as much to real interest rate changes in low-income countries as in higher-income ones. A recent IMF study's results imply that "the effective mobilization of domestic savings through changes in savings incentives is likely to require changes in the real interest rates, which, given the existing constraints, may prove unfeasible, especially in low-income developing countries" (Rossi, 1988, p. 126).

There also remains some uncertainty as to the implications of segmented and imperfect capital markets. Conventional analysis has often assumed away the extensive network of informal (or curb) credit markets. Yet careful modelling of real/financial interactions in Korea, allowing for the distinction between "curb" and regulated financial markets there, generated "unconventional" results from orthodox monetary and interest rate policies: higher (regulated) interest rates and monetary restraint led, in combination, to a serious slowdown in investment and growth, the effects of which exceeded any positive effects for household savings (Van Wijnbergen, 1983).

Nor are the advantages of financial liberalization for overcoming "financial repression" unambiguously favourable. Painful experience with overenthusiastic financial liberalization in the Southern Cone has bred a new respect for governmental supervision and control of the domestic financial system, and caution in respect of external capital market "opening" (Diaz-Alejandro, 1985).

II.   LONGER-TERM ISSUES: MEASUREMENT AND SUSTAINABILITY

Let me use the rest of my time to address some longer-term issues in development economics, and development studies more generally, that have recently been emerging or *re*emerging in policy discussions.

The first is one to which that late and great curmudgeon in development economics, Dudley Seers, directed major attention in the late 1960s and early 1970s: "What," he asked in 1972, "are we trying to measure?" His question, following earlier reflections on the meaning of "development," related to overall measures of economic development, and it was part of an effort that some described at the time as "dethroning GNP" (Seers, 1969, 1972). Twenty years later, I am not sure that there has been a satisfactory answer. And yet the 1980s have brought terrible new urgency to the basic question he asked.

Seers' main concern was with the proper consideration of poverty, unemployment, and equality in the measurement of overall development. Subsequent thinking generated suggestions for different ways of calculating overall economic growth rates—allowing equal weight for the income growth of each individual (instead of recording each extra dollar of total income as equal, regardless of who earns or receives it, as current GNP estimation procedures require), or even introducing "poverty weights" so as to assign higher weight to increases in the income of those at the bottom end of the income distribution than to those of the more fortunate at higher levels. These suggested alterations of estimating procedures were, in my judgment, good ideas. With the reduced fashion for distributional concern in the major industrialised countries in the 1980s, they have been more or less forgotten. But they remain good ideas. The renewed interest and debate in the latter half of the 1980s over the poverty and distributional implications of stabilization and adjustment programs—"adjustment with a human face"—provides an opportunity for their resurrection. The Ghanaian economy is said to be growing again; yet the suffering of the poorest and most vulnerable continues, and donors construct a PAMSCAD ("Program to Mitigate the Social Consequences of Adjustment"). And the poverty impact of the recession of the early 1980s, continued balance of payments and debt crises in subsequent years, and declining net international resource transfers (negative 6–7% of GDP in Latin America in recent years) is only now being fully understood. I therefore suggest a conscious effort, once again, to introduce distributional components into our commonest measures of economic performance, both at the national and the global level. (At the global level, the relatively good performance of poor and populous China and India may make global poverty-sensitive aggregate performance indicators for the 1980s look *better* than many think.)

The treatment of poverty and income distribution is important, but it is not the only aggregative measurement problem. And many others, of course, have addressed these and other measurement issues. The UN Research Institute for Social Development, for instance, developed a whole set of socioeconomic indicators of development in the 1960s (UNRISD, 1970). Adelman and Morris (1967) also made early efforts to incorporate noneconomic variables into overall measures of development. Another Morris fixed on only three indicators—infant mortality, literacy, and life expectancy—and proclaimed his "physical quality of life" (PQLI) index (1978), which was effectively popularised by Washington's Overseas Development Council. And these few references barely scratch the surface of the relevant literature. (Baster, 1972, is a good reference to the early literature on development indicators.)

On one aspect of the development question the social scientists most concerned with the measurement of development have, until very recently, had *very* little to say.

And the time has come for them to say a little more. It has been left to physical scientists, environmentalists, and ecologists to worry about "sustainability." The Brundtland Commission Report and other events have forced many more of us to devote attention to this hitherto relatively neglected dimension of development. Before Brundtland, increasing concern was expressed in many quarters about the longer-run implications of short-term survival strategies in ecologically fragile parts of the developing world, notably in drought-prone Africa. The short-term cutbacks necessitated by the trauma of the 1980s in most of sub-Saharan Africa and Latin America intensified these concerns. What would be the longer-run consequences of failure to maintain current social infrastructure—roads, buildings, schools, hospitals, etc.—not to speak of directly productive capital stock? And, even more frightening, what would be the longer-run consequence of failure to provide minimal nutrition for pregnant women and children in their crucial early years? Brundtland's concern for the environment expands these questions to the infinitely broader realm of planetary equilibrium.

That any of these "sustainability" issues should be seen as "new" to measurement-minded social scientists is, on the face of it, very odd. In the first place, those who specialize in national income accounting describe their favourite summary indicator as *Gross* National Product for a reason. The GNP is, conceptually, a measure that abstracts from longer-run consequences of current economic activities in that those who estimate it *consciously* do *not* deduct the costs of maintaining the current physical capital stock, let alone the human capital stock. *No* account is taken, that is to say, of "depreciation." No self-respecting private company or homeowner would draw conclusions as to successful performance without taking depreciation into account. Indeed our tax laws frequently invite us to err on the conservative side when doing so. Why do we not then take depreciation into account and record the *net* national product in our growth statistics and international comparisons? The conventional and simple answer is that it is far too difficult. It is worth noting that the same answer is usually offered whenever questions are asked about improved measurement of the distribution of income within nations, the same nations that routinely measure their GNP on a quarterly basis.

There can be little doubt that the data on depreciation *are* at present very weak. To generate such data would, certainly, in our present state of knowledge, require large numbers of fairly arbitrary assumptions. But anyone with more than superficial knowledge of the methodology of national income accounting knows that such assumptions and conventions abound already. Thirty years ago Kuznets asked, for instance, whether it would not be better to *deduct* such expenditures as commuter transport, police services, and national defence from the national product (gross or net) rather than adding them in. (Among other places he discusses such arbitrary choices in measurement in his masterful *Modern Economic Growth,* pp. 20–26.) The treatment of household services and a host of other arbitrarily treated items also continue to delight first year economics students around the world. In the early 1950s, the first national income estimates for Nigeria attempted to recognize some purported elements of its culture by estimating the annual number of marriages, multiplying them by the average bride price, and adding the product to the GNP—thereby treating women, for GNP purposes, as consumer durables (Prest and Stewart, 1953). Surely the question must be, again, "what are we trying to measure?"

Secondly, and probably ultimately more important, how we measure development, and, particularly, in the current context, how we treat depreciation, is profoundly based upon our value judgments. Our conventional GNP measure reduces all goods and services to a common money numeraire, established by using market prices (or the nearest possible equivalent). But relative prices are themselves highly variable across countries and over time; and they are also dependent, in part, on government policy. In the discussions over the appropriate treatment of distributional considerations it is generally recognized that prices will themselves alter when income distribution changes; a more equitable distribution will raise the relative price of food and lower that of Cadillacs, other things being equal in the short to medium term. The employment of market prices thus carries with it the implicit value judgment not only that prices are appropriate measures of social "value," but also that the current distribution of income is acceptable, both fairly strong and arbitrary assumptions.

Our twentieth-century market-oriented materialist culture is obviously not the only conceivable way in which human beings may organize themselves or pursue their own welfare. Some social scientists—evidently not usually economists—have repeatedly called attention to these value differences over the years. In the traditional culture of many North American native peoples, for instance, there is a conception of man-in-nature and the need for "sustainability" which appears fundamentally at variance with traditional economistic approaches. Land and resources, in some cultures, are to be left in the state in which they are found. The interests of future generations—of the rest of nature as well as of humanity—are to be respected as a matter of *highest* priority. It is not therefore possible to rationalize the "mining" of the environment via an interest rate at which the interests of future generations are discounted to the present. In effect, the *first* claim upon current income is the need to make up for depreciation. (More about the interest rate below.)

It seems to me that our new concern for "sustainability" requires that we look again at the measurement of depreciation and net national product (and net capital formation) (Bartelmus, 1987). If reputable scientists believe that we are now running down our assets—polluting the water and atmosphere, using up nonrenewable resources, reducing forest cover to a degree that engenders soil erosion and desertification—we should surely be accounting for it in our measures of developmental performance. It seems particularly perverse to record as extra income (gross) the expenditures on the inputs we devote to trying to offset some of these effects, as our current conventions require us to do. When depreciation is fully accounted for—and deducted from our gross measures of production—we are likely to find ourselves, if I read the Brundtland Commission correctly, doing much less well than we thought, particularly so in many of the developing countries. The high measured growth rates of the 1960s may have been, to a significant degree, illusory and the current setbacks in sub-Saharan Africa and Latin America are probably much more serious than previously thought.

Our new knowledge of the longer-run implications of nutritional deficiency will, I am afraid, generate even more depressing conclusions. When we *both* treat depreciation appropriately *and* take better account of the distribution of net income gains, we are likely to find the developing world, overall, to have been barely holding its own in the best cases, and moving significantly backward in all too many others. Quite possibly, we shall be seen to be moving backward at the global level as well.

The world's apparent new concern for sustainability and the environment raises further questions for traditional techniques of economic analysis, particularly development project analysis. The context in which development economists previously commonly encountered the notion of "sustainable" economic growth, ironically, was in that of traditional IMF programs. Conservative fiscal and monetary policies are the only ones, the IMF usually intones, that are "sustainable." The government of Peru in recent years, for instance, over IMF opposition, expanded demand (and reduced its external debt service payments), thereby immediately achieving rapid growth in employment and income. But few expected these gains to last. "Sustainability" is a central element in IMF objectives for the member countries it advises.

"Sustainability" *is* basically a conservative concept. And environmentalists, like the IMF, have long been seen by policymakers and thinkers in the developing countries as too cautious and insensitive to human development imperatives. Developmentalists and politicians, in developing countries, have often been prepared to take more risks. And rationales have been constructed for the realization of such gains as can be realised in the short run, much more generally, on the view that the long run is, after all, only a series of short runs. If the World Bank now adds environmental objectives and sustainability to its list of conditions on its loans, will this necessarily be good for human welfare in the short run in the developing countries?

An interesting paper in a recent issue of *World Development* notes that economists, in particular, have devoted relatively little attention to "sustainability." They are inherently suspicious of absolute objectives—specializing as they do in the logic of trade-offs. In particular, their benefit-cost methodology does not offer any premium for policies or projects that provide a "sustainable" income as opposed to those creating high income in the early years and less thereafter. "Economic principles tend to suggest that the 'mining,' depletion, or elimination of living resources is justifiable from an economic point of view and that unsustainable productive activities may be economically rational" (Tisdell, 1988, p. 381). The reason for this is that economic methodology assesses the value of contributions to future income (whether positive or negative) by discounting them to the present at some agreed (national) interest rate that is intended to represent the "social rate of discount." There has been no shortage of discussions of the selection of an appropriate rate for discounting the future. Yet, though it is crucially important to economic decision making, we do not have a good "fix" on what it should be in different times and places. (In practice, development agencies frequently just lick a finger, hold it to the wind, and declare it to be 10%.)

At a discount (interest) rate of 10%, the present value of a dollar's worth of costs incurred thirty years from now is less than 6¢. Who will act in anticipation of effects thirty years hence when they use such a calculus of benefits and costs? Who will worry about effects that are sixty years away? And how many years does it take to obtain returns from the crucial environmental investments upon which the future viability may depend? When investments at last appear profitable will it already be too late? These are matters of development policy with which the World Bank, newly concerned, and the research community have scarcely begun to wrestle. (See Leslie, 1987, for a forester's perspective on these issues.)

In a world increasingly concerned with the longer-term consequences of current decisions and with the possibility of "irreversibilities" and "threshold effects" in the environment, this methodology—with its implied discounting of the future at rates that are in dispute but are nowhere seen as zero—may be, at least for some purposes, profoundly wrong. Societies making their decisions on the basis of maintaining resources for their children in the same form in which they were received, and implicitly using zero rates of discounting the future, however "economically irrational," may be those that survive. It is noteworthy that Marxist economic practices have traditionally been ridiculed because of their inability to factor in this cost of capital, or "waiting," in their project analysis. Indeed so have early Christian and Islamic doctrines.

The ethics of intergenerational transfer are even more dubious than the economics of intertemporal comparisons. As the Brundtland Commission puts it, there may be "profits on the balance sheets of our generation, but our children will inherit the losses. We borrow environmental capital from future generations with no intention or prospect of repaying. . . . We act as we do because we can get away with it; future generations do not vote; they have no political or financial power; they cannot challenge our decisions" (p. 8). Rawls also noted the fundamental justice issue raised by such decisions (1971).

The author of the paper to which I referred earlier suggests that the risk of a system's collapse under stress-catastrophe must be factored into policymakers' calculations more effectively. Natural resource systems are especially prone to such irreversibilities, going well beyond the hysteresis effects, now fashionable to model in some other branches of economics, to the actual blocking of returns to previous potential equilibria. Developing countries may be ready to take greater risks in their pursuit of rapid development. On the other hand their poorest inhabitants cannot afford to take even minimal chances of unexpected losses and they and their children will bear the brunt of systemic deterioration or collapse; they may therefore be highly risk-averse. At a minimum, I believe, we need to take account of his conclusion:

> Despite continuing differences between economists and ecologists on the desirability of sustainable productive systems and the desirability of sustainable development, it would seem unwise for economists and others undertaking social cost-benefit analysis of projects for LDCs to ignore ecological considerations and spillovers. Indeed the claims in the traditional economic manuals for project evaluation in LDCs that such matters are likely to be unimportant is a serious shortcoming. The ecological consequences of many projects and developments in LDCs have been far from minor" (pp. 381–382).

CONCLUSION

This address has no conclusion. I have attempted to highlight some of the areas of our greatest conventional foolishness and some of our greatest areas of ignorance en route to whatever kind of global transformation and development we may be seeking. Frankly, I still see much ignorance about the key requirements for economic growth and development. Even within the context of current efforts at growth-oriented structural adjustment, we simply do not know enough about many of the issues: for instance, the implications for gender distribution of income (and therefore also for child welfare) of changing production structure (notably the shift towards export activity); the relative stability characteristics of Islamic financial systems (on the face of it, the international debt crisis would almost certainly not have arisen in an Islamic system); the potential for export expansion as the escape route for more than a handful of developing countries; the potential for a renewed socialism or other collective forms in the Third World after their many recent apparent setbacks; or the crucial requirements for technical progress.

It is for this conference to seek to generate greater wisdom and to begin to overcome at least a few of these and other areas of ignorance. Knowing so many of the participants as I do, I have every expectation that it will do both. Thank you very much for the opportunity of kicking it off in this way.

REFERENCES

Adelman, I., and Morris, C. T. *Society, Politics and Economic Development.* Baltimore: The Johns Hopkins University Press, 1967.

Bartelmus, Peter. "Accounting for Sustainable Development," Department of International Economic and Social Affairs, United Nations, Working Paper No. 8, November 1987.

Baster, Nancy (ed.). "Special Issue on Development Indicators." *Journal of Development Studies,* 8, 3 (April 1972).

Bhagwati, Jagdish. "Outward Orientation: Trade Issues." In Vittorio Corbo, Morris Goldstein, and Mohsin Khan (eds.), *Growth-Oriented Adjustment Programs.* Washington, D.C.: International Monetary Fund and World Bank, 1987.

Cornia, G. A., Jolly Richard, and Stewart, Frances (eds.). *Adjustment with a Human Face.* Oxford: Clarendon Press, 1987.

Diaz-Alejandro, Carlos F. "Goodbye Financial Repression, Hello Financial Crash," *Journal of Development Economics,* 19, 1–2 (September–October 1985).

Economic Council of Canada. *Venturing Forth, an Assessment of the Canada–U.S. Trade Agreement.* Ottawa, 1988.

Feinberg, Richard et al. *Between Two Worlds: The World Bank's Next Decade.* Washington, D.C.: Overseas Development Council, 1986.

Khan, Mohsin S., and Malcolm D. Knight. "Fund-Supported Adjustment Programs and Economic Growth." *IMF Occasional Paper* 41, November 1985.

Krugman, Paul. "Is Free Trade Passé?" *Journal of Economic Perspectives.* American Economic Association, 1, 2 (Fall 1987).

Kuznets, Simon. *Modern Economic Growth: Rate, Structure and Spread.* New Haven: Yale University Press, 1966.

Landau, Daniel, "Government and Economic Growth in the Less Developed Countries: An Empirical Study for 1960–1980." *Economic Development and Cultural Change,* 35, 11 (October 1986): 35–75.

Leslie, A. J. "A Second Look at the Economics of Natural Management Systems in Tropical Mixed Forests." *Unasilva,* 39, 1 (1987).

Michalopoulos, Constantine. "World Bank Programs for Adjustment and Growth." In Vittorio Corbo, Morris Goldstein, and Mohsin Khan (eds.), *Growth-Oriented Adjustment Programs.* Washington, D.C.: International Monetary Fund and the World Bank, 1987.

Moran, Theodore H. "Overview: The Future of Foreign Direct Investment in the Third World." In T. H. Moran et al., *Investing in Development: New Roles for Private Capital?* Washington, D.C.: Overseas Development Council, 1986.

Morris, Morris D. *Measuring the Condition of the World's Poor: The Physical Quality of Life Index.* Washington, D.C.: Overseas Development Council, 1978.

Prest, A. R., and Stewart, I. G. *The National Income of Nigeria, 1950–51.* London: H.M.S.O., Colonial Research Studies No. 11, 1953.

Ram, Rati. "Government Size and Economic Growth: A New Framework and Some Evidence from Cross-Section and Time-Series Data." *American Economic Review,* 76, 1 (March 1986).

Rawls, J. *A Theory of Justice.* Cambridge, Mass.: Harvard University Press, 1971.

Rossi, Nicola. "Government Spending, the Real Interest Rate, and the Behavior of Liquidity-Constrained Consumers in Developing Countries." *IMF Staff Papers,* 35, 1 (March 1988): 104–140.

Sachs, Jeffrey D. "Trade and Exchange Rate Policies in Growth-Oriented Adjustment Programs." In Vittorio Corbo, Morris Goldstein, and Mohsin Khan (eds.). *Growth-Oriented Adjustment Programs.* Washington, D.C.: International Monetary Fund and the World Bank, 1987, pp. 291–325.

Seers, Dudley. "The Meaning of Development." *International Development Review,* 11, 4 (1969).

———. "What Are We Trying to Measure?" *Journal of Development Studies,* 8, 3 (April 1972).

Taylor, Lance. *Varieties of Stabilization Experience.* Oxford: Clarendon Press, 1988.

Tisdell, Clem. "Sustainable Development: Differing Perspectives of Ecologists and Economists, and Relevance to LDCs." *World Development,* 16, 3 (March 1988): 373–384.

CHAPTER 4

"LIMITS TO GROWTH" AND "SUSTAINABLE DEVELOPMENT": GRAPPLING WITH ECOLOGICAL REALITIES

Paul Ekins

Department of Economics, Birkbeck College

1. INTRODUCTION

Following on from the 1992 Earth Summit, the UN Conference on Environment and Development (UNCED) in Brazil, it is perhaps worth reflecting on what is perhaps the major change in approach over the 20 years since the 1972 UN Conference on the Environment in Stockholm. Today the key phrase is 'sustainable development'. Then it was 'limits to growth'. The purpose of this paper is to examine and relate these two concepts; to see whether they are compatible and on what terms, and to judge which provides a more realistic approach to the environmental economic problems of the present time.

2. THE ECONOMIC GROWTH DEBATE

In order to shed light on the arguments for and against 'limits to growth' that raged so heatedly in the 1970s, not just among economists but in society at large, it is necessary to unpack the concept, in particular by asking 'what sort of limits?' and 'limits to what kind of growth?' At the outset it should be observed that the limits in question can be either ecological or social; while the growth in question can be that of the throughput of physical resources, GNP or welfare.

The term 'limits to growth' itself was the title of a book by Donella and Dennis Meadows and a team from the Massachusetts Institute of Technology (MIT), which was the principal fuel for the subsequent debate. For the Meadows team the limits

Ecological Economics, 8 (1993) 269–288. © 1993—Elsevier Science Publishers B.V. All rights reserved.

were ecological limits, and they applied to economic growth, understood as growth in production as measured by GNP, which they assumed implied a similar increase in the consumption of resources. They concluded that (Meadows et al., 1972, p. 23):

> The most probable result (of reaching the limits to growth) will be a rather sudden and uncontrollable decline in both population and industrial capacity.

The Meadows' model assumed that population and industrial capital would grow exponentially, leading to a similar growth in demand for food and non-renewables and in pollution. The supply of food and non-renewable resources were, however, taken to be absolutely finite. Not surprisingly, exponential growth within finite limits resulted in systematic breakdown; the expansive nature of compound growth also meant that the finite limits could be raised by a factor of four without significantly affecting the results.

While the 'limits to growth' thesis struck a chord with the general public, economists and other scientists were quick to seek to discredit it. One of the most comprehensive rebuttals came from a team at Sussex University's Science Policy Research Unit (Cole et al., 1973). They criticised the relationships in Meadows' model, the assumptions on which the model was based and the emphasis on purely physical parameters.

On the basis of their critique, Cole et al. re-ran Meadows' model with different assumptions and produced quite different results. This was also not a priori surprising because the key assumption they replaced was that of absolute limits by introducing ongoing exponential increases in available resources (through discovery and recycling) and the ability to control pollution. "To postpone collapse indefinitely these rates of improvement must obviously be competitive with growth rates of population and consumption so that even if the overall growth is rapid, it is also 'balanced'. In this case some kind of stable but dynamic equilibrium is obtained" (Cole et al., 1973, p. 119). The authors also claimed that, at 1% and 2%, the actual numerical values used as improvement rates for the various technologies were compatible with historical experience.

Lecomber (1975) admirably expresses the difference between resource optimists, such as Cole et al., and pessimists such as the Meadows' team. He identifies the three key effects that can reduce depletion or pollution: changes in composition of output, substitution between factor inputs, and technical progress (more efficient use of the same input). If these three effects add up to a shift away from the limiting resource or pollutant equal to or greater than the rate of growth, then the limits to growth are put back indefinitely. But, Lecomber (1975, p. 42) warns: "[This] establishes the *logical* conceivability, not the certainty, probability or even the possibility in practice, of growth continuing indefinitely. Everything hinges on the rate of technical progress and possibilities of substitution. This is perhaps the main issue that separates resource optimists and resource pessimists. The optimist believes in the power of human inventiveness to solve whatever problems are thrown in its way, as apparently it has done in the past. The pessimist questions the success of these past technological solutions and fears that future problems may be more intractable." Lecomber looks for evidence in an effort to judge between these two positions, but without success. "The central feature of technical advance is indeed its uncertainty" (Lecomber, 1975, p. 45). This conclusion is of relevance to the contemporary situation with sustainable development, as will be seen.

Many of the same points as those of Cole et al. (1973) are made, and the same beliefs about the efficiency of future technical change are held, by Wilfred Beckerman (1974) in his defense of economic growth. However, Beckerman also introduces several other arguments not related to technology. Firstly Beckerman (1974, pp. 18, 20) stresses: "It is essential not to confuse the issue of how consumption should be spread over time, which is the growth issue, with that of how resources should be used at any moment of time. The fact that resources are misallocated at any moment of time on account of failure to correct for externalities does not necessarily mean that the growth rate is wrong." Beckerman's point is that insofar as environmental degradation is caused by externalities, or 'spillover effects', which are failures of resource allocation, they cannot be solved by tinkering with rates of economic growth. This is true as far as it goes, but misses the important point that if these externalities persist to any given extent, their absolute effect in a large economy will be greater than in a small one. Given that failures to remedy externalities are common, due not least to the power of the vested interests that are causing them, opposition to the economic growth that amplifies them would seem a not irrational position on the part of those adversely affected.

The other point about rectifying resource misallocations is that per se it may reduce GNP growth. Lecomber (1975, p. 59) says: "It is misleading to regard environmental policies of this sort as *alternatives* to reducing economic growth since this would be their incidental effect. Benefits which are not included in GNP would be traded for other (smaller) benefits which are. GNP would fall and, during the period of transition to such policies, growth would fall, probably substantially." Of course, there is no certainty that correcting resource misallocations reduces growth, but if they could be corrected at zero net cost, which is what no reduction in growth implies, then there was no economic rationale for them in the first place. While such singular misallocations may exist, it is highly unlikely that the enormous externalities reflected in current environmental degradation are of this sort.

Whatever the potential of technological change, there are certain physical constraints, defined by the laws of thermodynamics, that cannot be circumvented. The Second Law—that all activity and transformation of energy or materials leads to an increase of entropy—has been most extensively related to economics by Georgescu-Roegen (1971).

In this analysis it is the increase of entropy that is the ultimate limit to growth. Economic activity increases entropy by depleting resources and producing wastes. Entropy on earth can only be decreased by importing low entropy resources (solar energy) from outside it. This energy can renew resources and neutralise and recycle wastes. To the extent that the human economy is powered by solar energy, it is limited only by the flow of that energy. Growth in physical production and throughput that is not based on solar energy must increase entropy and make environmental problems worse, implying an eventual limit to such growth. Growth in physical production based on solar energy is limited by the quantity and concentration of that energy. GNP can free itself from these limits only to the extent that it 'decouples' itself from growth in physical production; what Daly (1977, p. 118) calls "Angelized GNP". As will be seen later, such decoupling has occurred to some extent, but the entropy law decrees that it can never be complete. As Daly (1977, p. 119) puts it: "It would be necessary for us to become angels in order to subsist on angelized GNP."

Another Beckerman position concerns the overall benefit of economic growth, still understood as growth in GNP: "A failure to maintain economic growth means continued poverty, deprivation, disease, squalor, degradation and slavery to soul-degrading toil for countless millions of the world's population" (Beckerman, 1974, p. 9) and "This book is chiefly about why economic growth is still an important source of increased welfare and why it can safely be pursued without fear of environmental catastrophe" (Beckerman, 1974, p. 35). In believing that GNP is designed to measure "changes in economic welfare" (rather than production or income), Beckerman differs from some economists, but he concedes that it may not be a very good measure of such changes (Beckerman, 1974, p. 77). However, he considers that there are significant positive as well as negative omissions from GNP and cites Nordhaus and Tobin's (1971) figures as showing that: "The absolute rise in the 'good' items that are normally excluded from GNP has exceeded the absolute rise in the 'bad' items (both those that are included and those that are excluded from GNP)" (Beckerman, 1974, p. 86).

Beckerman's argument is therefore twofold: poor countries need economic growth to pull them out of poverty; rich countries pursue economic growth because of the net benefits it brings. With regard to the first of these arguments, there is now some doubt, rather more than when Beckerman was writing, whether economic growth per se is what poor people in poor countries need to improve their life prospects. Using the terminology introduced by Sen (1983, p. 754), entitlements such as ensured access to resources and capabilities to use those resources, neither of which are the automatic results of economic growth, may be even more important. Where these lead to more secure but non-market subsistence, they will not even show up as economic growth.

With regard to the second argument, it is a view which is diametrically opposed to the views of E.J. Mishan. In the works so far surveyed the emphasis has been on the feasibility or otherwise of economic growth. Its desirability has either been a moot point or, as with Beckerman, strongly asserted. It was the institutionalist economist K.W. Kapp who made the first thorough-going exploration of the social costs of the growth process (Kapp, 1950), but it was E.J. Mishan (1967, 1977) who first brought these costs to widespread public notice. Mishan (1977, p. 10) identified them thus:

> The uglification of once handsome cities the world over continues unabated. Noise levels and gas levels are still rising and, despite the erection of concrete freeways over city centres, unending processions of motorised traffic lurch through its main thoroughfares. Areas of outstanding natural beauty are still being sacrificed to the tourist trade and traditional communities to the exigencies of 'development'. Pollution of air, soil and oceans spreads over the globe . . . The upward movement in the indicators of social disintegration—divorce, suicide, delinquency, petty theft, drug taking, sexual deviance, crime and violence—has never faltered over the last two decades.

It is Mishan's thesis that these and other ill effects are the results of economic growth and far outweigh its benefits. Mishan sees the pursuit of such growth as leading Western civilisation to its nemesis. As long as these effects remain important, as they undoubtedly still do, Mishan's thesis stands unfalsified. Whether he will be proved right is, of course, a different matter.

The ecologists' concern was with the physical limits to economic growth. Mishan's focus is on the limits to social welfare that can be derived from growth. Hirsch (1976, p. 4) adds to the picture by postulating social limits to growth, distancing himself from the ecologists' critique with the words: "The concern with the limits to growth that has been voiced by and through the Club of Rome (Meadows et al., 1972) is strikingly misplaced. It focuses on distant and uncertain physical limits and overlooks the immediate if less apocalyptic presence of social limits to growth."

Hirsch's social limits derive from two causes: the increasing importance of positional goods; and the breakdown of individual morality in an affluent, growing economy. The positional economy "relates to all aspects of goods, services, work positions, and other social relationships that are either (1) scarce in some absolute or socially imposed sense or (2) subject to congestion or crowding through more extensive use" (Hirsch, 1976, p. 27). As incomes rise, the demand for positional goods increases; with fixed or very inelastic supply, the goods are either rationed through price (e.g., desirable resort properties) or criteria of eligibility (e.g., more stringent examinations) or their quality is degraded through overcrowding (e.g., roads). The effect is either to reduce growth, or the welfare to be derived from it or both.

On the subject of morality, Hirsch (1976, p. 141) writes: "The point is that conventional, mutual standards of honesty and trust are public goods that are necessary inputs for much of economic output. . . . Truth, trust, acceptance, restraint, obligation, these are among the social virtues which are also now seen to play a central role in the functioning of an individualistic contractual economy." Yet, Hirsch (1976, p. 175) asserts, these are precisely the virtues that are undermined by the selfsame individualism. "Economic growth undermines its social foundations."

Daly (1977, pp. 170, 176) brings the argument full circle by indicting "growthmania" for errors in both the ecological and moral spheres: "Economics has overlooked ecological and moral facts of life that have now come home to haunt us in the form of increasing ecological scarcity and increasing existential scarcity. . . . Ultimate means have been treated as if they were limitless, and the Ultimate End as if it were unreal."

Daly's solution to growthmania is the Steady-State Economy, "an economy with constant stocks of people and artifacts, maintained at some desired, sufficient levels by low rates of maintenance 'throughput'" (Daly, 1977, p. 17). The throughput is limited by strict quotas, auctioned by the government, on depletion of resources. The population is limited by the equal per capita issue of transferable birth licences. And inequality of income and wealth is limited by the setting of maximum and minimum levels, with redistribution from rich to poor. The dual ecological and social components of Daly's steady-state are explicit in the subtitle to his book: 'The Economics of Biophysical Equilibrium and Moral Growth'.

3. FROM LIMITS TO GROWTH TO SUSTAINABLE DEVELOPMENT

The 1970s' limits to growth critiques, both physical and social, failed to dent the social consensus in favour of economic growth, so that by the time the Brundtland Commission produced its report, *Our Common Future* (WCED, 1987), on environment and development, the emphasis was placed on a perceived complementarity between growth and environment. In her introduction to the report, Mrs. Brundtland calls for "a new era of economic growth—growth that is forceful and at the same time socially and environmentally sustainable" (WCED, 1987, p. xii).

This bullish attitude was justified by statistics which showed that over the period 1972–1986 the relationship between energy use and economic growth in industrial countries had undergone a significant change from the broadly proportional relation that had pertained before. In the US, energy intensity (the amount of energy used per unit of GDP) from 1973–1986 diminished by 25%. Over the OECD as a whole, it fell by 20% from 1973–85. In the same period for countries belonging to the International Energy Agency, GDP grew by nearly 32%, but energy use only by 5% (WRI, 1990, p. 146). A 'decoupling' of economic growth from energy consumption was proclaimed.

A major difference in the environmental debate since the publication of the Brundtland Report has been the positive engagement of business, which in the 1970s was still broadly unconvinced that there was a problem. Two significant international business initiatives have been launched, the 'Business Charter for Sustainable Development' for the International Chamber of Commerce (ICC) and the Business Council for Sustainable Development (BCSD), formed to give advice from a business perspective to the 1992 UN Conference on Environment and Development.

Both these initiatives believe environmental sustainability to be compatible with growth: "Economic growth provides the conditions in which protection of the environment can best be achieved, and environmental protection, in balance with other human goals, is necessary to achieve growth that is sustainable" (ICC, 1990). The BCSD view on the compatibility of growth and environmental protection is somewhat more ambivalent, as expressed in its report to UNCED in May 1992. In this report the relationship of compatibility is in one place characterised as extremely problematic, thus: "The requirement for clean, equitable economic growth remains the biggest single difficulty with the larger challenge of sustainable development. Proving that such growth is possible is certainly the greatest task for business and industry" (Schmidheiny, 1992, p. 9). Elsewhere the relationship (with trade thrown in) is characterised not just as compatibility but as complementarity: "Taking a long-term perspective, it follows then that economic growth, trade expansion and environmental protection are goals that can only be reached in conjunction" (Schmidheiny, 1992, p. 70).

In a new and even more optimistic twist to this debate, Bernstam (1991) postulates that industrialisation under free market conditions exhibits a characteristic relationship between growth and the environment: in the early days there is a negative trade-off at the expense of the environment. This effect diminishes as industrialisation proceeds and, at a certain historical moment, there is a positive relationship between the two. At this point "economic growth can reduce pollution if it increases the productivity of resources (that is, reduces wastes) faster than both resource output and population growth" (Bernstam, 1991, pp. 33, 34).

Bernstam (1991, p. 40) asserts that in industrial market economies this condition is now being met by the operation of what he calls the "Invisible Environmental Hand." I have subjected this assertion to detailed criticism elsewhere (Ekins, 1992), but the most important point is that it remains at the level of pure conjecture. In fact, it is flatly contradicted by trends in energy use since 1986. US energy intensity actually increased (that is, more energy was used per unit of GDP) in 1987 and 1988, as did that of several European countries (WRI, 1990, p. 146). Despite some limited evidence on air pollution (World Bank, 1992), there is no evidence that, over a prolonged period, Bernstam's condition for growth to reduce overall environmental impacts is being met.

Beckerman (1992), arguing for economic growth in developing countries, adopts the same line of argument as Bernstam (1991) with an intriguing difference. Bernstam's thesis was that continuing economic growth in industrial countries would reduce their contribution to global pollution, which would go some way towards compensating for the inevitable rise in pollution from growth in developing countries. Beckerman contends that it is *developing countries* that need economic growth to improve their environments, at least in important areas such as access to drinking water, sanitation and air quality. He concludes: "In the longer run, the surest way to improve your environment is to become rich" (Beckerman, 1992, p. 491). Beckerman is roundly dismissive of the whole debate around sustainability: "The aggregative concept of global sustainability . . . seems to be either morally indefensible or devoid of operational value," while the question "how do we achieve sustainable development?" is "unanswerable and meaningless" (Beckerman, 1992, pp. 491–492).

Beckerman's is not the only important voice from the 1970s debate to have restated their essential conclusions in the 1990s. A new report from Meadows et al. (1992, p. 12) states: "[The possible paths into the future] do not include continuous growth. The choices are to bring the burden of human activities upon the earth down to a sustainable level through human choice, human technology and human organisation, or to let nature force the reduction through lack of food, energy or materials, or an increasingly unsound environment."

The emphasis on continuing limits to growth is also echoed in a publication which includes contributions by two Nobel laureates in economics, one of whom writes: "Saving the environment will certainly check production growth and probably lead to lower levels of national income. This outcome can hardly surprise. Many have known for a long time that population growth and rising production and consumption cannot be sustained forever in a finite world" (Tinbergen and Hueting, 1991, p. 38).

It will be noticed that, while the resource pessimists' conclusions are essentially unchanged, and with the exception of the Bernstam/Beckerman views, there has been a significant shift in the resource optimists' position since the 1970s. Then, environmental limits were perceived to be either non-existent or automatically self-delimiting. Now the consensus among the mainstream optimists, as expressed in the Brundtland, WRI or BSCD reports, is that environmental problems are real and threatening and that to be reconciled with continuing economic expansion *active policy* on the part of both business and government will be required.

This consensus position received one of its most sophisticated restatements in the *World Development Report 1992* (World Bank, 1992). This report accepts the gravity of the environmental situation. Further, it accepts that some environmental problems are "exacerbated by the *growth* of economic activity" (p. 7, original emphasis). Exploring the implications of a 3.5-times rise in world output by 2030, it acknowledges that "If environmental pollution and degradation were to rise in step with such a rise in output, the result would be appalling environmental pollution and damage" (p. 9).

The Report recommends a twin strategy to achieve both growth and environmental conservation. Most importantly, "Some problems are associated with the *lack* of economic development; inadequate sanitation and clean water, indoor air pollution from biomass burning, and many types of land degradation in developing countries have poverty as their root cause. Here the challenge is to accelerate equitable income growth . . ." (p. 7, original emphasis). The Report accepts that "these 'win-win' policies will not be enough" (p. 5) and that, in other cases, "there may be trade-offs between income growth and environmental protection" (p. 1). However, "The evidence indicates that the gains from protecting the environment are often high, and that the costs in foregone income are modest if appropriate policies are adopted" (p. 1). The gains from 'win-win' opportunities on the one hand, and only modest costs on the other, could, on this analysis, result in both the 3.5-times rise in world output and "better environmental protection, cleaner air and water, and the virtual elimination of acute poverty" (p. 2).

The greater acceptance of environmental threat by policy-makers and academics than in the 1970s has also led to an explosion in research activity focused on the concept of 'sustainable development' that has been popularised by the Brundtland Report. By 1989 the literature had generated "a gallery of definitions" (Pearce et al., 1989, pp. 173–185). Such diversity of meaning clearly militates against clarity of discourse, to the extent that one survey of the sustainable development scene was led to conclude (Lele, 1991, p. 613):

> [Sustainable development] is a "metafix" that will unite everybody from the profit-minded industrialist and risk-minimising subsistence farmer to the equity-seeking social worker, the pollution-concerned or wildlife-loving First Worlder, the growth-maximising policy-maker, the goal-oriented bureaucrat and, therefore, the vote-counting politician.

Not surprisingly perhaps, Lele (1991, p. 613) finds that this all-inclusive formulation "suffers from significant weaknesses in:

(a) its characterisation of the problems of poverty and environmental degradation;

(b) its conceptualisation of the objectives of development, sustainability and participation; and

(c) the strategy it has adopted in the face of incomplete knowledge and uncertainty."

Notwithstanding these weaknesses, it is possible to identify several strands in recent writing about the economy and the environment, which do shed further light on the growth/environment relation. These strands can be identified as an increasing awareness of the extent of environmental externalities and a consequent stress on the need for environmental evaluation; a new perception of the differences, and therefore of the need to distinguish, between natural and man-made capital; an emphasis on John Hicks' original definition of income as production remaining net of capital depreciation, i.e., income is *defined* as a sustainable quantity; and a concern to reflect these issues and effects in quantitative economic analysis and especially to incorporate them in the System of National Accounts.

Each of these subjects now has a substantial literature, which can be no more than hinted at here. The extent of externalities in a modern industrial economy was explored by Leipert (1989) in his study for West Germany of the 'defensive expenditures' to which they give rise. Leipert classified these expenditures in six areas—the environment, transport, housing, security, health and work—and found that they had increased from an equivalent of 5% to an equivalent of 10% of West German GNP between 1970 and 1985, even ignoring global effects such as ozone depletion and climate change, and the environmental impacts of West German production and consumption on other countries.

The measurement of environmental damages is discussed in Pearce and Turner (1990, pp. 120–158) where they seek to make operational the concept of total economic value as actual use value plus option value plus existence value. There is still considerable controversy surrounding the reliability and appropriateness in many environmental contexts of the principal method discussed, contingent valuation (Hueting, 1989; Common and Blamey, 1992).

The relationship between natural and man-made capital is explored in Pearce et al. (1989, pp. 34 ff.) and Pearce and Turner (1990, pp. 43 ff.). Taking sustainability to mean a non-declining capital stock, this can be taken to refer to total capital stock or to man-made and natural capital stocks separately (the 'weak' and 'strong' sustainability condition, respectively). Which of these conditions is appropriate depends on the degree of substitutability of the two kinds of capital, which itself depends on issues of uncertainty, irreversibility and uniqueness. Daly (1991) argues that, in fact, "natural capital (natural resources) and man-made capital are complements rather than substitutes" (p. 20).

The essential sustainability of the Hicksian concept of income was stressed in several papers in Ahmad et al. (1989) and clearly demands that, in calculations of income, depreciation of natural capital should be deducted from gross production. That this is not done in the case of National Income has attracted increasing concern, with many writers advocating reform to the System of National Accounts. Ahmad, et al. (1989) contains several suggested approaches as to how this might be achieved.

Notwithstanding the theoretical and (rather less) practical progress that has been made on these issues, it is true to say that it has not been able to create a consensus over the relationship between environmental sustainability and economic growth. As Costanza has written: "The bottom line is that there is still enormous uncertainty about the impacts of energy and resource constraints . . . Ultimately, no one knows. Both sides argue as if they were certain, but the most insidious form of certainty is misplaced ignorance" (Costanza, 1989, p. 3). This sentiment is echoed by Pearce and Turner (1990) who, reviewing the 'limits to growth' issue, write: "Our belief is that only by improving substantially our understanding of economy–environment interactions will we get a better grasp of these wider issues" (p. 28).

Modesty in the face of uncertainty is, doubtless, laudable but it can all too easily lead to inaction or mere calls for more research. It is possible that UNCED's very modest achievements may lead to just that. Maurice Strong, UNCED's Secretary-General who also organised the 1972 Stockholm Environment Conference, summed up the post-UNCED danger in the words: "We don't have another twenty years now. I believe we are on the road to tragedy" (reported in Meadows, 1992). What, then, might be a prudent course of action with regard to economic growth and the environment, in the face of radical uncertainty?

4. ACHIEVING SUSTAINABILITY

At its simplest, the sustainability of something is its capacity for continuance into the future. Where economic activity or, more generally, a way of human life, is concerned, this sustainability will depend on economic, social (including cultural and ethical), and ecological factors. These factors are themselves interdependent, so, for example, ecological sustainability (the absence of ecological constraints on the capacity for continuance) will be influenced by social arrangements (Lele, 1991, pp. 609–610; Pezzey, 1992). The interdependence of these factors, and their change over time, is captured by Norgaard's concept of 'co-evolution' (Norgaard, 1992).

As we have seen, there is now widespread agreement, which formed the basis of UNCED, that most current economic development is not ecologically sustainable and that the unchecked consequences of this are likely to be unpleasant and perhaps catastrophic. The core of continuing disagreement lies in the extent to which new technologies can resolve problems of ecological unsustainability, while permitting continuing growth of GNP. The disagreement derives from differing positions of technological optimism and pessimism.

It is now clear that this issue will not be resolved theoretically. It is essentially an empirical question. But there is no reason for the lack of a priori theoretical agreement on this point to impede practical implementation of a policy which all sides agree to be desirable on both ecological and economic grounds; namely, the internalisation of environmental externalities and/or their reduction through the determined introduction of technologies to reduce environmental impacts. If the optimists are proved right, so much the better; if the pessimists are nearer the mark, at least environmental calamity will have been averted.

Achieving this technological transformation, however, and being able to respond further should it prove insufficient to adequately reduce environmental damage, depends in my view on two radical shifts in orientation: the adoption of ecological sustainability as the principal economic objective in place of economic growth, and the development of a new accounting system to reflect the ecological contributions to and impacts of economic activity, and to clarify the relationship of production growth to economic welfare.

Shifting the Policy Emphasis from Growth to Sustainability

I have argued in detail elsewhere on the need for a shift in policy emphasis from growth to sustainability if environmental problems are to be adequately addressed (Ekins, 1989). Maintaining the current orientation towards growth, with all its concomitant pressures towards business as usual, is much less likely to introduce the changes for ecological sustainability that are necessary.

An equation used by Paul and Anne Ehrlich (1990, p. 58) indicates the scale of the technological challenge if both sustainability and GNP growth are to be achieved. The equation relates environmental impact *(I)* to the product of three variables: population *(P)*, consumption per capita *(C)*, and the environmental intensity of consumption (the environmental damage per unit of GDP, *T*). This last variable captures all the changes in technology, factor inputs, and the composition of GNP. Thus:

$$I = PCT$$

In accordance with the widespread agreement at UNCED, it is assumed that current levels of *I* are unsustainable. With regard to energy consumption and climate change, the Intergovernmental Panel on Climate Change (IPCC) calculates that carbon dioxide emissions will quickly have to fall by a minimum of 60% to halt global warming. Three other greenhouse gases—N_2O, CFC-11, CFC-12—also need cuts of more than 70% (Houghton et al., 1990, p. xviii). With regard to other environmental problems, the Dutch National Environmental Policy Plan (MOHPPE, 1988) argues for cuts in emissions of 80–90% for SO_2, NO_x, NH_3 and waste-dumping, 80% for hydrocarbons and 100% for CFCs. Thus with regard to *I* overall, it seems conservative to suggest that sustainability demands that it should fall by at least 50%. With regard to population, the UN's recent projections indicate a global figure of 10 billion by about 2050 (Sadik, 1991, p. 3), about twice today's level. With regard to consumption, what is considered a moderate economic growth rate of 2–3% results in a quadrupling of output over 50 years. Thus, where subscript 1 indicates the quantity now and the subscript 2 indicates the quantity in 50 years time, we have:

$$I_2 = 1/2 \times I_1 \text{ (for sustainability)}$$
$$\left. \begin{array}{l} P_2 = 2P_1 \\ C_2 = 4C_1 \end{array} \right\} \text{(by assumption)}$$

For the Ehrlich equation to hold, this means that $T_2 = 1/16\ T_1$. In other words the environmental impact of each unit of consumption would need to fall by 93% over the next 50 years to meet the rather conservative condition for sustainability that has been adopted. Moreover, in order not to check GNP growth, the technological innovation involved would have to be non-inflationary. Tinbergen and Hueting (1991, p. 37) are openly sceptical of the possibility of this: "Saving the environment without causing a rise in prices and subsequent check of production growth is only possible if a technology is invented that is sufficiently clean, reduces the use of space sufficiently, leaves the soil intact, does not deplete energy and resources . . . *and* is cheaper (or at least not more expensive) than current technology. This is hardly imaginable for our whole range of current activities." One does not have to be a technological pessimist to share their doubts.

The extent to which growth itself undercuts improvements in environmental technology is illustrated by the Fraunhofer Institute's study on the macroeconomic effects on the (West) German economy of measures to prevent global warming, preliminarily reported in Schoen (1992). While technical measures were estimated to be able to cut

CO_2 emissions from industry by 81.2 million tons per annum from 1987 levels by the year 2005, increased production over that period (taking into account intersectoral changes in favor of less energy-intensive sectors) resulted in more CO_2 emissions of 64 million tons p.a. Thus only 17.2 million tons p.a., or 21% of the technical potential, actually shows up as reduced emissions. The rest simply goes to counteract the increased emissions due to production growth (Schoen, 1992, p. 7).

Elsewhere (Ekins, 1991a), I have performed another calculation on the basis of the Ehrlich equation using different assumptions and the following figures in World Bank (1990, table 1, pp. 178–179):

1988 GNP/Capital *(C)* in High-Income Countries = $17080
1988 Population *(P)* in High-Income Countries = 784.2 million (m)
1988 GNP/Capita in Low- and Middle-Income Countries = $750
1988 Population in Low- and Middle-Income Countries = 3952 m

The different assumptions for 50 years on were: that I must still be halved; that P will double, with all the increase in the Third World; that C will quadruple in the Third World (low- and middle-income countries), but stay constant in high-income countries. These assumptions yield the following figures for the year 2038 (1988 + 50):

2038 GNP/Capita *(C)* in High-Income Countries = $17080
2038 Population *(P)* in High-Income Countries = 784.2 m
2038 $C \times P$ in High-Income Countries = $13.4 tr (all as before)
2038 World Population $(P_2) = 2P_1 = 9472$ m
2038 Population in Low- and Middle-Income countries = 8688 m
2038 GNP/Capita in Low- and Middle-Income Countries = $3000
2038 $C \times P$ in Low- and Middle-Income Countries = $26.06 tr

With $P_2 = 2 P_1$, $I_2 = 1/2\ I_1$ (by assumption), it is easily verified from the Ehrlich equation that $T_2 = 0.21\ T_1$. This means that T in this case would need to fall by 79%.

The difference between the two figures with and without Northern income growth (93% and 79%) is further evidence of the enormously skewed nature of current consumption patterns. With *no* increase in consumption anywhere in the world, but with other assumptions unchanged, the Ehrlich equation indicates a necessary cut in environmental intensity of 75%. Allowing the Third World, with three quarters of the world's population, to more than double its population and quadruple its consumption per head (when its average level becomes still only about 20% of that in the First World) only raises the figure to 79%. But quadrupling the much larger consumption of First World countries as well raises it to 93%.

Such considerations suggest that the best and perhaps the only strategy for achieving ecological sustainability involves differentiating between North and South. In the South, very considerable percentage increases in current very low per capita income levels would appear to be compatible with environmental sustainability, even allowing for forecast population growth, provided that this is accomplished using the most environmentally advanced technologies, although the problems of transferring the technologies between different economic and cultural milieux should not be underestimated. There should also be a determined programme of ecological regeneration in the South through afforestation, soil conservation and small-scale irrigation, which could increase production there and simultaneously increase the natural resource base.

In the North the sustainability problem is quite different. High levels of per capita income mean that relatively small percentage growth rates result in large absolute increases in consumption and, therefore, in associated environmental impacts. That production growth in the North does not necessarily alleviate poverty there is shown by the evidence of the 1980s, which indicates that the number of people below the poverty line in some countries (e.g., the US and UK) increased despite growth in GDP (UNDP, 1991, pp. 30–31). Further, Goodland and Daly (1992) from the World Bank give ten reasons why growth in the North is also not the solution to poverty in the South. This decoupling of Northern growth from poverty alleviation, and the fact that such growth greatly increases the demands on environmental technologies in the resolution of environmental problems, strengthens the argument for a wholesale shift of objectives in the North from growth to sustainability, through the radical ecological transformation of production and consumption. Any production growth that may still result would have to be compensated for by even greater falls in environmental intensity.

A further condition for sustainable development in North and South is a restructuring of the economic relations between them; a complex issue I have discussed in Ekins (1991b), but which can be no more than mentioned here.

Providing More Rigorous Indicators of Welfare and Production

Economic growth and growth in GNP are usually taken to be synonymous. Thence the positive link with social welfare is also normally taken for granted. As we have seen, a key theme in the limits to growth debate has been a rejection of this positive link between growth and welfare. A more recent development has been a challenge of the identification of economic growth with growth in GNP, and a determined effort to reform GNP to take account of environmental impacts.

Hueting (1986; Hueting and Leipert, 1990) has consistently denied that economic growth means growth in GNP. His argument is that the purpose of the economy, and therefore the proper subject of economics, is the promotion, not of production and consumption, but of *welfare* (to which, of course, production and consumption may contribute). Logically, therefore, economic growth should mean an increase in welfare, which could have a variety of components of which Hueting (1986, pp. 243–244) identifies seven: production, environment, employment, leisure, working conditions, income distribution, and safety of the future. GNP growth at best is an indicator of production growth (but see below); economic growth should mean that welfare has increased, implying ideally that the contributions of all the above have been taken into account.

It is to make operational such a broader notion of economic growth that various different indicator systems have recently been proposed, including the Human Development Index (UNDP, 1990, 1991, 1992), Daly and Cobb's (1989) Index of Sustainable Economic Welfare and Victor Anderson's (1991) Global Report indicators. For further discussion of these issues and the elaboration of a four-component indicator framework, see Ekins (1990) and Ekins and Max-Neef (1992).

If the link between GNP growth and welfare is problematic, GNP's status even as an indicator of economic production is increasingly being called into question. GNP is supposed, of course, to measure, as a triple identity, production, expenditure and income. One problem already mentioned is the important and growing level of 'defensive expenditures', which are more in the nature of intermediate costs and should therefore not appear in GNP, although many are currently classed as final expenditure and therefore do so. Moreover, if GNP is to be a true figure of income, then not only does the depreciation of physical capital need to be deducted, as occurs in the computation of Net National Product (NNP), but the depletion of natural capital, or the costs of replacing such depletion with renewable substitutes, needs also to be subtracted if the (sustainable) income is not to be overstated. Finally, to the extent that the economy has become unsustainable, this represents accumulated costs in the past that should have been deducted from GNP, but were not.

Hueting et al. (1991) recommends that over all areas where environmental unsustainability is apparent, sustainability standards should be set and the cost of attaining them be deducted from GNP. Pearce et al. (1989, p. 108) recommends that for GNP to approach an indicator of sustainable income (or production, but not welfare), it should be subject to four subtractions: depreciation of manufactured capital, depletion of natural capital, household defensive expenditures, and the monetary value of residual pollution.

Were such adjustments to be made comprehensively, then much of the context of the 'limits to growth' debate would disappear because the new adjusted GNP simply would not grow in an economy that was fast depleting natural-capital or generating social and environmental externalities.

4. CONCLUSION

The debate about economic growth has focused attention on three extremely important sets of questions, which remain unanswered and extremely relevant today, concerning the current level and likely future increase of human economic activity. These questions are:

(a) Is such activity having an environmental impact which, at best, reduces the economic possibilities in the future and, at worst, is likely to precipitate widespread collapse? (The ecological sustainability debate.)

(b) Is such activity generating a range of negative social and environmental effects that actually outweigh many of the benefits of current affluence and of its nominal increase? (The welfare-from-growth debate.)

(c) Is such activity in market economies producing intense competitive and individualistic pressures that not only prevent individuals from enjoying their affluence, as in (b), but also undermine the cultural and moral fabric of society on which the economy itself actually depends? (The social sustainability debate.)

In the twenty years or so since these debates began in earnest, none of these questions have been conclusively answered in the negative. On the contrary, (a) now commands an almost universal positive response, which has given rise to UNCED, the largest inter-governmental conference ever held, and the ongoing concern with sustainable development. However, the debates have so far yielded nothing approaching consensus as to the ultimate relationships between economic growth and welfare or environmental or social sustainability.

It has, however, clarified some of the key parameters of these relationships. First, with regard to the environment, World Bank (1992, p. 9) sums up the basic conclusion thus: "Whether the limitations (of the earth's 'sources' and 'sinks') will place bounds on the growth of human activity will depend on the scope for substitution, technical progress and structural change."

It has been argued here that achieving possible reductions in environmental intensity and sustainable development will require different strategies in the North and South: more emphasis in the former on sustainability as a policy objective than on economic growth; and an emphasis in the latter on growth that is equitable and minimally environmentally damaging, with a combined focus on environmental regeneration, social reforms and careful industrialisation using the most environmentally advanced technologies. Such Southern growth will only be achieved in the context of reformed North–South economic relations. Maintaining the current undifferentiated emphasis on growth in both North and South is likely to increase unsustainability whatever the rhetorical commitments in favour of sustainable development.

Second, with regard to welfare, there can be no presumption that GNP growth, especially if it increases environmental destruction but even if it does not, increases social welfare. The relationship between GNP growth and welfare can only be elucidated by placing GNP in an operational indicator framework of economic welfare that goes well beyond it.

Third, with regard to social sustainability, it is quite possible that the type and pace of technological change required to make GDP growth and environmental protection compatible objectives, will exacerbate the sort of social problems identified by Mishan and Hirsch, with unpredictable results. These problems can only be addressed by explicitly exploring the moral and cultural issues raised by the predominant emphasis in economic thinking on individual preferences, self-interest, and competitive growth.

Such approaches provide an opportunity to invest the term 'sustainable development' with some deeper human, social and institutional significance, which may prove as important to its realisation as the mere development of and implementation of eco-technologies.

REFERENCES

Ahmad, Y., El Serafy, S. and Lutz, E. (Editors), 1989. *Environmental Accounting for Sustainable Development.* World Bank, Washington, DC.

Anderson, V., 1991. *Alternative Economic Indicators.* Routledge, London.

Beckerman, W., 1974. *In Defence of Economic Growth.* Jonathan Cape, London.

Beckerman, W., 1992. "Economic growth and the environment: whose growth? whose environment?" *World Development,* 20 (4): 481–496.

Bernstam, M., 1991. *The Wealth of Nations and the Environment.* Institute for Economic Affairs, London.

Cole, H.S.D., Freeman, C., Jahoda, M. and Pavitt, K.L.R. (Editors), 1973. *Thinking about the Future: a Critique of the Limits to Growth.* Chatto and Windus for Sussex University Press, London.

Common, M.S. and Blamey, J., 1992. *Sustainability and the limits to pseudo-market evaluation.* Centre for Resource and Environmental Studies, Australian National University, paper presented at 2nd meeting of International Society for Ecological Economics, Stockholm, Sweden, August 1992.

Costanza, R., 1989. "What is ecological economics?" *Ecological Economics,* 1: 1–7.

Daly, H.E., 1977. *Steady-State Economics.* W.H. Freeman, San Francisco, CA.

Daly, H.E., 1991. From empty world economics to full world economics. In: R. Goodland, H.E. Daly and S. El Serafy (Editors), *Environmentally Sustainable Economic Development: Building on Brundtland.* Environment Working Paper No. 46, World Bank, Washington, DC.

Daly, H.E. and Cobb, J., 1989. *For the Common Good.* Beacon Press, Boston.

Ehrlich, P. and Ehrlich, A., 1990. *The Population Explosion.* Hutchinson, London.

Ekins, P., 1989. "Beyond growth: the real priorities of sustainable development." *Environmental Conserv.,* 16 (1): 5–6, 12.

Ekins, P., 1990. "An indicator framework for economic progress." *Development,* 1990 (3/4): 92–98.

Ekins, P., 1991a. "The sustainable consumer society: a contradiction in terms"? *International Environmental Affairs,* 3 (4): 243–258.

Ekins, P., 1991b. "A strategy for global environmental development." *Development,* 1991 (2): 64–73.

Ekins, P., 1992. "Environmental head of government," review of Bernstam 1991. *Science and Public Policy,* 19 (1): 61–63.

Ekins, P. and Max-Neef, M. (Editors), 1992. *Real-Life Economics.* Routledge, London.

Georgescu-Roegen, N., 1971. *The Entropy Law and the Economic Process.* Harvard University Press, Cambridge MA.

Goodland, R. and Daly, H.E., 1992. "Ten reasons why Northern income growth is not the solution to Southern poverty." Environment Department, World Bank, Washington, DC.

Hirsch, F., 1976. *Social Limits to Growth.* Harvard University Press, Cambridge, MA.

Houghton, J., Jenkins, G. and Ephraums, J. (Editors), 1990. *Climate Change: the IPCC Scientific Assessment.* Cambridge University Press (for the IPCC—Intergovernmental Panel on Climate Change), Cambridge.

Hueting, R., 1986. "An economic scenario for a conserver economy". In: P. Ekins (Editor), *The Living Economy: a New Economics in the Making.* Routledge, London, pp. 242–256.

Hueting R., 1989. "Correcting national income for environmental losses: toward a practical solution." In: Y. Ahmad, S. El Serafy and E. Lutz (Editors), *Environmental Accounting for Sustainable Development.* World Bank, Washington, DC, pp. 32–39.

Hueting, R. and Leipert, C., 1990. "Economic growth, national income and the blocked choices for the environment." *Environmentalist,* 10 (1): 25–38.

Hueting, R., Bosch, P. and de Boer, B., 1991. *Methodology for the Calculation of Sustainable National Income.* Netherlands Central Bureau of Statistics, Voorburg.

ICC (International Chamber of Commerce), 1990. *The Business Charter for Sustainable Development: Principles for Environmental Management.* ICC, Paris.

Kapp, K.W., 1950. *The Social Costs of Private Enterprise.* Harvard University Press, Cambridge, MA.

Lecomber, R., 1975. *Economic Growth Versus the Environment.* Macmillan, London.

Leipert, C., 1989. "Social costs of the economic process and national accounts: the example of defensive expenditures." *Journal Interdisciplinary Economics,* 3 (1): 27–46.

Lele, S., 1991. "Sustainable development: a critical review." *World Development,* 19 (6): 607–621.

Meadows, D.H., 1992. *Rio: triumph of consciousness-raising.* Valley News, Plainfield, NH.

Meadows, D.H., Meadows, D.L., Randers, J. and Behrens, W., 1972. *The Limits to Growth.* Universe Books, New York.

Meadows, D.H., Meadows, D.L. and Randers, J., 1992. *Beyond the Limits: Global Collapse or a Sustainable Future.* Earthscan, London.

Mishan, E.J., 1967. *The Costs of Economic Growth.* Staples Press, London.

Mishan, E.J., 1977. *The Economic Growth Debate: an Assessment.* George Allen and Unwin, London.

MOHPPE (Ministry of Housing, Physical Planning and Environment), 1988. *To Choose or to Lose: National Environmental Policy Plan.* MOHPPE, The Hague.

Nordhaus, W. and Tobin, J., 1971. "Is growth obsolete?" In: M. Moss (Editor), *The Measurement of Economic and Social Performance.* Princeton University Press, pp. 509–532.

Norgaard, R., 1992. Co-evolution of economy, society and environment. In: P. Ekins and M. Max-Neef (Editors), *Real-Life Economics.* Routledge, London, pp. 76–86.

Pearce, D. and Turner, R.K., 1990. *The Economics of Natural Resources and the Environment.* Harvester Wheatsheaf, Hemel Hempstead, UK.

Pearce, D., Markandya, A. and Barbier, E., 1989. *Blueprint for a Green Economy.* Earthscan, London.

Pezzey, J., 1992. "Sustainability: an interdisciplinary guide." *Environmental Values,* 1 (4).

Sadik, N., 1991. *The State of the World Population 1991.* UNFPA (UN Fund for Population Activities), New York.

Schmidheiny, S., 1992. *Changing Course: A Global Business Perspective on Development and the Environment.* MIT Press, Cambridge, MA.

Schoen, M., 1992. "Macroeconomic effects of measures to affect global warming." Fraunhofer Institut, Karlsruhe, paper presented at 2nd meeting of International Society for Ecological Economics, Stockholm, Sweden.

Sen, A., 1983. "Development: which way now? *Economic Journal,*" 93: 745–762.

Tinbergen, J. and Hueting, R., 1991. "GNP and market prices: wrong signals for sustainable economic success that mask environmental destruction." In: R. Goodland, H.E. Daly and S. El Serafy (Editors), *Environmentally Sustainable Economic Development: Building on Brundtland.* Environment Working Paper No. 46, World Bank, Washington, DC, pp. 36–42.

UNDP, 1990. *Human Development Report 1990.* Oxford University Press, Oxford.

UNDP, 1991. *Human Development Report 1991.* Oxford University Press, Oxford.

UNDP, 1992. *Human Development Report 1992.* Oxford University Press, Oxford.

WCED (World Commission on Environment and Development), 1987. *Our Common Future* (The Brundtland Report). Oxford University Press, Oxford.

World Bank, 1990. *World Development Report 1990.* Oxford University Press, Oxford.

World Bank, 1992. *World Development Report 1992.* Oxford University Press, Oxford.

WRI (World Resources Institute), 1990. *World Resources 1990–91.* WRI, Washington, DC.

CHAPTER **5**

GENDER-AWARE ANALYSIS AND DEVELOPMENT ECONOMICS

Diane Elson

Department of Economics, University of Manchester

1. INTRODUCTION

Economic analysis that is gender-aware, in the sense of recognizing that all economic activity works through and within gendered relationships, has the potential to generate both a better understanding of the development process and a better understanding of the policies required to diminish gender inequality. This paper examines some of the factors that hinder the production of a fully gender-aware development economics and suggests ways in which improvements can be made.[1]

The concept of gender in this paper refers to the social differentiation of women and men through processes which are learned, changeable over time and vary within and between cultures. At the economic level, gender appears as a sexual division of labour in which some types of work are strongly associated with women and some types with men. The costs and benefits of the sexual division of labour are unequally shared between men and women to the disadvantage of the latter.[2]

2. GENDER-AWARENESS IN NEOCLASSICAL DEVELOPMENT ECONOMICS

At the macro level most analysis lacks gender-awareness but appears to be quite gender neutral. Women do not appear—but neither do men. The emphasis is rather on monetary aggregates, prices and quantities of commodities. Microeconomics does permit the introduction of women and men because it focuses on economic agents making

Journal of International Development: Vol. 5, No. 2, 237–247 (1993). © 1993 by John Wiley & Sons, Ltd.

choices, and these agents can be differentiated as female and male. However, it will be argued here that both at macro and micro levels, neoclassical economics tends to have insufficient gender-awareness; at the macro level because gender is not taken into account; and at the micro level because of the particular way that gender is taken into account.

The inadequacy of macroeconomics stems from its neglect of one whole area of production, the unpaid production of human resources; and from ignoring the interdependence between this area of production and the areas that macroeconomics is concerned with. This neglect tells against women in a variety of ways because such unpaid production is largely women's work; and also means that the theory gives an inadequate analysis of real economic processes.

The omission of women's unpaid work in human resource production is not simply the result of the conceptual complexities and practical difficulties of measuring it. It is also the result of implicit assumptions built into the theory of the determinants of the level and pattern of economic activity. If women's capacity to undertake unpaid domestic labour is implicitly treated as infinitely elastic, able to stretch so as to make up for any shortfalls in purchased inputs required to sustain human resources, without diminishing women's ability to undertake other forms of production, it will not have any determining effect upon the level and composition of overall national output or rate of growth, and there seems no need for macroeconomic analysis to take it into account.[3]

There *is* some justification for treating the process of production of human resources as rather different from the production of any other kind of resource. It does not tend to respond to economic signals in quite the same way,[4] because human resources have an intrinsic and not merely instrumental value. However, there are limits to the time and effort women can supply. When there are substantial falls in the level of national output and disruptive changes in its sectoral composition, breaking point may be reached, and women's capacity to care adequately for their families may collapse, undermining the human resource base of economic activity (for a good example, see Moser's (1989) study of a low-income urban community in Ecuador in conditions of recession and structural adjustment).

This in turn is likely to have a negative feedback on economic growth and the balance of payments, directly through shortfalls in human skills, and indirectly through the diversion of public expenditure from more directly productive uses to the tasks of policing, and repairing the damaged fabric of society through 'social work'. This may not show up immediately and may be difficult to measure, but in the longer run will hamper development.

A major reason for this constraint is inflexibility in the sexual division of labour. Studies available to date suggest that, even under the pressure of structural adjustment and economic crisis, the burden of caring for others remains largely with women, even when men are unemployed. The extent of this burden is directly related to macroeconomic policies. Public expenditure on social services such as health, education, and on social infrastructure such as sanitation and transport, and on food subsidies for the poor, tends to reduce this burden; and cuts in public expenditure on these items tend to increase this burden. Increasing women's domestic burdens is not only detrimental to women; it can also be detrimental to immediate macroeconomic goals if it impedes women's ability to produce the output that *is* counted as part of GNP.[5]

The key issue at the macro level is thus the *interdependence* between the output that macro analysis does take into account—marketed output—and the output that macro analysis does not take into account—the unpaid domestic labour that is critical for human resource production. A gender-aware approach recognizes the significance of this interdependence.

Unpaid domestic labour is not neglected in the same way in neoclassical microeconomics. There is a large literature on households and labour markets which incorporates discussion of it and offers explanations of why it is largely done by women. Here the problem is the *way* in which it is treated, as the outcome of the free choices of economic agents specializing according to their innate comparative advantage.

A good example is the 'new household economics'.[6] This theory is consistent with observable patterns of gender differentiation but that does not make it a good *explanation* of how such differentiation comes about; nor does it *justify* the treatment of households as unities for policy purposes (Folbre, 1986a, b).

Other explanations may also be consistent with observable patterns of gender differentiation. Sen (1990) develops an alternative theory of 'cooperative conflict'. In this view of the household, women and men gain from cooperating with one another in joint living arrangements because this increases the capabilities of the household as a whole; but the division of the fruits of cooperation is a source of conflict. Women are at a disadvantage in bargaining because their fall-back position tends to be worse; that is, if they try to live independently of men, they tend to experience poverty and social disapproval.[7] Sen goes beyond the usual bargaining approach by also raising the question of what determines preferences. He argues that people's perceptions of their interests, of what they want, and can legitimately claim, are shaped by their upbringing and the social context in which they find themselves.

On this basis he suggests that women, in the context of a society characterized by gender inequality, tend not to have such sharp perceptions as men of their own interests, needs, rights or deserts, and this further disables women in intra-household arrangements. This is a point which undermines the basic starting point of the neoclassical approach—the idea of the individual as characterized by the well-defined preference function. This depiction of the individual represents as universal, characteristics that are more likely to be the (learned) characteristics of men than of women.

Neoclassical analysis does recognize that some of the gender differentiation in paid work results from inequality. This is conceptualized as stemming from discrimination against women, variously attributed to prejudice (dislike of working with or for women; dislike of managing women); persistence of outmoded 'noneconomic' traditions; or to inadequate information about women (for instance, a mistaken belief that women lack certain abilities, such as the ability to make rational decisions, or acquire technical skills). Much econometric effort has gone into trying to determine how much of the gender differentiation in labour markets is due to discrimination and how much is 'legitimate' because it stems from differences in aspirations, qualifications, seniority, absenteeism, etc. (for example, Birdsall and Sabot, 1991). Women's lower aspirations, attributed to their lack of role models to copy, is emphasized as an explanatory variable in a study of gender in the labour market in Cote d'Ivoire, Kenya and Tanzania undertaken for the World Bank by Collier *et al.* (1991). The literature which emphasizes women's lower aspirations pays little attention to the pressures which may restrict women's aspirations. Lack of suitable role models may well play a part; but more potent is likely to be the disapproval expressed by many men of women who seek to achieve, a disapproval which may extend as far as physical violence.

The neoclassical analysis of gender discrimination in labour markets is limited in its ability to produce a fully gender-aware analysis by its 'choice-theoretic' basis. Aspirations, qualifications, labour market attachment, and quality of work done are all conceptualized as determined by preferences. The role of social structures is underplayed. As a result, responsibility for a considerable degree of inequality is placed on women themselves: thus a study by Birdsall and Fox (1991) of the substantial income differential between male and female school teachers in Brazil concludes that there is some evidence of discrimination but 'the real problem is rooted in the decisions of women to seek more restrictive training than men.' The 'choice-theoretic' approach begs all the important questions about how 'choosing subjects' are constituted and choice sets constrained. Because of this it can achieve only a very limited degree of gender-awareness.

3.   GENDER-AWARENESS IN STRUCTURALIST APPROACHES TO DEVELOPMENT ECONOMICS

Despite the critical stance of the structuralist approach it has tended to share with neoclassical economics a disregard of gender at the macro level. Structuralist macroeconomics recognizes that the level of economic activity and the effect of fiscal and monetary policy is partly determined by the 'social matrix' (Taylor, 1991: 21). But the components of the social matrix are identified only in class terms (Taylor, 1991: 22–23). Structuralist macroeconomics emphasizes changes in income distribution against labour as the hidden 'equilibrating factor' bringing aggregate supply into equality with aggregate demand in stabilization programmes (Taylor, 1991: 28). But there is no recognition that 'labour' is gendered and that declines in income of poorer households may fall more heavily on women and children than on men. There is now a wealth of evidence which shows that household income is not fully pooled and shared (Dwyer and Bruce, (eds.) 1988). Women typically bear the responsibility for managing household income and expenditure so as to meet the day-to-day needs of household members. But they do not control access to all the resources they require to discharge these responsibilities, and are thus dependent on transfers from male household members. A general finding from studies from all major regions of the Third World, as well as from many developed countries, is that whereas women's income is almost exclusively used to meet collective household needs, men tend to retain a considerable portion of their income for personal spending. The hidden 'equilibrating factor' is women's ability to absorb the shocks of stabilization programmes, through more work and 'making do' on limited incomes.

At the micro level, much structuralist criticism has been addressed to the 'elasticity optimism' of neoclassical analysis; for instance, to the assumption that higher prices for farmers will result in a higher total agricultural output rather than a switching from some crops to others. But the emphasis in such criticism is on the barriers to supply response which result from lack of investment in infrastructure and complementary inputs. The barrier that is caused by the pattern of gender relations in agriculture is usually neglected. Here limitations of the analysis again stem from omission—a failure to disaggregate the farming household.

Gendered patterns of resource control in rural households are likely to hinder supply response in many sub-Saharan countries (Elson, 1987; Palmer, 1991). For example, a study by Schoepf and Engundu (1991) found that in response to rising maize prices in Zaïre, men sought to increase maize cropping in fields under their control. But although men manage and control maize production, receiving the cash when the crop is sold, the sexual division of labour is such that many of the labour inputs are supplied by their wives. However, the women also have the responsibility of growing manioc to feed the family and provide cash to buy items such as clothing, salt, soap and fish. Thus maize and manioc compete for women's time; and whereas the proceeds from the sale of maize are controlled by men, women control the use of the manioc crop. In some areas in Zaïre, women have resisted men's demands for more inputs to maize production to enable them to go on cultivating manioc, thus restricting the maize supply response.[8]

Of course, incentives could be provided directly to the women for their labour input into crops managed by their husbands, if marketing agents were to make payments to women as well as men. This was suggested in Tanzania as a way of improving tea supply, but was resisted by both local development planning agencies and international development agencies as too radical: as one official put it, 'whatever happens, we do not want a revolution. If women have their own money, why will they marry?' (Mbilinyi, 1988).

Though gender issues are absent from most of the critiques of 'elasticity optimism' in policy towards agriculture, they do make an appearance in some of the critiques of World Bank structural adjustment programmes. Here, a limitation is that 'women' are merely added on as an additional category, usually as a 'vulnerable group', as in 'adjustment with a human face' (Cornia *et al.*, 1987).

The African Alternative Framework for structural adjustment with transformation (ECA, 1989) goes beyond a 'welfare' approach, and does begin to address some important imbalances in power, calling for cuts in military spending, greater accountability of the public sector, and an 'increased role of the people' to 'safeguard against bureaucratic excesses'. But it does not directly address the issue of male power and fails to recognize gender relations as one of the important disabling structures in need of transformation if development in Africa is to get back on track.

The limitations of the structuralist approach may be summarized as follows: though this approach does emphasize the importance of social relations ('social matrix', 'social structure') in shaping development, it only gets as far as incorporating 'women' into the analysis as a 'vulnerable group'. It does not recognize unequal gender relations as one of the key structures which determine how the economy functions.

4. GENDER-AWARE ANALYSIS OF DEVELOPMENT PROCESSES

Two examples of gender-aware analysis are discussed in this section. The first, by Palmer (1991), is a feminist adaptation of the neoclassical framework; the second, by

Mackintosh (1989), is feminist political economy which draws on aspects of struc-turalist and Marxist approaches.

Palmer's work is concerned with the impact of gender relations on the process of structural adjustment in sub-Saharan Africa. Her basic argument is that 'without a gen-der frame in the analysis, certain significant costs of economic inefficiency and resource misallocation are likely to persist, and that this will impair the chances of achieving sustainable growth' (p. 1). She brings a gender frame in to the analysis through the concept of 'gender-based market distortions' (p. 3), deliberately making comparison with the neoclassical concept of 'price distortions'. These distortions, in her analysis, go beyond discrimination, to encompass women's unpaid work in reproduc-tion and family maintenance, which Palmer conceptualizes as a tax (the 'reproduction labour tax') that women must pay before they can devote time to income-generating work. Distortions also include unequal terms of exchange of resources between women and men in households—Palmer conceptualizes this in terms of intra-household markets in which the terms of trade are biased against women.

Palmer concludes that gender-based market distortions are likely to be reinforced rather than weakened in the course of structural adjustment. To counteract this a vari-ety of policies are recommended. Palmer emphasizes that, in the long term, economic efficiency requires reforms in women's rights to property (i.e. in inheritance and mar-riage laws). 'This cuts deep into men's authority over women, and there is no question that it will be resisted. Yet it is crucial to economic transformation and dynamic efficiency. Women must be able to raise capital as easily as men if capital resources are to be efficiently distributed' (p. 140). To deal with the distortion caused by the 'reproduction labour tax' on women, Palmer recommends that the unpaid work of human resource production should be 'opened up to market forces' (p. 141) and com-moditized, with more child-care and household services being undertaken by paid workers. The payments are envisaged as coming not mainly from the pockets of indi-vidual women but from an employment tax on all registered companies to be paid into a national provident fund; and a sales tax on selected cash crops.

The strength of Palmer's approach is that she shows how a better analysis of current adjustment programmes and a more effective approach to designing alterna-tives can come from incorporating a conceptualization of gender relations into the investigation right from the start, rather than adding-on 'women' as an afterthought. She rejects the neoclassical view that analysis at the macro level need not be con-cerned with the unpaid work of human resource production, and that at the micro level, patterns of gender-differentiation are the result of choice. However, she retains the neoclassical view that markets in themselves are capable of being unbi-ased and of providing a 'true costing' of resources; and, in particular, she sees the development of extensive rural labour markets as being a way to both greater efficiency and greater gender equity (p. 124). A much less optimistic view of the role of markets is taken by Mackintosh (1989) in her study of gender, class and rural transition in Senegal.

Mackintosh (1989) provides an historically grounded analysis of agribusiness and the food crisis in Senegal, which shows how gender relations are crucial variables mediating the impact of commercialization of agriculture. Though the horticultural estates she studied employed large numbers of women, unpaid domestic work remained the responsibility of women, and the form of adaptation to wage work involved a redivision of labour between women, not a change in the sexual division of labour. However, 'individualized access to cash income introduced new contradictions within the households concerning the level of mutual obligations among members' (p. 163) and the sharpness of these contradictions influenced the way in which people acted in relation to growing food to supply their own needs. With the availability of wage work, as relations within households and between households became monetized, women ceased to be willing to do agricultural work unpaid. 'And once labour had to be paid, farming became a matter of individual commercial calculation, in which food growing inevitably lost out to cash crops given the relative prices' (p. 144) with important implications for household food security.

Mackintosh differs from Palmer in taking up a critical attitude to the new wage employment opportunities provided for women by agribusiness, arguing that their effects were contradictory: 'On the one hand there was an awareness among the women of the importance of their work and incomes, and a resulting confidence especially among some of the younger women. On the other hand there was also the contradictory trend, emerging out of the same set of circumstances, of husbands seeking to assert more control than had previously been acceptable over the incomes of their wives' (p. 171). Moreover, 'certain jobs, classified as women's jobs, had come to have attached to them lower pay and worse conditions than the jobs predominantly done by men' (p. 172). Women's work was entirely casualized and 'the hiring had a number of the corrupt features one might expect when young male team leaders are responsible for the hiring of women' (p. 173). While men were generally paid the minimum wage, women generally received less than this; and the expenditures that they had to make to discharge their obligations to nurture their families increased.

Where Mackintosh's analysis might be criticized is in not going far enough in explaining how the new wages and jobs came to be structured by gender inequality. She emphasizes the constraints of women's domestic obligations and the perceptions of management and workers about women's abilities, but this (like the neoclassical economics of gender discrimination) locates the source of gender differentiation outside the dynamic of commercialization. To take the analysis further requires investigations of the operation of markets and the management of commercial enterprises to reveal what is intrinsic to them that permits them to become gendered, and to be vehicles for the perpetuation of gender inequality.

5.   INCREASING GENDER-AWARENESS IN DEVELOPMENT ECONOMICS

The primary requirement is to examine the interaction of the production of goods and services and the production of human resources in the context of the sexual division of labour. This necessitates *gender disaggregation*. At the occupational level, farmers need to be disaggregated into male and female farmers; workers need to be disaggregated into male and female workers; traders and merchants need to be disaggregated into male and female traders and merchants, etc. This must be done at the outset of the analysis, rather than adding on 'women farmers', 'women workers' etc., as an after-thought.

It is particularly important that the *household should be disaggregated* and not treated as a unity, so that the cooperative conflicts and separate economic accounting units it may contain are revealed. The need to distinguish between female-headed and male-headed households seems to be widely appreciated, but not the need to distinguish between male and female patterns of resource control, work and expenditure within households containing both men and women. Even if income is redistributed within households so that everyone's material needs are met, it is important to know whether this is a stressful or peaceful process, one achieved in a way at odds or compatible with the autonomy and dignity of household members.

Disaggregation is not, however, enough. The level of gender-awareness will remain seriously inadequate without an attempt to go beyond the view that commercial processes are themselves gender-neutral and only become contaminated with male bias as a result of 'extraneous' removable factors such as prejudice and tradition.

A basis on which to build is provided by critical institutional economics,[9] which emphasizes the necessary incompleteness of contracts in an uncertain world, and the way in which the operation of markets, formation of prices and the organization of commercial production must necessarily rely on the operation of social institutions and norms—institutions and norms which are by no means necessarily socially optimal, though they may serve the interests of particular groups (for examples, see Bowles, 1985; Hodgson, 1988; Elster, 1989; Bardhan, 1989).

There is a gap in contracts to buy and sell which has to be filled by a mixture of mutuality, goodwill, trust, and power, coercion, and submission—a kind of 'moral economy' interacting with the monetary economy, embodied in routines, habits, customs, linking economic agents through cooperative networks as well as through cash. These are not regrettable 'traditions' which could be swept away by more thoroughgoing commercialization. Commercialization can change the forms and content of this 'moral economy' but cannot obliterate the need for it.

Critical analysis of markets and workplaces reveals that their norms and institutions are related to patterns of entitlements and power (Bowles, 1985; Mackintosh, 1990; Harriss, 1990). For instance, a study of the export trade in Jamaica found that although women entrepreneurs were involved in exporting, they were disadvantaged by not being part of the 'informal referral networks and business–social organizations where exchanges of information occur' (Commonwealth Secretariat, 1990: 48). The indispensable mutuality, goodwill and trust and access to information which such networks foster is often facilitated by discouraging 'outsiders'—optimal for those already members, but not for new entrants, nor for society as a whole.

Similarly, in labour markets, bias against women may boost profits by facilitating the construction of institutions and norms in the workplace that enable employers to maximize the amount of work that they can extract. Strategies of discipline, control and motivation may be built on the gendering of jobs to the disadvantage of women (Humphrey, 1985; Cockburn, 1985). As Humphrey (1985) discovered in his study of Brazilian factories, 'the supposedly objective economic laws of market competition work through and within gendered structures' (p. 219).

The presence of gender bias is not something that can be eliminated by trying to make markets more 'objective' because the incompleteness of contracts can never be overcome. But nor is such bias a *socially* optimal adaptation for dealing with incompleteness. It can be functional for the achievement of commercial objectives of particular groups (as well as for the perpetuation of male bias) but, at the same time, dysfunctional for the achievement of development objectives for society as a whole, as has been suggested in this paper.

One major implication is that policy analysis must encompass the design of institutional changes. Alternatives are available. The sphere of trust, goodwill, team spirit, could be extended if entitlements were more equally distributed and business networks were opened up to wider participation; the quality of work could be improved and maintained through more participatory and democratic structures.[10] The ability of men and women to respond to, and benefit from, new market opportunities in ways that do not jeopardize the production of human resources and the satisfaction of needs for things besides money, could be enhanced by changing the ways in which getting a living is integrated with raising children and looking after family members.

A development economics constituted on this basis would be capable of contributing more effectively to both the reduction of gender inequality and the achievement of other, more specifically economic, objectives.

NOTES

1 The scope of this paper is constrained by the limited space made available for it. It does not attempt to survey the whole of the relevant literature nor to substantiate each argument in detail. The interested, or sceptical, reader is invited to consult Elson (1991b) where the argument is more fully developed.

2 For further discussion of this point see Mackintosh (1981). For evidence, see United Nations (1991).

3 For more detailed discussion of these points see Elson (1991a), Ch. 7.

4 This is not to say that economic calculations do not play a role in decisions to bear children—or decisions about how, or indeed whether, they should be reared. The 'human capital' approach is useful in drawing attention to such calculations—but misguided when it elides all distinction between human resources and capital and consumption goods.

5 This has been explored at some length in some of the literature on gender and structural adjustment—see, for instance, Elson (1987, 1989, 1991a); Commonwealth Expert Group (1989); Palmer (1991).

6 For a useful critical exposition see Evans (1989).

7 Sen has been criticized by Kabeer (1991) for paying insufficient attention to how cooperative conflicts within households are enacted. She suggests that in regions of 'classic patriarchy' (i.e. North Africa, Middle East, South Asia) there is unlikely to be any open bargaining—here women are constrained to adopt submissive and self-sacrificing behaviour. However, in regions where women have more autonomy, such as much of sub-Saharan Africa, there is more overt bargaining and conflict.

8 This problem may be seen in neoclassical terms as an example of the 'principal-agent' problem (Collier, 1990).

9 There are two strands (at least) in the 'new institutional economics'—a neoclassical strand which explains institutional change in terms of changes in relative prices, and takes the persistence of an institution as evidence of its optimality; and a critical strand which emphasizes power and unequal entitlements in the explanation of institutions. For some discussion of the differences, see Bardhan (1989).

10 A similar point is made by Bardhan (1989) (though not in relation to male bias) when he writes: 'in transaction cost and imperfect information theories demonstrating the economic rationale of some existing institutions in terms of transaction costs and moral hazard, it is under-emphasized that a more democratic organization of the work process (following Bowles) or a more egalitarian distribution of assets (following Roemer) might have significantly reduced (not eliminated) the informational constraints and Hobbesian malfeasance problems which form the staple of much of the principal-agent games in the literature' (p. 1394).

REFERENCES

Bardhan, P. (1989). 'The new institutional economics and development theory: a brief critical assessment', *World Development,* 17(9), pp. 1389–1395.

Birdsall, N. and Fox, L. (1991). 'Why males earn more: location and training of Brazilian schoolteachers'. In Birdsall, N. and Sabot, R. (eds), *Unfair Advantage . . .* Washington, DC: World Bank, pp. 121–146.

Birdsall, N. and Sabot, R. (1991). *Unfair Advantage: Labor Market Discrimination in Developing Countries.* Washington, DC: World Bank.

Bowles, S. (1985). 'The production process in a competitive economy: Walrasian, neo-Hobbesian and Marxian models', *American Economic Review,* 75, pp. 16–36.

Cockburn, C. (1985). *Machinery of Dominance: Women, Men and Technical Know-How.* London: Pluto Press.

Collier, P. (1990). *Women and structural adjustment.* World Bank Economic Development Institute. Washington, DC: World Bank.

Collier, P., Appleton, S., Bevan, D. L., Burger, K., Gunning, J. W., Haddad, I., and Hoddinott, J. (1991). *Public Services and Household Allocation in Africa: Does Gender Matter?,* Report for Women and Development Unit. Washington, DC: World Bank.

Commonwealth Expert Group (1989). *Engendering Adjustment for the 1990s.* London: Commonwealth Secretariat.

Commonwealth Secretariat (1990). *Women in Export Development: Studies on Kenya, Ghana, Jamaica and Solomon Islands.* Export Market Development Division. London: Commonwealth Secretariat.

Cornia, G., Jolly, R. and Stewart, F. (eds) (1987). *Adjustment with a Human Face.* Oxford: Oxford University Press.

Dwyer, D. and Bruce, J. (eds) (1988). *A Home Divided—Women and Income in the Third World.* Stanford: Stanford University Press.

Economic Commission for Africa (1989). *African Alternative Framework.* Addis Ababa: United Nations.

Elson, D. (1987). 'The impact of structural adjustment on women: concepts and issues'. Paper prepared for Commonwealth Secretariat, London: Commonwealth Secretariat.

Elson, D. (1989). 'The impact of structural adjustment on women: concepts and issues'. In B. Onimode (ed.). *The IMF, the World Bank and the African Debt,* Vol. 2, *The Social and Political Impact.* London: Zed Books.

Elson, D. (ed.) (1991a). *Male Bias in the Development Process.* Manchester: Manchester University Press.

Elson, D. (1991b). *Gender Analysis and Economics in the Context of Africa.* Manchester Discussion Paper in Development Studies, No. 9103. Manchester: International Development Centre.

Elster, J. (1989). 'Social norms and economic theory', *Journal of Economic Perspectives,* 3(4), pp. 85–98.

Evans, A. (1989). 'Gender issues in rural household economics'. Institute of Development Studies Discussion Paper no. 254, Brighton: Institute of Development Studies.

Folbre, N. (1986a). 'Hearts and spades: paradigms of household economics', *World Development,* 14(2), pp. 245–255.

Folbre, N. (1986b). 'Cleaning house: new perspectives on households and economic development', *Journal of Development Economics,* 22, 5–40.

Harriss, B. (1990). 'Another awkward class: merchants and agrarian change in India'. In H. Bernstein, B. Crow, M. Mackintosh and C. Martin (eds), *The Food Question.* London: Earthscan, pp. 91–103.

Hodgson, G. (1988). *Economics and Institutions.* Cambridge: Polity Press.

Humphrey, J. (1985). 'Gender, pay and skill: manual workers in Brazilian industry'. In H. Afshar (ed.), *Women, Work and Ideology in the Third World.* London: Tavistock, pp. 214–231.

Kabeer, N. (1991). 'Gender, production and well-being: rethinking the household economy'. Institute of Development Studies Discussion Paper no. 288. Brighton: Institute of Development Studies.

Mackintosh, M. (1981). 'The sexual division of labour and the subordination of women'. In K. Young, C. Wolkovitz and R. McCullagh (eds), *Of Marriage and the Market.* London: CSE Books.

Mackintosh, M. (1989). *Gender, Class and Rural Transition—Agribusiness and the Food Crisis in Senegal.* London: Zed Books.

Mackintosh, M. (1990). 'Abstract markets and real needs'. In H. Bernstein, B. Crow, M. Mackintosh and C. Martin (eds), *The Food Question.* London: Earthscan, pp. 43–53.

Mbilinyi, M. (1988). 'The invention of female farming systems in Africa: structural adjustment in Tanzania'. Workshop on Economic Crisis, Household Strategies and Women's Work, Cornell University, Ithaca.

Moser, C. (1989). 'The impact of recession and structural adjustment policies at the microlevel: low income women and their households in Guayquil, Ecuador', *Invisible Adjustment,* Vol. 2. UNICEF.

Palmer, I. (1991). *Gender and Population in the Adjustment of African Economies: Planning for Change.* Geneva: ILO.

Schoepf, B. and Engundu, W. (1991). 'Women and structural adjustment in Zaire'. In C. H. Gladwin (ed.), *Structural Adjustment and African Women Farmers.* Gainsville. University of Florida Press, pp. 151–168.

Sen, A. K. (1990). 'Gender and cooperative conflicts'. In I. Tinker (ed.), *Persistent Inequalities—Women and World Development.* Oxford: Oxford University Press, pp. 123–149.

Taylor, L. (1991). *Varieties of Stabilisation Experience.* WIDER Studies in Development Economics. Oxford: Clarendon Press.

United Nations (1991). *The World's Women: Trends and Statistics, 1970–1990.* New York. United Nations.

PART TWO

ECONOMIC DEVELOPMENT AND UNDERDEVELOPMENT IN HISTORICAL PERSPECTIVE

Since the essence of development is rapid and discontinuous change in institutions and in economic relations, it is impossible to construct a rigorous and determinate model of that process. Such a model would necessarily omit too many of the significant variables in development. Instead a less rigorous but more richly textured approach that accounts for the most important socioeconomic variables must be constructed. For this we turn to history.

One of the greatest weaknesses of mainstream economic theorists is their lack of understanding of the process of development in the West between the seventeenth and twentieth centuries. "Liberalization" and "letting the market work" have become virtual mantras to be intoned for any question or problem. However, successful development historically put definite limits on these processes and incorporated an important role for social institutions, such as government. The development of capitalism in the West required change in the existing social structure, so that the progress-oriented middle class could become the leaders of society. This change often involved a violent struggle for supremacy between the old social order and the emerging new one. In the English Revolution of 1640, ending with the Supremacy of Parliament Act in 1688, the landed gentry and the urban middle class replaced the feudal lords as the dominant classes, thus preparing the way for later economic change. The French Revolution of 1789 replaced the old aristocracy with the new middle class; the absence of such social change was a major factor in the economic stagnation of Spain after the seventeenth century.

This change in social structure allowed productive use of the "social surplus," that part of society's total product remaining after basic consumption needs are met. How a society chooses to use this net product of its labor—squandering it in luxury consumption and military adventure or adding to the country's capital stock—conditions the pattern of development. Of critical importance is who controls the surplus. Are decisions made to favor the elite or is the social surplus distributed widely and used to develop society for the good of all?

Because the Western capitalist model forms the core of most current development strategies, it is important to have a clear sense of the dynamics of early capitalism and how it relates to development today. Dudley Dillard's article outlines the crucial elements in the historical development of capitalism in the West. He writes: "Productive use of the 'social surplus' was the special virtue that enabled capitalism to outstrip all prior economic systems." He also makes clear that this was not a simple and automatic process, not the result of laissez-faire; it resulted from struggle and succeeded when a virtual social revolution brought a broad-based progressive movement to power. Dillard also notes the historical alternation between government involvement and market supremacy. Since his article was written, the pendulum has swung away from directed government involvement, toward the free market. This will certainly not be its last swing.

Paul A. Baran's article argues the virtual impossibility of "capitalist" development in the South. For Baran, continuous capitalist development is implausible for the South because of the power configuration between foreign and domestic decision makers and the people. Capitalism entered most underdeveloped countries the "Prussian Way," that is, not through the growth of small, competitive enterprise, but through the transfer from abroad of advanced, monopolistic business. The history of the South has not seen the growth of a strong, property-owning middle class and the overthrow of landlord domination of society. Instead, an accommodation was reached between the newly arrived monopolistic business class and the socially and politically entrenched agrarian aristocracy. Korea and Taiwan are exceptions, but they prove the rule. Their domination by Japanese imperialism broke their ruling class, and in both cases land reform soon after World War II established a broad base of land ownership.

In countries with the historical experience of imposed capitalism, the actual social surplus was much lower than the potential social surplus. A large share of the potential social surplus was used by aristocratic landlords on excess consumption and the maintenance of unproductive laborers, by owners for quick profits or by the wealthy to accumulate assets abroad as a hedge against domestic social and political hazards. The actual social surplus was further reduced by the resources used to maintain elaborate and inefficient bureaucratic and military establishments, to guarantee control.

The Andre Gunder Frank article shows that stagnation in the periphery was generated by the same historical process as successful capitalist development in the center. Frank concentrates on the nation-state and the incorporation of Latin America and other peripheral economies into the world capitalist order. Hierarchical relations between the First World (North) and Third World (South) prevented sustained, dynamic capitalist development for the periphery. Integration into the global economy was achieved through an intermediate metropolis-satellite chain, in which the surplus generated at each stage was successively drawn to the center. The most underdeveloped regions are therefore those with the strongest past ties to the center; the strongest developing economies are those which, usually through some crisis, had looser colonial ties. Again, Japanese colonization differed in being more recent and shorter, in its attempt to develop the colony into a component of a "co-prosperity sphere," and by ending at the close of World War II. This accounts for some of the difference in performance of contemporary Asian countries.

The part concludes with two historical studies of the processes of development or underdevelopment. Lucile Brockway documents the formative influence of Britain's Kew Gardens on world agricultural production. Her study gives historical flavor to Frank's "center-periphery" distinction and shows how any initial capitalist dynamics in the South were hampered by conscious British policy and power. Through theft and deception Britain and other European countries were able to establish the productive base of their colonial empires, dividing the world into metropolis and satellite in Frank's terms. The Brockway story has a contemporary ring as ethnobotanists scour the world to preserve biological specimens that are threatened by economic expansion; in the process they may provide the basis for future agricultural development. However, it is not at all certain that the countries that harbor or "own" the exemplars of genetic diversity will receive any benefits from their biological resources.

The final article is E. Bradford Burns's study of El Salvador, a historical case study of modernization without development, which tangibly illustrates the points made earlier by Dillard, Baran, and Frank. El Salvador is a striking example of how the rapid and profound modernization of a once-neglected outpost of the Spanish empire was accompanied by increasing impoverishment of the majority of the inhabitants, that is, the development of underdevelopment. This history resulted in the Salvadoran civil war that continued from 1979 into the 1990s. The Escuela Militar, mentioned by Burns, provided one of the worst moments of the war when personnel who were trained there played a central role in the cold-blooded murder of six Jesuit priests, their housekeeper, and her daughter in 1989. After a truce and relatively fair elections, there is hope for improvement in El Salvador, although continued political assassinations by the right and an absence of fundamental change in power relations must temper any optimism. Conditions developed during many decades of history cannot be changed overnight.

With these readings you will have a sense of the historical play that has unfolded since the "rise of the West" destabilized the world after 1500. This will allow a better understanding of the richness of the development process that will be illustrated in the remaining parts of the book.

CHAPTER 6

CAPITALISM

Dudley Dillard

University of Maryland

Capitalism [is] a term used to denote the economic system that has been dominant in the Western world since the breakup of feudalism. Fundamental to any system called capitalist are the relations between private owners of nonpersonal means of production (land, mines, industrial plants, etc., collectively known as capital) and free but capitalless workers, who sell their labour services to employers. Under capitalism, decisions concerning production are made by private businessmen operating for private profit. Labourers are free in the sense that they cannot legally be compelled to work for the owners of the means of production. However, since labourers do not possess the means of production required for self-employment, they must, of economic necessity, offer their services on some terms to employers who do control the means of production. The resulting wage bargains determine the proportion in which the total product of society will be shared between the class of labourers and the class of capitalist entrepreneurs.

· · · · · ·

HISTORICAL DEVELOPMENT

1. Origins of Capitalism

Although the continuous development of capitalism as a system dates only from the 16th century, antecedents of capitalist institutions existed in the ancient world, and

Reprinted from *Encyclopaedia Britannica*, pp. 839–842, by permission of the publisher and the author. Copyright © *Encyclopaedia Britannica*, 1972.

flourishing pockets of capitalism were present during the later middle ages. One strategic external force contributing to the breakup of medieval economic institutions was the growing volume of long-distance trade between capitalist centres, carried on with capitalist techniques in a capitalist spirit. Specialized industries grew up to serve long-distance trade, and the resulting commercial and industrial towns gradually exerted pressures which weakened the internal structure of agriculture based on serfdom, the hallmark of the feudal regime. Changes in trade, industry, and agriculture were taking place simultaneously and interacting with one another in highly complex actual relations, but it was chiefly long-distance trade which set in motion changes that spread throughout the medieval economy and finally transformed it into a new type of economic society.

Flanders in the 13th century and Florence in the 14th century were two capitalist pockets of special interest. Their histories shed light on the conditions that were essential to the development of capitalism in England. The great enterprise of late medieval and early modern Europe was the woolen industry, and most of the business arrangements that later characterized capitalism developed in connection with long-distance trade in wool and cloth.

In Flanders revolutionary conflict raged between plebeian craftsmen and patrician merchant-manufacturers. The workers succeeded in destroying the concentration of economic and political power in the hands of cloth magnates, only to be crushed in turn by a violent counterrevolution that destroyed the woolen industry and brought ruin to both groups. A similar performance was repeated in Florence, which became one of the great industrial cities of Europe during the 14th century. Restless, revolutionary urban workers overthrew the ruling hierarchy of merchants, manufacturers, and bankers, and were in turn crushed in a bloody counterrevolution. Thus both Flanders and Florence failed to perpetuate their great industries because they failed to solve the social problem arising from conflicting claims of small numbers of rich capitalists and large numbers of poor workers.

2. Early Capitalism (1500–1750)

By the end of the middle ages the English cloth industry had become the greatest in Europe. Because of the domestic availability of raw wool and the innovation of simple mechanical fulling mills, the English cloth industry had established itself in certain rural areas where it avoided the violent social strife that had destroyed the urban industries of Flanders and Florence. Although it was subject to many problems and difficulties, the English rural cloth industry continued to grow at a rapid rate during the 16th, 17th and 18th centuries. Hence, it was the woolen industry that spearheaded capitalism as a social and economic system and rooted it for the first time in English soil.

Productive use of the "social surplus" was the special virtue that enabled capitalism to outstrip all prior economic systems. Instead of building pyramids and cathedrals, those in command of the social surplus chose to invest in ships, warehouses, raw materials, finished goods, and other material forms of wealth. The social surplus was thus converted into enlarged productive capacity. Among the historical events and circumstances that significantly influenced capital formation in western Europe in the early stage of capitalist development, three merit special attention: (1) religious sanction for hard work and frugality; (2) the impact of precious metals from the new world on the relative shares of income going to wages, profits, and rents; and (3) the role of national states in fostering and directly providing capital formation in the form of general-purpose capital goods.

Capitalist Spirit   The economic ethics taught by medieval Catholicism presented obstacles to capitalist ideology and development. Hostility to material wealth carried forward the teachings of the Christian fathers against mammonism. Saint Jerome said, "A rich man is either a thief or the son of a thief." Saint Augustine felt that trade was bad because it turned men away from the search for God. Down through the middle ages commerce and banking were viewed, at best, as necessary evils. Moneylending was for a time confined to non-Christians because it was considered unworthy of Christians. Interest on loans was unlawful under the anti-usury laws of both church and secular authorities. Speculation and profiteering violated the central medieval economic doctrine of just price.

Expansion of commerce in the later middle ages stirred controversies and led to attempts to reconcile theological doctrines with economic realities. In Venice, Florence, Augsburg, and Antwerp—all Catholic cities—capitalists violated the spirit and circumvented the letter of the prohibitions against interest. On the eve of the Protestant Reformation capitalists, who still laboured under the shadow of the sin of avarice, had by their deeds become indispensable to lay rulers and to large numbers of people who were dependent upon them for employment.

The Protestant Reformation of the 16th and 17th centuries developed alongside economic changes which resulted in the spread of capitalism in northern Europe, especially in the Netherlands and England. This chronological and geographical correlation between the new religion and economic development has led to the suggestion that Protestantism had causal significance for the rise of modern capitalism. Without in any sense being the "cause" of capitalism, which already existed on a wide and expanding horizon, the Protestant ethic proved a bracing stimulant to the new economic order. Doctrinal revision or interpretation seemed not only to exonerate capitalists from the sin of avarice but even to give divine sanction to their way of life. In the ordinary conduct of life, a new type of worldly asceticism emerged, one that meant hard work, frugality, sobriety, and efficiency in one's calling in the marketplace similar to that of the monastery. Applied in the environment of expanding trade and industry, the Protestant creed taught that accumulated wealth should be used to produce more wealth.

Acceptance of the Protestant ethic also eased the way to systematic organization of free labour. By definition, free labourers could not be compelled by force to work in the service of others. Moreover, the use of force would have violated the freedom of one's calling. Psychological compulsion arising from religious belief was the answer to the paradox. Every occupation was said to be noble in God's eyes. For those with limited talents, Christian conscience demanded unstinting labour even at low wages in the service of God—and, incidentally, of employers. It was an easy step to justify economic inequality because it would hasten the accumulation of wealth by placing it under the guardianship of the most virtuous (who were, incidentally, the wealthiest) and remove temptation from weaker persons who could not withstand the allurements associated with wealth. After all, it did not much matter who held legal title to wealth, for it was not for enjoyment. The rich like the poor were to live frugally all the days of their lives. Thus the capitalist system found a justification that was intended to make inequality tolerable to the working classes.

The Price Revolution   Meanwhile treasure from the new world had a profound impact on European capitalism, on economic classes, and on the distribution of income in Europe. Gold and silver from the mines of Mexico, Peru, and Bolivia increased Europe's supply of precious metals sevenfold and raised prices two- or threefold between 1540 and 1640. The significance of the increased supply of money lay not so much in the rise in prices as in its effect on the social and economic classes of Europe. Landlords, the older ruling class, suffered because money rents failed to rise as rapidly as the cost of living. The more aggressive landlords raised rents and introduced capitalistic practices into agriculture. In England the enclosure movement, which developed with ever increasing momentum and vigour during the 17th and 18th centuries, encouraged sheep raising to supply wool to the expanding woolen industry. Among labourers, money wages failed to keep pace with the cost of living, causing real wages to fall during the price revolution. The chief beneficiaries of this century-long inflation were capitalists, including merchants, manufacturers, and other employ-ers. High prices and low wages resulted in profit inflation, which in turn contributed to larger savings and capital accumulation. Profit inflation and wage deflation created a more unequal distribution of income. Wage earners got less and capitalists got more of the total product than they would have received in the absence of inflation. Had the new increments of wealth gone to wage earners instead of to capitalists, most of it would have been consumed rather than invested, and hence the working classes of the 16th century would have eaten better, but the future would have inherited less accumu-lated wealth.

Mercantilism   Early capitalism (1500–1750) also witnessed in western Europe the rise of strong national states pursuing mercantilist policies. Critics have tended to identify mercantilism with amassing silver and gold by having a so-called favourable balance of exports over imports in trading relations with other nations and communi-ties, but the positive contribution and historic significance of mercantilism lay in the creation of conditions necessary for rapid and cumulative economic change in the countries of western Europe. At the end of the middle ages western Europe stood about where many underdeveloped countries stand in the 20th century. In underdevel-oped economies the difficult task of statesmanship is to get under way a cumulative process of economic development, for once a certain momentum is attained, further advances appear to follow more or less automatically. Achieving such sustained growth requires virtually a social revolution.

Power must be transferred from reactionary to progressive classes; new energies must be released, often by uprooting the old order; the prevailing religious outlook may constitute a barrier to material advancement. A new social and political frame-work must be created within which cumulative economic change can take place.

Among the tasks which private capitalists were either unable or unwilling to perform were the creation of a domestic market free of tolls and other barriers to trade within the nation's borders; a uniform monetary system; a legal code appropriate to capitalistic progress; a skilled and disciplined labour force; safeguards against internal violence; national defense against attack; sufficient literacy and education among business classes to use credit instruments, contracts and other documents required of a commercial civilization; basic facilities for communication and transportation and harbour installations. A strong government and an adequate supply of economic resources were required to create most of these conditions, which constitute the "social overhead capital" needed in a productive economy. Because the returns from them, however great, cannot be narrowly channeled for private gain, such investments must normally be made by the government and must be paid for out of public revenues.

Preoccupation with productive use of the social surplus led mercantilist commentators to advocate low wages and long hours for labour. Consumption in excess of bare subsistence was viewed as a tax on progress and therefore contrary to the national interest. Mercantilist society was not a welfare state; it could not afford to be. Luxury consumption was condemned as a dissipation of the social surplus. Restrictions on imports were directed especially at luxury consumption.

Opportunities for profitable private investment multiplied rapidly as mercantilist policy succeeded in providing the basic social overhead capital. Rather paradoxically, it was because the state had made such an important contribution to economic development that the ideology of laissez-faire could later crystallise. When that occurred, dedication to capital accumulation remained a basic principle of capitalism, but the shift from public to private initiative marked the passage from the early state of capitalism and the beginning of the next stage, the classical period.

3.   Classical Capitalism (1750–1914)

In England, beginning in the 18th century, the focus of capitalist development shifted from commerce to industry. The Industrial Revolution may be defined as the period of transition from a dominance of commercial over industrial capital to a dominance of industrial over commercial capital. Preparation for this shift began long before the invention of the flying shuttle, the water frame and the steam engine, but the technological changes of the 18th century made the transition dramatically evident.

The rural and household character of the English textile industry continued only as long as the amount of fixed capital required for efficient production remained relatively small. Changes in technology and organization shifted industry again to urban centres in the course of the Industrial Revolution, although not to the old commercial urban centres. Two or three centuries of steady capital accumulation began to pay off handsomely in the 18th century. Now it became feasible to make practical use of technical knowledge which had been accumulating over the centuries. Capitalism became a powerful promoter of technological change because the accumulation of capital made possible the use of inventions which poorer societies could not have afforded. Inventors and innovators like James Watt found business partners who were able to finance their inventions through lean years of experimentation and discouragement to ultimate commercial success. Aggressive entrepreneurs like Richard Arkwright found capital to finance the factory type of organization required for the utilization of new machines. Wealthy societies had existed before capitalism, but none had managed their wealth in a manner that enabled them to take advantage of the more efficient methods of production which an increasing mastery over nature made physically possible.

Adam Smith's great *Inquiry Into the Nature and Causes of the Wealth of Nations* (1776) expressed the ideology of classical capitalism. Smith recommended dismantling the state bureaucracy and leaving economic decisions to the free play of self-regulating market forces. While Smith recognized the faults of businessmen, he contended they could do little harm in a world of freely competitive enterprise. In Smith's opinion, private profit and public welfare would become reconciled through impersonal forces of market competition. After the French Revolution and the Napoleonic wars had swept the remnants of feudalism into oblivion and rapidly undermined mercantilist fetters, Smith's policies were put into practice. Laissez-faire policies of 19th-century political liberalism included free trade, sound money (the gold standard), balanced budgets, minimum poor relief—in brief, the principle of leaving individuals to themselves and of trusting that their unregulated interactions would produce socially desirable results. No new conceptions of society arose immediately to challenge seriously what had become, in fact, a capitalist civilization.

This system, though well-defined and logically coherent, must be understood as a system of tendencies only. The heritage of the past and other obstructions prevented any full realization of the principles except in a few cases of which the English free trade movement, crystallised by the repeal of the Corn Laws in 1846, is the most important. Such as they were, however, both tendencies and realizations bear the unmistakable stamp of the businessman's interests and still more the businessman's type of mind. Moreover, it was not only policy but the philosophy of national and individual life, the scheme of cultural values, that bore that stamp. Its materialistic utilitarianism, its naive confidence in progress of a certain type, its actual achievements in the field of pure and applied science, the temper of its artistic creations, may all be traced to the spirit of rationalism that emanates from the businessman's office. For much of the time and in many countries the businessman did not rule politically. But even noncapitalist rulers espoused his interests and adopted his views. They were what they had not been before, his agents.

More definitely than in any other historical epoch these developments can be explained by purely economic causes. It was the success of capitalist enterprise that raised the bourgeoisie to its position of temporary ascendancy. Economic success produced political power, which in turn produced policies congenial to the capitalist process. Thus the English industrialists obtained free trade, and free trade in turn was a major factor in a period of unprecedented economic expansion.

The partition of Africa and the carving out of spheres of influence in Asia by European powers in the decades preceding World War I led critics of capitalism to develop, on a Marxist basis, a theory of economic imperialism. According to this doctrine, competition among capitalist firms tends to eliminate all but a small number of giant concerns. Because of the inadequate purchasing power of the masses, these concerns find themselves unable to use the productive capacity they have built. They are, therefore, driven to invade foreign markets and to exclude foreign products from their own markets through protective tariffs. This situation produces aggressive colonial and foreign policies and "imperialist" wars, which the proletariat, if organized, turn into civil wars for socialist revolution. Like other doctrines of such sweeping character, this theory of imperialism is probably not capable of either exact proof or disproof. Three points, however, may be recorded in its favour; first, it does attempt what no other theory has attempted, namely, to subject the whole of the economic, political, and cultural patterns of the epoch that began during the long depression (1873–96) to comprehensive analysis by means of a clear-cut plan; second, on the surface at least, it seems to be confirmed by some of the outstanding manifestations of this pattern and some of the greatest events of this epoch; third, whatever may be wrong with its interpretations, it certainly starts from a fact that is beyond challenge—the capitalist tendency toward industrial combination and the emergence of giant firms. Though cartels and trusts antedate the epoch, at least so far as the United States is concerned, the role of what is popularly called "big business" has increased so much as to constitute one of the outstanding characteristics of recent capitalism.

4.   The Later Phase (Since 1914)

World War I marked a turning point in the development of capitalism in general and of European capitalism in particular. The period since 1914 has witnessed a reversal of the public attitude toward capitalism and of almost all the tendencies of the liberal epoch which preceded the war. In the prewar decades, European capitalism exercised vigorous leadership in the international economic community. World markets expanded, the gold standard became almost universal, Europe served as the world's banker, Africa became a European colony, Asia was divided into spheres of influence under the domination of European powers, and Europe remained the centre of a growing volume of international trade.

After World War I, however, these trends were reversed. International markets shrank, the gold standard was abandoned in favour of managed national currencies, banking hegemony passed from Europe to the United States, African and Asian peoples began successful revolts against European colonialism, and trade barriers multiplied. Western Europe as an entity declined, and in eastern Europe capitalism began to disintegrate. The Russian Revolution, a result of the war, uprooted over a vast area not only the basic capitalist institution of private property in the means of production, but the class structure, the traditional forms of government, and the established religion. Moreover, the juggernaut unleashed by the Russian Revolution was destined to challenge the historic superiority of capitalist organization as a system of production within less than half a century. Meanwhile, the inner structure of West European economies was tending away from the traditional forms of capitalism. Above all, laissez-faire, the accepted policy of the 19th century, was discredited by the war and postwar experience.

Statesmen and businessmen in capitalist nations were slow to appreciate the turn of events precipitated by World War I and consequently they misdirected their efforts during the 1920s by seeking a "return to prewar normalcy." Among major capitalist countries, the United Kingdom failed conspicuously to achieve prosperity at any time during the interwar period. Other capitalist nations enjoyed a brief prosperity in the 1920s only to be confronted in the 1930s with the great depression, which rocked the capitalist system to its foundations. Laissez-faire received a crushing blow from President Franklin D. Roosevelt's New Deal in the United States. The gold standard collapsed completely. Free trade was abandoned in its classic home, Great Britain. Even the classical principle of sound finance, the annually balanced governmental budget, gave way in both practice and theory to planned deficits during periods of depressed economic activity. Retreat from the free market philosophy was nearly complete in Mussolini's Italy and Hitler's Germany. When World War II opened in 1939, the future of capitalism looked bleak indeed. This trend seemed confirmed at the end of the war when the British Labour party won a decisive victory at the polls and proceeded to nationalize basic industries, including coal, transportation, communication, public utilities, and the Bank of England. Yet a judgment that capitalism had at last run its course would have been premature. Capitalist enterprise managed to survive in Great Britain, the United States, western Germany, Japan, and other nations [with a] remarkable show of vitality in the postwar world.

CHAPTER 7

ON THE POLITICAL ECONOMY OF BACKWARDNESS

Paul A. Baran

I

The capitalist mode of production and the social and political order concomitant with it provided, during the latter part of the eighteenth century, and still more during the entire nineteenth century, a framework for a continuous and, in spite of cyclical disturbances and setbacks, momentous expansion of productivity and material welfare. The relevant facts are well known and call for no elaboration. Yet this material (and cultural) progress was not only spotty in time but most unevenly distributed in space. It was confined to the Western world, and did not affect even all of this territorially and demographically relatively small sector of the inhabited globe.

• • • • • •

Tardy and skimpy as the benefits of capitalism may have been with respect to the lower classes even in most of the leading industrial countries, they were all but negligible in the less privileged parts of the world. There productivity remained low, and rapid increases in population pushed living standards from bad to worse. The dreams of the prophets of capitalist harmony remained on paper. Capital either did not move from countries where its marginal productivity was low to countries where it could be expected to be high, or if it did, it moved there mainly in order to extract profits from backward countries that frequently accounted for a lion's share of the increments in total output caused by the original investments. Where an increase in the aggregate national product of an underdeveloped country took place, the existing distribution of income prevented this increment from raising the living standards of the broad masses

Reprinted from *The Manchester School* (January 1952), pp. 66–84, by permission of the publisher.

of the population. Like all general statements, this one is obviously open to criticism based on particular cases. There were, no doubt, colonies and dependencies where the populations profited from inflow of foreign capital. These benefits, however, were few and far between, while exploitation and stagnation were the prevailing rule.

But if Western capitalism failed to improve materially the lot of the peoples inhabiting most backward areas, it accomplished something that profoundly affected the social and political conditions in underdeveloped countries. It introduced there, with amazing rapidity, all the economic and social tensions inherent in the capitalist order. It effectively disrupted whatever was left of the "feudal" coherence of the backward societies. It substituted market contracts for such paternalistic relationships as still survived from century to century. It reoriented the partly or wholly self-sufficient economies of agricultural countries toward the production of marketable commodities. It linked their economic fate with the vagaries of the world market and connected it with the fever curve of international price movements.

A *complete* substitution of capitalist market rationality for the rigidities of feudal or semifeudal servitude would have represented, in spite of all the pains of transition, an important step in the direction of progress. Yet all that happened was that the age-old exploitation of the population of underdeveloped countries by their domestic overlords was freed of the mitigating constraints inherited from the feudal transition. This superimposition of business mores over ancient oppression by landed gentries resulted in compounded exploitation, more outrageous corruption, and more glaring injustice.

Nor is this by any means the end of the story. Such export of capital and capitalism as has taken place had not only far-reaching implications of a social nature. It was accompanied by important physical and technical processes. Modern machines and products of advanced industries reached the poverty-stricken backyards of the world. To be sure most, if not all, of these machines worked for their foreign owners—or at least were believed by the population to be working for no one else—and the new refined appurtenances of the good life belonged to foreign businessmen and their domestic counterparts. The bonanza that was capitalism, the fullness of things that was modern industrial civilization, were crowding the display windows—they were protected by barbed wire from the anxious grip of the starving and desperate man in the street.

But they have drastically changed his outlook. Broadening and deepening his economic horizon, they aroused aspirations, envies, and hopes. Young intellectuals filled with zeal and patriotic devotion traveled from the underdeveloped lands to Berlin and London, to Paris and New York, and returned home with the "message of the possible."

Fascinated by the advances and accomplishments observed in the centers of modern industry, they developed and propagandized the image of what could be attained in their home countries under a more rational economic and social order. The dissatisfaction with the stagnation (or at best, barely perceptible growth) that ripened gradually under the still-calm political and social surface was given an articulate expression. This dissatisfaction was not nurtured by a comparison of reality with a vision of a socialist society. It found sufficient fuel in the confrontation of what was actually happening with what could be accomplished under capitalist institutions of the Western type.

II

The establishment of such institutions was, however, beyond the reach of the tiny middle classes of most backward areas. The inherited backwardness and poverty of their countries never gave them an opportunity to gather the economic strength, the insight, and the self-confidence needed for the assumption of a leading role in society. For centuries under feudal rule they themselves assimilated the political, moral, and cultural values of the dominating class.

While in advanced countries, such as France or Great Britain, the economically ascending middle classes developed at an early stage a new rational world outlook, which they proudly opposed to the medieval obscurantism of the feudal age, the poor, fledgling bourgeoisie of the underdeveloped countries sought nothing but accommodation to the prevailing order. Living in societies based on privilege, they strove for a share in the existing sinecures. They made political and economic deals with their domestic feudal overlords or with powerful foreign investors, and what industry and commerce developed in backward areas in the course of the last hundred years was rapidly moulded in the straitjacket of monopoly—the plutocratic partner of the aristocratic rulers. What resulted was an economic and political amalgam combining the worst features of both worlds—feudalism and capitalism—and blocking effectively all possibilities of economic growth.

It is quite conceivable that a "conservative" exit from this impasse might have been found in the course of time. A younger generation of enterprising and enlightened businessmen and intellectuals allied with moderate leaders of workers and peasants—a "Young Turk" movement of some sort—might have succeeded in breaking the deadlock, in loosening the hide-bound social and political structure of their countries and in creating the institutional arrangements indispensable for a measure of social and economic progress.

Yet in our rapid age history accorded no time for such a gradual transition. Popular pressures for an amelioration of economic and social conditions, or at least for some perceptible movement in that direction, steadily gained in intensity. To be sure, the growing restiveness of the underprivileged was not directed against the ephemeral principles of a hardly yet existing capitalist order. Its objects were parasitic feudal overlords appropriating large slices of the national product and wasting them on extravagant living; a government machinery protecting and abetting the dominant interests; wealthy businessmen reaping immense profits and not utilizing them for productive purposes; last but not least, foreign colonizers extracting or believed to be extracting vast gains from their "developmental" operations.

This popular movement had thus essentially bourgeois, democratic, anti-feudal, anti-imperialist tenets. It found outlets in agrarian egalitarianism; it incorporated "muckraker" elements denouncing monopoly; it strove for national independence and freedom from foreign exploitation.

For the native capitalist middle classes to assume the leadership of these popular forces and to direct them into the channels of bourgeois democracy—as has happened in Western Europe—they had to identify themselves with the common man. They had to break away from the political, economic, and ideological leadership of the feudal crust and the monopolists allied with it; and they had to demonstrate to the nation as a whole that they had the knowledge, the courage, and the determination to undertake and to carry to victorious conclusion the struggle for economic and social improvement.

In hardly any underdeveloped country were the middle classes capable of living up to this historical challenge. Some of the reasons for this portentous failure, reasons connected with the internal make-up of the business class itself, were briefly mentioned above. Of equal importance was, however, an "outside" factor. It was the spectacular growth of the international labor movement in Europe that offered the popular forces in backward areas ideological and political leadership that was denied to them by the native bourgeoisie. It pushed the goals and targets of the popular movements far beyond their original limited objectives.

This liaison of labor radicalism and populist revolt painted on the wall the imminent danger of a social revolution. Whether this danger was real or imaginary matters very little. What was essential is that the awareness of this threat effectively determined political and social action. It destroyed whatever chances there were of the capitalist classes joining and leading the popular anti-feudal, anti-monopolist movement. By instilling a mortal fear of expropriation and extinction in the minds of *all* property-owning groups the rise of socialist radicalism, and in particular the Bolshevik Revolution in Russia, tended to drive all more or less privileged, more or less well-to-do elements in the society into one "counterrevolutionary" coalition. Whatever differences and antagonisms existed between large and small landowners, between monopolistic and competitive business, between liberal bourgeois and reactionary feudal overlords, between domestic and foreign interests, were largely submerged on all important occasions by the over-riding *common* interest in staving off socialism.

The possibility of solving the economic and political deadlock prevailing in the underdeveloped countries on lines of a progressive capitalism all but disappeared. Entering the alliance with all other segments of the ruling class, the capitalist middle classes yielded one strategic position after another. Afraid that a quarrel with the landed gentry might be exploited by the radical populist movement, the middle classes abandoned all progressive attitudes in agrarian matters. Afraid that a conflict with the church and the military might weaken the political authority of the government, the middle classes moved away from all liberal and pacifist currents. Afraid that hostility toward foreign interests might deprive them of foreign support in a case of a revolutionary emergency, the native capitalists deserted their previous anti-imperialist, nationalist platforms.

The peculiar mechanisms of political interaction characteristic of all underdeveloped (and perhaps not only underdeveloped) countries thus operated at full speed. The aboriginal failure of the middle classes to provide inspiration and leadership to the popular masses pushed those masses into the camp of socialist radicalism. The growth of radicalism pushed the middle classes into an alliance with the aristocratic and monopolistic reaction. This alliance, cemented by common interest and common fear, pushed the populist forces still further along the road of radicalism and revolt. The outcome was a polarization of society with very little left between the poles. By permitting this polarization to develop, by abandoning the common man and resigning the task of reorganizing society on new, progressive lines, the capitalist middle classes threw away their historical chance of assuming effective control over the destinies of their nations, and of directing the gathering popular storm against the fortresses of feudalism and reaction. Its blazing fire turned thus against the entirety of existing economic and social institutions.

III

The economic and political order maintained by the ruling coalition of owning classes finds itself invariably at odds with all the urgent needs of the underdeveloped countries. Neither the social fabric that it embodies nor the institutions that rest upon it are conducive to progressive economic development. The only way to provide for economic growth and to prevent a continuous deterioration of living standards (apart from mass emigration unacceptable to other countries) is to assure a steady increase of total output—at least large enough to offset the rapid growth of population.

An obvious source of such an increase is the utilization of available unutilized or underutilized resources. A large part of this reservoir of dormant productive potentialities is the vast multitude of entirely unemployed or ineffectively employed manpower. There is no way of employing it usefully in agriculture, where the marginal productivity of labor tends to zero. They could be provided with opportunities for productive work only by transfer to industrial pursuits. For this to be feasible large investments in industrial plant and facilities have to be undertaken. Under prevailing conditions such investments are not forthcoming for a number of important and interrelated reasons.

With a very uneven distribution of a very small aggregate income (and wealth), large individual incomes exceeding what could be regarded as "reasonable" requirements for current consumption accrue as a rule to a relatively small group of high-income receivers. Many of them are large landowners maintaining a feudal style of life with large outlays on housing, servants, travel, and other luxuries. Their "requirements for consumption" are so high that there is only little room for savings. Only relatively insignificant amounts are left to be spent on improvements of agricultural estates.

Other members of the "upper crust" receiving incomes markedly surpassing "reasonable" levels of consumption are wealthy businessmen. For social reasons briefly mentioned above, their consumption too is very much larger than it would have been were they brought up in the puritan tradition of a bourgeois civilization. Their drive to accumulate and to expand their enterprises is continuously counteracted by the urgent desire to imitate in their living habits the socially dominant "old families," to prove by their conspicuous outlays on the amenities of rich life that they are socially (and therefore also politically) not inferior to their aristocratic partners in the ruling coalition.

But if this tendency curtails the volume of savings that could have been amassed by the urban high-income receivers, their will to reinvest their funds in productive enterprises is effectively curbed by a strong reluctance to damage their carefully erected monopolistic market positions through creation of additional productive capacity, and by absence of suitable investment opportunities—paradoxical as this may sound with reference to underdeveloped countries.

The deficiency of investment opportunities stems to a large extent from the structure and the limitations of the existing effective demand. With very low living standards the bulk of the aggregate money income of the population is spent on food and relatively primitive items of clothing and household necessities. These are available at low prices, and investment of large funds in plant and facilities that could produce this type of commodities more cheaply rarely promises attractive returns. Nor does it appear profitable to develop major enterprises the output of which would cater to the requirements of the rich. Large as their individual purchases of various luxuries may be, their aggregate spending on each of them is not sufficient to support the development of an elaborate luxury industry—in particular since the "snob" character of prevailing tastes renders only imported luxury articles true marks of social distinction.

Finally, the limited demand for investment goods precludes the building up of a machinery or equipment industry. Such mass consumption goods as are lacking, and such quantities of luxury goods as are purchased by the well-to-do, as well as the comparatively small quantities of investment goods needed by industry, are thus imported from abroad in exchange for domestic agricultural products and raw materials.

This leaves the expansion of exportable raw materials output as a major outlet for investment activities. There the possibilities are greatly influenced, however, by the technology of the production of most raw materials as well as by the nature of the markets to be served. Many raw materials, in particular oil, metals, certain industrial crops, have to be produced on a large scale if costs are to be kept low and satisfactory returns assured. Large-scale production, however, calls for large investments, so large indeed as to exceed the potentialities of the native capitalists in backward countries. Production of raw materials for a distant market entails, moreover, much larger risks than those encountered in domestic business. The difficulty of foreseeing accurately such things as receptiveness of the world markets, prices obtainable in competition with other countries, volume of output in other parts of the world, etc., sharply reduces the interest of native capitalists in these lines of business. They become to a predominant extent the domain of foreigners who, financially stronger, have at the same time much closer contacts with foreign outlets of their products.

The shortage of investible funds and the lack of investment opportunities represent two aspects of the same problem. A great number of investment projects, unprofitable under prevailing conditions, could be most promising in a general environment of economic expansion.

In backward areas a new industrial venture must frequently, if not always, break virgin ground. It has no functioning economic system to draw upon. It has to organize with its own efforts not only the productive process *within* its own confines, it must provide in addition for all the necessary *outside* arrangements essential to its operations. It does not enjoy the benefits of "external economies."

There can be no doubt that the absence of external economies, the inadequacy of the economic milieu in underdeveloped countries, constituted everywhere an important deterrent to investment in industrial projects. There is no way of rapidly bridging the gap. Large-scale investment is predicated upon large-scale investment. Roads, electric power stations, railroads, and houses have to be built *before* businessmen find it profitable to erect factories, to invest their funds in new industrial enterprises.

Yet investing in road building, financing construction of canals and power stations, organizing large housing projects, etc., transcend by far the financial and mental horizon of capitalists in underdeveloped countries. Not only are their financial resources too small for such ambitious projects, but their background and habits militate against entering commitments of this type. Brought up in the tradition of merchandizing and manufacturing consumers' goods—as is characteristic of an early phase of capitalist development—businessmen in underdeveloped countries are accustomed to rapid turnover, large but short-term risks, and correspondingly high rates of profit. Sinking funds in enterprises where profitability could manifest itself only in the course of many years is a largely unknown and unattractive departure. The difference between social and private rationality that exists in any market and profit-determined economy is thus particularly striking in underdeveloped countries.

· · · · · ·

But could not the required increase in total output be attained by better utilization of land—another unutilized or inadequately utilized productive factor?

There is usually no land that is both fit for agricultural purposes and at the same time readily accessible. Such terrain as could be cultivated but is actually not being tilled would usually require considerable investment before becoming suitable for settlement. In underdeveloped countries such outlays for agricultural purposes are just as unattractive to private interests as they are for industrial purposes.

On the other hand, more adequate employment of land that is already used in agriculture runs into considerable difficulties. Very few improvements that would be necessary in order to increase productivity can be carried out within the narrow confines of small-peasant holdings. Not only are the peasants in underdeveloped countries utterly unable to pay for such innovations, but the size of their lots offers no justification for their introduction.

Owners of large estates are in a sense in no better position. With limited savings at their disposal they do not have the funds to finance expensive improvements in their enterprises, nor do such projects appear profitable in view of the high prices of imported equipment in relation to prices of agricultural produce and wages of agricultural labor.

Approached thus via agriculture, an expansion of total output would also seem to be attainable only through the development of industry. Only through increase of industrial productivity could agricultural machinery, fertilizers, electric power, etc., be brought within the reach of the agricultural producer. Only through an increased demand for labor could agricultural wages be raised and a stimulus provided for a modernization of the agricultural economy. Only through the growth of industrial production could agricultural labor displaced by the machine be absorbed in productive employment.

Monopolistic market structures, shortage of savings, lack of external economies, the divergence of social and private rationalities do not exhaust, however, the list of obstacles blocking the way of privately organized industrial expansion in underdeveloped countries. Those obstacles have to be considered against the background of the general feeling of uncertainty prevailing in all backward areas. The coalition of the owning classes formed under pressure of fear, and held together by the real or imagined danger of social upheavals, provokes continuously more or less threatening rumblings under the outwardly calm political surface. The social and political tensions to which that coalition is a political response are not liquidated by the prevailing system; they are only repressed. Normal and quiet as the daily routine frequently appears, the more enlightened and understanding members of the ruling groups in underdeveloped countries sense the inherent instability of the political and social order. Occasional outbursts of popular dissatisfaction assuming the form of peasant uprisings, violent strikes, or local guerrilla warfare serve from time to time as grim reminders of the latent crisis.

In such a climate there is no will to invest on the part of monied people; in such a climate there is no enthusiasm for long-term projects; in such a climate the motto of all participants in the privileges offered by society is *carpe diem.*

IV

Could not, however, an appropriate policy on the part of the governments involved change the political climate and facilitate economic growth? In our time, when faith in the manipulative omnipotence of the State has all but displaced analysis of its social structure and understanding of its political and economic functions, the tendency is obviously to answer these questions in the affirmative.

Looking at the matter purely mechanically, it would appear indeed that much could be done by a well-advised regime in an underdeveloped country to provide for a relatively rapid increase of total output, accompanied by an improvement of the living standards of the population. There are a number of measures that the government could take in an effort to overcome backwardness. A fiscal policy could be adopted that by means of capital levies and a highly progressive tax system would syphon off all surplus purchasing power, and in this way eliminate nonessential consumption. The savings thus enforced could be channelled by the government into productive investment. Power stations, railroads, highways, irrigation systems, and soil improvements could be organized by the State with a view to creating an economic environment conducive to the growth of productivity. Technical schools on various levels could be set up by the public authority to furnish industrial training to young people as well as to adult workers and the unemployed. A system of scholarships could be introduced rendering acquisition of skills accessible to low-income strata.

Wherever private capital refrains from undertaking certain industrial projects, or wherever monopolistic controls block the necessary expansion of plant and facilities in particular industries, the government could step in and make the requisite investments. Where developmental possibilities that are rewarding in the long run appear unprofitable during the initial period of gestation and learning, and are therefore beyond the horizon of private businessmen, the government could undertake to shoulder the short-run losses.

In addition an entire arsenal of "preventive" devices is at the disposal of the authorities. Inflationary pressures resulting from developmental activities (private and public) could be reduced or even eliminated, if outlays on investment projects could be offset by a corresponding and simultaneous contraction of spending elsewhere in the economic system. What this would call for is a taxation policy that would effectively remove from the income stream amounts sufficient to neutralize the investment-caused expansion of aggregate money income.

In the interim, and as a supplement, speculation in scarce goods and excessive profiteering in essential commodities could be suppressed by rigorous price controls. An equitable distribution of mass consumption goods in short supply could be assured by rationing. Diversion of resources in high demand to luxury purposes could be prevented by allocation and priority schemes. Strict supervision of transactions involving foreign exchanges could render capital flight, expenditure of limited foreign funds on luxury imports, pleasure trips abroad, and the like, impossible.

What the combination of these measures would accomplish is a radical change in the structure of effective demand in the underdeveloped country, and a reallocation of productive resources to satisfy society's need for economic development. By curtailing consumption of the higher-income groups, the amounts of savings available for investment purposes could be markedly increased. The squandering of limited supplies of foreign exchange on capital flight, or on importation of redundant foreign goods and services, could be prevented, and the foreign funds thus saved could be used for the acquisition of foreign-made machinery needed for economic development. The reluctance of private interests to engage in enterprises that are socially necessary, but may not promise rich returns in the short run, would be prevented from determining the economic life of the backward country.

The mere listing of the steps that would have to be undertaken, in order to assure an expansion of output and income in an underdeveloped country, reveals the utter implausibility of the view that they could be carried out by the governments existing in most underdeveloped countries. The reason for this inability is only to a negligible extent the nonexistence of the competent and honest civil service needed for the administration of the program. A symptom itself of the political and social marasmus prevailing in underdeveloped countries, this lack cannot be remedied without attacking the underlying causes. Nor does it touch anything near the roots of the matter to lament the lack of satisfactory tax policies in backward countries, or to deplore the absence of tax "morale" and "discipline" among the civic virtues of their populations.

The crucial fact rendering the realization of a developmental program illusory is the political and social structure of the government in power. . . . Set up to guard and to abet the existing property rights and privileges, it cannot become the architect of a policy calculated to destroy the privileges standing in the way of economic progress and to place the property and the incomes derived from it at the service of society as a whole.

Nor is there much to be said for the "intermediate" position which, granting the essential incompatibility of a well-conceived and vigorously executed developmental program with the political and social institutions prevailing in most underdeveloped countries, insists that at least *some* of the requisite measures could be carried out by the existing political authorities. This school of thought overlooks entirely the weakness, if not the complete absence, of social and political forces that could induce the necessary concessions on the part of the ruling coalition. By background and political upbringing, too myopic and self-interested to permit the slightest encroachments upon their inherited positions and cherished privileges, the upper classes in underdeveloped countries resist doggedly all pressures in that direction. Every time such pressures grow in strength they succeed in cementing anew the alliance of all conservative elements, by decrying all attempts at reform as assaults on the very foundations of society.

Even if measures like progressive taxation, capital levies, and foreign exchange controls could be enforced by the corrupt officials operating in the demoralized business communities of underdeveloped countries, such enforcement would to a large extent defeat its original purpose. Where businessmen do not invest, unless in expectation of lavish profits, a taxation system succeeding in confiscating large parts of these profits is bound to kill private investment. Where doing business or operating landed estates is attractive mainly because it permits luxurious living, foreign exchange controls preventing the importation of luxury goods are bound to blight enterprise. Where the only stimulus to hard work on the part of intellectuals, technicians, and civil servants is the chance of partaking in the privileges of the ruling class, a policy aiming at the reduction of inequality of social status and income is bound to smother effort.

The injection of planning into a society living in the twilight between feudalism and capitalism cannot but result in additional corruption, larger and more artful evasions of the law, and more brazen abuses of authority.

V

There would seem to be no exit from the impasse. The ruling coalition of interests does not abdicate of its own volition, nor does it change its character in response to incantation. Although its individual members occasionally leave the sinking ship physically or financially (or in both ways), the property-owning classes as a whole are as a rule grimly determined to hold fast to their political and economic entrenchments.

If the threat of social upheaval assumes dangerous proportions, they tighten their grip on political life and move rapidly in the direction of unbridled reaction and military dictatorship. Making use of favourable international opportunities and of ideological and social affinities to ruling groups in other countries, they solicit foreign economic and sometimes military aid in their efforts to stave off the impending disaster.

Such aid is likely to be given to them by foreign governments regarding them as an evil less to be feared than the social revolution that would sweep them out of power. This attitude of their friends and protectors abroad is no less shortsighted than their own.

The adjustment of the social and political conditions in underdeveloped countries to the urgent needs of economic development can be postponed; it cannot be indefinitely avoided. In the past, it could have been delayed by decades or even centuries. In our age it is a matter of years. Bolstering the political system of power existing in backward countries by providing it with military support may temporarily block the eruption of the volcano; it cannot stop the subterranean gathering of explosive forces.

Economic help in the form of loans and grants given to the governments of backward countries, to enable them to promote a measure of economic progress, is no substitute for the domestic changes that are mandatory if economic development is to be attained.

Such help, in fact, may actually do more harm than good. Possibly permitting the importation of some foreign-made machinery and equipment for government or business sponsored investment projects, but not accompanied by any of the steps that are needed to assure healthy economic growth, foreign assistance thus supplied may set off an inflationary spiral increasing and aggravating the existing social and economic tensions in underdeveloped countries.

If, as is frequently the case, these loans or grants from abroad are tied to the fulfillment of certain conditions on the part of the receiving country regarding their use, the resulting investment may be directed in such channels as to conform more to the interests of the lending than to those of the borrowing country. Where economic advice as a form of "technical assistance" is supplied to the underdeveloped country, and its acceptance is made a prerequisite to eligibility for financial aid, this advice often pushes the governments of underdeveloped countries toward policies, ideologically or otherwise attractive to the foreign experts dispensing economic counsel, but not necessarily conducive to economic development of the "benefitted" countries. Nationalism and xenophobia are thus strengthened in backward areas—additional fuel for political restiveness.

For backward countries to enter the road of economic growth and social progress, the political framework of their existence has to be drastically revamped. The alliance between feudal landlords, industrial royalists, and the capitalist middle classes has to be broken. The keepers of the past cannot be the builders of the future. Such progressive and enterprising elements as exist in backward societies have to obtain the possibility of leading their countries in the direction of economic and social growth.

What France, Britain, and America have accomplished through their own revolutions has to be attained in backward countries by a combined effort of popular forces, enlightened government, and unselfish foreign help. This combined effort must sweep away the holdover institutions of a defunct age, must change the political and social climate in the underdeveloped countries, and must imbue their nations with a new spirit of enterprise and freedom.

Should it prove too late in the historical process for the bourgeoisie to rise to its responsibilities in backward areas, should the long experience of servitude and accommodation to the feudal past have reduced the forces of progressive capitalism to impotence, the backward countries of the world will inevitably turn to economic planning and social collectivism. If the capitalist world outlook of economic and social progress, propelled by enlightened self-interest, should prove unable to triumph over the conservatism of inherited positions and traditional privileges, if the capitalist promise of advance and reward to the efficient, the industrious, the able, should not displace the feudal assurance of security and power to the well-bred, the well-connected, and the conformist—a new social ethos will become the spirit and guide of a new age. It will be the ethos of the collective effort, the creed of the predominance of the interests of society over the interests of selected few.

The transition may be abrupt and painful. The land not given to the peasants legally may be taken by them forcibly. High incomes not confiscated through taxation may be eliminated by outright expropriation. Corrupt officials not retired in orderly fashion may be removed by violent action.

Which way the historical wheel will turn and in which way the crisis in the backward countries will find its final solution will depend in the main on whether the capitalist middle classes in the backward areas, and the rulers of the advanced industrial nations of the world, overcome their fear and myopia. Or are they too spellbound by their narrowly conceived selfish interests, too blinded by their hatred of progress, grown so senile in these latter days of the capitalist age, as to commit suicide out of fear of death?

CHAPTER 8

THE DEVELOPMENT
OF UNDERDEVELOPMENT

Andre Gunder Frank

University of Amsterdam

I

We cannot hope to formulate adequate development theory and policy for the majority of the world's population who suffer from underdevelopment without first learning how their past economic and social history gave rise to their present underdevelopment. Yet most historians study only the developed metropolitan countries and pay scant attention to the colonial and underdeveloped lands. For this reason most of our theoretical categories and guides to development policy have been distilled exclusively from the historical experience of the European and North American advanced capitalist nations.

Since the historical experience of the colonial and underdeveloped countries has demonstrably been quite different, available theory therefore fails to reflect the past of the underdeveloped part of the world entirely, and reflects the past of the world as a whole only in part. More important, our ignorance of the underdeveloped countries' history leads us to assume that their past and indeed their present resembles earlier stages of the history of the now developed countries. This ignorance and this assumption lead us into serious misconceptions about contemporary underdevelopment and development. Further, most studies of development and underdevelopment fail to take account of the economic and other relations between the metropolis and its economic colonies throughout the history of the worldwide expansion and development of the mercantilist and capitalist system. Consequently, most of our theory fails to explain the structure and development of the capitalist system as a whole and to account for its

Reprinted from *Monthly Review,* 18, 4 (September 1966), pp. 17–31, by permission of Monthly Review Press. Copyright © 1969 by Andre Gunder Frank. All rights reserved.

simultaneous generation of underdevelopment in some of its parts and of economic development in others.

It is generally held that economic development occurs in a succession of capitalist stages and that today's underdeveloped countries are still in a stage, sometimes depicted as an original stage of history, through which the now developed countries passed long ago. Yet even a modest acquaintance with history shows that underdevelopment is not original or traditional and that neither the past nor the present of the underdeveloped countries resembles in any important respect the past of the now developed countries. The now developed countries were never *under*developed, though they may have been *un*developed. It is also widely believed that the contemporary underdevelopment of a country can be understood as the product or reflection solely of its own economic, political, social, and cultural characteristics or structure. Yet historical research demonstrates that contemporary underdevelopment is in large part the historical product of past and continuing economic and other relations between the satellite underdeveloped and the now developed metropolitan countries. Furthermore, these relations are an essential part of the structure and development of the capitalist system on a world scale as a whole. A related and also largely erroneous view is that the development of these underdeveloped countries and, within them of their most underdeveloped domestic areas, must and will be generated or stimulated by diffusing capital, institutions, values, etc., to them from the international and national capitalist metropoles. Historical perspective based on the underdeveloped countries' past experience suggests that on the contrary in the underdeveloped countries economic development can now occur only independently of most of these relations of diffusion.

Evident inequalities of income and differences in culture have led many observers to see "dual" societies and economies in the underdeveloped countries. Each of the two parts is supposed to have a history of its own, a structure, and a contemporary dynamic largely independent of the other. Supposedly, only one part of the economy and society has been importantly affected by intimate economic relations with the "outside" capitalist world; and that part, it is held, became modern, capitalist, and relatively developed precisely because of this contact. The other part is widely regarded as variously isolated, subsistence-based, feudal, or precapitalist, and therefore more underdeveloped.

I believe on the contrary that the entire "dual society" thesis is false and that the policy recommendations to which it leads will, if acted upon, serve only to intensify and perpetuate the very conditions of underdevelopment they are supposedly designed to remedy.

A mounting body of evidence suggests, and I am confident that future historical research will confirm, that the expansion of the capitalist system over the past centuries effectively and entirely penetrated even the apparently most isolated sectors of the underdeveloped world. Therefore, the economic, political, social, and cultural institutions and relations we now observe there are the products of the historical development of the capitalist system no less than are the seemingly more modern or capitalist features of the national metropoles of these underdeveloped countries. Analogously to the relations between development and underdevelopment on the international level, the contemporary underdeveloped institutions of the so-called backward or feudal domestic areas of an underdeveloped country are no less the product of the single historical process of capitalist development than are the so-called capitalist institutions of the supposedly more progressive areas. In this paper I should like to sketch the kinds of evidence which support this thesis and at the same time indicate lines along which further study and research could fruitfully proceed.

II

The secretary general of the Latin American Center of Research in the Social Sciences writes in that center's journal: "The privileged position of the city has its origin in the colonial period. It was founded by the Conqueror to serve the same ends that it still serves today; to incorporate the indigenous population into the economy brought and developed by that Conqueror and his descendants. The regional city was an instrument of conquest and is still today an instrument of domination."[1] The Instituto Nacional Indigenista (National Indian Institute) of Mexico confirms this observation when it notes that "the mestizo population, in fact, always lives in a city, a center of an intercultural region, which acts as the metropolis of a zone of indigenous population and which maintains with the underdeveloped communities an intimate relation which links the center with the satellite communities."[2] The institute goes on to point out that "between the mestizos who live in the nuclear city of the region and the Indians who live in the peasant hinterland there is in reality a closer economic and social interdependence than might at first glance appear" and that the provincial metropoles "by being centers of intercourse are also centers of exploitation."[3]

Thus these metropolis-satellite relations are not limited to the imperial or international level but penetrate and structure the very economic, political, and social life of the Latin American colonies and countries. Just as the colonial and national capital and its export sector become the satellite of the Iberian (and later of other) metropoles of the world economic system, this satellite immediately becomes a colonial and then a national metropolis with respect to the productive sectors and population of the interior. Furthermore, the provincial capitals, which thus are themselves satellites of the national metropolis—and through the latter of the world metropolis—are in turn provincial centers around which their own local satellites orbit. Thus, a whole chain of constellations of metropoles and satellites relates all parts of the whole system from its metropolitan center in Europe or the United States to the farthest outpost in the Latin American countryside.

When we examine this metropolis-satellite structure, we find that each of the satellites, including now-underdeveloped Spain and Portugal, serves as an instrument to suck capital or economic surplus out of its own satellites and to channel part of this surplus to the world metropolis of which all are satellites. Moreover, each national and local metropolis serves to impose and maintain the monopolistic structure and exploitative relationship of this system (as the Instituto Nacional Indigenista of Mexico calls it) as long as it serves the interest of the metropoles which take advantage of this global, national, and local structure to promote their own development and the enrichment of their ruling classes.

These are the principal and still surviving structural characteristics which were implanted in Latin America by the Conquest. Beyond examining the establishment of this colonial structure in its historical context, the proposed approach calls for study of the development—and underdevelopment—of these metropoles and satellites of Latin America throughout the following and still continuing historical process. In this way we can understand why there were and still are tendencies in the Latin American and world capitalist structure which seem to lead to the development of the metropolis and the underdevelopment of the satellite and why, particularly, the satellized national, regional, and local metropoles in Latin America find that their economic development is at best a limited or underdeveloped development.

III

That present underdevelopment of Latin America is the result of its centuries-long participation in the process of world capitalist development, I believe I have shown in my case studies of the economic and social histories of Chile and Brazil.[4] My study of Chilean history suggests that the Conquest not only incorporated this country fully into the expansion and development of the world mercantile and later industrial capitalist system but that it also introduced the monopolistic metropolis-satellite structure and development of capitalism into the Chilean domestic economy and society itself. This structure then penetrated and permeated all of Chile very quickly. Since that time and in the course of world and Chilean history during the epochs of colonialism, free trade, imperialism, and the present, Chile has become increasingly marked by the economic, social, and political structure of satellite underdevelopment. This development of underdevelopment continues today, both in Chile's still increasing satellization by the world metropolis and through the ever more acute polarization of Chile's domestic economy.

The history of Brazil is perhaps the clearest case of both national and regional development of underdevelopment. The expansion of the world economy since the beginning of the sixteenth century successively converted the Northeast, the Minas Gerais interior, the North, and the Center-South (Rio de Janeiro, São Paulo, and Paraná) into export economies and incorporated them into the structure and development of the world capitalist system. Each of these regions experienced what may have appeared as economic development during the period of its respective golden age. But it was a satellite development which was neither self-generating nor self-perpetuating. As the market or the productivity of the first three regions declined, foreign and domestic economic interest in them waned; and they were left to develop the underdevelopment they live today. In the fourth region, the coffee economy experienced a similar though not yet quite as serious fate (though the development of a synthetic coffee substitute promises to deal it a mortal blow in the not too distant future). All of this historical evidence contradicts the generally accepted theses that Latin America suffers from a dual society or from the survival of feudal institutions and that these are important obstacles to its economic development.

IV

During the First World War, however, and even more during the Great Depression and the Second World War, São Paulo began to build up an industrial establishment which is the largest in Latin America today. The question arises whether this industrial development did or can break Brazil out of the cycle of satellite development and underdevelopment which has characterized its other regions and national history within the capitalist system so far. I believe that the answer is no. Domestically the evidence so far is fairly clear. The development of industry in São Paulo has not brought greater riches to the other regions of Brazil. Instead, it converted them into internal colonial satellites, decapitalized them further, and consolidated or even deepened their underdevelopment. There is little evidence to suggest that this process is likely to be reversed in the foreseeable future except insofar as the provincial poor migrate and become the poor of the metropolitan cities. Externally, the evidence is that although the initial development of São Paulo's industry was relatively autonomous it is being increasingly satellized by the world capitalist metropolis and its future development possibilities are increasingly restricted.[5] This development, my studies lead me to believe, also appears destined to limited or underdeveloped development as long as it takes place in the present economic, political, and social framework.

We must conclude, in short, that underdevelopment is not due to the survival of archaic institutions and the existence of capital shortage in regions that have remained isolated from the stream of world history. On the contrary, underdevelopment was and still is generated by the very same historical process which also generated economic development: the development of capitalism itself. This view, I am glad to say, is gaining adherents among students of Latin America and is proving its worth in shedding new light on the problems of the area and in affording a better perspective for the formulation of theory and policy.[6]

V

The same historical and structural approach can also lead to better development theory and policy by generating a series of hypotheses about development and underdevelopment such as those I am testing in my current research. The hypotheses are derived from the empirical observation and theoretical assumption that within this world-embracing metropolis-satellite structure the metropoles tend to develop and the satellites to underdevelop. The first hypothesis has already been mentioned above: that in contrast to the development of the world metropolis which is no one's satellite, the development of the national and other subordinate metropoles is limited by their satellite status. It is perhaps more difficult to test this hypothesis than the following ones because part of its confirmation depends on the test of the other hypotheses. Nonetheless, this hypothesis appears to be generally confirmed by the nonautonomous and unsatisfactory economic and especially industrial development of Latin America's national metropoles, as documented in the studies already cited. The most important and at the same time most confirmatory examples are the metropolitan regions of Buenos Aires and São Paulo whose growth only began in the nineteenth century, was therefore largely untrammelled by any colonial heritage, but was and remains a satellite development largely dependent on the outside metropolis, first of Britain and then of the United States.

A second hypothesis is that the satellites experience their greatest economic development and especially their most classically capitalist industrial development if and when their ties to their metropolis are weakest. This hypothesis is almost diametrically opposed to the generally accepted thesis that development in the underdeveloped countries follows from the greatest degree of contact with and diffusion from the metropolitan developed countries. This hypothesis seems to be confirmed by two kinds of relative isolation that Latin America has experienced in the course of its history. One is the temporary isolation caused by the crises of war or depression in the world metropolis. Apart from minor ones, five periods of such major crises stand out and seem to confirm the hypothesis. These are: the European (and especially Spanish) Depression of the seventeenth century, the Napoleonic Wars, the First World War, the Depression of the 1930s, and the Second World War. It is clearly established and generally recognized that the most important recent industrial development—especially of Argentina, Brazil, and Mexico, but also of other countries such as Chile—has taken place precisely during the periods of the two World Wars and the intervening Depression. Thanks to the consequent loosening of trade and investment ties during these periods, the satellites initiated marked autonomous industrialization and growth. Historical research demonstrates that the same thing happened in Latin America during Europe's seventeenth-century depression. Manufacturing grew in the Latin American countries, and several of them such as Chile became exporters of manufactured goods. The Napoleonic Wars gave rise to independence movements in Latin America, and these should perhaps also be interpreted as confirming the development hypothesis in part.

The other kind of isolation which tends to confirm the second hypothesis is the geographic and economic isolation of regions which at one time were relatively weakly tied to and poorly integrated into the mercantilist and capitalist system. My preliminary research suggests that in Latin America it was these regions which initiated and experienced the most promising self-generating economic development of the classical industrial capitalist type. The most important regional cases probably are Tucumán and Asunción, as well as other cities such as Mendoza and Rosario, in the interior of Argentina and Paraguay during the end of the eighteenth and the beginning of the nineteenth centuries. Seventeenth- and eighteenth-century São Paulo, long before coffee was grown there, is another example. Perhaps Antioquia in Colombia and Puebla and Querétaro in Mexico are other examples. In its own way, Chile was also an example since, before the sea route around the Horn was opened, this country was relatively isolated at the end of the long voyage from Europe via Panama. All of these regions became manufacturing centers and even exporters, usually of textiles, during the periods preceding their effective incorporation as satellites into the colonial, national, and world capitalist system.

Internationally, of course, the classic case of industrialization through nonparticipation as a satellite in the capitalist world system is obviously that of Japan after the Meiji Restoration. Why, one may ask, was resource-poor but unsatellized Japan able to industrialize so quickly at the end of the century while resource-rich Latin American countries and Russia were not able to do so and the latter was easily beaten by Japan in the War of 1904 after the same forty years of development efforts? The second hypothesis suggests that the fundamental reason is that Japan was not satellized either during the Tokugawa or Meiji period and therefore did not have its development structurally limited as did the countries which were so satellized.

VI

A corollary of the second hypothesis is that when the metropolis recovers from its crisis and reestablishes the trade and investment ties which fully reincorporate the satellites into the system, or when the metropolis expands to incorporate previously isolated regions into the worldwide system, the previous development and industrialization of these regions is choked off or channelled into directions which are not self-perpetuating and promising. This happened after each of the five crises cited above. The renewed expansion of trade and the spread of economic liberalism in the eighteenth and nineteenth centuries choked off and reversed the manufacturing development which Latin America had experienced during the seventeenth century, and in some places at the beginning of the nineteenth. After the First World War, the new national industry of Brazil suffered serious consequences from American economic invasion. The increase in the growth rate of Gross National Product and particularly of industrialization throughout Latin America was again reversed and industry became increasingly satellized after the Second World War and especially after the post–Korean War recovery and expansion of the metropolis. Far from having become more developed since then, industrial sectors of Brazil and most conspicuously of Argentina have become structurally more and more underdeveloped and less and less able to generate continued industrialization and/or sustain development of the economy. This process, from which India also suffers, is reflected in a whole gamut of balance of payments, inflationary, and other economic and political difficulties, and promises to yield to no solution short of far-reaching structural change.

Our hypothesis suggests that fundamentally the same process occurred even more dramatically with the incorporation into the system of previously unsatellized regions. The expansion of Buenos Aires as a satellite of Great Britain and the introduction of free trade in the interest of the ruling groups of both metropoles destroyed the manufacturing and much of the remainder of the economic base of the previously relatively prosperous interior almost entirely. Manufacturing was destroyed by foreign competition, lands were taken and concentrated into latifundia by the rapaciously growing export economy, intraregional distribution of income became much more unequal, and the previously developing regions became simple satellites of Buenos Aires and through it of London. The provincial centers did not yield to satellization without a struggle. This metropolis-satellite conflict was much of the cause of the long political and armed struggle between the Unitarists in Buenos Aires and the Federalists in the provinces, and it may be said to have been the sole important cause of the War of the Triple Alliance in which Buenos Aires, Montevideo, and Rio de Janeiro, encouraged and helped by London, destroyed not only the autonomously developing economy of Paraguay but killed off nearly all of its population which was unwilling to give in.

Though this is no doubt the most spectacular example which tends to confirm the hypothesis, I believe that historical research on the satellization of previously relatively independent yeoman-farming and incipient manufacturing regions such as the Caribbean islands will confirm it further.[7] These regions did not have a chance against the forces of expanding and developing capitalism, and their own development had to be sacrificed to that of others. The economy and industry of Argentina, Brazil, and other countries which have experienced the effects of metropolitan recovery since the Second World War are today suffering much the same fate, if fortunately still in lesser degree.

VII

A third major hypothesis derived from the metropolis-satellite structure is that the regions which are the most underdeveloped and feudal-seeming today are the ones which had the closest ties to the metropolis in the past. They are the regions which were the greatest exporters of primary products to and the biggest sources of capital for the world metropolis and which were abandoned by the metropolis when for one reason or another business fell off. This hypothesis also contradicts the generally held thesis that the source of a region's underdevelopment is its isolation and its precapitalist institutions.

This hypothesis seems to be amply confirmed by the former super-satellite development and present ultra-underdevelopment of the once sugar-exporting West Indies, northeastern Brazil, the ex-mining districts of Minas Gerais in Brazil, highland Peru, and Bolivia, and the central Mexican states of Guanajuato, Zacatecas, and others whose names were made world famous centuries ago by their silver. There surely are no major regions in Latin America which are today more cursed by underdevelopment and poverty; yet all of these regions, like Bengal in India, once provided the life blood of mercantile and industrial capitalist development—in the metropolis. These regions' participation in the development of the world capitalist system gave them, already in their golden age, the typical structure of underdevelopment of a capitalist export economy. When the market for their sugar or the wealth of their mines disappeared and the metropolis abandoned them to their own devices, the already existing economic, political, and social structure of these regions prohibited autonomous generation of economic development and left them no alternative but to turn in upon themselves and to degenerate into the ultra-underdevelopment we find there today.

VIII

These considerations suggest two further and related hypotheses. One is that the latifundium, irrespective of whether it appears as a plantation or a hacienda today, was typically born as a commercial enterprise which created for itself the institutions which permitted it to respond to increased demand in the world or national market by expanding the amount of its land, capital, and labor and to increase the supply of its products. The fifth hypothesis is that the latifundia which appear isolated, subsistence-based, and semi-feudal today saw the demand for their products or their productive capacity decline and that they are to be found principally in the above-named former agricultural and mining export regions whose economic activity declined in general. These two hypotheses run counter to the notions of most people, and even to the opinions of some historians and other students of the subject, according to whom the historical roots and socioeconomic causes of Latin American latifundia and agrarian institutions are to be found in the transfer of feudal institutions from Europe and/or in economic depression.

The evidence to test these hypotheses is not open to easy general inspection and requires detailed analyses of many cases. Nonetheless, some important confirmatory evidence is available. The growth of the latifundium in nineteenth-century Argentina and Cuba is a clear case in support of the fourth hypothesis and can in no way be attributed to the transfer of feudal institutions during colonial times. The same is evidently the case of the postrevolutionary and contemporary resurgence of latifundia particularly in the north of Mexico, which produce for the American market, and of similar ones on the coast of Peru and the new coffee regions of Brazil. The conversion of previously yeoman-farming Caribbean islands, such as Barbados, into sugar-exporting economies at various times between the seventeenth and twentieth centuries and the resulting rise of the latifundia in these islands would seem to confirm the fourth hypothesis as well. In Chile, the rise of the latifundium and the creation of the institutions of servitude which later came to be called feudal occurred in the eighteenth century and have been conclusively shown to be the result of and response to the opening of a market for Chilean wheat in Lima.[8] Even the growth and consolidation of the latifundium in seventeenth-century Mexico—which most expert students have attributed to a depression of the economy caused by the decline of mining and a shortage of Indian labor and to a consequent turning in upon itself and ruralization of the economy—occurred at a time when urban population and demand were growing, food shortages became acute, food prices skyrocketed, and the profitability of other economic activities such as mining and foreign trade declined.[9] All of these and other factors rendered hacienda agriculture more profitable. Thus, even this case would seem to confirm the hypothesis that the growth of the latifundium and its feudal-seeming conditions of servitude in Latin America has always been and still is the commercial response to increased demand and that it does not represent the transfer or survival of alien institutions that have remained beyond the reach of capitalist development. The emergence of latifundia, which today really are more or less (though not entirely) isolated, might then be attributed to the causes advanced in the fifth hypothesis—i.e., the decline of previously profitable agricultural enterprises whose capital was, and whose currently produced economic surplus still is, transferred elsewhere by owners and merchants who frequently are the same persons or families. Testing this hypothesis requires still more detailed analysis, some of which I have undertaken in a study on Brazilian agriculture.[10]

IX

All of these hypotheses and studies suggest that the global extension and unity of the capitalist system, its monopoly structure and uneven development throughout its history, and the resulting persistence of commercial rather than industrial capitalism in the underdeveloped world (including its most industrially advanced countries) deserve much more attention in the study of economic development and cultural change than they have hitherto received. Though science and truth know no national boundaries, it is probably new generations of scientists from the underdeveloped countries themselves who most need to, and best can, devote the necessary attention to these problems and clarify the process of underdevelopment and development. It is their people who in the last analysis face the task of changing this no longer acceptable process and eliminating this miserable reality.

They will not be able to accomplish these goals by importing sterile stereotypes from the metropolis which do not correspond to their satellite economic reality and do not respond to their liberating political needs. To change their reality they must understand it. For this reason, I hope that better confirmation of these hypotheses and further pursuit of the proposed historical, holistic, and structural approach may help the peoples of the underdeveloped countries to understand the causes and eliminate the reality of their development of underdevelopment and their underdevelopment of development.

NOTES

1 *América Latina,* 6, 4 (October–December 1963): p. 8.
2 Instituto Nacional Indigenista, *Los Centros Coordinadores Indigenistas,* Mexico, 1962, p. 34.
3 Ibid., pp. 33–34, 88.
4 "Capitalist Development and Underdevelopment in Chile" and "Capitalist Development and Underdevelopment in Brazil" in *Capitalism and Underdevelopment in Latin America* (New York: Monthly Review Press, 1967).
5 Also see, "The Growth and Decline of Import Substitution," *Economic Bulletin for Latin America,* New York, 9, 1, March 1964; and Celso Furtado, *Dialectica do Desenvolvimiento* (Rio de Janeiro: Fundo de Cultura, 1964).
6 Others who use a similar approach, though their ideologies do not permit them to derive the logically following conclusions, are Aníbal Pinto S.C., *Chile: Un Caso de Desarrollo Frustrado* (Santiago: Editorial Universitaria, 1957); Celso Furtado, *A Formącao Económica do Brasil* (Rio de Janeiro: Fundo de Cultura, 1959) (recently translated into English and published under the title *The Economic Growth of Brazil* by the University of California Press); and Caio Prado Junior, *Historia Económica do Brasil,* 7th ed., (São Paulo: Editora Brasiliense, 1962).
7 See for instance Ramón Guerra y Sánchez, *Azúcar y Población en las Antillas,* 2d ed., (Havana, 1942), also published as *Sugar and Society in the Caribbean* (New Haven: Yale University Press, 1964).
8 Mario Góngora, *Origen de los "inquilinos" de Chile central* (Santiago Editorial Universitaria, 1960); Jean Borde and Mario Góngora, *Evolución de la propiedad rural en el Valle del Puango* (Santiago: Instituto de Sociología de la Universidad de Chile); Sergio Sepúlveda, *El trigo chileno en el mercado mundial* (Santiago Editorial Universitaria, 1959).
9 Woodrow Borah makes depression the centerpiece of his explanation in "New Spain's Century of Depression," *Ibero-Americana,* Berkeley, 35, 1951. François Chevalier

speaks of turning in upon itself in the most authoritative study of the subject, "La for-
mación de los grandes latifundios en México," *Problemas Agrícolas e Industriales de
México,* 8, 1, 1956 (translated from the French and recently published by the University
of California Press). The data which provide the basis for my contrary interpretation
are supplied by these authors themselves. This problem is discussed in my "Con qué
modo de producción convierte la gallina maíz en huevos de oro?" *El Gallo Ilustrado,*
Suplemento de *El Día,* Mexico, nos. 175 and 179, October 31 and November 28, 1965;
and it is further analyzed in a study of Mexican agriculture under preparation by the
author.

10 "Capitalism and the Myth of Feudalism in Brazilian Agriculture," in *Capitalism and
Underdevelopment in Latin America,* cited in note 4 above.

CHAPTER 9

PLANT IMPERIALISM

Lucile Brockway

"The greatest service which can be rendered to any country is to add a useful plant to its culture," wrote Thomas Jefferson. The movement of plants by human agency has affected the course of history. New staples have prevented famines, as when New World maize and sweet potato were introduced into China in the sixteenth century; they have supported population explosions, as when the Andean white potato spread throughout northern Europe in the eighteenth and nineteenth centuries and fed the workers in the burgeoning industrial cities. New plantation crops have helped to make some nations rich and others poorer, when a local plant-based industry was undermined by a plant transfer.

Seeds have been one of the most precious and easily transported cultural artefacts. They have been exchanged in local and long distance trade, have prompted voyages of discovery, and have been carried thousands of miles by migrating peoples. Only one hundred years ago, the "Turkey red" strain of hard winter wheat, a basic bread wheat, was brought to the United States by German Mennonite immigrants from the Russian Crimea, who carried the seeds in earthenware jars across the Atlantic to their new home in Kansas.

The archaeologist, Kent Flannery, suggests that transhumant bands of food collectors were instrumental in domesticating the first grains in the Middle East over ten thousand years ago by the simple process of carrying them from a niche that was hard to reach, such as the talus slope below a limestone cliff, and planting them in one that was more accessible, such as the disturbed soil around their camp on a stream terrace.

From *History Today,* 33 (July 1983), pp. 31–36. Copyright © *History Today,* 4 Wood Street, London EC2U 7JB.

In the new niche, the pressures of natural selection were relaxed and human selection was applied. This principle underlies all successful plant transfers. In a new environment selected and shaped by humans, the plant's natural enemies are left behind, and human attention tries to ward off new ones.

Natural plant monopolies have been short-lived. Being small and easily concealed, like diamonds or gold, seeds have often been smuggled. Until very recently, plant hunters and their sponsors, whether national governments, botanic gardens, commercial nurseries, or pharmaceutical houses, have treated plants as part of nature's bounty, theirs for the taking. Yet any plant worth taking has already been identified and put to use in a local ecosystem. Modern ethnobotanists are more ready than old-time plant hunters to acknowledge the scientific value of local lore, to consult with local experts, and to make suitable arrangements with local or national institutions. It is now generally agreed that rare plants, like minerals, are part of the natural resources of the country in which they are discovered, and are not to be removed without permission and recompense, perhaps merely an exchange of scientific information, perhaps a joint development of the resource. The concept of "ownership" of plants is intimately tied to the rise of the nation-state, to the idea of territorial sovereignty and to respect for the rights of weak and underdeveloped societies.

But in the eighteenth and nineteenth centuries botany was an ally of the expanding European empires. Botanists sailed on the great exploratory voyages of Captain Cook and his successors, collecting plants in the name of science and for the benefit of the mother country. Sir Joseph Banks, amateur botanist, president of the Royal Society, privy councillor to the King, who had sailed as a young man on Cook's first voyage and had participated in the discovery of Botany Bay, was influential in promoting the settlement of Australia to fill the need for a British naval base in the Far East during the Anglo-French struggle for India. Banks had noted the tall pines and wild flax on Norfolk Island and envisaged an Australian colony where settlers would grow provisions and make masts, spars, and sails. Botanists went with the earliest expeditions up the Niger, the Limpopo, the Zambezi. A botanist ran border surveys in the Himalayas and returned with a collection of nearly 7,000 plants. A botanist in the employ of the British East India Company learned the secrets of tea cultivation, and shipped out 2,000 tea plants and 17,000 tea seeds to start the tea industry in India.

"Well-ripened seeds of rarities will always be acceptable. Simply address Hooker at Kew," wrote the director of Kew Gardens in his annual report of 1851. Under William J. Hooker's direction Kew Gardens became a depôt for the exchange of plants within the Empire, receiving seeds from its collectors, propagating them in Kew greenhouses, and sending those plants with economic possibilities to colonies with suitable climates. Cork oaks were sent to the Punjab, ipecac, mahogany, and papyrus to India, West Indian pineapples to the Straits Settlements, tea plants to Jamaica, an improved strain of tobacco to Natal. Plant transfer is as old as the practice of agriculture, but it had never before been undertaken on such a scale.

Victorian botanists were so imbued with the imperialist ethos of the times that in some instances of plant transfer they failed to respect the rights of independent states with whom their government had diplomatic relations, and they gave little thought to the loss sustained by the country of origin. Historians of Kew Gardens never discuss in print the subterfuges and downright illegalities practiced by the Kew collectors in the transfers of cinchona from the Andean republics of Colombia, Ecuador, Peru, and Bolivia in the 1860s, and rubber from Brazil in 1876. They speak only of the humanitarian aspect of the one—quinine from cinchona to treat malaria—and the economic triumph of the other—the great rubber plantations of India, Ceylon, and Malaya. "Many countries owe a great debt, now rarely acknowledged, to those industrious men of Kew who gave their work and often their lives to foster the trade which began their economic development," says Ronald King, Secretary of the Royal Botanic Gardens, the latest in a long line of Kew's praise-singers.

In trying to list those countries that can be said to owe a debt to the Kew collectors, however, it soon appears that they are mostly former British colonies—India, Malaysia, Sri Lanka (Ceylon), Kenya, Zimbabwe (Rhodesia). The rubber plantations of Java, Sumatra, and Borneo, now in the Republic of Indonesia, and of Laos and Vietnam, formerly French Indochina, were all started from descendants of the rubber seeds which the British removed from Brazil, using grafting, planting, and tapping methods developed by British and Dutch botanists in the colonial botanic gardens. This seed transfer and others like it were undertaken primarily to provide the mother countries of northwestern Europe with tropical commodities produced under their administrative, financial, and judicial control.

In the early days of European expansion, the movement of plantation crops was from the Old World to the New, when the plant riches of the East were carried to the new found lands. On his second voyage, in 1494, Columbus brought sugar cane cuttings to Hispaniola, along with citrus fruits, grape vines, olives, melons, onions, and radishes. Although many of these plants failed in the climate of the Antilles, this was the first step in a two-way transfer of useful plants which A. J. Crosby, Jr., has aptly called "the Columbian exchange." European settlers brought wheat for their daily bread, and New World corn, manioc, peanuts, and sweet potatoes were carried eastward to become the dietary staples of subsistence farmers in many parts of Africa, Asia, and Oceania. But it was the luxuries derived from tropical plants—the nonessential foodstuffs that made a pleasurable addition to the diet, the dyes, and the fibres that had hitherto been available only through trade with the Arabs—that excited the imagination of European traders and governments, and fostered the plantation system in the new tropical colonies.

Sugar cane, originally domesticated in Southeast Asia, was transferred by Arab traders and farmers to Syria and Egypt, and by the tenth century to the islands of the Mediterranean. By the fourteenth century Venetians had learned its culture and the plantation system from the Arabs whom they had displaced. Spaniards and Portuguese carried plantation sugar to the Atlantic Islands (Madeira, the Canaries, the Azores), thence to the Caribbean and Brazil. In 1640 sugar arrived on Barbados, and with it the slave trade and 150 years of prosperity for the West Indian planters, the merchants at home, and the home governments.

The Arabs domesticated coffee, a tree native to the Ethiopian highlands, and introduced it to India, where the Dutch found it and planted it on Ceylon in 1659 and on Java in 1696. One coffee plant from Java reached the Amsterdam Botanic Garden in 1706 and from this one tree most of the coffee plantations of the New World are descended. Seeds from this tree were sent to Suriname (Dutch Guiana) in about 1715; coffee trees went from Suriname to French Guiana and, in 1727, to Brazil, where a great coffee industry was founded that lasts to this day. In the nineteenth century both coffee and cocoa, a native American plant, were taken to the West African colonies to be grown on plantations and by small farmers. Ghana, especially, became dependent on its cocoa exports for foreign exchange and has suffered recently from a drop in the price of cocoa.

Nineteen-year-old Eliza Lucas was responsible for the introduction of indigo to the American mainland. Plants of the genus *Indigofera* have been grown since at least 2000 BC in India to produce a blue dye. Northern Europe did not use indigo in textile dyeing until the seventeenth century when the British and Dutch East India Companies imported it and displaced the woad producers. In the eighteenth century, the French planted indigo in the French Antilles and exported the processed dye cakes, but the process was a closely held secret. A governor of nearby British Antigua, Colonel George Lucas, sent indigo seeds to his daughter, who managed his three South Carolina plantations in his absence. Although the overseer who was sent with the seeds deliberately spoiled the first batches of dye out of loyalty to his home island and fear of ruining its trade, Governor Lucas sent a black slave from one of the French islands, and with his help Eliza Lucas succeeded in mastering the process. In 1744 she sent a sample of six pounds of indigo cakes to London, and distributed the rest of the seeds of the 1744 crop to her neighbours. Three years later, South Carolina sent 135,000 pounds of indigo cakes to London. Parliament voted a bounty on indigo processed in British territories. A French embargo, making exportation of indigo seeds a capital crime, came too late to save their monopoly.

In 1770, Pierre Poivre, Intendant of Île de France (Mauritius), an island in the Indian Ocean on the sea route to India and Indonesia, sent expeditions to the uncharted coasts of the Moluccas to bring back cloves and nutmeg, which he planted in the island's Jardin Royal de Pamplemousses. As a young man Poivre had made a voyage to China and Indochina, was wounded, and lost an arm in Batavia. His enforced stay on Java gave him an opportunity to study the spice trade, which the Dutch had successfully monopolised since the seventeenth century. They regulated production to maintain artificially high prices and kept all foreigners out of their spice islands. In 1755 Poivre had smuggled pepper and cinnamon to Île de France and was ennobled by his king. Britain took the island from the French in the Napoleonic Wars, sent cloves to Zanzibar and Pemba off the East African coast, and nutmeg to Grenada in the West Indies. Grenada is now called "the Spice Island," instead of the Moluccas.

Many important plant sources changed hands through the vagaries of European politics. In 1796 Britain took Ceylon from the Dutch and gained access to the cinnamon monopoly. In the seventeenth century she had acquired Bombay, with its pepper trade, as part of the dowry of Catherine of Braganza, the Portuguese princess who married Charles II. Plants followed the flag, as the European powers fought among themselves for control of Asia, and later Africa.

The situation was quite different when Europeans decided in the nineteenth century that they wanted certain plants native to areas of Latin America which by that time were postcolonial, independent nation-states. Europeans could not bring in their armies, or steal plants from each other. Diplomatic pressure was tried, or subterfuge, or both, as in case of cinchona.

Cinchona's only natural habitat is on the eastern slopes of the Andes, where the bark was collected by forest-dwelling Indians working for absentee land owners. When European observers like the famous naturalist Alexander von Humboldt saw the Indians cutting down whole trees to strip bark, they were convinced that this "wasteful harvesting practice" would kill the industry. In point of fact, the barkless trunks would have been eaten by insects, whereas in six years new shoots sprouting from the roots were ready for cutting. The cinchona transfer is one of the most intrigue-filled tales in plant history, with both the British and the Dutch trying to get seeds out of the Andean republics, and later vying for control of the Asian-based trade. The Andean republics, newly liberated from Spain and plagued by counterrevolution, were too weak to protect their infant cinchona bark industry.

Charles Hasskarl, director of the Dutch Buitenzorg Gardens on Java, penetrated the Caravaya region of Peru and Bolivia in 1854 under an assumed name. Clements Markham, leader of the British expedition in 1860, fled with his seeds from irate local authorities across southern Peru, avoiding the towns, with only a compass to guide him. Richard Spruce, a renowned explorer and botanist who had worked his way up the Amazon headwaters to Ecuador before being hired as a Kew Gardens cinchona collector, set up camp in a remote mountain valley, collected 100,000 dried seeds, and grew over 600 cinchona seedlings. He successfully transported them by raft down to the coast, but these endeavours cost him his health and he never walked again. These efforts, however, yielded few living plants, except for Spruce's "red cinchonas," which supplied the stock for thousands of cinchona trees planted in the hilly areas of India and Ceylon. Ironically, this "red bark" of commerce proved to be inferior in quinine content to the Ledger varieties grown by the Dutch on Java from seeds purchased in 1865 from an English trader, whose Aymara servant smuggled them out of Bolivia, was imprisoned for his treason, and died from prison hardships.

In addition to this piece of luck as regards species, the Dutch program of intensive care of the cinchona trees gave them a further advantage over the British planters, and by the 1890s a cartel of Dutch quinine processors had control of the market. Many British planters in India and Ceylon switched to tea. The market for South American wild bark had already dwindled to near zero, from a high point of nine million kilos of bark in 1881 before plantation bark had come on the market in quantity.

But those who contend that the British cinchona coup turned out to be a costly fiasco miss the point. The British government did not undertake the cinchona transfer for the benefit of planters, but because it wanted to protect the health of its troops and civil administrators in India, where British rule had been severely shaken by the Sepoy Mutiny of 1857. And this was accomplished: British-made quinine and quinidine were reserved for the representatives of the British *raj,* and Britain's grip on India was made more secure by an influx of soldiers and civil servants who no longer feared "the deadly climate."

The much-vaunted program to sell government-made "totaquine," a less refined and cheaper antimalarial derived from cinchona bark, 'at every post office in Bengal' was never pursued with vigour and was soon allowed to lapse. European quinine processors made big profits from plantation-grown cinchona bark in South Asia. Quinine became a more and more expensive drug, mostly beyond the purse of the indigenous peoples of malarial areas, but useful to their Western masters, and especially to Western armies. In the First World War the Allies faced a shortage of quinine, since the neutral Netherlands sold bark and quinine to Germany. A representative of Howard & Sons, the British quinine processing firm, negotiated an agreement to pool Allied resources and to get access to the Java bark. He also "saved" the output of British cinchona estates from going to the India office, hence to the Indian public. In 1942 when the worst combined famine and malaria epidemic hit India and Ceylon, taking over two million lives, the British would not release quinine stockpiled in India to the civilian population. The cinchona plantations of Java were at that time in the hands of the Japanese and constituted one of the great prizes of their conquest of Southeast Asia. The United States, also desperately in need of quinine for its military forces in the South Pacific, instituted a successful crash program to rehabilitate the wild cinchona of the Andes. In two and a half years 18,000 tons of cinchona bark were harvested for processing in the United States.

Quinine was also essential to the British, French, and Germans in their "scramble for Africa," where appalling death rates had confined Europeans to the coast until quinine prophylaxis was adopted. It seems no coincidence that the New Imperialism of the late nineteenth century represented a European expansion into parts of the world where malaria was hyperendemic.

In the post–Second World War era, synthetic drugs largely replaced quinine in the Western world, but there was still a market for the drug. In 1959 a new cartel of Dutch, German, French, and British quinine processing companies was formed to control every aspect of the production and distribution of the world's supply of quinine, with reserved geographic markets for each firm and a uniform system of pricing. The main objective of this cartel was to eliminate competition, both among themselves and from outsiders, in bidding for the huge United States stockpile of bulk quinine, surplus war material then being put on the market. Members of the cartel agreed not to buy quinine from the Bandoeng factory in the Republic of Indonesia, a legacy from Dutch colonial days and the largest non-European processor of cinchona bark. By restricting its market, the cartel also gained access to Javanese cinchona bark which would otherwise have gone to the Bandoeng factory.

The celebrated rubber transfer occurred in 1876 when Henry Wickham, an English adventurer in the employ of Kew Gardens and the India Office, made off with a boatload of about 70,000 Hevea rubber seeds. Wickham hoodwinked the Brazilian customs officer, telling him that he had a cargo of "exceedingly delicate botanical specimens specially designated for delivery to Her Britannic Majesty's own Royal Gardens of Kew." The precious seeds were soon planted in Kew's greenhouses, and in a few months 1,900 rubber seedlings were en route to the Peradeniya Gardens in Ceylon. Seeds from Ceylon were sent to the Singapore Gardens, where Henry Ridley, a Kew-trained botanist, worked out the wound response method of tapping. He was called "Mad Ridley" or "Rubber Ridley" for his pains, but in 1895 he finally persuaded a few British planters in Malaya to try the new crop.

At the turn of the century 98 percent of the world's rubber came from Brazil. By 1919 the Brazilian rubber industry was dead. Singapore was thereafter the rubber capital of the world. In the 1930s, before the end of the colonial era, 75 percent of the world's rubber, by that time a vital strategic resource in both peace and war, came from British-owned plantations. Indentured Chinese labourers opened up the forests in Malaya; impoverished Tamils from India came across the straits to Malaya and Ceylon to work rubber and got caught up in debt peonage. The old agrarian empires of Asia supplied a docile and inexhaustible labour force.

In the early 1870s when Kew Gardens and the India Office first began trying to get rubber seeds out of Brazil (the first three attempts were failures because the seeds did not germinate), the wild rubber trade did not suffer from the cartel conditions that developed later. Britain had no conceivable reason of national security for invading Brazil's sovereignty by the surreptitious removal of one of its natural resources, merely an economic incentive, and in the preautomotive era, not a very strong one at that. Yet because the motorised West has depended heavily in this century on rubber emanating from Asian plantations, the rubber seed transfer, when it is remembered, is generally treated as an admirable exploit. Wickham's deceit of Brazilian authorities is not mentioned.

After the rubber coup of 1876 Kew Gardens did not undertake any organised expedition in contravention of laws prohibiting the exportation of Latin American plants, nor has any subsequent plant removal had the economic and political importance of rubber. But Britain still urged her consular officials to send home specimens of protected plants and reports on their propagation and processing, and Kew Gardens continued to seek such plants for study and to print such trade secrets in the name of science.

A case in point is sisal, a hard fibre suitable for making twine and rope. Sisal is obtained from the leaves of agave species native to the dry areas of Central America. The fibre was known and used by the Mayan Indians. In the 1830s commercial production was begun on the great *haciendas* of northern Yucatan. The Indian labour force was attached to the *haciendas* by debt peonage, easily enforced because Ladino appropriation of the water holes made independent village life impossible. After 1875, when grain production was intensified on the American plains, the Argentine pampas, and in eastern Europe to feed the growing urban populations of both North Atlantic seaboards, sisal was in great demand as a binder twine for wheat sheaves. The sisal plantations of Yucatan became vast agricultural factories, with American capital supplying machines to strip the fibre from the waste pulp, and railroads to take the sisal to the ports. Yucatan, once Mexico's poorest state, became its richest, and Mérida a glittering city.

Kew's interest was aroused. It was thought that sisal would do very well in the Bahamas and the other drier islands of the West Indies, which were languishing in postsugar, pretourist doldrums, as well as in Fiji, Mauritius, and perhaps India. But Mexico would not export its plants, nor give away its trade secrets. In 1890, however, the British consul in Vera Cruz obliged by sending Kew two lots of sisal plants, many of which were "dead on arrival," to quote a Kew report. Specimens were sent to the botanic gardens of Antigua, Fiji, and Singapore. In 1892 Kew published, in its *Bulletin of Miscellaneous Information,* a series of articles describing in detail the production and processing of Mexican sisal. Kew had done its part, according to its charter, in "aiding the Mother Country in everything that is useful in the vegetable Kingdom."

But the British plans miscarried. Scientific information travels easily to peoples culturally prepared to receive it. A German agronomist working for the German East Africa Company read the *Kew Bulletin* articles and found there, in a report of the director of the Trinidad garden, the name of a sisal bulbil supplier in Florida, where sisal plants had grown wild since 1840. Dr. Henry Perrine, former United States consul in Campeche, Mexico, had received from Congress in 1836 a grant of land on Biscayne Bay on which he intended to establish a botanic garden of exotic plants. While waiting for the Seminole War to be over, he settled with his family and his plants on Indian Key. Among the plants he brought from Mexico were figs, indigo, mulberry, tamarinds, mangoes (all originally from the East), and agaves. He had been given permission to take the agaves out of Yucatan in appreciation of his personal services to the community of Campeche during a cholera epidemic. In 1840 Dr. Perrine was killed in an Indian raid and his abandoned plants spread to the mainland.

A sisal industry never developed in Florida, but descendants of Perrine's sisal plants furnished the start of a thriving industry in East Africa, where German colonists adopted modern methods of planting, harvesting, and processing sisal, using a labour force of native tribesmen coerced into labour by land alienation and head-tax payments. Kenya, just to the north, started a similar industry from purchases of German bulbils, before a 1908 German embargo on their sale. Britain acquired German East Africa under the terms of the Versailles Treaty in 1919, and with the colony (then Tanganyika, now Tanzania) its sisal industry. Between the world wars, Java had huge sisal plantations. By the 1960s Mexico's share of the world's hard fibre trade had dropped to 12 percent; Manila hemp accounted for 13 percent; most of the rest was East African sisal. Another Latin American plant-based industry had been undermined in favour of European colonies in the Eastern hemisphere.

The white settlers in the East African highlands also grew coffee, tea, and maize for export to Europe. The agricultural value of the East African colonies rested entirely on introduced plants. The political repercussions of this imposed agricultural system are still reverberating today. But their contribution to the prosperity of the Empire was minor in comparison to that of the South Asian colonies, especially Malaya with its rubber, and Ceylon with rubber and tea. Java under the Dutch was the richest jewel in any colonial crown, with its plantations of rubber, cinchona, coffee, tea, sisal, and tobacco.

The partnership between colonising governments and botanic gardens in the transfer and scientific development of useful plants was mutually beneficial. State subsidy supported the science of botany, pure and applied. Botanic gardens repaid the national investment many times over, in the form of new plantation crops and improved yields. Tropical monoculture under European direction wrested an enormous bounty from the earth, but it also produced political and ecological imbalances with which the modern world must struggle.

FOR FURTHER READING

The Columbian Exchange by Alfred W. Crosby, Jr. (Greenwood Press, Westport, Conn.) is
a delightful short work on the two-way seed transfers between the Old and New Worlds.

A good introduction to the important food and fibre cultivars is *Plants and Civilization* by Herbert G. Baker (Wadsworth, Calif.) or *Seeds and Civilization* by Charles B. Heiser, Jr. (Freeman, San Francisco, Calif.). Clements Markham (John Murray, 1860 and John Murray, 1882) and Henry Wickham (Kegan Paul, 1908) have published accounts of their efforts and adventures as Kew collectors in Latin America; the journal of the great botanist Richard Spruce, edited by Alfred Russel Wallace, was published posthumously (Macmillan, 1908). The role of botanic gardens in seed transfer and development is treated in *Science and Colonial Expansion* by Lucile H. Brockway (Academic Press, 1979).

CHAPTER **10**

THE MODERNIZATION OF UNDERDEVELOPMENT: EL SALVADOR, 1858–1931

E. Bradford Burns

UCLA

"What most strikes me on arriving from Europe is the absence of all extreme poverty," Mrs. Henry Grant Foote observed approvingly of El Salvador in the mid-nineteenth century.[1] The British diplomat's wife concluded that Southern Europe and the major cities of England suffered far worse poverty and human misery than the diminutive— and other observers would add "backward"—Central American republic. These first impressions of the country, to which Queen Victoria's government had posted Mrs. Foote's husband in 1853, were also her conclusions strengthened by eight years of residence there.

Her memoir revealed at least one explanation for the satisfactory quality of life: people enjoyed access to land. The large Indian population still possessed a part of its communal lands, ranked by Mrs. Foote as among the "most fertile" areas of El Salvador.[2] Those who chose not to live in the communities, she noted, "generally have their own little piece of land and a house on it."[3] The outskirts of the capital, San Salvador, seemed almost Edenic in her prose: "The environs of the city are very beautiful, being one mass of luxuriant orange and mango trees, bending beneath their load of fruit, and the cottages of the poor people are remarkably neat and clean, each surrounded by its own beautiful shrubbery of fruit trees."[4] These observations buttressed her conclusion of the ready availability of food. The simple society excluded sharp distinctions between rich and poor. The Englishwoman praised the practical modesty among the upper class, although its humility sometimes bemused her. At one point she chuckled: "One custom struck us as very peculiar in this state. Everyone, from Presi-

From *Journal of Developing Areas*, no. 18 (April 1984), pp. 293–316. Copyright © 1984 by Western Illinois University.

dent downwards keeps a shop, and no one objects to appear behind his counter and sell you a reel of cotton, the wives and daughters officiating in the same capacity."[5] She left an incomplete although suggestive portrait of the new nation, characterizing life as bucolic, devoid of social and economic extremes.

Around the middle of the century, a small group of foreign travelers and diplomats, among them John Baily, E. G. Squier, Carl Scherzer, and G. F. Von Tempsky, visited El Salvador.[6] Their accounts corroborated Mrs. Foote's. Although those visitors considered the small nation to be overcrowded even then, they agreed that most of the population owned land, either individually or collectively. The large hacienda existed but did not monopolize the rural economy. Squier noted, "There is little public and unclaimed land in the state, and few large tracts held by single individuals."[7] He contrasted that aspect of land tenure favorably with the experience of other nations he knew. The Indians, who at midcentury comprised at least a quarter of the population, worked either their communal lands or individual plots. A large number of them exclusively inhabited a Pacific coastal area of 50 by 20 miles between the ports of La Libertad and Acajutla, "retaining habits but little changed from what they were at the period of conquest," according to Squier.[8] All the travelers lauded the generosity of nature and spoke of the abundance of food. Von Tempsky recalled that the Indian village, Chinameca, he visited in 1855 was "well supplied with the necessaries of life."[9] Particularly impressed with the region of Sonsonate, Scherzer lauded the abundance, variety, and low price of food.[10] None mentioned either malnutrition or starvation.

The largely subsistence economy produced rather leisurely for the world market. Indigo, traditionally a principal export, earned $700,000 of $1,200,000 from foreign sales in 1851. Minerals, balsams, skins, rice, sugar, cotton, and cacao accounted for much of the rest.

Even though the foreign visitors waxed eloquent about some idyllic aspects of life as they lived and perceived it in El Salvador, not one pretended that the isolated nation was a rustic paradise. Problems existed. The visitors lamented the disease and political turmoil. Still, even if life did not mirror the ideal, a socioeconomic pattern that benefited many had emerged in the long colonial period and much briefer national period: food was produced in sufficient quantity to feed the population, the economy was varied, little emphasis fell on the export sector, the land was reasonably well distributed, the foreign debt was low, and the absence of the extremes of poverty and wealth spoke of a vague degree of equality. Having endured for some time, however, by the 1850s such characteristics were about to disappear. The El Salvador those foreigners observed was on the threshold of change and a rather rapid and dramatic change at that.

Over the course of three centuries, Spain had implanted its political, economic, social, and cultural institutions in its vast American empire with varying degrees of effectiveness. Those regions nearest the viceregal capitals or well integrated into imperial trade patterns bore the most vivid testimony to their successful implantation. Consequently, no matter what great distances might have separated Lima from Mexico City, the gold mines of Colombia from the silver mines of Bolivia, or the sugar plantations of Cuba from the cacao estates of Venezuela, similarities in economic and political structures outweighed inevitable local variations. Historiographic studies tend to

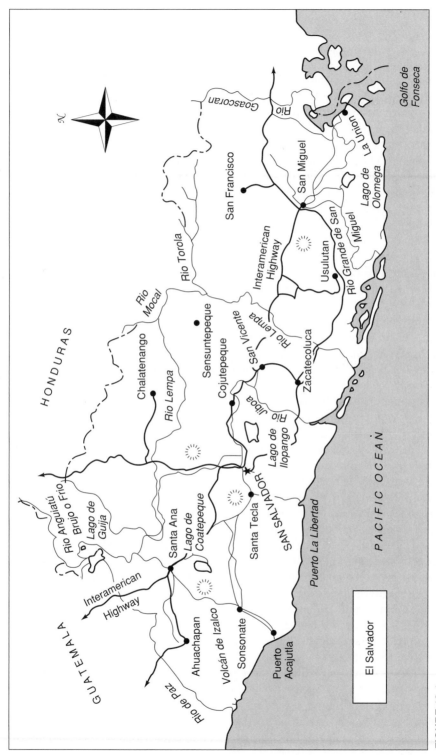

FIGURE 10-1
EL SALVADOR.

127

dwell on the relative changelessness and continuity of some of those institutions over half a millenium. The institutions surrounding the use of land and labor are two useful examples; the concentration and authoritarian exercise of political power is another. Still, the metropolitan institutions did not fully penetrate every part of Spanish America. To the degree they did not, those regions remained marginal to international trade and isolated from the primary preoccupations of the crown. Fusing Iberian, Indian, and African cultures and institutions, such regions remained nominally subordinate to a distant monarch but for practical purposes more responsive to local conditions.

More regional diversity existed in Spanish America during the period when the colonies obtained their independence, 1808–1824, than there would be at the end of the century. The reasons for the rapid homogenization during the nineteenth century are not difficult to find. Many of the elites in all the newly independent governments had embraced or would embrace the ideas that sprang from the European Enlightenment. They admired French culture, while they looked to England for their economic vigor. As the nineteenth century waxed, their collective desire grew to create in the New World a replica of Europe north of the Pyrenees. To emulate the "progress" the elites believed characteristic of their model nations, they needed capital. They obtained it through loans, investments, and trade, all three of which linked them ever more closely to North Atlantic capitalism. Marvelous advances in communication and transportation facilitated the growing conformity forged by common goals and trade patterns. One major consequence was that as the new nations neared the first centenary of their independence, the institutional patterns of Latin America reflected a more striking similarity than they had after more than three centuries of Iberian domination. To achieve conformity required certain areas and nations, those that once had been marginal to Spanish interests and thus most superficially incorporated into European commercial patterns, to change dramatically. A predominately export-oriented economy linked to international capitalism became the dynamo propelling that profound, rapid change. In certain cases, radical transformation—almost revolutionary in some instances—challenged the stereotypes of "changelessness" and "continuity" often applied to the entire area.

One of the new nations, El Salvador, provides a striking example of the rapid and profound change of a once-neglected outpost of the Spanish empire. Further, its experience with progress or modernization accompanied by the increasing impoverishment of the majority of the inhabitants illustrates how a Latin American nation could modernize without developing.[11]

Spanish institutions had imperfectly penetrated El Salvador. Throughout the colonial period that small area bore a closer resemblance to its Indian past than to any of the bustling centers of colonial Spanish America. Like the other Central Americans, the Salvadorans remained geographically isolated and largely self-sufficient. As Adriaan C. van Oss convincingly argued, the Central Americans had "turned their backs on the coasts and thereby on intensive commerce with the motherland."[12] Yet, within the short span of three decades, roughly between 1860 and 1890, El Salvador acquired the economic, political, and social institutions characterizing the rest of Latin America. These included a dynamic and modernizing export sector based on monoculture and the predominance of the large estate producing for foreign trade; a subservient, impoverished, landless rural labor force; concentration of economic and political power within the hands of the principal planters who exercised it from a single dominant city, the capital, which, if it fell short of duplicating its urban model, Paris, nonetheless contained districts reflecting the architectural influence of nineteenth-century Europe; and a political understanding and tolerance between an increasingly professional military and politicoeconomic elites. In a number of fundamental aspects, El Salvador became nearly indistinguishable from the other Spanish-speaking nations. The process by which that formerly isolated and singular state acquired institutions characteristic of the rest of Spanish America as well as the consequences of that process merit study.

For three centuries Central America formed part of the Spanish empire before it fell briefly under Mexican rule. A shaky confederation, the United Provinces of Central America, emerged in 1824 but crumbled under political rivalries a decade and a half later. In 1839, some of the leading citizens of San Salvador declared the independence of El Salvador, although the vision of a greater Central American fatherland remained constant in El Salvador. Promulgating a constitution in 1841, the Salvadorans embarked on a tempestuous political journey. The population of the new republic, estimated in 1855 to be 394,000, consisted largely of Indians and mestizos with a small minority of whites, blacks, and mulattoes (see Table 10-1). Most of the population lived in the countryside.

The economic structures characteristic of the long colonial past remained intact during the first half of the nineteenth century. El Salvador continued to export in small quantities marginal products of limited demand. The Spanish mercantilist legacy rested lightly on the region because of its isolation and economic insignificance. The land-use patterns accommodated both Spanish and Indian practices. The Indian villages held the land they needed; the traditional Indian communities survived. The

TABLE 10-1
ESTIMATES OF THE POPULATION
OF EL SALVADOR, 1821–1930

Year	Population
1821	250,000
1855	394,000
1878	554,000
1882	612,943
1892	703,500
1900	783,433
1910	986,537
1920	1,178,665
1930	1,353,170

Source: Jeffry Royle Gibson, "A Demographic Analysis of Urbanization: Evolution of a System of Cities in Honduras, El Salvador, and Costa Rica," Ph.D. diss., Cornell University, 1970, p. 80.

haciendas, the large estates owned by Spaniards and their descendants, also existed. In the early nineteenth century, there were approximately 440 haciendas averaging close to 2,000 acres each.[13] They accounted for one-third of the land area. The Indian communities produced food for local consumption. So did the haciendas, but they also grew the principal export crops, foremost of which was indigo.

Indigo production required both a regular and a seasonal labor force. The haciendas drew their workers from neighboring Indian communities. They also slowly but steadily encroached on Indian lands. The control of the political institutions of the new republic by a small merchant and planter class complemented those trends. The new national elite fully understood the importance to their own prosperity of controlling land and labor. No longer did a distant Spanish crown thwart them. For the time being, however, certain other realities inhibited their economic expansion. The frequent wars in Central America, a scarcity of capital and credit, a disruption of trade routes and patterns, and the lack of any products in high demand in foreign markets caused a general economic decline throughout much of the first half of the nineteenth century. Those political and economic realities enforced a kind of balance between the Indian communities and the haciendas. Both seemed to provide satisfactory, if very modest, lifestyles. Such was the El Salvador described by Foote, Squier, Von Tempsky, Scherzer, and Baily.

After 1858, new socioeconomic patterns took shape. Greater political stability and closer contact with the North Atlantic nations, principally the United States, France, and Great Britain, partially explain the emergence of the new patterns. Very importantly, the elite found a new crop, coffee, that the country could grow and profitably sell abroad. More than anything else, concentration on the growth and export of that single crop altered old institutions. Before the end of the century, the new coffee estates became the base of economic production, political power, and social organization. The coffee planters emerged as the powerful economic, political, and social elite.

Instrumental in initiating the challenge to the old system, President Gerardo Barrios (1858–1863) directed the fledgling nation's first steps toward modernization and change. A trip through Europe in the early 1850s had influenced him profoundly. In one letter back to El Salvador, he proclaimed his mission: "I urgently needed this trip to correct my ideas and to be useful to my country. . . . I will return to preach to my fellow countrymen what we Central Americans are and what we can become."[14] He did. He informed the legislative assembly in 1860 that he intended to "regenerate" the nation.[15]

In a pattern already becoming familiar throughout Latin America, those who would "regenerate" their society advocated rather uncritically the models provided by the leading capitalist nations of the North Atlantic. Their agrarian, industrial, and technological advances awed the Latin American elites. Those nations seemed to have found the sure road to "progress," a gloriously nineteenth-century notion for which the current social science concept "modernization" is synonymous. In the minds of the elites, "to progress" came to mean to re-create the European model in Latin America. Carried to its extreme, it even signified the encouragement of European immigration to replace the Indian and African peoples of the New World. Within a broad Latin American perspective, Barrios was by no means unique in either his discovery of Europe or his hope of recreating his nation in its image. Within the narrow confines of bucolic El Salvador, however, he seemed to be something of a visionary ready to deny the past in order to participate in an alluring if uncertain future.

Barrios characterized the nation he governed as one that was "backward," "destitute," and "misgoverned," and into which he believed he introduced "progress."[16] Both a military commander and the owner of a medium-sized estate, the president represented the nascent middle class in his lifestyle, outlook, and aspirations. His government vaguely encompassed a liberalism characteristic of later nineteenth-century Salvadoran politics. He favored individual liberties, opposed dictatorial rule, and sought to end the neofeudalism dominating the countryside. He succeeded in accelerating a rural shift from neofeudalism to neocapitalism. In a not unfamiliar pattern in nineteenth-century Latin America, however, liberty during the Barrios years—as thereafter—smiled exclusively on the elites, and authoritarian rule remained the practice despite rhetoric to the contrary.

A devoted francophile, President Barrios incorporated Liberal and Positivist ideas into his policies to turn his country from its Iberian and Indian past to a closer approximation of a rapidly changing Western Europe. In 1860, the first program he announced for his government included these five goals: promotion of agriculture, industry, and commerce; introduction into El Salvador of the progress that distinguished other nations; encouragement of immigration; reform of the educational system in accordance with the latest European ideas; and construction of roads and ports to facilitate international communication and transportation. Such goals typified the modernizers of nineteenth-century Latin America. Soon after the announcement of his program, the president promulgated the nation's first civil code and a new educational plan, both of which inevitably drew on the latest European models. In true Positivist fashion, Barrios believed the government should play a direct role in encouraging exports.[17] The most immediate results of his policies were to facilitate the growth of capitalism and to promote foreign commerce. Indeed, exports doubled between 1860 and 1862.[18]

Barrios appreciated the incipient agrarian and commercial changes already under way in El Salvador. In 1853, steamship service had been inaugurated between El Salvador and California. Six years later, the government began to pay a subsidy to the Pacific Mail Steamship Company to service the Salvadoran ports. As one immediate consequence, sugar and rum exports rose, a trend Barrios applauded. United States diplomats stationed in San Salvador also spoke enthusiastically about the rising export trade facilitated by the steamships.[19] President Barrios not only encouraged the growth of crops with an international demand but favored land and labor laws complementary to such agrarian enterprise.

Understanding the importance of coffee on the world market and the suitability of El Salvador's rich volcanic soil to produce it, the president promoted its production.[20] Farmers had first started to grow small amounts of coffee for local consumption in the eighteenth century. Governmental encouragement of its production dated from 1846, without noticeable results. Barrios assumed a vigorous role in its promotion in order both to diversify exports and to increase national income. Under his direction, coffee exports had their modest beginnings. In his presidential address to the legislative assembly on January 29, 1862, he emphasized the impetus his government gave coffee, predicting (incorrectly) that within two years El Salvador would be the major coffee producer in Central America.[21]

In the decades after Barrios (really even including the Conservative government of Francisco Duenas, 1863–1871),[22] the Liberals articulated a program of goals focusing on the modernization of the transportation and communication infrastructures, the expansion of coffee exports, the adoption of European models, and the strengthening of governmental power. Never loath to use force to implement their program, they extended their authority from the presidential palace to the most remote hamlet.

The relatively complex process of coffee production engendered a series of crises in the traditional neo-Hispanic and neo-Indian institutions that had adequately served a society whose economy leisurely grew indigo and food crops.[23] The eventual triumph of coffee, a kind of victory of modern capitalism, necessitated new institutional arrangements.

Coffee production differed significantly from indigo, traditionally the primary export. The indigo plant grew without need of a great deal of care or investment. Within a year, the farmer could harvest it, although the amount of pigment increased if harvest could be delayed two or even three years. Indigo production required a small permanent work force supplemented during the harvesting and processing, both of which were relatively uncomplicated. Coffee could be grown under a variety of conditions on lands ranging from a small plot or a few acres to vast extensions of land. Small coffee planters seemed to flourish in some parts of Latin America. Colombia provided a useful example. In El Salvador, however, the growing and most especially the processing of coffee took place on medium-sized and large estates. Care, conservation, and fertilizing of the land and preparation of the coffee, including drying, processing, and sacking, required considerable capital and a large permanent work force generously augmented during the harvest season. Coffee planters waited three to five years for the first harvest. They required considerably more capital, patience, and skill than the producers of indigo. Those requirements severely limited the number of coffee growers but particularly the number of processors. Handsome profits, however, reimbursed the few who met the requirements.

The lure of a lucrative market prompted those planters who could bear the financial burden to expand their estates, which grew at the expense of communal landholdings and small landowners. The shift in landowning patterns fundamentally altered the lifestyle of the majority. The governments enthusiastically encouraged this change: they facilitated the concentration of land into fewer and fewer hands. Thus, in the decades between 1860 and 1890, the landholding patterns came to resemble the commercial capitalistic models characteristic of plantation economies elsewhere in the world. The first step was to label the Indian communal lands as retrograde, antiprogressive. They stood accused of the heinous crime of delaying or even preventing modernization. In short, they preserved the "backward" past. President Barrios initiated the legal attack on the *ejidos,* landholding communities, and the *tierras communales,* municipally owned and worked lands. His policies forced part of those lands onto the market, just as ambitious entrepreneurs sought more acres for coffee trees.

An official governmental land survey in 1879 revealed that only a quarter of the land still belonged to the villages.[24] The government of President Rafael Zaldivar (1876–1885) promptly oversaw the disposal of those remaining lands. Zaldivar proudly wore the modernizing mantle of Barrios, demonstrating his admiration for his predecessor by erecting an imposing mausoleum for him. An editorial in the *Diario Oficial* in early 1880 summarized the official attitude toward the communal lands, revealing once again the ideological continuity of the governments after 1858:

> On the one hand, we see virgin fertile lands that are calling for the application of capital and labor to reap the wealth that is promised; while on the other, we see the majority of the inhabitants of our villages content to grow crops of maize and beans that will never raise this miserable people above their sorry position. They will remain in the same wretched state they endured in colonial times. . . . The government is determined to transform the Republic, to make each one of the villages, yesterday sad and miserable, into lively centers of work, wealth, and comfort.[25]

Action followed. In early 1881, the government abolished the tierras communales. With far-reaching consequences, the decree denounced ancient practices to declare unequivocally the economic policy in vogue for some decades dramatically enforced after 1881: "The existence of lands under the ownership of *Communidades* impedes agricultural development, obstructs the circulation of wealth, and weakens family bonds and the independence of the individual. Their existence is contrary to the economic and social principles that the Republic has accepted." A year later, a law dissolved the ejidos for the same reason: they were "an obstacle to our agricultural development [and] contrary to our economic principles."[26] The communidades and ejidos bore the blame, according to official thinking, of thwarting "progress," meaning, of course, the expansion of coffee culture. In both cases, the lands were divided among community members. Such actions disoriented the Indian and folk populations, which had little concept of private ownership of land. Quite the contrary, they identified the community and the land as one: the land existed for the commonweal of the group. The community cared for the land in an almost religious fashion. Cooperation rather than competition governed the economic behavior of those populations. In the government's judgment, the Indians and rural folk obviously were not prepared to contribute to El Salvador's capitalist future.

Once the communal lands were distributed into small plots, the coffee planters set about acquiring the land. Experience proved that it was easier to befuddle and buy out the new, small landowner than the well-entrenched and tradition-oriented community.[27] The emerging rural class system, increasingly characterized by a small group of wealthy coffee planters and processors on the one hand and a large body of ill-paid laborers on the other, contrasted sharply with the more equalitarian structures of rural El Salvador prior to 1860.

Export patterns altered radically during the same decades. From the colonial period into the early 1880s, El Salvador had enjoyed varied agrarian production and export: maize, indigo, tobacco, sugar, cacao, coffee, cotton, and tropical fruits. The midcentury invention of synthetic dyes doomed the most important of those exports, indigo. Coffee more than made up for its demise. The export statistics tell the tale. In 1860, coffee composed but 1 percent of the exports; in 1865, 8 percent; and in 1870, 17 percent. In 1875, for the first time, the value of coffee exports exceeded indigo exports, quite a change from 1865 when the value of indigo exports amounted to 15 times that of coffee. Table 10-2 indicates the changing nature of El Salvador's exports during the critical 1864–1875 period. In 1879, coffee accounted for 48.5 percent of the total value of all exports. By 1910, it accounted for $4,661,440 of exports totaling $5,696,706. Indigo by then earned only $107,936 on the world markets. During the decade of the 1880s, El Salvador became virtually a monoagricultural exporting nation, its economic prosperity largely dependent on the purchase of coffee by three or four nations, which, in turn, supplied investments, technology, and manufactured goods in quantities commensurate with the profits from coffee sales.

The domination of the national economy by coffee obviously affected the rural folk, the overwhelming majority of the population. The expanding coffee estates continued to dispossess vast numbers of them of their lands. They, then, depended on the coffee plantations for work and, to the relief of the coffee planters, formed a sizable pool of unemployed and underemployed who could be hired at meager wages. At the same time, the increasingly unstable position of larger numbers of the rural population created discontent and unrest among them. The rural poor protested their deteriorating situation. Major uprisings occurred in 1872, 1875, 1880, 1885, and 1898. The planter-dominated governments addressed the problem of maintaining order not only to assure tranquillity but just as importantly to ensure a docile and plentiful labor supply. Threatening fines, arrests, and punishments, the Vagrancy Laws of 1881 required the populace to work. The Agrarian Law of 1907 further regulated the rural working class, while it authorized the organization of a rural constabulary to provide the physical protection the landowners' demanded. Agricultural judges—in a fashion somewhat reminiscent of the Spanish *repartimiento* system—made certain that the labor force was available when and where the planters needed it. The new rural police enforced the judges' decisions, intimidated the workers, protected the planters, and guaranteed the type of rural order the planters believed essential to their prosperity. They already had closely identified national well-being with their own.

By the end of the century, coffee had transformed El Salvador. The landowning structures, the land-use patterns, and the relationship of the workers to the land were radically different. Whereas in 1858, there existed a reasonable balance between large estates, small landholdings, and ejidos, by 1890, the large estate dominated. The increasing accumulation of capital in a few hands strengthened the coffee estate, improved coffee processing, and further facilitated coffee exportation.

A tiny but significant group of capitalists appeared by the end of the century. Foreign immigrants, who invariably married into the leading Salvadoran families, played a disproportionately important role among them. They skillfully combined their wider knowledge of North Atlantic capitalism with local needs. A small number of Salvadoran capitalists from both the upper and middle classes and the local representatives of British capitalists joined them. Some of them controlled the processing and/or export sectors of the coffee industry, highly lucrative and strategic enterprises. Their interests obviously intertwined with those of the coffee planters.

Political stability accompanied economic growth and change. Beginning with the government of Barrios in 1858 and ending with that of General Antonio Gutierrez in 1898, the chiefs-of-state stayed in office longer than their predecessors. In that 39-year time span, 7 presidents governed for an average of 5.7 years each, more than double the time the chiefs-of-state between 1839 and 1858 had served. Five of the presidents

TABLE 10-2
VALUE OF EXPORTS, 1854–1875
(In Silver Pesos)

Year	Total value of exports	Value of indigo exports	Percentage of exports	Value of coffee exports	Percentage of exports	Value of all other exports	Percentage of exports
1864	—	1,129,105	—	80,105	—	—	—
1865	2,765,260	1,357,400	49.0	138,263	1.5	1,369,597	49.5
1866	2,463,437	1,548,000	64.3	197,075	8.1	682,362	27.6
1867	3,056,388	1,979,850	64.7	275,075	9.1	801,463	26.2
1868	3,521,020	2,131,500	60.5	528,153	15.0	861,367	24.5
1869	3,906,100	2,447,550	62.7	507,793	13.0	950,767	24.8
1870	3,902,041	2,619,749	67.1	663,347	17.0	618,945	15.9
1871	3,896,588	2,308,317	59.2	662,420	17.0	925,851	23.8
1872	3,763,838	2,786,574	74.0	489,299	13.0	487,965	13.0
1873	3,521,096	1,808,037	51.2	1,056,329	30.0	662,730	18.8
1874	3,949,858	1,721,378	43.5	1,342,952	34.0	885,528	22.5
1875	5,070,172	1,160,700	22.9	1,673,157	33.0	2,236,351	44.1

Source: Rafael Menjívar, *Acumulación Originaria y Desarrollo del Capitalismo en El Salvador* (San Jose, Costa Rica: Editorial Universitaria Centroamérica, 1980), p. 35.

135

had military backgrounds. Force dislodged each president from office. The administration of Tomás Regalado, 1898–1903, marked a transition. General Regalado came to power through force, regularized his position through election, served the constitutional four-year term, and then stepped down from the presidency at the end of that term.[28]

The coffee elites had codified the political rules for their domination in the Constitution of 1886. It remained in force until 1939, the longest lived of El Salvador's many constitutions. Suppressing communal landownership, it emphasized the inviolability of private property. Within the classic framework of nineteenth-century liberalism, the document valued the individual over the collective. It enfranchised literate male adults, a minority in a land where illiteracy prevailed. Characterized as authoritarian and elitist, it served the planters handsomely during the half-century it was in force, defining the political boundaries of the "modern" state they sought to create.[29] It contributed significantly to the new political stability.

Increasing political stability, rising exports and income, economic growth, and a careful attention to the servicing of foreign debts nominated El Salvador as a candidate for foreign loans used to purchase a wide variety of consumer items the coffee class fancied, to introduce foreign technology, and to modernize the economy. Not unnaturally, a government in the service of the planters favored investment in and modernization of the infrastructure servicing the coffee industry. Renovation of two important ports, La Libertad and Acajutla, was completed in the 1860s. The first bank opened its doors in 1872, and they multiplied in number during the decade of the 1880s. The republic entered the railroad era in 1882 with the opening of a modest 12-mile line between Sonsonate, a departmental capital and one of the principal commercial centers, and Acajutla. The line facilitated the export of the varied local products, among which coffee was rapidly becoming the most important. English loans in 1889 promoted the expansion of an incipient railroad system that also fell under English administration.

British investments accompanied loans and together they assured Britain's economic preeminence. Besides railroads, mining attracted British capital. In 1888, the English established the Divisadero Gold and Silver Mining Company and the following year, the Butters Salvador Mines. The British began to enter the banking business in El Salvador in 1893.

The coffee interests also appreciated the importance of a modern capital, the symbol of their prosperity, as tribute to their "progressive" inclinations, and the focal point of their political authority. By the end of the century larger numbers of the richest families were building comfortable, in some cases even palatial, homes in the capital. They broke some of their immediate ties with the countryside and the provincial cities to become a more national elite centered in San Salvador.

A sleepy capital of 25,000 in 1860, San Salvador boasted of no pretensions. A visitor in the mid-1880s remembered: "There is very little architectural taste shown in the construction of the dwellings or of the public buildings . . . the streets are dull and unattractive. . . . The public buildings are of insignificant appearance."[30] It compared unfavorably with the cities of similar size in Latin America. Sensitive to that reality, the newly prosperous coffee elites resolved to renovate the capital, expunging the somnolent past in favor of the envisioned vigor of the future. The city took on new airs as the center of a booming economy. By 1910, the population numbered more than 32,000. The central streets had all been paved and electricity illuminated the city. An excellent drainage system ensured the good health of the inhabitants. A series of new buildings, among them a commodious headquarters for the governmental ministries, a cathedral, and a market, added to the modernity. The elites boasted of attractive homes in the capital. The new and beautiful Avenida de la Independencia combined with ample parks and plazas to provide grace and spaciousness to the city. The modern, still somewhat quiet capital made a favorable impression on visitors. Above all else it spoke of—and symbolized—the prosperity that coffee afforded the nation.[31]

The very restricted democracy fostered by the Constitution of 1886 functioned smoothly in the early decades of the twentieth century. From 1903 to 1931, each president was elected in the approved fashion—selected by his predecessor and ratified by a limited electorate—and served for the constitutional mandate of four years. The politicians respected the doctrine of "no reelection." Peaceful selection and rotation of presidents contrasted sharply with the violence characteristic of the change of governments in the nineteenth century. The preponderance of civilian presidents was also unique. Of the eight men elected to the presidency during the 1903–1931 period, only one was a military officer, General Fernando Figueroa (1907–1911).

The prosperity and power of the coffee planters reached their culmination during the years 1913–1929, an economic and political period referred to as the Melendez-Quiñonez dynasty because of the two related families that held the presidency. Those families ranked among the largest coffee producers. When an assassin felled President Manuel Enrique Araujo in 1913, Vice-President Carlos Melendez assumed the presidency as the constitution provided and then won the presidency in his own right during the elections the following year. In 1919, his brother, Jorge Melendez, succeeded him for four years, followed by his brother-in-law, Alfonso Quiñonez Molina, for another quadrennial. This tightly knit family political dynasty demonstrated the ease incumbent presidents enjoyed in manipulating elections to select their successors. It further illustrated the increasingly narrow political base of the coffee planters. Indeed, fewer and fewer men controlled the thriving coffee industry, particularly the processing and export. During the dynasty, perhaps more than at any other period, those linked to coffee exports were able to monopolize both economic and political power. One obviously enhanced the other. Wealth conferred the prestige that facilitated political manipulation. In turn, their control of the government complemented their economic interests. During those years, the planters successfully held the small but aggressive urban middle class at bay, repressed or manipulated the impoverished majority—both the rural masses and the growing urban working class—and neutralized the military, from whose ranks had arisen so many of the nineteenth-century presidents.

The actual exercise of political power by the coffee class forged a unique chapter in Salvadoran history: prolonged civilian rule. When General Figueroa, a constitutionally elected president, left the presidential palace in 1911, civilian politicians occupied it for the succeeding two decades, a remarkable record, never equaled before or since.

Of course the economic strength, political influence, and social domination of the coffee elites had been a reality since the last decades of the nineteenth century. From the beginning of their rise to economic and political power in the 1860s and 1870s they had enjoyed amiable relations with the military. The planters counted on the military to support a political system complementary to coffee exports. Economic prosperity, after all, facilitated the modernization and professionalization of the army. The easy shift from military to civilian presidents manifested the harmonious relations between the planters and the officers.

The army had won its laurels on the battlefield. Nearly a century of international struggles—the frequent wars against Guatemala, Honduras, Nicaragua, and assorted foreign filibusters—and of civil wars created a strong and reasonably efficient army, perhaps the best in Central America. A prudent government pampered the military. A military academy to train officers functioned sporadically. In 1900, the third such school, the Escuela Politécnica Militar, opened, only to be closed in 1927. Five years later the government inaugurated the Escuela Militar, still functioning. Thus, for most of the years of the twentieth century, a professional academy existed. In 1909, the government contracted with Chile for a military mission to improve the training of officers. The Escuela Politécnica Militar and the Escuela Militar provided a reasonable-to-good education for the cadets and fostered the corporate interests of an officer class. Increasingly the academy drew its cadets from the urban middle and lower middle classes, two groups enthusiastically advocating the modernization of the country.[32] While the officers' concept of modernization tended to parallel that of the planters, it also emphasized the need for up-to-date military training and equipment, manifested a growing faith in industrialization, and responded to the vague but powerful force of nationalism.

In 1910, the government reported that its army consisted of an impressive 78 staff officers, 512 officers, and 15,554 troops on active duty (a figure that seems to be inflated).[33] Percy F. Martin, in his exhaustive study of El Salvador in 1911, reported: "The Government . . . have [sic] devoted the closest care and attention to the question of military instruction, and the system at present in force is the outcome of the intelligent study of similar systems in force in other countries, and the adaptation of the best features existing in each. A very high esprit de corps exists among the Salvadoran troops, and, for the most part, they enter upon their schooling and training with both zeal and interest."[34] The government favored the officers with good pay, rapid promotion, and a host of benefits. Martin marveled at the comforts provided by one of the officers' clubs: "For the use of officers there exists a very agreeable Club, at which they can procure their full meals and all kinds of light refreshments at moderate prices: while the usual amusements such as drafts, cards, billiards, etc., are provided for them. So comfortable is this Club made that officers, as a rule, find very little inducement to visit the larger towns in search of their amusements."[35] A contented military was the logical corollary to planter prosperity.

The further solidification of the corporate interests of the military was encouraged by the establishment in 1919 of a periodical for and about the military and in 1922 of a mutual aid society, the *Círculo Militar.* More than an economic association, it encouraged the moral, physical, and intellectual improvement of its members. One knowledgeable visitor to Central America in 1928 claimed that El Salvador had the best-trained army in the region.[36]

Peace and order at home combined with increasing demands for coffee ensured a heady prosperity for the planters and their government. With the exception of an occasional poor year, usually due to adverse weather, production moved upward after 1926 toward an annual harvest of 130,000,000–140,000,000 pounds, as Table 10-3 illustrates. After 1904, El Salvador produced at least one-third of Central America's coffee, its closest competitors being first Guatemala and second Costa Rica. After 1924, Salvadoran production surpassed that of Guatemala to hold first place in quantity (and many would add quality) in Central America. The elites and the government became increasingly dependent on income from coffee production.

A significant change in El Salvador's international trade pattern also took place. In the nineteenth century, El Salvador sold much of its exports to the United States and bought most of its imports from Europe. In the twentieth century, that triangular pattern became increasingly bilateral due to a closer trade relationship with the United States, which bought more Salvadoran exports than any other nation and began to furnish most of its imports as well.

Growing U.S. investments in El Salvador further linked the two nations economically. Prior to the opening of the twentieth century, U.S. investments had been practically nonexistent. In 1908, they totaled a modest $1.8 million, but they rose rapidly thereafter: $6.6 in 1914; $12.8 in 1919; and $24.8 in 1929. While these sums were insignificant in terms of total U.S. investments abroad, which in Latin America alone accounted for over $1.6 billion by the end of 1914, they represented a sizable proportion of the foreign investments in El Salvador by 1929. United States investors conse-

TABLE 10-3
COFFEE PRODUCTION,
1924–1935

Year	Pounds
1924–1925	95,020,000
1925–1926	101,413,000
1926–1927	66,139,000
1927–1928	149,474,000
1928–1929	134,042,000
1929–1930	143,301,000
1930–1931	165,347,000
1931–1932	105,822,000
1932–1933	141,096,000
1933–1934	127,869,000
1934–1935	130,073,000

Source: Edelberto Torres Rivas, *Interpretación del Desarrollo Social Centroamericano* (San José, Costa Rica: Editorial Universitaria Centroamérica, 1973), pp. 284–85.

quently began to exert influence over the Salvadoran economy. The pro-U.S. attitudes of the presidents of the Melendez-Quiñonez dynasty greatly facilitated the penetration of North American interests into El Salvador, while World War I reduced the British presence.[37]

The coffee planters and their allies exuded confidence. Coffee prices, land devoted to coffee production, coffee exports, and coffee income all rose impressively after 1920. At no time from 1922 through 1935 did coffee represent less than 88 percent of the total value of exports. During three of those years, 1926, 1931, and 1934, it accounted for 95 percent. The amount of land producing coffee increased from 170,000 acres in the early 1920s to 262,000 acres in the early 1930s. Meanwhile, coffee growing and processing concentrated in ever fewer hands with no more than 350 growers controlling the industry by the mid-1920s. The largest enjoyed annual incomes of $200,000.[38]

Ruling from their comfortable and modern capital, the planters and their allies were creating an impressive infrastructure of roads, railroads, and ports as well as a telegraphic and telephone communication network. The plantations, the government, and the army were efficiently run. In their own terms, the elites were highly successful. Still, they nurtured visions of further change. Some fretted over the dependence on coffee for prosperity and talked of the need to diversify agriculture. A few experimented with cotton as an alternate export. Others spoke in terms of industrialization, and limited amounts of capital did support an incipient manufacturing sector. The elites even discussed the extension of democratization and the inclusion of the lower classes in the political process. It was the talk of a contented minority that wanted to perfect their political and economic systems. Benefiting from the great changes wrought by transforming a largely peasant and subsistence economy into a plantation and export economy, the coffee elites assumed that their own prosperity reflected the well-being of the nation they governed.

While the shift to coffee culture may have created an aura of progress around the plantation homes and the privileged areas of the capital, it proved increasingly detrimental to the quality of life of the majority. One U.S. observer contrasted the lifestyles of the classes in 1931:

> There is practically no middle class between the very rich and the very poor. From the people with whom I talked, I learned that roughly ninety percent of the wealth of the country is held by about half of one percent of the population. Thirty or forty families own nearly everything in the country. They live in almost regal splendor with many attendants, send their children to Europe or the United States to be educated, and spend money lavishly (on themselves). The rest of the population has practically nothing. These poor people work for a few cents a day and exist as best they can.[39]

This grim observation was by no means novel. After a tour of Central America in 1912, Charles Domville-Fife concluded that "there are more comparatively poor people in this country [El Salvador] than there are in some of the larger states."[40] An academic study of the 1919–1935 period speaks of "recurrent food shortages" and "economic desperation" among the masses in a period of high living costs and low wages.[41] The cost of basic foods skyrocketed between 1922 and 1926: corn prices, 100 percent; beans, 225 percent; and rice, 300 percent. The importation of those foods, once negligible, became significant in 1929.[42]

An analysis of the class structure in 1930 suggests the concentration of wealth: it categorized 0.2 percent of the population as upper class.[43] An accelerating rate of population increase accentuated the problems of poverty. The population reached 1,443,000 by 1930. The vast majority was rural. Yet, only 8.2 percent could be classified as landowners.[44]

The very changes that facilitated the concentration of land into fewer hands also precipitated the social and economic disintegration of the lifestyle of the overwhelming majority of the Salvadorans. The changes squeezed off the land those who grew food for their own consumption and sold their surpluses in local marketplaces. The relative ease of access to land—hence, food—depicted by the five travelers in the 1850s was no longer accurate after 1900. The dispossessed depended on seasonal plantation jobs. Some began to trickle into the towns and capital propelled by rural poverty and the search for urban jobs, which either did not exist or for which they were unprepared. The extent of the new social and economic disequilibrium was not immediately appreciated. Impressive economic growth masked for a time the weakness of the increasingly narrow, inflexible, and dependent economy.

As is true in such overly dependent economies, events in distant marketplaces would reveal local weaknesses. By the end of the 1920s, the capitalist world teetered on the edge of a major economic collapse whose reverberations would shake not only the economic but also the political foundations of El Salvador.

With his term of office nearing an end in 1927, President Quiñonez picked his own brother-in-law, Pio Romero Bosque, to succeed him, a choice with significant consequences. Don Pio, as Salvadorans invariably refer to him, turned out to be more liberal, less conventional, and highly unpredictable in comparison with his three predecessors of the Melendez-Quiñonez dynasty. He entered office riding high on the wave of coffee prosperity, but the international financial crisis that began in 1929–1930 soon tossed his government into a trough of economic troubles, testing all his skills in navigating the ship of state.

The dynamic sector of the economy suffered the vicissitudes common to nations dependent on the export of a single product. In an indictment before the Legislative Assembly, Minister of Finance José Esperanza Suay pointed out the cause of the nation's economic plight: "The coffee crisis that this year [1929] has alarmed everyone clearly indicates the dangers for our national economy of monoculture, the domination coffee asserts over agrarian production."[45] El Salvador may have been an efficient coffee producer, but it was not the only one. In fact, exporters were beginning to outnumber importers. The economic prosperity of at least ten Latin American nations, of which Brazil was by far the most important, also depended on coffee sales. At the same time, a few African areas were producing coffee for export. Demand fell while supplies remained constant or even increased in some instances. Consequently the price dropped drastically. In 1928, El Salvador sold its coffee for $15.75 per hundred kilograms—in 1932, for $5.97. The financial consequences for El Salvador can readily be perceived in an economy in which coffee constituted 90 percent of the exports and 80 percent of the national income. Not surprisingly therefore, government revenues plummeted 50 percent between 1928 and 1932. El Salvador witnessed the highest index of rural unemployment in Central America. Small coffee growers suffered severely. Their loss of land through bankruptcy and foreclosure—an estimated 28 percent of the coffee holdings—augmented the estates of the large landowners. The problems revealed a modernized but underdeveloped economy, one that readily responded to foreign whims but failed to serve Salvadoran needs.

The planters' reaction to the mounting problems exacerbated the nation's economic woes. They increased the amount of land devoted to coffee in an effort to make up for falling prices. The consequences of that trend were as obvious as they were disastrous: the economy depended more than ever on coffee, more peasants lost their land, rural unemployment rose, and food production for internal consumption declined.[46]

President Romero Bosque tried valiantly to ride out the economic storm. Politically he fared better. Practicing the liberal ideology he preached, he permitted the full play of those liberties authorized by the Constitution of 1886 but hitherto suppressed. His administrative talent and his unimpeachable honesty impressed his fellow countrymen. He determined to make honest men of politicians. He turned on his less-than-scrupulous predecessors and even sent Quiñonez into exile. Those actions heightened his popularity despite the economic crisis.

To the amazement of all and the consternation of the professional politicians, Don Pio decided to hold an honest presidential election in 1931. Contrary to all previous political practices, the president advanced no candidate. It was indeed a historical first. Since no political parties existed, a few hastily organized to take advantage of the unprecedented opportunity to electioneer.

The six new parties represented the interests of the working, professional, middle, and planter classes and thereby reflected the social changes overtaking El Salvador.[47] A small but vocal urban working class had emerged in the 1920s, flexing its muscle in several important strikes. The presidents of the dynasty flirted occasionally with that potential source of political power. Their policies gyrated from wooing the workers to repressing them. In 1925, some workers and intellectuals, with the assistance of communist leaders from Guatemala, founded the Communist party of El Salvador. In the excitement of preparation for the 1931 election, a Labor party also emerged. It nominated Arturo Araujo, who enjoyed a genuinely popular following. The candidate sought to distance himself from his more radical supporters, the foremost of whom, Agustín Farabundo Martí, was busy organizing rural labor, an activity guaranteed to disturb landlords and arouse the suspicion of the military.

To avoid any of the international influences among the Labor party members, most notably of communism, Araujo turned to the ideas of Alberto Masferrer to enhance his party's program. An intellectual, philosopher, and writer, Masferrer dominated Salvadoran letters.[48] The strongest voice of the newly invigorated nationalism in El Salvador, he criticized the institutions that had been shaped by the coffee class and called for greater social justice. In Patria, the prestigious and lively newspaper he founded on April 27, 1928, Masferrer protested against the presence of foreign companies, the lack of decent housing, and the high cost of living. He advocated industrialization and the protection of national resources from foreign exploitation. He denounced those "who have the souls of a checkbook and the conscience of an account ledger," those who kept "the people in misery, who kill by hunger thousands of persons, and who cause more than half the workers to die due to lack of food, shelter, or rest before they reach the age of thirty."[49] Both the extreme left and right verbally assaulted Masferrer. The right labeled him a dangerous Bolshevik, criminal agitator, and subversive. The left attacked him as a demagogue, traitor, and right-wing socialist.

For his campaign, Araujo adopted Masferrer's program of *vitalismo,* the "vital minimum" that the philosopher defined as "the sure and constant satisfaction of our basic needs."[50] Thus, Araujo campaigned for the nine major points advocated by vitalismo, among them: hygenic, honest, and fairly remunerated work; medical care, potable water, and decent sanitation; a varied, adequate, and nutritious diet; decent housing; sufficient clothing; expedient and honest justice; education; and rest and recreation. Within the context of Salvadoran society in late 1930 and early 1931, Araujo ventilated some "revolutionary" views. Vitalismo, he declared, would be financed by transferring funds from the military budget to social expenditures. One can but speculate about the reaction to such a proposition within the confines of those comfortable officers' clubs.

Masferrer himself held some unconventional ideas about the role of the military within Salvadoran society. That fully one-sixth of the national budget went to the army in 1929 disturbed him. It was not productive investment; it did not contribute to national development. "For a country that no longer fights wars, our army is extraordinarily expensive. . . . And, if there are no longer any wars to fight, why should the state maintain such a burdensome institution?" he asked.[51] The army could serve much more useful national goals if it added to its traditional roles of protection from foreign invaders and the maintenance of internal order those of building and maintaining roads, providing water to the villages, improving the health of the inhabitants through sanitation campaigns, protecting the forests, and helping the population in times of natural disaster.

Araujo also heeded Masferrer's call for land reform. The philosopher advocated the nationalization of the land and its redistribution.[52] He classified the landowning system as well as the relations between the landlords and rural workers as "feudal": "The lord in this case is the landowner, he who gives and takes, he who permits the worker to reside on his lands or expels whoever does not obey or please him."[53] Araujo planned to have the government buy the land from the rich and redistribute it to the poor.

With its platform firmly buttressed by the ideas of Masferrer, the Labor party aroused the enthusiasm of large numbers of people who viewed its program as the means to solve the deepening economic difficulties and to create a more just society. For his running mate, Araujo chose a military man, General Maximiliano Hernandez Martinez. The general had borne the presidential standard of the small National Republican party before he joined forces with Araujo. First as a presidential candidate and later as a vice-presidential candidate, Martinez appealed to the popular classes on social issues.

Honoring his promises, Don Pio remained impartial during the selection of presidential candidates and the campaign. The elections took place in early January 1931. Araujo won. He confronted an impossible task. Somehow he had to reconcile the vast differences among the Labor party, the coffee planters, the military, and the newly emergent middle class. He had to accomplish his miracle in the midst of the worst—

and what would be the longest—economic crisis in modern Salvadoran history. The problems cried for bold action; an irresolute president proved to be incapable of acting. He ignored the "vital minimum" program that he had supported during the campaign. His inaction confounded and then alienated his followers. Frustrations mounted daily; unrest resulted.

On December 2, 1931, the military responded to the crises precipitated by economic collapse and political unrest. The soldiers turned out of office the first and thus far only freely elected president, who fled the country after less than one year in office. The military coup was the first in 33 years—since November 1898, when General Tomás Regalado seized power—and the first staged by professional army officers who did not come from the dominant socioeconomic class.[54] Three days later the military junta turned power over to the constitutional vice-president, General Hernandez Martinez, who also had served as minister of war.[55] His exact role in the coup d'etat still remains unexplained. Invested with power, he governed energetically for the next 13 years, a record of political longevity in El Salvador.

Most sectors of society greeted the military seizure of power with relief. It had become painfully apparent to all that President Araujo, immobilized by the economic debacle and the inability of the national institutions to respond to new demands, could not govern. The majority thought the young officers who carried out his overthrow would be able to resolve the crises threatening to destroy the nation. Rightly or wrongly, the populace put trust and hope in those officers. The Marxist student newspaper *Estrella Roja* congratulated the military on the coup d'etat. It reiterated the belief that the incompetence of Araujo "imposed a moral obligation on the military to remove him from office." The newspaper quickly pointed out, however, that the coup itself could resolve few of the nation's fundamental problems:

> Pardon our skepticism. We do not believe that the coup will end the Salvadoran crisis which is far more transcendental than a mere change of government. The crisis has deeper roots than the incapacity of Don Arturo. It results from the domination of a capitalist class that owns all the land and means of production and has dedicated itself to coffee monoculture.[56]

Although no profound institutional changes were forthcoming, Araujo's downfall represented something more than "a mere change of government." It initiated new alliances and a sharing of power. In short, it ended the coffee planters' monopoly of economic and political power.

The economic collapse alone had not triggered the coup. The causes of the political change also included the growing social, economic, and political complexities engendered by incipient industrialization and growing urbanization, more intensive nationalism, the roles played by immigrants, an urban proletariat, an expanding middle class, and professional military officers in an increasingly varied society, improved transportation and communication, and efforts to diversify the economy. Further, any explanation of the coup must take into account the inability of President Araujo to govern, an unfortunate reality in the country's first democratic experiment, which may have revealed as much about institutional structures as it did about the chief executive.

The demands on the government varied, and while some could be reconciled, others could not. The rural folk looked to the communal past for a solution to their plight. They wanted the government to return land to them. The planter elites obviously favored the present land distribution and the export economy from which they had extracted so many benefits for such a long period. The expanding middle class and the professional military thought in nationalistic terms that included a reduction in the level of dependency, a wider sharing of social benefits, and industrialization. Their solutions to the crises lay in the cities. Urban growth had been slow, and, as Table 10-4 shows, the populations of the five largest cities remained relatively small. Urban dwellers accounted for only 15 percent of the population. Yet, they provided many of the leaders advocating innovations.

The events of 1931 brought to a close a dynamic period in the history of El Salvador during which the coffee planters had gained economic and political ascendancy to dominate the nation. Stresses during the preceding decade demonstrated the increasing difficulty the coffee planters experienced in governing the nation. The brief political experiment under Don Pio and Don Arturo had been sufficient to prove that a functioning, pluralistic democracy would not work to the planters' best advantage. They lost their political monopoly. The coup in 1931 signified that they would not regain it. They understood by then that they would benefit most from an authoritarian government managed by the military and complementary to some of the goals of the middle class, which wanted access to the national institutions and upward mobility. Those groups worked out a suitable arrangement to the exclusion of the rural masses and the urban working class. They divided the tasks of government after December 5, 1931: the military exercised political power, while the landowners, in alliance with sympathetic bankers, merchants, exporters, and segments of the urban middle class, controlled the economy. Each respected the other. General Martinez succeeded in reestablishing oligarchical control, although he could not return the nation to the status quo ante 1931. El Salvador was entering a new phase of history.

During the 1858–1931 period, El Salvador reshaped its institutions in order better to export coffee; modernization had taken place, producing some of the advantages its advocates had predicted. There were more and better roads, a modest railroad system,

TABLE 10-4
POPULATIONS OF THE FIVE
LARGEST CITIES, 1930

City	Population
San Salvador	89,385
Santa Ana	39,825
Santa Tecla	20,049
San Miguel	17,330
Sonsonate	15,260

Source: Gibson, "A Demographic Analysis of Urbanization," p. 338.

efficient ports, and a capital city with sections boasting all the amenities of its European or U.S. counterparts. Almost everything connected with the export of coffee and the lifestyles of the elites seemed up to date, indistinguishable from what one might find in the capitals of the major industrial nations. Impressive growth had taken place. The statistics measuring population, coffee production, and foreign investments had risen impressively, and, until 1929, so had national income. An observer could conclude that certain aspects of national life had progressed in the course of seven decades, that the "progressive" El Salvador of 1931 differed considerably from the "backward" nation Barrios had resolved to "regenerate" in 1858.

National life was different, but not always in a positive way. Quite another legacy of growth and progress was the nation's acute dependence on the export of a single product, coffee, for its prosperity. Monoculture and plantations were some of the results, and they dominated the economy. The efficient production of coffee did not extend to foodstuffs. The countryside fed the population less adequately than before. By the end of the 1920s, El Salvador began to import food, not because the land could not feed the people—the hoary excuse of overpopulation has been disproven—but rather because the planters used it to grow export crops.[57] On several levels, the nation had lost control of its own economy. By 1931, El Salvador confronted a series of political and economic crises, the consequences of the type of modernization its governments had imposed.

The perceptive observations of two commentators, widely spaced in time, reveal the basic difference separating the El Salvador of the end of the 1850s from that of the end of the 1920s. Mrs. Foote had lived among a well-fed population. Large estates, small farms, and communal lands coexisted. The relatively varied export sector had played a significant but not the dominant role in the economy. The critical eye of Alberto Masferrer viewed quite a different situation. He assessed the state of Salvadoran society in 1928 in this way:

> There are no longer crises; instead, there are chronic illnesses and endemic hunger. . . . El Salvador no longer has wild fruits and vegetables that once everyone could harvest, nor even cultivated fruits that once were inexpensive. . . . Today there are the coffee estates and they grow only coffee. . . . Where there is now a voracious estate that consumes hundreds and hundreds of acres, before there were two hundred small farmers whose plots produced corn, rice, beans, fruits, and vegetables. Now the highlands support only coffee estates and the lowlands cattle ranches. The cornfields are disappearing. And where will the corn come from? The coffee planter is not going to grow it because his profits are greater growing coffee. If he harvests enough coffee and it sells for a good price, he can import corn and it will cost him less than if he sacrifices coffee trees in order to grow it. . . . Who will grow corn and where? . . . Any nation that cannot assure the production and regulate the price of the most vital crop, the daily food of the people, has no right to regard itself as sovereign. . . . Such has become the case of our nation.[58]

In vivid contrast to Mrs. Foote's earlier observations, Masferrer saw a hungry population with limited access to the use of land, a population whose basic need for food was subordinated to the demands of an export-oriented economy. The "progress" charted by the Salvadoran elites had failed to benefit the overwhelming majority of the citizens.[59] Prosperity for a few cost the well-being of the many.

The contrasts between Foote's and Masferrer's observations suggest that little or no development had taken place, if one measures development by a rising quality of life index and the maximum use of resources, natural and human, for the well-being of the majority. Thus, the contrasts provoke serious questions about the wisdom of the type of modernization and economic growth El Salvador pursued after 1858, since neither addressed the needs of the majority of the Salvadorans. Rather, they left a legacy of poverty, dependency, and class conflict that succeeding generations of generals, politicians, and planters have not been able to resolve.

NOTES

1 Mrs. H. G. Foote, *Recollections of Central America and the West Coast of Africa* (London: Newby, 1869), p. 101.
2 Ibid., p. 84.
3 Ibid., p. 61.
4 Ibid., pp. 54–55.
5 Ibid., p. 60.
6 John Baily, *Central America: Describing Each of the States of Guatemala, Honduras, Salvador, Nicaragua, and Costa Rica* (London: Saunders, 1850); E. G. Squier, *Notes on Central America, Particularly the States of Honduras and Salvador* (New York: Harper, 1855); Carl Scherzer, *Travels in the Free States of Central America: Nicaragua, Honduras, and San Salvador,* 2 vols. (London: Longman, 1857); G. F. Von Tempsky, *Mitla: A Narrative of Incidents and Personal Adventures on a Journey in Mexico, Guatemala, and Salvador in the Years 1853–1855* (London: Longman, 1858). In a much later and certainly more scholarly study, David Browning tends to confirm the main theses of these more impressionistic travelers: *El Salvador: Landscape and Society* (Oxford: Oxford University Press, 1971).
7 Squier, *Notes on Central America,* p. 326.
8 Ibid., p. 331.
9 Von Tempsky, *Mitla,* p. 424.
10 Scherzer, *Travels in the Free States,* vol. 2, pp. 148, 195–96.
11 For a series of useful case studies of the effects of the penetration of international capitalism upon the local economies during the nineteenth century, see Roberto Cortes Conde, *The First States of Modernization in Spanish America* (New York: Harper, 1974).
12 Adriaan C. van Oss, "El Régimen Autosuficiente de España en Centro América," *Mesoamérica* (Guatemala) 3 (June 1982): 68.
13 Browning, *El Salvador,* pp. 85, 87.
14 Letter of General Gerardo Barrios, Rome, November 21, 1853, printed in the *Revista del Departamento de Historia y Hemeroteca Nacional* (San Salvador) 11 (March 1939): 42.
15 That speech is printed in Joaquin Parada Aparicio, *Discursos Médico-Historicos Salvadoreños* (San Salvador: Editorial Ungo, 1942), p. 222.
16 Address to the General Assembly, January 29, 1862, printed in Italo Lopez Vallecillos, *Gerardo Barrios y su Tiempo,* vol. 2 (San Salvador: Ministerio de Educación, 1967), p. 219.
17 Gary G. Kuhn, "El Positivismo de Gerardo Barrios," *Revista del Pensamiento Centroamericano* (Managua), 36 (July–December 1981): 88. For a more general statement

on Positivism in El Salvador see Patricia A. Andrews, "El Liberalismo en El Salvador a Finales del Siglo XIX," ibid., pp. 89–93.

18 Kuhn, "El Positivismo," p. 87.

19 ". . . the commerce of the Central American States has wonderfully increased, and especially within fifteen years and since the establishment of the line of steamers from Panama. This has introduced and established regularity, certainty, and dispatch in their communication with the rest of the world. It has organized and maintained a mail service and secured a rapid, sure, and safe mode of commercial intercourse and exchange. In the interests which are thus growing up into importance, *[sic]* and wealth and commanding influence will be found the means of counteracting the unfortunate results of their political systems, and those interests must soon be powerful and widespread enough to be able to finally put down the political system which retards or hinders their development. . . . Since the establishment of the Panama Company's Steamers, the Revenues from the Custom House in . . . Salvador have more than quadrupled. The foreign commerce of all the Republics, which, previous thereto, was in the hands of a few who could afford to import cargoes around Cape Horn, has been opened to all. . . . The growth of California and the States on the Pacific has opened new courses for their trade" (James R. Partridge to Secretary of State, April 22, 1865, Diplomatic Dispatches from U.S. Ministers to Central America, General Records of the Department of State, National Archives of the United States of America). "The Republic of Salvador, though territorially much the smallest of the five Central American States, is *first* in the amount of exports and only *second* in population. It has three seaports on the Pacific, La Unión, La Libertad, and Acajutla, at all of which the Panama Railroad Steamers stop twice a month, up and down, and at which American vessels land and receive freight and passengers. In the other Central American States these steamers land only at one port" (A. S. Williams to Secretary of State, March 27, 1867, ibid.).

20 Lopez Vallecillos, *Gerardo Barrios,* pp. 127–28, 216–18.

21 Ibid., pp. 216–17.

22 This interpretation of the Duenas administration rests on the assessments of Derek N. Kerr, "La Edad de Oro del Café en El Salvador, 1863–1885," *Mesoamérica* (Guatemala) 3 (June 1982): 4, 7, as well as on the diplomatic dispatches of A. S. Williams. In particular, see his dispatches of January 12 and February 8, 1969, to the U.S. Secretary of State, Diplomatic Dispatches from U.S. Ministers to Central America, General Records of the Department of State, National Archives of the United States of America.

23 For an understanding of the negative effect the introduction of coffee culture had on the peasantry of Costa Rica and Guatemala, see Mitchell A. Seligson, *Peasants of Costa Rica and the Development of Agrarian Capitalism* (Madison: University of Wisconsin Press, 1980); and David J. McCreery, "Coffee and Class: The Structure of Development in Liberal Guatemala," *Hispanic American Historical Review,* 56 (August 1976): 438–60.

24 Browning, *El Salvador,* p. 190.

25 Ibid., p. 173.

26 The quotations from the Law for Extinction of Communal Lands, February 26, 1881, and the Law for the Extinction of Public Lands, March 2, 1882, are found in William H. Durham, *Scarcity and Survival in Central America: Ecological Origins of the Soccer War* (Stanford, Calif.: Stanford University Press, 1979), p. 42.

27 This trend was almost universal throughout Latin America. For the general discussion consult E. Bradford Burns, *The Poverty of Progress: Latin America in the Nineteenth*

Century (Berkeley and Los Angeles: University of California Press, 1980), particularly pp. 132–54. For specific discussions of El Salvador see Browning, *El Salvador,* particularly pp. 146, 147, 167, 173, 175, and 214; Alastair White, *El Salvador* (Boulder, Colo.: Westview, 1982), p. 93; and Rafael Menjivar, *Acumulación Originaria y Desarrollo del Capitalismo en El Salvador* (San José, Costa Rica: Editorial Universitaria Centroamericana, 1980), pp. 123–27.

28 Jorge Larde y Larín, *Guía Histórica de El Salvador* (San Salvador: Ministerio de Cultura, 1958), pp. 32–43.

29 Rafael Guidos Vejar, *El Ascenso del Militarismo en El Salvador* (San Salvador: UCA/Editores 1980), p. 65.

30 William Eleroy Curtis, *The Capitals of Spanish America* (New York: Harper, 1888), 180–81.

31 Percy F. Martin, *Salvador in the XXth Century* (London: Arnold, 1911), pp. 256–75.

32 The role of the military in El Salvador, 1858–1931, and the relations between civilian politicians and military officers adhere in general terms to the broad observations made by Edwin Lieuwen concerning the behavioral pattern of the military throughout Latin America in the nineteenth and early twentieth centuries. See his *Arms and Politics in Latin America* (New York: Praeger, 1961), pp. 17–35. Vejar provides the details and some general conclusions for the study of the Salvadoran military in the nineteenth and early twentieth centuries in *El Ascenso del Militarismo.*

33 Martin, *Salvador,* p. 86.

34 Ibid., p. 87.

35 Ibid., p. 88.

36 Arthur J. Ruhl, *The Central American* (New York: Scribner's, 1928), p. 174.

37 Rafael Menjivar covers the topic and statistics of growing U.S. investments in *Acumulación Originaria,* pp. 55–81.

38 The statistical data in this paragraph are drawn largely from Everett A. Wilson, "The Crisis of National Integration in El Salvador, 1919–1935" (Ph.D. diss., Stanford University, 1969), pp. 108–41.

39 Major A. R. Harris, U.S. Military Attache to Central America, December 22, 1931, National Archives of the United States, R. G. 59, File 816.00/828, as quoted in Thomas P. Anderson, *Matanza: El Salvador's Communist Revolt of 1932* (Lincoln: University of Nebraska Press, 1971), pp. 83–4.

40 Charles W. Domville-Fife, *Guatemala and the States of Central America* (London: Francis Griffiths, 1913), pp. 285–86.

41 Wilson, "Crisis of National Integration," pp. 29, 115, 128.

42 Ibid., pp. 126–27; Durham, *Scarcity and Survival,* p. 36.

43 Alejandro R. Marroquín, "Estudio Sobre la Crísis de los Años Treinta en El Salvador," *Anuario de Estudios Centroamericanos,* 3 (1977): 118.

44 Ibid.

45 Quoted in ibid., p. 121.

46 Vejar, *Ascenso del Militarismo,* pp. 102, 100.

47 These parties were the Partido Evolución Nacional (National Evolution party), representing the most conservative and economically powerful groups; the Partido Zaratista (party of Alberto Gomez Zarate), grouping together the urban supporters of Zarate who favored the policies of the "Dynasty"; the Partido Constitucional (Constitutional party), sharing much of the conservative philosophy of the National Evolution party and appealing largely to the same groups; the Partido Fraternal Progresista (Progressive Fraternal party), directed by a general and enjoying military support, appealed to the rural workers in a paternalistic way; Partido Nacional Republicano (National Republican party), also directed by a general, Maximiliano Hernandez Martinez, and uniting professionals, students, workers, and some coffee growers; and the Partido Laborista (Labor party), appealing to the urban and rural workers as well as to smaller farmers. Ibid., pp. 113–14.

48 Hugo Lindo, "El Año de Alberto Masferrer," *Inter-American Review of Bibliography,* 29 (July–September, 1969): 263–77. His biographers tend to be uncritical. One, Matilde Elena Lopez, characterized him as Central America's "broadest thinker," one of the "most illustrious men of the continent," and a "revolutionary." *Masferrer: Alto Pensador de Centroamérica: Ensayo Biográfico* (Guatemala City: Editorial del Ministerio de Educación, 1954), p. 9.

49 Quoted in Marroquin, "Estudio Sobre la Crisis," p. 144.

50 Alberto Masferrer, *Patria* (San Salvador: Editorial Universitaria, 1960), p. 83. The first edition of *El Minimum Vital* appeared in 1929. This essay draws on Masferrer's newspaper discussions of his idea and on the definitive textual edition: *Minimum Vital y Otras Obras de Carácter Sociológico* (Guatamela City: Ediciones del Gobierno, 1950), pp. 179–210.

51 Masferrer, *Patria,* p. 219.

52 Ibid., 189–90.

53 Quoted in Marroquín, "Estudio Sobre la Crisis," p. 145.

54 Vejar, *Ascenso del Militarismo,* p. 12.

55 There is no doubt that Maximiliano Hernandez Martinez is a controversial figure in Salvadoran historiography, generally denounced as an "eccentric"—if not "insane"—dictator. Two scholars of twentieth-century Salvadoran history, Everett A. Wilson and Robert V. Elam, suggest that some revisionist assessments of Martinez may be in order. Wilson concludes, "There are several indications that Martinez, in spite of the notorious eccentricity and brutality of his long regime, presided over significant national reconstruction in the early 1930's" ("Crisis of National Integration," p. 233). Elam emphasizes, "Perhaps no president in this nation's history began with a broader base of support than that enjoyed by Maximiliano Hernandez Martinez in 1932" ["Appeal to Arms: The Army and Politics in El Salvador, 1931–1964" (Ph.D. diss., University of New Mexico, 1968), p. 45].

56 Vejar, *Ascenso del Militarismo,* p. 131.

57 A major theme of William H. Durham, *Scarcity and Survival in Central America,* is that if Salvadorans would make more efficient use of their land, they would be able to feed themselves well.

58 Masferrer, *Patria,* pp. 179–82.

59 The Salvadoran situation amply illustrates the theme of the impoverishment of the majority as Latin America "progressed" or "modernized" in the nineteenth century set forth in Burns, *The Poverty of Progress.* For an economist's view of that theme, consult Robert E. Gamer, *The Developing Nations: A Comparative Perspective* (Boston: Allyn and Bacon, 1976). Another useful economic analysis, but with a contemporary emphasis, is: David Felix, "Income Distribution and the Quality of Life in Latin America: Patterns, Trends, and Policy Implications," *Latin American Research Review,* 18, 2 (1983): 3–34.

PART THREE

RESTRUCTURING THE WORLD: DEMOCRACY, DEBT, AND DIFFERENTIATION

Eastern Europe was the focus of much early modern thinking on issues of development. Its level of development notably lagged the remainder of Europe, and the experiences of both Europe and of the Soviet Union seemed to provide guidance in solving its problems. After following the Soviet model of development since 1945, the Eastern European countries have reappeared as the newest "developing countries," and are again at the center of the development debate. Their 1989 revolutions separated them from the Soviet bloc and permitted alternative development models, new forms of government, and new possibilities for integrating into the world system.

Eastern Europe is the clearest example of heightened international instability during the 1990s. A listing of other examples would be quite long: the ethnic strife in the former Yugoslavia, the waves of refugees in the Caribbean emanating from Haiti and Cuba, the turmoil and virtual genocide in Rwanda, political instability in Japan and the Koreas, the fall of the apartheid regime in South Africa, the demise of the Soviet Union, accelerated by its defeat in Afghanistan . . . just add your own examples. Many factors are contributing to this situation, but the decline in U.S. ability to enforce its policies in the West and the demise of Russian dominance of the East are central. This has left a vacuum in the international system that the United Nations has often been called on to fill. In 1990 as intervention was prepared to push Iraq out of Kuwait, then-President Bush spoke of a "new world order," based on international law, with the United Nations at the center of its legitimacy and enforcement. There have been some modest successes, for example, organizing relief for Rwanda refugees. Most experiences have not been particularly salutary, however, for example, the U.N. involvement in stabilizing Somalia, which failed, and the longstanding impasse in Bosnia. The conclusion of Burg (1993, p. 363) is persuasive: "The wars in the former

Yugoslavia have made it clear that the principles and practices that provided a stable framework for international security in an era of the cold war are no longer sufficient to preserve the peace."

Not all of the instability has been of a negative sort, however. The apartheid regime in South Africa fell and ushered in a black majority government under Nelson Mandela, thus avoiding what many observers feared would be an extremely bloody period of strife. Palestinians have attained control over the West Bank and Gaza in the Middle East. Jordan and Israel have reached a peace agreement, diminishing a flash point for many recent armed confrontations. And throughout the entire world there has been a movement to supplant dictatorial, nondemocratic regimes with new democratic governments, more responsive to the citizens of all countries.

Political instability in the 1990s is surely linked with the economic instability of the 1980s and the deterioration of economic performance in all areas save East Asia. By 1995 differentiation among the various areas of the South had increased, with East Asia becoming ever more prosperous and Africa on the whole becoming poorer. Latin America and Eastern Europe saw their level of economic development decline, although there are signs of recovery as the decade continues, despite the unsolved problem of the debt. The same process of differentiation was occurring within most regions and most countries; liberalization and market allocation created winners and losers, with governments less able to cushion the fall of the losers.

Underlying these tendencies and changes is an effort to find a new approach to a world system, to find order and direction in a world of instability. The one certainty is that global integration will continue its accelerating path and will put its stamp on the outcome. Richard Falk (1993) sees globalization occurring from two directions: from above through markets and leading states, but also from below through grassroots democratic forces. The outcome, especially for the South, will depend on the balance between these two tendencies. It is unclear where this process will lead. That is the fundamental question for development today, and by decade's end we will have initial answers. The articles in this part highlight both how the world is being reshaped and the most important factors in the increasing differentiation of the South.

The first three articles examine the adjustments and adaptations to the new conditions, first in Greater Central Asia, then in governmental forms and the extension of democracy, and finally in the new Eastern Europe and its economics and politics. The next three articles examine the differentiated economic performance of the decade, first with the success of East Asia, next with Africa whose poor economic performance shows no sign of changing dramatically, and finally with Latin America which still must deal with the effect of its debt on economic performance.

Robert L. Canfield's article places Greater Central Asia in an historical context, showing how geopolitical decisions placed Afghanistan as a buffer between Russia and the West and influenced transportation and communication in the area. With the failure of the Soviet effort to exert direct control in Afghanistan, that buffer role has disappeared and the area is undergoing a fundamental reorganization. Its outlines will be largely determined by changing political relations as well as by technology-driven developments in transportation and communication. The final outline of the area is unclear, but Canfield's conclusion that the power of the state is not favored by the "new" technologies (including "low tech" examples such as the radio) emphasizes the need to think beyond traditional categories.[1]

Terry Lynn Karl and Philippe C. Schmitter's treatment of the wave of democratization examines one of the most positive elements of this time of instability. Globalization based on responsive democratic governments is more likely to lead to human development. For example, Karl and Schmitter point out that democracies do not go to war with other democracies.[2] The process of democratization is quite complex and it differs dramatically across geographical regions. Nonetheless, the article suggests that this "fourth wave" of democratization shows signs of being more lasting, especially in cases of "consolidated democracy," and opens the possibility for improved international relations.

Ronald H. Linden's article first describes the post-1945 evolution of Eastern Europe and gives a basis for understanding the reorientation and restructuring that is currently underway. These states have been buffers, much like Afghanistan, and the collapse of the Soviet bloc has induced a rapid turn to the West. However, many difficulties remain and there is no evidence that the fundamental development problems of Eastern Europe will be solved by this step. There are continued examples of countries slowing or even reversing their policies, and there are as many political and economic failures as successes. At the same time, traditional ethnic and regional conflicts are far from solved and can dominate the entire process at times, as in the former Yugoslavia.

The second set of three articles treat the differentiation among the areas of the South that accelerated during the 1980s. John Page's article on East Asia is a story of constant and steady change and development. Those countries' policy, based on "economic fundamentals" and government intervention, led to rapid growth between 1965 and 1990, accompanied by improvements in the distribution of income. At one level, this experience provides some answers to the problem of development; at another level, the success of the Asian countries has contributed to the widening gaps in the South and to unprecedented differentiation across geographical areas. This situation will frame the challenge for development policy and thinking in coming decades.

The next two articles, J. Barry Riddell's on sub-Saharan Africa and Robert Devlin's on Latin America and debt, treat the two geographic areas that were hurt most by the international instability of the 1980s. They analyze the two cases in their international context, the international lending organizations and their influence on domestic policy (in the case of Africa) and the international financial system (in the case of Latin America).

Riddell describes the stabilization packages that the World Bank and IMF require of countries who wish access to their capital funds. He is quite critical of the direct effects on the economies and suggests that the continent is being reshaped by these external forces. The impact on the role of the state, on the environment, on poverty and development are all profound, and in Riddell's eyes not positive. One effect will be a further distancing of Africa's economic performance from that of other areas of the South.

Devlin describes the debt situation in Latin America, its detrimental effects on those economies, and the role played by banks and governments. He then details the deterioration in economic performance in Latin America. It was exacerbated by the resource transfer from those countries through the debt overhang, a transfer of $179 billion between 1982 and 1988. Devlin attributes this sorry outcome to half-hearted international public policy, and he details the steps that have been taken to confront this continuing problem. He is cautiously optimistic that the international financial system can adjust and begin to make a positive contribution to Latin American development. The recurrence of Mexico's debt problem in 1994 to 1995 shows that any optimism must be tempered.

The Appendix by John Clark and Eliot Kalter update the approaches to working with the debt. The situation has stabilized and there are now positive capital flows to many Latin American countries; however, the drain of the debt continues as a weight on Latin American and African development efforts. And any disruption in the new flows of capital to those areas would rekindle the problems of the 1980s.

There are many sources and sites of instability in our contemporary world. This section and its articles highlight how the world is being reshaped and how a notable differentiation among areas of the South is occurring. As such they provide a basis for viewing the decade of the 1990s and beyond.

NOTES

1   "Low tech" communication innovations have played important roles in many of the cases of instability. The Hutu civilians in Rwanda who participated in the genocidal murders had been terribly frightened by their government's incessant radio-borne predictions of Tutsi atrocities on a Tutsi rebel victory. They responded to government radio transmitted calls to take the initiative by attacking Tutsi's. The nationalist fervor created in Serbia and Croatia owed much to government control of the media and exclusion of less nationalist perspectives from dissemination and discussion.

2   Sen's article in Part One showed the link between democracy, a free press, and famine prevention.

REFERENCES

Burg, Steven. "Why Yugoslavia Fell Apart," *Current History* (November 1993): pp. 357–63.
Falk, Richard. "In Search of a New World Model," *Current History* (April 1993): 145–49.

CHAPTER 11

RESTRUCTURING IN GREATER CENTRAL ASIA: CHANGING POLITICAL CONFIGURATIONS

Robert L. Canfield

Department of Anthropology, Washington University, St. Louis

Central, Southwest, and South Asia—Greater Central Asia—seem to be restructuring. However, defining the emerging political situation in this vast region and estimating the future direction of developments are impossible tasks if events are viewed merely as unrelated and disparate. A longer view may expose a broad pattern. In this article I venture a tentative and provisional interpretation of events in this region and suggest a trajectory of change whose features should become more clear over the next few decades.[1]

Structural change, I presume, is impelled by influences that are not always obvious, indexed in events that collectively reveal that a new turn in relationships is taking place. If we are to identify a trajectory of change in Greater Central Asia in our time, we must look for the "physics" of policy changes, the forces that are now acting upon people and changing the contexts within which policies are set, decisions made, and actions taken.[2] But identifying such forces requires the favoring of particular developments that seem critical or determinative. I will here stress the importance of certain technologies. Technological innovations build upon one another to give a directional animus to events, and they transform social and political conditions by introducing new possibilities for social and political interaction. This is what seems to be happening in Greater Central Asia in our time; certain technological changes are being introduced that will transform the possibilities for social and political action in the region.

The particular technologies I emphasize here are transportation and communications, which influence social and political affairs in similar ways as both are means of

From *Asian Survey,* no. 32 (October 1992), pp. 875–887. © 1992 by The Regents of the University of California.

overcoming the social barrier of distance. I will consider the particular ways that these technologies have affected economic and political affairs in the past in Greater Central Asia and how other innovations, as they come into use, will likewise affect the course of affairs in the future. Our task is to consider what those effects might be. A great deal, however, must remain unexamined in this analysis. Nothing will be said about the possible social effects of the rapid growth of population in this region, or the declining average age, or the declining quality of life; nothing about the disastrous environmental and health problems, the abundance of modern weaponry in the region, or the growing narcotics industry.

In the first section, I briefly summarize the political effects of transport and communications technologies in the past; in the subsequent sections I examine the emerging patterns of political relations in our time in relation to the technological conditions coming into use in the region, and then consider possible directions in the future. I will argue that the long established geopolitical configuration in this region that recently collapsed was affected by changes in transport facilities and communications devices, and that the new geopolitical configuration will take form in respect to other changes in these facilities and devices.

TECHNOLOGICAL INNOVATIONS AND TRANSFORMATION OF GEOPOLITICAL PATTERNS

European Imperial Power

In the history of Central Asia, certain transport or communications innovations have established new possibilities for social alignment and political behavior. One of these was the development of sea transport between Europe and Asia that deprived Central Asia of the locational advantage it had previously enjoyed. Before the sixteenth century, Greater Central Asia was the locus of heavily traveled routes of traffic between the denser population centers of Eurasia. But when the Europeans found a sea route,[3] the wealth of Asia began to move on the high seas and the economy of Central Asia seriously declined.

The political impact on the region was a gradual weakening of the Central Asian rulerships, and over the next several centuries they became vulnerable to pressures that were gathering strength in the northwest. In the sixteenth century Muscovite czars began to expand their influence into the inland territories of Asia. With increasing pace in the next century, Russians spread across Siberia to the Pacific and in the eighteenth and nineteenth centuries they were pressing southward into Kazakhstan and Central Asia; they reached the north banks of the upper Oxus River by 1900.

In the meantime, the British, who had become the preeminent sea-based imperial presence in South Asia, had advanced northward along the Indo-Gangetic plain into the southern foothills of the Hindu Kush mountains. The Russians and British began to confront each other in the region in the nineteenth century; their rivalry over the intermediate territory gave Central Asia its modern identity as a marginal zone, for their conflicting interests pulled the interior of Asia into two main sectors. In a swath of territory that lay outside the firm control of both, the nation-state of Afghanistan took form toward the end of the century. Because both powers feared the advance of the other in the region, Afghanistan became the locus of anxious counter-political activity. Eventually, in 1907, the empires agreed on a definition of their respective inner Asian spheres of interest. The agreement excluded both from Afghanistan's internal affairs, in effect leaving the country as a zone of underdevelopment separating their domains.

Railroad Imperialism

The second technical innovation that affected Greater Central Asia's political shape was railroads. In the second half of the nineteenth century, the British and Russians both believed that "railways, rather than warships and mass armies, would decide the fate of India, and ultimately of Asia and Africa."[4] Rails became "the bloodstream of the [British] Raj," reducing by 1869 the travel time between Calcutta and the Northwest Frontier, India's gateway to Central Asia, from three months by road and barge to only three days by rail (it is now two days).[5] The Russians introduced railroads somewhat later but eventually were laying track at unprecedented speed, dramatically extending their reach across Asia.

As Afghanistan was the natural point of confrontation between the two powers, the rivalry between the Russians and British shaped that country's political relations with the outside world. The conflicts of interest worked to ensure that Afghanistan remained underdeveloped. The British wanted it "to be inaccessible and impermeable, denying the possibility of swift, surprise movements across its frontier." The Russians saw Afghanistan as the crucial route of access into the subcontinent, and in the final years of the nineteenth century made several proposals to construct railroads that would connect key points in Russian Central Asia to India's northwest frontier. All these proposals were rejected by the British because of "past history," they said, and the "prejudices of the two countries."[6] The Afghans, for their part, wanted both the British and the Russians to stay outside their borders, and according to Ispahani, by a series of policy decisions "denied themselves an advanced, large-scale routing network in order to preserve their freedom."[7] The tension between the Russians and British over control of Central Asia and the suspicions of the Afghans over foreign intrusion worked to solidify Afghanistan's geopolitical function as a zone of separation between Russian and British spheres of control. The railhead at the borders of Afghanistan materially evinced the political imperatives that shaped affairs in the region.

As a result of these conflicting interests, certain Russian schemes for the further advance of rail in the region were never realized, at least not at that time. Besides those that would have connected Central and South Asia through Afghanistan, there were plans for a north-south trans-Persian railway connecting Central Asia to the Indian Ocean. Such a line would have transformed Bandar Abbas, in the words of a Russian author, into a "Russian Vladivostock in the Persian Gulf"—or, in the words of a worried British historian, into "a second Port Arthur."[8] This line—at least the Trans-Iranian Railway part between Bandar Shapur and Julfa—was eventually built after World War I and was in place in time to serve a purpose for which no one had dreamed—to carry American lend-lease supplies to the Soviet Red Army in World War II.

Communications Innovations and Populist Movements

The third kind of innovation that shaped politics in Greater Central Asia was the communication devices that began to be introduced after about 1850. The telegraph and later the telephone (devices that transmitted information from point to point faster than people or goods could travel) and the printing press and later the radio (devices that disseminated information to masses of people) dramatically altered the possibilities for social interaction over great distances and among large populations. They made information an increasing factor in public affairs. Through these devices, growing numbers of people became aware of each other's opinions and in other respects developed a sense of shared interests and an ability to cooperate in a common cause.

After about 1880, populations all over Asia began to coordinate and organize activities that became a growing problem to the established empires. Peoples in South Asia, Central Asia, and West Asia began to agitate for such social innovations as a free press, independent local governments, the use of local rather than imperial languages, broadening of education to the masses, and so on. The consequence was a major assault on the imperial governments of Asia. Popular movements gained strength in the latter part of the nineteenth century, were seemingly quenched by the suppressive measures of the imperial regimes, then by the second decade of this century were again rising to a new crescendo. All over Asia, as imperial regimes tottered, new populist movements dominated the political discourse as "nationalist" elites spoke out on behalf of large publics. In India new popular assemblies were instituted as growing numbers of communities became self-conscious and worked in concert. In North Asia, of course, the Russian czars were replaced by the Bolsheviks. In West Asia the Ottoman empire finally collapsed, to be replaced by powerful local movements seeking to establish populist governments.

Throughout the world, information technology was opening new resources for exploitation by government as well as populist leaders. The loudspeaker was being used in Germany with great effect by Hitler, the radio in the United States by Roosevelt and, notably, by Churchill during World War II. In India the British continued to vacillate, as they had for decades, over how free the local press might be. In the emerging Soviet Union, information control became a vital concern. The Soviets not only used the new devices to project their propaganda but also resolutely sought to control from the center the flow of information among the Soviet masses, matching their plans to develop a centrally controlled economy. It was in the wake of the German collapse after World War II that Winston Churchill dubbed the information barrier around the Soviet bloc the "Iron Curtain."

The configuration of power in Greater Central Asia after World War II, therefore, resembled that which had existed for over a century—except that the dominant powers were different. The Soviet Union was ensconced in the north and the successor states of the British empire were situated in South Asia. The United States, taking up the regional concerns of the British, made several attempts to form the states of Southwest Asia into an alliance, a "northern tier" that would serve as a barricade against potential Soviet advances to the south. The Soviets, as the Cold War became more strident, intensified their efforts to seal their populations from outside influences, not only censoring news but also jamming foreign broadcasts. Afghanistan, in the meantime, continued to serve as a buffer state between the Soviet Union and the "northern tier" nations along its southern flank.

THE WEAKENING OF THE NORTH-SOUTH BOUNDARY

This configuration of alignments was being undermined by incremental changes after World War II. The Soviets invested in an advanced infrastructure in their Central Asian republics in order to exploit their mineral and oil resources. They added new rail lines, improved the roads, introduced pipelines for the shipment of oil and coal (in slurry form), increased the number of navigable miles on the rivers, installed electric power lines, and constructed airports. The Central Asian republics were thereby drawn more tightly into the Soviet metropolis, and in the process were made less self-sufficient.[9] In the southern sector of Greater Central Asia, other improvements in the transport and communications infrastructure were being made, most notably the improvement and extension of highways and rail lines in Iran. Plans for the railways entailed the laying of 10,000 km. of new track that would eventually connect to other countries—to Zahedan, which was already linked into Pakistan's railway system; to Sarakhs in Turkmenia; and to two port cities on the Indian Ocean—Bandar Abbas and Chah Bahar. By the time of the demise of the Shah's government in 1979, a new agreement had been signed to build a connecting railway system within Afghanistan.

It was the improvement of the transport and communications infrastructure within Afghanistan in the period after World War II that most dramatically marked the changing possibilities for the alignment of powers in Greater Central Asia. In the period from about 1955 to 1979, the government of Afghanistan, aided by the Americans, the Soviets, and other European nations, invested heavily in an improved transport and communications infrastructure. It constructed hydroelectric dams, large canals and irrigation systems, telegraph and telephone systems, airports capable of servicing large commercial aircraft and, eventually, airstrips in the provincial capitals for a newly established internal airline company, an extensive system of paved highways, and a national radio station. Through this aggressive program of development, many of the dispersed and isolated populations of the country became much more accessible to each other, the central government, and the outside world. With little notice, Soviet Central Asia and South Asia, which had formerly been separated by a zone of underdevelopment, were becoming more accessible to each other through technological improvements within Afghanistan and Iran. By the 1970s, the setting for a major geopolitical restructuring was in place.

The Breach of the Afghanistan Barricade

The most notable events that exposed the new spatial structure in Greater Central Asia were, of course, the Iranian Revolution and the Soviet-Afghanistan War. The revolution in Iran marked the collapse of the "northern tier" policy, humiliated the United States, and inspired Islamic activists all over the Muslim world. It was mainly owing to concern about the strength of the uprisings against a new Marxist regime in Kabul that the Soviets decided to intervene in Afghanistan. That decision turned out to be catastrophic, as the war that ensued broke open the Soviet side of the barricade and became an increasing embarrassment to the Soviets.

Gholam Ali Ayeen[10] has pointed out that empires characteristically have maintained control through intimidation and an appearance of invincibility. But embarrassing defeats, even if militarily inconsequential, have weakened the strands that bonded empires, exposing frailties in their systems and emboldening disaffected elements to express their frustrations openly, in some cases to revolt. The Afghanistan resistance inspired disaffected elements within the Soviet bloc to test the power and resolve of the central administration. The Eastern Europeans were in fact watching the Afghanistan resistance with great interest in the early 1980s and took heart for their own causes. The Poles were the first to express their dissent, soon to be followed by many other dissenting groups who collectively undermined the integrity of the Soviet system.

Perhaps the main contribution of the Afghanistan war to this process was the breakdown of Soviet information management.[11] Frustration and disenchantment grew among the Soviet peoples as increasing numbers of dead soldiers were brought back from the war and as the surviving veterans returned with stories differing markedly from official reports. Also, by the mid-1980s Afghan resistance groups were injecting their own propaganda among the Muslim peoples of Central Asia by means of cassette tapes and tracts. These informal sources of uncensored information opened a rift in the Iron Curtain. Gorbachev's *glasnost* policy was obliged in part by the rising flow of uncontrolled information about Afghanistan. As the Soviets withdrew their troops in 1988 and 1989, they also introduced radical policies inside the Soviet Union, easing censorship and ceasing to jam foreign broadcasts. The Soviet peoples, for the first time under Soviet rule, had relatively free access to outside and inside news. The Iron Curtain was finished.

THE JOINING OF NORTH AND SOUTH CENTRAL ASIA

At this writing, further evidence is appearing of the collapse of the once firm boundary between the northern and southern portions of Greater Central Asia. Political and commercial ties are developing among various nation-states across this divide, surely to be followed by infrastructural investments that will materially bridge it. Indeed, the nineteenth century vision of a network of rail lines connecting Europe, India, and the Russian "heartland" would seem to be an emerging reality. Iran is making plans to lay the tracks that will be the final links in the system as originally conceived. In May 1990 it inaugurated a project to build a rail line between Bafq and Bandar Abbas that will connect the existing system to the Indian Ocean, and in 1991 Pakistan and Iran agreed to improve and expand their highway and railroad interconnections. Once these are completed, Pakistan will enjoy direct rail access to West Asia and Europe, and Iran will have direct access to South Asia. Indeed, the agreement was made in the context of a more general agenda, which was to foster closer cooperation among these two nations and the new republics of Central Asia.

These moves are being made as a growing number of business interests and governments in the world are examining possibilities for investment and development in the Central Asian republics. The several nations in southern and western Asia vying to establish profitable ties to the newly formed successor states of the Soviet empire are establishing relations that will become materially evident in improved transport facilities, some of which will reach across the divide between North and South Asia. Turkey has offered help to the republics of Azerbaijan, Uzbekistan, Turkmenia, and Kazakhstan in the financing and construction of new transport linkages to the West. The Iranians are introducing textile mills, rebuilding mosques and madrasas, turning Tashkent into an airline hub in Central Asia, instituting development projects in Azerbaijan and Turkmenia, and installing direct telephone connections to, as well as opening a consular office in Tajikistan. Before his eviction from office, President Najibullah of Afghanistan was making overtures to the successor states in Central Asia—not to offer help, of course, but to obtain it. And Pakistan as early as 1990 was arranging with Uzbekistan to facilitate religious publication, educate students, and exchange Islamic scholars through its International Islamic University in Islamabad.[12]

A most striking indication that the former north-south divide is being bridged is Pakistan's new policy toward Afghanistan. Pakistan decided in early 1992 to try to persuade its Afghan clients, who have been the most intransigent Islamists among the *mujahedin* resistance groups, to come to terms with the Kabul regime. Prime Minister Nawaz Sharif's administration has even distanced itself from Pakistan's own Islamists, once a vital base of his support. The impulse behind this policy shift is the desire to develop ties to the Central Asian republics, whose leaders are essentially secularists and regard Islamism as potentially disruptive and destabilizing; clearly, they would not welcome a radical Islamist regime in Kabul. In addition, Nawaz Sharif's government has been retouching its image to project a more moderate Muslim appearance, more like Turkey than Saudi Arabia, and stressing its strong Sunni heritage, like the Central Asians and unlike the Shiite Iranians. Pakistan's new interest in Central Asia could eventually be expressed materially in improved transport facilities, including (according to some official statements) railroads. This change in policy expresses how definitely the configuration of strategic options has changed. In its own interest, Pakistan must tie its economic future to Central Asia. The republics, for their part, are interested in access to the international commercial system, which is possible through Pakistan.[13]

If railroads are constructed between Pakistan and Central Asia, the easiest route would be through Afghanistan—either via Kandahar and Herat to Kushka or the more challenging route through Kabul and Salang to Termez. The current political uncertainties in the country will delay infrastructural decisions by the Afghans, but assuming the country remains intact, whenever the situation stabilizes the new leadership will be faced with outside offers to assist in reconstruction. As long as unresolved internal issues override external concerns, the government could take different postures toward neighboring countries, depending on its internal composition: a Tajik-Uzbek coalition in Kabul would favor the Central Asian neighbors, whereas a Pushtun coalition would likely favor Pakistan. But once a government is firmly ensconced in Afghanistan, its policies will be shaped by international issues. Whatever its initial inclinations might be, the new Afghanistan government will be inclined to keep its stronger neighbors at bay even as it accepts their economic support.

Historically, Afghanistan has looked to India to counter the influence of Pakistan and to other nations of the Middle East, notably Turkey, to counter the influence of Iran. Relations with India are tense at present, as the *mujahedin* leadership in Kabul is furious with India for siding with the Afghan Marxists. The imperatives of Afghanistan's external politics will, over the long term, likely induce the new Afghan leaders, whoever they are, to develop stronger ties with Turkey and eventually even with India. In any case, as the critical problem of legitimacy is resolved and a government firmly established, the Afghans will become attracted to the possibilities of development. Because of its strategic location, Afghanistan will eventually welcome aid to improve its infrastructure; as that takes form, the country could become a vital bridge between the northern and southern sectors of Asia.

The trajectory of change in Greater Central Asia is toward infrastructural improvements that will give the region a more central place in the transport pattern of Eurasia. Elsewhere in Asia there are other plans for development that will add further importance to the location of Greater Central Asia. That is, in the distant future, the United Nations' proposed Tumen River basin project in Korea and China—which is supposed to create a kind of Rotterdam on the Pacific—could increase substantially the overland traffic between East Asia and other parts of Eurasia. Already Japan has become Pakistan's largest trading partner, and as the infrastructure of overland transport improves in Central Asia it will be more heavily used. The South Koreans are already a major source of high-tech investment in Kazakhstan and Kirghizia, and their interests will likely enlarge as the region develops.

As new ties are formed between Turkey, Iran, Afghanistan, Pakistan, and the Central Asian republics, Greater Central Asia will become strategic to the formation of a huge economic trading region. It could regain an importance it has lacked since before the rise of maritime trade in the sixteenth century. The emerging political restructuring of the region will be manifested in, and further enhanced by improvements in transport and communications facilities. The vestiges of the once critical boundary between northern and southern Eurasia will disappear as large capital investments in transport and communications facilities connect the several isolated parts of the region with each other and the wider world. The populations of South Asia, Europe, and East Asia will have faster and cheaper access to each other by land through this intermediate zone. What was once a boundary will become a corridor.

NEW TECHNOLOGIES OF CULTURAL TRANSMISSION AND THEIR POTENTIAL IMPACT ON POPULAR CONSCIOUSNESS

Improvements in the transport infrastructures of Central Asia constitute one kind of innovation that is opening up new possibilities for political and social interaction in Greater Central Asia. Other innovations now, or soon to be, diffusing into the region are the new technologies of communications—cassette tapes, television, videos, copiers, computers, microchip telecommunications systems, and other information technologies. These devices are transforming the ways information and other cultural materials are managed and disseminated. All over the world they are creating new industries, new forms of enterprise, new forms of social relations, new elites, and new means of exerting influence. Although they already seem to be considerable, the precise social and political effects of these devices over a long period are as yet unclear anywhere in the world.

The broadcast media—radio and television—which are becoming more widely available to the populations of Greater Central Asia, have been in use for some time, of course, but the programming now coming into use is relatively new and different.[14] Now that Soviet jamming of the radio frequencies has ceased, the BBC, Voice of America, Radio Free Europe, and Radio Liberty are widely heard as well as the "official" state radio broadcasts. Not only have more radio sources of information become available, but for the time being many of those sources appear to be carrying more reliable information. Millions of people in this part of the world are becoming more aware of developments elsewhere through these less controlled broadcast media, and aware of how their local interests are affected by events elsewhere.

Radio is the important broadcast medium in the region now, but television is becoming more available. The privately owned AsiaSat I satellite has a footprint stretching from Iran to Japan and a potential audience of 2.3 billion people. Its signal can be captured by anyone with a dish larger than 2.5 meters in diameter. Already the demand has escalated. The Gulf War generated a huge appetite for outside news, and this was quickly followed by a demand for more entertainment. CNN, the BBC's World Service Television, and local channels based on AsiaSat I are already operating. Local entrepreneurs in India have begun to set up privately owned satellite dishes in order to sell cable television to their neighbors. Recently, when U.S. Secretary of State Baker visited the republics, virtually all the Central Asian leaders wanted to know how to get access to CNN.

Radio and television are broadcast technologies that can reach large and dispersed audiences sharing a common language. Just as the advance of printing enabled elites to reach wide audiences and eventually helped nationalities become self-aware and organize into powerful social movements, the broadcast technologies, through their ability to reach larger audiences, similarly will affect the political sensibilities of the peoples of Greater Central Asia. These media will enable the scattered populations of the region—the Turkic speakers (Uzbeks, Turkmens, Kirghiz, Kazakhs, and Azerbaijanis) and speakers of the Persian dialects (Farsi, Tajik, Dari)—to become more aware of commonalities.

Television is the more powerful medium. As it becomes more available, it will strongly affect the public consciousness of the peoples of Greater Central Asia as it has done elsewhere, introducing new tastes, ambitions, heroic images, and expectations. So far, the programming has been government controlled and almost universally boring, but other sources of the kind of television programming that has been popular elsewhere, much of it produced in the West, are becoming available in South Asia and will soon come on line in Central Asia as well. The introduction of the stylized caricatures so effectively portrayed on the screen will give a new shape to popular tastes and virtual images.

But not everyone will accept Western programming, which will necessarily challenge and sometimes offend the sensibilities of people in these cultures. One of the motivating impulses of the Islamic "fundamentalist" movements has been frustration over the growing influence of Western culture on popular tastes in the Muslim world. "Television comes in for most of the blame," says Immanuel Sivan, "because it brings the modernist message in the most effective, audiovisual form into the very bastion of Islam—family and home. But the same holds true for radio and for tape cassettes."[15]

Cassette recorders, along with videos and telephones, are "narrowcasting" devices, that is, means of making direct contact with specific individuals and audiences. They are also different from national radio and television broadcasting systems in that they are less expensive and more accessible to the private sector and to individual use. These "low tech" devices are becoming more available all over Greater Central Asia. Cassette tape recordings have already been an inexpensive means of distributing recorded sermons, lectures, recited poetry, and speeches, not to mention music. But the content of such tapes is not limited to religious or political topics; cassette recordings of Michael Jackson are reportedly popular in Central Asia.[16] Videos, although less accessible in Central Asia itself, are well entrenched elsewhere in Eurasia and cannot be but a few years from being standard fare all over the Asian continent. The video industry is already booming in India, where one can buy videos produced locally and also videos of films and television programs filched from satellite broadcasts.

The social and political consequences of the introduction of these "low tech," narrowcast technologies are hard to predict. Narrowcast technologies enable self-conscious and special interest groups to disseminate their ideas to targeted individuals and communities. They can be effective in socializing new recruits and are already being used by the various Islamic interest groups such as the Shia, the Ismailis, the Sufi orders, and other activist groups.[17] But broadcast and narrowcast technologies are potentially alike in one respect: they can weaken loyalty to nation-states. Neither of these technologies favor the interests of states. State boundaries that do not coincide with linguistic boundaries are easily bridged by broadcasting, and governments can no longer effectively jam broadcast signals as was done before; also, narrowcasting devices are easily smuggled across state lines. In the emerging world, governments will likely be unable to control the flow of information as before; indeed, nation-states will likely find these devices a threat to their ability to manage their internal affairs. Perhaps a historian in the future will see in retrospect what our generation can grasp only vaguely: that we also are as strongly "acted upon" as have been the generations of the past.

NOTES

1 Some recent considerations of developments in the region are by Graham Fuller, "The Emergence of Central Asia," *Foreign Policy* 78 (Spring 1990), pp. 49–67, and Andre Gunder Frank, *The Centrality of Central Asia,* Comparative Asian Studies, no. 8 (Amsterdam: V.U. University Press, 1992).

2 Fernand Braudel described the "physics" of policy change operating in 16th century Spain in *The Mediterranean and the Mediterranean World in the Age of Philip II,* vol. 1 (New York: Harper, 1972), p. 19.

3 Janet Abu Loghud explains that the real change was less a matter of improved sea-going technology than of the aggressive orientation of the Europeans on the Indian Ocean (*Before European Hegemony* [Oxford: Oxford University Press, 1989]). In any case, from the point of view of Central Asia, it was a shift in technology as well as the route of travel.

4 Milan Hauner, *What is Asia to Us? Russia's Asian Heartland Yesterday and Today* (Boston: Unwin Hyman, 1990), p. 103.

5 Michael Satow, "38,000 Miles of Track: India's Railway Lifeline," *National Geographic,* 165:6 (1984), pp. 744–49; Paul Theroux, "Foward" in Michael Satow and Ray Desmond, *Railways of the Raj* (New York: New York University Press, 1980).

6 Mahnaz Ispahani, *Roads and Rivals: The Political Uses of Access in the Borderlands of Asia* (Ithaca, N.Y.: Cornell University Press, 1989), p. 95.

7 Ibid., p. 96, also ff.

8 Hauner, *What is Asia to Us?,* pp. 103, 105.

9 Victor Mote, "Afghanistan and the Transport Infrastructures of Turkestan," in Milan Hauner and Robert L. Canfield, eds., *Afghanistan and the Soviet Union: Collision and Transformation* (Boulder, Colo.: Westview Press, 1989). This is not to say that the population was integrated into the wider Soviet society (see William Fierman, ed., *Soviet Central Asia: The Failed Transformation* (Boulder, Colo.: Westview Press, 1991).

10 Gholam Ali Ayeen, "Afghanistan wa Sarnawisht-i Imperaturiha! Aya Tarikh Tikrar Khahad Shud?"[Afghanistan and the destiny of empires! Is history repeating itself?]. *Mujahed Wollas,* vol. 5.

11 Many Afghans believe that their resistance *caused* the collapse of the Soviet Union. This is hubris, but the effect of that prolonged and painful war on the Soviet people should not be minimized.

12 These new alliances are not without their contradictions. Iran can cultivate the Azeris as Shiite Muslims but not as Turkic peoples, for the Turkic-Persian divide within Iran is still sensitive. For the leaders of the Central Asian republics, who are essentially secularists, the development of ties with Iran or Pakistan could invite problems with the Islamicist elements within those countries.

13 Apart from attempts to develop ties by government leaders in the nations of Greater Central Asia, various other elements of the successor republics have tried on their own to develop ties with other societies. Opposition groups in Azerbaijan, Uzbekistan, and Tajikistan, for instance, have been looking for help from the outside. Also, there are natural affinities for similar cultural groups on the opposite sides of boundaries and a growing interest in knowing cultural compatriots. The Tajiks have a natural interest in the Persian speakers in Iran and Afghanistan, where the old Persianate tradition persists in a less diluted form than in their homeland; and the Turkic peoples of Uzbekistan, Turkmenia, and Kirghizia have a strong sense of cultural affiliation with each other as well as with Turkey.

14 Chingiz Aitmatov, "The Influence of Information Technology on the Economic and Cultural Life of Soviet Central Asia," *Impact of Science on Society,* no. 146 (1987), pp. 183–87) is an obviously idealized report but it contains some interesting information.

15 Immanuel Sivan, *Radical Islam: Medieval Theology and Modern Politics* (New Haven: Yale University Press, 1985), p. 3.

16 Mark Saroyan, "Waiting for the Islamic Revolution in Soviet Central Asia," First annual Nava'i Lecture in Central Asian Studies, Georgetown University, 1991, p. 3.

17 David Edwards, "Summoning Muslims: Print, Politics, and Religious Ideology in Afghanistan," paper presented at the annual meeting, American Anthropological Assn., 1987.

CHAPTER 12

DEMOCRATIZATION AROUND THE GLOBE: OPPORTUNITIES AND RISKS

Terry Lynn Karl and Philippe C. Schmitter

Stanford University   University of Chicago

On April 25, 1974, a conspiracy of young military officers overthrew the authoritarian regime that had been ruling Portugal for forty years. At the time, no one imagined that this isolated and unexpected event would be followed in relatively short order by the demise of over *forty* other autocracies. This wave of democratization spread first to the neighboring, semiperipheral, Southern European countries of the First World, and later to almost the entire continent of Latin America.[1] In the mid-1980s, it reached Asia, beginning with "people power" in the Philippines, then extending to South Korea, Taiwan, Thailand, and even to some elites in China.[2] Surprising as these regime changes were to most of the actors involved and to all of the academics observing them, they pale in comparison to the shock produced by the sudden collapse of Soviet-style regimes during 1989–1990. This event resounded dramatically in Africa, where by 1991 eight countries could be considered democratic.[3]

Communism's "grand failure" also led to triumphalist claims of the "unabashed victory of economic and political liberalism."[4] Indeed, the end of the Cold War, the collapse of the Soviet Empire, and the virtual elimination of a viable alternative to capitalist development sparked extraordinarily hopeful prescriptions regarding the prospects for democracy in the future. But are such prescriptions warranted? And what are the implications of this democratic sweep for the international system?

In this chapter, we will first explore the dynamics of the "wave" of regime transformations that has engulfed the world since 1974 and then discuss the differences in its impact upon world regions. We pay particular attention to the peculiarities of Eastern

© Michael Klare and Daniel Thomas, eds., *World Security: Challenge for a New Century,* 2nd ed. (New York: St. Martin's Press, 1994). Reprinted with permission of St. Martin's Press, Inc.

Europe, where democratization is inextricably linked to the collapse of the planned economy. Finally, we ask some questions about the prospects for the eventual consolidation of these experiments with democracy and the risks and opportunities that they pose for the international system.

A GLOBAL WAVE OF DEMOCRATIZATION?

We are currently witnessing the fourth historical wave of democratization.[5] The first wave, often marked by the introduction of universal suffrage (initially limited to white male property-owners) in the United States in the late 1820s, lasted until the so-called "Springtime of Freedom" that engulfed Europe in 1848–49 and then receded quickly, leaving relatively few democracies in its wake. The second corresponded to World War I and its aftermath, although this too met with a reverse wave initiated by Mussolini's termination of Italy's fragile democracy. The third took place during World War II and its aftermath, and eventually included countries as diverse as West Germany, Italy, Austria, Japan, South Korea, Brazil, and Costa Rica.

The second and third waves had a more lasting impact on the global distribution of political regimes, especially the latter, which triggered a veritable avalanche of decolonization. Not all of these ex-British, French, Dutch, Belgian, U.S., and Japanese colonies in Africa, Asia, the Caribbean, and the Pacific remained democratic for a long time, but a few did: India, Jamaica, Trinidad and Tobago, Malta, Botswana, the Gambia, Malaysia, and Sri Lanka. Yet here, too, democratization was followed by a reverse wave. Most of the newly independent Third World countries descended into various forms of single-party and personal autocracy during the 1960s, an authoritarian trend that was dramatically intensified in Latin America as first Peru, then Brazil, Bolivia, Argentina, Ecuador, and finally the long-standing democracies of Uruguay and Chile fell under military rule. The global swing away from democracy also swept Asia (especially South Korea, Indonesia, and the Philippines), the Mediterranean (Greece and Turkey), and Africa, where the largest proliferation of authoritarian governments occurred.[6]

Compared to these previous waves, the fourth one is distinctive in two respects:

1 It is not the result of a cataclysmic exogenous event, that is, worldwide or regional warfare. While this wave was produced in part by common causes affecting many countries, there is no single event of the scope and scale of World War I or World War II that provoked democratization. Instead, a variety of factors, ranging from the numerous economic and military failures of authoritarian rulers to the changing policies of external actors like the Catholic Church, the European Community, the former Soviet Union, and the United States, have played significant roles in bringing about these new transitions.7

2 It has been much more global in its reach. It began in Southern Europe, spread to Latin America, affected some Asian countries, and literally swept through Eastern Europe. Even Africa, often considered too poor to produce democracies, is currently experiencing its effects. Moreover, from Mongolia to Mali, Madagascar to Mexico— in countries that are experimenting with liberalization rather than full-blown democra-

tization—important changes are still in the offing. Only the Arab countries of North Africa and the Middle East seem to have remained immune, although some democratic momentum has occurred in Algeria, Tunisia, and Jordan. As a consequence, the fourth wave has affected far more countries and been more thorough in its regional impact than its predecessors. Some parts of the world that were previously almost uniformly autocratic are now almost equally democratic.

Diffusion is the most obvious hypothesis for explaining these differences. Where diffusion occurs, the successful example of one country's transition establishes it as a "model" to imitate. Once a given region is sufficiently saturated with this mode of political domination, pressure will mount to compel the remaining autocracies to conform to the newly established norm. Democratic "contagion" of this sort occurred in past waves, but it was confined to the exchanges between countries that were geographically proximate and culturally comparable. Researchers once found empirical proof of its presence by tracking the spread of political innovation from nearby units to those farther away. Such tests are no longer adequate in light of the global development of "complex communicative interdependence." Today people from China to Chile simultaneously are exposed to pictures of "people power" in the Philippines, and democratization can "leapfrog" from Southern Europe to Latin America without first affecting nearby North Africa or Eastern Europe. With the spread of television and communications satellites in the 1970s and short-wave radios and fax machines in the 1980s, authoritarian governments have found it increasingly difficult to control the information available to their subjects. Global communications networks not only demonstrate to people in one country that autocrats can be successfully removed in another; they often show just how it can be done!

Diffusion is thus a particularly appealing explanation for the contemporary wave of democratization. It does not illuminate why a wave a democratization may start in the first place, but it helps to understand how and why it may spread. Because modern systems of communication are not spatially bound and may not even be culturally confined, their new reach suggests the likelihood that the relevance of the international context will increase steadily with each successive instance of successful regime change. Those coming later in the wave will be more influenced by those that preceded them. Whether later transitions can be expected to learn from mistakes made earlier is perhaps less predictable, but there may be an advantage to "delayed democratization"—just as it has been argued that "late economic development" occasionally had its advantages. There is already some evidence to support this supposition. Spaniards were profoundly affected by the end of forty-five years of Portuguese dictatorship prior to the death of Franco, and democratizers there shaped their strategies accordingly. The Spanish transition, in turn, was very influential in Latin America, especially Argentina and Chile. Today, democrats in Eastern Europe eagerly seek lessons from these prior transitions that might be applicable in their own very different context.

Such diffusion does not rely upon the development and spread of communications alone. Particular to the fourth wave of democratization is another phenomenon that has fostered this demonstration effect and that may have less to do with contagion than with what could be called consent. Each successive case of democratization has contributed more and more to the development of formal nongovernmental organizations and informal informational networks devoted to the promotion of human rights, protection of minorities, monitoring of elections, provision of economic advice, and fostering of exchanges among academics and intellectuals—all intended to promote further democratization. In the initial cases of Portugal, Greece, and Spain, this sort of an international infrastructure hardly existed. Indeed, some of the key lessons were learned from these experiences and subsequently applied elsewhere. By now, there exists an extraordinary variety of international parties, associations, foundations, religious and social movements, networks, and firms ready to share practical advice on "how to" democratize or to intervene either to promote or to protect democracy.

Their efficacy is enhanced by regional and international organizations that have been revitalized with the end of the Cold War and that have adopted democratic promotion as a means of keeping the peace. Nowhere is this more notable than in Nicaragua and El Salvador, where for the first time the United Nations, backed by a thick network of democratic contacts, has presided over demilitarization and fair elections, mediated human rights disputes, and negotiated peace agreements.[8] This suggests a second hypothesis: the international context surrounding democratization may have shifted from a primary reliance on public, bilateral intergovernmental channels of influence "downward," on the one hand, toward an increased involvement of private, nongovernmental organizations, and "upwards," on the other hand, toward a greater role for international organizations. If so, it may be the concrete activity of these agents of consent, rather than the abstract process of contagion, that accounts for the "global reach" of regime change and the fact that so few regressions to autocracy have thus far occurred.

Yet, even if the world has become a sort of global village in which democratic norms, practices, and experiences are more widely shared, the argument for "contagion" is especially persuasive within specific regional contexts. In Latin America, for example, the unexpected (and highly controlled) transition in Paraguay seems to have been influenced by the fact that the country was surrounded by nascent democracies, although Chile under Pinochet held out successfully against such pressures for a period during the 1980s. Shortly after the Catholic Church played a major role in the downfall of the Marcos regime in the Philippines in 1986, Cardinal Kim called for democracy in South Korea, and it is probable that events in these two countries subsequently influenced the push toward liberalization in China, Burma, and Taiwan.

Eastern Europe provides the best possible case for contagion, even though the initial impetus for regime change was given by an exogenous event, that is, the shift in Soviet foreign and defense policy towards the region. No one can question the accelerating flow of messages and images that went from Poland to Hungary to East Germany to Czechoslovakia to Romania to Bulgaria and, eventually, to Albania, or the impact that successive declarations of national independence had upon the member republics of the Soviet Union. Indeed, the experiences of Eastern Europe, and to a lesser extent Central America, suggest that the lessons of contagion and the mechanisms of consent seem to function better at the regional, rather than the binational or global, level.[9]

ONE ROAD TO DEMOCRACY OR A CONTRAST BETWEEN CONTINENTS?

Global democratization—whatever its extent (or, as we shall see, its durability)—has been a very diverse process. There is no "standard" context in which autocracies become politically vulnerable, nor is there a single "modal" way of removing autocrats from office. The early democratizations of the fourth wave were the result of a variety of factors: an unwinnable colonial war, a military defeat in Cyprus, and the death of Franco precipitated transitions respectively in Portugal, Greece, and Spain. Once they occurred, however, the changes in these "leaders" helped to stimulate and shape events elsewhere. Subsequent democratizations have been at least indirectly interconnected, and one can find a substantial amount of overlap between each of the world regions. Still, it is possible to distinguish four contrasts between the regime changes that have occurred in Southern and Eastern Europe, South and Central America, Asia and, most recently, in Africa in: (1) their respective points of departure; (2) their modes of transition from autocratic rule; (3) the significance of external actors for triggering and guiding the events; and (4) the variety and sequencing of their transformative processes.

The Points of Departure

The classical contention that differences in level of development, literacy, urbanization, and so forth could explain the emergence of democratization has not stood up well during the fourth wave of democratization. While it is true that most of the societies involved were in the "middle-range" on most of these aggregate indicators, only three, Spain, South Korea, and Taiwan, were close to being full members of the exclusive club of advanced industrial countries. The others were strung out across a broad spectrum ranging from the relatively industrialized and highly literate ex-Communist systems of Czechoslovakia, Hungary, and Poland to such relatively impoverished and illiterate capitalist systems as Bolivia, Paraguay, Honduras, Peru, Benin, and Pakistan—with a large group of countries lying somewhere in between on one or another of the development indicators: for example, Brazil, Uruguay, Chile, Argentina, Portugal, Greece, Turkey, Romania, Bulgaria, Estonia, Latvia, Georgia, and Lithuania. If democratization should occur in one of the real "outlyers" in the development process, (e.g., Haiti, Albania, Mongolia, Mali, the Congo, Namibia, and Ethiopia), then a whole generation of theorizing about economic development as its major precondition will have to be rejected!

Points of departure may also be distinguished by the nature of the previous autocracy. These regimes have come in a great variety of types: from civilian to military, personal to institutional, and authoritarian to totalitarian. Under the pressure of the contemporary wave, all possible permutations of these types have collapsed. Romania was "civilian/personal/totalitarian"; Brazil was "military/institutional/authoritarian." As we shall see, there is some reason to suspect that the mode of transition may be related to these distinctions. In Romania, where power was concentrated in one individual, Ceaucescu was overthrown violently within a very short time; in contrast, the Brazilian generals presided over a peaceful and long, drawn out, regime change largely under their control.

Policymakers and scholars generally assume that the starkest contrast should be between "the East" and "the South," that is, between communist/totalitarianism and capitalist/authoritarianism systems, given the extreme differences in their modern histories. In fact, most of these Eastern political systems had long since degenerated into some form of authoritarian rule, not that far removed from the ways in which their Southern brethren were governed. Romania and Albania were obvious exceptions, although their high degree of personalization of power suggests a possible analogy with such cases of "sultanism" as Somoza's Nicaragua, Trujillo's Dominican Republic, Stroessner's Paraguay, or Mobutu's Zaire. What did remain a distinctive attribute of the East, however, was the monopolistic fusion of political and economic power into a party-state apparatus, the so-called *nomenklatura,* which (with the exception of Cuba and possibly Mexico) has had little parallel in the autocracies of Latin America, Asia, and Africa.

But what is most striking between the East and the South are the differences in point of departure in socio-occupational structure as the result of so many years of policies in the East designed to compress class and sectoral distinctions, equalize material rewards and, of course, eliminate the diversity of property relations under communism. Except where a "second economy" had emerged earlier and prospered commercially (e.g., Hungary), Eastern social systems seem very "amorphous" in their social structure, and it is difficult to imagine how the parties and interest associations that are so characteristic of all types of "Western" democracy could emerge, stabilize their respective publics, and contribute to the general consolidation of the regime. While the greater equality of the East puts these countries at a certain advantage when compared to the highly inequitable countries of Latin America, it is simultaneously a great disadvantage. Without more substantial and more stable class and sectoral differences, the politics of these neodemocracies are likely to be driven by other, much less tractable, cleavages, especially ethnicity or religious identity. In this sense Eastern Europe resembles Africa, where ethnic and other conflicts based upon identity have generally predominated.

The Modes of Transition

Regime changes are "produced" by actors who choose strategies that lead from one kind of regime to another. They are constrained in the choices available to them by their point of departure, that is, their prevailing social, economic, and political structures, and by the tremendous uncertainty that characterizes any regime change. The interaction of their strategies may often result in outcomes that no one initially preferred. But the identity of these political actors and the concrete strategies they collectively choose combine to define which type of transition will occur in a particular country.

Different modes of transition are depicted in Figure 12-1.[10] Simplifying a very complex choice on the horizontal axis, *strategies of transition* can vary along a continuum that runs from unilateral recourse to force to multilateral willingness to compromise. In short, transitions can be "ordered" or they can be bargained. In between lies a muddled and ambiguous zone of action in which mutual threats are exchanged, acts of physical intimidation and coercion may be committed, and substantial mobilizations of support may occur. The vertical axis distinguishes between cases in which most, if not all, of the impetus for change comes "from below," that is, from actors in subordinate or excluded positions in the social, economic, and political order of the ancien régime, and those in which elite actors "from above," that is, from within the dominant institutions of authoritarian rule, social prestige, and/or economic exploitation, play the leading role in moving the system toward some form of democracy. Again, it is important to note that the range of variation cannot be collapsed into a neat dichotomy, thus the diagram leaves room for a "messy" intermediate category in which elites and nonelites mingle and compete for the direction of the transition. Actors coming "from outside" may intervene directly and significantly on either axis—encouraging compromise or force, on the one hand, and mass activity or elite actions, on the other. As the democratization of Japan and Germany illustrate, they can play an especially significant role when they have defeated the previous authoritarian regime in international warfare!

FIGURE 12-1
MODES OF TRANSITION: THE DISTRIBUTION OF RECENT CASES.

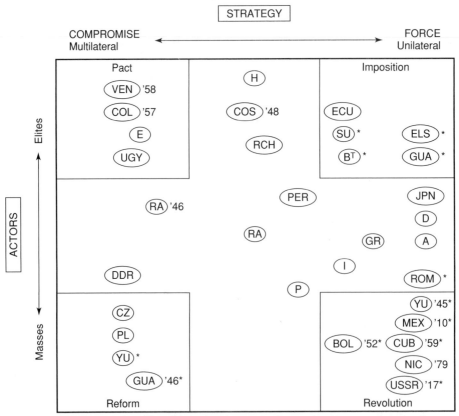

* These countries either did not then become or have not yet become democracies.

From the four "extreme" corners of the plot in Figure 12-1 emerge four ideal types of regime transition: (1) *pact,* when elites agree upon a multilateral compromise among themselves (e.g., Spain, Uruguay, Colombia, Venezuela); (2) *imposition,* when elites use force unilaterally and effectively to bring about a regime change against the resistance of some incumbents (e.g., Brazil, Ecuador, Turkey, Soviet Union); (3) *reform,* when masses mobilize from below and impose a compromised outcome without resorting to violence (e.g., Czechoslovakia, Poland, Yugoslavia, and Guatemala in 1946); and (4) *revolution,* when masses rise up in arms and defeat the previous authoritarian rulers militarily (e.g., Nicaragua). In the capacious space between the four extremes lie presumably a large number of situations in which both the identity of the relevant actors and the selection of strategies are "mixed." Violence is tempered by compromise before it becomes dominant; masses are aroused and active, but still under the control of previous elites; and domestic actors and strategies are significant, but the outcome hinges critically on what foreign occupiers or intervenors do.

Countries seldom fit neatly into boxes, so it is not always easy to classify specific cases according to the coordinates of Figure 12-1. Take, for example, Poland's transition. It began in 1980 in the *reform* box with the rise of Solidarnosc—a mass-based movement advocating regime change by nonviolent means. This "phase" ended with a *pact* in 1981, which was subsequently broken by the *imposition* of a military regime— whose temporary effect was to abort the transition process altogether. In 1989 these autocratic rulers chose, under pressure from two successive strike waves but without being compelled to do so by the organized violence of their adversaries, to enter into "roundtable" negotiations that subsequently produced another *pact,* which in turn led to restricted elections in June that brought to power a mass-based *reform* government. Since its transition began and ended in the *reform* box, and since it was conditioned all along by the presence of a mass movement, we place Poland there—in effect, ignoring the tortuous path by which it left and returned.[11]

Portugal is another hard case to classify. It began its 1974 transition suddenly and unexpectedly by imposition—a coup d'état launched by junior military officers in the context of impending military defeat in Guinea-Bissau. Virtually overnight, the successful seizure of power triggered a mass response that first pushed the process in a reformist direction and, then, in the spring and summer of 1975, seemed to be leading toward a revolutionary outcome. The defeat of radical military elements in November prevented that and for some time the Portuguese polity remained suspended between reform and imposition (efforts to negotiate pacts failed), until the elections of 1987 and consequent changes in the constitution placed the country at last on the road to consolidation.[12]

Other countries show similar "mixed" modes of transition. Chile was firmly (and protractedly) entrenched in the imposition mode until General Pinochet misjudged his capacity to win a key plebiscite in 1988. Subsequently, its revived civilian politicians opted for a pacted transition based on a "grand alliance" of all opposition parties. Hungary is a somewhat similar case in which the initial impetus came from within the dominant party, but these elites lost control and were forced to "roundtable" with opposition groups who, themselves, aroused little popular support. The German Democratic Republic would have been a standard case of reform from below were it not for the substantial interference of elites from the neighboring Federal Republic at key moments in its transition. Similarly, Romania may have first undergone an accelerated regime change under revolutionary conditions of violence and mass involvement, but the (unclear) role of the Soviet Union and the subsequent recuperation of the *nomenklatura* and military apparatus resemble the imposition mode.[13]

One major East-South difference that seems to emerge, irrespective of the mode of transition, is the extent of collapse of the previous regime. Not only were the Eastern European regime changes less "preannounced" and the opposition forces less "preprepared" to rule than in the South, but once new governments were formed the role of previous power-holders declined much more precipitously and significantly than it has elsewhere. There were a few exceptions where rebaptized (and possibly reformed) communists managed to do well in the initial "founding elections" and to hold on as a group to key executive positions, but even then they often proved incapable of governing effectively and were displaced in relatively short order, vide Albania, Bulgaria, and Estonia. By our calculation, only in Romania, Mongolia, Ukraine, Azerbaijan, Lithuania, and Serbia are previous communists continuing to play a significant role, either as a party governing alone or a party in alliance with others.

This contrasts with Southern Europe and Latin America, where neodemocracies were often governed initially by centrist or rightist parties that had important elements (and persons) from the previous regime in their ranks, and where "traditional" powers such as the armed forces or the police retained very significant power to intervene in policy-making and affect the choice of institutions. Spain, Brazil, and Chile may be the most extreme cases, but almost everywhere the transition takes place in the shadow—if not under the auspices—of the ancien régime. This is also the case in Africa, where the armed forces remain a "veto" force even when they have withdrawn from direct rule. In contrast, given the virtual abdication of their previous rulers, Eastern Europeans could harbor the (momentary) illusion of a tabula rasa upon which to build new rules and practices, rather than behave as if they had to cautiously wend their way through a "living museum" of powerful actors from the past.

The Role of External Actors

One of the more confident generalizations of the early literature on democratization emphasized the much greater importance of domestic forces and calculations, as opposed to foreign influences, in determining the nature and timing of regime transition. It was hinted, however, that the latter might play a more significant role, subsequently, in the consolidation phase.[14] This observation, which was based on the experiences of Southern Europe and South America, does not fit either Eastern Europe or Central America. Without a previously announced and credible shift in the foreign and security policies of the Soviet Union, and a less dramatic though equally telling change in U.S. policy toward its neighbors, neither the timing nor the occurrence of regime change would be easily explicable in these two regions.

Moreover, there is much more evidence of "contagion" within these two regions, that is, of events in one country accelerating a response in its neighbors. Unlike Southern Europe, South America, and Asia, where democratization did not substantially alter long-standing commercial relations or international alliances, the regime changes in Eastern Europe triggered a major collapse in intraregional trade and the dissolution of the Warsaw Pact. Into this vacuum moved an extraordinary variety of Western advisors and promoters—binational and multilateral. In Central America as well, external actors have imposed political "conditionality" upon the process of consolidation, linking specific rewards explicitly to the meeting of specific norms, or even to the selection of specific institutions.[15]

The Sequence of Transformations

All of the above differences pale in importance before the sequence of transformations, in our opinion. In none of the Southern European, South American, or African cases did the regime change from autocracy to democracy occur alone, in complete isolation from other much-needed military, social, and economic transformations. Except in Central America and Eastern Europe, it was usually possible to deal with these variegated demands sequentially; that is, a change in the polity did not immediately call into question the economic model or the existence of the military. In some especially favored cases, major structural changes had already been accomplished under the previous autocracies. For example, most of these transitions "inherited" acceptable national identities and boundaries—even if the degree of local or regional autonomy remained contested. In a few, the military had already been largely subordinated to civilian control (e.g., Spain under Franco), or the economy had undergone substantial restructuring to make it more internationally competitive (e.g., Chile under Pinochet).

In Eastern Europe, by contrast, not only are such major transformations all on the agenda for collective action and choice, but very little authoritative capacity exists for asserting priorities among them. This *simultaneity* means that there is a great deal more to do than in the South, and it seems as if it must be done at once. Many decisions have to be made in the same time frame, and their uncontrolled interactions tend to produce unanticipated (and usually unwanted) effects. Even within a given issue area, the absence of historical precedents makes it difficult to assert theoretically what should come first: holding elections or forming a provisional government? drafting a national constitution or encouraging local autonomy? releasing prices or controlling budget deficits? privatizing state industries or allowing collective bargaining? creating a capital market or sustaining a realistic exchange rate?, and the list could continue indefinitely.

Even if "transition theory" can offer a few generic insights strictly within the political domain, these risk being quite irrelevant given simultaneous—rather than sequential—demands for changes in major economic, social, cultural/national, and military institutions. For example, one knows in the abstract that the formation of provisional governments can be a bad thing, especially before the configuration of national party systems is evident, but what if (as seems to have been the case in Czechoslovakia) it is necessary to head off a polarized conflict among nationalities? In retrospect, it seems to have been a crucial error for Gorbachev to have convoked (or tolerated) elections at the level of republics *before* holding a national election that would have legitimated his own position and, with it, the All-Union framework of territorial authority, but this was presumably necessitated by the correlation of forces within the Communist party and the military at the time.

One thing is becoming abundantly clear—and this was observed already in the classic article of Dankwert Rustow that lies at the origin of much of today's work on transition:[16] that without some prior consensus on overarching national identity and boundaries little or nothing can be accomplished to move the system out of the protracted uncertainty of democratic transition into the relative calm (and even boredom) of consolidation. This places the former Soviet Union and Yugoslavia in a radically different sequence, and it is not inconceivable that all of their "successor republics" will be paralyzed by a similar imperative. It also bodes ill for Africa, where borders drawn by colonizers are likely to be contested in the future regardless of the firm intentions of African governments to the contrary.

A VARYING RANGE OF OUTCOMES?

Different modes of transition from authoritarian rule do not necessarily lead to democracy. Indeed, *consolidated democracy* is only one possible outcome. Democracy can be defined in generic terms as "a system of governance in which rulers are held accountable for their actions in the public realm by citizens, acting indirectly through the competition and cooperation of their representative."[17] For this arrangement to work, certain procedural norms must be met,[18] including: (1) control over decisions by elected officials; (2) regular and fair elections; (3) adult suffrage; (4) widespread eligibility to run for office; (5) rights to free expression, speech, and petition; (6) access to alternative sources of information; (7) rights to form/join associations and parties; and (8) civilian control over the military. Where these procedural norms exist and are respected through regularized and fair "rules of the game" based on political competition, consolidated democracies can be found.

But some of these procedural norms can also be found in a context in which actors may not have been successful in producing a stable and legitimate form of governance, that is, in establishing a type of democracy that is appropriate for and accepted by a given population. Thus, a second possible outcome is *unconsolidated democracy*. Another way of putting the point is that democracy, in its most generic sense, may persist after the demise of autocracy, but not be consolidated into a specific and reliable set of rules or institutions. Some countries (Argentina is most frequently cited, but Botswana is another case) may be "condemned" for the foreseeable future to remain democratic only because no feasible alternative mode of domination is (presently) available. Elections are held; associations are tolerated; rights may even be respected to some extent; the procedural minima are met with some degree of regularity, but the *ensemble* of rules and institutions do not jell into regular, acceptable and predictable patterns that can reproduce themselves over time and command the allegiance of citizens. "Democracy" is not replaced by something else—say, the old form of autocratic rule—it just persists by reacting in ad hoc and ad hominem ways to successive problems. Under these circumstances, there is no underlying agreement to govern the relationship between parties, organized interests, and ethnic or religious groups.

A third possible outcome of transition is the formation of a *hybrid regime,* that is, a polity which cannot meet the procedural minima of democracy but also does not return to the status quo ante. These have been referred to as *dictablandas,* authoritarian regimes that recognize some rights and protection for the individual but do not permit political competition, and *democraduras,* regimes which often severely restrict popular participation but do allow a degree of political competition.[19] They have become increasingly common, especially in Central America and Africa, as authoritarian rulers seek to introduce democratic mechanisms into their polities in order to assuage international forces encouraging democratization. El Salvador, where elections since 1982 have been held in the context of the systematic violation of political and human rights, is one such *democradura,* although it may cross the threshold to democracy if UN-negotiated peace accords guarantee a different context for the 1994 elections. The Ivory Coast and Gabon are others. Hybrid regimes are unlikely to provide a stable political solution after transition, and thus may be more usefully viewed as an interim stage before a return to full authoritarianism or progress toward democracy.

Finally, a fourth possible outcome of transition is *regression to authoritarian rule.* Statistical data from the prior three waves of democratization suggest that this may be the most probable result. Indeed, each earlier wave was followed by a reverse wave of authoritarian rule that eliminated many (but not all) of the previous transitions to democracy. In 1990, at the height of transitions, roughly 45 percent of all independent countries were democratic, the same percentage as in 1922.[20] Still, each wave of democratizations has left more democracies in place, and there have been relatively few regressions to date. Haiti, Peru, Thailand, and Nigeria are the most evident cases of regression, while the very start of a transition has been blocked in Burma and China and stalled in Algeria. For whatever reason, democratic waves seem to last approximately two decades, so the extent of regression may not be known until the end of the 1990s—a factor that makes the recent military coup attempts in democratic Venezuela especially troubling.

Even where some form of democracy does result from the demise of authoritarian rule, new democracies face distinctive problems related to both the timing and nature of their transitions. On the one hand, political democracy in the contemporary period may be rooted in a fundamental paradox: the modes of transition that appear to enhance initial survivability may preclude the democratic self-transformation of the economy or polity further down the road. Transitions are highly uncertain moments; for democracies to emerge from them, actors must often limit uncertainty by entering into bargains that protect the privileges of those who formerly supported authoritarian rule. In Chile, for example, democratizers had to accept a constitution imposed by the Pinochet regime that contained blatantly antidemocratic provisions, including a guarantee for the military of 10 percent of all copper revenues over and above its normal budget. Cruelly, these bargains, while permitting democracies to persist in the short run, may constrain their potential for resolving the problems of poverty and inequality that continue to plague them. They may be especially costly during the present time of economic hardship, when virtually all new democracies are coping with crises in growth, employment, foreign-exchange earnings, debt repayment, and so forth.

Such trade-offs are especially evident in elite-dominated processes of democratization, which are unilaterally imposed by authoritarians in power. Pacted and reform democracies, whatever their defects, have been honed through compromise between at least two powerful contending actors, thus their institutions tend to be more flexible when faced with future bargaining over substantive issues and/or demands for the revision of existing rules. In Uruguay, for example, while the agreed-upon rules made it very difficult to challenge agreements between the military and the political parties on the issue of amnesty for crimes committed during authoritarian rule, the left opposition, excluded from this accord, was nevertheless able to force the convocation of a plebiscite on this major issue—which it subsequently lost. It is difficult to imagine that anything similar could occur in Brazil. Because the Brazilian armed forces exerted almost complete control over the timing and content of the transition, they never curtailed their own prerogatives nor fully agreed to the principle of civilian control and they have not been compelled to adopt institutional rules reflecting the need for compromise.

It is reasonable to hypothesize that what occurs in the phase of transition or early consolidation may involve a significant trade-off between some form of political democracy, on the one hand, and equity, on the other. The contrast between the cases of Uruguay and Brazil suggests the reasoning behind this hypothesis: where transitions are unilaterally imposed by armed forces who are not compelled to enter into compromises, they threaten to evolve into civilian governments controlled by authoritarian elements who are unlikely to push for greater participation, accountability, or equity for the majority of their citizens. Paradoxically, in other words, the heritage left by what some would call "successful" authoritarian experiences, that is, those characterized by relatively moderate levels of repression and economic success that has left the military establishment relatively intact, may prove to be the major obstacle to future democratic self-transformation.[21] This same danger exists, albeit to a lesser extent, in civilian-directed unilaterally imposed transitions, for example, Mexico under Salinas, because the institutional rules are likely to be systematically rigged to favor incumbents and to permit less scope for contestation.

Thus, even though the emergence of new and stable democracies is by far the most desirable of the four outcomes sketched above, they confront significant problems in their struggle to consolidate rather than collapse. They must establish new constitutional and electoral systems; abolish authoritarian bastions, like death squads or secret police; establish a professional pattern of civil-military relations and a reduced role for the military; cope with torturers; design forums for interaction between business, government, and labor; and contain ethnic or regional conflict—all in the context of economic hardship. In some cases, as Eastern Europe so painfully demonstrates, the mere fact of democratization, that is, the promise of free expression for the first time, unleashes pent-up forces previously suppressed by coercion that threaten the stability of both states and regimes. These democracies guarantee a greater respect for law and human dignity when compared to their authoritarian predecessors, but they may be unable to carry out substantive reforms that address the lot of their poorest or most oppressed citizens.

NEW REWARDS AND RISKS
FOR THE INTERNATIONAL SYSTEM?

We now return to our initial questions: What are the prospects for consolidating the regime changes of this fourth wave of democratization? And what implications will these changes have for the international system as a whole?

One can point to some optimistic features of the present context. According to Freedom House, which has been surveying the progress of human and political rights since the early 1970s, more people live under freedom than ever before.[22] Although democracies can abuse individual and collective freedoms, especially those of ethnic minorities, they tend to respect rights much more predictably and extensively than their authoritarian counterparts. To the extent that they are consolidated, they also provide regular channels for the expression of dissent and offer reliable mechanisms for peacefully changing their government leaders and policies.

Moreover, the proliferation of popularly accountable government has direct implications for peace and security. One of the few "laws" of international relations that seems to hold invariably is that democracies do not go to war with other democracies. Autocracies have frequently fought each other as well as democracies; and democracies have invaded authoritarian regimes, even small ones where the national security threat is questionable at best—vide the recent cases of the United States in Grenada and Panama—but a world or a region populated by consolidated democracies is definitely likely to be less insecure and violent. Its member states will still have international conflicts, but where two democracies are concerned, they are much more likely to resort to compromise, mediation, and adjudication in resolving them.[23]

There is also reason to believe that the fourth wave may be followed by less regressions to authoritarian rule than the past three. To no small degree, this can be attributed to the steady growth of international nongovernmental organizations (NGOs) that provide services for neodemocracies and monitor their performance in elections and human rights, as well as mobilize support for them when threatened by military coups, rigged elections, or arbitrary government action. Complementing this development of an embryonic "transnational civil society" is the strengthening of the role of international, intergovernmental organizations (IGOs), either at the global level in the United Nations and its specialized agencies or at the regional level through such entities as the European Community, the Organization of American States, or the Association of Southeast Asian Nations. The "political conditionality" they have imposed, along with the material support they have mobilized or the collective sanctions they have applied, has not always been sufficient to prevent regression to autocracy and violence—witness the sad cases of Burma, Haiti, and Bosnia-Herzegovina; but they have led to some important successes in Nicaragua, El Salvador, and Namibia. There is little question that the growing strength of these transnational forces makes it more difficult for authoritarian rulers to anoint themselves as self-appointed "saviors of the fatherland."

But there are also good reasons to avoid the triumphalism of those who believe that the demise of communism and the exhaustion of utopian ideologies heralds the definitive victory for democratization. All previous waves of regime change eventually receded—and it simply may be too early to tell how many polities will be dragged back to autocracy this time. Certainly the fact that most neodemocracies are simultaneously having to cope with declining economic performance, accelerating inflation rates, heavy external indebtedness, severe fiscal crises, insistent demands for industrial restructuring to meet increased international competition, and persistent capital flight is not making their task easier. Although citizens in new democracies thus far have responded to these strains of economic austerity and adjustment by focusing their discontent on specific governments rather than on the notion of democracy itself, it is uncertain how long they can "punishment vote" parties out of office or remove corrupt officials from their positions before the regime itself is questioned.

Indeed, there are growing signs of what the Spaniards have called *desencanto* (disenchantment) with democracy itself. The perception that democratization can increase corruption, that professional politicians have arrogated disproportionate salaries and perquisites to themselves, that policies imposing burdens on privileged groups do not get applied, that such entrenched powers as the military have protected and even increased their share of the public budget, that crime has increased, that arbitrary violations of human rights by police forces persist, that the tax burden is unfairly distributed or collected, that unsavory nationals or even foreigners are reaping too many of the benefits from policies of privatization and deregulation—some or all of these complaints have emerged with regularity in nascent democracies. They have been taken up by opportunistic demagogues or populists who promise that the "temporary" use of exceptional powers and suspension of civil and human rights will right all these wrongs and return the polity to a "better" democracy. The recent attempted coups in Venezuela, or Peruvian President Fujimori's suspension of the legislature in 1992, his subsequent rule by decree and eventual convocation of a controlled election to draft a new (and, presumably, more authoritarian) constitution, may well be harbingers of future developments.

But these problems of economic suffering and political disappointment pale when compared to those of cultural conflict. One frequent characteristic of autocracies is their tendency to suppress or manipulate ethnolinguistic minorities. The nascent democracies that succeed them inherit these accumulated resentments and provide the discriminated groups with the freedom to openly express their demands. In Southern Europe and Latin America, where national borders were relatively secure before the transition, demands by subnational groups have met with repression and violence, but conflicts have remained relatively confined, if no less brutal. In Eastern Europe and Africa, where historical resentments run deep and existing borders often divide rather than unite nations, mobilization along ethnolinguistic lines is especially explosive and threatens to overwhelm the usual bases of social cleavage: class, status, generation, gender, and so forth, which underlie stable party and interest-group systems. The sad fact is that democracy depends on the *prior* existence of a legitimate political unit—and this can only be accomplished by complex and often lengthy historical processes. There is no democratic way of deciding what the physical and cultural boundaries of that unit should be. Slogans such as the self-determination of peoples, and devices such as plebiscites or referenda, simply beg the question of who is eligible to vote and whether the majority can legitimately impose its will on the minority.

The contemporary international system will be deeply affected by this fourth wave of democratization, but not in a single or predictable way. What is certain is that multilateral organizations and transnational forces will be called upon to deal with more and more issues, including many that were previously regarded as lying exclusively under the jurisdiction of national states. Traditional notions of sovereignty will be increasingly questioned as international actors monitor domestic elections, verify human-rights conditions, and demobilize national armies. Whether such organizations will slide down a "slippery slope" toward operational overload, or can find ways to successfully circumscribe their involvements, remains to be seen.[24]

At the same time, long-established democracies like the United States will be pushed to decide whether or not to make the promotion and sustenance of democracy a central foreign policy goal. In this debate, detractors will point to the poor performance record of the past, especially in Latin America, while proponents will put their faith in "political conditionality," aimed at linking the provision of international aid to the fulfillment of specific democratic objectives within and between states.[25] Sanctions may be more frequently applied to those who dramatically and systematically violate widespread norms of human rights. The fact that democratic practices and respect for fundamental rights stands as an explicit requirement for membership in the European Community, that the United States has begun to explore the prospect of making democratization a condition for assistance, and that financial and technological aid is increasingly available from autonomous democratic organizations, creates new incentives to sustain the fourth wave. Yet, it also carries the danger that big-power faith in political engineering seeks to impose a uniform political model that ignores the broad variations in local circumstances among countries. What ultimately will determine the efficacy of these external incentives depends as much upon the sensitive recognition by "conditioners" that democracies come in diverse types, by various routes, from different points of departure, and under different constraints, as it does upon the actions taken by authoritarians reluctant to reform.

NOTES

1 For a discussion of the initial sweep of democratization across Southern Europe and Latin America, see the four-volume study by Guillermo O'Donnell, Philippe C. Schmitter, and Laurence Whitehead, eds., *Transitions from Authoritarian Rule* (Baltimore: Johns Hopkins University Press, 1986).

2 For a discussion of democratization in Asia, see Larry Diamond, Juan J. Linz, and Seymour Martin Lipset, eds., *Democracy in Developing Countries: Asia* (Boulder, CO: Lynne Rienner Publishers, 1989).

3 These are Benin, Botswana, Cape Verde, Gambia, Mauritius, Namibia, Sao Tome and Principe, and Zambia. By 1992, Mali had joined these ranks, and important negotiations toward democracy were occurring in South Africa as well. See Larry J. Diamond, "International and Domestic Factors in Africa's Trend Toward Democracy" (Stanford: Hoover Institution, Working Papers in International Studies, 1992).

4 See Zbigniew Brzezinski, *The Grand Failure: The Birth and Death of Communism in the Twentieth Century* (New York: Charles Scribner's Sons, 1989) and Francis Fukuyama, "The End of History?" *The National Interest,* 16 (Summer 1989), p. 3.

5 Samuel Huntington contends that this is actually the third wave of democratization, with the first one lasting almost one hundred years, from 1828–1926. This seems excessively long, especially because, by our criteria, a wave involves interactive and interdependent choices across national boundaries within a more compressed period of time. Hence, below we distinguish an earlier wave in the first part of the nineteenth century from the wave that surrounded World War I. See his *The Third Wave: Democratization in the Late Twentieth Century* (Norman and London: University of Oklahoma Press, 1991).

6 By some counts, one-third of the globe's democracies had fallen under authoritarian rule by the mid-1970s. See Juan Linz and Alfred Stepan, "Political Crafting of Democratic Consolidation or Destruction: European and South American Comparisons," in Robert A. Pastor, ed., *Democracy in the Americas: Stopping the Pendulum* (New York: Holmes and Meier, 1989), p. 47.

7 This observation lends weight to the contention that no single factor is adequate to explain the emergence of new democracies. On this point, see Terry Lynn Karl, "Dilemmas of Democratization in Latin America," *Comparative Politics,* Vol. 23, No. 1 (October 1990).

8 In Nicaragua, the UN monitored internal elections for the first time and oversaw the demobilization of the contras. It subsequently expanded its role in El Salvador from electoral supervision and peacekeeping to actual peacemaking. For a discussion of its role in this latter country, see Terry Karl, "El Salvador's Negotiated Revolution," *Foreign Affairs,* Vol. 7, No. 2 (Spring 1992). For an excellent discussion of the changing role of the United Nations and the challenges facing it, see Ernst B. Haas, "Collective Conflict Management: Evidence for a New World Order?" in Thomas G. Weiss, ed., *Collective Security in a Changed World* (Providence, RI: Brown University, World Peace Foundation and the Thomas J. Watson Institute for International Studies and World Peace, 1992).

9 Extraregional powers seem to have learned this lesson. Most of the U.S. intervention in the delicate early years of the Portuguese transition was channelled through friendly European powers, just as much of the American aid for Eastern Europe is slated to pass through the European Bank for Reconstruction and Development.

10 This depiction of different modes of democratic transition originally appeared in Terry Lynn Karl, "Dilemmas of Democratization in Latin America," op.cit.

11 For a detailed discussion of these later events, see Marjorie Castle, "A Successfully Failed Pact? The Polish Roundtable of 1989," Ph.D. dissertation (Stanford University, 1993).

12 See Philippe C. Schmitter, "Liberation by *Golpe:* Retrospective Thoughts about the Demise of Authoritarian Rule in Portugal," *Armed Forces and Society,* Vol. 2, No. 1 (Fall 1975).

13 Cf. Michel Castex, *Un mensonge gros comme le siècle: Roumanie, histoire d'une manipulation* (Paris: Albin Michel, 1990); also "Enigmas of a Revolution," *The Economist* (January 6, 1990).

14 For the initial observation, see Guillermo O'Donnell and Philippe C. Schmitter, *Transitions from Authoritarian Rule: Tentative Conclusions about Uncertain Democracies* (Baltimore: Johns Hopkins Press, 1986), pp. 17–21. It should be noted that the cases upon which this generalization was based did not include those of Central America. In that subregion, external influence and intromission has been (and continues to be) much more significant. For a criticism with regard to Southern Europe, see Geoffrey

Pridham, ed., *Encouraging Democracy: The International Context of Regime Transition in Southern Europe* (Leicester: Leicester University Press, 1991).

15 The changing international context for democratization is discussed at greater length in Philippe C. Schmitter, "The International Context for Contemporary Democratization: Constraints and Opportunities upon the Choice of National Institutions and Policies," paper presented at the East-South Systems Tranformation (ESST) Conference, 4–7 January 1992, Toledo.

16 Dankwart Rustow, "Transitions to Democracy," *Comparative Politics,* 2 (1970), pp. 337–363.

17 For a more detailed explication of this definition, see Philippe C. Schmitter and Terry Karl, "What Democracy is . . . and is not," *Journal of Democracy,* Vol. 2, No. 3 (Summer 1991), pp. 75–88.

18 These have been explored most thoroughly in the work of Robert Dahl, especially, in his *Dilemmas of Pluralist Democracy* (New Haven: Yale University Press, 1982). In the above-cited article by Schmitter and Karl, two additional criteria for assessing the existence of democracy have been added to Dahl's original seven.

19 Guillermo O'Donnell and Philippe C. Schmitter, op.cit.

20 Huntington, op.cit., p. 25.

21 The notion that especially "successful" authoritarian regimes paradoxically may pose important obstacles for democratization can be found in Anita Isaacs, "Dancing with the People: The Politics of Military Rule in Ecuador, 1972–1979," Ph.D. thesis, Oxford University (1986) and Guillermo O'Donnell, "Challenges to Democratization in Brazil," *World Policy Journal,* Vol. V, No. 2, (Spring 1988), pp. 281–300.

22 Cf. Freedom House, *Freedom in the World: Political Rights and Civil Liberties, 1990–1991* (New York: Freedom House, 1991) and previous editions. For a more general discussion of the problem of measuring democracy and its change over time, see the articles in the special number of *Studies in Comparative International Development,* Vol. 25 (1990) by Alex Inkeles, "Introduction: On Measuring Democracy," pp. 6–14 and R. D. Gastil, "The Comparative Survey of Freedom: Experiences and Suggestions," pp. 25–50.

23 See Michael W. Doyle, "Liberalism and World Politics," *American Political Science Review,* 80 (December 1986) and Bruce Russett, "Politics and Alternative Security: Towards a More Democratic Therefore More Peaceful World," in Burns H. Weston, ed., *Alternative Security: Living Without Nuclear Deterrence* (Boulder, CO: Westview Press, 1990).

24 Ernest Haas warns that if these organizations try to address all of these tasks simultaneously, they invite failure. See his "Beware the Slippery Slope: Notes Towards the Definition of Justifiable Intervention," prepared for the Committee on International Security Studies of the American Academy of Arts and Sciences, January 5, 1993.

25 In summing up the record of the United States in Latin America, Abraham Lowenthal warns that efforts to promote democracy "have rarely been successful, and then only in a narrow range of circumstances." See "The United States and Latin American Democracy: Learning from History," in his edited volume, *Exporting Democracy: The United States and Latin America* (Baltimore: Johns Hopkins Press, 1991). For a proponent's view, see Larry Diamond, "Promoting Democracy," *Foreign Policy,* No. 87 (Summer 1992).

CHAPTER **13**

THE NEW INTERNATIONAL POLITICAL ECONOMY OF EAST EUROPE

Ronald H. Linden

Department of Anthropology
Washington University, St. Louis

The revolutions of 1989 in East Europe and the political changes which followed altered not only the domestic but also the international situation for the East European states. The states of the region are being pushed towards greater economic interaction with the West by, *inter alia,* the new regimes' desire to jettison their socialist, state-dominated economic systems and reap the benefits of world and domestic market trading. Some are being helped and welcomed by Western institutions, while others are finding themselves the target of a multinational form of "differentiation." At the same time, for all of the new democracies there are powerful factors inhibiting their "move West."

THE REGION BEFORE THE REVOLUTIONS

Prior to 1989 the politics and the economics of the states of East Europe were dominated by Soviet concerns. These involved maintaining the political compliance and military security of the region and thereby maintaining its service in the larger sphere of Soviet foreign policy. That service consisted of: (1) demonstrating and validating the position of the Soviet Union as a world power; (2) insuring its ability to play a major role in determining the future of Germany and of Europe; (3) helping to protect the USSR in the event of a physical attack from the West; and (4) satisfying the economic needs of the Soviet economy.

The forms this dominance took were both bilateral and multilateral and included a preponderance of political, economic, and military Soviet influence in the region. This

Reprinted with permission from STUDIES IN COMPARATIVE COMMUNISM, VOL. XXV, No. 1, MARCH 1992, 3–21, Butterworth Heinemann, Oxford, England.

did not mean that throughout the region the East European states were always dutiful servants of Soviet will or that the political and economic systems of each were uniformly and totally tied to the Soviet system. There was in fact a range of behavior displayed by the East European states in many spheres within an overarching Soviet hegemony.[1]

The trade of all of the states was dominated by the Soviet Union. The USSR was for each of the East European states the single largest supplier and importer of their goods, controlling anywhere from 20 per cent to nearly 60 per cent of their junior partner's trade as late as 1989. In the supply of energy and raw materials the dominance was even more pronounced, except for Romania which was able until the mid-1980s largely to avoid dependence on Soviet supply.[2] Some of the other East European states managed to avoid the position of Bulgaria, more than half of whose trade was with Moscow, by cultivating ties in certain sectors with the West, or with developing countries. Poland and Romania both developed the former before the dislocations of the 1980s and Romania consistently pursued economic ties with the latter, in an attempt to secure energy supplies.[3] The economic arrangement was not always a positive sum game for the USSR. As Marrese and Vanous have shown, the supply of energy to East Europe at less than world prices in return for the purchase of overpriced manufactured goods constituted a substantial subsidy to the East European economies by the Soviet Union, something which was eventually accepted by Soviet analysts.[4]

Politically, all were ruled by a communist party which secured for itself a monopoly on legitimate political activity. From the Soviet point of view this not only mimicked the system in place in the USSR, but proved immensely advantageous in other ways. First, it allowed the Soviet leadership to bring its influence to bear on the leadership of the East European country by working through a single elite-dominated party whose decisions and policies were not subject to public input. There was little need for these parties to try to achieve mass public support. In addition, parties and movements offering alternative visions of the country's present and future were kept from sanctioned public access, essentially leaving Soviet supported views in a dominant position in media discussion. Second, through the ideological and personnel screening practiced by the *nomenklatura* of East Europe, the USSR could see to it that leaders attentive to and usually supportive of Soviet interests came to and held power. Third, the economic dependency of the leaders of the region's parties tended to make them compliant to Soviet demands for economic resources and supportive of the USSR internationally.

Still, the East European response was not uniform across the region or over time. Soviet support did not insure against—and indeed even provoked—occasionally tumultuous expressions of public displeasure. These episodes, such as occurred in Czechoslovakia in 1968 and in Poland several times, placed the local regime in the position of trying to survive between the pressure of its own population's desires and those of Moscow. This situation produced several changes of leadership, occasional threats of Soviet intervention, and two full scale invasions. Less dramatically, room for autonomy in certain spheres of domestic or foreign policy did evolve. Poland, for example retained private farms and an influential Catholic church; Hungary moved forward with economic reform well before the USSR; and Romania pursued a calculatedly deviant foreign policy.[5]

Overwhelmingly, Soviet dominance of the region was carried out through bilateral means, through direct representations, visits, and agreements. But this system was supplemented and legitimated by multilateral institutions which were intended to broaden the structure of Soviet influence and act as a counter to nominally similar institutions which had arisen in the West. The Warsaw Pact was formed in 1955 in response to West German entry into NATO and served to legitimate Soviet military presence and, in the case of Czechoslovakia in 1968, actions, while insuring full coordination and subservience of the combined militaries to the Soviet Union in time of war. Through its Political Consultative Committee (made up of the party first secretaries of the Pact states) and frequent summits, the Pact also acted to support and broaden the appeal of various Soviet foreign policy initiatives over the years.[6]

The Council for Mutual Economic Assistance (CMEA) was founded in 1949, but remained largely a paper organization for more than a decade. In the early 1960s Nikita Khrushchev sought to strengthen the organization's ability to direct and coordinate the economic plans of its members (read: the East European states) in response to the strength and vigor of the European Economic Community and the rising political challenge from China. This organization never achieved the status of a multilateral economic community, however, and instead provided further mechanisms by which the East Europeans could be isolated from the world economy. Trade among the CMEA members was conducted on a barter basis using an artifact known as the "transferrable ruble" as an accounting device. None of the countries' currencies were convertible even among themselves, nor was there any method of settling up with finality one country's yearly deficit with another. Various attempts were launched to "strengthen cooperation" among the organizations members in order to achieve something close to economic integration but these produced few results.[7]

It was, however, bilateral Soviet economic dominance which affected the most significant isolation of the states from the world economy. This operated in several ways. The USSRs possession of the preponderance of the energy sources of the region made the CMEA states—and even those only associated with them such as Yugoslavia—dependent on a steady supply of Soviet natural resources. These were supplied at lower than world "friendship" prices which, though adjusted, still typically lagged behind world prices. This, plus the widespread if erroneous Western perception of a Soviet "umbrella" over growing East European debt, allowed the states of East Europe to avoid the painful adjustment which the global energy trade was forcing on more vulnerable market economies.[8] Second, the East European states' economies, like that of the USSR itself, were driven not by the demands or opportunities of an internal or external market, but by the capacities and exigencies of the Soviet supply system. Hoarding resources and meeting quotas were more important than satisfying—much less creating—a market. Enterprise and sector losses were made up by the state budget. These were not just "shortage economies," in Janos Kornai's famous phrase, but internationally dependent shortage economies because they depended on one key supplier for their input, a supplier which had every reason to continue rather than to attenuate that dependency.

Third, and critical to the present attempt to enter into the global economy, the purchases of the USSR dominated East European export sales. The industrial structure of the East European states was geared toward supplying the Soviet Union. As an undemanding and seemingly inexhaustible market, the USSR exacted less in the way of production standards from the suppliers of East Europe than a global market would have. The need to supply the Soviet economy had its origins in politics—specifically Moscow's desire for a supportive international orientation of the region. Satisfying the Soviet market kept the regional hegemon satisfied, for the most part, and also the East European labor force employed. But there were economic consequences. The needs of the Soviet economy were not comparable to those of western industrialized countries. Feeding the eastern "market" kept East European industry less competitive, a fact which was not crucial until interaction with the West increased, first in particular countries and industries, then all at once in the wake of the revolutions of 1989.

SINCE THE REVOLUTIONS: THE PUSH TOWARD THE WEST

The Return to Europe

The revolutionary changes which occurred throughout East Europe during 1989–1990 involved two related processes: (1) the sweeping from power of the one-party rule of Soviet-supported communist parties; and (2) the establishment of processes for the holding of broadly competitive elections. The first process removed the major indigenous element holding the region to the Soviet economic and political spheres of influence, the East European communist parties. The second process started the states on the road toward establishing or broadening ties to the rest of the world which are replacing those that have held sway for more than four decades.

In general, the new democracies of East Europe are being pushed toward greater involvement with the Western economic system by the expressed preferences of their population for what they perceive as the advantages of western style capitalism and their rejection of the failings of the Soviet style socialism. While the pace and manner of the revolutions varied across the region, the overthrow of communist dominance was a movement *against* the existing system, both politically and economically. In Czechoslovakia, for example, that meant the pervasive political control of the communist party and continued repression by its police. In Romania it meant the overthrow of the leader who had himself replaced the power of the communist party, Nicolae Ceausescu. While the particular catalysts differed—emigration in East Germany, police repression in Czechoslovakia—the dynamic in most cases included pressure on the regimes to begin or to broaden genuine political consultation, to remove top elites, and eventually to make themselves vulnerable to public approbation.

At the same time the movement against the system was in most cases complemented by a movement *for* something: the European model. The most powerful force exerted both on the political systems and the peoples of East Europe was the pull of the idea of Europe itself. As the revolutions of 1989 spread, the sentiment was increasingly voiced by those making the changes that they wanted their country to be "European", to join or rejoin a political continent from which they had been forcibly cut off. The systems being created to replace the former dominance of the communist party were explicitly parliamentarian, multi-party, and based on the political systems and values demonstrated and practiced throughout Western Europe.[9]

The European "model" has been put in place, with national variations, throughout the region, with the encouragement and often explicit assistance of the leaders, governments, and parties of Western Europe. The creation of election systems was aided vigorously by many West European parties, especially the German CDU and SPD, but also British conservatives and American Democratic and Republican strategists. This guidance, plus the clear draw of the European idea itself, accounts for the extraordinary speed with which parliamentary systems and multiparty and multiround elections took shape in East Europe. What has been created in Europe now is what natural scientists might call a collection of "more similar systems." The "East" and the "West" have much more in common now than they have had at any time since World War II.

International Economic Ties

The return to Europe has been most evident in the rapid expansion of various forms of economic ties.

Trade   Trade between the developed countries of the West and most of the East European countries had peaked in 1980 and declined thereafter in response to tightening credit conditions, the worsening debt position of the East, and the effects on both the western and eastern economies of the second oil shock. Still, western trade had begun to recover by 1987 for all except Romania which continued to cut its imports as part of a drastic strategy to pay off its hard currency debt.[10]

Western trade with Poland, East Germany, Hungary, and Czechoslovakia was thus already increasing at the time of the 1989 upheavals. The more developed of the region's states were modestly increasing their purchase of western goods, with Hungary's imports 8.4 per cent higher in 1989 than 1988, East Germany's nearly 6.7 per cent higher, and Poland's 4.4 per cent higher. Hungary and East Germany also registered healthy increases in exports to the West, 7.4 per cent and 9.5 per cent respectively, while Poland managed a 1.9 per cent increase. Czechoslovakia's performance was more erratic with a substantial increase in exports (10.8 per cent) but a slight drop in imports (1.6 per cent). Romania continued to cut its imports (2.6 per cent), but for the first time also displayed a fall (of 3.6 per cent) in exports to the West.[11]

Those states whose relations with the West were already on the upswing continued this movement after the revolutions, in some cases dramatically. Polish exports to the West grew by more than 41 per cent in 1990, to the point where this region accounted for two-thirds of all Polish trade. Nor was this gain accounted for by simply selling more Polish coal. The country's export of machinery, which has been steadily increasing, is its biggest export item, accounting for nearly twice the convertible currency value of coal exports. Czechoslovakia saw a similar jump over the first half of 1990 and, unlike Poland, whose debt forced it to sharply limit its imports of western goods, Czechoslovak imports from the developed West grew by more than 50 per cent. By the end of 1990 the developed West's share of Czechoslovakia's trade exceeded 40 per cent. Hungary's exports to the developed countries grew by more than 17 per cent and its imports by 5.6 per cent in the first six months of 1990. East Germany before its absorption was moving in a similar direction: exports to the developed West were up

9.5 per cent in the first third of 1990 and imports were up 6.7 per cent. Romania reversed its restrictions on imports and those from the West grew to take a share of more than 30 per cent. But the disastrous state of the economy meant that exports for 1990 to all regions, including the West, fell. For most of the region the expansion of favorable trading opportunities, such as the extension of Most Favored Nation (MFN) trade status by the United States and the relaxing of export controls by the multilateral coordinating committee (COCOM) partners, eased this western reorientation of trading opportunities.[12]

Most of the East European states saw an increase in their imports from developing countries, accounted for chiefly but not entirely by oil imports as the Soviet economy sputtered. Because of the difficulties and then disintegration of the Soviet economy, Soviet-East European trade fell even more sharply in 1991. Exports to East Europe fell by 45 per cent in the first six months of 1991 (compared to the first six months of 1990) while imports declined by 55 per cent over the comparable period.

Aid and Credits   The increase in trade with the West was accompanied by an outpouring of various forms of aid from the western industrialized nations. The Soviet Union had received more than 16 000 tons of food and other aid by December, 1990, in the face of reports of food shortages.[13] During 1990 the European Community pledged more than US$1.3 billion for the East European states under its PHARE program (Polish and Hungarian Assistance for the Reconstruction of Europe), plus another US$1.5 billion for currency stabilization funds for Hungary and Czechoslovakia, a separate US$1 billion in direct loans to Hungary, and other loans through the European Bank for Reconstruction and Development (EBRD) to Poland and Hungary. The Community also agreed to lend Yugoslavia more than US$1 billion over five years.[14] In all, the group of 24 western industrial nations offered a program of more than US$21 billion.[15] Individual countries of the West have been offering expanded bilateral aid and credits, most of which are tied to the economies of the givers and all of which serves to expand the level and breadth of connections between their economies. Germany, the most powerful of the European economies, has gone furthest in this regard, absorbing the entire economy of what used to be East Germany. But it has also pledged to the USSR some US$3 billion in guaranteed loans plus an additional US$8 billion to cover the costs of the withdrawal of over 360 000 troops plus dependents from former East German territory. In December, 1990, Germany agreed to a US$67 million aid and loan package for Hungary. France, Spain, and Italy all offered aid or credit packages to the USSR tied to their own countries' economies.[16]

The Role of the Clubs   In addition to functioning as a general model, the European ideal is embodied in a number of powerful international institutions. Some, such as the Council of Europe, are the institutional representation of the legal and political ideals to which the governments and systems of Europe have pledged themselves, e.g. parliamentary democracy, full expression of human and civil rights. Others, such as the European Community, are the result of a more laborious process of making an economic entity out of political affinity. Still others, such as NATO, include significant and powerful non-European components. Each of these organizations represents a successful, even if incomplete, institutionalization of common values—in stark contrast to the hegemonic imposition of organizational structures which has been common in the East.

As such, they exercise a powerful pull on the newly "rejoined" states of the East. Some hold out the promise of full membership which, when it happens, signals acceptance. The Council of Europe for example in 1989 extended guest status to Bulgaria, Hungary, Poland, the Soviet Union, and Yugoslavia, sent missions to observe elections in several states during 1990 and in October, 1990, formally accepted its first East European state, Hungary. At the same time the Council held out the prospect of membership to Poland, with an explicit condition: the holding of fully free national elections. The new East European leaderships made it clear that they see entrance into the Council of Europe as representing their acceptance into the European community of values. And they have not been shy about indicating that they see this action as merely a first step to more fully joining Europe by, for example, joining the European Community.[17]

Some of these organizations offer other concrete but less than full forms of association to the East European states. The European Community began discussions about establishing "association" agreements with Czechoslovakia, Poland, and Hungary.[18] NATO was cool to the possibility of having East European states join but nevertheless engendered discussions about expanding NATO's role, to make it more expressly political.[19] Meanwhile NATO Secretary General Manfred Woerner has been extremely active in organizational diplomacy throughout the region.[20]

Probably the most powerful of the "clubs," and the one exercising the most direct effect on the recreation of market-like economies in East Europe, is the IMF. While no stranger to the region—IMF programs were negotiated with Romania, Hungary, and Yugoslavia during the 1980s—the organization is now offering funds and guidance to virtually all the East European states. Most of the East European countries have shown themselves eager to tap the resources of the organization and willing to implement the specific policies the IMF insists on. Because an IMF program is usually a condition for further negotiations on outstanding debt issues by western creditors, the IMF's clout in the most debt ridden is enormous. In December, 1990, for example, the Hungarian government reformulated its 1991 budget to produce one with a substantially reduced deficit, in order to qualify for a US$1 billion credit extended by the IMF for that year.[21] In February, 1991, Bulgaria—which had stopped payments on its debt—raised its prime interest rate by a factor of three and removed most price controls in order to secure approval of an IMF package.[22]

Transnational Ties Helping this process of integration along is a greatly expanded openness of borders, tourist traffic, and the steady hectoring by members of what might be termed the world capitalist university: economic advisors, bankers, lawyers, theorists, specialists, and company presidents who have been jamming the outer offices of policymakers in East Europe. Their steady provision of dollars and *diktat* encourages the replication of non-communist economic systems and their further interconnection with those of the West.[23]

Probably the most visible of the transnational contacts lies in the area of joint ventures. Western—and predominantly West European[24]—businesses have moved quickly to explore opportunities in East Europe and the USSR. Some high profile deals have been struck, such as the purchase of Hungary's Tungsram by General Electric and the awarding of a share of Czechoslovakia's Skoda autoworks to Volkswagen. By one estimate some 10 000 joint venture contracts had been signed by the end of 1990. The proportion of those actually functioning however is much smaller, less than half, for example, in Poland.[25] But in response to clearly expressed preferences, all of the East European states have promised or enacted new legislation removing some of the more troublesome aspects of joint venture legislation. Romania, for example, adopted new rules expanding the areas of permitted operation of joint ventures, removing import duties on capital imported for such operations, allowing tax holidays and reductions for reinvestment, and allowing limited repatriation of profits in hard currency. At the end of 1990, Hungary removed its authorization requirements for joint ventures with Hungarian non-state companies or for those which did not involve more than 10 per cent of state assets.[26]

The Uses of Foreign Policy

The new governments of East Europe have found themselves somewhat adrift with the collapse of the Soviet-created system of European and international ties. The parameters of foreign policy action had been circumscribed in the past and several international issues were muted altogether by Soviet hegemony. Approaches to the West were possible, depending on who made them, but expressions of Soviet displeasure ranging from concern to active intervention could be counted on. Romanian recognition of West Germany in 1967, for example, provoked a hasty Warsaw Pact summit at which the next likely suitors Czechoslovakia and Hungary were restrained. And from time to time the Kremlin attempted to orchestrate a more unified front against Chinese hostility.

The disappearance of such parameters meant opportunities for the new East European governments to pursue ties in accordance with goals determined at home, and in accordance with their expressed desire to "join Europe." This spawned, for example, the active diplomacy of Vaclav Havel and of both President Arpad Goncz and Prime Minister Jozef Antall of Hungary, and the wooing of the West European multilateral organizations mentioned above.[27] The purpose of such activity is not simply to take advantage of long denied opportunities. It is designed to provide the new regimes with a new type of security in two senses. First—and this is especially evident in central Europe—it represents a *search for a new constituency,* a new reference group for the states involved. No longer within the Soviet family, the governments of these states seek to reduce not just their isolation, but their vulnerability to being forced to return to that family. In 1989 and 1990, the changes in East Europe outpaced those in the Soviet Union from whence they had sprung. Given the history of Soviet-East European relations, there remained the possibility that Moscow would try to reverse this progress. Especially after the resignation of Foreign Minister Edvard Shevardnadze and many others associated with reform in the USSR, the apparent rise of conservative influence around Mikhail Gorbachev during the end of 1990 and in particular the use of military force against the independence movements in the Baltic states at the beginning of 1991 concern increased. From the East European point of view, then, the sooner Poland, Hungary, and Czechoslovakia negotiated the removal of Soviet troops from their territories and their own acceptance into the West, the better.[28] The more they become part of the West, part of an active international group which welcomes them and supports them, the less chance there will be that if something untoward should happen in Moscow—or Minsk—they will be pulled back into the East. The people and leaders of this region have seen enough evidence of the fact that shifts in developments can have dramatic consequences for them[29] to fear that if a retrograde leadership were to come to power in certain powerful states of the Commonwealth (e.g. Russia, Ukraine), their situation could become more dangerous.

Several East European states moved to partly mitigate these possible effects of Soviet disaggregation by direct arrangements with republics and through the search for new trade partners. In the autumn of 1990, Hungary announced the establishment of consular relations and the intention to establish full diplomatic relations with Ukraine; Poland signed similar declarations with the Russian Federation and with Ukraine.[30]

In addition, the disaggregation of the Soviet Union as an economic entity poses enormous dangers for East Europe. As can be seen in the oil trade, the difficulties in its own system—which have been compounded by autarchic tendencies in the republics—are causing the East European states difficulties even apart from those related to transition. For the same reason, several countries became active in securing oil supplies directly from Soviet republics or from other suppliers. Czechoslovakia, for example, purchased 200 000 tons of oil directly from the Tyumen oblast in Siberia and moved to secure new gas supplies from Algeria and oil from Iran.[31]

The disintegration or collapse of the major successor states could have catastrophic consequences for these small states and economies.[32] The possibility of a massive emigration from the USSR into East Europe prompted Poland and Czechoslovakia among others to prepare contingency measures to accept the refugees many of whom would not be able to pass on to what is presumed to be their final destination, West Europe.[33] The burden of these people—added to numerous East European refugees moving from south to north[34]—will increase the cost and decrease the flexibility of the East European states.

The search for a new constituency is also behind several foreign policy initiatives involving former East European states which cut across former cold war boundaries. Hungary and Czechoslovakia have been active in the creation of the so-called "Pentagonal Initiative." This intermittent conference, involving these two states plus Yugoslavia, Italy, and Austria, cuts across former bloc lines and is aimed at increasing cooperation in key areas such as transportation and environmental protection.[35] A similar initiative has grown up around the Black Sea,[36] and in February, 1991, the presidents of Hungary, Poland, and Czechoslovakia met at Visegrad, Hungary, to pledge joint cooperation in a number of areas.[37]

A second form of security derives from uses of foreign policy domestically The new governments of East Europe came to power with a popularity and a legitimacy based on having made—or steered—the revolution. Yet all were faced with the immense task of not only constructing a plausible democratic system, but also restoring their countries to economic health. While East Germany had the popular and ultimately irresistable option of being absorbed by the West, such a course was not available elsewhere. Instead, painful and difficult choices were needed. These involved for-mulating policies which sounded like what people said they wanted ("a market econ-omy") but which also sounded like what they did *not* want (unemployment, inflation). The drastic measures instituted by Poland at the beginning of 1990 and the electoral results seemed to illustrate both the pain and the gain of an abrupt switch.

Faced with such tasks, the new governments have found that foreign policy offers an effective tool for achieving or retaining some of the popularity which domestic pol-icy actions do not. They can do things abroad which will win them acclaim—espe-cially if they reverse long held communist policies to which people objected. Hungary, for example, began to speak out much more sharply on the status of the Hungarian minority in Romania. Czechoslovakia (and all the other states) resumed diplomatic relations with Israel. Hungary, Czechoslovakia, and, more slowly, Poland began nego-tiations to remove Soviet troops from their countries. Hungary vigorously pushed for the reformation of the Warsaw Pact and announced that in any case it was leaving the military arm of the organization.[38] These actions not only moved these central Euro-pean states toward membership in a different constituency, but were popular at home and allowed the build up of something the previous regimes never held—political legitimacy.

Moreover these policies accord with those of the West in most cases and bring the East European states in closer international political alignment with them. This con-tributes to their appearance as more "similar systems" and in some cases improves their chance for increasing economic support. For example, all of the East European states lined up behind United Nations sanctions imposed on Iraq because of its August, 1990, invasion of Kuwait and the war which began in January, 1991. All also approved the sending of medical or chemical warfare support groups to the Persian Gulf.[39] This placed them, for the first time for most of them, clearly on the side of the West in a major international dispute and moreover allowed them to put forth claims for the sub-stantial losses suffered as a result of this allegiance. These include losses of debt repayments, the cost of securing higher priced oil and the estimated loss of expected exports. Romania, Poland, and Bulgaria were especially hard hit; for all of the East European states the World Bank estimated the cost to be US$15 billion. The USSR estimated its own losses at US$10 billion.[40]

Increased Vulnerability

The losses arising from the crisis in the Persian Gulf illustrate starkly a key aspect of the region's movement west: the increase in its vulnerability. The states of East Europe spent most of the post-war period relatively isolated from the vicissitudes of the capi-talist global economy. Their relatively closed planning-dominated and Soviet oriented systems could not protect them forever from the changing dynamics of the world economy. And those who had ventured furthest tended to be those that suffered the most serious negative consequences, with Poland being the best example.[41]

The new situation means that as the restrictions of the former "closed" system depart, so too will its protection. This is most evident in the area of price and supply of commodities. With an eagerness bordering on naivete, the new governments of East

Europe in late 1989 pushed the Soviet Union to move CMEA trading to world prices denominated in hard currencies. Most were at the time running trade surpluses with the USSR. At the January, 1990, summit meeting of the CMEA it was decided to move in this direction, which Moscow quickly realized would work to its advantage. The switch to hard currency pricing and accounting in 1991 (including for some barter trade which remains) would have benefitted the USSR. The brief increase in the price of oil caused by the tensions in the Persian Gulf was estimated to have cost the East European states some US$3.5 billion in 1990 alone. But a drop in Soviet oil production attributable to problems in the Soviet economy[42] and sharp cuts in oil exports to the East European states—by an average 30 per cent—meant that these states had to seek other suppliers. By mid-1991, for example, Saudi Arabia had become Romania's chief source of crude oil.[43]

The switch in trade also hurts the East European states whose overpriced, Soviet-oriented manufactured goods have to be greatly reduced in price or greatly improved, or both, if they are to be sold in the West. This need has been made all the greater by the severe drop in Soviet imports of East European goods. Some of the East European states, for example Poland, have been able to maintain trade surpluses with the West. But others, such as Bulgaria, suffering serious dislocations, needing more imports—which now have to be paid for at world prices in hard currency—but having less to sell themselves for hard currency are incurring unwelcome burdens of deficits and debt.

This kind of vulnerability reinforces the desire on the part of the Central European governments to increase their integration with the West—even while it makes them politically vulnerable (see below). The need to improve quality and the capacity of production means a greater need to attract western capital, technology, and know-how in order to allow their economies to compete. Hence the expanded interest in western joint venture partners.

There Goes the Neighborhood

One of the other reasons for the rapid movement West is that there is no place to go home to. CMEA, never very vigorous before the revolutions, was pronounced dead less than a year after.[44] Moreover, the dominant economy of the organization, that of the Soviet Union, was in no position to continue exercising the influence it once did as even its own republics pursue increasingly autarchic economic policies.

Similarly, the Warsaw Pact lost its political base—which never went lower than the collective leadership of the states in any case—and even its *raison d'etre,* with the reunification of Germany to which the USSR acquiesced. Those Central European states which had formed the "iron triangle" against a supposed western invasion indicated their desire to either leave the organization or to so transform it as to render it unrecognizable. The Pact's most important—and explosive—function had always been to symbolize, and on occasion to protect, Soviet security interests in the region. When in 1989 Mikhail Gorbachev made it clear that this would no longer be the case, even the unacknowledged rationale for the presence of Soviet troops in the region (the "Brezhnev doctrine") disappeared.[45]

NOT SO FAST . . .

As eager as the new governments appear to be to move their economies and policies into step with the West and as impossible as retreat to the East appears to be, progress has been uneven. Several factors contribute to restrain integration of East with West.

The Costs

Chief among these is the sheer cost of wrenching these economies out of state socialism. To compete internationally requires substantial new investment, most of which cannot be financed by the countries themselves. Economies already groaning under the burden of debt have to take on even more in order to put a firm ground under their transition. Some have commodities or products to sell on the world market which will enable them to earn their own funds—for example Poland earned a US$4.7 billion surplus in hard currency trade in 1990. But others—especially those without natural resource endowments—will find themselves well behind in the race for sales, especially in the higher profit manufactured goods areas. In addition, all face the double burden of having to finance both redevelopment and environmental cleanup.[46]

Domestically, establishing prices which reflect production costs, relative scarcity, and the price of inputs (especially those from abroad) means dramatic increases in the prices of rents, food, fuel, and virtually anything else not subsidized by the government. All of the East European states either instituted state-mandated price increases or allowed prices to float freely during 1990 and 1991. This produced inflation rates ranging from roughly 20 per cent in Romania to 70 per cent in Poland.[47]

Such increases hit the newly liberated consumers of East Europe with a double blow. First, in anticipation of price increases typically announced in advance by nervous governments, suppliers hold back and the market becomes even more barren. Then when increases come into effect, goods return but at prices which shock societies accustomed to poor supply but low relative prices. Gains in time for the consumer allowed by the elimination of lines or the need for scavenging the city for goods— what economists call the increased "efficiency of money"—may be insufficient to offset the shock of higher prices.[48] The governments of East Europe thus are faced with the choice of keeping up subsidies—which is part of the reason their predecessors got into trouble in the first place—or abandoning them and suffering the political consequences.

The size of the need may also act as a brake to the development of full and rapid ties. The European Bank for Reconstruction and Development has only been modestly capitalized (US$12 billion) and will almost certainly sustain substantial losses at first. Founding members were slow to pass the national legislation necessary for ratifying the bank charter and filling key positions has been difficult.[49] The United States, the largest western economy, has been parsimonious in its promise of economic aid, pledging roughly US$400 million for East Europe in 1990 and 1991. Criticisms and calls for greater involvement have been frequent.[50] The BIS estimates that the difference between aid offered and East Europe's needs for 1991 alone will be US$7 billion.[51] The ability and interest of the West in aiding the East European recovery may be further inhibited by the costs to the western economies of the disruption in oil price and supply caused by the Gulf crisis. This contributed to recessionary directions in most western economies. During the first nine months of 1990 the Bank for International Settlements reported a 7 per cent drop in western lending to East Europe.[52] Moreover the country with one of the strongest economies, Germany, has directed its considerable resources towards the absorption and reconstruction of East Germany and at shoring up the crumbling Soviet economy.

By the same token it has always been the USSR which has represented the great prize to the West because of the size of its natural resources and potential market, plus its political power. Western states and others dealt with select East European states, of course, usually in pursuit of specific policy goals, e.g. free emigration, or the overall aim of eroding Soviet dominance and the division of Europe. Now, it is clearly not in the interest of these same states to have the new commonwealth break up suddenly and violently. Nor, evidently, do many in the west want the countries, broken up or not, to sink into abject economic chaos or poverty. The Western response to the Russian food crisis and the push on the part of the European Community and the United States to generate aid demonstrate that. If this continues, and given the size and scope of the Commonwealth's needs, what will be left for the states of East Europe?

Nor is the West necessarily welcoming all with open arms. Reference has already been made to the economic burdens. Politically the institutions which function in Europe have been engaged in a multisided debate of their own over how to parcel out the responsibility for the new "European architecture." The Council of Europe has been lobbying for a key role in the civic and political rights dimension to which the CSCE (Conference on Security and Cooperation in Europe) actors are also staking a claim.[53] The former has kept clear standards of admission to the new supplicants of East Europe. As of early 1991 only Hungary and Czechoslovakia had been admitted as full members.

More restrained yet has been the response of the European Community to the prospect of eastern members. The transformations of 1992 are bearing down on the organization and significant political struggles are still going on related to issues such as agricultural prices. Moreover the indirect absorption of East Germany has only just begun. Rapid entrance into the Community by many East European states is unlikely.[54] To these preoccupations of the EC is added their own fear that economic transformation in East Europe and the USSR will unleash a flood of immigrants who will burden the economies of the EC. Such apprehensions will make favorable policy moves on issues such as borders more difficult and retard the overall process of "connecting" the East with the West.[55] To some extent the cost of remaining outside can be mitigated by special arrangements, such as those that were for years in force between East Europe and Yugoslavia. But the full integration of the economies of the East will be hindered as long as they remain outside such community arrangements as the free movement of labor or the common agricultural policy.

Stragglers on the Road

In any case not all the East European states will enjoy the "simultaneous transition" to capitalism. While Poland, Hungary, and Czechoslovakia have enjoyed the loud cheering and significant support of the West, Bulgaria and Romania find themselves waiting in the ante room. Both countries elected parties and people who were members of the former communist regime, and both moved noticeably slowly toward formulating or implementing economic reform. Romania in particular alienated much of the western community because of the use by President Ion Iliescu of miners and "miners" to attack and disrupt a long standing anti-government demonstration in Bucharest in June, 1990. Judging by the external balance sheet of the country, with little or no hard currency debt and the presence of natural resources, Romania could be an attractive target for investment and involvement. But retrograde actions like the use of the miners and the apparent lack of a functioning political or parliamentary opposition have slowed down the acceptance.[56]

The Trials of Economic Reform

Probably the most important inhibiting factor in the short run will not be international at all but, as with the revolutions themselves, domestic. The "movement West" while reflecting a broad consensus, is not embraced everywhere and in all countries with equal vigor.

In Central Europe there are disagreements over how far and how fast the transformation should go. Privatization of assets, among other issues, has produced substantial debate, especially over the question of sale of the countries' assets to foreign investors. In Hungary the rapid sale of several hotels and newspapers to western chains at prices considered too low and with too little consultation prompted new laws and the creation of new agencies to oversee privatization.[57] One of the charges levelled by returning emigre presidential candidate Stanislaw Tyminski against the government of Polish Prime Minister Tadeusz Mazowiecki was that Mazowiecki had sold the country's business to foreigners too cheaply. Tyminski was unable to substantiate this charge and indeed few Polish businesses had been sold at all by that time, but the charge contributed to his unexpected second place finish in the first round of the Polish elections and the defeat of Mazowiecki in that election.[58]

Controversy has also grown substantially in the past year over the speed and cost of economic adjustment plans. This is most evident in the sphere of economic reform, to which all of the new governments are nominally committed. Only in Poland was rapid, comprehensive reform of the system of subsidies, guaranteed employment, and state planning and direction instituted immediately. The result, in some respects have been impressive, a stable, realistic value for the Polish zloty, the return of goods to the stores, a hard currency trade surplus, and a dramatic cut in the inflation rate. On the other hand, the appearance and rapid increase in unemployment, and the disparity which remains between the price of goods and the average Pole's salary provided a broad basis of political support for criticism of the reform policies and the government which instituted it, that of Tadeusz Mazowiecki. His defeat in the first round of the presidential election in November, 1990—not just by Lech Walesa but by a political unknown Stanislaw Tyminski—demonstrates the risk to any East European government bent on rapid economic reform.

Despite the long history of economic reform in Hungary and the apparent electoral mandate of the Hungarian Democratic Forum elected in the spring of 1990, this government was unable to institute a gasoline price rise in October, as a truck and taxi driver strike blocked roads throughout the country. Within two months of the strike, State Secretary for Economic Policy Gyorgy Matolcsy and Finance Minister Ferenc Rabar resigned as a result of a dispute over the pace of economic reform.[59]

Such a dispute was also evident in Czechoslovakia, where Finance Minister Vaclav Klaus needed to lobby vigorously, secure the backing of the country's most influential politician, Vaclav Havel, and carve a committed political force out of the ruling coalition in order to begin broader economic reform.[60] Small-scale privatization and, as noted, price increases, have begun. But the country's ability to follow through with a coherent national program has been called into question by the need to forge an effective federal system of government that will balance the demands for control coming from Slovakia with countervailing concerns in the Czech Republic.

Progress toward economic reform has been only halting in Bulgaria and Romania. The election of the Bulgarian Socialists (formerly communists) in June, 1990, provided a very small majority in the legislature (211 of 400 seats) and magnified the sharp polarization between those supporting the former ruling party and those supporting the opposition Union of Democratic Forces. Two successive governments headed by Andrey Lukanov presented two successive economic programs that failed to find legislative support. The second of these programs, presented in November, 1990, led to nationwide strikes and to the downfall of the government.[61]

In Romania, the National Salvation Front which replaced Nicolae Ceausescu won a resounding parliamentary victory (66 per cent) by offering only vague indications of transformation of the economic system and playing on the fears of the population of the pain of a "Polish solution." In the autumn, strikes and threatened strikes forced the government of Prime Minister Petre Roman to put off broadening the range of price increases that had begun in November, 1990, and were due to encompass food and other basic products in January, 1991. In both Bulgaria and Romania price increases were eventually implemented; in the former under a new government led by an opposition prime minister, in the latter after the prime minister secured the commitment of his ruling party to the process. But in both cases other key aspects of the process—especially privatization of assets—lagged behind.

At the level of society, policies which increase social stratification and are blamed for introducing unemployment, poverty, and crime are not likely to meet with universal acceptance. Forty years of socialism has instilled strong support for egalitarianism in the work force. Moreover, while the power and dominance of the communist parties were smashed in most cases, the nominal values and successor political organizations supporting them did not disappear. Communist candidates won 13 to 15 per cent of the vote in the national election in East Germany, Czechoslovakia, and Hungary during 1990; a successor party was in power in Bulgaria until late 1991 and still holds the majority in parliament in Romania. While firm conclusions must await stronger evidence, these results suggest a residual of support for both the ideals and the parties of communism. This would be strengthened by a painful or unsuccessful economic transformation.[62]

Finally, the expansion of the political stage throughout the region has allowed a strong upsurge of regional or ethnically based interests to assert themselves in several states. This has been most dramatic in the Soviet Union itself and in Yugoslavia, but regional prerogatives have been asserted in Czechoslovakia as well, for example over control of the country's oil and gas pipeline and its profitable arms industry.[63]

Even in those parts of Central and Eastern Europe where ethnic divisions are not predominant, local councils and communities have begun to assert their prerogatives on key issues, such as the use of national resources, economic investment, and ecological destruction.[64] In Poland farmers were the first to express their displeasure with the Mazowiecki government, and elections there showed Stanislaw Tyminski drawing the bulk of his support from rural districts.

The rural–urban split has already shown itself to be a critical fissure. Parliamentary election results in both Romania and Bulgaria showed, for example, much stronger support for the successor parties, the National Salvation Front and the Bulgarian Socialist party, in the countryside than in the cities. Partly this reflects an intense suspicion of "the city"—its intellectuals, its lifestyle, its political power—by much of the rural population.[65] For virtually all of the countries of East Europe this will mean opposition in the countryside to actions taken by reformers in "the center," based on the strong desire of a population now empowered to determine the effect of policies on their daily lives and communities.

CONCLUSION

From this analysis of roughly the first two years of shifting international connections and their impact on the new East Europe, it is evident that the "move west" is strong and is having a clear effect on the foreign policy of some of these states, in particular Poland, Czechoslovakia, and Hungary. All have found themselves vulnerable to international economic dislocation in a way they did not before and for most, foreign policy provides a more attractive and effective way to build and keep legitimacy than does making difficult choices dealing with the domestic economy.

A differentiation is evident in both domestic and foreign policy between the states of Central Europe and those of southeastern Europe, i.e. Romania and Bulgaria. The slower movement in the latter two is mirrored in the cooler reactions of western political and economic institutions to these regimes. But even in Central Europe, where the political commitment to radical reform is more evident, the burden of debt, the costs of transformation, the loss of the secure Soviet source of supply and purchase, and, most importantly, the difficulty of implementing a complicated and painful transition from planned to market economy act as powerful inhibiting factors.

The East European states have succeeded in producing democratic processes and institutions faster than they can be wielded. Within one year of the extraordinary revolutions of 1989 competitively elected national legislatures were in place in all but Poland and presidents elected by the people or parliament were in place in all. But precisely because of the competitiveness, the openness, the very democracy of the new systems, the economic rejoining of Europe may take a bit longer.

NOTES

1 For reviews of Soviet-East European relations see Zbigniew Brzezinski, *The Soviet Bloc: Unity and Conflict,* rev. ed. (Cambridge, MA: Harvard University Press, 1971);

James F. Brown, *Relations Between the Soviet Union and its East European Allies* (Santa Monica, CA: Rand Corp, 1975); Ronald H. Linden, *Bear and Foxes; the International Relations of the East European States* (Boulder, CO: East European Quarterly, 1979); Sarah M. Terry, *Soviet Policy in Eastern Europe* (New Haven, CT: Yale University Press, 1984); Charles Gati, *Hungary and the Soviet Bloc* (Durham, NC: Duke University Press, 1986).

2 United Nations, Economic Commission for Europe. *Economic Survey of Europe in 1986–1987* (New York: United Nations, 1987), p. 202. On earlier trade dominance and an illustration focusing on Poland, see Zbigniew Fallenbuchl, "The Commodity Composition of Intra-Comecon Trade and the Industrial Structure of the Member Countries," in NATO-Directorate of Economic Affairs, *Comecon: Progress and Prospects* (Brussels: NATO, 1977), pp. 103–134. On Romania see Ronald H. Linden, *Communist States and International Change: Romania and Yugoslavia in Comparative Perspective* (Boston, MA: Allen and Unwin, 1987), pp. 48–60, 69–84.

3 Gary Teske, "Poland's Trade with the Industrialized West: Performance, Problems and Prospects." Joint Economic Committee, *East European Economic Assessment,* pt. 1, "Country Studies, 1980" 97th Congress, pp. 72–95. John M. Montias, "Romania's Foreign Trade: An Overview," in Joint Economic Committee, *Eastern European Economics Post Helsinki,* 95th Congress (Washington, DC: USGPO, 1977), pp. 865–885. Ronald H. Linden, "Romania: The Search for Economic Sovereignty" in Joint Economic Committee, *Pressures for Reform in the East European Economics,* Vol. 1, "Study Papers," 101st Congress (Washington, DC: USGPO, 1989), pp. 291–306.

4 Michael Marrese and Jan Vanous, *Soviet Subsidization of Trade with Eastern Europe: A Soviet Perspective* (Berkeley, CA: University of California, Institute of International Studies, 1983). For a discussion of the challenges to Marrese and Vanous' analysis see Charles Gati, *The Bloc That Failed* (Bloomington, IN: Indiana Press, 1990), pp. 119–124. For a Soviet discussion see E. Sheynin, "Sotsialisticheskaya ekonomicheskaya integratsia: realnost' i vymysli"[Socialist economic integration: reality and falsehoods], *Vneshnaya Trogovlaia,* Vol. 3 (1986), pp. 38–42.

5 See the review of developments pre-1989 in James F. Brown, *Eastern Europe and Communist Rule* (Durham, NC: Duke University Press, 1988).

6 See Linden, *op. cit.,* note 1, pp. 53–176.

7 William Y. Wallace and Roger A. Clarke, *Comecon, Trade and the West* (London: Frances Pinter, 1986). Zbigniew Fallenbuchl, "The Council for Mutual Economic Assistance and Eastern Europe," *International Journal,* Vol. XLIII, No. 1 (Winter 1987–1988), pp. 106–126.

8 Egon Neuberger, Richard Portes, and Laura D. Tyson, "The Impact of International Economic Disturbances on the Soviet Union and Eastern Europe: A Survey," Joint Economic Committee, *East European Economic Assessment,* Part 2, Regional Assessment, 97th Congress (Washington DC, 1981), pp. 128–147. Laura D'Andrea Tyson, "The Debt Crisis and Adjustment Responses in Eastern Europe: a Comparative Perspective," *International Organization,* Vol. 40, No. 2 (Spring, 1986), pp. 239–285.

9 For a review of the developments of 1989 see "1989: A Year of Upheaval" *Report on Eastern Europe,* Vol. 1, No. 1 (January 5, 1990); on the establishment of parliaments and elections see "Toward Democracy in Eastern Europe," *Report on Eastern Europe,* Vol. 1, No. 28 (July 13, 1990). For an example of a statement reflecting this view, see the interview with Bulgarian Prime Minister Dimitar Popov in *Die Welt,* December 27, 1990.

10 Bulgarian exports, which had never been very robust, also did not increase. See Leyla Woods, "East European Trade with the Industrial West," in Joint Economic Committee, *Pressures for Reform in the East European Economies,* Vol. 2, "Study Papers," 101st Congress (Washington, USGPO, 1989), pp. 408–419.

11 Statistics in this section are drawn from data in *PlanEcon Report,* numbers 30–31, 37–38, and 39 for 1991; 13, 14–15, 18–19 and 44–45 for 1990; and 44–45 for 1989. The discussion of Soviet trade is drawn from *PlanEcon Report,* No. 51–52 (January 10, 1992), pp. 2–7.

12 In December, 1990, for example, the COCOM agreed to a special exemption for Hungary in advanced of reductions in controls expected to follow. By the end of 1991 all the East European countries had received MFN from the United States except Albania and Romania.

13 The largest donor by far was Germany which also planned to ship to the USSR its entire stock of food and other items stored in Berlin against the possibility of another blockade. *AP,* November 30, 1990.

14 *RFE* Correspondent's Report (Brussels), December 20, 1990.

15 For a review of western actions see J.M.C. Rollo, *The New Eastern Europe: Western Responses* (London: Frances Pinter, 1990), pp. 116–132.

16 *AFP,* October 29, 1990; *International Herald Tribune,* October 29, 1990; *Commersant,* November 26, 1990, p. 6.

17 Richard Weitz, "The Council of Europe and the East," *Report on Eastern Europe,* Vol. 1, No. 34 (August 24, 1990), pp. 50–51; *RFE* correspondent's report (Strasbourg), October 2, 1990.

18 *DPA,* December 18, 1990. Association Agreements were signed in December, 1991.

19 This was reflected in the final statement of the heads of state of NATO who met in London in July, 1990 (*AP,* July 6, 1990) and of the foreign ministers who met in Brussels in December (*AFP,* December 18, 1990). For NATO's reaction to possible Bulgarian membership see *Reuter,* November 27, 1990. NATO's parliament, the North Atlantic Assembly did grant "associate delegate" status to Bulgaria, Czechoslovakia, Hungary, Poland, and the USSR in November, 1990.

20 Woerner visited Moscow in July, Prague and Warsaw in September, and Budapest in November, 1990. In addition, the Conference on Security and Cooperation in Europe (CSCE), which already included all the East European states as members, began developing new institutions, such as a secretariat based in Prague, in an attempt to take a more permanent and visible role in building the new Europe. In September, 1990 it did act as a gatekeeper by accepting as an observer the one European state which heretofore had declined to join, Albania.

21 *AP,* December 31, 1990; *Radio Budapest,* January 2, 1991. For a review of IMF lending see *Handelsblatt,* December 31, 1990. In January, 1991, Albania announced its intention to apply for IMF membership (*DPA,* January 13, 1991).

22 *AP,* February 2, 1991.

23 Such traffic also proceeds in the other direction. Miklos Nemeth, prime minister of Hungary during 1989–1990 and Boris Fedorov, once the minister of finance for the Russian federation of the USSR, joined the new European Bank for Reconstruction and Development.

24 During the first three-quarters of 1990 the United States accounted for only 3 per cent of the acquisition made by foreigners in East Europe and the Soviet Union and only 14 per cent of the joint ventures. It ranked third behind Germany and France. *New York Times,* December 23, 1990.

25 Marvin Jackson, "The International Economic Situation and Eastern Europe," *Report on Eastern Europe,* Vol. 1. No. 52 (December 28, 1990) p. 39.

26 *Monitorul Oficial al Romaniei,* Annul II, Nr. 37, March 20, 1990. *Business East Europe,* January 14, 1991, p. 12; *Hungarian Rules of Law in Force,* Nr. 11/5, 1991.

27 See Jan Obrman, "Foreign Policy: Sources, Concepts, Problems," *Report on Eastern Europe,* Vol. 1, No. 37 (September 14, 1990), pp. 6–16; Jan Obrman, "Putting the Country Back on the Map," *Report on Eastern Europe,* Vol. 1, No. 52 (December 28, 1990), pp. 10–14; Alfred Reisch, "The Hungarian Dilemma: After the Warsaw Pact, Neutrality or NATO?" *Report on Eastern Europe,* Vol. 1, No. 15 (April 13, 1990), pp. 16–22; Alfred Reisch, "Primary Foreign Policy Objective to Rejoin Europe," *Report on Eastern Europe,* Vol. 1. No. 52 (December 28, 1990), pp. 15–20.

28 For a review of East European reactions to the crackdown in the Baltics see *Report on Eastern Europe,* Vol. 2, No. 6 (February 8, 1991), pp. 23–37.

29 See, for example, Charles Gati, *op. cit.* note 1, pp. 127–155.

30 *Tass,* September 27, 1990; *East European Markets,* October 19, 1990, p. 14.

31 *Financial Times,* December 19, 1990; *Radio Prague,* November 15, 1990; *Radio Czechoslovakia,* December 2, 1990. Hungary and Romania also made deals with Iran; *MTI* (in English), January 30, 1991; *Radio Bucharest,* February 20, 1991.

32 See for example the statement by Col. Zbigniev Skoczylas, the director of a new bureau opened at the Polish ministry of the interior to deal with the possibility of up to two million refugees leaving the USSR: "If this horror was to happen," Skoczylas said, "Poland would fall apart as a state, as an economic system, in two or three months." *AP,* December 7, 1990. Similar sentiments were voiced in Czechoslovakia; see *Ceteka* (in English), December 10, 1990.

33 Poland set up a special office in the interior ministry; Czechoslovakia began to set up camps near the Soviet border and both these countries and Hungary redeployed troops to handle an expected flow of refugees. *Ceteka* (in English), December 20, 1990; *The Times* (London) December 27, 1990; *Washington Post,* December 24, 1990; *Die Welt,* February 8, 1991.

34 Poland reported nearly one million more visitors in 1990 than in 1989 and estimated that some 25 000 refugees from Romania alone were in the country. *New York Times,* December 26, 1990.

35 *MTI* (in English), July 30, 1990; see also, Patrick Moore, "New Dimensions for the Alpine–Adria Project," *Report on Eastern Europe,* Vol. 1, No. 9 (March 2, 1990), pp. 53–56. In mid-1991 the group became the "Hexagonale" when Poland joined.

36 In December, 1990, Turkey, the USSR, Bulgaria, and Romania met in Ankara to discuss the possibility of establishing a Black Sea "economic cooperation region." *Reuter,* December 19, 1990.

37 See the text of the Visegrad declaration, *MTI,* February 15, 1991.

38 *Financial Times,* June 11, 1990; *Reuter,* June 26, 1990 and November 20, 1990.

39 Saudi Arabia did not approve the sending of the Bulgarian contingent. Czechoslovakia also sold Saudi Arabia six planeloads of gas masks; Bulgaria and Romania offered US troops the use of holiday resort facilities.

40 *Reuter,* October 23, 1990; *TASS,* October 28, 1990. In addition to other forms of aid received from the European Community, Bulgaria was designated as a recipient of aid from the United Nations designed to reduce the losses suffered from the sanctions. *AP,* November 28, 1990; *Radio Sofia,* December 12 and 13, 1990.

41 See Teske, *op. cit.,* note 3.

42 By mid-1991 Soviet oil production had fallen from 12.5 million barrels per day (mbd) to 10 mbd; *Financial Times,* September 9, 1991, see the discussion in *PlanEcon Report,* No. 46–47 (November 23, 1990), pp. 20–23 and the report on an interview with Soviet minister of gas and oil, Leonid Filimonov, *TASS,* February 6, 1991.

43 *PlanEcon Report,* No. 39 (October 31, 1991), p. 9.

44 A new organization, originally called the Organization for International Economic Cooperation, was supposed to replace CMEA according to the communique of the CMEA Executive Council, *CTK* (in English), January 5, 1991. In June, 1991, a renamed Economic Forum met in Sofia; BTA, June 28, 1991 (*Foreign Broadcast Information Service,* July 10, 1991, p.1).

45 In February, 1991 the six remaining Warsaw Pact states dismantled the military cooperation mechanisms of the Pact and declared their intention to end political aspects as well by the end of the year. *Reuter,* February 25, 1991.

46 Hilary F. French, *Green Revolutions: Environmental Reconstruction in Eastern Europe and the Soviet Union.* Worldwatch Paper 99 (Washington, DC: Worldwatch Institute, 1990); "The Soviet Union and Eastern Europe," *Environmental Policy Review,* Vol. 4, No. 2 (July, 1990), entire issue.

47 See Marvin Jackson, "The Economic Situation in Eastern Europe 1990," *Report on Eastern Europe,* Vol. 2, No. 1 (January 4, 1991), pp. 55.

48 I am indebted to Marvin Jackson for alerting me to this point.

49 *Reuter,* October 18, 1990; *AP,* November 27, 1990.

50 See the Statement by Czechoslovak President Vaclav Havel, *AP,* October 29, 1990.

51 *AP,* October 23, 1990.

52 *AP,* February 14, 1991.

53 In September, 1990, the Council of Europe was host to a colloquy on "Europe: the roads to democracy, The Council of Europe and the 'architecture' of Europe." Strasbourg, France, September 18–19, 1990. In November, 1990, the CSCE nations held a summit at which a new "Charter of Paris for a new Europe," a treaty on conventional forces and a joint non-aggression declaration were signed. For texts of Charter and declaration, see *NATO Review,* No. 6 (December, 1990), pp. 26–31.

54 See, for example, the statement by German Chancellor Helmut Kohl warning against early entry of East European states into the EC; *Reuter,* September 27, 1990.

55 One of the first acts of the new united German government was to reinstate visa requirements for citizens of Poland. The requirements were lifted by Germany and five other EC countries in March, 1991.

56 Mark Almond, "Romania Since the Revolution," *Government and Opposition,* Vol. 25, No. 4 (1990), pp. 484–496. Romania was granted guest status in the Council of Europe and included in G-24 aid programs only in January, 1991.

57 *Financial Times,* September 20, 1990; *Los Angeles Times,* May 19, 1990; *New York Times,* September 9, 1990.

58 See Louisa Vinton, "Walesa and Tyminski in the Second Round," *Report on Eastern Europe,* Vol. 1, No. 51 (December 21, 1990), pp. 10–13. See also Anne Applebaum, "Who Owns Central Europe?" *The American Spectator,* Vol. 24, No. 2 (February 1991), pp. 14–16.

59 *Radio Budapest,* November 28 and December 12, 1990. Gasoline and transportation prices were eventually increased in January, 1991. *Radio Budapest,* December 20, 1990, *MTI* (in English), January 15, 1991.

60 *Die Presse,* December 14, 1990; *Financial Times,* October 24 and November 19, 1990. Jiri Pehe, "The Civic Forum Splits into Two Groups," *Report on Eastern Europe,* Vol. 2, No. 10 (March 8, 1991), pp. 11–14.

61 Duncan Perry, "Lukanov's Government Resigns: New Prime Minister Nominated," *Report on Eastern Europe,* No. 51 (December 21, 1990), pp. 1–5.

62 See the statement by Czechoslovak communist party leader Vasil Mohorita about the party's intent to fight economic reform: the *Daily Telegraph,* October 9, 1990. See also the statement of the Czechoslovak communist party congress (November, 1990). *CTK* (in English), November 4, 1990. In February, 1991, a leaflet circulating in Pleven, Bulgaria, listed three columns of prices for food, one under the Bulgarian communist party, one under the Socialists and one under the Presidency of Zhelyu Zhelev, who headed the opposition Union of Democratic Forces. *Radio Sofia,* February 7, 1991.

63 *Reuter,* December 12, 1990: *Financial Times,* January 22, 1991.

64 See for example, "Local Councils Worry Investors," *East European Markets,* October 5, 1990. In December, 1990, representatives of the Federation of Free Trade Unions from Timisoara, Romania, demanded economic independence for the region. *AFP,* December 30, 1990.

65 See, for example, Rada Nikolaev, "Results of the National Elections," *Report on Eastern Europe,* No. 26 (June 29, 1990); Mark Baskin, "Bulgaria" Paper delivered at annual meeting of the American Association for the Advancement of Slavic Studies, Washington, DC, October 19, 1990. Mihnea Berindei and Ariadna Combes, "An Analysis of the Romanian Elections," *Uncaptive Minds,* Vol. II. No. 4 (1990), pp. 21–23.

CHAPTER 14

THE EAST ASIAN MIRACLE: BUILDING A BASIS FOR GROWTH

John Page

Outsiders have pondered the success of East Asia—what some call a "miracle"—with wonder and admiration. Never before have countries expanded so fast for so long. From 1965 to 1990, the region's 23 economies grew faster than those of all other regions (see Figure 14-1), and income inequality declined, sometimes dramatically. Most of this achievement can be attributed to the stellar growth performance of eight economies: Japan; the "four tigers"—Hong Kong, the Republic of Korea, Singapore, and Taiwan Province of China; and the three newly industrializing economies (NIEs) of Southeast Asia—Indonesia, Malaysia, and Thailand.

Moreover, these eight economies share other characteristics that set them apart from other developing economies. These include:

- more rapid output and productivity growth in agriculture;
- higher rates of growth of manufactured exports, with their share of world exports of manufactures leaping from 9 percent in 1965 to 21 percent in 1990;
- earlier and steeper declines in fertility;
- higher growth rates of physical capital, exceeding 20 percent of GDP on average between 1960 and 1990, supported by higher rates of domestic savings (see Figure 14-2);
- higher initial levels and growth rates of human capital; and
- generally higher rates of productivity growth.

For a comprehensive discussion, see *The East Asian Miracle: Economic Growth and Public Policy,* a World Bank Policy Research Report published by the Oxford University Press, New York, NY, USA, 1993. This report was prepared by a team led by John Page and comprising Nancy Birdsall, Ed Campos, W. Max Corden, Chang-Shik Kim, Lawrence MacDonald, Howard Pack, Richard Sabot, Joseph Stiglitz, and Marilou Uy.

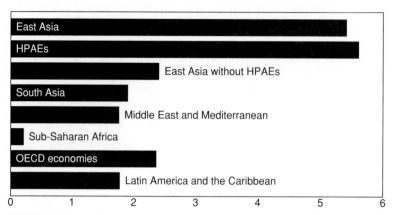

FIGURE 14-1
EAST ASIA'S STELLAR PERFORMANCE.
(average GNP per capita growth rate, in percent, 1965-90)

As other developing countries debate whether they can emulate East Asia's success, key questions arise. What were the sources of East Asia's success? What was the role of public policy in fostering growth? Can policies that were successful in East Asia be replicated by other economies?

In an effort to answer these questions, the World Bank undertook a major comparative study of economic growth and public policy in East Asia, *The East Asian Miracle* (see box). One of the key findings is that East Asia succeeded because it got the economic policy fundamentals right. Macroeconomic performance was unusually stable, providing the necessary framework for private investment. Policies to increase the integrity of the banking system and make it more accessible to nontraditional savers increased the levels of financial savings. Education policies that focused on primary and secondary education generated rapid increases in labor force skills. Agricultural policies stressed productivity change and did not tax the rural economy excessively. All of these economies kept price distortions within reasonable bounds and were open to foreign ideas and technology. To this extent, there was no economic "miracle"; East Asia's success simply reflects sound economics.

But these economic fundamentals do not tell the entire story. Almost all of the East Asian economies engaged, at one time or another, in some form of policy interventions—one of the most controversial aspects of development policy. Selective interventions took many forms, including mild repression of interest rates, directed credit, selective industrial promotion, and trade policies that pushed manufactured exports.

What was the relative role of economic fundamentals and intervention in East Asia's success? The study maintains that East Asian economies thrived because governments used a combination of fundamental and interventionist policies to (1) accumulate physical and human capital; (2) allocate this capital to highly productive investments; and (3) acquire and master technology and achieve rapid productivity growth.

Gross domestic investment

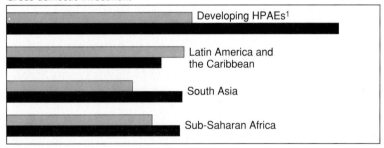

Gross domestic savings

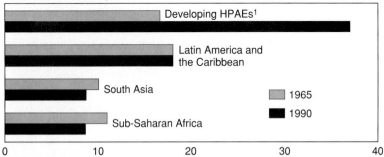

FIGURE 14-2
EXCEPTIONAL SAVINGS AND INVESTMENT RATES.
(percent of GDP)
Source: World Bank.
Note: The regional averages are unweighted.
[1] High performing Asian economies (HPAEs): Indonesia, Hong Kong, Japan, Malaysia, the Republic of Korea, Singapore, Taiwan Province of China, and Thailand.

ACCUMULATING CAPITAL

The East Asian economies accumulated both physical and human capital much more rapidly and consistently than other economies, accounting for a large portion of their superior performance.

Building Human Capital

East Asia began its rapid growth with an educational advantage over other developing economies and sustained that advantage through explicit policies of investing in basic education. Primary and secondary education levels were higher in these economies in the 1960s than in other low- and middle-income economies. Public spending concentrated on primary and secondary education. For example, in the mid-1980s, Indonesia, Korea, and Thailand devoted more than 80 percent of their education budget to basic education. Declining fertility and rapid economic growth meant that, even when education investment as a share of GDP remained constant, more resources were available per child in East Asia than in other developing regions.

The limited public funding for postsecondary education was used primarily for science and technological education (including engineering), while university education in the humanities and social sciences was handled through the private system. Some of these economies also imported educational services on a large scale, particularly for disciplines requiring specialized skills.

Creating Effective and Secure Financial Systems

Financial sector policies in these economies were designed to encourage savings and channel the funds into activities with high social returns.

Increasing Savings   The East Asian economies increased savings by ensuring generally positive real interest rates on deposits and creating secure bank-based financial systems through strong prudential regulation, good supervision, and institutional reforms. In addition, Japan and Taiwan established postal savings systems to attract small savers. These systems offered small savers greater security and lower transaction costs than the private sector and made substantial resources available to government.

Some governments also used a variety of more interventionist mechanisms to increase savings. Malaysia and Singapore guaranteed high minimum private savings rates through mandatory provident fund contributions. Japan, Korea, and Taiwan all imposed stringent controls and high interest rates on loans for consumer items as well as stiff taxes on so-called luxury consumption.

Increasing Investment   The East Asian economies encouraged investment by several means. First, they did a better job than most developing economies of creating infrastructure complementary to private investment. Second, they created an investment-friendly environment through a combination of tax policies and measures that kept the relative prices of capital goods low, largely by maintaining low tariffs on imported capital goods. These fundamental policies had an important impact on private investment. Third, and more controversial, most of these economies kept deposit and lending rates below market-clearing levels, a practice known as financial repression.

Japan, Korea, Malaysia, Taiwan, and Thailand experienced extended periods of mild financial repression. In these economies, real deposit rates were zero or mildly positive and stable, but because savings were not very responsive to changes in real interest rates (above zero), governments could mildly repress interest rates on deposits with a minimal impact on savings and pass the lower rates to final borrowers, thus subsidizing corporations. This policy of mild financial repression differed significantly from the repressed financial regimes of other low- and middle-income countries because interest rates were both more stable and positive in real terms.

ALLOCATING CAPITAL

But high levels of physical and human capital are not a guarantee for success. Resources, once accumulated, need to be allocated to high-yielding activities. Again, these economies used a combination of market mechanisms and government intervention to guide allocative decisions in both the labor and capital markets. Labor market policies tended to use the market and reinforce its flexibility. In the capital market, governments intervened systematically both to control interest rates and to direct credit but did so within a framework of generally low subsidies to borrowers, targeting of allocations to areas of presumed market failure, and careful monitoring.

Letting Markets Work: Flexible Labor Markets

Government roles in labor markets in the successful Asian economies contrast sharply with the situation in most other developing countries. The governments in these economies have generally been less vulnerable and less responsive than other developing country governments to organized labor demands to legislate a minimum wage. Rather, they have focused their efforts on generating jobs, effectively boosting the demand for workers. As a result, employment levels have risen first, followed by market- and productivity-driven increases in wage levels. Because wages, or at least wage-rate increases, have been downwardly flexible in response to changes in the demand for labor, adjustment to macroeconomic shocks has generally been quicker and less painful in East Asia than in other developing regions.

Assisting the Market: Capital Markets

Capital markets serve to allocate funds to competing investments. Each of the Asian economies made some attempts to direct credit to priority activities; all except Hong Kong gave automatic access to credit for exporters. Housing was a priority in Hong Kong and Singapore, while agriculture and small and medium-size enterprises were targeted sectors in Indonesia, Malaysia, and Thailand. Taiwan has recently targeted technological development. Japan and Korea have at various times used credit as a tool of industrial policy to promote the shipbuilding, chemical, and automobile industries.

The implicit subsidy of directed credit programs in the East Asian economies was generally small, especially in comparison with other developing economies, but access to credit and the signal of government support to favored sectors or enterprises were important. In Korea, the subsidy from preferential credit was large during the 1970s, reflected in a large gap between bank and curb market interest rates. This gap has declined sharply in recent years, as Korea has shifted away from heavy credit subsidies to selected sectors. In Japan implicit subsidies were small, and the direction of credit may have been more important as a signaling and insurance mechanism than as an incentive.

Although East Asia's directed credit programs were designed to achieve policy objectives, they nevertheless included strict performance criteria. In Japan, public bank managers employed rigorous economic and financial evaluations to select among applicants from sectors that were being targeted by the government. In Korea, the government individually monitored the large conglomerates using market-oriented criteria, such as exports and profitability. Recent assessments of some directed credit programs in Japan and Korea provide microeconomic evidence that they increased investment, promoted new activities and borrowers, and were directed at firms with high potential for technological spillovers (see "The Role of Credit Policies in Japan and Korea" in this issue).

Directed credit programs without strong performance-based allocation and monitoring—as in some other East Asian economies—have been largely unsuccessful. The changing level of financial sector development and the increasing openness of these economies to international capital flows have caused directed credit programs to decline in importance.

PROMOTING PRODUCTIVITY

The East Asian economies used several strategies for increasing productivity growth, including absorbing foreign technology, employing selective industrial policies, and encouraging rapid export growth.

Absorbing Foreign Technology

These economies actively sought foreign technology through a variety of mechanisms. All welcomed technology transfers in the form of licenses, capital goods imports, and foreign training. Openness to foreign direct investment speeded technology acquisition in Hong Kong, Malaysia, Singapore, and, more recently, Indonesia and Thailand. Japan, Korea, and, to a lesser extent, Taiwan restricted foreign direct investment but offset this disadvantage by aggressively acquiring foreign knowledge through licenses, overseas education, and capital goods imports.

Promoting Specific Industries

Most East Asian governments have pursued sector-specific industrial policies to some degree. The best known instances include Japan's policies to promote heavy industry in the 1950s and the subsequent imitation of these policies in Korea. These policies included import protection as well as subsidies for capital and other imported inputs. Malaysia, Singapore, Taiwan, and even Hong Kong have also established programs— typically with more moderate incentives—to accelerate the development of advanced industries. Despite these actions, there is little evidence that industrial policies have affected either the sectoral structure of industry or rates of productivity change (see "Roots of East Asia's Success" in this issue).

Encouraging Export Strategies

The active promotion of manufactured exports was a significant source of these economies' rapid productivity change. Although all of them except Hong Kong passed through an import-substitution phase, with high and variable protection of domestic import substitutes, these periods ended earlier than in other economies. Hong Kong, Malaysia, and Singapore adopted trade regimes that were close to free trade.

Japan, Korea, and Taiwan halted import liberalization, often for extended periods, and heavily promoted exports. Thus, while incentives were largely equal, they were the result of countervailing subsidies rather than of trade neutrality; promotion of exports coexisted with some protection of the domestic market. In the Southeast Asian economies, in contrast, governments gradually but continuously liberalized the trade regime, supplemented by institutional support for exporters, to achieve the export push. Exchange rate policies in all economies were liberalized and currencies frequently devalued to support export growth. Because governments were credibly committed to the export push strategy, producers, even those in the protected domestic market, knew that sooner or later their time to export would come.

Manufactured export growth provided a powerful mechanism for technological upgrading. Because world markets for technology are imperfect, firms that export have greater access to technology than those that produce import substitutes or nontraded goods. Exports can confer benefits to the enterprise and spillovers to the rest of the economy that are not reflected in market prices. These information-related spillover effects are an important source of rapid total factor productivity growth. Both cross-economy evidence and more detailed studies of total factor productivity performance of industries in Japan, Korea, and Taiwan confirm the significance of exports for rapid productivity growth.

OTHER INNOVATIVE FEATURES

The success of the East Asian economies stems partly from the policies they adopted and partly from the institutional mechanisms they created to implement them. The context within which growth-oriented policies were undertaken differs from that of most other low- and middle-income countries in two important respects. First, political leadership adopted the principle of shared economic growth as a major social goal, and, second, governments relied on the private sector.

The Principle of Shared Growth

To win the support of the society at large, East Asian leaders supported the principle of shared growth, promising, in effect, that as the economy expanded, all groups would benefit. But sharing growth raised complex coordination problems. First, leaders had to convince economic elites to support pro-growth policies. Then they had to persuade the elites to share the benefits of growth with the middle class and the poor. Finally, to win the cooperation of the middle class and the poor, leaders had to show them that they would indeed benefit from future growth.

Very explicit mechanisms were used to demonstrate that all would have a share of future wealth. Korea and Taiwan carried out comprehensive land reform programs; Indonesia used rice and fertilizer price policies to raise rural incomes; Malaysia introduced explicit wealth-sharing programs to improve the lot of ethnic Malays vis-à-vis the better-off ethnic Chinese; Hong Kong and Singapore undertook massive public housing programs. In several economies, governments assisted workers' cooperatives and established programs to encourage small and medium-size enterprises. Whatever the form, these programs demonstrated that the government intended for all to share in the benefits of growth.

Role of the Private Sector

Private, not public, investment was the major engine of rapid growth in these economies. Between 1970 and 1990, virtually all of the difference in investment between these economies and other low- and middle-income economies was due to their much higher levels of private investment (see Figure 14-3).

Responsible macroeconomic management, particularly low inflation and small fiscal deficits, encouraged long-term planning and investment and may have been responsible as well for exceptional savings rates. East Asian leaders built a business-friendly environment, of which a major element was a legal and regulatory structure that was generally hospitable to private investment. But beyond this, these economies have, with varying degrees of success, focused on enhancing communications between business and government. Japan, Korea, Malaysia, and Singapore have established forums, called deliberation councils, to enable private sector groups to influence the formulation and implementation of government policies relevant to their interests. In contrast to lobbying, where rules are murky and groups seek secret advantage over one another, the deliberation councils made the allocation rules clear to all participants.

Some of these economies have gone a step further, creating "contests" that combined competition with the benefits of cooperation among firms and between government and the private sector. Such contests range from very simple nonmarket allocation rules, such as access to rationed credit for exporters, to very complex coordination of private investment in the government-business deliberation councils of Japan and Korea. The key feature of each contest, however, is that the government distributes rewards—access to credit or foreign exchange—based on performance, which the government and competing firms monitor.

WHAT CAN EAST ASIA TEACH?

To what extent does East Asia offer lessons for other developing economies? The diversity of experience, the variety of institutions, and the great variation in policies mean that there is no one model for success. Rather, each of the eight economies studied used a combination of policies at different times to perform the functions needed for rapid growth: rapid accumulation, efficient allocation, and higher productivity growth.

While the fundamental, market-oriented economic policies can be recommended without reservation, the efficacy of more institutionally demanding strategies has not been established in other settings and is clearly difficult to imitate when the fundamentals are not securely in place. The problem is not only to try to understand which specific policies may have contributed to growth but also to understand the institutional and economic circumstances that made them viable.

The research results indicate that promoting specific individual industries was generally not successful and therefore holds little promise for other developing

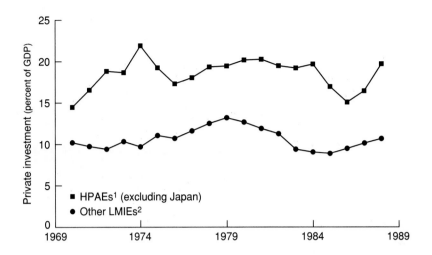

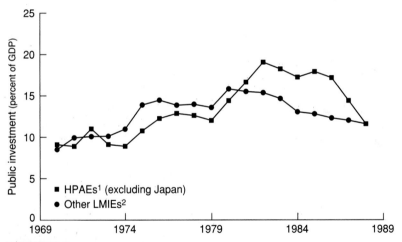

FIGURE 14-3
HIGH SHARE OF PRIVATE INVESTMENT
Source: World Bank.
[1] High performing Asian economies (HPAEs): Indonesia, Hong Kong, Japan, Malaysia, the Republic of Korea, Singapore, Taiwan Province of China, and Thailand.
[2] LMIEs: low- and middle-income economies.

economies. Mild financial repression, combined with directed credit, has worked in some circumstances. Strategies to promote exports and to adapt and improve the technology available in industrial countries have been by far the most generally successful selective approaches used by these economies and hold the greatest promise for other developing economies.

CHAPTER 15

THINGS FALL APART AGAIN: STRUCTURAL ADJUSTMENT PROGRAMMES IN SUB-SAHARAN AFRICA

J. Barry Riddell

Department of Geography, Queens University, Kingston,
Ontario, Canada

International economics and global politics are unfamiliar territory for many. However, the operations of institutions such as the World Bank and the International Monetary Fund (I.M.F.) have profound impacts upon the countries with which they treat, and these extend beyond financial issues and geo-politics. This article indicates how the I.M.F. has imposed 'conditionalities' in sub-Saharan Africa as integral elements of Structural Adjustment Programmes (S.A.P.s) that affect not only the lives of all the inhabitants, but also the nature and landscapes of the nations concerned—their very geographical composition.

Although the specifics of S.A.P.s differ, four basic elements are always present: currency devaluation, the removal/reduction of the state from the workings of the economy, the elimination of subsidies in an attempt to reduce expenditures, and trade liberalisation. Such prerequisites are intended to lead to the 'adjustment' of malfunctioning economies in order that they become viable components of a global system. However, at the same time, the countries themselves are altered in certain fundamental ways. These involve the organisation of the state, the character of the environment, the supply of food, the meaning of development, urban–rural interaction, and distinctly different future prospects for the several areas that comprise the Third World.

Two tasks are undertaken in this study. First, the voluminous and difficult literature on S.A.P.s, as they apply to the countries of sub-Saharan Africa, is summarised and rendered in a non-obscuring vocabulary. Secondly, an indication is given of the outcome of I.M.F. conditions and adjustments. In these manners, global political economy is translated into its geographical expression.

Reprinted with permission of Cambridge University Press from *The Journal of Modern African Studies,* 30, 1 (1992), pp. 53–68.

DEVELOPMENT AND DEBT: THE NATURE OF ADJUSTMENT PROGRAMMES

In the years following independence in Africa there was a feeling of hope and expectation among the citizens of the new nations and their leaders. The rewards of economic development and growth were about to be obtained and seemed just around the corner. The formula for advance was known; it was only a matter of time and effort. Freedom from the colonial yoke meant that advance was on the horizon. However, today there is a growing sense of failure throughout much of sub-Saharan Africa, whether it is Ethiopia in the midst of political and ecological strife, Zambia experiencing economic decline, Somalia being torn apart by rival factions, or Liberia's débâcle. The world has fallen apart for most of the continent's citizens, ranging from public servants in the growing urban centres to peasants in the often declining rural areas.

The debt crisis dominates national life: unemployment is increasing, food and fuel are in short supply, availability of services has deteriorated, and standards of living are falling. It is more than a matter of export earnings not meeting the financial obligations of debt-servicing and the costs of imports, for the situation is exacerbated by rapid population growth, environmental deterioration, over-urbanisation, unemployment, and AIDS. The extent of the problem has been described succinctly in the preface to a recent collection of essays on the economic emergency facing the Third World:

> Between 1982 and 1987, according to IMF statistics, the developing countries have paid back to their creditors a little over 700 billion US dollars . . . [meanwhile] their total long-term debt rose from 568 billion US dollars to 1190 billion, which is roughly half of their national incomes and one-and-a-half times their annual exports.[1]

Compounded by the repatriation of profits by multinational companies and by other 'flights of capital', as well as by declining terms-of-trade, the resultant scenario suggests that the biblical 'Four Horsemen of the Apocalypse'—war, famine, disease, and pestilence—have been let loose on the continent. According to Susan George, 'Financial Low Intensity Conflict (FLIC)' is taking place.[2]

Chinua Achebe wrote *Things Fall Apart* (London, 1958) in order to describe the disasters which befell African society and economy with the onset of colonialism. Financial stringency is leading to similar results again almost a century later. The exigency means that the economies of the newly independent states are in decline,[3] with little or no hope for the immediate future despite the rhetoric of international institutions.

Although Africa's financial crisis is rooted in factors that are both endogenous (e.g. misallocation of funds, excessive military spending) and exogenous (e.g. declining terms-of-trade, all-too-frequent droughts), the immediate albeit temporary 'fix' is to obtain a loan from the global organisation which facilitates international trade and finance.[4] The I.M.F. is concerned that heavily-indebted nations make the adjustments that are needed in order to become viable members of the international economy, and hence insists upon certain 'conditionalities' which must be met by the borrowing régimes, not least in the hope and/or expectation that they will be able to meet their debt obligations if they return to a 'proper' economic path.

Naturally, the international financial institutions foresee great difficulties, not least in the actual implementation of S.A.P.s. However, their publications rarely raise doubts about ultimate long-term success, despite crucial short-term problems.[5] Table 15-1 indicates the large number of adjustment programmes instituted in sub-Saharan Africa by the I.M.F. over the last 12 years. Although the imposed conditions are arranged on a country-by-country basis, they contain certain common characteristics.

1. Currency Devaluation

One of the basic notions of structural adjustment is that local purchasing power has been 'over-valued' as regards its international worth. The effect of devaluation is to reduce the value of the local currency in terms of imported items, including such basic necessities as fuel, medicine, and food, and to make exported goods cheaper (and thus increase their demand). Because of 'knock-on' effects, the prices of non-traded items are also adversely affected.

The consequence is that all-too-many Africans experience a dramatic reduction in their standard of living as the cost of previously affordable household necessities suddenly become too expensive to purchase. For example, the following price increases occurred in Freetown immediately after devaluation in 1986: a bar of soap, from 0.50 to 2.00 *leone*; a bunch of fire wood, from 1.50 to 4.00 *leone*; a gallon of kerosene, from 9.00 to 23.00 *leone*: and a chicken, from 20.00 to 80.00 *leone.* The reaction of Sierra Leoneans was not surprising. As explained by Ankie Hoogvelt, 'It was . . . as if "tiefs" had come in the night, "all de money done"'.[6]

Devaluation also increases the cost of many other essential items, including farm and factory inputs, the medicines provided by the health-care system, and the piped water brought by development projects. The list goes on and the impact is felt throughout the entire national economy, especially because of the increased cost of transport.

2. Removal of Government Involvement

As an arm of a neo-classical economic system, the I.M.F. wants the removal of state interference in order to 'free-up' capitalism and allow the market mechanism to operate through the impersonal forces of supply and demand. In Africa, the intervention of governments in the market has a lengthy pedigree, being a legacy of the colonial past, albeit becoming more and more associated with corruption, inefficiency, and ineptitude since independence. The rôle of the state is most explicit in national development plans, and in ubiquitous parastatal organisations such as produce marketing boards. African régimes have felt the need to become heavily involved in the promotion, management, and manipulation of their economies, primarily in order that they operate in the interest of local people, and so that certain basic infrastructural provisions be made.

Now that the state is being forcibly prevented from influencing the working of the economy, the lives of a great many Africans are being negatively affected, particularly since the greatest source of employment is to be found in the public sector. In addition, because of the declining capacity of many governments, infrastructure and services have been reduced, especially education and health care.

TABLE 15-I
I.M.F. PROGRAMMES IN SUB-SAHARAN AFRICA, 1980–91

Nation	80	81	82	83	84	85	86	87	88	89
Angola										
Benin									×	
Botswana										
Burkina Faso										
Burundi							×		×	×
Cameroon									×	
Central African R.	×	×		×	×	×		×	×	
Chad		×				×		×		×
Congo							×			
Côte d'Ivoire		×		×	×	×	×	×	×	×
Djibouti										
Equatorial Guinea	×	×				×			×	
Ethiopia		×					×			
Gabon	×						×			×
Gambia, The		×	×		×		×	×	×	×
Ghana				×	×		×	×	×	×
Guinea			×				×	×		×
Guinea-Bissau		×						×		×
Kenya	×		×	×		×		×	×	×
Lesotho									×	×
Liberia	×	×	×	×			I	×		
Madagascar	×	×	×		×	×	×	×	×	×
Malawi	×		×	×	×			×	×	×
Mali	×		×	×		×			×	
Mauritania	×	C				×	×	×		×
Mauritius	×	×		×		×		×		
Mozambique								×	×	×
Niger				×	×		×	×	×	
Nigeria								×		×
Rwanda										
São Tomé & Príncipe										×
Senegal	×	×	×	×		×	×	×	×	×
Sierra Leone		×	C	×	×		×	S	I	
Somalia	×	×	×			×		×	I	
Sudan	×	×	×	×	×		I	×		
Swaziland				×						
Tanzania	×	×					×	×	×	
Togo		×		×	×	×	×	×	×	×
Uganda	×	×	×	×				×	×	×
Zaïre		×	×	×	×	×	×	×		×
Zambia		×	×	×				I		
Zimbabwe		×		×						

*a*Source: International Monetary Fund, *IMF Survey* (Washington, D.C.), publish annually, 1 January 1980 to 31 December 1991. × : at least one programme begun Compensatory Financing Facility (C.F.F.), Compensatory and Contingency Finance (C.C.F.F.), Structural Adjustment Facility (S.A.F.), or Extended S.A.F. (E.S.A.F.). C.: programme cancelled. I: declared ineligible by the I.M.F. S: declared suspended by N: declaration of non-co-operation.

3. Elimination of Subsidies

African régimes have also interfered with prices in a variety of ways, especially by means of expensive subsidies in respect of food and petroleum in order to lower the rising cost of living of the inhabitants, notably the urban poor. However, these measures have helped to distort and destroy market mechanisms, and hence the I.M.F. insists upon the removal of price controls and alterations. The result is double edged: on the one hand, such action reduces living standards, often pushing the purchase of food beyond the reach of the poor; and on the other, the repercussions of the increased costs of movement are felt throughout the society as virtually every item and service is affected, either directly or indirectly.

4. Liberalisation of Trade

The I.M.F. is attempting to reintegrate the nations of Africa into the international economy, especially via the intensification of export agriculture. Attempts are being made to turn the clock back to the type of economic system which most governments have been trying to restructure since independence—the production of cheap raw materials for the developed parts of the world in exchange for more expensive processed goods. The most dramatic effect in Africa has been to reduce/remove the protection of the local industries that were supposed to lead to economic advance because of their forward and backward linkages. The I.M.F. views these enterprises as over-priced producers, burdened by corruption, ineptitude, and overstaffing. The loss of employment is as devastating as the removal of the perceived path to development and growth.

THE GEOGRAPHICAL IMPACT OF ADJUSTMENT

The result of such *first*-round effects is that the geography of the continent is being reshaped by external forces and decisions. This is the second time in about a century that such changes have occurred, because colonial contacts also led to profound alterations. It must be underlined that the effects of the current internationalisation are generally not in the interests of most Africans, and the outcome is often greatly resented. The most obvious expressions of the resultant disquiet are the riots and organised protests which have taken place in many countries, albeit only briefly reported in either newspapers or on radio/television.[7] However, these disturbances are but the most visible means of protest against what is widely considered to be a series of unfair, uncaring, and inefficient measures of adjustment.[8]

The fact of the matter is that tropical Africa is being dramatically altered by the following *second*-round effects that S.A.P.s have on (1) the future of the state, (2) the environment, (3) differentiation in third-world scenarios, (4) food availability, (5) urban rural disparities, and (6) poverty and underdevelopment.

1. The Future of the State[9]

It is possible that smaller and more meaningful entities operating within larger regional structures may sooner or later replace a number of African states.[10] After all, most are really artificial creations of the colonial powers, and it is not known how many Africans would mourn their passing. Certainly, few régimes have represented those they rule, and are unable to control the economy within which they operate as they become increasingly politically irrelevant. Without any positive influence upon national development their continuation is in doubt. To understand the failure of such states, three issues need to be considered.

(i) States Without Citizens   The present reality in sub-Saharan Africa is that people are withdrawing from a political system which is uncaring, corrupt, inept, predatory, and unrepresentative, and from an economy which operates to the advantage of élites and in the interests of the developed world. The result is that governments and their administrations are avoided and ignored by increasing numbers in both the countryside and the city as a 'second economy' emerges.[11]

Most peasants participate more or less simultaneously in two types of exchange. In order to reap the advantage of selling their produce or their labour, and in return, purchasing their necessities, they work within the market system, dominated by the impersonal forces of supply and demand. However, they also act within a social exchange system whereby goods and services are transferred by mechanisms such as reciprocity and redistribution.[12] In addition, the vast majority in the rural areas obtain their supplies of food through subsistence production.

Africans have alternated between the market and social exchange systems through both time and space according to needs, prices, ecological conditions, and social obligations. However, as the terms-of-trade have worsened such that the cost of food in the market has become prohibitive, peasants have increasingly moved back into the so-called 'economy of affection'. Here, conditions may not be ideal, but at least there is some food to eat, and security can be found while meaningful kinship, locality, and ethnicity relationships are being fulfilled. Elsewhere this has been termed the 'exit option',[13] whereby peasants distance themselves from an impersonal market that appears to have acted against them like a 'robber'. This is a simple act of avoiding exploitation.

At the same time, persons residing in urban centres have increased their involvement in the informal economy, formerly conceived of as peripheral and as 'soaking up' (in an employment sense) the 'surplus' supply of labour. However, there has been such an expansion in the small-scale production and marketing of petty commodities, as well as in the provisions of numerous services, that in many third-world cities over half of the labour force is now absorbed in this sector.[14] This is an urban parallel to the peasant's 'exit option', in that more and more are moving to escape from an economic system which is regulated and taxed by African governments, and which is not only shrinking but also failing to deliver any rewards.

Thus, the state is becoming virtually irrelevant to an increasing number of what might be described as its 'former' citizens. Mounting portions of both the rural and urban economies extend beyond its control as disengagement gathers pace.[15]

(ii) Problems in African State / I.M.F. Relationships   At least three difficulties make interaction futile. The first is the too-frequent assumption by the Fund that the market permeates everywhere. However, although mechanisms for buying and selling dominate exchange in the so-called 'islands of development',[16] and although part of the story of the expansion of colonialism was the spread of the market throughout Africa, most of the inhabitants retain ties, if only partial, to a holistic culture with social exchange, such as reciprocity and redistribution, being an integral part. In this sense, most peasants are not fully integrated into the market.

The second difficulty is that the governments through which the I.M.F. operate rarely represent all their inhabitants. Democracy is found in only a few countries in the continent, with the norm being some form of dictatorial rule by either military or one-party leaders.

Finally, there is the curious paradox whereby the I.M.F. requires a strong state in order to implement structural adjustment programmes, while weakening the government with its conditionalities.[17]

(iii) Reduction in the State's Ability to Operate   Most régimes in sub-Saharan Africa operate some type of patron-client system. They provide their supporters and other members of the élite or potential competitors with jobs (including many specially created), import quotas, contract allocations, access to government projects, funds for the military and police, as well as parastatal organisations, etcetera.[18] However, with increasingly limited financial ability such traditional mechanisms of patronage disintegrate. At the same time, the decline in services, the lack of employment, and the decay in infrastructure enhances the perception by the majority of the population that they are not responsible for the nation's debt and have not partaken in any rewards.

The result of the above is the collapse of the African state as more and more of its citizens 'depart', despite many heavy-handed attempts to create a form of national unity. The poor in both the city and the countryside are heard to mutter phrases such as: 'things can't be worse than they are already', and 'why should I be expected to pay back loans which have enriched others'.

2. The Environment

As pressures mount for a more prosperous economic system in order to reduce the burden of debt and to feed the growing population, additional strains are placed on the resources of the environment.[19] This takes place in two main ways: by the construction of mega-sized projects which have to be financed, and by the repayment of the service charges on the borrowings of the past. Both imply increased government earnings which come about by more production for sale.

The negative effects of large dams have been well documented elsewhere,[20] and expanded agricultural output means the increased use of land and labour. Both magnify the vulnerability of the inhabitants,[21] thereby further reducing their ability to cope with 'natural' disasters. Lest the 'debt-for-nature swaps' be seen as a saviour on the horizon,[22] it must be pointed out that the financial benefits of such exchanges are only minor.[23] Forest cover is reduced, erosion removes ever-increasing volumes of precious soil, and desertification is accelerated in many drier parts of the continent.

Such ecological damage has already led to a redistribution over time (to the next generation) and over space (from the Third to the First World). Indeed, 'development' is so chimerical in many parts of sub-Saharan Africa that the process taking place should be more realistically termed 'underdevelopment'.[24] Land degradation cannot be ignored because many environments are not resilient. While the Brundtland Commission talked of sustainable development as being necessary,[25] it should be reiterated that much export agriculture in Africa tends to be of the 'extraction' type.

These environmental problems are made more severe by two related crises. The rapid population growth being experienced by many African countries means increased demands upon the land base, especially for food. In addition, there is the emergency of fuel availability. As most people are unable to afford kerosene for cooking and heating, they use whatever fuelwood they can obtain. However, this formerly abundant resource is become more and more scarce because of the excessive removal/harvesting of trees, especially in drier areas and in the environs of cities.[26] The potential saviour, electricity, is generally very expensive to produce and distribute.

3. Differentiation in Third-World Scenarios

Regardless of whether or not the Third World should be viewed as a meaningful totality, it was widely assumed for many years that the various developmental routes being followed by different nations would all lead to a better future.[27] This universal projection of the 1960s has been discredited in the light of so many setbacks, especially in Africa, in contrast to the spectacular economic progress achieved by the Newly Industrialising Countries (N.I.C.s), albeit confused by the advance of certain members of O.P.E.C. (Organisation of the Petroleum Exporting Countries).

At present there appear to be three distinct groups in the so-called 'South' (as opposed to the developed 'North'). The first, mainly in Asia, will continue to experience economic advance that is associated with hardship for many. The second will struggle on in poverty, moving from crisis to crisis, while the third, mainly in sub-Saharan Africa, will experience collapse under the burden of debts which cannot be repaid. In this sense, the World Bank studies which began in the 1980s will doubtless be continued,[28] because some states will collapse and the international community will be busy searching for new financial intermediaries.

4. Food Availability[29]

The continent's food crises have worsened over the past 25 years and no solution is in sight.[30] It might be hypothesised that the devaluation demanded by the S.A.P.s will serve to spur production, because lowering the international value of a country's currency means the reduction/removal of cheaper imported food. This often leads to better prices for local farmers who, in turn, will be stimulated to increase their output. In this sense, it is certainly possible that the supply of food *per capita* may cease the downward progression of the past.

However, there will be two forces acting against such a scenario. The 'uncaptured peasantry' can be expected to use the 'exit option' indicated above, if the prices obtained in the market do not appear to justify the labour expended. In addition, the S.A.P.s stress agricultural exports and, as has been the case in the past, land and labour are thereby removed from the cultivation of crops for domestic consumption.

In other words, the future of food availability is unclear, with marked variations from one situation to another. Urban centres will be most affected if/when peasant producers lose interest in the market. In contrast, the countryside will become more self-sufficient as an increasing portion of rural dwellers become less dependent upon the mechanisms of supply and demand. Further, as the price of marketed food rises, this becomes less accessible to poor people.

5. Urban-Rural Disparities

The 'urban bias' of the post-independence years is likely to be modified by the removal or reduction of the state's redistribution ability.[31] The quality of life in many towns and cities will fall as the cost-of-living rises, as the provision of services worsens, as unemployment increases, as wages decline, and as subsidies on items such as food and fuel are removed. At the same time, the rural areas will benefit, at least to some extent, from the fact that the I.M.F. usually insists upon higher producer prices to stimulate production. Moreover, because the rôle of the state is being down-graded in importance, so also are many of the policies, programmes, and plans which led to urban centres being favoured in previous decades; and the taxing effects of produce marketing boards are being eliminated as these parastal organisations disappear.

Despite these improvements and considerable variations in the quality of life, the scales are likely to remain tilted in favour of the city. Upcountry roads have fallen into disrepair, and little money is available for restoration. The cost of moving produce has risen with the price of fuel, and shortages have become common. Farm inputs, such as seeds, fertiliser, credit, and tools, are increasingly expensive and scarce. Services such as extension, credit, water, health, and education have declined or become non-existent. Finally, the augmented 'farm gate' prices are virtually worthless when peasants find little or nothing to purchase in the market.

6. Poverty and Underdevelopment

There can be little doubt that the effects of S.A.P.s in Africa have led to worsened conditions. Poverty has increased, and it no longer sounds radical to describe the process taking place in many countries as 'underdevelopment'. The quality of life had declined as prices have risen, as infrastructures have crumbled, as services have deteriorated, and as employment opportunities have been reduced. Almost everyone has suffered, but rural peasants, urban slum dwellers, female-headed households, and the children of the poor have felt the negative effects of adjustment most severely, especially when their conditions are exacerbated by drought and conflict.

It is in recognition of the existence of particularly vulnerable groups that many seminars have been held, and many words written, in an attempt to find a solution to their plight. Unfortunately, it is probable that the latest strategy, known as 'adjustment with a human face',[32] will become yet another in the array of temporary and ineffective in phrases of the 'development business' in the Third World like 'basic needs', 'trickle-down', 'redistribution with growth', 'development from below', 'self-reliance', etcetera.

Africa's human capital has declined dramatically in recent years. Apart from the new catastrophy of AIDS, once-conquered diseases are reappearing, the standards if not the quantity of a lot of education have deteriorated, levels of nutrition have fallen, and certain other quality-of-life indicators are worsening, including infant mortality and life expectancy.[33] Many of the advances achieved in the first two decades of independence have been reversed.[34]

Not so long ago, 'development' in the continent was associated with a more urban and industrial society, in which poverty, inequality, and employment improved, and the relative importance of raw material exports declined. Today, 'underdevelopment' involves a return from the city and factory back to the mines and fields. Things in too many parts of the Third World have fallen apart. Africa is suffering from 'Silent Violence', and 'Financial Low Intensity Conflict'.[35]

CONCLUSION

Two quotations from what is arguably the best book to have been written about the effects of the I.M.F.'s structural adjustment programmes provide a sad endnote to this tale of woe. In the words of Susan George, 'the debt crisis is too serious to be left to financiers and economists', and 'Economic policies are not neutral. Contrary to received opinion, they can even kill.'[36] Such statements serve to underline the significance of the continental alterations indicated above, by suggesting that both the nature and attempted management of the debt crisis are causing profound, life-threatening changes which extend beyond the sphere of so-called 'experts'. Development, in the final analysis, is about humans. The debt crisis is not simply a matter of economics; health, education, employment, poverty, standard of living, diet, politics, and the nature of society are also integral elements.

Of course, adjustments *are* necessary because financial debts have crippled virtually every African country, but an I.M.F.-approved programme ought not to be the prerequisite for all other major sources of funding. The fact is that too many members of that Washington-based organisation are oblivious to the reality of Africa and its people—at least in terms of their actions, despite an obscuring rhetoric. As claimed by George:

> The Fund lives in a never-never land of perfect competition and perfect trading opportunities, where dwell no monopolies, no transnational corporations with captive markets, no protectionism, no powerful nations getting their own first.[37]

As a result, the policies followed over the past decade are leading to the destruction of the continent in several fundamental ways, with the failure of the state being an immediate outcome and environmental deterioration being devastating in the long run. The lesson is that if this takes place in Africa, it will occur elsewhere in the Third World, and soon, because of interdependency, the entire global economy will be altered.

It is little wonder that some Africans refer bitterly to an international authoritarianism that reminds them of the way that external decisions are imposed upon their countries in the colonial past. According to President Julius Nyerere in 1985:

> The developed countries have a very large measure of control over the world economy. They act as a group, and make decisions which they see as in their own interests. The leadership of the group is in the hands of the nation with the most powerful economy—USA . . . The IMF has become largely an instrument for economic and ideological control of poor countries by the rich ones . . . in enforcing the unilateral will of the powerful.[38]

There is more than anger and rhetoric in such remarks, because excessive power does reside in external financial institutions and donor agencies; national control of the economy, an important achievement of the independence struggle, has disappeared. Moreover, it was the apparatus of the state and its public enterprises which served to shelter the poor of African countries from the inequalities of private business, and to provide the services and infrastructure that have been associated with post-colonial developments.

A drastic revision in the workings of the global economy is urgently needed, but many of the suggested schemes do little more than delay the day of reckoning. These include plans which envisage enhanced monetary inputs, as well as either writing off or further rescheduling some debts and/or easing their terms of repayment.[39] At the same time, more promising but radical schemes are ignored or given a polite rhetorical response, including George's 3-D strategy (debt, democracy, development) and the African Alternative Framework of the U.N. Economic Commission for Africa.[40] Default bears tremendous costs, and 'home-grown' adjustments generally serve only to delay the intervention of international financial institutions.

If collapse is to be avoided, more attention must be given to devising programmes which will actually improve not worsen the condition of the poor, and above all address the issue of capital flight, whereby those who continue to benefit most from the continent's crisis are made to return their gains. If this scenario appears unrealistic, recall that it took hundreds of economists over a quarter of a century to work out the S.A.P.s which have led to so much chaos and misery in sub-Saharan Africa.

NOTES

1 H. W. Singer and Surya Sharma (eds.), *Economic Development and World Debt* (London, 1989), pp. xix–xx.

2 Susan George, *A Fate Worse than Debt: a radical new analysis of the Third World debt crisis* (London, 1988). The crisis has become pervasive enough to be highlighted and treated as 'The Debt Police', in *Time International* (New York), 31 July 1989, pp. 32–8. A recent report in *West Africa* (London), 13–19 January 1992, p. 72, indicates that Nigeria's $34,000 million external debt is acting as a stranglehold on development.

3 According to the World Bank, *Sub-Saharan Africa. From Crisis to Sustainable Growth: a long-term perspective study* (Washington, D.C., 1989), p. 221, sub-Saharan Africa has experienced increasingly unfavourable rates of average annual G.N.P. *per capita* growth compared to all low-income countries (figures in brackets) during the following periods: 1965–73, 2.9 (3.3)%; 1973–80, 0.1 (2.6)%; 1980–7, −2.8 (4.0)%.

4 The 1980s witnessed a complicated convergence between the I.M.F. and the World Bank in the evolution of S.A.P.s that address the twin issues of debt and economic growth. Previously, the Fund was mainly concerned with currencies and international trade, whereas the interests of the World Bank centred upon poverty and development. See the special issue of *Geoforum* (Elmsford, NY, and Oxford), 19, 1, 1988, pp. 1–131, on 'The Debt Crisis', edited by Stuart Corbridge, and also Bonnie Campbell, 'Indebtedness in Africa: consequence, cause or symptom of the crisis?', in Bade Onimode (ed.), *The IMF, the World Bank and the African Debt*, Vol. 2, *The Social and Political Impact* (London and New Jersey, 1989), pp. 17–30.

5 Cf. various articles in the quarterly publication of the I.M.F. and the World Bank,

Finance and Development (Washington, D.C.). When their combined resources, journals, access to the media, and economic expertise are considered, it would be fair to suggest that the perceptions, opinions, and programmes of these two international organisations overwhelm those of the African continent.

6 Ankie Hoogvelt, 'The Crime of Conditionality: open letter to the Managing Director of the International Monetary Fund (IMF)', in *Review of African Political Economy* (Sheffield), 38, 1987, p. 80.

7 At the annual meeting of the Canadian Association of African Studies held in 1990 at Dalhousie University, Halifax, Nova Scotia, the World Bank representative was roundly booed by the banquet audience when attempting to justify S.A.P.s that are known to have caused widespread misery and destruction.

8 J.C. Scott, *Weapons of the Weak: everyday forms of peasant resistance* (New Haven and London, 1985).

9 See, *inter alia*, A. O. Hirschman, *Exit, Voice, and Loyalty: responses to decline in firms, organizations, and states* (Cambridge, MA, 1970); Robert H. Bates, *Markets and States in Tropical Africa: the political basis of agricultural policies* (Berkeley and Los Angeles, 1981); Richard Sandbrook with Judith Barker, *The Politics of Africa's Economic Stagnation* (Cambridge, 1985); Gerald K. Helleiner, *Africa and the International Monetary Fund* (Washington, D.C., 1986); Victor Azarya, 'Reordering State-Society Relations: incorporation and disengagement', in Donald Rothchild and Naomi Chazan (eds.), *The Precarious Balance: state and society in Africa* (Boulder and London, 1988), pp. 3–21; Bade Onimode, *A Political Economy of the African Crisis* (London and New Jersey, 1988); Robert H. Bates, 'The Reality of Structural Adjustment: a sceptical appraisal', in Simon Commander (ed.), *Structural Adjustment and Agriculture: theory and practice in Africa and Latin America* (London and Portsmouth, NH, 1989), pp. 221–7; Bonnie K. Campbell (ed.), *Political Dimensions to the International Debt Crisis* (London, 1989); Reginald Herbold Green, 'Articulating Stabilisation Programmes and Structural Adjustment: sub-Saharan Africa', in Commander (ed.), op. cit. pp. 35–54; Tony Killick, *A Reaction Too Far: economic theory and the role of the state in developing countries* (London, 1989); Trevor W. Parfitt and Stephen P. Riley, *The African Debt Crisis* (London and New York, 1989); Thomas J. Biersteker, 'Reducing the Role of the State in the Economy: a conceptual exploration of IMF and World Bank prescriptions', in *International Studies Quarterly* (Guildford, Surrey), 34, 1990, pp. 477–92; Thomas M. Callaghy, 'Lost Between State and Market: the politics of economic adjustment in Ghana, Zambia, and Nigeria', in J. M. Nelson (ed.), *Economic Crisis and Policy Change* (Princeton, 1990), pp. 259–319; J. M. Nelson 'Introduction', in Nelson (ed.), op. cit. pp. 3–32; and Richard Sandbrook, 'Taming the African Leviathan', in *World Policy Journal* (New York), Fall 1990, pp. 673–701.

10 For example, given the recent (and continuing?) collapse of the state in Liberia, Somalia, or Ethiopia, who can be certain that they will survive indefinitely? Others are also experiencing the most severe financial constraints, including Sierra Leone, Mali, and Zambia.

11 Janet MacGaffey, *Entrepreneurs and Parasites: the struggle for indigenous capitalism in Zaïre* (Cambridge, 1987).

12 Paul Bohannan and George Dalton (eds.), *Markets in Africa* (Evanston, 1962).

13 Goran Hyden, *Beyond Ujamaa in Tanzania: underdevelopment and an uncaptured peasantry* (London, Berkeley, and Los Angeles, 1980).

14 David Drakakis-Smith, *The Third World City* (London and New York, 1987), p. 66.

15 For example, T. L. Maliyamkono and M. S. D. Bagachwa, *The Second Economy in*

Tanzania (London and Dar es Salaam, 1990), pp. 134–5, report that only 20–30 per cent of food staples pass through official channels in that country.

16 William A. Hance, V. Kotshar, and R. J. Peterec, 'Source Areas of Export Production in Tropical Africa', in *Geographical Review* (New York), 51, 1961, pp. 487–99.

17 This supposed paradox is resolved when the rôle of the state is decomposed into its six separate components. See Biersteker, loc. cit.

18 Parfitt and Riley, op. cit.

19 Piers Blaikie, *The Political Economy of Soil Erosion in Developing Countries* (London and New York, 1985).

20 W. M. Adams, 'The Environmental Effects of Dam Construction in Tropical Africa: impacts and planning procedures', in *Geoforum,* 17, 1986, pp. 403–10, and 'The Downstream Impact of Dam Construction: a case study from Nigeria', in *Transactions, Institute of British Geographers* (London), 10, 1985, pp. 292–302.

21 The analogy to the colonial half-truth of 'vent for surplus' is apt. For a nuanced analysis of the complementarity *versus* competition debate regarding cash crop production, see T. J. Bassett, 'Development Theory and Reality: the World Bank in northern Ivory Coast', in *Review of African Political Economy,* 41, 1988, pp. 45–59.

22 Africa's first Environmental Action Plan (E.A.P), in Madagascar, was announced in 1990.

23 Deborah Burand and Carol Barton, 'Debt-for-Nature Swaps', in[U.N.] *Development Forum* (Washington, D.C.), 17, 4, July–August 1989, pp. 12–13, and John Cartwright, 'Conserving Nature, Decreasing Debt', in *Third World Quarterly* (London), 11, 2, April 1989, pp. 114–27.

24 Cf. David Kimble, *The Consolidation and Effectiveness of the University* (Zomba, 1984), p. 15: 'we mislead ourselves by using a *paranymn*—namely, a word which signifies the opposite of that suggested by its user. Hence the need to put "so-called" before "developing"[countries] '.

25 The World Commission on Environment and Development,   *Our Common Future* (Oxford and New York, 1987).

26 See Gene Ellis, 'In Search of a Development Paradigm: two tales of a city', in *The Journal of Modern African Studies* (Cambridge), 26, 4, December 1988, pp. 677–83, for evidence of the Ethiopian Government's inability, 13 years after its nationalisation of trees, to sustain a viable fuelwood-supply forest for Addis Ababa. See also, Barry Munslow et al., *The Fuelwood Trap: a study of the SADCC region* (London, 1988).

27 See the debate between R. M. Auty, 'Worlds within the Third World', in *Area* (London), 11, 1979, pp. 232–5, and Jonathan Crush and J. Barry Riddell, 'Third World Misunderstanding?', in ibid. 12, 1980, pp. 204–6.

28 The key World Bank studies in the 1980s were *Accelerated Development in Sub-Saharan Africa: an agenda for action* (1981), *Sub-Saharan Africa: progress report on development prospects and programs* (1983), *Toward Sustained Development in Sub-Saharan Africa: a joint program of action* (1984), *Financing Adjustment with Growth in Sub-Saharan Africa* (1986), and *Sub-Saharan Africa: from crisis to sustainable growth* (1989).

29 See Lionel Demery and Tony Addison, 'Food Insecurity and Adjustment Policies in Sub-Saharan Africa: a review of the evidence', in *Development Policy Review* (London), 5, 1987, pp. 177–96; Randolph C. Kent, 'Food, Famine and Future Prospects for Africa', in *Third World Quarterly,* 10, 1, January 1988, pp. 373–81; Gavin Williams, 'The World Bank in Rural Africa, Revisited: a review of the World Bank's Nigeria agricultural sector review, 1987', in *Review of African Political Economy,* 43, 1988,

pp. 42–67; Reginald Herbold Green, 'The Broken Pot: the social fabric, economic disaster and adjustment in Africa', in Onimode (ed.), op. cit. Vol. 2, pp. 31–55; and John Loxley, 'Structural Adjustment in Africa: reflections on Ghana and Zambia', in *Review of African Political Economy,* 47, 1990, pp. 8–27.

30 J. Barry Riddell, 'The African Malaise', in *Canadian Journal of Development Studies* (Ottawa), 8, 1987, pp. 387–92, and Michael Watts, 'The Agrarian Crisis in Africa: debating the crisis', in *Progress in Human Geography* (London), 13, 1989, pp. 1–41.

31 J. Barry Riddell, 'Urban Bias in Underdevelopment: appropriation from the countryside in post-colonial Sierra Leone', in *Tijdschrift voor Economische en Sociale Geografie* (Amsterdam), 23, 1985, pp. 36–41.

32 Many of the policies and programmes suggested in the collection edited by Giovanni Andrea Cornia, Richard Jolly, and Frances Stewart, *Adjustment with a Human Face,* Vol. 1, *Protecting the Vulnerable and Promoting Growth,* and Vol. 2, *Country Case Studies* (Oxford, 1987 and 1988), are unrealistic in the reality of the political economy in Africa and the international trading system.

33 C. A. Anyinam, 'The Social Costs of the International Monetary Fund's Adjustment Programs for Poverty: the case of health care development in Ghana', in *International Journal of Health Services* (Farmingdale, NY), 19, 1989, pp. 531–47, and Hugh McCullum, 'Africa's Debt: the children pay', in *The United Church Observer* (Toronto), N.S. 52, June 1989, pp. 18–24.

34 Richard Longhurst, Samura Kamara, and Joseph Mensurah, 'Structural Adjustment and Vulnerable Groups in Sierra Leone', in *IDS Bulletin* (Brighton), 19, 1, January 1988, pp. 25–30, and Bonnie K. Campbell and John Loxley (eds.), *Structural Adjustment in Africa* (London, 1989).

35 Michael Watts, *Silent Violence: food, famine and peasantry in northern Nigeria* (Berkeley, 1983), and George, op. cit.

36 George, op. cit. pp. 4 and 6.

37 Ibid. p. 56. This is enhanced by I.M.F. 'holier than thou' writing.

38 Julius K. Nyerere, 'Africa and the Debt Crisis', in *African Affairs* (London), 84, 337, October 1985, pp. 493–4.

39 Such pardons only serve to allow the élite to resume the past agendas which led to the current crises of the continent—in other words, they indicate to people like President Mobuto of Zaïre that they can renew their plunder because the day of reckoning has been delayed.

40 U.N. E.C.A., *African Alternative Framework to Structural Adjustment Programmes for Socio-Economic Recovery and Transformation* (Addis Ababa, 1989), E/ECA/CM.15/6/Rev.3.

CHAPTER 16

OPTIONS FOR TACKLING THE EXTERNAL DEBT PROBLEM

Robert Devlin

UN Economic Commission for Latin America and the Caribbean

I. THE CURRENT SITUATION

1. Searching for Progress

Looking to the North, one sees the OECD economies out of recession, and indeed enjoying one of the longest periods of noninflationary economic expansion in their modern history.[1] A highly decentralized international lender-of-last-resort facility (composed of the IMF, World Bank, Bank for International Settlements, OECD central banks, treasuries, export credit agencies, and the private banks themselves) has proved its effectiveness in averting the destabilizing defaults in Latin America that threatened to emerge from the systemic payments crisis of that region.[2] Thus, in the middle of the worst financial crisis since the 1930s, private banks have generally performed remarkably well. For example, throughout the crisis years of 1982–1986 the international earnings of United States banks remained buoyant, and indeed their overall growth of net income accelerated as these institutions diversified into new profit opportunities at home (Table 16-1). Negative earnings manifested themselves only in 1987, on account of the first large-scale allocation of reserves against possible losses on the Latin American portfolio.[3] The industry, however, rebounded in the first half of 1988, reporting a strong recovery of earnings.[4]

Moreover, behind this strong earnings performance an impressive "growth-oriented adjustment" of the banks' loan portfolio in Latin America is under way. Again the United States banks are illustrative: by March 1988, they had reduced their absolute exposure in the region by 12% with respect to June 1982 (Table 16-2), while doubling

From *CEPAL Review, 37* (April 1989), pp. 27–34.

TABLE 16-1

UNITED STATES BANKING: SELECTED INDICATORS
(Percentage of Total Average Assets)

	1980	1981	1982	1983	1984	1985	1986	1987
Net interest revenue	2.8	2.8	3.1	3.3	3.4	3.6	3.6	3.4
Money centre banks	2.4	2.4	2.8	2.9	3.1	3.2	3.2	2.9
Regional banks	3.4	3.3	3.4	3.7	3.9	4.1	4.0	3.0
Net income	0.62	0.59	0.59	0.67	0.65	0.66	0.67	−0.31
Money centre banks	0.51	0.52	0.54	0.64	0.60	0.69	0.70	−0.65
Regional banks	0.76	0.67	0.66	0.69	0.70	0.64	0.65	0.01
International earnings	—	—	—	—	—	—	—	—
Money centre banks	0.27	0.30	0.32	0.29	0.27	0.26	0.22	−1.33
Regional banks	—	—	—	—	—	—	—	—

Source: ECLAC, on the basis of data in Thomas Hanley et al., *A Review of Bank Performance* (various editions), New York: Salomon Brothers.

their primary capital, all of which enabled them to cut in half their Latin American loan-to-capital ratio, from a precarious 124% to a much more manageable 58% (Table 16-3). United States money centre banks now have 25–30% of their LDC portfolio backed by loan loss reserves, while many United States regional and continental European banks have a corresponding coverage of 50% or more (Table 16-4).[5] In sum, the international management of the payments difficulties in Latin America has helped the bankers to convert a situation which was originally, for them, a severe "crisis" into something more akin to a "problem." Indeed, the success of the bankers' adjustment is reflected in signs of complacency in financial circles about the Latin American situation: in the view of some experts, a refusal to pay by any one of the major debtors— Brazil, Mexico, Argentina, or Venezuela—would not now create undue stress in the world banking system.[6]

The creditors' diagnosis of the problem in Latin America is also certainly more realistic now than it was at the outset. Gone are the rosy scenarios about a short-term liquidity crisis; most creditors now recognize that the problem in Latin America is structural, because time-consuming internal economic and social transformations are needed in most debtor countries to competitively produce and sell the tradeable goods required to generate foreign exchange for normal servicing of the debt. Likewise, there is now recognition that protracted belt tightening in the debtor countries is counterproductive: in order to politically legitimize necessary reforms and to raise the mass of domestic savings available for investment and debt service, countries clearly must achieve a sustained expansion of their economies.

TABLE 16-2
EXPOSURE OF UNITED STATES BANKS IN LATIN AMERICA

| | Millions of dollars | | | | | | | | | Annual growth rates (total exposure) | | |
| | June 1982 | | | December 1987 | | | March 1988 | | | 1986 | 1987 | March 88/ June 82 |
	Top 9	Rest	Total	Top 9	Rest	Total	Top 9	Rest	Total			
Latin America	48,714	33,368	82,082	49,757	24,720	74,477	49,015	23,116	72,311	-3.0	-5.4	-11.9
Oil-exporting countries	23,567	17,285	40,852	20,699	12,446	33,145	20,066	11,621	31,867	-6.0	-6.7	-22.0
Bolivia	231	137	368	39	24	63	38	20	58	-13.6	-29.2	-84.2
Ecuador	1,257	910	2,167	1,137	650	1,787	1,119	586	1,705	3.1	-11.4	-21.3
Mexico	13,602	11,619	25,221	13,396	9,002	22,398	12,848	8,240	21,088	-3.7	-4.9	-16.4
Peru	1,330	1,017	2,347	441	400	841	390	392	782	-23.3	-27.4	-66.7
Venezuela	7,147	3,602	10,749	5,686	2,370	8,056	5,671	2,383	8,054	-10.8	-7.8	-25.1
Non-oil-exporting countries	25,147	16,083	41,230	29,058	12,274	41,332	28,949	11,495	40,444	-0.3	-4.2	-1.9
Argentina	5,595	3,212	8,807	6,709	2,521	9,230	6,766	2,452	9,281	3.5	2.0	4.7
Brazil	12,336	8,179	20,515	15,763	6,507	22,270	15,754	5,986	21,740	0.2	-5.7	6.0
Colombia	2,075	961	3,036	1,398	675	2,073	1,350	700	2,050	-15.0	-3.8	-32.5
Costa Rica	221	259	480	178	139	317	176	133	309	-5.2	-20.6	-25.6
Chile	3,314	2,761	6,075	3,907	1,964	5,871	3,841	1,778	5,619	0.1	-6.1	-7.5
El Salvador	53	16	69	8	41	49	6	46	52	12.2	-10.9	-24.6
Guatemala	96	53	149	29	19	48	29	12	41	-32.4	4.3	-72.5
Honduras	139	64	203	42	64	106	36	68	104	-9.3	—	-48.8
Nicaragua	257	168	425	13	30	43	13	28	41	-26.7	-34.8	-90.3
Paraguay	299	28	327	60	17	77	58	12	70	-37.4	-28.0	-78.6
Dominican Republic	338	108	446	263	80	343	263	82	345	-6.6	-14.0	-22.6
Uruguay	424	274	698	688	217	905	657	198	855	0.8	1.8	22.5

Source: ECLAC, on the basis of United States Federal Financial Institutions Examination Council, *Statistical Release*, various numbers.

TABLE 16-3
UNITED STATES BANKING: LATIN AMERICAN EXPOSURE AS A PERCENTAGE
OF PRIMARY CAPITAL

	June 1982			March 1988		
	Top 9	Rest	Total	Top 9	Rest	Total
Latin America	180.0	85.4	124.0	96.7	31.8	57.7
Oil-exporters	87.1	44.2	61.8	40.2	16.1	25.7
Non-oil-exporters	93.0	41.2	62.2	56.5	15.7	32.0
Memo item:						
Primary capital[a]	27.1	39.1	66.2	51.5	77.7	129.1

[a]Billions of dollars.
Source: ECLAC, on the basis of data from the United States Federal Financial Institutions Examination Council, *Statistical Release,* various numbers.

TABLE 16-4
UNITED STATES BANKING: RESERVES SET ASIDE ON LDC PORTFOLIO
(Millions of Dollars)

	Reserving 1987			Total estimated reserves	Percentage of LDC portfolio
	II Quarter	IV Quarter	Total		
Money centre banks					
Bankers Trust	700	—	700	1,000	25
Chase Manhattan	1,600	—	1,600	2,000	25
Chemical Bank	1,100	—	1,100	1,360	25
Citicorp	3,000	—	3,000	3,325	25
Manufacturers Hanover	1,700	—	1,700	1,787	25
J.P. Morgan and Co.	850	—	850	1,330	25
Republic N.Y. Corp.	100	10	110	200	40
Bank of Boston Corp.	300	200	500	430[a]	55[a]
First Chicago	780	240	1,020	1,132	39
Selected regional banks					
Bank of New England	97	100	197	192[a]	75[a]
Midlantic Corp.	30	25	55	54[a]	63[a]
Mellon Bank	290	180	470	621[a]	45[a]
Banc One Corp.	53	—	53	7	67
NBD Bancorp.	54	—	54	106	50
Sovran Financial	—	—	—	44	45
First Union Corp.	25	—	25	28	49
First Republic Bank	275	—	275	350	26
Bank America Corp.	1,100	—	1,100	2,004	20
First Interstate	500	180	680	612[a]	54[a]
Security Pacific	558	350	908	980[a]	54[a]
Wells Fargo	550	39	589	850[a]	50[a]
First Wachovia Corp.	50	31	81	55	60

[a]Medium- and long-term loans.
Source: ECLAC, on the basis of data in Thomas Hanley and others, *A Review of Bank Performance: 1988 Edition,* New York, Salomon Brothers, 1988.

The more realistic diagnosis has also led to more realistic responses. Some banks, recognizing that the "time" implicit in the restructuring process erodes some of the present value of the income stream of their assets in Latin America, began in 1987 to more aggressively adjust downward the valuation of their loans in the region.[7] Moreover, the devaluation of assets has sometimes resulted in relief for the debtors as banks now show an increasing willingness to accept formal debt reduction schemes through direct or indirect participation in debt-equity swaps,[8] the purchase of below market interest rate exit bonds,[9] the conversion of debt into bonds at a discount,[10] direct buy-backs,[11] etc.

The new diagnosis likewise has induced better responses from the multilateral lenders. The recognition of the structural problem has brought the World Bank from the background of the international debt strategy to the centre of the playing field.[12] Meanwhile, the IMF has accommodated to the new realities by extending its adjustment programs to up to four years, lengthening the period of review of its performance criteria to six months, as well as creating a new expanded contingency financing facility.

Turning South, one finds that the crisis has coincided with some positive changes in Latin America. There are today thirteen democratic governments in the region compared to only four in the late 1970s.[13] On the economic front, the severity of the crisis in Latin America has certainly broken the back of the dogmatism sometimes attached to import substitution development strategies and so-called inward-looking development. Indeed, one senses the emergence of a new pragmatism in the formulation of development policy. While eschewing some of the more simplistic prescriptions for economic liberalization emanating from the North, the achievement of international competitiveness is now a central preoccupation of the authorities of the region. Most countries are manifestly eager to learn the art of producing and selling for highly competitive international markets. The popular notion of the State as the handmaiden of development also has undergone reassessment; there is a general awareness that government resources are inefficiently deployed and that private initiative offers more potential for development.[14]

Good intentions obviously are not enough. However, while Latin America's efforts to alter the direction of its development policy and restore creditworthiness do not warrant unreserved applause, it would be equally unfair to ignore the great adjustments that have actually been undertaken and the sacrifices they have involved. Between 1982 and 1988 the region transferred US$179 billion to its creditor countries.[15] Moreover, that outward net transfer of resources from Latin America was policy-induced, for it was made possible only because the region rapidly converted a longstanding trade deficit—averaging nearly US$2 billion per annum in 1978–1981— into a massive trade surplus that averaged US$26 billion per annum in 1982–1988. The trade surpluses, in turn, could not have come about without exchange rate devaluations, adjustments of domestic interest rates, fiscal correction (including the selling off of State enterprises), compression of real wages, etc.[16] Also, the domestic effort must be evaluated in the light of an unhelpful external environment. Aside from protectionism, exports have been hindered by historically low average unit prices, which have caused the value of exports to expand by only a small fraction of the recorded growth of export volume (Table 16-5).

TABLE 16-5
LATIN AMERICA: EXPORTS OF GOODS
(Index, 1980 = 100)

	Value			Volume			Variation[a]	
	Annual averages			Annual averages			Value	Volume
	1978–1981	1982–1987	1988[b]	1978–1981	1982–1987	1988[b]		
Latin America	85	99	115	96	126	156	52.7	
Oil-exporters	82	95	87	95	125	152	50.5	
Bolivia	86	70	56	99	74	69	(73.7)	
Ecuador	87	95	89	102	128	159	35.7	
Mexico	81	131	134	93	181	228	65.2	
Peru	81	75	68	98	94	71	(180.5)	
Venezuela	82	70	54	104	85	106	(79.8)	
Non-oil-exporters	88	103	139	98	127	159	57.8	
Argentina	97	94	94	114	124	131	—	
Brazil	89	119	166	95	144	197	65.3	
Colombia	86	103	150	95	114	174	99.0	
Costa Rica	95	97	120	107	114	121	32.3	
Chile	79	87	146	93	130	158	23.1	
El Salvador	88	66	59	96	79	78	(141.2)	
Guatemala	84	71	73	91	83	83	(176.1)	
Haiti	76	93	83	85	112	82	70.4	
Honduras	89	92	115	95	96	106	309.1	
Nicaragua	123	76	48	144	87	45	(102.3)	
Panama	—	—	—	—	—	—	—	
Paraguay	96	136	251	93	132	239	99.5	
Dominican Republic	96	80	85	103	103	107	—	
Uruguay	89	102	130	97	121	130	59.1	

[a]Variation between annual average of 1978–1981 and 1982–1987. Numbers in parentheses refer to cases where both value and volume declined over the two periods.
[b]1988 data estimate from ECLAC, *Preliminary Overview of the Latin American Economy* (LC/G.1536), Santiago, Chile, January 1989, table 8.
Source: Calculated from data of ECLAC Division of Statistics and Quantitative Analysis.

2. Itemizing the Setbacks

While there have been signs of progress on some fronts, there have also been setbacks of major importance. In the last six years, the North has lost export markets,[17] and hence jobs and GNP growth, due to a reduced capacity to import in Latin America. OECD firms with direct investments in Latin America have not been able to escape the crisis; their profitability has fallen and corporate uncertainties in Latin America are certainly up.[18] United States banks, which are those with the greatest exposure in Latin America, have lost ground in the international race for dominance of financial markets: expansion into a world of financial liberalization is a capital-intensive endeavour, and the time and resources United States banks must allocate to propping up their slumping Latin American portfolio has clearly put them at a competitive disadvantage. Moreover, although it is difficult to prove definite links, it is also suspected that the increased supply of illicit drugs from Latin America is at least partially linked to shortages of foreign exchange in the region.

The North may also have suffered a serious erosion of the value of its "goodwill" in Latin America. On the one hand, creditors have repeatedly failed to keep their promises of new financing for the debtors; most recently the Baker Plan's 1985 commitment to mobilize US$20 billion of new bank finance and US$9 billion of official loans over three years has remained unfulfilled. Multilateral net disbursements to the region have declined rather than increased, while private bank loans have been few and far between, and heavily concentrated in the hands of only a lucky few within the so-called Baker 15 (Tables 16-6 and 16-7). Meanwhile, the IMF's credibility has been further tarnished over the last few years because its programs continue to be associated with economic recession; this has caused more countries to distance themselves from the Fund exactly when in principle the need for its guidance is greater than ever (Table 16-8). The 1988 Toronto Summit's priority attention to Africa's debt problem, contrasting with the continued inertia on the Latin American front, was also not very helpful.[19] Finally, the United States administration's often unconstructive approach to the InterAmerican Development Bank's problems has been a severe source of contention in hemispheric relations.

The setbacks for Latin America since the outbreak of the crisis have been very dramatic. Who would have imagined back in 1982 that by 1988 Latin America's per capita gross domestic product would be nearly 7% below the 1980 figure?[20] While domestic savings have been higher than ever before, since 1982 the region's domestic investment—vital to any serious campaign to make Latin America's goods and services more internationally competitive—has been 22% below the average annual level recorded in 1978–1981 (Table 16-9). On a per capita basis the investment performance has been even worse: in 1987 such outlays were the highest of the six years of the crisis, yet even so per capita investment in that year was the lowest since 1971![21] Inflation has increased spectacularly in Latin America; the regional average was nearly 500% in 1988, with rates reaching three digits for two countries (Argentina and Brazil) and four digits for another two (Nicaragua and Peru). Real wages have for the most part been depressed, while official unemployment is disturbingly high.[22] Although the social repercussions of the crisis are hard to quantify, there are studies

TABLE 16-6
15 BAKER PLAN COUNTRIES: MEDIUM-TERM BANK CREDITS, 1986–1988[a]
(Millions of Dollars)

	1986	1987	January–August 1988
Total	483	10,004	6,250
Argentina	17	2,100	—
Bolivia	—	—	—
Brazil	—	—	5,200
Chile	—	—[a]	—
Colombia	201	87	1,000
Cote d'Ivoire	—		—
Ecuador	220	32;(300)[b]	—
Mexico	—	7,700	—
Morocco	—	25	50
Nigeria	—	—	—
Peru	—	—	—
Philippines	—	—	—
Uruguay	45	—	—
Venezuela	—	30	—
Yugoslavia	—	20	—

[a]In a rescheduling in 1987 Chile secured a "retiming" of its interest payments which saved the country about US$450 million in 1988.
[b]Cancelled.
Source: OECD, *Financial Statistics Monthly,* various numbers, Paris, and ECLAC, Economic Development Division.

TABLE 16-7
IMF, WORLD BANK, AND IDB: NET TRANSFERS TO LATIN AMERICA
(Billions of Dollars)

	1980	1981	1982	1983	1984	1985	1986	1987
1. Net disbursements	2.3	2.7	4.0	8.8	7.4	5.3	4.4	2.1
IMF	−0.1	0.1	1.2	5.7	3.3	1.5	0.2	−0.5
World Bank	1.2	1.3	1.4	1.7	2.1	1.9	2.7	1.6
IDB	1.2	1.3	1.4	1.4	2.0	1.9	1.5	1.0
2. Interest charges	1.0	1.2	1.3	1.7	2.2	2.7	3.6	4.0
IMF	0.1	0.1	0.1	0.3	0.6	0.9	0.9	0.8
World Bank	0.6	0.7	0.8	0.9	1.0	1.1	1.7	2.1
IDB	0.3	0.4	0.4	0.5	0.6	0.7	1.0	1.1
3. Net transfers (1–2)[a]	1.1	1.5	2.8	7.2	5.2	2.6	0.7	−1.9
IMF	−0.2	—	1.2	5.4	2.7	0.6	−0.8	−1.3
World Bank	0.5	0.6	0.6	0.8	1.1	0.8	1.0	−0.5
IDB	0.8	0.9	1.0	1.0	1.4	1.2	0.5	−0.1

[a]May not sum properly due to rounding.
Source: Calculated from data provided by SELA.

TABLE 16-8
LATIN AMERICA: PARTICIPATION IN MULTILATERAL ADJUSTMENT PROGRAMS

	IMF		World Bank	
	1982–1983	1987	1982–1983	1987
Total	13	6	1	9
Oil-exporters	3	2	—	3
Bolivia	—	x	—	x
Ecuador	x	—	—	x
Mexico	x	x	—	x
Peru	x	—	—	—
Venezuela	—	—	—	—
Non-oil-exporters	10	4	1	6
Argentina	x	x[a]	—	x
Brazil	x	—[b]	x	x
Colombia	—	—	—	x
Costa Rica	x	x	—	x
Chile	x	x	—	x
El Salvador	—	—	—	—
Guatemala	x	—	—	—
Haiti	x	—	—	—
Honduras	x	—	—	—
Nicaragua	—	—	—	—
Panama	x	—	—	—
Paraguay	—	—	—	—
Dominican Republic	x	—	—	—
Uruguay	x	x	—	x

[a]"Out," at least transitorily in 1988.
[b]"In" in 1988.
Source: ECLAC, Economic Development Division, based on the respective institution's data.

which suggest an important deterioration on many fronts and confirm what the casual observer senses when visiting almost any Latin American capital city.[23]

Finally, the evolution of the debt burden indicators has not been entirely encouraging. After seven years of costly adjustments the region's debt-to-export ratio in 1988 (339%) was 60% higher than in 1980. On the other hand, the interest/exports ratio had fallen to 28% by 1988, and although that was still extremely burdensome, it was nevertheless the lowest level recorded since 1981 (Table 16-10).

II.   WHY THE SKEWED DISTRIBUTION OF COSTS BETWEEN CREDITORS AND DEBTORS?

The review of the situation since 1982 suggests some improvements, but also points to serious setbacks for the creditor and debtor countries alike. Yet the review also highlights a distribution of benefits and costs that is clearly skewed against the debtor countries. In effect, thanks to a growth-oriented adjustment, private banks now only

TABLE 16-9
GROSS DOMESTIC SAVINGS AND INVESTMENT IN LATIN AMERICA[a]

	Savings Index 1980 = 100		Investment Index 1980 = 100	
	1978–1981	1982–1987	1978–1981	1982–1987
Latin America	96	107	94	73
Oil-exporters	—	—	—	—
Bolivia	91	57	129	64
Ecuador	92	114	93	74
Mexico	94	113	92	69
Peru	95	79	89	80
Venezuela	107	83	117	74
Non-oil-exporters	—	—	—	—
Argentina	112	104	88	51
Brazil	90	110	91	78
Colombia	97	113	99	110
Costa Rica	103	184	85	70
Chile	82	122	90	57
El Salvador	85	74	134	85
Guatemala	94	98	117	77
Haiti	91	150	96	107
Honduras	101	83	98	63
Nicaragua	—	—	93	134
Panama	80	100	94	86
Paraguay	83	69	93	85
Dominican Republic	107	151	92	95
Uruguay	123	155	91	50

[a]Market prices and 1980 dollars.
Source: Calculated from data of ECLAC, Division of Statistics and Quantitative Analysis.

have a problem in Latin America; the countries of the region, in contrast, have a development crisis of ever deepening proportions. Why?

Impatient creditors often point to: (i) bad economic policies in the debtor countries, coupled with their excessive debt accumulation in the 1970s; and (ii) an unwillingness in the 1980s to make and persist with the hard economic decisions needed to turn the Latin American economies around. Moreover, there often exists by implication the notion that if creditors provide comprehensive relief for the debtors this will raise moral hazard, as well as giving rise to a tendency to abuse the degrees of freedom won thanks to the relaxation of the efforts to restructure the region's economies and make them more competitive internationally.

The debtors, on the other hand, tend to focus on the harsh external environment and the weight of the outward transfer of resources.[24] The argument is by now well developed. Expenditure switching policies normally take a great deal of time to work their way through the economies, especially in structurally uncompetitive ones. Thus, the large trade surplus needed to effectively service debts at high real rates of interest can

TABLE 16-10
LATIN AMERICA: EXTERNAL DEBT

	Debt[a] 1988[b]	Debt/exports 1981	Debt/exports 1988[b]	Debt/GDP 1981	Debt/GDP 1988	Interest/exports 1981	Interest/exports 1988[b]	Arrears 1987	Arrears Sept. 1988
Latin America	401.4	247	339	46	53	28	28	x	x
Oil-exporters	159.2	220	343	—	—	23	28	x	x
Bolivia	3.9	348	595	—	—	35	35	x	x
Ecuador	105	202	388	51	80	23	33	x	x
Mexico	96.7	259	339	52	62	29	29	—	—
Peru	16.2	239	442	45	70	24	22	x	x
Venezuela	31.9	160	290	56	49	13	26	—	—
Non-oil-exporters	242.1	273	337	—	—	34	28	x	x
Argentina	56.8	329	541	55	81	36	40	—	x
Brazil	114.6	313	321	39	42	40	30	x	—
Colombia	15.9	199	218	24	33	22	21	—	—
Costa Rica	4.1	229	260	90	108	28	20	x	x
Chile	19.1	311	236	73	74	39	23	—	—
Cuba	(5.7)[c]	—	—	—	—	—	—	x	x
El Salvador	1.9	174	185	—	—	8	10	—	—
Guatemala	2.8	96	225	—	—	8	13	x	x
Haiti	0.8	155	276	—	—	3	7	—	x
Honduras	3.2	180	290	—	—	14	14	x	x
Nicaragua	6.7	464	2068	—	—	37	103	x	x
Panama	4.2	92	—	—	—	—	—	—	x
Paraguay	2.2	171	324	—	—	15	12	x	x
Dominican Republic	3.8	168	220	—	—	19	13	x	x
Uruguay	6.1	183	354	51	97	13	23	—	—

[a]Billions of dollars.
[b]ECLAC, *Preliminary Overview of the Latin American Economy, 1988* (LC/G.1536), Santiago, Chile, January 1989.
[c]Excluded from totals. Represents debt with so-called market countries in 1987.
Source: ECLAC, Economic Development Division.

be achieved in the short term only with a disproportionate amount of import compression and domestic economic recession. Moreover, since it is inherently difficult for developing countries to quickly raise domestic savings (especially during an economic slowdown), the outward transfer of resources tends to have its counterpart in reduced investment and social expenditure, which is counterproductive, because it hampers economic restructuring and future capacity to service debts. Furthermore, the changing of relative prices for the purpose of making an external transfer tends to aggravate inflationary pressures. This situation is complicated by the fact that debt servicing is largely the responsibility of the public sector, giving rise to an internal budgetary transfer problem. As demonstrated even in the United States, tax and public expenditure decisions belong in extremely delicate political terrain. If there is no broad domestic political consensus to accept a decisive increase in taxes and a lowering of public expenditure to accommodate the transfer, the State must mobilize the necessary resources through an inflationary tax. This is a risky strategy that can easily degenerate into hyperinflation.[25]

As in most polarizing issues, the truth probably lies in between the extremes of the arguments of the two groups. To overcome the development crisis and put Latin American debtors back on track, adequate and sustained internal effort is unquestionably a necessary first step in a successful restructuring process. Thus far the internal efforts have been of varying intensity and duration in the region, but such efforts have certainly been made. As mentioned earlier, domestic policy has induced a transfer of resources to the creditor countries of US$179 billion, or more than 4% of GDP per annum. To illustrate the magnitude of the transfer, suffice it to recall that this exceeds the outward net transfer forced on defeated Germany under the 1919 Treaty of Versailles (2.5%) and defeated France under the 1871 Treaty of Frankfurt (2.3%).[26] The debtors also deserve some patience from the creditor countries: to turn around a development strategy that worked reasonably well for 50-odd years is much more than a six-year project.[27] In addition, the economic transformation is being attempted simultaneously with a fragile transition to political democracy. A peripatetic course might be a likely feature of any process of economic transformation built on a very weak and emerging institutional framework.

Moreover, it is always difficult to isolate the contribution made to economic recovery by domestic efforts from the effects of the external environment. If that environment had been clearly supportive of the debtors' efforts to adjust and restructure, one could more comfortably point an accusing finger at lack of serious domestic effort. But in most respects the external environment has been extremely unsupportive of Latin America's adjustment policies. Of critical importance in this regard is the fact that the region's adjustment process has been badly underfinanced from the outset of the crisis.[28] Indeed, whether it be the formula of 7% annual expansion of bank lending that emerged in 1982, or the Baker Plan's 2 1/2% per annum formula, financing volumes have not satisfied the modest targets that the creditors have variously committed themselves to.[29] Underfinancing for the debtors translates into overtransferring of resources to creditors. The transfer problem is therefore a real one that has undermined the efficiency of the debtor countries' policies for adjustment and restructuring.

III. THE MOST CONSPICUOUS WEAK LINK: HALF-HEARTED INTERNATIONAL PUBLIC POLICY

A systemic debt crisis is a collective problem. In these circumstances, negative externalities emanating from the private market are notoriously indiscriminating, drawing into the problem prudent and imprudent lenders/borrowers alike, and even passing serious costs onto those not even remotely involved in the problem.[30] Moreover, rational individual responses to the situation can be very damaging to the collective good and escalate the costs for all. Hence the need for public intervention in the marketplace, first, to stabilize private expectations, and second to assist in restructuring the market agents (borrowers, lenders, or both) in a way that is functional to the renewed solvency of the system and to global recovery with minimum social disruption. Given the opportunities for "free riding" when externalities exist, and its adverse effects on the efficiency of any institutional arrangement, effective public solutions often are to varying degrees coercive in nature.[31] All these principles are usually put into practice when severe financial strain emerges in the domestic markets of the creditor countries.[32]

The international debt crisis that emerged in 1982 has in fact been subject to international public management.[33] Yet, the effectiveness of the latter as an instrument in the promotion of global prosperity and development in an interdependent world has been severely limited. This is because the international debt management strategy has not evolved much beyond a lender-of-last-resort function designed to keep the Northern banking system stable. Indeed, with time it has become increasingly obvious that it is the sporadic threat of a destabilizing default, rather than the sustained requirements of financing economic restructuring in the debtor country, that brings forth new credits. The faster the banks have strengthened their balance sheets, the tighter external financing has become. Meanwhile, however, official lenders have not been given the means to pick up the slack; indeed, they are aggravating the problem as the net flow of resources from these institutions has now turned negative (Table 16-7).

The latest phase of the international debt strategy—the so-called Market Menu Approach—does not rectify the situation. To the extent that it represents a public policy initiative at all, it repeats the basic flaw of the earlier stages: the day to day mechanics of a supposedly multilateral debt management program remain biased toward the narrow objective of securing an orderly adjustment of private financial portfolios in the North.

The initial phase of the debt management strategy was characterized by a "holding action" designed to enable the international financial system to avoid accounting losses via commercially priced reschedulings and new money packages. Now, the latest phase is primarily oriented to the gradual adjustment of the banks' asset values and enhanced risk diversification through schemes involving debt swaps and securitization. As for the macroeconomic issue of finance to support economic reforms, investment, growth, and restored creditworthiness in the debtor countries, it largely remains a passive residual to this process. It is in this sense that the Market Menu is basically a private creditors' menu.

As ECLAC has shown in a recent study, from the perspective of the debtors' macroeconomic needs the Market Menu may list some interesting "appetizers," but the "main entrées" simply are not there.[34] The market-based approach of the menu relies on the principle of voluntary responses from the individual creditors, with little more than moral support from their governments. However, conventional market financing is procyclical in nature and therefore new capital will be unlikely to flow spontaneously to Latin America in a macroeconomically significant volume as long as potential creditors see big discounts of 50% or more on existing debt.

As for the new and more exotic instruments designed around portfolio adjustments, their natural development will be only gradual. It is well known that private markets operate at the margin and each new instrument must start small even under favourable circumstances.[35] In Latin America advance is further slowed by complex free rider and international legal, tax, and accounting problems in the market, as well as many institutional investors' lack of familiarity with the region. There are also demand constraints in Latin America as questions of sovereignty and monetary control limit the potential expansion of some of the creditors' preferred instruments in the Market Menu.[36]

Another consideration is that the bulk of the proposed debt reduction instruments in the menu act on the principal. Since countries are not amortizing debt anyway, the immediate impact of the transaction on the balance of payments is indirect, in the form of reduced interest payments; hence relief will be marginal until the cumulative scope of the reduction of the principal becomes very large.[37] The menu also has the serious drawback that voluntary market transactions are effected only sporadically, making it difficult to predict the timing of conversions, their distribution among the different countries, the amount of relief for the balance of payments, and the effectiveness of the conversion with respect to the support of a domestic program for economic reform and restructuring.

In sum, when left to their own devices, private markets naturally unwind from a large debt overhang only slowly. The amount of debt swapped and converted at a discount into other types of assets will undoubtedly rise markedly in the years ahead.[38] Yet for the immediate future the Market Menu Approach—at least as currently formulated—will only chip away at the corners of the region's problems because it does not address the urgent central macroeconomic issue of today: how to finance in a sustained and predictable way the economic reforms and new investments that Latin America will need to initiate growth now and begin to restore its capacity to service foreign debts. From the standpoint of a collective economic problem and collective solutions, the Market Menu Approach therefore clearly represents unambitious public policy. Indeed, in some essential ways the market menu seems to have thrust us back to the 1930s, when debtor countries and private creditors groped inefficiently for 20 years for a way to unwind from the debt overhang of that period.[39]

IV. WHERE DO WE GO FROM HERE?

The Latin American debt problem should be viewed in its proper context, as a collective international problem: at a time when private sources of credit for Latin America have collapsed, the reliance on voluntary private "micro" responses from the menu to resolve a systemic macroeconomic financial problem promises to delay the adjustment of both debtor and creditor countries and raise costs for the international community as a whole. The systemic aspects of the problem give theoretical and practical support to the idea that there is a need for more aggressive production of international public goods designed to accelerate the adjustment of debtor and creditor countries alike, as well as to ensure that costs are distributed in such a way that they can be paid for out of future growth of the global economic system.

The reason why the proposal for a multilateral debt conversion facility has repeatedly appeared in the debate about debt, and will not go away despite rather heated rejections by the leaders of the international debt strategy, is that it is the most complete expression of the systemic nature of the debt problem in the Western Hemisphere and the social efficacy of a collective solution.[40] Obviously, many of the details of such a complex facility, as well as auxiliary regulatory, accounting, and tax measures, need to be refined, but the basic thrust of the proposed initiative—an orderly and macroeconomically significant reduction of the present value of debt in return for orderly adjustment of economic policy—is in the best spirit of good public economic policymaking in an interdependent world. As an interim step to negotiating such a complex facility, one could envision—under the auspices of IMF-approved exchange restrictions within the context of an official standby program—an immediate temporary freezing of interest payments (with forced capitalization of the difference) at levels consistent with specified targets of investment and growth in the debtor economies.

A less ambitious public policy could consist simply of the approval of ad hoc public guarantees on bank loans and market debt reduction instruments, coupled with supportive modification of tax and accounting rules for the banks. This could grant the credit enhancement needed to bring a volume of conversions and buybacks sufficient to generate rapid and significant balance-of-payments financing for the debtor countries. Bolivia's recent debt buyback at 11 cents on the dollar is a good example of how ambitious intervention by the international public sector can bring about a quick and substantial reduction of the debt overhang.

Ad hoc guarantees, while more effective than the hands-off approach of the current Market Menu, are not without their drawbacks, however. On the one hand, the distribution of relief among countries may be arbitrarily based on political factors, while the timing of that relief remains uncertain. On the other, since ad hoc arrangements tackle free rider problems and other negative externalities only in a piecemeal fashion, their cumulative cost over the medium term could be actually more than a full-fledged debt reduction facility today.

Should Latin America promote these and other collective international initiatives? Certainly yes. Should Latin America bank its future development on the imminent emergence of comprehensive public initiatives? Probably not. Collective solutions for a large number of individual economic agents are notoriously difficult to organize when customs, traditions, legal standards, strategies, and economic circumstances differ. To act collectively, there must be a common sense of extreme stress. This sense of stress existed in Northern financial circles in 1982 when virtually all national banking systems were vulnerable to defaults in Latin America; this explains the amazingly quick and extraordinarily tight global coordination among the creditors to avoid default in the early years of the crisis.[41] However, as the banks' vulnerability to default has receded, and as interest in Latin America's markets has become increasingly over-shadowed by developments in vibrant Asia, as well as in the emerging new Common Market of Europe and the free trade area of North America, even that limited coordination has broken down into an extremely muddled approach, where each creditor is now increasingly set free to cut its own deal. Indeed, in most respects the so-called Market Menu legitimizes the serious de facto breakdown in coordination among creditors and their governments and multilateral agencies.[42]

Collective solutions also typically have immediate costs, whereas the benefits are spread out more gradually. Serious financial and external adjustment problems limit the United States' ability to respond to difficulties in the hemisphere with new money, at least on the scale that we had become accustomed to in the 1950s and 1960s. Meanwhile, it remains to be seen to what degree Japan and Europe will be willing to fill the financial void in the region, and whether this can be done without creating serious conflict over the traditional distribution of political spheres of influence.

New public initiatives therefore could be very slow in emerging, or else they could be of insufficient scale to tackle the development crisis in the region. But this does not mean that the Market Menu is the only game in town. Indeed, the debtors have gradually developed their own menu of options which includes various types of moratoria on debt service payments. Notwithstanding recent developments in Brazil, more than half of the countries in Latin America are now deploying this latter approach (Table 16-10). It is also important to remember that most of the recent debt restructurings carried out under the official Market Menu have evolved out of concessions by the creditors, designed to either coax a country out of a moratorium, or prevent it from entering one.[43] Moreover, these agreements can represent more than a temporary respite from a threat of future moratorium only to the degree that they adequately address the underlying capacity to pay of the debtor. So far, only the recent Bolivian agreement would unequivocally fall into this category.

The debtors' menu of options should not be underestimated. In the past an organized formal or informal threat to impose full or partial limits on payments has proven difficult partly because of the lack of internal consensus on what to do about the outward net transfer of resources. It is possible to observe, however, a series of interesting shifts in political alliances in a number of important debtor countries which suggest that that consensus may now be emerging in more countries as we move into the seventh year of the development crisis of the region.

In addition, the debtor countries will gradually learn the secrets of how to sustain growth in a state of full or partial moratorium. Most earlier limits on payments evolved out of the force of events, set off by a poor domestic economic policy, or were mistakenly conceived as an end in and of itself, which only served to stimulate self-defeating populism. Now, however, there are signs of greater sophistication. Perhaps because of some recent bad experiences, more countries seem to realize that, in order to be a successful instrument for economic recovery, a temporary moratorium must evolve out of a coherent economic program designed to vigorously correct internal and external disequilibria. Furthermore, the limit on payments must be partial and conciliatory in nature, with lines of communication to the creditors kept open and constructive proposals offered to them for resolving the problem in a context compatible with an explicit growth-oriented economic reform program of the debtor country. To the extent that debt service is forcibly rechannelled into a coherent and sustainable economic program and gratuitous conflict is avoided, the country enhances the possibility of eventually winning a more realistic settlement on the outstanding debt.

V. CONCLUSIONS

We have seen that the outward transfer of resources from Latin America hinders adjustment, growth, and economic restructuring through its aggravation of either the foreign exchange constraint, the savings/fiscal constraint, or both. In the absence of systematic payment guarantees from the creditor governments, the voluntary market options in the Menu Approach promise to reduce that transfer burden only gradually over a long haul and with a high degree of uncertainty regarding the amount and timing of relief, as well as its distribution among the debtors. In the meantime, the external finance requirements for supporting macroeconomic programs of growth and restructuring remain unsatisfied. It is thus no surprise that there are very few countries in Latin America which have so far been able to sustain a process of adequate growth with price stability.

An international strategy for growth and reconstruction which benefits only a few problem debtors is clearly a half-hearted international public policy. Yet, it could be unproductive for the debtor countries of Latin America to sit back and wait for the creditor governments to rescue them from their plight with more ambitious international public initiatives. We have seen that collective solutions to a systemic problem emerge more out of a sense of urgency than a sense of good will. As long as the Northern financial systems can successfully adjust to the debt overhang with minimum public assistance, and as long as the economic problems of the region do not provoke open manifestations of political radicalization in the debtor countries, it will be difficult for a comprehensive public policy response to emerge from the heterogeneous bloc of creditor countries. Clearly, then, the solution to Latin America's crisis of debt and development must, more than ever, come from "inside" the region. This approach is moreover aided today by the serious cracks and disputes that have been developing in the creditors' negotiating bloc, coupled with the lessening importance of the Latin American portfolio in the global economy, because this state of affairs affords more freedom to the debtor countries regarding the formulation of policies designed to lower the outward transfer of resources.

Countries undoubtedly will want to approach the reduction of this transfer in different ways. A minority of countries will find it appropriate to work entirely within the official framework of the Market Menu Approach, periodically rescheduling debts on commercial terms, seeking involuntary loans, and participating in debt reduction schemes voluntarily sanctioned by the creditors. Other countries, however, will decide, or be forced by events, to limit the transfer through a partial or total stoppage of payments. In some cases the limit (or threat of a limit) on debt service will be a very transitory bargaining tactic designed to achieve more favourable conditions within the officially sanctioned debt management scheme, but in others it will be a longer-term policy stance designed to force the creditors to share in the costs of a medium-term program of economic growth and restructuring.[44] A prolonged partial or full moratorium will, of course, drive down secondary market prices of the debt to the floor and thereby give the countries more leverage in establishing the pace and discounted terms of eventual debt settlements.[45]

As for cooperation among the debtor countries of the region, past experience suggests that this can be only of very limited scope in view of the heterogeneous conditions of the borrowers. However, as the common stress of the development crisis intensifies, the barriers standing in the way of regional cooperation may be overcome, bringing forth more effective joint initiatives to reduce the net outward transfer of resources.

In sum, the classic market mechanism for resolving a debt overhang—default—was temporarily suspended by the unprecedented international debt management strategy of the early 1980s. However, as we move through the seventh year of the region's debt servicing difficulties, some of the classic market dynamics of the 1930s seem to be taking hold. Private credit markets have failed and do not discriminate well among the debtors, while new credit is withheld regardless of the countries' economic policies and capacity to pay. Just as in the 1930s, some countries in Latin America are normally servicing their foreign debt without much refinancing, but most are not. Trading of debt paper has accelerated, and secondary market prices reflect large discounts. Some of the debtors' economies manage to overcome the external constraints, while others do not. This is clearly a very unsatisfactory solution to the debt overhang, with unnecessary costs for debtors and creditors alike. However, it is the only realistic option until there is more far-sighted political leadership in the creditor countries.

NOTES

1 During 1983–1988 growth of GNP in the industrialized countries averaged 3.5% per annum. Given the voters' preference for continuity in the political leadership of the North, this rate of growth would seem to be satisfactory. However, as Sidney Dell remarked to the author, the performance is not satisfactory when viewed from the needs of an interdependent world: OECD economic growth has been highly volatile, uncertain as to its sustainability, and has imparted relatively little buoyancy to the debtor's terms of trade. The growth rate is calculated from data in IMF, *World Economic Outlook,* advance copy (Washington, D.C.: IMF September 25, 1988), p. 71.

2 For an analysis of these international facilities see Philip Wellons, *Passing the Buck* (Boston: Harvard Business School Press, 1987), chap. 7. For an analysis of how these facilities were applied during the Latin American crisis see ECLAC, *External Debt in Latin America* (Boulder, Colo.: Lynne Rienner Publishers, 1985), chap. 3, and ECLAC, *The Evolution of the External Debt Problem in Latin America and the Caribbean,* Estudios e Informes de la CEPAL series, no. 72 (LC/G.1487/Rev.1–P), Santiago, Chile, 1988, United Nations publication, sales no.: E.88.II.G.10, chap. 1.

3 The increase in loan loss reserves was induced by actions of Citibank, which raised reserves by US$3 billion in the second quarter of 1987. For competitive reasons, most other United States banks with Latin American exposure copied Citibank to one degree or another. Consequently, United States banks reported US$11 billion in losses in the second quarter, which represented the industry's worst performance since the 1930s.

See ECLAC, "Economic Survey of the United States of America," Washington Office, August 24, 1988, p. 29, published later as *Economic Survey of the United States, 1987* (LC/G.1477; LC/WAS/L.3/Rev.1), Santiago, Chile, February 1989.

4 See Thomas Hanley et al., *Developing Country Exposures—Have Investors Recognized the Degree of Progress Made by Money Center Banks?* (New York: Salomon Brothers, July 21, 1988), p. 2.

5 For the situation of European banks, see Gunner Wiegand, *Western Europe and the Latin American Debt Crisis,* working paper no. 12, Madrid, 1988, p. 20.

6 *Daily Telegraph* (UK), "Time to Break the Cycle of Third World Debt," August 30, 1988.

7 At the beginning of 1988 this process further intensified. In April–June 1988 the largest United States banks had loan charge-offs of US$0.9 billion, up from US$0.6 billion in the first quarter of the year. See T. Hanley and others, op. cit., p. 2.

8 Debt/equity swaps in Argentina, Brazil, Chile, and Mexico totalled US$5 billion in 1987. Peter Truell, "Cutting Losses," *Wall Street Journal,* September 23, 1988, supplement, p. 10 R.

9 In the 1988 debt rescheduling of Brazil roughly 100 banks subscribed to exit bonds amounting to about US$1 billion. The bonds carried a 6% interest rate for 25 years.

10 Early in 1988 Mexico converted US$3.67 billion of commercial bank debt into US$2.56 billion of bonds, which represented a 30% discount. The bonds had a single 20-year maturity and carried an interest rate of 1.63% over LIBOR. The principal of the bond was secured by the government's purchase of a 20-year United States Treasury zero-coupon bond for an amount equivalent to the outstanding Mexican government bonds.

11 In March 1988 Bolivia arranged to buy back US$318 million of its public commercial bank debt—nearly 50% of the total with these lenders—at a price of 11 cents on the dollar. The resources for the buyback arrangement came from OECD countries. The operation was facilitated by the establishment of a special escrow account in the IMF for the depositing of OECD contributions. Meanwhile, in mid-1988 Chile negotiated with its banks an arrangement to use up to US$500 million of its international reserves to buy back bank debt at a discount. In November 1988 Chile bought back US$299 million of bank debt at 56 cents on the dollar.

12 The most recent manifestation of this was the willingness of the World Bank to sponsor a restructuring loan for the government of Argentina even though the Argentine economic authorities could not reach prior terms with the IMF for a standby agreement. See Stephen Fidler, "World Bank Agrees Argentine Loan," *Financial Times,* September 26, 1988.

13 The four democratic governments in the 1970s were Colombia, Costa Rica, the Dominican Republic, and Venezuela. It should be added that Ecuador's democratic institutions were restored in April 1979.

14 Commercial bankers recognize the emergence of this new consensus in the region. See, for instance, John Reed, "New Money in New Ways," *International Economy* (October/November 1987): 50.

15 See ECLAC, *Preliminary Overview of the Latin American Economy, 1988* (LC/G.1536), Santiago, Chile, January 3, 1989, table 15.

16 For a detailed analysis of the process of adjustment in Latin America, see Andrés Bianchi, Robert Devlin, and Joseph Ramos, "El Proceso de Ajuste en la América Latina," *El Trimestre Económico,* 44, 216 (October/December 1987).

17 One study has shown that by 1985 United States exports to Latin America were 28% below levels recorded in 1981 and 47% below the potential export level. The latter is defined as maintenance of a constant export share vis-à-vis GDP. See Joint Economic Committee, United States Congress, "Trade Deficits, Foreign Debt and Sagging Growth," Washington, D.C., September 1986, table 6.

18 For example, rates of return on United States direct investment in Latin America declined from an average of 17% in 1980–1981 to 6% in 1982–1985. See United Nations Centre on Transnational Corporations, *Transnational Corporations in World Development: Trends and Prospects* (ST/CTC/89), New York, 1988, United Nations publication, sales no. 88.II.A.7, p. 82.

19 The scheme for African debtors allows creditor governments to write off one-third of the debts, or cut interest rates by half or 3.5 percentage points, or lengthen the amortization period to 25 years. The plan has been criticized as not being radical enough for these problem debtors. See *Financial Times,* "Africa's Debt Burden," September 30, 1988, p. 18.

20 ECLAC, *Preliminary Overview,* op. cit., table 3.

21 ECLAC, Division of Statistics and Quantitative Analysis.

22 Data from ECLAC, *Preliminary Overview,* op. cit.

23 World Bank, "Poverty in Latin America: The Impact of Depression," Washington, D.C., 1986.

24 For a more complete analysis see ECLAC, *Restrictions on Sustained Development in Latin America and the Caribbean and the Requisites for Overcoming Them* (LC/G.1488(SES.22/3)/Rev. 1), Santiago, Chile, February 9, 1988. The study that helped to shift the analytical focus of the debt debate to the question of the transfer problem is Helmut Reisen and Axel Van Trotsenberg, *The Budgetary and Transfer Problem,* Paris, Organization for Economic Co-operation and Development (OECD), 1988.

25 An analysis of the complex relationship between debt service and inflation can be found in Rudiger Dornbusch, "Debt, Inflation and Growth: The Case of Argentina," Washington, D.C., International Monetary Fund, February 16, 1988.

26 See Bianchi, Devlin and Ramos, op. cit., p. 891.

27 The per capita GDP in Latin America grew by a respectable 3% per annum over 1950–1980.

28 Ground has focussed on this issue. Conventional criteria suggest that the transitory components of external shocks should be financed. However, according to Ground's estimates, the external finance made available to Latin America over 1982–1985 covered only 37%, 25%, 36%, and 16% of the respective transitory components of the adverse external shocks in that period. See Richard Ground, "The origin and magnitude of the recessionary adjustment in Latin America," *CEPAL Review,* no. 30 (LC/G.1441), Santiago, Chile, December 1986, p. 72.

29 When the crisis first broke out, private banks, in conjunction with the IMF, committed themselves to an annual expansion of 7% in their credit exposure in the region. The actual expansion in the first round of reschedulings came closer to 6% and fell dramatically thereafter. Then, in September 1985, Secretary Baker of the United States Treasury established a new target for bank credit expansion of 2 1/2% per annum for 3 years. This goal was not fulfilled; indeed, the response of the banks was to begin a sustained reduction of their exposure in the region. Moreover, the slack was not picked up by multilateral and bilateral lenders.

30 Colombia is a good illustration of this problem: with a debt-to-export ratio of only a little over 2:1 and a debt-to-GDP ratio of 34%, it has had tremendous difficulty securing fresh credit from the private banks.

31 Detailed analysis of the problems of collective action and public goods can be found in James Buchanan, *The Demand and Supply of Public Goods* (Chicago: Rand McNally and Co., 1968), chap. 5.

32 The collective nature of the problem even manifests itself in isolated payments crises of individual firms. Because of this, bankruptcy laws often impose collective solutions upon a firm's creditors. See Thomas Jackson, *The Logic and Limits of Bankruptcy Law* (Cambridge, Mass.: Harvard University Press, 1986).

33 By now the nature of the coordinated policies of the IMF, OECD Central Banks, and Treasuries with the creditor banks and debtor governments is so well known that it is not necessary to summarize it here. If desired, however, details may be found in ECLAC, *External Debt in Latin America,* op.cit., pp. 47–86.

34 ECLAC, *The Evolution,* op. cit., chapter 11.

35 See Mahesh Kotecha, "Repackaging Third World Debt," *Standard and Poor's International Credit Week,* August 1987, p. 9; and Kenneth Telljohann, "Analytical Framework," *Prospects for Securitization of Less Developed Country Loan* (New York: Salomon Brothers, June 1987), p. 11.

36 "Negative side effects" are particularly complex in the popular debt-equity swaps. See Group of Thirty, *Finance for Developing Countries,* New York, 1987.

37 As an illustration, the original goal of the Mexican-Morgan Guaranty bond operation of early 1988 was to convert US$20 billion of debt. If this goal had been attained at an average (rather optimistic) discount of 40%, something of the order of US$350 million of net interest payments would have been saved. While this type of operation had many merits, including the banks' formal recognition of market discounts, its significance as a vehicle for macroeconomic financing is less apparent in view of the US$7 billion interest burden with the private lenders. In any event, as mentioned in note 10, the banks' reception to the plan was less enthusiastic than had originally been hoped for. A detailed analysis of the Mexican bond offer can be found in Kenneth Telljohann and Richard Buckholz, *The Mexican Bond Exchange Offer* (New York, Salomon Brothers, January 1988).

38 The volume of secondary market trading in 1987 is estimated to have been about US$12 billion. Some expect that figure to rise to US$25 billion in 1988. To put these figures in perspective it must be remembered that they include considerable double counting and therefore do not mirror actual debt conversions. The figures also are still small relative to the estimated US$300–350 billion of problem LDC debt in the international commercial banking system. See Richard Lawrence, "Banker Proposes Solution to Argentina, Brazilian Debt," *Journal of Commerce,* September 28, 1988; and Eugenio Lahera, *La Conversión de la Deuda Externa: Antecedentes, Evolución y Pérspectivas* (LC/R.614), UNDP/ECLAC Project "Finance for Development," Santiago, Chile, ECLAC, September 1987.

39 For a good review of the portfolio adjustments of debtors and creditors in the 1930s and 1940s, see Marilyn Skiles, *Latin American International Loan Defaults in the 1930s: Lessons for the 1980s?,* Federal Reserve Bank of New York, research paper no. 8812, April 1988.

40 In the contemporary debate early proposals were made by Peter Kenen and Richard Weinert. Kenen proposed conversion at a discount, while Weinert proposed conversion at par with below-market interest rates, on the grounds that this would spread the banks' losses over time. See Peter Kenen, "A Bailout for the Banks," *The New York Times,* March 1983 and Richard Weinert, "Banks and Bankruptcy," *Foreign Policy,* no. 50, Second Quarter, 1983, pp. 128–149. Kenen has recently updated and expanded his proposal. See Peter Kenen, "A Proposal for Reducing the Debt Burden of Developing Countries," Princeton, N.J., Princeton University, March 1987. Other people proposing a global debt conversion facility are: John La Falce, "Third World Debt Crises: The Urgent Need to Confront Reality," *Congressional Record,* Washington, D.C., 133, 34, (March 5, 1987); Don Pease, "A Congressional Plan to Solve the Debt Problem," *International Economy* (March/April 1988): 98–105; James Robinson, "A Comprehensive Agenda for LDC Debt and World Trade Growth," London, American Express Bank, March 1988; Percy Mistry, "Third World Debt," May 1987; and Arjun Sengupta, "A Proposal for a Debt Adjustment Facility," Washington, D.C., IMF, March 8, 1988.

41 The coordination was so good that Latin Americans began to perceive the formation of a creditors' cartel. See OAS, "Desarrollo Integral y Democracia en América Latina y el Caribe: Ideas y Agenda para la Acción," Washington, D.C., September 28, 1987, p. 23.

42 The breakdown of the cartel reflects itself in the growing disputes among all parties in the creditor bloc about how to share responsibilities in the management of the debt issue. Serious public disagreements have broken out among the private banks, between the banks, their governments, and the multilateral lenders, among the creditor governments, between the creditor governments and multilateral lenders, and even between the World Bank and IMF (over the recent World Bank loan program in Argentina, mentioned in note 12). For an analysis of the breakdown of the creditor coordination, see ECLAC, *The Evolution,* op. cit.

43 This manifested itself clearly during the fourth round of reschedulings. See ECLAC, *Economic Survey of Latin America and the Caribbean, 1987: Advance Summary* (LC/G.1511), Santiago, Chile, pp. 42–60.

44 There are various ways a moratorium can be established. For some techniques that draw partially on the experience of the 1930s, see ECLAC, ibid.

45 Again, this is what happened in the 1930s. Indeed, some countries stopped debt service to accumulate resources for a buyback of debt at very low market prices. See M. Skiles, op. cit.

APPENDIX

RECENT INNOVATIONS IN DEBT RESTRUCTURING

John Clark and Eliot Kalter

International Monetary Fund

The recent agreements with commercial banks on debt reduction packages for Argentina and Brazil and the implementation by Paris Club creditors of a menu of enhanced concessions in reschedulings for low-income countries have made headlines. These are, however, only the latest steps in a series of debt restructuring innovations aimed at facilitating the resolution of debt servicing problems for countries carrying out strong adjustment and reform programs. This article reviews the experience with these innovations and looks at prospects for the many developing countries that still face heavy debt burdens.

The shift in approach toward debt reduction since the late 1980s reflected widespread appreciation that the existing strategy needed to be reinforced. Expectations in the early years of the debt crisis that debtor countries would be able to resume normal debt servicing within a short period of time were not borne out. Meanwhile, with repeated reschedulings of principal and consolidations of interest, the stock of debt continued to grow, impairing domestic confidence and undermining countries' adjustment efforts. Moreover, the refinancing of interest on bank claims through new money packages became increasingly difficult to negotiate as the financial position of commercial bank creditors strengthened.

BANK DEBT RESTRUCTURINGS

Against this background, in March 1989, US Treasury Secretary Brady proposed that official support be provided to countries to finance the restructuring of commercial

From Finance & Development, *September 1992, pp. 6–8.*

250

bank debt through comprehensive packages involving a "menu" of market-based debt and debt service reduction options. The main condition for this support was that the debtor be implementing a strong set of adjustment and reform policies that, combined with debt operations, would provide for substantial progress toward external viability. Under this approach, banks can choose among a range of options previously agreed between the borrower and a committee of the country's leading bank creditors. Among the options, buybacks have allowed banks to exit by selling their claims back to the borrower at a discount. Under more complex bond exchanges, existing loans have been swapped for bonds with a reduced principal amount (discount exchanges), or predetermined sub-market interest rates (par exchanges). In addition, the repayment period on the remaining obligations has been extended, reaching up to 30 years.

To encourage creditors to participate in debt exchanges, they were given the opportunity to convert their loans into less easily rescheduled securities and to attach collateral accounts—often funded with the assistance of official creditors—to guarantee the payment of the principal and/or a portion of the interest on the new bonds. Because the collateral is refundable (or can be drawn to cancel liabilities), such guarantees provide an additional effective reduction in claims payable to banks by effectively prepaying a portion of the remaining obligations through the collateral accounts.

The menu approach has facilitated nearly universal participation by banks in debt packages and has lowered costs by allowing banks to select options that best suit their particular tax, regulatory, and accounting situations, as well as their views on the future path of interest rates and the country's prospects. Experience has shown that despite the variety of instruments and menus, in general, the amount of debt reduction achieved through each of the packages has been broadly consistent with—and generally somewhat greater than—what might have been achieved through buybacks at the secondary market prices prevailing when agreement was reached.

Implementation of these debt restructurings has been time-consuming, but progress has been fairly steady. Agreements have now been reached covering about three-fourths of bank claims on countries that had experienced recent debt servicing difficulties. Packages have been completed for six countries—Costa Rica, Mexico, Nigeria, the Philippines, Uruguay, and Venezuela. A second package is in the process of being completed for the Philippines, while agreements in principle have been reached for Argentina and Brazil, and negotiations are in progress in a number of other cases.

Taking the packages already completed, claims to be paid to commercial banks by debtor countries have been reduced in present value terms by about $38 billion since 1989, cutting these countries' medium and long-term bank debt by roughly two-fifths (see Table 16-11). Associated interest relief in relation to GDP has varied, depending, among other things, on the size of the bank debt involved, but has generally been around $\frac{1}{2}$ of 1 percent of GDP for the major debtors. Required funding for these operations has totaled around $14 billion, of which the IMF and the World Bank, in connection with borrowers' economic adjustment programs, have each lent around $2\frac{1}{4}$–$2\frac{1}{2}$ billion. The remainder has come from bilateral loans and grants and the countries' own reserves. Officially supported debt reduction has been complemented by a continued role for debt-equity conversions, with over $24 billion of debt converted under official schemes during 1989–91, bringing the total to about $40 billion since 1984.

TABLE 16-11
BRINGING THE DEBT DOWN *Commercial Bank Debt Restructuring, 1987–June 1992*
(In billions of US dollars)

	Debt restructured[1]	Debt reduction		Debt-service reduction[3]	Pre-payments	Total reduction in claims payable to banks[4]
		Buy back[2/3]	Discount exchange[2/3]			
Bolivia (1987)	0.5	0.3	0.2	0	...	0.5
Chile (1988 and 1989)	0.4	0.4	—	—	—	0.4
Costa Rica (1990)	1.6	1.0	—	0.2	...	1.2
Mexico (1988 and 1990)	46.7	—	7.9	7.0	7.7	22.6
Mozambique (1991)	0.2	0.2	—	—	—	0.1
Niger (1991)	0.1	0.1	—	—	—	0.1
Nigeria (1991)	5.4	3.4	—	0.6	0.4	4.3
Philippines (1990 and 1992)[5]	5.2	2.6	—	0.7	0.5	3.9
Uruguay (1991)	1.2	0.6	—	0.2	0.1	0.9
Venezuela (1990)	13.5	1.4	0.5	2.7	1.7	6.3
Total	74.7	10.0	8.6	11.3	10.3	40.2
Of which:						
Since March 1989	70.3	9.4	7.3	11.3	9.8	37.8

Source: IMF staff estimates.
[1] Under debt and debt-service reduction operations; includes associated past due interest but excludes debt restructured under new money options.
[2] Excludes prepayment of principal and interest through guarantees.
[3] Adjusted for the impact of value recovery clauses.
[4] Does not include new debt incurred to finance these operations.
[5] Reflects impact of debt exchange expected to be completed after June 30, 1992.

In addition to the middle-income countries cited above, a number of low-income countries—in particular Bolivia, Mozambique, and Niger—have completed buybacks at deep discounts that have greatly reduced the commercial bank debt of these countries. Given the countries' generally weak external positions and low income levels, these operations have been financed with concessional resources. These countries have also benefited from various types of debt for development conversions (e.g., debt-for-environment, debt-for-health, and debt-for-education). However, for most low-income countries facing debt servicing difficulties, debt to commercial banks accounts for a relatively small proportion of the total, and the treatment of bilateral official debt, which often accounts for the preponderant share, is an important aspect of their efforts to regain external viability.

BILATERAL OFFICIAL CREDITORS

Over the past decade, bilateral official creditors have assisted developing countries encountering debt servicing difficulties through a wide range of instruments, including new financing through officially supported export credits and direct bilateral loans and grants, debt service restructuring, and bilateral ODA (official development assistance) debt forgiveness initiatives. A key feature of the approach taken by bilateral official creditors has been to exclude short-term debts and new (post-cutoff date) claims from reschedulings. This strategy—which has effectively given seniority to these claims—has been crucial to the continuation of new official support. As a result, net resource flows to developing countries from official creditors remained positive and even increased in many cases over the past decade. Moreover, resources were provided on increasingly concessional terms.

Notwithstanding these efforts, low-income countries in particular found increasing difficulties in meeting the terms of previous reschedulings. In addition, the growing need for cash-flow relief required increasingly comprehensive consolidations, which in turn contributed to a growth in the stock of debt. The Paris Club initially responded by lengthening the repayment periods for these countries from ten years to up to twenty years (and the grace periods from five years to up to ten years), beginning in 1987. A second and more decisive step was taken in late 1988, when Paris Club creditors adopted a menu approach with concessional options ("Toronto terms"). Through 1991, 20 debtor countries had obtained 28 reschedulings on Toronto terms, consolidating debt obligations of some $6 billion with an average grant element of over 20 percent on nonconcessional debt (see Table16-12).

While reschedulings under Toronto terms brought some low-income countries closer to a graduation from the rescheduling process, creditors recognized that more far-reaching concessions would be required for most other low-income rescheduling countries to achieve a sustained improvement in their debt situation. Creditors agreed in December 1991 to implement a new menu incorporating enhanced concessions in reschedulings for low-income countries. This new menu provides for a 50 percent reduction (in net present value terms) of debt service payments consolidated on non-ODA debts and a graduated repayment schedule over 23 years, through either an outright cancellation of 50 percent of the consolidated claims or a resched-

TABLE 16-12
OFFICIAL FINANCING THROUGH PARIS CLUB RESCHEDULINGS

	1986	1987	1988	1989	1990	1991	1992
							Jan.–June
	(Amount consolidated in billions of US dollars)						
Low-income countries [1]	9.2	1.5	1.2	3.0	2.8	0.9	0.9
Of which under:							
Toronto terms	—	—	0.5	2.0	2.8	0.2	—
Enhanced concessions	—	—	—	—	—	0.8	0.9
Middle-income countries	3.9	23.9	8.2	15.6	13.7	72.6	13.8
Of which:							
Poland and Egypt	—	15.4	—	—	10.4	57.8 [2]	—
Cumulative total							
amount consolidated [3]	50.7	76.2	85.6	104.2	120.7	194.2	208.9
	(Number of reschedulings)						
Low-income countries [1]	12	7	9	13	10	4	5
Middle-income countries	4	10	6	11	8	12	5
Cumulative total number							
of reschedulings [3]	83	100	115	139	157	173	183
Cumulative total number of							
rescheduling countries [3]	40	42	43	50	52	55	55

Source: *Paris Club Agreed Minutes; and IMF staff estimates.*
[1] *SAF/ESAF eligible.*
[2] *Total value of debt restructured.*
[3] *Cumulative since 1980.*

uling at concessional interest rates. The menu also includes the nonconcessional option available under Toronto terms. With respect to concessional loans, creditors agreed to graduate payments and to maintain concessional interest rates to achieve the same proportion of effective debt reduction.

To date, seven countries have benefited from the new rescheduling terms—Benin, Bolivia, Equatorial Guinea, Nicaragua, Tanzania, Togo, and Uganda. The amount consolidated under these terms has totaled about $1¾ billion, with an average grant element of around 45 percent on nonconcessional debt, reflecting the use of the nonconcessional option by some creditors.

Under the new approach, Paris Club creditors have continued their practice of rescheduling only those obligations falling due during a concurrent arrangement with the IMF. However, the agreements also provide for the possibility that the remaining stock of debt might be similarly restructured and reduced after a period of three to four years, provided that previous reschedulings are fully implemented, other nonmultilateral creditors grant comparable relief, and appropriate arrangements with the IMF are continued. The terms of these operations have yet to be settled; nonetheless, creditors have in principle indicated readiness to provide a definitive resolution to the problem of bilateral official debt.

For middle-income countries, bilateral official debt usually accounts for a smaller share of total debt than for low-income countries and actions by bilateral official creditors on debt are less decisive in affecting these countries' medium-term prospects for viability. In light of the difficulties faced by some of these countries, since 1990 Paris Club creditors have granted heavily indebted lower middle-income countries longer repayment terms, while selectively permitting voluntary swaps of debt for local currency obligations, such as debt-for-nature swaps. These new terms have been obtained by 15 heavily indebted lower middle-income countries, helping to reduce their number to a point where an exit from the rescheduling process is now in sight. Others, however, continue to face uncertain prospects. The July 1992 industrial country economic summit communiqué encouraged the Paris Club to recognize the special situation of some highly indebted, lower middle-income countries on a case-by-case basis.

In the meantime, bilateral official creditors have also dealt with the exceptional situations of Poland and Egypt. In each case, the Paris Club agreed to restructure the entire stock of debt (totaling a combined $58 billion) and to reduce the present value of the debt by 50 percent through a menu of options. An important feature of both agreements is that they provide for staged implementation, with some reduction taking place at the outset and the remainder taking place based on developments under the IMF arrangements supporting these countries' adjustment efforts.

FUTURE PROSPECTS

The combination of officially supported debt reduction, extended repayment schedules, and strengthened policy implementation has brought impressive and hopefully lasting results in a number of middle-income debtor countries. With a return to more normal creditor/debtor relations, costly and difficult concerted refinancing exercises are no longer needed, arrears have been eliminated, and investor confidence has been restored. As a result, discounts on the debt of these countries in the secondary market have declined, access to private financing (mainly through securities markets) has increased significantly, capital flight has been reversed, and growth prospects have improved. Mexico, Chile, and Venezuela have been in the forefront of this process of market re-entry; recently, Argentina and Brazil have also been able to gain access to sizable flows, even though they have yet to finalize debt restructurings.

For heavily indebted low-income countries, the new approach by Paris Club creditors provides the potential means for countries to exit from the rescheduling process. Some are already on the verge of achieving that goal, although they will continue to rely on appropriate concessional financing. For others, however, as well as for some lower middle-income countries, the current debt burden is such that their balance of payments situation will still remain difficult over the medium term.

Despite the benefits of debt reduction, the debt burdens of most restructuring countries remain significant. The authorities of these countries must continue to implement sound macroeconomic policies—complemented by further structural measures where necessary—to maintain confidence and ensure that new flows will be appropriately channeled into productive investment. A number of countries that have been experiencing continued debt-servicing difficulties have yet to gain access to the new restructuring terms potentially available to them on their commercial bank and bilateral official debt. For some of these countries, a renewed adjustment effort will be needed to address the internal and external imbalances that constrain their growth prospects. The favorable impact that the combination of strengthened policy implementation and the broadened menu of restructuring options have already had on the prospects of some countries demonstrates the benefits that potentially await them.

PART FOUR

AGRICULTURE
IN DEVELOPMENT

Development theorists have always assigned the agriculture sector a central role in the development process, and our understanding of that role has evolved with time. Early writers emphasized industrialization, although they counted on agriculture to provide the necessary output of food and raw materials, along with the labor force that would gradually be transferred into industrial production. Later thinking moved agriculture to the center of the development process; the hopes for technical change in agriculture and the "green revolution" suggested that agriculture could be the dynamo for growth. Indeed, growth of agricultural output reached historical highs throughout the world, for example, cereal production increased an average of 2.5 percent per year in the world between 1965 and 1989 (World Bank, 1992). Processed agricultural products were important contributors to the export-led growth pattern of countries such as Taiwan. Chile's growth during the past decade was largely through agricultural exports.

Agriculture continues to be important in virtually all developing countries and will play a central role in any development process. In 1990 agriculture contributed 31 percent of total output in low-income economies and 17 percent in lower-middle-income countries (World Bank, 1992).[1] The rural population still bulks large in most countries, for example, 80 percent in Kenya, 77 percent in India, and 59 percent in Guatemala.

Changes in individual countries and in the world economy have stimulated rethinking of the role of agriculture in development, and the articles in this section reflect that effort. They should be read in the context of the growing concern with "sustainable development" introduced in the articles in earlier parts. It is highly questionable that the rapid rate of increase in food production is sustainable. There is already evidence that yields are dropping in many areas of the world and environmental degradation is threatening production in others. The UN Conference on Population and Development in Cairo in 1994 highlighted the pressure population increases are placing on natural resources and emphasized the necessity of a broad-based development which can balance the carrying capacity of resources and the demands placed on them. The following articles present elements of the agricultural system that will influence any effort to adjust to this new reality and to embody agriculture in a true development process.

Derek Byerlee examines the long-run effect of the international economy on agriculture and on food production and trade. The article continues the theme of the last section, for the reshaping and restructuring of the world economy will undoubtedly affect the agricultural sectors of developing economies. Byerlee's focus is international trade in one staple commodity, wheat, which has taken on a peculiar importance in agriculture trade. There are twenty-six developing countries that do not produce wheat, and twenty more who import more than half of their consumption. In addition, wheat exports are dominated by developed countries and wheat imports by developing countries doubled during the 1970s. The impact was profound, affecting domestic food production, changing domestic food consumption patterns, and often leading to balance-of-payments pressures and overprotected domestic processing industries. The effects varied across the world. For example, the East Asian economies ensured that the increase in wheat consumption was not primarily from imports and that a protected domestic processing industry did not develop. Byerlee documents the important role that wheat has played in the entire agricultural system, the result of international trading relations. Wheat is certainly the best example, but the entire trajectory of agricultural development in the South is largely determined by the mode of insertion of these countries in the international economy.

Joseph E. Stiglitz turns our point of view to the domestic economy and how we can understand the behavior of that large majority of the population of many countries that still works in agriculture. He employs a modification of the standard neoclassical model to explain the persistence of a rudimentary (and "inefficient") form of organizing agricultural production, sharecropping. Stiglitz's "new development economics" is an attempt to generalize across all countries in the mode of early development thinkers. He assumes rational individual behavior and competition, but modifies that familiar model by assuming that information is costly, and therefore less than perfect, and that institutions adapt to reflect these costs. The modified model allows him to describe or explain sharecropping, cost-sharing between sharecropper and landlord, the dual role of landlord and credit provider, and some elements of technical change. The article is especially provocative in the challenge it presents to other theories of the peasant; and Stiglitz attempts to set out the criteria for choosing among the competing theories.

Judith A. Carney provides another ground-level view of agriculture in the South in her historical overview of changes in agriculture in the Gambia in Africa, and more specifically in the effect they have had on women. Her study reinforces Diane Elson's point in Part One that including gender in issues of development is central to any successful development program. Anyone interested in seeing the same case made for Central America should read Yudelman (1993).

Agricultural policy in the Gambia has attempted to expand irrigation into rice and vegetable production, two products traditionally grown by women. The first rice program foundered by interfering with the carefully balanced traditions of women's land access and work obligations and it left a legacy of tensions in producing areas. The second rice irrigation scheme resulted in women losing access to individual plots and led them to pool their labor in a novel fashion to raise the wage they could obtain. It also turned them into sharecroppers with male household heads. Finally, projects to produce vegetables for export to Europe provided another option for periurban women. Again the labor demands and the weak bargaining power of the women resulted in low incomes for the producers. So these efforts at agricultural development showed at best mixed results, largely because of their failure to understand clearly the factors that affect the welfare of women in the Gambia.

Finally, Gene Ellis's "Two Tales of a City" (Addis Ababa in Ethiopia) is a cautionary tale, illustrating the fragile balance between human activity and nature, by focusing on the urban eucalyptus forest of Addis. Ellis combines historical information with satellite observations of the urban forest to document a 33 percent decline in the forest in a period of three years after new policies were implemented in 1974. The result has been ecological disruption, forcing the use of much less appropriate fuels and requiring the exploitation of more distant sources of fuelwood. Parallel examples could be found in many countries under many different types of governments, and the yearly publication of the Worldwatch Institute, *The State of the World,* provides ample documentation of the many environmental threats. Ellis's tale reemphasizes the point that development can succeed only if it is "sustainable," if the environment can accommodate the changes. This must be a starting point in any view of the role of agriculture in development.

The combination of the articles in Part Four provides an up-to-date overview of the agricultural sector in development. Each national economy has an agricultural sector which is quite varied and complex and which remains an important element of the development process. Not even the newly industrializing countries (NICs) are exceptions. And the subsistence or peasant sector continues to absorb large portions of the population in many countries. However, the internationalization of agriculture has a profound impact in all countries, and its effects have been quite mixed.

NOTE

1 At the same time it must be realized that agriculture's share is declining. In 1965 it contributed 41 percent of output in low-income economies and 22 percent in lower-middle-income countries.

REFERENCES

The World Bank. *The World Development Report, 1992.* New York: Oxford University Press, 1992.

Yudelman, Sally. "Women Farmers in Central America." *Grassroots Development,* 17, 2 (1994): 2–13.

CHAPTER 17

THE POLITICAL ECONOMY OF THIRD WORLD FOOD IMPORTS: THE CASE OF WHEAT

Derek Byerlee

The World Bank

INTRODUCTION

Much attention has been focused on the increase in food imports by Third World countries during the last decade. This increase is usually equated with a growing gap between food production and consumption in developing countries. Yet projections, whether based on simple projection methods or more formal econometric models, have consistently underestimated imports by developing countries. For example, FAO and USDA forecasts of wheat imports by developing countries for 1985 (made in 1977–78) had already been exceeded by 20%–25% in 1981.[1]

This paper takes a new look at trends in food imports by developing countries. It focuses on wheat imports in the context of the wider food policy, institutional, and external trade environment in which these imports occur. It departs substantially from the traditional econometric approaches, which emphasize regional aggregates, to analyze evidence at the country level, where national food policies are made. An analysis across countries interpreted in the light of national and international policies provides fresh insights into the political economy of rapidly increasing wheat imports.

Wheat has special significance in the analysis of food policy and food imports in the Third World. First, cereals constitute the bulk of Third World food imports, and, among cereals, wheat is by far the dominant food grain import. In 1980, wheat accounted for an estimated 86% of food grain imports by Third World countries.[2] Since the postwar years, when Europe was the major wheat buyer in international markets, wheat imports have been increasingly destined for the Third World (including

Economic Development and Cultural Change, 35, 2 (January 1987), pp. 307–328. Copyright © 1987 by The University of Chicago.

China), which now accounts for two-thirds of total world wheat imports. In particular, in the last decade, wheat imports by developing countries have expanded extremely rapidly, doubling from 1970 to 1981. Second, unlike rice, world wheat *exports* are dominated by developed countries, which produced about two-thirds of the world's wheat and accounted for about 95% of total exports in 1979–81. Third, a significant group of 84 developing countries lying in the tropical belt between 23 degrees south latitude and 23 degrees north latitude currently do not produce wheat. Hence, there is a basic inconsistency between the traditional food staple (i.e., rice, coarse grains, or roots and tubers) and the importation of wheat, a nontraditional staple with little immediate prospects for local production. Finally, wheat—more than any other cereal staple—usually undergoes a greater degree of commercial processing before being consumed. This means that transportation, processing, and marketing costs make up a larger proportion of final consumer prices (over 80% for bread), and consumer prices are more sensitive to the influence of policy interventions and market distortions at each stage of the process.

This paper begins by summarizing recent patterns in wheat consumption and imports in the Third World. A framework is then developed to explain these trends in light of both national food policies and policies of the exporting countries. The framework is applied in a cross-country analysis of wheat imports and policy interventions. The evidence on biases in national and international food policies in favor of wheat products is developed in some detail, and policy measures to arrest growing dependence on food imports are discussed.

RECENT TRENDS IN CONSUMPTION AND IMPORTS

During the last 2 decades, wheat has shown a remarkably rapid and widespread increase in its contribution to diets in the Third World. Data from FAO indicate that, in all major regions, wheat consumption has increased more than any other food staple in both a relative and absolute sense (see Table 17-1). Consumption of rice has also increased but to a much smaller extent than that for wheat. To a large extent increased wheat consumption reflects a widespread substitution for so called inferior food staples—coarse grains and roots and tubers—whose per capita consumption has declined (Table 17-1). These trends in consumption patterns have accelerated during the 1970s, when wheat consumption in the Third World grew at an annual rate of 5.4%. An estimated 80% of the increase in world wheat consumption in this period occurred in the developing world.[3]

Although these changing consumption patterns were general across countries, there is a sharp division between countries in the extent to which increased wheat consumption was supplied by domestic production or by imports. For the largest wheat producers (China, India, Pakistan, and Turkey), rapid increases in domestic production have supported increased consumption and in some cases allowed for import substitution. For all other regions, increased consumption has largely been met by imports (Table 17-2). This includes those regions where wheat is a traditional food but import dependence is high (e.g., over 100 kilograms per capita of wheat is imported by countries of North Africa) and the tropical zone, where wheat consumption is much lower but almost all wheat is imported (e.g., Southeast Asia and sub-Saharan Africa).[4] Many countries in the

TABLE 17-1
AGGREGATE CHANGES IN CONSUMPTION OF FOOD STAPLES, BY REGION (%)

	Staple food calories provided by wheat, 1975–77	Annual growth rate in per capita availability of staple foods for human consumption, 1961–77			
		Wheat	Rice	Coarse grains	Roots and tubers
1. Countries where wheat is the traditional food staple[a]	72	1.3	2.0	−1.2	−.1
2. Large mixed-cereal economies (India, China, Mexico)	28	2.8	.4	−.7	−2.1
3. Tropical belt of countries where wheat is not a traditional staple[b]	15	2.7	.8	−.6	−.5

[a]Includes countries from Morocco to Pakistan and the Southern Cone of Latin America.
[b]Includes countries lying between 23 degrees north latitude and 23 degrees south latitude.
Source: Calculated from FAO, *Food Balance Sheets* (Rome: FAO, 1981).

tropical belt now have per capita wheat imports (and consumption) of 30–50 kilograms per year.

In summary, in 1978–80 there was a total of 65 developing countries consuming over 100,000 tons of wheat annually. Forty-six of these countries were less than 50% self-sufficient in wheat and 26 (i.e., those in the tropical belt) did not produce wheat (i.e., less than 20,000 hectares). Wheat import dependence has increased in almost all Third World countries (except the four largest producers) to reach high levels by the 1980s.

A FRAMEWORK FOR ANALYZING THE DYNAMICS OF WHEAT IMPORTS

Figure 17-1 is a schematic representation of the complex of factors underlying the dynamics of wheat consumption and imports in the Third World. Both domestic and international actors operate to influence wheat consumption. On the domestic side, the main actors are *(a)* producers; *(b)* consumers; and *(c)* local grain-transport, storage, and processing industries. The main international actors are private and public agencies involved in the world wheat trade. In some cases, such as grain shipment and processing, international and domestic actors may be closely linked.

It is hypothesized that "natural" market forces operating on both the demand and supply sides tend to promote wheat consumption. With increasing incomes, consumer preferences are expected to favor wheat, especially in countries where wheat is not a traditional staple and consumers seek to diversify diets. The world supply of wheat

TABLE 17-2
RELATIONSHIP BETWEEN WHEAT CONSUMPTION, PRODUCTION, AND IMPORTS IN MAJOR DEVELOPING COUNTRY REGIONS

	Wheat consumption per capita, 1978–80 (kg)	Wheat imports per capita, 1978–80 (kg)	Increase in wheat consumption per capita, 1961–65 1978–80 (kg)	Increased consumption supplied by imports (%)	Growth rate 1961–65 to 1978–80 (% year)	
					Wheat consumption per capita	Wheat production per capita
Eastern and Southern Africa	16	8	4.1	66	1.8	0
Western Africa	13	13	8.6	100	6.6	[a]
North Africa	184	118	54.0	90	2.2	-1.6
Middle East (except Turkey)	167	54	39.0	51	1.2	0
South Asia	52	4	16.2	0[b]	2.3	4.0
Southeast Asia	13	13	7.4	100	5.3	[a]
East Asia	69	12	32.8	17	4.0	4.1
Mexico, Central America	50	27	13.1	70	1.9	-.2
Andes	38	35	4.5	100[c]	.8	-6.2
Southern Cone (except Argentina)	67	38	16.3	59	3.3	1.3
All developing countries[d]	61	14	20.0	26	2.5	2.4

[a] Non-wheat-producing regions.
[b] Production increased faster than consumption so that imports decreased.
[c] Production decreased so that imports increased to maintain per capita consumption.
[d] Includes Argentina and Turkey.
Source: Calculated from FAO Tapes of Production and Trade Statistics.

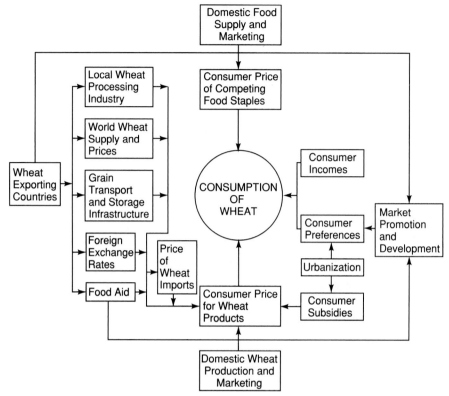

FIGURE 17-1
MAJOR INFLUENCES ON WHEAT CONSUMPTION AND IMPORTS IN THE THIRD WORLD.

and world market prices are also expected to be favorable to consumption of wheat products because of rapid technological change in some major wheat-producing countries (e.g., the United States, India, and China).

A central thesis of this paper is that governments, in both importing and exporting countries, have been key actors, whose interventions in wheat markets have consistently reinforced market phenomena and rapidly accelerated the substitution of wheat products for traditional staples. Government interventions on the domestic side are shown toward the right-hand side of Figure 17-1. These include *(a)* interventions in production of wheat and competing food staples; *(b)* investments, taxes and subsidies, and controls on the marketing and processing of wheat, both domestic and imported; *(c)* explicit consumer subsidies on wheat products; and *(d)* influences on consumers' preferences through market promotion and development. Interventions by governments of both the importing and exporting countries also influence the price of *imported* wheat, including *(a)* trade and exchange rate policies of both importers and exporters, *(b)* subsidies and credit facilities for wheat exports, *(c)* the provision of food aid (largely wheat), and *(d)* marketing and promotion policies by private and public agencies of exporting countries.

Finally, it is hypothesized that a number of influential interest groups have been important in biasing policy interventions toward wheat consumption and imports. These include the influence of middle-income urban consumers in food policy decisions, the vested interests and market power of the wheat-processing sector, and the linkages of this sector with exporting interests in developed countries, such as grain exporters or milling and shipping industries. Interest groups in exporting countries have also succeeded in distorting the policies of these countries toward wheat exports to the Third World. To a large extent, all of these interest groups reinforce each other in promoting wheat consumption.

Clearly, a comprehensive analysis of all of these factors and their linkages is beyond the scope of this paper. My focus is largely on the domestic policy environment with somewhat less attention to the international environment.

THE DOMESTIC POLICY ENVIRONMENT AND WHEAT CONSUMPTION

The Urban Bias of Wheat Consumption

Increased wheat consumption in the developing world has to a large extent occurred in urban areas. This is less so in the traditional wheat-consuming countries of the Middle East/North Africa, but even in that region there is a tendency to switch from coarse grains (such as barley) to wheat with migration to urban areas. Table 17-3 shows wheat consumption by rural and urban areas in three groups of countries. In countries where wheat consumption is relatively low, consumption is more strongly biased to urban areas. Furthermore, for this group of countries, wheat consumption is biased toward middle- and upper-income groups. Typically, the richest 25% of households have a per capita consumption of wheat twice that of the poorest 25%.[5] Income elasticities of demand in these countries generally range from 0.5 to 1.0 and are higher than for any other cereal staple. This underlines the important effect of incomes on wheat consumption and its substitution for other cereals.

There is considerable evidence that wheat is preferred as a convenience food. In urban areas, there is a strong tendency to switch to processed products, which require less preparation and reduce costs of cooking fuel. The data for Egypt (Table 17-4) vividly show these trends. There is also some evidence that women's participation in the labor force increases bread consumption.[6]

Biases in Consumer Pricing Policy toward Wheat Imports

A major factor in increased wheat consumption in urban areas has been the widespread intervention by governments in food marketing, resulting in reduced prices of wheat products to urban consumers. The most common and direct intervention has been to subsidize wheat flour or bread to consumers. In the traditional wheat-consuming countries of the Middle East/North Africa, these subsidies often represent 50% or more of the total cost of providing flour (based on imported wheat) to consumers or bakers (Table 17-5). Subsidies also occur in most of the mixed cereal economies of South and East Asia (e.g., China and India), although they are often lower (20%–30%) and in

TABLE 17-3

CONSUMPTION OF WHEAT PRODUCTS IN RURAL AND URBAN AREAS
IN SELECTED COUNTRIES

Country or region	Year	Annual per capita consumption of wheat products (kg/year)	
		Rural areas	Urban areas
High wheat consumption (>100 kg/capita/year):			
India, Punjab State	1974–75	130	117
Egypt	1974–75	109	178
Pakistan	1982	150	100
Intermediate wheat consumption (30–100 kg/capita/year):			
Peru	1972–73	28	43
Sri Lanka	1981	26	57
India, Bihar State	1974–75	39	57
Sudan	1982	25	84
Low wheat consumption (<30 kg/capita/year):			
Brazil	1975	9	29
Indonesia, Java	1980	3	32
Philippines	1975–79	5	18
Kenya	1974–75	10	30
India, Andhra Pradesh State	1974–75	2	9

Source: Government of India, *National Sample Survey: 28th Round, Oct. 73–June 74* (New Delhi: Department of Statistics, 1977); H. Alderman, J. von Braun, and S. A. Sakr, *Egypt's Food Subsidy and Rationing System: A Description,* Research Report no. 34 (Washington, D.C.: IFPRI, 1982); P. A. Cornelisse and S. N. H. Naqvi, *The Anatomy of the Wheat Market in Pakistan* (Islamabad and Rotterdam: Pakistan Institute for Development Economics and Erasumus University, 1984); Fundação Instituto Brasileiro de Geografia e Estatistica, *Estudo Nacional da Despesa Familiar* (Rio de Janeiro, 1978); P. Lizardo de las Casas Maya, "A Theoretical and Applied Approach to the Formulation of Alternative Agricultural Sector Policies" (Ph.D. diss., Iowa State University, 1977); D. I. Steinberg et al., *Sri Lanka: The Impact of PL480 Title I Food Assistance,* AID Impact Evaluation no. 39 (Washington, D.C.: USAID, 1982); D. Franklin, M. P. Demousin, and M. W. Harrell, *Consumption Effects of Agricultural Policies: Bread Prices in the Sudan* (Raleigh, N.C.: Sigma One Corp., 1982); S. L. Magiera, *The Role of Wheat in the Indonesian Food Sector,* Foreign Agricultural Economics Report no. 170 (Washington, D.C.: USDA, 1981); M. E. C. Bennagen, "Staple Food Consumption in the Philippines," Working Paper no. 5 (Washington, D.C.: IFPRI, 1982); N. Shah and K. Frohberg, "Food Consumption Patterns—Rural and Urban Kenya," Working Paper (Vienna: IIASA, 1980); FAO, *Review of Food Consumption Surveys,* vol. 2, *Africa, Latin America, Near East, Far East* (Rome, 1977).

India are targeted to low-income consumers through ration shops. Wheat-producing countries of Latin America, such as Mexico and Brazil, also had high subsidy levels (see Table 17-5). Even a number of non-wheat-producing countries—such as Sri Lanka, Cuba, and the Ivory Coast—have had substantial consumer subsidies on wheat products. Overall, over half of the 56 countries for which data were available had consumer subsidies on wheat products. In most cases, these subsidies are specific to

TABLE 17-4

COMPOSITION OF RETAIL PURCHASES OF WHEAT AND WHEAT PRODUCTS
BY RURAL AND URBAN AREAS, EGYPT (%)

Wheat product	1954–55		1974–75	
	Rural	Urban	Rural	Urban
Grain[a]	75	9	49	4
Flour	17	23	33	14
Bread	7	68	18	81
Total	100	100	100	100

[a]Includes consumption of home-grown grain.

Source: H. Alderman, J. von Braun, and S. A. Sakr, *Egypt's Food Subsidy and Rationing System: A Description,* Research Report no. 34 (Washington, D.C.: International Food Policy Research Institute, 1982).

TABLE 17-5

CLASSIFICATION OF COUNTRIES ACCORDING TO LEVEL OF CONSUMER SUBSIDY
ON WHEAT PRODUCTS, 1980–81

	High subsidy (>40%)	Moderate subsidy (10%–40%)	No significant subsidy	Significant tax on wheat products (>20%)
Sub-Saharan Africa	2	6	3	1
Middle East/North Africa	9	4	—	—
Far East, wheat-producing	1	3	—	—
Far East, non-wheat-producing	—	2	6	3
Latin America	4	4	6	2
All countries for which data available	16	19	15	6

Note: Column entries are number of countries and are based on subsidies on imported wheat. In most cases, subsidies on domestically produced wheat are somewhat higher.

Source: D. Byerlee, *The Increasing Role of Wheat Consumption and Imports in the Developing World,* CIMMYT Economics Paper no. 5/83 (El Batan, Mexico: CIMMYT, 1983).

wheat. Rice is also subsidized in a number of countries, whereas subsidies on maize and other coarse grains exist in only a handful of countries (e.g., Mexico).

In a few countries (e.g., Pakistan, Egypt, and Mexico in some years), low consumer prices for wheat products result from policies that reduce producer prices for wheat below world prices, although in almost all these cases direct government subsidies have played a more important role than low farm prices (see Table 17-6). Aside from these countries, there is little evidence in favor of the conventional wisdom that governments have maintained low producer prices in order to favor urban consumer-interest groups.[7]

TABLE 17-6
CLASSIFICATION OF COUNTRIES BY NOMINAL PROTECTION COEFFICIENTS
FOR PRODUCERS AND CONSUMERS, EARLY 1980s
(% of Countries)

	NPC for consumers			
	<.85	.85–1.15	>1.15	Total
NPC for producers:				
<.85	31	11	0	42
.85–1.15	12	11	0	23
>1.15	19	0	15	34
Total	62	23	15	100

Note: The NPC (Nominal Protection Coefficient) is the ratio of domestic prices (converted at the official exchange rate) to world prices adjusted by marketing and transport costs. Adjusted NPCs, calculated at shadow exchange rates by correcting for differential domestic and international inflation, indicated a lower percentage of countries subsidizing producers (i.e., 23% of countries with NPC > 1.15).

Source: D. Byerlee and G. Sain, "Food Pricing Policy in Developing Countries: Bias against Agriculture or for Urban Consumers?" *American Journal of Agricultural Economics,* 68 (1986), pp. 961–969.

Trade and exchange-rate policies also often favor low wheat prices to consumers, relative to competing staples. Because wheat is regarded as an industrial input (i.e., to the milling industry), explicit or implicit tariffs for wheat are typically kept low. Meanwhile, other staple foods are protected either by tariffs (in the case of cereals) or by high international transport costs (for roots and tubers). At the same time, many countries, especially in sub-Saharan Africa, have maintained overvalued exchange rates, which have reduced the cost of wheat imports relative to domestically produced staples. A number of countries have also recently established two-tiered exchange rates under which wheat is invariably classified as an "essential" item and imported at the cheaper rate (e.g., Ecuador).

The effect of these various policy interventions on prices of wheat products have been threefold. First, the absolute price of wheat products to consumers is often low. Table 17-7 shows the distribution of bread prices in wheat-importing countries in relation to a "world" price based on imported wheat in economies such as Panama and Hong Kong with relatively free markets. For most countries, especially the major wheat importers of the Middle East/North Africa and Mexico and Brazil, consumer bread prices are low; for many, bread prices are less than one-half of world prices. Second, the price of wheat products is often low in relation to competing food staples. I have estimated that, for consumer prices based on imported grains, the ratio of the price of wheat flour to rice should be slightly less than 1.0 in a free-trading country. For wheat flour to maize, the price ratio should be close to 2.0.[8] In many countries of sub-Saharan Africa and Latin America where coarse grains are an important staple (e.g., Ivory Coast, Ghana, Nigeria, Egypt, Sudan, Ecuador, and Brazil), wheat flour based on imported wheat was cheaper than the locally produced coarse grain staple in 1980–81. Likewise in East Asia (e.g., Korea and Japan), wheat flour was much cheaper than rice (the local staple) because of high protection to

TABLE 17-7
DISTRIBUTION OF BREAD PRICES BY DEVELOPING COUNTRY REGION, 1980–81
(No. of Countries)

	Low prices (<US$.60/kg)	"Normal" prices[a] (US$.60–1.00/kg)	High prices (>US$1.00/kg)
Sub-Saharan Africa	7	10	5
Middle East/North Africa	11	—	—
South Asia	4	1	—
Southeast and East Asia	—	3	5
Latin America	6	6	5
Total	28	20	15

Note: Based on conversion at the official exchange rate. Overvalued exchange rates reduced real prices further in a number of countries, especially in sub-Saharan Africa.

[a]"Normal" bread prices are based on prices in importing countries with relatively free trade policies. In Hong Kong, Panama, and Singapore, bread prices were approximately US$.80/kg. A 25% variation in this price has been selected to allow for differences in local processing costs.

Source: Calculated from data reported in ILO, *Bulletin of Labour Statistics* (various issues), supplemented and edited by the author.

domestic rice production. However, in some rice-producing countries, the price of wheat products relative to rice was high due to high tariffs on imported wheat (e.g., Colombia) and/or subsidies or export taxes on rice (e.g., Thailand). No country for which data are available had high wheat flour prices relative to maize (i.e., a ratio of 2:1 or above). Third, policy interventions in favor of wheat have resulted in declining *real* consumer prices for wheat products, both absolutely and relatively, over a wide array of countries (Tables 17-8 and 17-9). The major exception once again has been in the rice economies of Southeast Asia, where real bread prices have increased significantly. In relatively "free market" economies, such as Hong Kong, real bread prices changed little in the 1970s.

There is ample evidence that wheat consumption is sensitive to prices, especially in countries where wheat is not a traditional staple. Estimated price elasticities in these countries usually exceed −0.5 (absolutely) with relatively high cross-price elasticities with respect to rice.[9] Declining real prices of wheat products may explain half or more of the rapid increase in per capita wheat consumption in many countries during the 1970s.[10]

Although the evidence on biases in consumer pricing policy across countries is overwhelming, the consequences of this bias and the reasons for its existence have not been sufficiently analyzed. Several factors appear to converge in favor of wheat. In a number of wheat-producing countries, such as Mexico, India, and China, distinct surplus wheat-producing regions exist where government grain-procurement agencies find it convenient to purchase urban food requirements. Hence it is relatively easy to control procurement prices. Rapid technological change and relatively stable yields in the largely irrigated wheat environments of these countries have also facilitated the growing importance of wheat in government procurement strategies. In wheat-importing countries, the fact that wheat is readily available in world markets and

TABLE 17-8
CLASSIFICATION OF COUNTRIES BY ANNUAL PERCENTAGE CHANGE IN REAL PRICES OF BREAD, 1971–81

Region	No. of countries where data available	Annual change in real price of bread (% of countries)					
		<-3%	-3%—-1%	-1%—1%	1%–3%	>3%	Total
Sub-Saharan Africa	17	35	18	18	18	12	100
Middle East/North Africa	8	50	38	—	12	—	100
South Asia/Southeast Asia	12	—	8	25	8	58	100
Latin America	16	44	12	—	6	38	100
All developing countries	53	32	17	11	11	28	100
Industrialized countries	13	—	8	31	62	—	100

Source: See Table 7. Consumer prices deflated by the consumer price index from IMF, *International Financial Statistics* (Washington, D.C.: various issues).

TABLE 17-9
CHANGES IN REAL PRICES OF WHEAT FLOUR, RICE, AND MAIZE IN SELECTED
COUNTRIES, 1970s

City and country	Period	Change in retail prices (%)		
		Wheat flour	Rice	Maize, other coarse grain
São Paulo, Brazil	1969–79	−46	−1	167
Cali, Colombia	1970–80	7	−3	62
Mexico City, Mexico	1970–80	−48	18	−19[a]
Khartoum, Sudan	1971–81	−44	—	1[b]
Djakarta, Indonesia	1969–79	−22	−8	9
Dakar, Senegal[c]	1970–80	163	−30	10[d]
Manila, Philippines[c]	1968–78	168	−19	7

Note: Annual average consumer prices deflated by the consumer price index.
[a]Maize tortillas.
[b]Sorghum.
[c]Bread subsidies were drastically cut in Senegal, and import protection increased in Philippines in the 1970s.
[d]Millet.
Source: See Table 5.

usually passes through a small number of mills makes it relatively easy to control prices.[11]

Perhaps more important, urban populations—particularly middle- and upper-income groups who consume much of the imported wheat—are an important political power base capable of influencing policy. In almost all countries, wheat subsidies have been captured largely by urban populations and in many cases by the middle- and upper-income urban groups. For example, Alvarez estimated that before Peru eliminated food subsidies in the late 1970s (60% of which went for wheat), 83% of the subsidies were received by the urban population and 40% by the middle- and upper-income groups of Lima who made up only 10% of the total population.[12] A similar situation prevailed in Brazil and Indonesia.[13] Only in South Asia (India, Sri Lanka, and Bangladesh) has there been an effort to target wheat subsidies to low-income consumers. Many subsidy programs were initiated in 1974–75 to protect consumers from high world wheat prices at that time. Other countries instituted subsidies when wheat food aid was eliminated or reduced.[14] Finally, many governments with strict consumer price controls for flour or bread have been reluctant to raise prices in line with inflation, which has led to rapid real price declines and increasing subsidy levels in countries with high inflation rates (e.g., Mexico and Brazil).

Urban Food Supplies and Wheat Imports

There are also a number of factors operating on the supply side that influence wheat consumption in urban areas. With strong preferences for wheat products, lagging domestic production of staple foods, and poor infrastructure for transporting and marketing domestic food production in urban areas, there has been a natural tendency to import wheat to feed urban consumers, especially in countries where large cities are located on the coast. This is evident in the relatively low year-to-year variability in wheat imports by most countries (Table 17-10). In most cases, wheat imports have steadily increased with little relationship to domestic cereal production except in some major wheat-producing countries. Also, wheat imports are relatively inelastic with respect to world prices since both consumer and producer prices are usually fixed by government policy and often do not reflect changes in world prices.[15] Rice imports, on the other hand, are more variable and depend on domestic rice production as well as fluctuations in world rice prices.[16] This strategy of relying on wheat imports to supply urban consumers is most advanced in Latin America, where close to two-thirds of the population now lives in urban areas. In the Andean region, wheat consumption has reached 40 kilograms per capita, over 90% of which is imported and most of which is consumed in urban areas.

Using wheat imports to feed urban consumers is to some extent reinforcing. A marketing, storage, and processing infrastructure has been developed accordingly. Because these investments are usually oriented toward port facilities and located in large coastal cities, they cannot be readily utilized to market domestic food production. In addition, the wheat-processing sector (i.e., milling and baking) is highly wheat specific and cannot be converted to processing domestically produced food because either mills are located at a substantial distance from the wheat-producing region or, more commonly, wheat is not produced locally and is not likely to be, in the near

TABLE 17-10

INDEX OF VARIABILITY IN WHEAT AND RICE IMPORTS: SELECTED
WHEAT-PRODUCING AND NON-WHEAT-PRODUCING COUNTRIES, 1966–80 (%)

Country	Wheat	Rice
Wheat-producing:		
Syria	54	32
Iran	44	49
Morocco	13	a
Mexico	82	a
Chile	31	62
Non-wheat-producing:		
Ghana	20	16
Indonesia	26	29
Philippines	12	a
Honduras	11	50
Venezuela	12	a

Note: Calculated as $I = CV \sqrt{1 - \bar{R}^2}$, where CV is the coefficient of variability and R is the corrected coefficient of determination from a linear time trend regression. The lower the index, I, the less the variability around the trend line.

[a]Not calculated because country is exporter or insignificant importer of that commodity.

Source: See J. D. A. Cuddy and P. A. Della Valle, "Measuring the Instability of Time Series Data," *Oxford Bulletin of Economics and Statistics,* 40 (1978): 79–85.

future, in the tropical belt of countries. Indeed, the wheat-processing sector in developing countries is often a powerful interest group able to influence and even control grain-procurement strategies.[17] This sector has grown very rapidly in the last 10–20 years so that the proportion of wheat flour in international wheat trade has declined.[18] The most rapid growth of the milling industry has occurred in the tropical belt, where countries such as Nigeria, Sri Lanka, and Indonesia—which were importing most of their wheat as flour in 1970—have recently become self-sufficient in flour production. Nigeria and Indonesia, in fact, have an excess of milling capacity beyond their annual consumption of 1.5–2.0 million tons of wheat. Ironically, the larger flour mills in the world are now located in these non-wheat-producing countries. While there are cost economies in grain versus flour transport, there is little evidence that it is an efficient use of resources to establish a capital- and foreign-exchange-intensive local milling industry in non-wheat-producing countries. This industry usually receives high tariff protection from imported flour (Table 17-11) and in many cases operates at a high margin relative to mills in developed countries.[19] More important, once established, the industry has a vested interest in continuing wheat imports, even if local production of cereals other than wheat offers the opportunity for import substitution. There are only a few cases in which wheat imports by non-wheat-producing countries have declined, and these have occurred in times of acute foreign exchange crises, such as in Sierra Leone, Guyana, and Ghana in 1982–83.

THE EXTERNAL INFLUENCES

World Wheat Prices and Policies of Exporting Countries

A number of external factors related to world wheat markets and policies of exporting countries have promoted wheat imports and consumption. The simplest of these is the

TABLE 17-11
EXAMPLES OF TARIFF PROTECTION PROVIDED TO WHEAT-MILLING INDUSTRY

		Import duty (%)	
	Year	Wheat grain	Wheat flour
Republic of Korea	1975	0	30
Philippines	1975	10	30
Kenya	1975	0	40
Sierra Leone	1974	0	167
Guatemala	1975	6	50
Ecuador	1979	0	70
Papua New Guinea	1982	0	Banned
Nigeria	1982	5	15

Source: Data for 1975 are from FAO, *Review of Agricultural Policies* (Rome: FAO, 1976). Other data were collected by the author.

fact that the price of wheat in international markets is significantly lower than the main competing food grain (i.e., rice), is less variable, and has tended to decline over time relative to rice.[20] Nonetheless, the costs of wheat imports are often underestimated since wheat is usually processed using foreign-exchange-intensive milling and baking methods and over one-quarter of the product (i.e., the bran) is used for animal feed.[21]

The lower price of wheat in world markets reflects rapid technological change in wheat-exporting countries as well as agricultural policies of exporting countries. The United States in the 1960s and the EEC in the 1970s have explicitly subsidized wheat exports. It is estimated that EEC export subsidies reduced the world market price of wheat by 11% in the 1970s.[22] In recent years, aggressive credit programs have provided attractive terms for purchase of wheat in world markets.

Food Aid

Food aid has also been a major external influence on wheat imports. Over 80% of cereal food aid is provided in the form of wheat or wheat flour, and this proportion holds for both countries where wheat is a traditional staple and countries where wheat is not a staple. Food aid originated with a specific objective of disposing of the surpluses of exporting countries and developing markets for commercial sales of these products. In the early 1960s, nearly 60% of Third World wheat imports (excluding China) were provided by food aid. In the 1970s, the amount of wheat food aid declined and now averages only 12% of total wheat imports of developing countries. Nonetheless, it remains important to some countries, such as Egypt, Sri Lanka, the Sudan, and Bolivia.

The impact of food aid on food imports and domestic cereal production is complex and country specific, and a full discussion is beyond the scope of this paper.[23] The most direct effect is to lower the real price of wheat imports (often to half or less than half of the price of commercial imports) and, in many cases, to provide wheat free of charge. Recent studies have shown that countries that receive significant amounts of wheat food aid (e.g., Bangladesh, Bolivia, and the Sudan) have higher per capita wheat imports than non-food-aid countries of comparable levels of income and urbanization.[24] Furthermore, current commercial imports of wheat by the tropical countries are positively related to the amount of wheat received as food aid in the past.[25] This long-run effect reflects several factors, such as (a) an established consumer exposure and even preference for wheat products, (b) market promotion activities often associated with food aid programs, (c) institutionalization of low wheat prices to urban consumers, and (d) establishment of a local wheat-processing industry to accommodate food aid imports.

Finally, the possible negative impact of food aid on domestic food production is a subject of continuing controversy. In the Andean region, domestic wheat production declined in response to reduced producer prices for wheat during the 1960s when most wheat was imported as food aid.[26] In other cases, such as Brazil, domestic producer prices for wheat were supported at a level above world prices, and domestic wheat production increased rapidly.[27]

Other External Influences

Wheat-exporting countries have actively promoted bread consumption in many countries. Private as well as public agencies of exporting countries have provided technical advice and training for the establishment of local milling and baking industries and for introducing new wheat products to consumers.[28] In contrast, export promotion efforts for rice and especially maize for food are relatively weak.

Furthermore, the milling and baking industry in many developing countries is owned or closely linked to the grain industry of the exporting countries. This is particularly the case in Latin America and Africa, where flour mills and large bakers or other manufacturing industries based on wheat (e.g., the biscuit industry) are frequently owned by multinational corporations with links to the grain-export business.[29] These industries often consist of one or a few firms that undertake sales and shipment of wheat as well as local processing and can exert considerable pressure on government policy. In some cases, foreign aid agencies of donor countries have actively supported the development of a baking industry.[30]

More recently, a fourth external influence, the International Monetary Fund, has exerted considerable pressure *against* the set of national policies discussed above.[31] With the current debt crisis, countries receiving loans from the IMF have committed themselves to more realistic exchange-rate policies and to elimination of bread subsidies. These policies have led to sharp increases in bread prices in 1982–83 in a number of countries, such as Brazil, Ecuador, and Nigeria. Nonetheless, the effect has been only partial, and growth of wheat consumption may have slowed but has not declined. Furthermore, the political significance of bread prices has recently been demonstrated by widespread protests in Tunisia and Morocco when bread subsidies were reduced in 1984. In both cases, governments reversed their decision to raise bread prices.

IMPLICATIONS FOR FOOD IMPORTS AND FOOD POLICY

The data presented here clearly demonstrate the special place of wheat in national and international food policy decisions. Governments have attempted to control both producer and consumer prices of wheat in almost all Third World countries. Relative to other food staples (except possibly rice), these policy interventions have been to a remarkable extent successful in controlling prices. With controlled producer and consumer prices, wheat imports have been the major instrument of food policy to equate supply and demand. Furthermore, while Third World food imports are often equated with efforts to reduce hunger and the interests of feeding the poor, the evidence of this paper suggests otherwise, especially in countries where wheat is not a traditional staple. Food imports in these countries represent a desire of middle-income urban consumers for a low-cost convenience food.

The size of the policy interventions and the number of countries involved are sufficient to account for much of the growth of food imports to the Third World in the last decade. Consumer subsidies alone account for a large share of wheat imports. Taking the large wheat importers alone (over 500,000 tons annually), the weighted average subsidy on wheat in 1981 was over 50% of consumer prices. Even assuming a relatively inelastic demand (−0.33), wheat imports by this group of countries would be at least one-third lower if market prices prevailed. These countries together make up well over half of commercial wheat imports by the Third World. This, together with wheat imports as food aid (over 6.0 million tons) and subsidized exports by the EEC (14 million tons), which are largely destined to Third World countries, suggests that a significant share of wheat imports by the Third World is accounted for by direct government interventions in wheat markets.

The regions with the strongest prospects for continuing rapid increases in wheat imports are the tropical belt of non-wheat-producing countries in Southeast Asia and sub-Saharan Africa. Here urbanization is still low but increasing rapidly. In sub-Saharan Africa, population growth in 35 major capitals now averages 9% annually.[32] At this rate, not only the marketed food surplus but also the associated marketing, transportation, and storage requirements must double in size every 8 years simply to maintain per capita food consumption in urban areas at current levels. The strategy of turning to imported wheat (reinforced by consumer pricing policies) to meet urban food supplies is likely to continue unless there is a drastic reversal in domestic food production and food policy. In Southeast Asia, pricing policies often lead to relatively high wheat prices, but rapidly rising incomes and urbanization still promote demand for wheat products.

Almost all Third World countries have expressed an objective of reducing food imports. For most countries, food policy measures are available to arrest the trend toward increased reliance on imported wheat. In the wheat-producing countries of the Middle East and North Africa, considerable potential exists for increasing domestic wheat production.[33] Targeting of urban consumer subsidies to the poor would also reduce demand and free resources for development of the domestic food sector.

For the non-wheat-producing countries of the tropics, substitution of wheat imports will require a combination of strategies including *(a)* increased domestic production of local food staples, *(b)* development of convenience food based on local staples (e.g., composite flours for bread), and *(c)* removal of policy-induced price disincentives against consumption of local staples. Sri Lanka, Colombia, and Senegal are examples of countries that reduced or eliminated bread subsidies in the 1970s. They are also among the handful of countries where per capita wheat consumption has declined. At the same time, acceptance of food aid in the form of local cereals will reduce the impact of wheat food aid (other than emergency aid) on consumer habits and slow the development of a wheat-processing industry. Importation of wheat as flour rather than grain would also provide a more temporary nature to wheat imports than the establishment of a local milling industry. The removal of tariff protection on wheat milling is probably sufficient in most countries to arrest the development of this industry.

There is now a renewed emphasis on finding ways to make local staples into acceptable convenience foods for urban consumers. This includes the numerous but not very successful attempts to produce composite flours by mixing local staples and wheat flour for bread making. In most cases, however, the major obstacle is pricing policy that maintains low wheat prices relative to local staples and provides no incentive to substitute for imported wheat.

All of these food policy alternatives to slow the trend in wheat imports are, of course, challenging the very interest groups that have led to the growth of wheat imports in the last 2 decades. Yet there is some hope for optimism, given the policy changes in a number of countries during the economic crisis of 1982–83. International and donor agencies can reinforce these trends through more appropriate food aid policies and more attention to the underlying causes of food imports. In particular, those charged with analyzing the "food gap" will need to pay more attention to variables such as urbanization and consumer price policies in making their projections. This argues for more analysis of food policy at the country level, which can then be built up into aggregate regional and world projections.

NOTES

1 See, e.g., projections in FAO, *Agriculture: Towards 2000* (Rome: FAO, 1979).
2 Imports of rice, the single most important food staple of developing countries, are only about one-sixth of wheat imports and have grown much more slowly. Imports of coarse grains by developing countries have risen rapidly, but almost all were destined to animal feed. See CIMMYT, *World Maize Facts and Trends,* Report no. 1 (El Batan, Mexico: CIMMYT, 1981).
3 D. Byerlee, *The Increasing Role of Wheat Consumption and Imports in the Developing World,* Economics Paper no. 5/83 (El Batan, Mexico: CIMMYT, 1983).
4 Throughout this paper, the term "tropical countries" refers to countries that are entirely or almost entirely within the latitude belt 23 degrees north to 23 degrees south.
5 Byerlee, (note 3 above).
6 D. Franklin, M. P. Demousin, and M. W. Harell, *Consumption Effects of Agricultural Policies: Bread Prices in the Sudan* (Raleigh, N.C.: Sigma One Corp., 1982).
7 This issue is analyzed in detail in D. Byerlee and G. Sain, "Food Pricing Policy in Developing Countries: Bias against Agriculture or for Urban Consumers?" *American Journal of Agricultural Economics,* 68 (1986), pp. 961–969. There is substantial evidence that producer pricing policy is more favorable to producers than earlier studies had indicated. For earlier evidence, see W. L. Peterson, "International Farm Prices and the Social Cost of Cheap Food Policies," *American Journal of Agricultural Economics,* 61 (1979): 12–21; and E. Lutz and P. L. Scandizzo, "Price Distortions in Developing Countries: A Bias against Agriculture," *European Review of Agricultural Economics,* 7 (1980): 5–27. However, the large size of consumer subsidies relative to government revenues has undoubtedly reduced government investments in promoting domestic food production.
8 Assumes export prices of wheat, rice, and maize of x, 2x, and 0.75x, respectively; international freight and handling 0.3x; marketing margin of 15% of CIF price; milling rate .72; and a 10% markup to represent the mill to retail margin. Margins were based on data from several countries. See Byerlee (note 3) for details.
9 Recent estimates of price elasticities for wheat products are as follows: −0.8 for the Philippines [H. Bouis, "Demand for Cereal Staples in the Philippines," unpublished paper (Washington, D.C.: IFPRI, 1982)]; −0.9 for Brazil [W. Gray, *Food Consumption Parameters for Brazil and Their Application to Food Policy,* Research Report no. 32 (Washington, D.C.: IFPRI, 1982)]; −0.4 for the Sudan (Franklin et al.); −1.8 for Indonesia [S. L. Magiera, *The Role of Wheat in the Indonesian Food Sector,* Foreign Agricultural Economics Report no. 170 (Washington, D.C.: USDA, 1981)]; and −1.1 for Sri Lanka [H. Alderman and C. P. Timmer, "Consumption Parameters for Sri Lankan Food Policy Analysis, *Sri Lankan Journal of Agrarian Studies,* 1 (1980): 1–12].

10 For evidence, see Franklin et al. on the Sudan and Gray on Brazil.

11 C. Hodges and T. Roe, "Government Intervention into the Market for Wheat in Four Low-Income Countries" (paper presented at the meeting of the American Agricultural Economics Society, Logan, Utah, 1982).

12 E. Alvarez, *Política Agraria y Estancamiento de la Agricultura, 1967–77* (Lima: Instituto de Estudios Peruanos, 1980).

13 For Brazil, see Gray. For Indonesia, see A. J. Nyberg, "Food Policy—Import Substitution or Import Dependence" (paper presented to the Third Biennial Meeting of the Agricultural Economics Association of Southeast Asia, Kuala Lumpur, 1979).

14 This is partially supported by a negative correlation of −.46 between current bread prices and wheat food aid per capita received during 1955–75 in a cross-sectional analysis of 39 tropical countries. See Byerlee (note 3 above).

15 Econometric analyses of wheat imports also support this view. See P. C. Abbott, "Modeling International Grain Trade with Government Controlled Markets," *American Journal of Agricultural Economics,* 61 (1979): 22–31; and C. L. Jabara, "Cross-Sectional Analysis of Wheat Import Demand among Middle-Income Developing Countries," *Agricultural Economics Research,* 34 (1982): 34–37.

16 W. P. Falcon and E. A. Monke, "International Trade in Rice," *Food Research Institute Studies,* 17 (1979–80): 176–306.

17 W. J. Carbonell and H. Rothman, "An Implicit Food Policy: Wheat Consumption Changes in Venezuela," *Food Policy,* 2 (1977): 305–17.

18 Wheat flour production increased at an annual rate of 23.4% in Brazil, 7.6% in Indonesia, 11.1% in Kenya, 11.7% in Cuba, 14.4% in Guatemala, and 7.2% in the Philippines between 1975 and 1980. See United Nations, *Monthly Bulletin of Statistics* (various issues).

19 Personal communication with mill operators in Ghana, Indonesia, Senegal, Mexico, and the Dominican Republic suggests that milling margins (ex-mill price of flour in wheat equivalent divided by mill delivery price of wheat) are often of the order of 20%–40% compared with margins close to zero in industrial countries where the value of by-products pays for the milling cost. See also Magiera (note 9 above).

20 R. Barker and R. W. Herdt, *The Asian Rice Economy* (Washington, D.C.: Resources for the Future, 1985); and Falcon and Monke (note 16 above).

21 Flour milling of imported wheat is usually undertaken in large, capital-intensive mills. Baking techniques, however, may range from very small scale, labor-intensive firms to large, capital-intensive industries. See E. Chuta, *Choice of Appropriate Technique in the African Bread Industry with Special Reference to Sierra Leone,* World Employment Program Working Paper (Geneva: International Labor Organization, 1981); and C. B. Baron, ed., *Technology, Employment and Basic Needs in Food Processing in Developing Countries* (New York: Pergamon Press, 1980).

22 V. Koester, *Policy Options for the Grain Economy of the European Community: Implications for Developing Countries,* Research Report no. 35 (Washington, D.C.: IFPRI, 1982).

23 For a recent review of effects of food aid, see C. Stevens, *Food Aid and the Developing World* (London: Croom Helm, 1979).

24 See Byerlee (note 3 above); Abbott (note 15 above); Hodges and Roe (note 11 above).

25 Byerlee (note 3 above).

26 L. Dudley and R. J. Sandilands, "The Side Effects of Foreign Aid: The Case of Public Law 480 Wheat in Colombia," *Economic Development and Cultural Change,* 23 (1975): 325–36; and M. Valderrama, "Effecto de las Exportaciones Norteamericanas de

Trigo a Bolivia, Perú, Ecuador y Colombia," *Estudios Rurales Latinoamericanos,* 2 (1979): 173–98.

27 L. Hall, "Evaluating the Effects of PL480 Wheat Imports on Brazil's Grain Sector," *American Journal of Agricultural Economics,* 62 (1980): 19–28.

28 See W. Wilson, "U.S. Wheat Associates: Recipe for Successful Marketing," *Foreign Agriculture,* 20 (1982): 18–19; "U.S. Export Development Programs," *Agriculture Abroad* (August 1981).

29 The large grain-exporting companies, Continental and Bunge, and U.S. flour millers such as General Mills, Pillsbury, and International Multifoods each own and operate flour mills in several Latin American countries. In West Africa, flour mills in Sierra Leone, Liberia, and Nigeria are owned by Seaboard Corporation, a grain-shipping company now linked to Cargill that also owns mills in Guyana and Ecuador. In Francophone countries, mills are owned by a French grain-marketing and milling cooperative. In many countries, such as Indonesia and Nigeria, the state also owns a significant interest in flour mills. See P. Barback and P. Flynn, *Agribusiness in the Americas* (New York: Monthly Review Press, 1980); M. Lajo, "Perú: Monopolio y Vulnerabilidad Almentaria," *Comercio Exterior* (Mexico City), 32 (1982): 84–94; D. Johnson, "International Multifoods Strategy in Venezuela," *Agribusiness Worldwide* (February 1981), pp. 38–42, and "Pillsbury's Involvement with the Saudi Arabian Flour Mills," *Agribusiness Worldwide* (October 1980), pp. 38–43.

30 L. Freeman, "CIDA, Wheat and Rural Development in Tanzania," *Canadian Journal of African Studies,* 16 (1982): 479–504. USAID involvement in a bakeries project is discussed in "Problems Delay Egyptian Plants," *Milling and Baking News* (Kansas City, Mo.), vol. 63 (October 4, 1983).

31 See D. K. Willis, "The Link between International Aid and Riots in African Streets," *Christian Science Monitor* (April 20–26, 1985).

32 J. Meerman and S. H. Cochrane, "Population Growth and Food Supply in Sub-Saharan Africa," *Finance and Development,* 19 (1982): 12–17.

33 See D. Byerlee and D. L. Winkelmann, *Accelerated Wheat Production in Semi-Arid Areas: Economic and Policy Issues,* Economics Working Paper no. 81/2 (El Batan, Mexico: CIMMYT, 1981).

CHAPTER 18

THE NEW DEVELOPMENT ECONOMICS

Joseph E. Stiglitz

Stanford University

1. INTRODUCTION

For the past 15 years, I have been attempting to construct a consistent view of less developed economies and the development process, to identify in what ways they are similar and in what ways (and why) they are different from more developed economies.[1] I cannot present even a summary of these views here. What I have been asked to do is to present one piece of that perspective, that relating to the organization of the rural sector, and to explain why I (or someone else) should "believe" these theories, or at least, why they are more plausible than several widely discussed alternative theories.

There are five central tenets of my approach:

1 Individuals (including peasants in the rural sectors of LDCs) are rational, that is, they act in a (reasonably) consistent manner, one which adapts to changes in circumstances.

2 Information is costly. This has numerous important implications: individuals do not acquire perfect information, and hence their behavior may differ markedly from what it would have been if they had perfect information. When individuals engage in a trade (buying labor services, extending credit, renting land or bullocks), there is imperfect information concerning the items to be traded; thus, transactions which would be desirable in the presence of perfect information may not occur. Similarly, certain contracts, e.g., performing certain services at a certain standard, may not be feasible, espe-

Reprinted with permission from *World Development,* 14, 2 (1986), pp. 257–65, Elsevier Science Ltd, Pergamon Imprint, Oxford, England.

cially if it is costly to ascertain, *ex post,* whether or how well those services have been performed.

3 Institutions adapt to reflect these information (and other transaction) costs. Thus, institutions are not to be taken as exogenous, but are endogenous, and changes in the environment may lead, with a lag, to changes in institutional structure.

4 The fact that individuals are rational and that institutions are adaptable does not, however, imply that the economy is (Pareto) efficient. The efficiency of market economies obtains only under the peculiar set of circumstances explored by Arrow and Debreu. These include a complete set of markets and perfect information, assumptions which, if questionable in more developed economies, are clearly irrelevant in LDCs. With imperfect information and incomplete markets, the economy is almost always constrained Pareto inefficient, i.e., there exists a set of taxes and subsidies which can make everyone better off (see Greenwald and Stiglitz, 1986).

5 This implies that there is a *potential* role for the government. That is, the government could effect a Pareto improvement if (i) it had sufficient knowledge of the structure of the economy; (ii) those responsible for implementing government policy had at least as much information as those in the private sector; (iii) those responsible for designing and implementing government policy had the incentives to direct policies to effect Pareto improvements, rather than, for instance, to redistribute income (either from the poor to the rich or vice versa, or from everyone else, to themselves), often at considerable loss to national output. Informational problems, including incentive problems, are no less important in the public sector than in the private; the fact that we have studied them well in the latter does not mean that they are not present in the former. The consequence of these remarks is to make us cautious in recommending particular government actions as remedies for certain observed deficiencies in the market.

2. THE BASIC OUTLINES OF THE THEORY OF RURAL ORGANIZATION

In this section, I wish to outline what the general approach presented above says about the economic organization of the rural sector. There are a wide variety of institutional arrangements observed in different LDCs. One set that has been of longstanding interest to economists is sharecropping. Earlier views of sharecropping held that it was an inefficient form of economic organization: the worker received less than the value of his marginal product, and thus he had insufficient incentives to exert effort. The question was, how could such a seemingly inefficient form of economic organization have survived for so long (and why should it be such a prevalent form of economic organization at so many different places at different times?). For those who believe in even a modicum of economic rationality, some explanation had to be found.

One explanation that comes to mind is that peasants are more risk averse than landlords: if workers rented the land from the landlords, they would have to bear all of the risk. Though workers' risk aversion is undoubtedly of importance, it cannot be the entire explanation: there are alternative (and perhaps more effective) risk-sharing arrangements. In particular, in the wage system, the landlord bears all of the risk, the worker none. Any degree of risk sharing between the landlord and the worker can be attained by the worker dividing his time between working as a wage-laborer and working on his own or rented land.[2]

The other central part of the explanation of sharecropping is that it provides an effective incentive system in the presence of costly supervision. Since in a wage system, the worker's compensation is not directly related to his output, the landlord must spend resources to ensure that the worker actually works. In a sharecropping system, since the worker's pay depends directly on his output, he has some incentives to work. The incentives may not be as strong as they would if he owned the land (since he receives, say, only half the product); but that is not the relevant alternative. Sharecropping thus represents a compromise between the rental system, in which incentives are "correct" but all the risk is borne by the worker, and the wage system, in which the landlord who is in a better position to bear risk, bears all the risk but in which effort can only be sustained through expenditures on supervision. This new view (Stiglitz, April 1974) turns the traditional criticism of sharecropping on its head: it is precisely because of its incentive properties, relative to the relevant alternative, the wage system, that the sharecropping system is employed.

The contention that the rental system provides correct incentives is, however, not quite correct. The rental system provides correct incentives for effort decisions. But tenants make many decisions other than those involving effort; they make decisions concerning the choice of technique, the use of fertilizer, the timing of harvest, etc. These decisions affect the riskiness of the outcomes. For instance, many of the high-yielding seed varieties have a higher mean output, but a greater sensitivity to rainfall. Whenever there is a finite probability of default (that is, the tenant not paying the promised rent), then tenants may not have, with the rental system, the correct incentives with respect to these decisions. Of course, with unlimited liability, the worker could be made to bear all of the costs. But since the tenant might be unable to pay his rent even if he had undertaken all of the "right" decisions, and since it is often difficult to ascertain whether the individual took "unnecessary" risks, most societies are reluctant to grant unlimited liability, or to use extreme measures like debtor prisons, to ensure that individuals do not take unnecessary risks.[3] Hence, in effect, part of the costs of risk taking by the tenant is borne by the landlord.[4] With sharecropping, both the landlord and the tenant face the same risks.[5]

Thus, sharecropping can be viewed as an institution which has developed in response to (1) risk aversion on the part of workers; (2) the limited ability (or desire) to force the tenant to pay back rents when he is clearly unable to do so; and (3) the limited ability to monitor the actions of the tenant (or the high costs of doing so).

The general theory has been extended in a number of directions, only three of which I can discuss here: cost sharing, interlinkage, and technical change.

In many situations, there are other important inputs besides labor and land, such as bullocks or fertilizer. How should these inputs be paid for? Clearly, if the worker pays all of the costs, but receives only a fraction of the benefits, he will have an insufficient incentive to supply these other inputs. Cost sharing is a proposed remedy. If the worker receives 50% of the output, and pays 50% of the cost, it would appear that he has the correct incentives: both benefits and costs have been cut in half.[6]

But in fact, though cost shares equal to output shares are common, they are far from universal. How do we explain these deviations from what seems both a simple, reasonable rule, and a rule which ensures economic efficiency? To find the answer, we again return to our general theoretical framework, which focuses on the role of imperfect information. First, it is clear that the landlord may want the tenant to supply more fertilizer than he would with a 50–50 rule, if increasing the fertilizer increases the marginal product of labor, and thus induces the worker to work harder. Remember, the central problem of the landlord is that he cannot directly control the actions of his worker; he must induce them to work hard. The reason that sharecropping was employed was to provide these additional incentives.

But if a cost-sharing arrangement can be implemented, it means that the expenditures can be monitored; and if the expenditures can be monitored, there is no necessity for engaging in cost sharing; rather the terms of the contract could simply specify the levels of various inputs. But workers typically have more information about current circumstances than the landlord (in the fashionable technical jargon, we say there is an asymmetry of information). A contract which specifies the level of inputs cannot adapt to the changing circumstances. Cost-sharing contracts provide the ability and incentives for these adaptations, and thus are more efficient contracts than contracts which simply specified the level of inputs.[7]

Another aspect of economic organization in many LDCs is the interlinkage of markets: the landlord may also supply credit (and he may also supply food and inputs). How can we explain this interlinkage? Some have claimed that it is simply another way that landlords exploit their workers. We shall comment later on these alternative explanations. For now, we simply note that our general theory can explain the prevalence of interlinkage (both under competitive and noncompetitive circumstances). We have repeatedly noted the problem of the landlord in inducing the worker both to work hard and to make the "correct" decisions from his point of view (with respect to choice of technique, etc.). Exactly analogous problems arise with respect to lenders. Their concern is that the borrower will default on the loan. The probability of a default depends in part on the actions taken by the borrower. The actions of the tenant-borrower thus affect both the lender and the landlord. Note too that the terms of the contract with the landlord will affect the lender, and vice versa: if the landlord can, for instance, reduce the probability of default by supplying more fertilizer, the lender is better off. The actions of the borrower (both with respect to effort and the choice of technique) may be affected by the individual's indebtedness, so that the landlord's (expected) income may be affected by the amount (and terms) of indebtedness. There appear to be clear and possibly significant externalities between the actions of the landlord and the actions of the lender. Whenever there are such externalities, a natural market solution is to internalize the externality, and that is precisely what the interlinkage of markets does.[8]

Thus, interlinkage is motivated by the desire for economic efficiency, not necessarily by the desire for further exploitation of the worker.

Interlinkage has, in turn, been linked to the incentives landlords have for resisting profitable innovations. Bhaduri[9] has argued, for instance, that landlords-cum-creditors may resist innovations, because innovations reduce the demand for credit, and thus the income which they receive in their capacity as creditors. Braverman and Stiglitz[10] have shown that there is no presumption that innovations result in a reduction in the demand for credit. Credit is used to smooth income across periods, and under quite plausible conditions, innovations may either increase or decrease the aggregate demand for credit. But they argue further that what happens to the demand for credit is beside the point.

The central question is simply whether the innovation moves the economically relevant utilities possibilities schedule outward or inward. The utilities possibilities schedule gives the maximum level of (expected) utility to one group (the landlord) given the level of (expected) utility of the other (the workers). The economically relevant utilities possibilities curve takes into account the information problems which have been the center of our discussion thus far, for instance, the fact that with sharecropping, individuals' incentives are different from what they would be with costless monitoring. The utilities possibilities schedule with costless monitoring might move one way, the economically relevant utilities possibilities schedule the other. Thus, for instance, there are innovations which, at each level of input, increase the output, but which, at the same time, exacerbate the incentives-monitoring problem. Such innovations would not be socially desirable. Landlords would resist such innovations, as well they should, though from an "engineering" point of view, such innovations might look desirable.

The consequences of interlinkage for the adoption of innovations, within this perspective, are ambiguous. There are innovations which would be adopted with interlinkage, but would not without it, and conversely; but the effect of the innovation on the demand for credit does not seem to play a central role.

Though the landlord correctly worries about the incentive-monitoring consequences of an innovation, one should not jump to the conclusions either that the landlords collectively make decisions which maximize their own welfare, or that the landlord always makes the socially efficient decision. The landlord, within a competitive environment, will adopt an innovation if at current prices (terms of contracts, etc.) it is profitable for him to do so. Of course, when all the landlords adopt the innovation, prices (terms of contracts) will change, and they may change in such a way that landlords are adversely affected.[11] In a competitive environment landlords cannot resist innovations simply because it is disadvantageous to them to do so. (By contrast, if they are in a "monopoly" position, they will not wish to resist such innovations, since presumably they will be able to capture all the surplus associated with the innovation.)

But just as the market allocation is not constrained Pareto efficient (even assuming a perfectly competitive economy) whenever there are problems of moral hazard, so too the market decisions concerning innovation are not constrained Pareto efficient. (We use the term constrained Pareto efficient to remind us that we are accounting for the limitations on information; we have not assumed the government has any information other than that possessed by private individuals.) Though in principle there exist government interventions which (accounting for the costs of information) could make everyone better off, whether such Pareto improving interventions are likely to emerge from the political process remains a moot question.

3. ALTERNATIVE THEORIES

In this section, I wish to present in summary form what I view to be the major competing approaches to understanding the organization of economic activity in the rural sector.

In many respects, I see my view as lying between other more extreme views. In one, the peasant is viewed as rational, working in an environment with reasonably complete information and complete and competitive markets. In this view, then, the differences between LDCs and more developed countries lies not so much in the difference between sophisticated, maximizing farmers and uneducated rule-bound peasants as it does in differences in the economic environments, the goods produced by these economies, their endowments, and how their endowments are used to produce goods. In this view, sharecropping is a rational response to the problems of risk sharing; but there is less concern about the incentive problems than I have expressed; with perfect information and perfect enforceability of contracts, the sharecropping contract can enforce the desired level of labor supply and the choice of technique which is efficient. These theories have had little to say about some of the other phenomena which I have discussed: interlinkage, technical change, cost sharing. Interlinkage might be explained in terms of the advantages in transactions costs, but if transactions costs were central, one should only have observed simple cost-sharing rules (with cost share equalling output share).

By contrast, there are those who view the peasant as irrational, with his behavior dictated by customs and institutions which may have served a useful function at some previous time but no longer do so. This approach (which I shall refer to, somewhat loosely, as the institutional-historical approach) may attempt to describe the kinds of LDCs in which there is sharecropping, interlinkage, or cost sharing. It may attempt to relate current practices to earlier practices. In particular, the institutional-historical approach may identify particular historical events which lead to the establishment of the sharecropping system, or the development of the credit system. But this leaves largely unanswered the question of why so many LDCs developed similar institutional structures, or why in some countries cost shares equal output shares, while in others the two differ. More fundamentally, a theory must explain how earlier practices developed; and to provide an explanation of these, one has to have recourse to one of the other theories. Thus, by itself, the institutional-historical approach is incomplete.

Still a third view emphasizes the departures from competitiveness in the rural sector, and the consequent ability of the landlords to exploit the workers. In some cases, workers are tied to their land; legal constraints may put the landlord in a position to exploit the worker. But in the absence of these legal constraints, one has to explain how the landlords exercise their allegedly coercive powers. In many LDCs there is a well-developed labor market. Many landlords need laborers at harvest time and at planting time. The worker chooses for whom he will work. It is important to recognize that the exploitation hypothesis fails to explain the mechanisms by which, in situations where there are many landlords, they exercise their exploitative power.[12] More generally, it fails to explain variations in the degree of exploitation over time and across countries. The fact that wages are low is not necessarily evidence of exploitation: the competitive market will yield low wages when the value of the marginal product of labor is low.

The exploitation hypothesis also fails to explain the detailed structure of rural organization: why cost shares are the way they are, or why (or how) landlords who can exploit their workers use the credit market to gain further exploitative capacity.

There may be some grain of truth in all these approaches. Important instances of currently dysfunctional institutions and customs can clearly be identified. Institutional structures clearly do not adapt instantaneously to changed circumstances. Yet, as social scientists, our objective is to identify the systematical components, the regularities of social behavior, to look for general principles underlying a variety of phenomena. It is useful to describe the institutions found in the rural sector of LDCs, but description is not enough.

Therefore, I view the rationality hypothesis as a convenient starting point, a simple and general principle with which to understand economic behavior. Important instances of departures from rationality may well be observed. As social scientists, our objective is to look for *systematic* departures. Some systematic departures have been noted, for instance in the work of Tversky, in individuals' judgments of probabilities, particularly of small probability events; but as Binswanger's 1978 study has noted, departures from the theory appear less important in "important" decisions than in less important decisions. Many of the seeming departures from "rationality" that have been noted can be interpreted as "rational" decision-making in the presence of imperfect information.

I also view the competitiveness hypothesis as a convenient starting point.[13] Many of the central phenomena of interest can be explained without recourse to the exploitation hypothesis. Some degree of imperfect competition is not inconsistent with the imperfect information paradigm: the imperfect information paradigm provides part of the explanation for the absence of perfect competition; it can help identify situations where the landlords may be in a better position to exploit the workers. Moreover, to the extent that imperfect information limits the extent to which even a monopoly landlord can extract surplus from his workers, the imperfect information paradigm can provide insights into how he can increase his monopoly profits. The theory of interlinkage we have developed can thus be applied to the behavior of a monopolist landlord.

There is one other approach that has received some attention that is, in fact, closely related to the one I have advocated: the transactions cost approach, which attempts to explicate economic relations by focusing on transactions costs. Information costs are an important part of transactions costs (though information problems arise in other contexts as well). My reservations concerning the transactions cost approach lie in its lack of specificity: while the information paradigm provides a well-defined structure which allows one to derive clear propositions concerning, for instance, the design of contracts, the transactions cost paradigm does not. Thus, the transactions cost approach might provide some insight into why cost sharing is employed, but not into the terms of the cost-sharing agreement. The transactions cost paradigm might say that economies of scope provide an explanation for why the landlord also supplies credit, but it does not provide insights into when the landlord-cum-creditor would subsidize credit, or when he would "tax" it. Moreover, while the information paradigm identifies parameters which affect the magnitude of the externalities between landlords and creditors, and thus enables, in principle, the identification of circumstances under which interlinkage is more likely to be observed, the transactions cost paradigm can do little more than to say that there are circumstances in which the diseconomies of scope exceed the economies, and in these circumstances there will not be interlinkage.

4. CRITERIA FOR EVALUATING ALTERNATIVE THEORIES

In the previous section, I discussed briefly some of the major competing hypotheses. In this section, I wish to outline a set of criteria for evaluating a theory, and to apply these criteria to these alternative theories. No novelty is claimed for the criteria; no attempt is made to provide a general epistemological theory.[14] These are presented more in the spirit of a "working man's" criteria.

We can divide the criteria into two groups: internal and external. The internal criteria include[15]:

1 *Internal consistency:* Are the axioms (underlying assumptions) mutually consistent, and do the conclusions follow from these assumptions?

2 *Simplicity:* In general, the fewer the assumptions required to explain the given phenomena, the better.

3 *Completeness:* The assumptions of the model should be as "primitive" as possible. Thus, in macroeconomics, a theory which explains unemployment in terms of wage rigidities is, in this sense, incomplete: it leaves open the question of why wages are rigid.

The external criteria include:

1 *Verifiability* (or falsifiability): The theory should have at least some implications which are verifiable or falsifiable, in principle; that is, it should at least be possible to design thought experiments under which some of the implications of the theory could be rejected.

2 *External consistency:* Are *all* the implications of the model consistent with observations? Note that among the (obvious and direct) implications of the model are those that directly follow from the assumptions; thus, if an assumption itself can be falsified, the model will not possess the property of external consistency. Friedman's contention that a theory should be judged only by the validity of its conclusions is, in this view, wrong. Theories whose assumptions seem unreasonable, i.e., whose assumptions themselves can be falsified or whose assumptions have other implications which seem unacceptable (i.e., can be falsified) should be rejected. *Some* of the implications of many "bad" theories may be correct; indeed, probably no theory that has received any attention has *all* of its implications inconsistent with (at least some interpretations of) the data. But a good theory should have no implication which is inconsistent with observations.

3 *External completeness:* The theory should have something to say about as many regularities that have been observed in the area of study as possible. Thus, a theory which explains both why there is sharecropping as well as the determinants of the shares is better than a theory which simply explains why there is sharecropping. This is closely related to the criteria of:

4 *Specificity:* A good theory should make as many specific predictions concerning particular phenomena as possible.

5 *Predictive power:* A good theory should not only be consistent with regularities which have already been noted, but also suggest new regularities which have not yet been noted.

6 *Generality:* The same general hypotheses should be able to explain phenomena in widely different contexts.

I now want to review the performance of the alternative theories in terms of these basic criteria. The imperfect information paradigm does well, I would argue, on all of the criteria. The work in this area has been marked by an attempt to state clearly the assumptions, and to derive its conclusions from the assumptions: it does well on the criterion of internal consistency. Similarly, it does well on the other two internal criteria: the assumptions are simple and are reasonably primitive. Though in most work, the information technology is taken as given, in some ongoing research (see, e.g., Braverman and Stiglitz, 1986b), even this is taken to be endogenously determined. The theory provides specific predictions which are verifiable, and indeed has something to say about virtually every aspect of rural economic organization. It makes predictions concerning a variety of regularities that should be found in LDCs, but unfortunately, these have not been subjected to rigorous testing. At the same time, there is no well-agreed upon regularity that seems inconsistent with the theory.

One of its most attractive properties, however, is that the information paradigm provides a general framework which is applicable to both developed and less developed economies. The concerns about effort and choice of technique which are central to sharecropping reappear, in somewhat modified form, in the analysis of labor and capital markets in more developed countries. It shares this property with the "rational peasant, with perfect markets and complete information" paradigm. But the latter theory fails to provide a good account of the differences between developed and less developed economies.

But my major objection to the rational peasant model with full information and complete markets (as with the corresponding theories of developed economies) is that it is inconsistent with many observations and it fails to provide explanations of others.

It does not explain why sharecropping is employed (with perfect information, there are a variety of equivalent contractual forms; if sharecropping were employed, the contract would specify the amount of labor to be supplied).

It fails to explain cost sharing, and in particular why cost shares should differ from output shares.

It assumes that there is a complete set of risk markets; it is clear that individuals cannot purchase insurance against many important risks and that this has important consequences for their behavior.

In most small villages, it is not reasonable to assume that if a landlord offered a rupee less to his wage laborers, he would obtain no workers. In many situations, there appear to be workers who are willing to work at the going wage, but fail to obtain employment: there appears to be involuntary unemployment, a phenomenon which seems inconsistent with the classical competitive models.

This theory can be adapted to make it at least seem to explain the phenomena under study and to make it seem less inconsistent with the facts[16]: indeed, our imperfect information paradigm can be thought of as one such adaptation. But we would argue that it is a fundamental alteration, one which affects our views of economic relations under a wide variety of circumstances. When a theory provides predictions which are inconsistent with the facts in a wide variety of circumstances, and when it fails to provide explanations of important regularities, what is needed is not an ad hoc modification of the model on a case-by-case basis, but rather a basic reformulation: the imperfect information paradigm provides such a reformulation.

The transactions cost approach represents another attempt to modify the basic theory in a consistent way. As we have commented above, information costs are a particular form of transaction costs, and I find many aspects of the transactions cost approach attractive.[17] But the theory fails on several of the critical external criteria: to the extent that the theory relies on unobservable transaction costs, it often seems to fail the test of falsifiability; just as the present set of economic relations is justified by current (unobservable) transaction costs, changes in the nature of economic relations are "explained" by reference to similarly unobservable changes in transaction costs. The theory also fails the test of specificity of predictions and of external completeness: as we noted, while it may provide an explanation for why sharecropping is employed, it cannot explain the nature of the cost-sharing arrangements and has little to say about other items of the sharecropping contract.

By contrast, the exploitation theory fails on both the internal and external criteria for judging theories. There is not a clearly stated set of primitive assumptions from which the conclusions logically follow. For instance, if the structure of economic relations is determined by the attempt of landlords to exploit their workers, what determines the limits on their capacities to do so? The theory fails to explain why sharecropping provides a better method of exploitation than other forms of contractual arrangements; it fails to explain why cost sharing enhances the ability of the landlord to exploit his workers. It fails to explain the circumstances under which cost shares would exceed output shares. And it fails to explain why providing credit enhances the ability of the landlord to exploit the peasant. When there are many landlords in a community, it fails to explain how they can act collusively together. The experience with cartels in other areas is that it is hard to maintain collusive arrangements voluntarily when the number of participants becomes more than a few. If this is true here, then the theory only provides an explanation of the structure of economic relations within communities with a limited number of landlords; if this is not true in LDCs, why?

To the extent that the theory relies on the notion of power which cannot be independently quantified, the theory is not falsifiable: one can always account for differences in the terms of the contract over time or geographically in terms of differences in power.[18] To the extent that the theory fails to provide answers to these questions, it is seriously incomplete.

5. CONCLUSIONS

The theory of rural organization which is based on rational peasants in environments in which information is imperfect and costly provides a simple explanation for a wide variety of phenomena in LDCs. It represents an important application of a more general paradigm, what I have referred loosely to as the "Imperfect Information Paradigm" which has been useful in explaining phenomena under a wide variety of settings, under competition, oligopoly, and monopoly, in labor markets, capital markets, insurance markets, and product markets. The richness of social phenomena is such as to make it unreasonable to expect any theory to explain all of the observed variations in institutions and behavior. But a theory should at least be able to explain the important regularities. Here, we are concerned with explaining sharecropping, both its widespread use, and the form it takes; it should explain cost sharing, with cost shares frequently differing from output shares, and the interlinkage of credit and land markets. This our theory does, and the competing theories fail to do. There is a rich set of further predictions emanating from our theory which have yet to be tested. Whether, when these tests are performed, the theory will still stand, or whether it will have to be modified, or abandoned, remains to be seen.

NOTES

1 For two surveys of certain aspects of this work, see Stiglitz (1982b, 1985).
2 See Stiglitz (April 1974).
3 Indeed, such extreme measures may have deleterious incentive effects, discouraging risk taking.
4 See Johnson (1950); Allen (1985).
5 This aspect of sharecropping has been emphasized by Johnson (1950), and by Braverman and Stiglitz (1982a). See also Stiglitz and Weiss (1981).
6 See Heady (1947).
7 See Braverman and Stiglitz (1982b).
8 See Braverman and Stiglitz (1982a). This problem is discussed in the more general information theoretic literature under the rubric of the multiple principle-agent problem. The externalities which we have discussed here arise in virtually all moral hazard problems. See Arnott and Stiglitz (1984).
9 See Bhaduri (1973).
10 Braverman and Stiglitz (1986b).
11 If the innovation, at the current prices, increases the demand for workers enough, then the terms of the contracts may shift sufficiently in workers' favor to make landlords worse off. This is analogous to what, in more simple contexts, is referred to as a Pigou land-saving innovation.
12 Note that recent advances in repeated games have shown how collusive outcomes can be attained even in noncooperative settings. Thus, landlords in rural economies where mobility is limited and in which there are only a few landlords in any community may well act collusively. The circumstances in which these noncooperative collusive arrangements work well has, however, not been well studied.
13 Indeed, with limited labor mobility, in small villages the labor markets are unlikely to be perfectly competitive; at the same time, the landlord is far from a labor monopolist.

The real world is probably better described by a model of "monopolistic competition" than either of the polar models, monopoly or perfect competition.

14 Similarly, this is not the place to provide an evaluation of alternative theories (e.g., the theories of Karl Popper).

15 This list is not meant to be exhaustive. An important criterion in other contexts is *robustness;* the conclusions of the theory should not be sensitive to small perturbations in the assumptions.

16 When the theory gets complicated by these ad hoc modifications it loses the property of simplicity, which was originally one of its main virtues.

17 It is sometimes suggested that, once transactions costs are accounted for, equilibrium with rational peasants will have all the standard efficiency properties that economies with no transactions costs have. This is another example where the conclusion does not follow logically from the assumptions; the conclusion is arrived at by reasoning by analogy. Transactions costs (including information costs) are "like" other production costs. Why, once these are appropriately accounted for, should not the economy still be efficient?

Unfortunately, it turns out that, in general, economies with imperfect information (or incomplete markets) are not constrained Pareto efficient (where the term "constrained" Pareto efficient simply reminds us that we have appropriately taken into account the transactions costs (information imperfection, incomplete markets). (See Greenwald and Stiglitz, (1986.) The formalization of Adam Smith's invisible hand conjecture is one of the great achievements of modern economic theory; the Fundamental theorem of economics, like any other theorem, depends on the assumptions. The assumptions concerning perfect information, no transactions costs, and complete markets are not innocuous assumptions, but are central to the validity of the result. Information costs may, in some respects, be like other costs of production, but the differences are sufficiently important to invalidate the Fundamental Theorem of Welfare Economics.

18 Thus, "power" is to the exploitation theory what transactions cost is to the transactions cost model.

REFERENCES

Allen, F. "The Fixed Nature of Sharecropping Contracts." *Journal of Public Economics* (March 1985): 30–48.

Arnott, R., and J. E. Stiglitz. "Equilibrium in Competitive Insurance Markets." Mimeo. (Princeton University, 1984).

Bhaduri, A. "Agricultural Backwardness under Semifeudalism." *Economic Journal* (1973).

Binswanger, H. P. "Attitudes Towards Risk: Experimental Measurement Evidence in Rural India." *American Journal of Agricultural Economics,* 62, 3 (August 1980): 395–407.

Binswanger, H. P. "Attitudes Towards Risk: Implications and Psychological Theories of an Experiment in Rural India." Yale University Economic Growth Center DP 286 (1978b).

Braverman, A., and J. E. Stiglitz. "Sharecropping and the Interlinking of Agrarian Markets." *American Economic Review,* 72, 4 (September 1982a): 695–715.

Braverman, A., and J. E. Stiglitz. "Moral hazard, incentive flexibility and risk: Cost sharing arrangements under sharecropping," Princeton University, Econometric Research Center Memorandum No. 298 (1982b).

Braverman, A., and J. E. Stiglitz. "Cost Sharing Arrangements under Sharecropping: Moral Hazard, Incentive Flexibility and Risk." *American Journal of Agricultural Economics,* 68, 3 (1986a): 642–52.

Braverman, A., and J. E. Stiglitz. "Landlords, Tenants and Technological Innovations." *Journal of Development Economics* 23, 2 (1986b): 313–32.

Greenwald, B., and J. E. Stiglitz, "Externalities in Economies with Imperfect Information and Incomplete Markets." *Quarterly Journal of Economics* 101, 2 (1986): 229–64.

Heady, E. "Economics of Farm Leasing System." *Journal of Farm Economics* (August 1947).

Johnson, D. Gale "Resource Allocation under Share Contracts." *Journal of Public Economics* (April 1950): 111–23.

Newbery, D., and J. E. Stiglitz. "Sharecropping, Risk Sharing, and the Importance of Imperfect Information," paper presented to a conference in Mexico City, March 1976, and published in Ja. A. Roumasset et al., eds., *Risk, Uncertainty and Development* (SEARCA, A/D/C, 1979), pp. 311–41.

Newbery, D., and J. E. Stiglitz. *The Theory of Commodity Price Stabilization* (Oxford University Press, 1981).

Newbery, D., and J. E. Stiglitz. "The Choice of Techniques and the Optimality of Market Equilibrium with Rational Expectations." *Journal of Political Economy,* 90, 2 (April 1982): 223–46.

Stiglitz, J. E. "Rural-Urban Migration, Surplus Labor and the Relationship between Urban and Rural Wages." *East African Economic Review,* 1–2 (December 1969): 1–27.

Stiglitz, J. E. "Alternate Theories of Wage Determination and Unemployment in LDCs: The Labor Turnover Model." *Quarterly Journal of Economics,* 87 (May 1974): 194–227.

Stiglitz, J. E. "Incentives and Risk Sharing in Sharecropping." *Review of Economic Studies,* 41 (April 1974): 219–55.

Stiglitz, J. E. "The Efficiency Wage Hypothesis, Surplus Labor and the Distribution of Income in LDCs." *Oxford Economic Papers,* 28, 2 (July 1976): 185–207.

Stiglitz, J. E. "Some Further Remarks on Cost-Benefit Analysis." In H. Schwartz and R. Berney, eds., *Social and Economic Dimensions of Project Evaluation* (IDB, 1977); Proceedings of the Symposium on Cost-Benefit Analysis, IDB, Washington, D.C., March 1973, pp. 253–82.

Stiglitz, J. E. "Alternative Theories of Wage Determination and Unemployment: The Efficiency Wage Model." In Gersovitz et al., eds., *The Theory and Experience of Economic Development: Essays in Honor of Sir W. Arthur Lewis* (London: George Allen & Unwin, 1982a), pp. 78–106.

Stiglitz, J. E. "Structure of Labor Markets and Shadow Prices in LDCs." Presented at World Bank Conference, February 1976, in R. Sabot, ed., *Migration and the Labor Market in Developing Countries* (Boulder, Colo.: Westview Press 1982b), pp. 13–64.

Stiglitz, J. E. "The Wage-Productivity Hypothesis: Its Economic Consequences and Policy Implications." Paper presented to the American Economic Association, 1982.

Stiglitz, J. E. "Economics of Information and the Theory of Economic Development." *Revista de Econometria.*

Stiglitz, J. E., and A. Weiss. "Credit Rationing in Markets with Imperfect Information." *American Economic Review,* 71, 3 (June 1981): 393–410.

Tversky, A. "Intransitivity of Preferences." *Psychological Review,* 76 (1969): 31–48.

CHAPTER 19

PEASANT WOMEN AND ECONOMIC TRANSFORMATION IN THE GAMBIA

Judith A. Carney

Department of Geography, UCLA

INTRODUCTION

The 1968–73 Sahelian drought ushered in a new era of agricultural development strategies in The Gambia which were to have far-reaching effects on peasant farmers generally and especially on women. International development agencies began 'drought proofing' regional economies by constructing irrigation infrastructures to extend agriculture for year-round cultivation (Franke and Chasin, 1980; Derman, 1984; CRED, 1985). The subsequent trajectory of Gambian irrigated agriculture has emphasized rice and vegetables, two crops traditionally grown by women.

Both crops have emerged as central to donor and state efforts towards economic restructuring. Rice and vegetables receive policy and funding support for their potential to improve foreign exchange reserves by reducing cereal imports and developing The Gambia's comparative advantage as a winter vegetable supplier to European markets. But the commercialization of these crops has proceeded amid a welter of conflicting productivity and equity objectives. Donor efforts to target Gambian women in the development process have become linked to the broader goal of restructuring the peasant labour process for year-round irrigated production. Contract farming has emerged as the instrument favoured by both multilateral donors and the state to achieve equity and productivity goals.

This article traces the convergence of contract farming with gender equity objectives in Gambian irrigated rice and vegetable production over the past decade to illuminate three issues: first, the specific position women are assuming in national

Reprinted with permission from *Development and Change,* Vol. 23 (1992) No. 2, 67–90, by permission of Sage Publications Ltd.

strategies of economic transformation; second, the way in which new forms of commoditization are heightening gender conflicts over access to productive resources; and, finally, the significance of women's struggles over land access for their participation in contract farming.

The article is divided into four parts. Following a brief commentary on contract farming, the discussion shifts in the next two sections to its emergence in irrigated rice development and, more recently, irrigated horticulture. The contradictions posed by contract farming for the gender equity objectives of international donors are discussed in the conclusion.

TRANSFORMING AGRICULTURAL PRODUCTION: CONTRACT FARMING

Over the past decade contract farming has received increasing support from the private sector and international donor community as a promising strategy to transform peasant farming from a static to a dynamic sector (World Bank, 1981; Glover, 1984; Williams and Karen, 1984).[1] Contract farming represents a distinct social organization of labour in which peasant producers are linked to either transnational corporations, private individuals or the state, to supply agricultural commodities to specifications established in advance by an oral or written contract (Jarosz, 1987; Watts et al., 1988; Watts, 1990). These arrangements often commit farmers to the use of specific inputs such as seeds, fertilizers and pesticides, in exchange for technical assistance and marketing outlets provided by suppliers (Jarosz, 1987: 3). By facilitating technology transfer to smallholders and improving their access to inputs and markets, contract farming is frequently presented as a contract of reciprocity, one of mutual benefit to producer and supplier (Clapp, 1988).

While the marketing and commodity characteristics of contract farming have received considerable research emphasis (Morrissy, 1974; Binswanger and Rosenzweig, 1986), less attention has focused on its impact on the peasant labour process (Buch-Hansen and Marcussen, 1982). Contract farming reorganizes agriculture to conform with production schedules that demand strict timing of peasant work routines. This labour-intensifying feature of contract farming is poorly researched, yet, as we shall see below, proved central to the conjunction of contract farming with gender equity objectives in The Gambia.

IRRIGATED RICE DEVELOPMENT: FOOD SECURITY OBJECTIVES

In 1966, just after independence, The Gambia began to realize an unfulfilled colonial policy objective: the development of pump-irrigated rice schemes. Over the next two decades more than 4000 ha of women's swamp rice land were converted to double-cropped irrigated perimeters (Figure 19-1). The impetus for this development was domestic substitution of imported rice, which had climbed to nearly 9000 tons per annum (Carney, 1986). Increased rice dependency was occurring at the same time that export values for the country's chief cash crop, peanuts, were declining; funding by

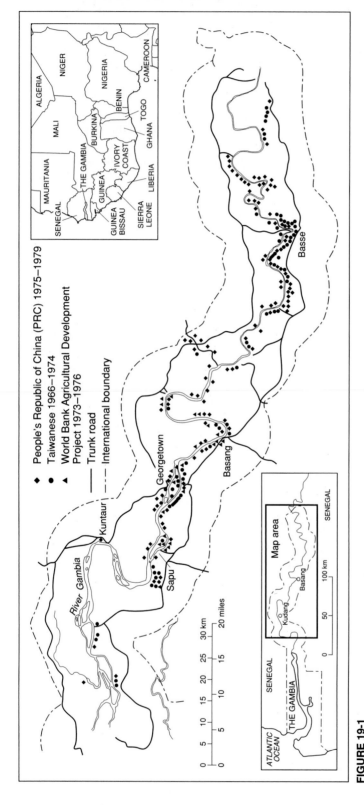

FIGURE 19-1
SMALL-SCALE IRRIGATED RICE SCHEMES: THE GAMBIA, 1966–80. (*Source:* Carney, 1986.)

Taiwan (1966–74), the World Bank (1973–6), and mainland China (1975–9) aimed to staunch foreign exchange losses by making the country self-reliant in production of the dietary staple (Carney, 1986).

The first phase of Gambian rice development lasted until 1980. Despite differing ideological perspectives, the donors followed a similar development strategy: implementing small-scale perimeters averaging 30 ha, in rural communities. Land was not alienated from the patrilocal, extended, polygynous family farm unit. Even though rice is traditionally a woman's crop in The Gambia, each donor agency introduced the green revolution production package to household heads, assuming family labour would be forthcoming for year-round cultivation. However, the donors' joint utility view of Gambian household-based production ignored four crucial characteristics of the farming system that had evolved among rice-growing ethnic groups. These factors, summarized below, were to frustrate double-cropping objectives.

1 A distinct gender division of labour by crop: in rice-growing areas, Gambian women traditionally grow rice while men cultivate rain-fed cereals (maize, millet and sorghum).

2 A spatial division of labour: women's agricultural production is concentrated chiefly in lowland swamps and men's on the uplands.

3 The predominance of men in export crop production: peanuts, The Gambia's principal export crop, are cultivated on sandy, free-draining upland soils and in rice-growing regions, primarily by men.[2]

4 A pattern of labour and property rights on the family land-holding that makes a distinction between production for communal subsistence needs and production for individual use or exchange.

Landholding in the Gambian household-based production system is divided into two types of land use categories that carry distinct labour obligations and crop rights.[3] The vast majority of plots constituting a farm holding are termed household fields, and their purpose is to meet the overall subsistence needs of the family unit. All able-bodied family members are required to provide labour on these fields, and the produce comes under control of the male household head who arranges storage and distribution to dependents and their families. In rice-growing regions women traditionally cultivate lowland rice on household fields while men use the uplands for planting cereals or peanuts, which can be converted to cash for supplemental food purchases by the family unit.

In return for labouring on household fields, dependent sons, their wives and older children are granted usufruct to a smaller portion of the household's farmholding. This subset of household land, referred to as individual fields, grants dependent family members plots for cash cropping. In rice-cultivation areas men grow peanuts for sale, as do women of the Fula and Serahuli ethnic groups. Women's economic activities among the dominant ethnic group, the Mandinka, however, centre on less remunerative rice cultivation. On individual plots family members control the products of their labour and realize the benefits from sale.[4]

The first phase of Gambian irrigated rice projects perturbed this land use production system in several critical ways. First, household heads, to whom the production package was introduced, termed the developed land 'household fields'. As the schemes incorporated many of the Mandinka women's former individual plots, the designation frequently left them with no land for cash crop production. Second, by introducing improved rice production to male household heads, the donors unwittingly established a tradition for men to assume control over technological change in a crop traditionally cultivated by women (Dey, 1980). Finally, although the schemes were established to generate surpluses through double cropping, household field labour obligations had developed traditionally in the context of *one* five-month agricultural season. Despite 'naming' pump-irrigated plots household fields, there was no precedent for household heads to invoke female labour obligations for *two* cropping seasons (Carney, 1986).

A major consequence of small-scale irrigated schemes was the evolution of a new land use pattern in the pumped plots which honoured women's customary land rights but conflicted with donor and state productivity objectives. During the dry season the plots functioned as intended and women discharged their household labour obligation. However, in the wet season men and Serahuli women turned to their more remunerative upland peanut crop.[5] Mandinka females, on the other hand, converted the irrigated plot to an individual field for rain-fed rice cultivation.[6] The initial phase of Gambian irrigated rice development consequently closed with several tensions that were to structure labour and land use in a subsequent large-scale project implemented in central Gambia: (1) women had become marginalized from technological improvement in a crop they traditionally cultivated; (2) Mandinka females' ability to exercise their crop rights depended on access to rice land; and (3) the emergent land use pattern that upheld women's crop rights conflicted with donor and state objectives to realize year-round pumped production.

At the close of the first phase of Gambian irrigated rice development, the country was far from its goal of food security. By 1980 milled imports accounted for 50 per cent of domestic consumption, which prompted the state to seek donor assistance for another form of irrigated rice production that would provide muscle to double-cropping objectives (Carney, 1988). The Jahaly-Pacharr irrigated rice project, which began operation in 1984 under the direction of the International Fund for Agricultural Development (IFAD), introduced significant changes over previous schemes (Figure 19-2).[7] Jahaly-Pacharr is a large-scale project that links 2000 households in seventy villages through a centralized pumping and water delivery system.[8] A network of tertiary and quaternary canals gives the Gambian management the means to control water deliveries to the basic 0.5 ha plot unit. The government made project implementation dependent on a land lease which it successfully negotiated with district authorities and village headmen. The land lease enables the management to tie plot usufruct to double cropping while contract farming has been deployed to recast household labour routines for strict production schedules. (See Figure 19-3 for comparative labour requirements between peanuts, swamp rice and cultivation on the project's pumped plots.) Participating households are advanced inputs on credit and are linked to marketing channels through the government's co-operatives.

The Jahaly-Pacharr project heralded yet another significant departure from the earlier phase of Gambian irrigated rice development. Aware of Dey's (1980, 1981)

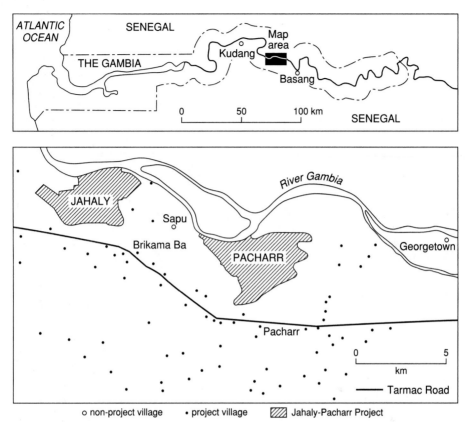

FIGURE 19-2
THE JAHALY-PACHARR PROJECT AREA. (*Source:* Adapted from Saine, 1988.)

research on the deleterious effects of previous irrigation schemes for women's economic opportunities, the donors proclaimed female rice farmers the principal
beneficiaries (IFAD, 1981)—an action that received international praise for gender
equity objectives (Rycroft, 1985; *African Business,* 1986). However, the donors' intent
conflicted with productivity goals fashioned by contract farming.

Project plot allocations had been made on the basis of household labour availability
and, significantly, women's pre-existing tillage rights. Production schedules were
adjusted to the disposition of family labour for double cropping and particularly, the
availability of female labour in the rice fields during the wet season when peanut cultivation commenced. While the donors registered the plots in female farmers' names, no
change was forthcoming in resource control. Male household heads, with support from
the Gambian management, invoked 'tradition' to claim the developed plots as household fields. Arguing that the household field designation provided the only institutional
means to recruit family labour for year-round paddy production mollified the donors
but obfuscated the important interests served by this decision. Political alliances by the

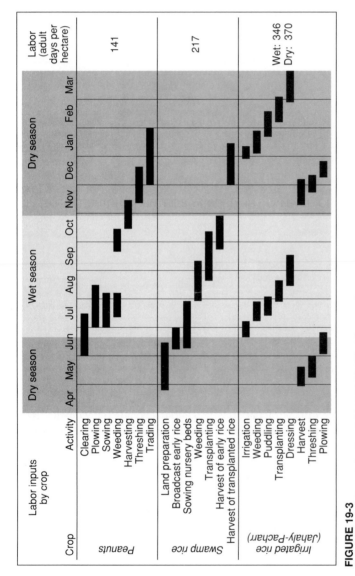

FIGURE 19-3
COMPARATIVE LABOUR REQUIREMENTS. (*Source:* Carney fieldwork data.)

ruling government party with district chiefs and village headmen were being cemented with project development, and would be disturbed by a shift in resource control to women.[9] The government's decision to raise the producer paddy rice with project development in tandem with the scheme's surplus-generating potential promised substantial profits which would come under control of the household head (Carney, 1986). The naming of the project's plots as household fields thus enabled the household head to make claims to women's unpaid labour when in practice the plot functions in part as his individual field capable of generating investable surpluses for accumulation (Carney, 1986, 1988).

Contract farming in irrigated rice resulted in dramatic changes in women's labour, access to land and economic opportunities. By absorbing pre-existing swamp rice fields, the project disenfranchised Mandinka female farmers from access to individual plots.[10] Their initial response revolved around getting the management to designate non-pumped project land as their individual fields, but they encountered little institutional support for their land rights. Their strategies consequently coalesced with those of the women of other ethnic groups who began demanding labour remuneration in paddy from the household head for wet season cultivation. As contract-farming production schedules and continued household participation in the project rely heavily on female labour availability, women in the vast majority of project households managed to negotiate recompense for their labour (Carney, 1988). Elementary share-cropping relations have developed between dependent females and the male household head with women receiving a portion of paddy production that averages about 10 per cent of total paddy output, with a value of US$30–85 (1987) per annum. But in about 20 per cent of project households, women were unable to negotiate labour remuneration.[11] As a consequence, they withdrew their labour from the households' irrigated plots. These Mandinka women have developed a number of alternative, albeit less satisfactory, income-generating alternatives which include: (1) marketing vegetables, condiments and prepared food; (2) vegetable gardening for sale; (3) planting peanuts when land is available; and (4) labour for wages. However, to improve daily wage rates women have converted their traditional reciprocal labour networks into work groups for hire during peak farming operations like weeding and transplanting. By pooling their labour for group hire, women have been able to push up their daily wage rates to about US$0.70 per day (Carney, 1987).

In sum, contract farming has shifted many women into sharecropping relations with male household heads, proletarianized others and converted some female rice farmers into wage workers on the project's plots. Where women formerly realized the benefits of their labour on individual plots directly, they are now dependent on the outcome of intra- and inter-household negotiations for income. Even though these strategies have sometimes resulted in improved wage rates, land loss remains for them the legacy of rice development projects and the basis for their struggles. One female farmer forcefully expressed this awareness in a BBC documentary filmed in the project area: 'we were asleep then, but now we are awake'.[12] A major outcome of women's experience with contract farming in the project area is the pursuit of collective strategies to re-establish long-term land access. Over the past five years these strategies have increasingly focused on establishing vegetable gardens in male-controlled uplands (Carney,

1986; Schroeder, 1989).[13] Market gardens are providing rural Gambian women with an avenue to reconstitute individual crop rights where land access has experienced considerable erosion—a process similar to that unfolding with female vegetable growers located along the country's coastal peri-urban corridor.

IRRIGATED HORTICULTURE: DEVELOPING THE GAMBIA'S COMPARATIVE ADVANTAGE

Although the policy emphasis on horticultural exports is fairly recent, Gambian women have long been involved in vegetable gardening for subsistence and exchange. The first European to describe The Gambia, Cadamosto, noted in 1455 an active dry season vegetable trade, while eighteenth-century travellers observed women cultivating vegetables in household gardens and in rotation with rice in lowland swamps (Crone, 1937; Adanson, 1759; Park, 1799). Vegetable gardening also received encouragement during the colonial period, but its expansion was limited by the elementary technology utilized to obtain water for dry season cultivation—*shadufs,* in which river water is fetched by hand for plot irrigation.[14]

The groundwork for the contemporary horticultural trade dates back to the 1970s when the state, in conjunction with private capital and international aid, began establishing boreholes, sprinkler systems and concrete-lined wells for dry season irrigated production.[15] A warm winter climate and geographic proximity to Europe (six hours by air) encouraged policy support for The Gambia's comparative advantage as a winter fruit and vegetable supplier to European markets, as did favourable tariffs and the removal of export taxes on fresh produce with IMF restructuring in 1985 (Government of The Gambia, 1987; Jack, 1990). In the five years following IMF economic reforms, annual vegetable and fruit exports to Europe have grown to 3000 tons with a value exceeding US$1 million (Jack, 1990).

While non-governmental organizations (NGOs) have been active in helping women's groups develop about 340 small-scale vegetable gardens (ca 0.5–2 ha) in rural Gambia (Nath, 1985; Sumberg and Okali, 1987; Schroeder, 1989; DeCosse and Camara, 1990), the export sector remains concentrated in the peri-urban corridor along the Atlantic coast near the capital and airport, where private land-holding is interspersed with communal tenure (Table 19-1).

Established women's vegetable gardening groups provided the basis for the development of the Gambian horticultural trade. In the early 1970s the Ministry of Agriculture established pilot onion-growing schemes with women's groups in the western region of the country, which proved the feasibility of dry season production for export. With the emergence of markets and fiscal incentives, the horticultural subsector expanded in the peri-urban area onto parastatals and farms owned by private individuals or senior government officials. In the 1980s private holdings devoted to mixed fruit and vegetable production increased with the entry of Gambian businessmen and residents of Levantine and South Asian origin. Production is currently dominated by about sixteen growers on 1000 ha of privately owned land. Most of the private holdings funnel their production to two exporters (a Lebanese and an East African Indian) who control 75 per cent of the air freight space to Europe (Jack, 1990, pers. comm.).

TABLE 19-1
STRUCTURE OF GAMBIAN VEGETABLE PRODUCTION

Type	No.	Approx. size (ha)	Tenure	Funding source	Water source	Market
Peri-urban						
1. Parastatal	1	200	State	State	Borehole	Export, hotels, supermarkets
2. Private	16	50–100	Individual	Private	Borehole	Export, hotels, supermarkets
3. Communal	13	3–15	Usufruct	Multilateral	Borehole or concrete-lined wells	Export, hotels, supermarkets
Rural						
1. Donor	340	0.5–2	Usufruct	NGO	Lined wells	Local
2. Non-donor	216			Women's groups	Unlined wells	

Source: Sumberg and Okali (1987); Planas (1990); DeCosse and Camara (1990); I. Jack (1990, pers. comm.).

Female labour has been critical to the development of export production on these commercial farms. In the initial transition when orchards were established in mangos, papayas, avocados and citrus, women's groups were often granted usufruct to a vegetable garden in return for watering the trees. But their land access frequently terminated when the fruit trees matured (Gaye et al., 1988). The conversion of state and private farms to year-round operations with boreholes and sprinkler systems, however, has created a demand for female labour in vegetable production. Women perform most of the labour-demanding farm operations such as sowing, transplanting, weeding, harvesting and grading produce quality. Employed on a wage or piece-work basis, women's seasonal incomes average US$70–80 (Table 19-2).

Since 1986 the 'women in development' international lobby has influenced three multilateral donors—the United Nations Development Programme (UNDP), the European Economic Community (EEC) and the Islamic Development Bank (IDB)—to target women in Gambian horticultural development by establishing thirteen smaller (5–15 ha) projects on communal land in the peri-urban corridor. Donor involvement has strengthened the efforts of women's groups to secure usufruct to village land for a communal garden through village headmen. Once established, women divide the garden plot into individual allocations. The donors subsidize the irrigation infrastructure, fencing and often in the initial years, inputs and credit. But vegetable gardening poses two major problems for female farmers. More labour intensive than cereal farming, horticultural production adds to women's agricultural and household work burdens. As a consequence, the marketing of highly perishable produce poses a considerable difficulty. Vegetable gardening, moreover, relies on expensive imported inputs like seeds, fertilizers and pesticides which must be purchased in advance of crop sales. Contract farming is viewed as a solution to these problems by the multilateral donors who, since 1989, have linked women's communal gardens to the credit and marketing channels organized by private growers (Gambian Horticultural Improvement Project, 1991).

TABLE 19-2
FEMALE LABOUR REMUNERATION BY VEGETABLE SCHEME TYPE

Type	Dominant labour system	Average dry season income per woman (dalasis)[a]
Peri-urban		
1. Parastatal	W	550
2. Private	W,P	500
3. Communal		
Borehole[b,c]	CF	500
Well[c]	CF	300
Rural		
NGO[c]	S	250
Non-NGO	S	100

W = wage; P = piece work; CF = contract farming; S = self.
Notes: [a] (1990) US$1 = 7 dalasis; [b]fuel costs subsidized; [c]inputs subsidized.
Source: Carney, 1990 fieldwork data.

On the surface contract farming appears to present advantages to both large-scale private growers and women's gardening groups. Contracting with a large grower enables women to obtain costly inputs on credit as well as securing market outlets for their produce. Conversely, contract farming enables large growers to augment produce supplies for export. However, the presumed reciprocity of this arrangement is cast into doubt upon review of the types of problems that surfaced between communal women's groups and large growers during 1989–90. These problems illustrate women's economic vulnerability with contract growing as well as highlighting the subsidy which their labour provides to the horticultural export sector.

Gambian horticultural contractors do not use written contracts with women's groups, preferring verbal arrangements in which the contractor promises to purchase a set quantity of a specific crop. These agreements may or may not include seed and credit advances. Verbal agreements, however, enable the contractor to shift the risks of export crop production onto the women as well as appropriate a large share of the value created by their labour. This occurs in several ways. When there is a market glut or shift in export demands, the contractor may forgo promised purchases. As local demand for specialty vegetables is limited, defaulted agreements leave women with few outlets for their produce.[16] Distress sales of highly perishable produce bring few financial rewards for a season's labour.[17] The failure of growers to honour purchases made through verbal agreements emerged as a recurrent problem in 1989–90.

A second abuse occurs when the contractor advances inputs on credit for repayment from sales. Women have little protection from being overcharged for the credit extended to them. One women's group, contracted to plant chillies in 1989, received only half the market rate after the costs of the inputs were discounted. This prompted them in the following season to procure their own seeds to bargain up the price of their chillies. The grower, however, budged little on his price offer. Already committed to planting chillies, the women's group had to accept his terms (Planas, 1990).

The buyer's right to determine quality grades for export operates as an additional means to depress women's returns from vegetable gardening. Many women's groups complain that high-quality produce is often graded at an inferior standard, which reduces the price they receive. The transfer of value from female producers to the contractor through grading practices is a frequently encountered abuse in contract farming.

Female gardeners, however, do not meekly accept such abuses; in fact, they have consistently pursued strategies to improve their position, including the threat of legal action. In 1989 when one contractor refused to honour his purchase agreement with a women's garden group, a donor representative had to step in to dissuade them from taking the grower to court. Not only were the women unlikely to get a hearing in the absence of a written contract, but attempted legal action would probably result in other export growers blacklisting the group (Planas, 1990).

Such conflicts seriously call into question the mutuality that presumably underlies contract farming production relations as well as its ability to improve women's welfare and income generation. By shifting marketing risks onto female growers, contractors reduce their losses as well as female returns to labour from export horticultural development in The Gambia. Annual incomes for women in communal gardens with contract farming average US$58–89 (see Table 19-3), far below the average per capita income of US$260. Whether working as hired hands on large farms or for themselves on individual plots in communal gardens, women's labour rates vary little, falling between 5 and 7 dalasis a day. This is low recompense for vegetable gardening, which is highly labour intensive, especially in women's sites, generally dependent upon wells for hand-watering. Gardens require two waterings a day which in areas of deep-dug wells average two hours per session, but may reach seven hours in rural areas with shallow wells (Smith et al., 1985).

Irrespective of where women's gardens are located, the additional labour of their daughters and co-wives is important in maintaining production schedules on a daily and seasonal basis. The IDB schemes, improved with a borehole and sprinkler system, provide the only exception to this general pattern. Since water is pumped, women do not have to journey daily to the garden. However, production costs of the borehole system are extremely high: 43 per cent of produce value (Table 19-3), with 96 per cent of those expenditures going on imported supplies like diesel.[18] Dependence on volatile import prices and irregular fuel oil deliveries into the country have reduced the benefits women receive on the borehole schemes, and raise serious questions regarding their long-term sustainability (Barrett and Browne, 1991).

With Gambian horticultural development, multilateral donors have once again implemented 'women in development' projects that champion contract farming for gender equity objectives. Credit advances and expanded marketing outlets have facilitated female entry into commercialized vegetable production. But vegetable cultivation is labour demanding and requires conformity with quality standards and tight production schedules for export that are regulated by private growers. Whether a woman works as a wage labourer on a state or private farm or as a contracted farmer

TABLE 19-3
WOMEN'S PER CAPITA INCOME: REPRESENTATIVE COMMUNAL GARDENS
PERI-URBAN AREA

	Wet season 1989	Dry season 1990	Annual income (dalasis)
IDB (borehole)			
Produce value	37,507	134,753	172,260
Production costs	−16,034	−56,608	−72,642
Net garden income	21,473	78,145	99,618
Per capita garden income (160 members)	134	488	622
UNDP (well)			
Produce value	58,375	142,200	200,575
Per capita garden income (490 members)	119	290	409

Source: Gambian Horticultural Improvement Project (1991).

on communal gardens, her income opportunities are severely limited. With daily labour rates that hover below US$1, female labour maintains The Gambia's edge in competitive export markets while subsidizing the profits accumulated by the private sector within the country.

CONCLUSION

The growing pressure of the 'women in development' group on international agencies to target female farmers by direct policy measures found expression in the 1980s through multilateral-funded development projects in The Gambia.[19] Women were to become the principal beneficiaries of Gambian irrigated rice and vegetable projects and thus benefit from commercialized production of their traditional crops. But the donors' equity concerns were inscribed within a broader policy context that aimed to restructure and intensify labour routines through contract farming. The convergence of equity with productivity objectives has unfolded with contradictory consequences for women's labour, income opportunities and access to land for independent farming.

Female labour and agronomic experience are crucial to contemporary strategies of economic transformation, yet women capture little of the value from their toil. They perform the labour-intensive field operations in both irrigated rice and vegetable production while most of the benefits derived from their labour flow to male household heads, the state or private contractors. Despite women's ongoing struggles with men to force up the value of their labour power, female income levels generally remain below the government minimum daily wage scale of 9 dalasis. With the returns to labour so meagre, these case studies suggest that more than the lack of alternative income-earning possibilities may be at play in women's participation in contract farming.

While contract farming provides Jahaly-Pacharr households with access to credit and markets, women's benefits are nominal and largely a reflection of the value they have managed to negotiate for their labour power. The value of female labour in the project area, however, was deeply imbricated with the issue of land access. Those Mandinka females made landless by project implementation were placed in a more vulnerable position than women of other ethnic groups whose upland individual fields were undisturbed by the scheme's development. Women's access to individual plots within the project area consequently proved pivotal to their ability to negotiate forms of labour remuneration. For Mandinka females, radical responses such as labour withdrawal and the formation of work groups for hire sometimes proved their only means to counter household pressures to toil all year round without compensation. While the Jahaly-Pacharr project involved women in contract farming through sale of their labour power or elementary share-cropping relations, its longer-lasting effect was to catapult women into organizing as a group for their common interests. A significant focus of Mandinka women's collective strategies over the past five years is their attempt to secure access to male-controlled uplands through NGO-supported vegetable gardens.

A concomitant process is under way with a different target group of women in the coastal peri-urban corridor where urbanization, tourist development and the proliferation of horticultural projects have increased the pace of land concentration over the past twenty years through private as well as communal landholdings, and led to a reduction in female access to farmland.[20] The availability of multilateral funding to women's groups for irrigated vegetable production has provided females with an important venue for negotiating land rights through village headmen. But their usufruct to upland areas for gardens remains tenuous.[21] Maintaining harmonious relations with donors and following their directives becomes instrumental in women's strategies to defend access to individual plots and figures prominently in female compliance with contract-farmed vegetable schemes.

Berry (1986) pointed out the centrality of access to and control over resources for understanding contemporary patterns of African agrarian transformation. Donor funding for Gambian irrigation projects over the past twenty-five years has triggered numerous struggles for control over productive resources at the state, regional and household levels. Land concentration has occurred in both private and communal holdings—a process that is increasing socio-economic differentiation as well as gender conflict. As land becomes scarce, women in farm households are particularly affected. By undermining women's access to resources for independent farming, female labour power is 'freed' for the accumulation objectives of husbands, village headmen, state officials and private entrepreneurs. But the deleterious effects of commoditization do not go unchallenged by women. New forms of incorporation into the international economy, like contract farming, explode with conflicts between men and women over household labour mobilization. Consequently, the issue of women's access to land for independent farming not only emerges as central to contemporary gender conflicts, but also underscores the crucial linkage of the changing sexual division of labour for emergent class structures in sub-Saharan Africa (Mackintosh, 1989).

A number of researchers have drawn attention to labour as the primary constraint in African agricultural development (Watts, 1983; Berry, 1986; Richards, 1986; Mbilinyi, 1988). By intensifying female labour demands and subordinating work routines to production schedules, contract farming exacerbates the comparative advantage of women's disadvantage (Staudt, 1987; Mackintosh, 1989). While the evidence collected in these Gambian case studies concurs with Kandiyoti's (1990) and Whitehead's (1990) observation that 'women in development' projects do not accord well with the implementation of more efficient forms of labour control, it also points to the significance of gender-based struggles over resources for the forms of female participation in contract farming.

NOTES

1 Contract farming, however, is not new to Africa; its antecedents date to the late colonial period. One of the earliest British attempts at contract farming occurred in The Gambia. During the 1950s the Colonial Development Corporation unsuccessfully attempted contract farming in a rice project (the Gambia Rice Farm) now a part of the Jahaly-Pacharr project (Dey, 1991, pers. comm.).

2 While this point is generally accurate, it should be noted that women of the Serahuli and Fula ethnic groups may also grow groundnuts in rice-growing areas. In non-rice farming regions women of any ethnic group may cultivate the leading cash crops, cotton and peanuts.

3 A more complete discussion of this landholding system is provided in Dey (1980 and 1982) and Carney (1994).

4 In rural Gambia a small percentage of rice plots may also be 'owned' by individuals. Individually owned plots, created by clearing and cultivating unclaimed land, are independent of household control. In the case of women, individually owned land is frequently inherited or passed on to daughters rather than daughters-in-law. For more detail see Dey (1980) and Webb (1989).

5 Again, this was a general pattern as some men did cultivate irrigated rice during the wet season. Factors affecting their decision to do so included: (1) relative shifts in producer prices that favoured rice over peanuts; (2) the availability of female labour for transplanting and weeding irrigated rice; and (3) plots with favourable drainage for water control.

6 The Gambia's population is distributed among five major ethnic groups: Mandinka (40 per cent), Fulani (16 per cent), Wolof (14 per cent), Jola (9 per cent) and Serahuli (8 per cent). All but the Wolof and Fulani traditionally cultivate rice. Jola rice-production systems are located in rain-fed and inland swamp areas of the western portion of the country. Pump-irrigated rice development has expanded in the freshwater tidal-irrigated areas of central and upper Gambia where Mandinka and Serahuli settlement is concentrated (Figure 19-1).

7 Other donors of the Jahaly-Pacharr project include the African Development Bank, the World Food Programme and the governments of the Netherlands and Germany.

8 The Jahaly-Pacharr project includes 1500 ha, of which 560 are pump irrigated and the remainder used for improved rain-fed and tidal cultivation during the wet season. This discussion focuses on contract farming on the pumped plots. See Carney (1994) for patterns of women's access to the non-pumped plots.

9 Male resistance to donor equity goals surfaced in the preliminary land distribution when men received 90 per cent of the project's plots. The donors intervened to reverse the process and register the plots in women's names. Men acquiesced only after local leaders received assurance from the Gambian management that the plots would come under control of the male household head (Carney, 1986).

10 See Carney (1994) for a discussion of ethnic factors regulating women's access to individual plots.

11 Ethnicity and the resource position of households were important variables in women's success in labour compensation (Carney, 1988).

12 A Mandinka project woman quoted in a BBC documentary, *The Lost Harvest*, produced by Sarah Hobson in 1983.

13 Some Mandinka project women are now growing peanuts on borrowed land over which they have no long-term claim. Attempts to re-establish long-term land claims for independent farming are instead focusing on an upland field, of 2 ha or less, for a village women's garden.

14 National Archives of The Gambia, files 2/961, 47/7 and 47/40.

15 Among the donors involved are several affiliates of the United Nations, the Club du Sahel/CILLS (Permanent Interstate Committee for Drought Control in the Sahel), the European Economic Community, the Islamic Development Bank, the German government and about six non-governmental organizations.

16 Local markets include sales to a small expatriate community, a few supermarkets and tourist hotels. The tourist hotels and supermarkets, however, rely on imported frozen vegetables and only purchase about 10 per cent of their supplies locally, chiefly fresh fruits, tomatoes and onions.

17 Producers earn about 25 per cent of the value from middlewomen's sales to hotels (Jack, 1990, pers. comm.).

18 For example, borehole gardens require 50 litres per day of imported diesel for dry season irrigation.

19 The multilateral donor emphasis on women continued into the 1990s with the World Bank's US$15 million pilot 'Women in Development' project in The Gambia, funded for a five-year period. Covering nearly every economic activity affecting women, the project also aims to strengthen the entrepreneurial skills of market middlewomen and private traders (World Bank, 1990).

20 Nearly 100,000 tourists (principally from England, Germany and Sweden) annually visit The Gambia between November and April. This provides a market for some locally produced fruits and vegetables, but most food items (including perishables) are imported. For a critical view of the weak linkages between the tourist sector and local production, see Lacville (1991).

21 See Schroeder and Watts (1990) for a discussion of men's attempts to regain control over some rural women's vegetable gardens by planting fruit trees, as well as Dey (1990) for a broader overview of the significance of gender issues for the design of sustainable irrigation schemes in Africa.

REFERENCES

Adanson, M. (1759) *A Voyage to Senegal, The Isle of Goree and the River Gambia.* London: Nourse.

African Business (1986) 'After Rice Success Will Bridge-Barrage Be Next?' (January) pp. 21–3.

Barrett, H. and Browne, A. (1991) 'Environmental and Economic Sustainability: Women's Horticultural Production in The Gambia', *Geography* 76(3): 241–8.

Berry, S. (1986) 'Concentration without Privatisation: Agrarian Consequences of Changing Patterns of Rural Land Control in Africa', paper presented at symposium on Agricultural Policy and African Food Security: Issues, Prospects and Constraints, Toward the Year 2000, University of Illinois, Center for African Studies, Champaign (24–6 April).

Binswanger, H. and Rosenzweig, M. (1986) 'Behavioral and Market Determinants of Production Relations in Agriculture', *The Journal of Development Studies* 22(3): 503–39.

Buch-Hansen, M. and Marcussen, H. (1982) 'Contract Farming and the Peasantry: Cases from Western Kenya', *Review of African Political Economy* 23:9–36.

Carney, J. (1986) 'The Social History of Gambian Rice Production: An Analysis of Food Security Strategies', PhD dissertation, Geography Department, University of California, Berkeley.

Carney, J. (1987) 'Contract Farming in Irrigated Rice Production: Jahaly Pacharr Project, The Gambia', Contract Farming in Africa Project, Working Paper No. 8. Binghamton, NY: Institute for Development Anthropology (IDA).

Carney, J. (1988) 'Struggles over Crop Rights and Labour within Contract Farming Households in a Gambian Irrigated Rice Project', *Journal of Peasant Studies* 15(3): 334–49.

Carney, J. (1994) 'Contracting A Food Staple in The Gambia', in P. Little and M. Watts (eds) *Living Under Contract: Contract Farming and Agrarian Transformation in Sub-Saharan Africa.* Madison: University of Wisconsin Press.

Clapp, R. (1988) 'Representing Reciprocity, Reproducing Domination: Ideology and the Labour Process in Latin American Contract Farming', *Journal of Peasant Studies* 16(1): 5–39.

CRED (Center for Research on Economic Development) (1985) *Rural Development in the Gambian River Basin.* Ann Arbor, MI: CRED.

Crone, G.R. (1937) *The Voyage of Cadamosto.* London: The Hakluyt Society.

DeCosse, P. and Camara, E. (1990) 'A Profile of the Horticultural Production Sector in The Gambia'. The Gambia: Department of Planning, Ministry of Agriculture.

Derman, W. (1984) 'USAID in the Sahel', in J. Barker (ed.) *The Politics of Agriculture in Tropical Africa,* pp. 77–97. Newbury Park, CA: Sage.

Dey, J. (1980) 'Women and Rice in The Gambia: The Impact of Irrigated Rice Development Projects in The Farming System', PhD dissertation, Sociology Department, University of Reading.

Dey, J. (1981) 'Gambian Women: Unequal Partners in Rice Development Projects?', *Journal of Development Studies* 17(3): 109–22.

Dey, J. (1982) 'Development Planning in The Gambia: The Gap Between Planners' and Farmers' Perceptions, Expectations and Objectives', *World Development* 10(5): 377–96.

Dey, J. (1990) 'Design for Sustainable Farmer-managed Irrigation Schemes in sub-Saharan Africa', paper for the International Workshop on Design for Sustainable Farmer-Managed Irrigation Schemes in Sub-Saharan Africa, Wageningen Agricultural University, Department of Irrigation and Soil and Water Conservation, The Netherlands (5–8 February).

Franke, R. and Chasin, B. (1980). *Seeds of Famine.* Totowa, NJ: Allanheld.

Gambian Horticultural Improvement Project (1991) '1990 Evaluation of Horticultural Extension Programmes and Operational Plan for 1991', GHIP, Yundum, The Gambia (mimeo).

Gaye, G.O., Jack, I. and Caldwell, J. (1988) 'Use of Farming Systems Research Extension (FSR/E) Methods to Identify Horticultural Research Priorities in The Gambia, West Africa', *Hortscience* 23(1): 21–5.

Glover, D. (1984) 'Contract Farming and Smallholder Outgrower Schemes in Less-Developed Countries', *World Development* 12(11–12): 1143–57.

Government of The Gambia (1987), 'Donors Conference on the Agricultural Sector in The Gambia'. The Gambia: Ministry of Agriculture.

IFAD (International Fund for Agricultural Development) (1981) *Jahaly and Pacharr Appraisal Report.* Rome: IFAD.

Jack, I. (1990) 'Export Constraints and Potentialities for Gambian Horticultural Produce', report prepared for the National Horticultural Policy Workshop, Banjul, The Gambia (3–5 December).

Jarosz, L. (1987) 'Contract Farming and Smallholder Households in Africa', MA thesis, Geography Department, University of California, Berkeley.

Kandiyoti, D. (1990) 'Women and Rural Development Policies: The Changing Agenda', *Development and Change* 21(1): 5–22.

Lacville, R. (1991) 'When Tourism's Profits Go Abroad', *Manchester Guardian Weekly* (May 26): 21.

Mackintosh, M. (1989) *Gender, Class and Rural Transition.* London: Zed.

Mbilinyi, M. (1988) 'Agribusiness and Women Peasants in Tanzania', *Development and Change* 19(4): 549–83.

Morrissy, D. (1974) *Agricultural Modernization through Production Contracting.* New York: Praeger.

Nath, K. (1985) 'Women and Vegetable Gardens in The Gambia: Action Aid and Rural Development', Working Paper No. 109. Boston, MA: African Studies Center, Boston University.

Park, M. (1799) *Travels into the Interior of Africa*. 1954 edition, London: Eland Books.

Planas, T. (1990) 'Women's Communal Vegetable Growing Schemes', paper presented at National Horticultural Policy Workshop, Banjul, The Gambia (3–5 December).

Richards, P. (1986) *Coping with Hunger*. London: Allen and Unwin.

Rycroft, C. (1985) 'How Women Were Involved in The Gambia', *International Agricultural Development* 5(1): 24.

Saine, M.D. (1988) Map of the Jahaly-Pacharr Project. Sapu, The Gambia.

Schroeder, R. (1989) 'Seasonality and Gender Conflict in Irrigated Agriculture: Mandinka Rice and Vegetable Production in The Gambia', Co-Evolutionary Terrains: History, Ecology and Practice in Malagasy and Gambia Rice Systems, Working Paper No. 4. New York: Rockefeller Foundation.

Schroeder, R. and Watts, M. (1990) 'Struggling over Strategies, Fighting over Food: Adjusting to Food Commercialization among Mandinka Peasants in The Gambia, West Africa', unpublished manuscript, Geography Department, University of California, Berkeley.

Smith, F., Jack, I. and Singh, R. (1985) *The Survey of Rural Women's Vegetable Growing and Marketing Program*. Banjul: Action Aid.

Staudt, K. (1987) 'Uncaptured or Unmotivated? Women and the Food Crisis in Africa', *Rural Sociology* 52(1): 37–55.

Sumberg, J. and Okali, C. (1987) 'Workshop on NGO-sponsored Vegetable Gardening Projects in The Gambia', Yundum, The Gambia: Horticultural Unit of Gambian Department of Agriculture and Oxfam America.

Watts, M. (1983) *Silent Violence: Food, Famine and Peasantry in Northern Nigeria*. Berkeley, CA: University of California Press.

Watts, M. (1990) 'Peasants Under Contract: Agro-Food Complexes in the Third World', in H. Bernstein, B. Crow, M. Mackintosh and C. Martin (eds) *The Food Question*, pp. 149–62. New York: Monthly Review.

Watts, M., Little, P., Mock, C., Billings, M. and Jaffee, S. (1988) *Contract Farming in Africa*, Vol. I. Binghamton, NY: IDA.

Webb, P. (1989) 'Intrahousehold Decisionmaking and Resource Control: The Effects of Rice Commercialization in West Africa', Working Paper on Commercialization of Agriculture and Nutrition, No. 3. Washington, DC: International Food Policy Research Institute.

Whitehead, A. (1990) 'Food Crisis and Gender Conflict in the African Countryside', in H. Bernstein, B. Crow, M. Mackintosh and C. Martin (eds) *The Food Question*, pp. 54–68. New York: Monthly Review.

Williams, S. and Karen, R. (1984) *Agribusiness and the Small-Scale Farmer: A Dynamic Partnership for Development*. Boulder, CO: Westview Press.

World Bank (1981) *Accelerated Development in Sub-Saharan Africa: An Agenda for Action*. Washington, DC: World Bank.

World Bank (1990) *Republic of The Gambia Women in Development Project*. Washington, DC: World Bank.

CHAPTER 20

IN SEARCH
OF A DEVELOPMENT
PARADIGM: TWO TALES
OF A CITY

Gene Ellis

University of Denver

One of the most pressing problems confronting development planners in Africa is how to increase local supplies of fuel wood. As explained in a donor-commissioned report at the beginning of the current decade:

1 Not nearly enough trees are being planted to meet future rural and urban needs: during the next 20 years, "annual fuel wood planting will need to increase by about 15 times over current levels," and even this assumes optimistically that "up to a fourth of future fuel wood demand will be met by conservation or . . . alternative fuels." In fact, negligible resources are being devoted to establishing new "plantations of any significant size."[1]

2 African governments cannot be expected to meet these needs because they "will obviously not have the funds from their own resources to pay for programs of this size."[2]

3 In many countries, "the necessary national cadres of foresters and/or extension agents simply do not exist . . . transportation and other logistic support is often lacking."[3]

4 Most governmental efforts to regulate access to land on which fuel wood is being grown have been ineffective, and to make matters worse the local inhabitants have often been alienated from forestry staff who have been placed in policing rôles, making cooperation in other initiatives less likely.

5 The costs of creating fuel wood projects have been high and variable: "Sahel (CILSS) is using an illustrated average of $725 per hectare for village woodlots based

From *The Journal of Modern African Studies*, 26, 4 (1988), pp. 677–83. Reprinted with the permission of Cambridge University Press.

on recent field experience . . . The World Bank's proposed five-year planting averages \$765/hectare in East Africa and over \$850/hectare in West Africa."[4]

The above-cited document noted that although a large-scale multi-purpose reafforestation project in Algeria had reported costs of only about \$300/hectare, a field study had revealed that as much as \$1,080 was required for labour alone, while the overall costs per hectare of reafforestation had been estimated to be as high as \$1,600 by the World Food Program.[5] It is small wonder that two American experts, asked separately which donor-supported forestry projects would be able to pay for themselves in the market-place if unsubsidised, both answered tersely, "None."

The almost universal conclusion seems to be that drawn by Frances Gulick in 1980, namely "that there must be massive fuelwood planting programs."[6] But in a situation where governments are without adequate resources, where skilled personnel are not available, where donors are increasingly constrained, and where marginal costs are high and rising, is not a strategy based on "more of the same" doomed to failure? Given the sheer magnitude of what needs to be done and the inadequacy of the public efforts which can be mounted, resources must be mobilised on a wider scale. Hence the search for responses which can and will be replicated by the process of what might be called "contagion."[7]

THE FIRST TALE: THE DEVELOPMENT OF THE ADDIS ABABA FOREST

Traditionally, the Imperial Court of Ethiopia had been a "moving capital," slowly transversing the Highlands, subjugating and taxing peoples and resources as it went.[8] However, having been influenced greatly by foreigners who hoped that it might be feasible to construct a railway that would "open up" the interior—not least by providing a suitable location for their missions—Emperor Menelik decided towards the close of the nineteenth century to create a permanent headquarters for his government and administration at Finfini, to be known as Addis Ababa, or "New Flower." The rapid build-up of facilities and population put extreme pressure on local forest supplies, and hence the inhabitants were ordered not to cut or burn down trees without permission, and to replant any areas that were so cleared.

The laws went unheeded and unenforced, and it was reported that travellers approaching Addis Ababa at the turn of the century had to do without wood for several days, so scarce was the supply.

After a few Europeans had brought in as many as 26 varieties of eucalyptus, Menelik threw his support behind their introduction by distributing seedlings at nominal prices, and by exempting any lands so planted from taxation. By 1899 a writer noted that the owners of small holdings were growing eucalyptus in hopes of high profits, and that many houses and roads were rapidly becoming surrounded by these trees. Indeed, such was the latter's popularity that when in 1913 the newly created Ministry of Agriculture ordered that these woodlands should be uprooted in the belief that eucalyptus dried up water supplies, the proclamation went unheeded.

The shortage of fuelwood had been eased by the 1920s, and by the Italian invasion in 1936 the Addis Ababa forest was estimated to cover not less than 4,000 hectares. Aerial photography showed that this had increased to 7,900 hectares in 1957, and to 10,400 hectares in 1964, roughly keeping pace with the growth of the population.

What are the main lessons that can be learnt from this successful indigenous enterprise?

1 The creation of the eucalyptus forest was an example of that ideal type of donor-assisted scheme in which those involved concentrate on "teaching how to fish" rather than on supplying the needy with food.

2 Although the external assistance was limited, it appears to have been a necessary ingredient. The eucalyptus seedlings were all exotic to Ethiopia, the costs of transportation were high relative to any expectation of private returns, the growth and organisation of the forest took several decades, and there were few if any chances of being able to create a monopoly of output that would be profitable enough to repay the total outlay.[9]

3 There were no long-term governmental inputs, unlike many modern forestry projects. Indeed, by the 1960s, eucalyptus was still considered to be a "plantation" tree and hence neglected by the Forestry Research Institute.[10]

4 The countryside remained denuded while the urban forest expanded. Jane Jacobs presents a convincing case that cities developed agriculture first, and exported it later to rural areas.[11] Certainly, in Ethiopia the information and techniques from abroad arrived first in Addis Ababa, where the location of the forest minimised transport and energy costs, and where the inhabitants then provided the demand. In addition, the counterproductive defects of the traditional land-tenure system were avoided.[12]

5 The lack of professional advice proved to be no disadvantage, and may have been a blessing in disguise. Despite the validity of certain scientific criticisms—for example, the stems were "neither pruned nor stripped of leaves,"[13] with the seedlings having been planted at a far higher density than would have been recommended by a "textbook forester"—the crude techniques proved to be enduring and economic. The explanation, of course, is that research conducted by experimental stations might seek to discover, for example, "optimal" watering rates for maximum growth according to the perceived standards of particular disciplines, whereas these might have little or no relation to what can best be done by peasants, given their circumstances and constraints.

6 The "running costs" of the forest were minimal. No expensive supervisors were needed (as thought necessary for a proposed F.A.O./U.N.D.P. project), and there were few transportation expenses. Many women were prepared to walk daily as far as 14 kilometres to purchase fuel from the wood-cutters and retail it in the city. Because of the forest's location, all parts of the trees (including twigs, leaves, and stems) were utilised. Of that which was trucked, the bulk was informally transported on top of contracted loads. It is doubtful if planners would have dared to devise a development project that required the bulk of forest products to be carried to the market on the backs of both animals and people, but this mode of carriage resulted in large-scale employment, and enabled bundles of wood to compete in the market with alternative fuels.

7 Lastly, the continuing viability of this early twentieth-century industry must be emphasised. It endured throughout an enemy invasion, and despite benign neglect by the Ethiopian authorities, in one of the poorest and least literate economies in the world.

Given that there will never be enough external assistance to fund all the reafforestation that is needed, whether in state plantations or in village woodlots, and given the limitations of indigenous governments as regards expertise, administrative and managerial talent, and especially finance, then the focus of the efforts of donors must be to complement and draw out the resources of the private sector, and not to compete with highly subsidised, nonreplicable efforts.

A SECOND, CAUTIONARY TALE: NEVER TROUBLE TROUBLE TILL TROUBLE TROUBLES YOU

In late 1974, the Imperial Government was overthrown by a coup d'état, and the following year the revolutionary leaders began implementing a program of extensive rural reforms, making "land to the tiller" for the first time a reality in Ethiopia. At about the same time, the new régime nationalised not only urban property but also woodlands and forests. This led to a great reduction in the number of seedlings that were being grown along the Awash river, so that far fewer were transported and transplanted to plots near the capital. In addition, the inhabitants were given strong incentives to cut down and market as many trees as possible before adequate policing powers to enforce the proclamation could be institutionalised.

The short-term impact of these changes was estimated by examining two high-level "photographs" of the eucalyptus forest of Addis Ababa that were taken on January 31, 1973 and February 11, 1976 by means of the "Landsat" remote sensing technology (Figure 20-1). In order to quantify the loss that had taken place, a grid containing 7,200 squares was established, and after these had been studied it became clear that the postrevolutionary photograph contained 32.8 percent fewer "dots," each representing approximately one acre or 0.4 hectare of eucalyptus forest-cover.[14] Although it seems indisputable that the forest did in fact recede (and by approximately this order) over the three-year period, it is open to debate what caused the losses. However, during several months in late 1975, Allan Hoben of Boston University and I were involved in an attempt to assess the effectiveness of the land reforms, and both the conversations by day and the sound of axes by night made us very aware of the negative reactions to the changes that had taken place in the system of incentives.

Of course, other influences were also at work, notably the severe transportation bottlenecks in the early stages of the revolution that diminished the flow of charcoal into Addis Ababa, thereby increasing the demand for locally produced fuelwood and the rate of exploitation. In addition, it must be admitted that the need to replant eucalyptus is reduced by the fact that it regularly "coppices"—i.e., sprouts from the severed stumps. It is nevertheless clear that there was a dramatic decrease in the Addis Ababa forest between the observations, and it seems certain that this can be attributed to the changed incentives.

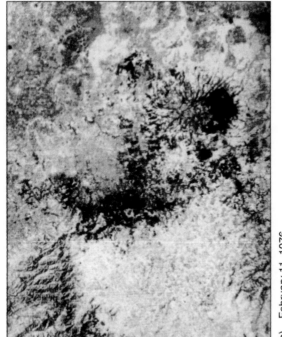

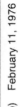

(a)   January 31, 1973

(b)   February 11, 1976

FIGURE 20-1
These photos were taken on January 31, 1973, and February 11, 1976. The dark crescent around Addis Ababa (1) is forested mountain slopes. Further south (2) is another mountain planted with eucalyptus. A large blow-up was used to divide the city into a grid from which forest losses could be determined. The photo with the largest forest is, of course, the "before" of 1973; that with the smallest, 1976.

• • • • • •

The presence of an extremely modest "external aid" project by foreign embassies in Addis Ababa at the turn of the century led to the introduction of eucalyptus into Ethiopia and to the beginnings of the forest that grew with the population over the years, and which supplied a major portion of the city's energy needs. Although aid was probably necessary for the creation of the forest, no long-term governmental inputs were required, in neither research nor support services. The point to emphasise is that the incentives provided by the urban market were sufficiently attractive to enable the efforts of large numbers of individuals to be organised productively by small profit-making entrepreneurs.

Throughout most of the continent it is *not* a case of "if it works, don't fix it," or that there is a "natural" system which will provide adequate incentives, because the energy sector in Africa can scarcely be described as "working." In the Ethiopian case, fuel-wood shortages did not readily give rise to rural forestry, given the constraints of the land-tenure system. The conclusions to be reached are rather that a forest must be designed which can reproduce itself, and that interventions likely to affect either the direct or indirect incentives should be examined carefully since they may have a devastating impact.

POSTSCRIPT

And how are things today, some 13 years after the nationalisation of trees? A recent report of the Ethiopian National Energy Authority summarises the present position.[15]

1 Despite the efforts of the government, 85 percent or more of the biomass fuels consumed in Addis Ababa have been supplied, transported, and marketed by small-scale entrepreneurs, most of whose activities are "illegal" in the sense that they have originated in the unauthorised cutting of trees.[16]

2 Whereas "fuels" such as canvas, rubber, and leather scraps were only used "years ago" in such small-scale industrial undertakings as brick-making, they are now burnt in households as well. As the report notes, this raises real health considerations: "their use at all demonstrates the delicate balance between supply and demand in Addis Ababa," and is a "real negative trend factor."[17] In addition, dung is increasingly used as a fuel in the city, as it has been for many years in the countryside.[18]

3 The price of wood fuel has risen sharply in Addis Ababa from an estimated Ethiopian $38.79 per metric ton in 1975 (the year of the revolution), to E.$101.92 in 1980, and to E.$250 in 1988. Although some of this increase has been caused by inflation (basic grain prices rose over this period by a factor of 4 or more), and some represents the increasing demand of the growing population, it is also evident (given the other indicators) that the supply constraints have become acute, and that the ready elasticity noted in the earlier city forest system has been lost.[19]

4 The private production of wood has been replaced by about 200 square kilometers of eucalyptus plantations around Addis Ababa that are managed by peasant associations. Unfortunately, their "enforcement activities . . . are not consistent in any way or place," with resulting uneven incentives, as well as uncertainties and disruptions in supply. The report calls attention also to the problems caused by the short growing rotations of 2–3 years, since 5–7 are needed if there is to be a proper maturation cycle. In addition, the illegal nature of much of the cutting, and the "nonconservation" orientation of legal harvesting (due to inadequate incentives offered by the present system of public ownership), are helping to cause excessive rates of stump mortality. Increasingly, roots are being sold in the urban market as firewood.[20]

5 The government has endeavoured to replace the private vendors of firewood, charcoal, and construction poles in Addis Ababa with as many as 31 biomass fuel depots that are "primarily a wholesale operation working under price-controlled conditions." The "in-forest" price for a 40-kilogram sack of charcoal is so low (E.$3.50), as against what it will fetch in the market (E.$21.29), that only very poor quality fuel is sold to the depots. Although the latter appear "to be reasonably managed and to have a grasp of the magnitude of the problems in Addis Ababa," the time taken between harvesting and transporting trees was so excessive that the depots sometimes received logs that had rotted and hence deteriorated in value.[21]

In summary, it is clear that the changes in the mid-1970s are still having a profound effect today, and that the government has not been able to create alternative incentives that will sustain a viable fuelwood-supplying forest. More importantly, in light of the limited resources at their command, the authorities have not yet devised a system which is "contagious" as regards the required behaviour of producers. Supply has not kept pace with demand, prices have risen, rotation times have been cut, and poor fuel substitutes with significant social costs (dung, rubber scraps) have been introduced. The crisis may have reached dangerous proportions:

> The 1986–87 price surge should be viewed as an indicator of just how fragile and volatile the fuelwood supply is. . . . Any supply disruption will likely lead to an immediate pricing reaction from the private sector, and spontaneous social turmoil could result. *Interventions will have to be well thought out and very carefully implemented* to not cause unnecessary perturbations.[22]

NOTES

1 Frances A. Gulick, "Suggested Approaches for CADA Initiatives in Fuelwood Production," U.S. A.I.D./Africa, Washington, D.C., October 18, 1980, p. iii, citing the World Bank's Renewable Energy Task Force survey of needs in 10 countries (Central African Republic, Chad, Ethiopia, Gabon, Mali, Rwanda, Somalia, Tanzania, Uganda, and Burkina Faso, then known as Upper Volta), where fuel wood accounts for 90 percent or more of all energy consumed.

2 Ibid., p. iv.

3 Ibid., p. 14. According to James W. Howe and Frances A. Gulick, "Firewood and Other Renewable Energies in Africa: A Progress Report on the Problem and the Response," Overseas Development Council, March 31, 1980, p. 21: "A recent case history from a Kougougou (Upper Volta) regional development project, assisted by FAO/UNDP funds, illustrates the fact that, without manpower, transport, and gasoline, foresters,

however well motivated, cannot be expected to service and supervise even small-scale planting programs successfully."

4 Gulick, op. cit., p. 12.

5 Fred Weber, "A Reforestation Project in Algeria: What It May Mean to Future Forestry and Conservation Activities in Sub-Saharan Africa," US AID/Africa, February 12, 1981. In Brazil, where the government had chosen to create plantations rather than follow the path of community forestry, the public subsidy alone ranged from $1,235 to $2,025 per hectare, thereby giving this plantation project "the dubious distinction of being one of the most costly man-made forests in the world," according to "The Socio-Economic Context of Fuelwood Use in Small Rural Communities," US AID Evaluation Special Study No. 1, August 1980, p. 113.

6 Gulick, op. cit., p. 13.

7 The term "contagion" refers to the spread of technologies by emulation alone, and was first used in this sense, as far as I know, by William Gross, then head of Volunteers for International Technical Assistance.

8 The information in this section is based on the following: Richard Pankhurst, *Economic History of Ethiopia, 1800–1935* (Addis Ababa, 1968), pp. 247, 705, and 707; the National Academy of Science's Ethiopian case-study, *Firewood Crops: Shrub and Tree Species for Energy* (Washington, D.C., 1981); Ronald J. Horvath, "Addis Ababa's Eucalyptus Forest," in *The Journal of Ethiopian Studies* (Addis Ababa), 6 (1968): 13–19; and from limited observations during fieldwork in 1970–1 and 1975.

9 There is evidence that all developed countries, whether socialist or capitalist, have found it necessary to provide public funds for agricultural research and development; apart from the fact that the initial costs are so high, the flow of information cannot readily be privatised to create sufficient incentives. For a discussion of the dilemma which the production and utilisation of knowledge creates for private enterprise, see Harry G. Johnson, "The Efficiency and Welfare Implications of the International Corporation," in Charles P. Kindleberger, ed., *The International Corporation: A Symposium* (Cambridge, Mass., 1970), pp. 35–56.

10 Horvath, loc. cit., p. 17.

11 Jane Jacobs, *The Economy of Cities* (New York, 1970), chap. 1.

12 See Allan Hoben, *Land Tenure among the Amhara of Ethiopia: The Dynamics of Cognatic Descent* (Chicago and London, 1973), and Dan Franz Bauer, *Household and Society in Ethiopia* (East Lansing, 1977), for an examination of several land-tenure systems and their impact on innovation.

13 *Firewood Crops*, p. 180.

14 For a description of the technology and uses of remote sensing, see Barry N. Haack, "Landsat: A Tool for Development," in *World Development* (Oxford), 10, 10, 1982, pp. 899–909. My thanks go to the Regional Remote Sensing Facility in Nairobi, which provided the photographs.

15 Ethiopian National Energy Authority, "Biomass Fuels Supply and Marketing Review. Interim Report on Biomass Fuels Production, End-Use Efficiency, and Sales Mechanisms," Addis Ababa, April 1988, written by Robert A. Chronowski, under the direction of Lemma Eshetu of ENEA. Although the authors clearly note that their findings are less than statistically robust because of the logistical difficulties encountered during the three-week survey, I have taken the view that the reported evidence is worth summarising.

16 Ibid., p. 1.

17 Ibid., p. 26.

18 Ibid., p. 15.
19 Ibid., p. 9. The price series upon which the data are based were taken from the World Bank and from the CEPPE. Addis Household Fuel Survey, Addis Ababa, 1986.
20 Ethiopian National Energy Authority, op. cit., pp. 3 and 13–14.
21 Ibid., pp. 3 and 10.
22 Ibid., p. 6, my emphasis.

PART FIVE

INDUSTRY IN DEVELOPMENT

One of the tenets of early development analysis, emphasized by Sen in Part One, was the fundamental importance of industrialization. Sen provided evidence that countries that have industrialized have performed better on many development indicators. The strongest evidence is provided by the newly industrialized countries (NICs), particularly Taiwan and South Korea, but also Singapore, Hong Kong, Brazil, and Mexico.

The one clear lesson of the forty years of development theory and policy is that there are no simple answers. By 1970 the industrialization of many countries reached its limit because substituting domestic production for imports could not generate the resources for a self-sustaining process, particularly if high-priced oil was among the imports. Often the industries were sustained only by government subsidies, or if they were state-owned enterprises, they became contributors to the fiscal deficit and to domestic inflationary pressures.

Even at its best, industry's effect on the domestic economy was not unambiguously positive. It often resulted in a protected sector, characterized by high incomes for only a few owners and high wages for a small elite labor force. For the most part, industries of the South remained dependent on international sources of technology, which reduced the dynamism they transmitted to the domestic economy. Industry still offered the possibilities of backward and forward linkages that were noted long ago by Albert Hirschman (1958), but their effect on most economies was neither uniform nor powerfully positive.

The evolution of the international economy has also affected the role of industrialization. Virtually every country in the world has made an effort to industrialize and to sell its industrial products in the world market. As a result, international competition has grown progressively more difficult. At the same time, control over technology and information has favored transnational corporations which are located primarily in the developed world. They have influenced the entire industrialization process, not always to the benefit of the South as a group and often to the detriment of a particular country, a group, or an area within a country.

As a result, we must rethink the role of industry in development, to take account of the contemporary situation. Industry will be central to any development process, but not in the manner the early development economists had envisioned. This updating is the task of this part.

The article by Helen Shapiro and Lance Taylor is an excellent summary of the status of thinking on industrialization today, and a good example of another approach to the "new development economics." Shapiro and Taylor assess the earlier debates on the role of industry and emphasize a central weakness: the theoretical nonexistence, or at least the superficial treatment, of the state. They draw on a wealth of empirical information from case studies of industry, the state, and development, in the North as well as the South, in the belief that "elements of the strategies appropriate to large and small countries are best described through empirical generalizations rather than the abstract model used by neoclassical theory." This methodology differs fundamentally from Stiglitz's "new development economics" in Part Four. They are able to specify seven boundary conditions for successful industrialization and then to make eleven generalizations that are useful for understanding that process and for developing policies toward industrialization. Although, as we might expect, there is no simple answer to the question of the role of industry in development, Shapiro and Taylor conclude that the experience of the past forty years does provide a basis for steps which can improve the contribution of industry to development.

The next two articles focus on the most dynamic focal point of industrialization in the South, that is, East Asia. The first article relates the East Asian experience to the possibilities for industrialization in eight countries of South and Southeast Asia. The second article provides more detail on the industrialization process and suggests that the pacific basin of East Asia and Latin America could become a fourth industrial power, joining the United States, Europe, and Japan. The careful reader will note that none of the articles deals specifically with Africa, the Middle East or Central Asia; these are not areas of notable industrialization at this time. This will reinforce the tendency to greater differentiation in the South, which was noted in Part Three.

Clive Hamilton provides an overview of the Asian development success stories, Taiwan, South Korea, Singapore, and Hong Kong, and then assesses the likelihood of similar industrialization in eight other countries of South and Southeast Asia. His framework could be applied to other countries of the South, and many of his lessons relate directly to the conclusions of Taylor and Shapiro. He finds that the ability of a country to follow the East Asian pattern of industrialization depends on international conditions, on internal economic conditions and policies, and finally on domestic politics and power and class relations. The first, international conditions, is not likely to be as benign as it has been in the past, given changes in international competition. The domestic requirements are formidable: to increase saving, to improve enterprise management, and to modernize the agricultural sector. Finally, the process is more likely to be successful if an industrial capitalist class dominates politics or is at least the major influence on state power. Hamilton then applies his analysis to the eight other countries. He finds the prospects poor for Indonesia, the Philippines, Nepal, and Bangladesh, doubtful for India and Pakistan, and favorable for Malaysia and Thailand.

Dae Won Chol's article provides a somewhat more technical and microeconomic perspective on the industrial performance of the four East Asian NICs (or NIEs, newly industrializing economies) and four of the other economies treated by Hamilton— Malaysia, Thailand, Indonesia, and the Philippines. He contrasts these countries' industrial development, based on the growth of new industries like electronics, with the growth in Europe and the United States of chemicals and so on, and then with Latin America's growth in raw-materials-based industries. After examining the change in economic relations between Latin America and East Asia, Chol concludes that there is potential for two areas to develop in complementary fashion during the 1990s and that Latin America could follow the pattern of East Asian industrialization.

The final two articles provide cautionary notes, as does Part Three on agriculture and the challenge of sustainable development. Guy Standing's article indicates that this same industrialization process has "feminized" international labor and has not measurably increased the security and stability of women's lives in the world. Robert Devlin deals with the rapid privatization of state enterprises that is occurring in Latin America, but also in Eastern Europe and Africa. Privatization has a number of goals and is highly ideologically tinged. The article examines its background and points out that conscious efforts must be undertaken to ensure that privatization not lead to social inequity, an experience that has become all too common across the world.

Standing's treatment of global feminization documents both the increased labor force participation of women and the accompanying decrease in the benefits that had traditionally accompanied industrial employment: job security, higher pay, job safety, and the security of insurance programs. His assessment is that the supply-side programs that have encouraged deregulation and cutthroat international competition have created a "cult of insecurity." The effect of development processes on women and on issues of gender has become an important concern of contemporary development economics. Standing's conclusion is that current industrial strategies are eroding their control in very important areas and are increasing women's vulnerability. He suggests a broad-based rethinking of industrial and labor policy to take these trends into account, and he claims that privatization is likely to affect women negatively since they are relatively better off in public enterprises.

This suggestion leads naturally to Devlin's article. The push to privatize state-owned enterprises has been an important component of neoconservative efforts to reduce the role of governments in the South. Devlin provides an overview of the magnitude of privatization in Latin America and then examines the many factors entering into this effort. Contrary to the euphoric pronouncements of free-enterprise economists who see privatization as the road to development, especially in Eastern Europe, he finds the process much more complex.

Nonetheless, there is scope in development efforts for privatization: there are state enterprises that are inefficient; there are areas where the private sector has matured and the human resource base has improved, often through government education policies, making greater private activity more feasible; and there are sectors in which the state should reduce its activity. The fiscal crisis faced by many developing countries will increase the pace of privatization when it can relieve fiscal pressures, and it is entirely likely that the decade will see a contraction in the role of government. It seems to us less likely that this is "the dawn of a new era of unfettered markets and private enterprise" than "one of adjustment in which the state seeks to redefine the instruments and scope of its intervention" (Bienen and Waterbury, 1989). The key problem continuing to face privatization efforts—whether in Eastern Europe, Africa, or Latin America—is their effect on social welfare. Devlin closes by suggesting that the fundamental element is to ensure that the gains from privatization be shared widely, rather than simply creating a private monopoly from the state monopoly.

As was the case with the agricultural sector, active rethinking of the industrial dimensions to development is under way, based on the wealth of experience that has been gained. The international context will have a major impact on any national development strategy that is undertaken, and success in establishing a viable set of domestic policies will affect the contribution that industry can make.

REFERENCES

Bienen, Henry, and John Waterbury. "The Political Economy of Privatization in Developing Countries." *World Development* 17, 5 (1989): 617–632.

Hirschman, Albert O. *The Strategy of Economic Development.* New Haven, Conn.: Yale University Press, 1958.

CHAPTER 21

THE STATE AND
INDUSTRIAL STRATEGY

Helen Shapiro

Harvard Business School, Boston, Massachusetts

Lance Taylor

New School for Social Research

1. INTRODUCTION

The debate about industrial strategy in the economic development literature has always been charged. During the past decade, the voltage rose as planners faced a rapidly changing global economy at the same time as their ability to act domestically was curtailed by fiscal constraints. Meanwhile, two neoclassically based attacks against state intervention were vigorously mounted in the 1970s and 1980s, and a reaction is getting under way. These shifts in objective circumstances and intellectual foundations notwithstanding, the fact remains that industrial strategies continue to be pursued—all governments intervene to shape their economies' productive structures by default or design.

The goal of this paper is to set out guidelines not only about how governments should select industrial strategies, but also how they should make the difficult transition from one policy regime to another when that becomes desirable or necessary. We begin our discussion by reviewing "old" views (circa 1960) of the role of the state, and the two waves of neoclassical attack. A countercritique is put forth, emphasizing the specificity of each country's industrial experience. "Boundary conditions" to successful policies are addressed, which lead to generalizations about the strategy lines different kinds of economies might pursue.

Reprinted with permission from *World Development,* 18, 6 (1990), pp. 861–78, Elsevier Science Ltd, Pergamon Imprest, Oxford, England.

2. THE ROLE OF THE STATE

Industrial strategy rests upon directed public interventions at the sectoral or firm level, aimed at stimulating particular lines of economic endeavor. Microeconomic "targeting" of policies toward particular sectors is necessarily involved. The state may also undertake economy-wide actions complementary to the sectoral thrusts. *All* governments engage in industrial strategy in this sense. Historically, no country has entered into modern economic growth without the state's targeted intervention or collaboration with large-scale private sector entities.

(a) Industrial Strategy: The Development Theorists' View

Alexander Gerschenkron (1962) was among the first to postulate conditions that lead economies to follow different strategy lines. Based on his study of European industrialization, he argued that a country's economic position relative to more advanced nations directly influenced the nature of the state's intervention in its development process. In particular, the English industrial revolution was not a model for those that followed. Its own success guaranteed that all subsequent attempts would significantly vary.

Because it came first and embodied relatively unsophisticated technology, England's industrialization was more gradual and less capital intensive than its followers. The rapid pace of technical change and the widening disparities between their actual and potential rates and levels of economic development dictated other paths for countries in the then-periphery. Germany, Italy, and Russia were likely to jump immediately into the most modern industrial sectors, characterized by capital intensity and scale economies. In these economies, however, capital was scarce and diffused, and the entrepreneurial class either risk averse or financially weak.

Different initial conditions engendered diverse institutional forms and sectoral compositions when industrial growth got under way. In the follower countries, Gerschenkron suggested that the state itself had to substitute for the market and "force" industrialization. Whereas the government's role in an "autonomous" development effort was largely restricted to creating a suitable environment for private capital, in the followers the state became more directly involved with the extraction and allocation of resources, and the establishment and management of firms. Greater "relative backwardness" led to more widespread public intervention to overcome economic inertia.

Throughout the 1960s, economists more directly concerned than Gerschenkron with development policy shared a consensus favoring state intervention, based on different but related criteria. The Keynesian revolution, which cast doubt on the market's ability to achieve optimal results, was used to legitimize economic planning. Keynes's emphasis on domestic economic prosperity as opposed to international concerns was extended to support national industrialization strategies in the Third World.

Development economics arose as a separate field of study following these Keynesian precepts. It also incorporated Schumpeter's (1934) distinction between structural economic change (or "development" in his usage) and mere growth. General equilibrium theory, it was argued, could not describe the dynamic heart of the process—long-run development would not automatically flow from decentralized, optimal decision making in the short run. Hirschman (1958) and others saw development as a sequence of punctuated disequilibria. An investment project could create opportunities for others elsewhere, either by raising profits for industries downstream by lowering their costs of production or by making it possible to take advantage of scale economies by expanding the market or inducing greater specialization among firms. An individual investor's profit and loss calculus could not adequately capture such social benefits (or costs). As Allyn Young (1928) had emphasized early on, dynamic externalities arising from investment could move the system away from equilibrium in ways that comparative static analysis could never take into account.

Scitovsky (1954) explained the conditions required for the price mechanism to achieve optional dynamic allocation: complete and functioning markets, an absence of increasing returns, and complete tradability. Empirical study showed that these conditions did not obtain in less developed countries (LDCs). Those economies were plagued with structural rigidities. Wages and exchange rates were singled out as not reflecting true opportunity costs. Private costs to investors supposedly exceeded social opportunity costs, understating industry's social return. Beginning with the work of Prebisch (1950), the Latin American structuralist school emphasized institutional barriers preventing free factor mobility and productivity growth. Development, therefore, would require creating the conditions under which capitalism could work, i.e., functioning labor and capital markets and national market integration.

From a planning perspective, Chenery (1961) and others showed how optimality of a free trade regime depended on the absence of market imperfections (including economies of scale). Singer (1950) and Prebisch (1959) embellished this work by arguing that static comparative advantage as revealed by current prices could not capture secular trends. Differences in price and income elasticities for primary and manufactured goods meant that raw material exports could not pay for manufactured imports in the long run. The supposed inevitability of future foreign exchange shortages provided an argument for industrialization not easily read from current relative prices.

Distinct viewpoints are evident in the 30-year-old literature, but a perception of development as a process of dynamic, nonmarginal change united all the authors. Required investments are lumpy and (in a poor country) large in comparison to savings flows or even the national capital stock. Although it may provide adequate signals for marginal changes, the price mechanism cannot guide "big" industrial decisions, nor can it be relied upon to induce the resource transfer necessary for industrialization. Public interventions are required both to support investors (via protection, subsidies, cheap credits, etc.) and to invest directly to break critical bottlenecks. A greater extent of market failure in less developed as opposed to richer economies provides the basic rationale for expanding the scope of state intervention.

These theoretical arguments also justified import-substitution schemes already in process. Export-led growth was inconceivable to Third World technocrats and politicians who had witnessed (and seen their economies strongly affected by) the collapse of raw material prices and world trade in the 1930s. Trade expansion continued to look bleak in the mid-1950s while Europe was rebuilding and its currencies were still not fully convertible. Confronting foreign exchange constraints, many countries shifted their economic focus to the domestic market. Industrialization was also in the interest of the political coalitions that emerged in newly formed states. In this environment, development banks, state-owned enterprises, and industrial targeting arose naturally in the developing world.

(b) Neoclassical Reactions

There were at least two major problems with the literature just reviewed. One is that while it was rich with diagnoses of why backward economies do not develop, it offered limited guidance as to how the government was to intervene to set things right. Planning tools such as social cost-benefit analysis and programming models soon proved unable to blueprint industrial growth. More fundamentally, the development theorists tacitly assumed that the state had unlimited capacity to intervene in the economic system. Its failure to carry out its assigned developmental role(s) became apparent, almost equally quickly. While doubt about the adequacy of the market was the main thrust of the first wave of dissent, the development economists' unstated beliefs about the nature of the state and its capacity to intervene became the target of the second attack.

P. T. Bauer (1972, 1984) was prescient in pointing out these problems. Generalizing from his experience in India, he had articulated most of the 1980s vintage criticisms of an expanded public sector 20 years before. He not only considered government failure, i.e., corruption and mismanagement, more critical than market failure, but reversed the direction of causality: intervention *caused* and did not cure market imperfections. Implicitly, he assumed the market mechanism capable of self-correction. Bauer was especially fearful of the adverse political consequences he thought were associated with concentration of economic power by the state.

Toye (1987) is correct in dubbing Bauer "a pioneer of the counterrevolution," but Bauer was distinctly a lone wolf until the first neoclassical reaction put traditional development economics squarely on the defensive. This initial blow was aimed at the state's capacity to guide structural change. Using new analytical tools from trade theory such as effective rates of protection and domestic resource costs, Little, Scitovsky, and Scott (1970) showed that industrial strategies were inefficient—the incentives they created were highly unequal for different economic actors. These authors and their successors sought (how successfully is taken up below) to correlate "distorted" policy regimes with poor economic performance. Read between the lines, they advocated laissez faire as the only viable alternative to an incentive mare's nest.

This neoclassical critique was bolstered by the success of export-oriented countries such as South Korea and Taiwan, which at the time were thought to have noninterventionist states. Their rapid growth in comparison to economies which followed import-substitution strategies seemed to provide empirical validation for Harry Johnson's (1967) earlier claims that dynamic gains could be had from free trade. An avid follower, Anne Krueger (1984) later explained that: "From a theory without any evidence in the early 1960's suggesting departures from free trade for dynamic reasons, the tables are turned; empirical evidence strongly suggests dynamic factors that may be associated with export-led growth" (p. 139). Export expansion somehow spurred by market liberalization became the industrialization strategy of choice.

Work around the turn of the decade by Krueger, Balassa (1971), and others was not so much anti-intervention as anti-import substitution. The debate between old-style development economists and more orthodox theorists still centered on market failure. It focused on whether to intervene, and with the exception of Bauer and a few isolated voices from the Left—Galbraith (1964) and Myrdal (1970)—the protagonists stopped well short of denying the state's political and institutional capacity to fulfill its pre-scribed role. That more radical claim came with the second phase of counterrevolu-tion.

The "neoclassical political economy" of the 1980s explicitly attacks the early development economists' implicit belief in the efficacy of government intervention. Lal (1983) is a representative introduction. Echoing Bauer, he contends that "bureau-cratic failure" may be worse than "market failure." Other authors set up formal models of the interaction between state and economy to show how government intervention is likely to produce inefficiencies. State policy is endogenized to the general equilibrium system by depicting it as the outcome of individual optimizing behavior in the political realm. Srinivasan (1985) classifies this effort under three heads: Mancur Olson's col-lective action framework, Buchanan's public choice school, and related work on trade, development, and economic history.

Olson (1982) argues that due to bargaining costs and the problem of free riders, individuals are unlikely to organize in their collective interest unless they are in small groups and/or can impose selective incentives on group members. Such coalitions of self-interested persons are likely to try to redistribute income toward themselves instead of working to raise efficiency and national income, the full benefits of which they will not receive. In stable (or static) societies, politics will increasingly be orga-nized to cater to these interests. Efficient resource allocation will be inhibited, and by extension there will be no incentives for Schumpeterian entrepreneurs to seek out technical innovations that might speed overall growth.

While Olson is primarily concerned with the implications of his coalitions for growth and social change, Buchanan (1980) is specific about the economic losses that result from profit seeking in the presence of the state. The "public choice" school argues that the emergence of monopoly and other distortions from public pol-icy does more than impose a deadweight loss on the economy (as measured by the famous "little triangles" of comparative statics). Competition for rents which accrue to the winners of government largesse turns into widespread "directly unproductive profit-seeking" (DUP, pronounced dupe) activities, in Bhagwati's (1982) phrase. Examples include lobbying, active politics, bribe paying, etc. Since almost any state intervention opens space for a rent (import quotas, traffic cops, defense contracts—the list is endless), the risk is that seeking government favors will override normal market activity. Rational rent seeking by individuals can produce extreme subopti-mality for the economy as a whole.

Krueger's (1974) article on rent seeking and Buchanan's extension of deadweight loss calculations have been widely applied in the trade and development area. Krueger emphasized quantitative restrictions placed on imports. Firms will compete for import licenses and their attached rents: "To the extent that rent-seeking is competitive, the welfare cost of import restrictions is equal to the welfare cost of the tariff equivalent *plus the additional cost of rent-seeking activities.*"

More recent contributions have attributed DUP activity to those seeking to set up particular policies in the first place. Actors within the government itself may enter the fray, as do bureaucrats in Bardhan's (1984) extension of this line of thought to the Indian state. In his view, conflicts between bureaucrats and industrialists over appropriation of rents interact with India's traditional rural-urban disparities to perpetuate stagnation. Like other explanations of the slow "Hindu rate of growth," Bardhan's theory is to an extent belied by the improved performance of the large, distorted, and closed Indian economy after the early 1980s.

With regard to industrial strategy, rent seeking has strong implications. Inward-oriented development, by definition, relies upon market restrictions and state intervention, which supposedly create an environment more congenial to DUP than a more open, export-promoting policy line. The theory thus arrives at another explanation for the relative success of export-promoting strategies: the state is less involved so the economy is less prone to DUP. A generalization is that freer trade and factor mobility reduce rent seeking by restraining the interests and making cartels harder to maintain. The success of South Korea, where everyone now admits that the government has been extremely interventionist, is explained by its use of policy tools associated with external orientation which allowed for greater market play. The pressures of international competition are supposed to mitigate the worst sort of rent seeking observed in countries practicing pure import-substituting industrialization (ISI).

Douglass North's (1981) work on economic history can serve as a final example of the new neoclassical approach. The state, for North, becomes its own "vested interest group," creating a tradeoff between economic efficiency and state power. Paul Kennedy's (1987) subsequent best-selling discourse on military spending twists this line of thought into a vicious circle—the effort to be a great power induces internal economic tensions which make great power status ever harder to sustain.

North argues that specification of property rights is the key explanatory variable for economic performance, subject to technological constraints. He arrives at this view via the well-known Coase (1937) theorem, which shows that if property rights are well-specified and transaction costs are zero, individuals will face correct incentives and free trade will lead to efficient resource allocation among them. North endogenizes institutional change and a theory of the state to account for the persistence of inefficient property rights: economic and political efficiency are equivalent only when this condition coincides with the state's objectives. For example, because of transaction costs such as monitoring, the state may choose to raise its revenue by creation and taxation (or direct management) of a monopoly. The state may marshal ideological arguments to support its ends, but be opposed by nonfavored firms or people who strive for an alternative regime. Tension is inevitable in the presence of a Northian (or Bardhanian) state.

To summarize, there is no question that the DUP school is correct in emphasizing that state intervention, for reasons both intended and unforeseen, does not necessarily lead to efficient outcomes, in either a static or dynamic sense. Moreover, the state's enormous presence means that its actions change the environment in which firms and people operate in unexpected (and unexpectable) ways. Ironically, the early development economists did not perceive these problems because they accepted the traditional neoclassical separation of the economic and political spheres. Basically, they did not contemplate a theory of the state.

Before the new critique surfaced, neoclassical theory at least assumed that markets function, presupposing a minimal "night watchman" role for the government. In contrast, the omission of the state as an explicit actor is a fundamental flaw in the development theorists' argument, since they relied upon the state as an agent of change and presumed that it had the requisite political autonomy and administrative tools to carry out the task. In the presence of widespread market failure, the superior capacity of government functionaries to allocate resources became an article of faith. The state's ability to undertake sectoral targeting and its fiscal capacity for direct intervention were taken for granted.

The question remains, however, whether the neoclassical political economy model is any more relevant than the one it seeks to discredit.

3.   ELEMENTS OF A CRITIQUE

The new literature reveals a number of shortcomings. We take up the economics of public intervention first, then go on to criticize the positive theory of the state that the neoclassical authors propose, and finally bring in perspectives on industrial strategy from other social sciences.

(a)   The Economics of State Interventions

As we observed in connection with Little, Scitovsky, and Scott's (1970) book, two linked ideas are central to the neoclassical perspective: (1) elimination of distortions will enhance economic efficiency in Pareto's sense, and (2) increased efficiency will in turn lead to better macroeconomic performance, conventionally measured by the rate of growth of GDP. Solid support for either proposition is difficult to find.

With regard to "getting the prices right," a balanced judgment is that such a step frequently may be a necessary condition for enhanced microeconomic supply performance, but is scarcely ever sufficient. For example, such findings appear in 18 country studies of stabilization and adjustment programs organized by the World Institute for Development Economics Research (WIDER), reviewed by Taylor (1988). Several country cases of trade improvements were associated with price reform *in conjunction with* public interventions such as aggregate demand manipulation, export subsidies, public investment, and barter trade deals, but in other countries price reform alone produced poor results.

At issue is Gerschenkron's long-forgotten point about backwardness and inertia: more than a market signal is required to displace the previous "equilibrium" in order to make nontraditional export markets and investment projects attractive. An established rule of thumb among agricultural economists is that an anticipated 30–40% rate of return plus other incentives are required to make farmers switch to a new, untried crop. Similar generalizations no doubt apply in industry; especially in poor countries, the state is (or was, in many parts of the world) the only entity with deep enough pockets to make beyond-market incentives sufficiently sweet. It is also the only entity with broad enough coercive powers to make credible threats to actors throughout the economy when they fail to perform.

Whether enhanced micro efficiency, if attained, significantly raises the growth rate is a methodologically thorny issue to address. Any quantitative judgment requires a counterfactual reference point. Little triangle estimates of the welfare gains from eliminating distortions have remained stubbornly small ever since Harberger (1959) broached the question in a serious way. One side effect of the invention of rent seeking was to increase the welfare gains by widening their base (*vide* the Krueger quotation above), but the Ptolemaic fallacy begins to arise: you add epicycles to the model to get the result you desire. Any moderately clever general equilibrium modeler can also make the triangles shrink.

As discussed in more detail below, econometric results are also not informative. Relating growth performance to increased exports (as a proxy for liberalization?) has become an active cottage industry. However, most regressions of the GDP growth rate on the export growth rate come up with a coefficient about the size of the export share (as would follow from differentiating the national product identity). Raising the coefficient by making export growth "explain" a Solow-Denison technical progress residual à la Feder (1983) is a regression fallacy: one trending variable relates to any other with close but meaningless goodness of fit.

More fundamentally, the neoclassical isomorphisms between absence of distortions, efficiency, and growth are ahistorical and timeless. They fail to account for the experience of the advanced capitalist economies, as Schumpeter with his emphasis on entrepreneurs and innovations recognized long ago. During the industrialization push in all now-rich countries, public interventions were rife. Horowitz (1977) shows that US courts restricted individuals' control over property; decisions came to favor community property over absolute domain. While the court actions served the general welfare, they violated Buchanan's strict conditions for Pareto optimality. The Handlins (1969) and Hartz (1948) demonstrate that although they were constrained by the constitution in their choice of instruments, US state legislatures controlled exports and granted monopoly power to public corporations.

At the federal level, industrial interventions in the United States during the nineteenth century were huge. The government targeted railroads and farmers with land give-aways (millions of acres to the railway companies and 240 acres to the farm families who avoided speculation), and was highly protectionist until after World War II. Following the Meiji Restoration, the Japanese state set itself up as entrepreneur, financier, and manager in several manufacturing lines. Its activist role continued throughout the militarist period and after World War II in the famous industrial programming of MITI. Although different in form and character, interventionist policies continue in the United States. Despite its pro-market rhetoric, the government continues to direct American production capacity and technical advance to support both military and economic ends. Boeing would not be Boeing, nor would IBM be IBM, in either military or commercial endeavors, without Pentagon contracts and civilian research support.

Returning to the developing economies, the key issue is what form the Gerschenkronian challenge to industrialize may take. At present, the international arena presents new opportunities (and constraints) to LDCs, but they can only be seized (and evaded) by timely and versatile policy moves. Dynamic gains from trade may not be available to, nor the export-promotion strategy warranted for, every economy. Fishlow (1986) and Cline (1982) propose a series of counterarguments about the institutional requirements for export-led growth, the nature of traditional exports (the elasticities, and much more important, as argued below, the possibilities of extending industrial activity downstream), and the potential fallacy of composition if all LDCs attempt trade expansion.

The success of an outward-oriented development scheme is contingent on structural conditions that cannot be taken for granted. Boratav's (1988) WIDER study shows that Turkey's export "miracle" in the first part of the 1980s rested upon a preexisting industrial base created by ISI, policies leading to contraction of domestic demand for manufactures, attempts at general price reform, subsidies of up to one-third of export sales plus related incentives, and rapid growth in demand for the products the country could produce by culturally compatible buyers in the region (the Gulf countries and both sides in the Iran-Iraq war). Had any one of these factors been missing, the boom probably would not have occurred.

Turkey's and other experiences with ISI suggest that this strategy need not lead to results as dismal as is often claimed. Fishlow (1986) shows how disaggregation reveals divergent histories in Latin America. During 1965–73, Brazil's GDP grew at 9.8% annually; Mexico's grew at 7.9%. For 1970–80, the rates were 8.4 and 5.2% respectively. Median growth rates for East Asia (South Korea, Taiwan, Indonesia, Malaysia, the Philippines, and Thailand) during these periods were 8.3 and 8.0%. More fundamentally, evaluating performance by comparing growth rates does not make a lot of sense—"fast" or "slow" growth depends on the basis for comparison and the relative stage of development. Brazil is not Korea; in another popular contrast, India is not Korea or even China.

The international environment also complicates the task of neoclassical political theory. In particular, domestic DUP activity is not the only distortion of free markets that occurs. The existence of transnational corporations (TNCs), strong oligopolies in certain world markets, unequal access to technology and other factors contradict the basic assumptions of free trade. Helleiner (1990) and other exponents of the strategic trade models that have recently appeared show how economic rents need not be competed away in the presence of economies of scale, and how intervention may be Pareto superior to laissez faire. Empirical studies demonstrate that these complications affect industrial structure and performance. The ways in which leading sectors develop change with the context, and correspondingly have different macro-level effects. The implications for DUP models are manifold. The need for the state to bargain effectively with the TNCs complicates North's story: the case studies in Newfarmer (1985) give a good feel for the difficulties that can arise. DeVries (1983) points out in criticizing Olson that coalitions may arise to meet challenges during periods of stagnation and not cause them.

The basic problem is again one of counterfactuals: in attacking the government, neoclassical political economy posits an idealized market in its stead. This easily manipulable base for comparisons simply does not exist, as numerous counterexamples show. TNCs may (or may not) enhance efficiency, but they surely carry economic and political clout. Chicago-based literature on regulation stresses that the market itself generates its own rent seeking entities and redistributions of income. There is a peculiar asymmetry in the DUP models, whereby individuals coalesce to force a political redistribution, but do not do the same in the marketplace. The political arena is depicted full of lobbyists and cartel builders, while the economy is presented as being more or less subject to competition. Despite greater putative openness under a liberal trade regime, there is no guarantee that an export-promotion strategy is any less subject to DUP activity than import substitution. So-called fictional exports mushroomed in Turkey during the 1980s, as firms bought up emigrant remittances to turn in the hard currency along with doctored invoices to skim extra profits off the spate of export subsidy flows.

(b) The Absent Neoclassical State

As they reify the market, the neoclassical political economists elide an explicit discussion of the state, despite their claim to making public action an endogenous variable. Their argument presupposes a passive, pluralist state that is acted upon by interest groups with equal access to its largesse. Indeed, the characteristics of the favors that it distributes are often not fully specified, although general equilibrium implications differ. Blomqvist and Mohammad (1986) show how levels of efficiency loss are affected by the line of production in which rent receivers engage, while Barbone (1985) argues that changes in the level of wealth implicit in the claim to an import quota affect aggregate demand.

Besides the nature of the state's favors, the specific groups to whom they are distributed will have economic and political implications. Bowles and Eatwell (1983), Barry (1983), and Cameron (1983) all argue that neoclassical political economy posits a peculiar counterfactual combining a nonpolitically organized society with an ideal liberal state, completely neutral with regard to distribution. Potential conflicts between universal suffrage and capitalism as well as the importance of liberal, democratic institutions for social (and therefore economic) stability are ignored.

The pluralist model is inapplicable to many developing countries, e.g., Brazil. There, throughout this century the state has never been the passive favor dispenser of the DUP literature. In the 1950s, it attempted to insulate itself from interest group pressure, but also created new interest groups by virtue of its interventions (Shapiro, 1988). If the state has some degree of autonomy, it need not resort to authoritarianism to eliminate DUP activity, as neoclassical authors like Lal (1983) suggest. Stable policy is another tool: if the government establishes credibility in its commitment to a particular policy line (e.g., expansion of the automobile industry in Brazil), DUP activity in that area will be ineffective and tend to wane.

Under certain conditions, the state itself may be able to extract rents from the private sector and shape investment behavior, possibilities that neoclassical political economy does not recognize (see Shapiro, 1988). Its standard assumption that individuals foresee the future perfectly with at most random errors flies in the face of the rigidities and risks of the Third World, where consequences of political and economic change are largely unknown. An important intervention, discussed more fully below, is public investment. Recent evidence suggests that public projects "crowd in" private investment via complementarities, rather than crowding it out by driving up interest rates (a market signal). In another area, one has to explain how both directed incentives and public investment have been orchestrated to transform ISI into export promotion in South Korea and elsewhere. Externalities and the uses of policies to reduce fundamental uncertainty about economic affairs have to be built explicitly into any credible theory of the developing country state.

As mentioned above, neoclassical authors lean toward authoritarianism as a device to preclude special interests from taking over the state. Lal's judgment is famous: "A courageous, ruthless, and perhaps undemocratic government is required to ride roughshod over these newly-created special interest groups" (1983, p. 33). Findlay (1986) blurs the issue but without explicitly discussing the nature of the state; he implies that the emergence of authoritarianism in South Korea and Brazil explained their shift toward export orientation. By contrast, from the field of political science, O'Donnell's (1973) bureaucratic-authoritarian model for Latin America at least tried to explain *why* military regimes were inclined to open their economies to international finance, and why democracy was no longer compatible with economic growth.

The underlying neoclassical suspicion that democracy is not compatible with economic growth unwittingly echoes some Marxist theories of the state. Offe (1974) and Offe and Ronge (1975) have analyzed the inherent contradiction between the capitalist state's primary concerns: accumulation of capital and political legitimacy. Fiscal crises along O'Connor's (1973) lines are brought forth. For example, an argument heard often in Brazil is that keeping up investment and satisfying popular demands under a fiscal constraint may simply be beyond the competence of the state (Weffort, 1978; Malloy, 1987).

The subtle difficulty with both the Marxist and neoclassical frameworks is that recognizing a potential contradiction between democracy and economic expansion in no way implies a logical affinity between authoritarian states and capitalist growth. Nor is democracy necessarily correlated with a poor growth record—there are at least moderately successful social democracies at all income levels around the world. The combination of dictatorship and outstanding economic performance, when it appears, is due to particular conditions in particular states, which must be specified. In his classic study of dictatorship and democracy, Barrington Moore (1966) saw affinities between the rise of democratic institutions and capitalism. Recent authors find an indeterminate relationship between economic policy and political regime, e.g., Haggard (1985) on the linkages between political regimes and the sorts of economic stabilization programs they apply.

The neoclassical faith in authoritarianism finally proves inconsistent in several ways. Lal (1983) is the first to point out that bureaucrats have no special talent for running an economy, but presumably they would be called upon to do so (at least at second hand) in his authoritarian state. They would have to be nonarbitrary in their use of concentrated power. Authoritarian regimes as actually observed do not behave in such ideal fashion. Latin American military rulers were not notably efficient, and demonstrated that the distribution of spoils is not a civilian monopoly. Olson (1982), predictably, sees the difficulties of Latin American states in exercising control as arising from excessively powerful interest groups seeking industrial protection to the detriment of agriculture. A more plausible view is that despite superficial regime changes, Latin America suffers from too much stability in its class and institutional structure.

(c) Other Perspectives

Briefly, it is worth noting that the social science literature outside of economics had drawn a whole different set of conclusions from the experience of later industrializers such as Japan (Johnson, 1982) and South Korea. This body of work frequently argues that sensible policy and the institutional means by which to implement it are the keys to a successful industrial strategy. In the tradition of Gerschenkron, effective institutional change is the critical explanatory factor for self-sustaining growth. From this angle, the debate about state intervention becomes sterile when it is waged entirely in market vs. nonmarket terms. Those who credit the invisible hand in all success cases have biased vision: if an economy grows rapidly, they see market forces in action; if it grows slowly, bad public policy is at fault. Those at the other extreme reduce economic development to a problem of domestic institution building. Structural constraints may be posed by the domestic and international economies, but they are ultimately nonbinding.

Such narrow frameworks are reminiscent of the earlier debate on mercantilism. Whether fiscalism built up national states at the expense of economic development was defined by Heckscher as a tradeoff between "power versus plenty." Along North's lines, a conflict of interest between the crown and the merchant class was presumed. But as Wilson (1967) remarks:

> It seems doubtful whether the controversy is a very fruitful one. For it becomes plain as soon as we try to define what "mercantilists" meant by "power" that they were thinking of a political system which rested on an economic base and had certain economic ends. Equally, "plenty" was thought of in relation to politics and strategy. "Wealth" was not merely an economic conception; it had to be of a character that would coincide with and reinforce the strength of the nation and its capacity to defend itself . . . "Power and Plenty," that is to say, were not mutually exclusive conceptions but complementary conceptions (p. 495).

The question becomes one of what conditions created the "fiscal desperation" (p. 494) of Spain, or the British fiscalism that "seemed to move in parallel with powerful private and public interests and was less evidently damaging to economic development . . ." (p. 521). What applies to visible fiscalism applies to the invisible hand as well.

4. BOUNDARY CONDITIONS

There are examples of successful industrial strategies in both the developed and developing economies, but many such initiatives have failed for both political and economic reasons. Some of the successes seem to be associated with authoritarian regimes, others with democratic institutions. Institutional responsiveness seems central to success.

Can anything more definite be said about sensible strategies in specific contexts in the developing world?

In this section, arguing mainly on economic grounds, we try to describe more concretely the circumstances in which certain industrial policies may (or may not) have a chance for success. The argument is organized in terms of context-dependent "patterns" of industrial change that have been observed, and associated "boundary conditions" delimiting the sort of policies that it makes sense to use in specific national cases. We concentrate on seven sets of conditions, discussed roughly in order of ease of quantification: country size, internal vs. external orientation, labor skills, wages and income distribution, the fiscal and managerial capacity of the state, the economy's industrial heritage, and productivity growth and access to technology. Other factors such as the nature of the bureaucracy also influence the prospects for successful policy implementation, as discussed by Evans (1989).

(a) Country Size

The size of a country, best measured by population, influences its industrial prospects. This insight is old (dating to Werner Sombart at least) and has been elaborated econometrically by Hollis Chenery and coauthors, e.g., Chenery, Robinson, and Syrquin (1986). Chenery's statistical approach relies on both continuous relationships and sample splits. His most fruitful division has been between "large" and "small" nations, with the frontier at a population of (say) 20 million. The equations fit better for large countries: they seem to follow a more uniform pattern of industrial change. This observation is consistent with the importance of specialized, niche-oriented industrial strategies for small, open economies, as discussed below.

The econometric results for a big country can be summarized as follows: it typically enters earlier into import substitution and has a higher manufacturing share of GDP than does a small country at the same per capita income level; it pursues import substitution further into intermediate and capital goods and producers' services. The statistically "typical" large country's import and export shares of GDP are likely to be around 10% (with a standard deviation of about the same size; Korea is far more open than the norm) while a small country's shares may be more than one-half.

Both the regressions and (more importantly) country histories suggest that big countries exploit import-substitute-then-export (ISTE) strategies in manufacturing. The basic premise is that big, protected markets permit economies of scale and scope. At the same time, they allow the luxury of allocative inefficiency for extended periods of time—high-cost production creates economic loss, but does not represent a binding restriction on inward-oriented growth. In a favorable context, a statically inefficient industrial sector may become the base for breaking into the world trade with import-substituting products, as Turkey's example in the 1980s suggests.

With due regard to our warnings about facile country comparisons, South Korea and Brazil make an interesting contrast. Korea, with its unusually high trade shares, has successfully designed policies to direct the transformation of domestic production for a protected local market into export capability. A highly skilled labor force and rapid growth of a capital stock embodying world-class technology have played a central role. Brazil has historically directed more of its output toward the domestic market and has lower trade shares, e.g., Brazilian commodity exports were about 8% of GDP in the early 1980s, as opposed to South Korea's 38%.

Brazil's industrial strategy has relied on rapid demand growth in the domestic market to generate scale economies and technical change. One disadvantage is that sales prospects at home are more limited than for the world as a whole, and a concentrated income distribution (as discussed below) may be required to support purchases of modern goods. Indeed, there is always a risk that the domestic market will become saturated. Without access to external credit, domestic demand in an ISI strategy cannot grow much faster than exports in the medium to long run, i.e., there are lower bounds on the ratio of imports to GDP. If foreign resource flows decline, the state may be forced to tighten fiscal policy as a "third gap" binds (Bacha, 1980, Taylor, 1989); we take up this problem below. Foreign obligations may be especially vexing if (as in Brazil's case) much technology was imported via TNCs.

An advantage of an inward-oriented industrialization strategy is that it may pay off in terms of an autonomous growth path (less subject to external shocks) in the long run, as Hughes and Singh (1987) emphasize in the cases of India and China. When they occur, external shocks can be offset via domestic recessions which force firms to seek export markets abroad, so long as they have enough dynamism to maintain international competitiveness. This is one of several areas in which industrial and macroeconomic policies interact, favorably in the short run but unfavorably in a longer period if continued recession holds down capital formation, making local production facilities increasingly noncompetitive in the world market (as may have happened in the late 1980s to automobile plants in Brazil).

Since small countries are far more open to foreign trade, they are likely to find the ISTE approach less fruitful. Sector-level inefficiencies can easily degenerate into a binding foreign resource constraint. With benefit of hindsight, one can see that now-prosperous small economies earned foreign exchange by exploiting niches in which they could be efficient producers for export trade, e.g., downstream expansion of forest products plus high-skill/high-tech manufacturing in Canada, Sweden, and Finland, shipping in Norway (before oil), high-tech industry and financial services in Switzerland, etc.

Following the Canadian "staple school" of economic historians (Innis, 1962; Watkins, 1963), Hirschman (1977) raised the practically important question of the growth potential of the resource base. Timber and oil may favor downstream industrial and marketing expansion more than, say, sugar and bauxite. In the long run, local production of such raw materials can lead to capacity to manufacture the relevant capital goods, e.g., paper machines and components for oil refineries or petrochemical plants with associated engineering skills. The policy issues center around manipulating effective protection for downstream activities so that they can develop in an effective fashion.

Building upon a "staple" service is also an option to be explored. Entrepôt trade can be an extremely productive base, as exemplified recently by Hong Kong, a small economy which skipped much import substitution (in part because the Shanghai textile industry migrated there in the wake of the Chinese revolution) and rapidly attained export capability in many lines. Its experience is hard to replicate, however, since Hong Kong follows a prosperous city-state model of great antiquity which is not open to the overwhelming majority of poor countries in the world. For a large nation, an industrial city selling largely to the internal market is a mixed blessing (because of regional disparities, migration flows, etc.) but it is also an omen for general growth—inwardlooking industrialization seems to need an "engine." Hong Kong's metropolitan economic numbers are not more striking than São Paulo's or Bombay's, even though the hinterlands of Brazil and India grow far more slowly than their national city-states.

A special political economy underlies the successful small country approach, as Katzenstein (1985) points out for the prosperous European economies. Historically, the private sector took the lead and absorbed the failures in opening niches, but bankruptcies were cushioned by "oligarchic" politics (close linkages among large industrial firms, labor unions organized from the top down, and a stable state) plus publicly supported safety nets. Small prosperous countries initially practiced protection, but now maintain undistorted trade regimes and adjust to rapid technical change through close cooperation among public, corporate, and labor elites. In Switzerland, Sweden, and the Netherlands, nationally based TNCs are the entrepreneurs in international markets, but depend on the rest of the system. These countries exploit niches not only in manufacturing, but also in financial and other services. Very few small developing economies have started such a transition—Singapore and Hong Kong are the recent success cases (entrepôt trade, finance, and low wage manufacturing) and, for internal political reasons, Lebanon appears to have failed.

(b) Internal vs. External Orientation

The degree of "openness" of an economy has at least two interpretations: the levels of its trade shares (obviously affected by the nation's size), and the comparative absence of interventionist commercial policies. On both definitions, openness has implications for industrial strategy. But, as we have already seen, just how it influences industrialization and growth is a topic of intense debate.

The mainstream view is that high foreign trade shares—especially exports—in GDP help industrialization; hence, policy should be directed toward eliminating barriers to trade. There is also an increasing body of literature supporting the opposite point of view, e.g., papers from WIDER on the topic include Taylor (1987), Chakravarty and Singh (1988), and Helleiner (1990). The best summary so far is that the debate is inconclusive: an a priori case for either an open or closed trade policy regime can never be fully proved.

As we observed above, this Scotch verdict also applies to the empirical evidence on the relationship between openness and growth (based largely on cross-sectional regressions and computable general equilibrium models in the absence of comparative historical studies). Chenery, Robinson, and Syrquin (1986) present cross-country regressions showing that within country groups based on population and trade specialization in manufactures and primary products, the early GDP growth rates of export-oriented economies were a few tenths of a percent above the overall average during the period 1950–83. Using another grouping based upon per capita GNP and observed growth rates, McCarthy, Taylor, and Talati (1987) show that fast-growing countries did not on average have either high or increasing shares of exports in GDP between 1962 and 1984. Examples are easy to cite: among middle-income countries, Jamaica (12%), Uruguay (5%) and Portugal (16%) have high industrial export shares of GDP and grow slowly; Colombia and Brazil have shares of 2 or 3% and their growth has historically been fast. Poorer countries' growth rates are more subject to the vagaries of capital inflows and primary product trade, but similar observations hold: Cameroon and Egypt have grown fairly rapidly with industrial export shares of about 1%, while slow-growing India (until recently) and Honduras both have shares of 3% or more.

Despite these inconclusive results, the empirical literature does present five boundary conditions that appear to apply fairly widely:

First, and least controversial, the ratios of manufactured to primary products both produced and exported tend to rise as per capita GDP goes up. In a broad sense, industrialization *is* concomitant to economic growth.

Second, trade and output data suggest that at the two-digit level of industrial classification, import substitution usually precedes production for exports, as we have already observed. The lag may be very short as in the case of South Korea (except for automobiles, where the transition took 20 years), but normally one must think in terms of quinquennia or decades. But this sector-average generalization does not rule out the possibility of a country's exporting a particular product the day it begins to be produced.

Third, both production and trade shares vary within narrower ranges in large countries than in small ones, emphasizing the importance of niche-seeking strategies for the great majority of economies in the world. The relatively few large economies that exist shape their industrial structures more in line with domestic demand.

Fourth, countries poor (rich) in natural resources tend to have high (low) shares of industry in both exports and GDP. Japan and Korea on the one hand, and the United States and Brazil on the other are obvious examples.

Finally, Fishlow (1985) raises a useful distinction between "export-led" and "export-adequate" growth. In terms of broad regional distinctions, the labels describe Asian (externally oriented) and Latin American (internally oriented) strategies. The current problem for countries pursuing the latter line is how to regain a viable growth process under fiscal duress.

To summarize, empirical regularities linking country size, observed trade shares, and economic performance help set limits on how policy can affect openness and growth. Boundary conditions suggest that the trade and production patterns of Costa Rica will never resemble Brazil's, for a variety of reasons. The implication is that policy should not be formed in one economy taking a vastly different one as a model. However, if some intervention is effective in (say) Jamaica, it might pay off in Costa Rica as well, since both small, open countries share many of the same limits to growth.

(c) Labor Skills

There is no question that high skills are required of workers in industrial modes of production—substantial literacy and numeracy are required to produce commodities ranging from Green Revolution wheat to computer codes for microprocessors. Successful industrializers since World War II exemplify the pattern—Korea has virtually complete literacy and world-class ratios of engineers and technically trained persons to the overall population.

The real policy question is how both formal education and on-the-job training can be geared toward industrialization, in a period of tightened budget constraints for most governments in the Third World. Quoting UNESCO data, Schultz (1988) observes that public expenditure on education per child more than doubled during the period 1970–80 in all developing regions, and then decreased in 1982. A fair guess is that educational spending in most poor countries in the late 1980s continued this tendency toward stagnation or decline. Even if industrial jobs can be successfully created, these data suggest that skill constraints may increasingly bind. In a time when most governments are short of cash, policies to encourage the private sector to shoulder a greater share of the national educational effort may be required. Regulatory action supporting on-the-job training and similar activities may partially counteract the state's inability to tax the private sector in this regard.

(d) Wages and Income Distribution

Evidence from the WIDER studies and elsewhere suggests that progressive income redistribution is likely to stimulate aggregate demand (Taylor, 1988). Compositional shifts may also occur, although country-level evidence suggests that the new commodity basket may be either more or less labor intensive (i.e., wealthier segments of the population who lose in the redistribution may bias their consumption toward either labor-intensive services or capital-intensive commodities, depending on context). There is also likely to be a reduction in import intensity of demand.

These compositional shifts are all relatively weak, so that the short-run effect of redistribution on industrial strategy can probably be ignored. The important conjunctural factor is the change in aggregate demand. It suggests that redistribution can only be pursued up to a certain point, beyond which balance of payments and/or inflation problems arise.

Beyond the conjuncture, dynamic feedbacks become important. Real wages are often central to the distributional process, and their secular growth may be necessary for industrialization in the long run. Now-popular efficiency wage arguments (Bowles and Boyer, 1988, give the radical version) suggest that worker motivation and efficiency depend on good pay. The bulk of demand for advanced products must come from exports or wage income. These linkages mean that which classes gain from productivity increases is an important question. On the one hand, worker motivation and internal demand require real wage increases; on the other, if real wages rise more slowly than productivity, unit labor costs fall, which can help trade. But it is clear that aiming for low wages alone is *not* a viable or sustainable strategy. South Korea would never have shifted its exports from human hair and cheap garments to automobiles and electronics had its wages stayed at the levels of 1955.

(e) Fiscal and Managerial Capability of the State

The WIDER studies emphasized how in many countries public investment stimulates private capital, via complementarities; the same point is also recognized by the International Monetary Fund (Blejer and Khan, 1984). Recent econometric results support the observation, e.g., Chakravarty (1987) estimates that the "crowding-in coefficient" for public on private investment in Indian agriculture lies between one and two, while Ortiz and Noriega (1988) find a Mexican economy-wide coefficient of one. For a 72-country international cross section, Barro (1989) gets a coefficient of one.

Despite the importance of crowding in, many governments currently find public investment impossible because (even with improved tax performance and current spending cuts) they are fiscally constrained. In the major debtor countries, the public sector owes 5% or more of GDP in external obligations each year—new projects are a luxury impossible to afford. In macro models with three or four gaps (investment crowding in and inflationary pressure can be added to the traditional savings and foreign exchange constraints), Bacha (1990) and Taylor (1989) show that reducing state capital formation may be the only plausible response to output losses and inflation stemming from a tightened foreign exchange constraint. The implications for long-term growth are, needless to say, poor.

Besides fiscal problems, an important empirical question is whether the state can in fact handle all the obligations we have discussed. Theories of how it functions aside, finding an existing government capable of making use of the local resource base, utilizing the advantages and avoiding the problems inherent in the country's size, maintaining an intelligent stance between import substitution and export promotion, seeking export niches, hastening skill creation, and dealing effectively with new technologies like microprocessors is not an easy task. Optimal performance in all areas is impossible. The question is whether the state can effectively cope. Its managerial capacity—even to supervise a regime of laissez faire—is perhaps the most important boundary condition of all.

Here, we can only flag the issue—Evans (1989) takes up some of the problems it creates. But one observation (especially relevant for Africa) follows naturally from the discussion earlier in this paper: arguments for liberal policies may be based on desperation about the capacity of the state. Since the public sector does so badly, the reasoning goes, an unfettered private sector couldn't possibly do worse. This view ignores the objective difficulties—unfavorable ecological conditions, plummeting export volumes and prices, political turmoil—that African and other poor countries have faced, as well as the historical fact that industrialization does not flourish in a fully free-market regime. However, the fact that the private sector is unlikely to create industrialization on its own does not answer the question about how state capacity can be improved. Even under favorable macroeconomic conditions, a painful learning process is likely to be involved.

(f) Industrial Heritage

As we have stressed, industrialization is a historical process: each country must be seen as traversing a particular dynamic path. For a poor country, its initial conditions obviously matter. South Korea in the 1950s had a low per capita income and little capital stock. However, there had been a recent, successful land reform, and the population was well educated and had been exposed to industrial culture during the colonial period under the Japanese. Ample human capital, generous foreign aid, privileged access to American and Japanese markets, and other intangible factors set the stage for the Korean industrial miracle. The contrast with African countries which still struggle with relics of a much more exploitative form of colonialism could not be sharper. Their lack of educational infrastructure and even rudimentary industrial experience stand out.

As a country pursues industrialization, transitions continue to occur. Toward the end, fully developed economies enter more or less competitively into world markets with levels of export subsidies, import barriers, and activities like dumping restrained to "normal" levels (with normality being a flexible concept, *vide* Japanese import restrictions and the increasing interest of the United States in "strategic trade"). In the developing world, the import-substitute-then-export strategy means that large economies may hold themselves (or at least many of their products) away from international competition for periods measured in decades. Small countries are necessarily more open to trade, and arguably have fewer opportunities for dynamic gains from distorting prices in the short run. Conceivably, their size deficiencies could be offset by regional production/trading groups, although their record of success so far is bleak. Flexible manufacturing processes as discussed by Piore and Sabel (1984) may also provide opportunities for surmounting problems posed by economies of scale, but they are just beginning to be applied in the developing world.

Neither import substitution nor the return toward international competitiveness is typically led by the invisible hand. Internally, as the small, prosperous European economies exemplify, an interlocking institutional network allows negotiation among well-organized groups—unionized labor, transnational companies, and big government. *Chaebol* and *zaibatsu* confronted by labor and activist states demonstrate the same tendencies in Korea and Japan. A key long-term result of a successful industrial strategy is a set of institutions conducive to high levels of investment and saving (undertaken, as Keynes observed, by different institutional groups whose actions have to be coordinated), absorption of technical change, and demand control mechanisms through which the government can support a steady pace of output growth.

Externally, an export push may be required to compensate (so to speak) for a period of import substitution. As we have observed, successful newly industrialized countries (NICs) often follow this pattern, although there are historical exceptions—the United States remained quite closed throughout its industrialization and India is now. But would both these economies improve their performance by pushing sales abroad?

The benefits of more exports are easy to enumerate. They can support the current account as imports are liberalized (except when there are negative domestic resource costs), and by simple arithmetic raising a modest export share of GDP toward unity is likely to be a less painful process than further reducing an already low import coefficient toward zero. Also, when world trade is expanding faster than world GDP, exports tap into a rising source of demand. As we have noted, the unknown for countries making the transition over the next decades is whether or not international trade will continue to grow as rapidly in the future as it has in the recent past. As Hobson (1902) observed long ago, progressive income redistribution and creation of a welfare state can also underwrite growth in demand.

Rapid export expansion aside, the "return" involves a transition from noncompetitive to competitive trade, as Chenery (1975) pointed out. On the export side, the emphasis shifts from primary products with a small internal market to manufactures and services sold both abroad and at home. Goods initially produced to substitute for imports (often creating a further dependence on imported intermediates and capital goods) must ultimately find external markets if world-class costs and variety are to be provided to domestic consumers. There is no reason why production for appropriate niches should not initially be supported by import barriers and export subsidies; indeed "opportunity costs" of not trading have to be ignored until learning and scale effects take hold. The point is that full industrialization only occurs after infant firms grow up, and can compete more or less effectively on international terms. The issues raised by DUP theorists are important in this context—why should a firm try to compete with foreigners instead of seeking national rents? Directed public interventions, social consensus, and profit opportunities in world-market competition necessarily must play a role in the difficult transition from noncompetitive to more competitive trade.

(g) Productivity Growth and Access to Technology

International competitiveness depends on steadily growing productivity and access to best-practice technology. With regard to productivity, it is useful to distinguish improvements due to better resource allocation and trend increases over time. In the mainstream view, liberalized trade and industrial policy should improve allocation. However, in a recent review article, Pack (1988) concludes that ". . . to date, there is no clear confirmation of the hypothesis that countries with an external orientation benefit from greater growth of technical efficiency in . . . manufacturing. When combined with the relatively small static costs of protection [i.e., small triangles], this finding leaves those with a predilection toward a neutral regime in a quandary" (p. 353). And again, "[c]omparisons of total factor productivity growth among countries pursuing different international trade orientations do not reveal systematic differences in productivity growth in manufacturing, nor do the time-series studies of individual countries that have experienced alternating trade regimes allow strong conclusions in this dimension" (p. 372). Allocative efficiency gains do not seem to result from liberal policy moves.

With respect to sources of productivity growth over time, Pack does observe that there are often large gaps between current LDC and international best-practice technology. Moreover, along Kaldor-Verdoorn lines, Amsden (1988), in her WIDER country study of South Korea, emphasizes that rapid output growth (perhaps coming largely from exports) can feed back positively into new, late vintage capital formation and productivity increases. As we have already observed, one source of Korean cost competitiveness is the fact that labor productivity grows faster than real wages, reducing unit labor costs. The virtuous circle to more exports, additional investment in export industries, and further productivity gains is successfully closed.

After the effects of formal schooling and on-the-job learning are taken into account, it is clear that if productivity is to be raised, new technology must be acquired. Despite isolated exceptions (e.g., Korean and Brazilian design of new models of cars and armored personnel carriers), little technical innovation occurs in the developing world. New technology must be obtained through deals with international suppliers, involving licensing and royalty costs, or via direct foreign investment on the part of transnational firms. Either route involves extensive bargaining between local public and private sector firms and external suppliers, under the aegis of the state.

The conditions of these bargains vary with a country's own industrial history and time. Dealing in the 1980s with Suzuki about setting up an automobile industry, India may have been in a weaker position than was Brazil when it dealt with Ford and Volkswagen 30 years before: the corporations were groping almost as blindly as their potential host at that stage. The main similarity is that a process beginning with assembly and leading toward rising domestic content is one policy goal. The time frame for such a change may be fairly short, since NIC industrial sophistication has by now reached the point at which international productivity levels in greenfield plants can be rapidly acquired, as in production of car engines during the past decade in Mexico.

Even this comfortable generalization breaks down, however, when new technologies like those based on microprocessors are at issue. Stimulating local applications rather than production of hardware has emerged as the relevant policy objective— Sweden, the most computerized economy in the world, does minimal local manufacture. In developing countries, pursuing computer literacy and familiarity emerges as the relevant policy goal. Traditional ISI strategies do not apply, but state and privately supported educational initiatives possibly may.

5. POLICIES IN ACTION

The discussion so far shows that forming industrial strategy (or reforming policies inherited from the past while growth and industrialization proceed apace) is a complex pursuit. Small wonder that practical policy advice in the area boils down to compiling lore about interventions that have (or have not) worked in one context, and trying to extrapolate about the outcomes they might provoke in another. In this spirit, we offer a few suggestions about possible approaches to strategy.

Before turning to specifics, a word about general orientations is in order. Industrial strategies can follow three broad lines—proactive state guidance of the economy, *laissez faire,* and a middle way.

The proactive industrializing state has fallen from fashion in recent years, especially in its traditional central planning attire. With party cadres calling the shots throughout the system under guidance from the top, planning did aid industrialization in big countries with simple economies and strong states—the Soviet Union in the

1930s and China two decades later. However, when production processes become more interlinked and technically harder to organize and consumers grow more sophisticated, absence of personal freedom and room for initiative handicaps adoption of new techniques and products, braking productivity growth. A rule-bound, rent-seeking bureaucracy becomes an additional fetter on change. The current wave of reforms in (ex?) socialist nations is aimed precisely at removing these obstacles to modern economic growth.

Proactive guidance can also take the form of widespread, intense industrial targeting. Such policies have been practiced with some success by the NICs in both their import-substitution and export-promotion phases. However, they fit less well into an economy that is small, open, and lacks industrial sophistication. In such a context, public participation in, but not direction of, the economy runs naturally between the free market and centrally planned extremes. As noted above, this road was taken by small country development "success cases" such as those in East Asia since World War II and in European social democracies after the turn of the century. For the reasons just discussed, elements of the strategies appropriate to large and small countries are best described through empirical generalizations rather than the abstract model used by neoclassical economic theory. They include the following:

1 Even with successfully interventionist strategies, the government generally guides but does not directly manage decentralized, market-responsive decision making at the firm level. Especially in developing economies where middle-level cadres are weak, highly able people to do the guiding from the top of both the state and key enterprises are essential. There do not have to be large forces of "planners," but they need political backing, which in turn rests upon effective state mediation among interest groups. Guidance takes place through continual consultation among the state and producer, export and labor organizations. It may be centralized as in the famous presidential Blue House export targeting in Korea or in MITI in Japan, or more widely spread as around the development banks, planning ministry, and producers' organizations in Brazil. The point is that flexible, institutionally appropriate channels are created.

2 Through the consultation process there is feedback from producers to the state, which centralizes information and selectively shares it among firms. National solidarity and an ideology of growth sanction such bureaucratic transgressions of the rules of the market game. If such forces do not coalesce behind an industrialization push, it is much more likely to fail.

3 The state also provides venture capital for new enterprises, often at highly favorable interest rates. This is a form of lending that traditional, garden-variety banks are usually not willing to undertake. Development banks, if aggressive, can play a key role in providing venture capital and long-term investment finance in general. Their project search and identification procedures have to take place at the micro level— among the 20,000 commodities in the seven-digit SITC. Economists' two-digit level computations of effective protection rates and domestic resource costs are not of great use in identifying potentially profitable niches and sources of productivity growth in detail. Market knowledge and intuition are essential to the decision process. A publicly backed private sector is the institution best suited to carry it out.

4 Targeting is universal, with the state giving support to "thrust industries." However, in success cases, incentives can be (and are) withdrawn if firms do not meet performance criteria such as export expansion or incorporation of best-practice techniques. When scale economies are possible, protection plus barriers to entry through firm licensing may be combined. If too many producers are in an already protected market, cost reductions due to rising output volume at the firm level may never be realized unless the state or a large private sector agent brings about consolidation. For an industry starting *ab initio,* the relative merits of a quota cum licensing and a tariff regime have to be weighed; the former may be essential only when an existing sector has to be rationalized.

5 The most effective incentives depend on context. Some drain and others add revenue to the treasury, and this dimension must be weighed. Some are administratively difficult, provide especially strong incentives for rent seeking, etc. Large countries on an ISTE path may opt for a Brazil-type "law of similars," banning any imports that compete closely with items produced at home; smaller economies might suffocate under such blanket provisions, but then they have to manage detailed import tariffs or quotas. Cheap credit is often an effective, easily administered incentive, but the government has to have the power (and the will) to cut it off if firms do not satisfy performance criteria.

6 The criteria themselves should be straight-forward and transparent—exports and technical advance. More theoretical considerations such as potential economies of scale may be used in selecting industries for targeting, but firms should perform according to simpler rules. "White elephants" grazing happily on state subsidies are not permitted to thrive in a well-run economy. In many cases, the monsters' pale hue is due to poor management, which can be changed. In situations where a bad investment decision was initially made or a good one was overtaken by external competition (e.g., Swedish shipyards), the government accepts an obligation to retrain and reemploy workers discharged in white elephant liquidations. Rapid overall growth lets this sort of transition hurt less.

7 The issue of who bears the costs of the policies just sketched must be addressed. Vicious DUP circles involving the government and specific social groups can always appear—a successfully industrializing state will cut such knots and with luck compensate the losers from the fruits of productivity growth (e.g., Korean real wages rise less rapidly than productivity, but they do rise). External circumstances may make interventionist strategies more feasible in some contexts than others. A government that is fiscally constrained because it pays interest on external debt has few degrees of freedom; indeed, pushing exports via domestic recession to transfer resources abroad may distort the whole economic system. Successful growth may be impossible in debtor economies without reduced payments, in which case foreign institutions would pay part of the adjustment cost.

8 There is often division of control, implicit or regulated through licensing, of sectoral production among national public and private enterprises and sometimes transnational corporations (or TNCs). Public enterprises do best in infrastructure, "base" industries, and sectors like oil and high-tech services in which, largely for social reasons, labor and management come to share a strong ethos of performance.

Parastatals become bureaucratized and do poorly in sectors where performance depends on complex product and process changes; private enterprise often does a better job of keeping up.

9 "Infrastructure" broadly construed includes health and education. As already noted, small European countries specializing in high productivity exports, Korea, and Japan all score high on indicators such as ratios of technical people to the overall population, student scores on international science examinations, and overall well-being of their residents. The educational system in many economically successful nations is geared more toward high average performance than individual brilliance.

10 In the rich small countries and the NICs, synergy between state and private sector extends to capital formation. As noted above, public investment often does not crowd out private investment from its assigned sectors, but in fact crowds it in. The implication is that state investment programs should be designed to raise productivity in both the public and private sectors. As noted above, a state-directed phase of growth is not likely to end successfully unless private institutions appear to sustain high investment levels and generate and channel savings flows to finance them.

11 Orthodox economic theory suggests that distortions should just be avoided—in practice this recommendation reduces to little more than common sense. Successful industrializers hold distortions in line, but their efforts in this direction should not be exaggerated. The NICs are not models of laissez faire; nor were the generations of successful economies preceding them. Long-term, large divergences from market signals are costly; in a shorter run they may stimulate entrepreneurship and productivity growth. Neoclassical theory mostly gives static allocation rules. They boil down to a list of "don'ts," useful curbs to exuberance in decision making but secondary to dynamic processes of change.

6. SUMMARY AND CONCLUSIONS

The early optimism of development economics was misplaced—in the competence of the state, in the effectiveness of its interventions, in the independence of the national growth project from international trade, technology, and capital markets. In contrast to their predecessors, the legacy of 1980s vintage development economists will be documentation of imperfect policy making. The operating assumption of imperfect markets has been replaced by the presumed inevitability of imperfect states. Many have concluded that the former is the lesser of two evils, the implication being that governments should get out of development altogether.

The difficulty with this largely neoclassical recommendation is that its attempt to frame the question of the role of the state as a choice between evils is fundamentally flawed. This perspective only reinforces the profession's tendency to view economics and politics as distinct spheres. When economists finally discovered the state, they found it wanting and tried to reason it away. In the new neoclassical synthesis, the political and economic sciences are once again divorced.

But the state cannot be dismissed so easily. As we have noted repeatedly, virtually all cases of successful economic development have involved state intervention and improvisation of an industrial strategy. Mainstream economists deny this reality, arguing that no political arrangement can exist under which the state's actions will not be vitiated by DUP. But on the other hand, they want that state to act by disengaging itself from the economy. A much more sophisticated political economy is required, to *explain* and not just postulate the relationship between state and society.

Beyond these theoretical issues, changing conditions also have to be recognized. Constraints on public action have become more binding in recent years. Both foreign debt obligations and policy pressures such as International Monetary Fund and World Bank conditionality impose limits and generate internal political realignments. Fiscal costs of subsidies become more irksome at the same time as globalization of industrial activity makes it harder to attract foreign investment simply to serve an internal, albeit protected, market.

The general lesson to be learned from experience is that there are no bags of policy tricks that work regardless of context. However, that does not mean the policy decisions are contingent only on internal and external political and economic conditions of individual countries. Comparative analysis helps explain *why* particular strategies perform well or poorly in particular contexts. We have seen that successful industrial strategies have respected the boundary conditions limiting economies in which they were applied, and have incorporated the context-dependent structures discussed above. They were also flexible and adaptive. By describing boundaries and institutional dynamics within a consistent framework, we have attempted to move the intellectual debate about the state's role in development toward a synthesis that policy makers can use.

REFERENCES

Amsden, Alice. "Republic of Korea." Stabilization and Adjustment Policies and Programmes Country Study No. 14. Helsinki: WIDER, 1988.

Bacha, Edmar L. "A Three-Gap Model of Foreign Transfers and the GDP Growth Rate in Developing Countries." *Journal of Development Economics* 32 (April, 1990), pp. 279–296.

Balassa, Bela. "Trade Policies in Developing Countries." *American Economic Review, Papers and Proceedings,* 61 (1971): 178–187.

Barbone, Luca. "Essays on Trade and Macro Policy in Developing Countries." Ph.D. dissertation. Cambridge, Mass.: Department of Economics, Massachusetts Institute of Technology, 1985.

Bardhan, Pranab K. *The Political Economy of Development in India.* Oxford: Basil Blackwell, 1984.

Barro, Robert. "A Cross-Country Study of Growth, Saving, and Government." NBER Working Paper No. 2885. Cambridge, Mass.: National Bureau of Economic Research, 1989.

Barry, Brian. "Some Questions about Explanation." *International Studies Quarterly,* 27 (1983): 17–27.

Bauer, P. T. *Reality and Rhetoric: Studies in the Economics of Development.* London: Weidenfield and Nicolson, 1984.

Bauer, P. T. *Dissent on Development.* London: Weidenfield and Nicolson, 1972.

Bhagwati, Jagdish N. "Directly Unproductive Profit Seeking (DUP) Activities." *Journal of Political Economy,* 90 (1982): 988–1002.

Blejer, Mario, and Mohsin Khan. "Government Policy and Private Investment in Developing Countries." *IMF Staff Papers,* 31 (1984): 379–403.

Blomqvist, Ake, and Sharif Mohammad. "Controls, Corruption, and Competitive Rent-Seeking in LDCs." *Journal of Development Economics,* 21 (1986): 161–80.

Boratav, Korkut. "Turkey," Stabilization and Adjustment Policies and Programmes Country Study No. 5. Helsinki: WIDER, 1988.

Bowles, Samuel, and Robert Boyer. "A Wage-Led Employment Regime: Income Distribution, Labor Discipline, and Aggregate Demand in Welfare Capitalism." Helsinki: WIDER, 1988.

Bowles, Samuel, and John Eatwell. "Between Two Worlds: Interest Groups, Class Structure, and Capitalist Growth." in Dennis C. Mueller (ed.), *The Political Economy of Growth.* New Haven, Conn.: Yale University Press, 1983.

Buchanan, James. "Rent Seeking and Profit Seeking." In J. M. Buchanan, R. D. Tollison, and G. Tullock (eds.), *Toward a Theory of Rent-Seeking Society.* College Station, TX: Texas A&M University Press, 1980.

Cameron, David R. "Creating Theory in Comparative Political Economy: On Mancur Olson's Explanation of Growth." Paper presented at the Annual Meeting of the American Political Science Association, Chicago: 1983.

Chakravarty, Sukhamoy. *Development Planning: The Indian Experience.* Oxford: Clarendon Press, 1987.

Chakravarty, Sukhamoy, and Ajit Singh. "The Desirable Forms of Economic Openness in the South." Helsinki: WIDER, 1988.

Chenery, Hollis B. "The Structuralist Approach to Development Policy." *American Economic Review, Papers and Proceedings,* 65 (1975): 310–16.

Chenery, Hollis B. "Comparative Advantage and Development Policy." *American Economic Review,* 51 (1961): 18–51.

Chenery, Hollis B., Sherman Robinson, and Moshe Syrquin. *Industrialization and Growth.* New York: Oxford University Press, 1986.

Cline, William. "Can the East Asian Model of Development Be Generalized?" *World Development,* 10 (1982): 81–90.

Coase, Ronald. "The Nature of the Firm." *Econometrica,* 4 (1937): 386–405.

DeVries, Jan. "The Rise and Decline of Nations in Historical Perspective." *International Studies Quarterly,* 27 (1983): 11–16.

Evans, Peter. "Predatory, Developmental and Other Apparatuses: A Comparative Analysis of the Third World State." *Sociological Forum,* 4, 4 (1989).

Feder, Gershon. "On Exports and Economic Growth." *Journal of Development Economics,* 12 (1983): 59–73.

Findlay, Ronald. "Trade, Development, and the State." Paper presented at the 25th Anniversary Symposium on the State of Development Economics. New Haven, Conn.: Economic Growth Center, Yale University, 1986.

Fishlow, Albert. "Brief Comparative Reflections on Latin American Economic Performance and Policy." Helsinki: WIDER, 1986.

Fishlow, Albert. "The State of Latin America Economics." In *Economic and Social Progress in Latin America.* Washington, D.C.: Inter-American Development Bank, 1985.

Galbraith, John Kenneth. *Economic Development in Perspective.* Cambridge, Mass.: Harvard University Press, 1964.

Gerschenkron, Alexander. *Economic Backwardness in Historical Perspective.* Cambridge, Mass.: Harvard University Press, 1962.

Handlin, Oscar, and Mary Flug Handlin. *Commonwealth: A Study of the Role of Govern-*

ment in the American Economy: Massachusetts 1774–1861 (revised edition). Cambridge, Mass.: Belknap Press of Harvard University Press, 1969.

Haggard, Stephan. "The Politics of Adjustment." *International Organization,* 39 (1985): 505–34.

Harberger, Arnold. "Using the Resources at Hand More Effectively." *American Economic Review, Papers and Proceedings.* 49 (1959): 134–46.

Hartz, Louis. *Economic Policy and Democratic Thought: Pennsylvania 1776–1860.* Cambridge, Mass.: Harvard University Press, 1948.

Helleiner, G. K. "Trade Strategy in Medium-Term Adjustment." *World Development,* 18, 6 (1990).

Hirschman, Albert O. "A Generalized Linkage Approach to Development, with Special Reference to Staples." *Economic Development and Cultural Change,* 25, Supplement (1977): 67–98.

Hirschman, Albert O. *The Strategy of Economic Development.* New Haven, Conn.: Yale University Press, 1958.

Hobson, John. *Imperialism: A Study.* London: J. Nisbet, 1902.

Horowitz, M. *The Transformation of American Law.* Cambridge, Mass.: Harvard University Press, 1977.

Hughes, Alan, and Ajit Singh. "The World Economic Slowdown and the Asian and Latin American Economies: A Comparative Analysis of Economic Structure, Policy and Performance." Helsinki: WIDER, 1987.

Innis, Harold A. *The Fur Trade in Canada* (revised edition). New Haven, Conn.: Yale University Press, 1962.

Johnson, Chalmers A. *MITI and the Japanese Miracle.* Stanford, Calif.: Stanford University Press, 1982.

Johnson, Harry G. *Economic Policies Toward Less Developed Countries.* Washington, D.C.: The Brookings Institution, 1967.

Katzenstein, Peter. *Small States in World Markets: Industrial Policy in Europe.* Ithaca, N.Y.: Cornell University Press, 1985.

Kennedy, Paul. *The Rise and Fall of the Great Powers.* New York: Random House, 1987.

Krueger, Anne O. "Comparative Advantage and Development Policy 20 Years Later." In Moshe Syrquin, Lance Taylor, and Larry Westphal (eds.), *Economic Structure and Performance: Essays in Honor of Hollis B. Chenery.* New York: Academic Press, 1984.

Krueger, Anne O. "The Political Economy of the Rent-Seeking Society." *American Economic Review,* 64 (1974): 291–303.

Lal, Deepak. *The Poverty of "Development Economics."* London: Institute of Economic Affairs, Hobart Paperback No. 16, 1983.

Little, Ian M. D., Tibor Scitovsky, and Maurice Scott. *Industry and Trade in Some Developing Countries: A Comparative Study.* London: Oxford University Press, 1970.

Malloy, James J. "The Politics of Transition in Latin America." In James M. Malloy and Mitchell A. Seligson (eds.), *Authoritarians and Democrats: Regime Transition in Latin America.* Pittsburgh: University of Pittsburgh Press, 1987.

McCarthy, F. Desmond, Lance Taylor, and Cyrus Talati. "Trade Patterns in Developing Countries, 1964–82." *Journal of Development Economics,* 27 (1987): 5–39.

Moore, Jr. Barrington. *Social Origins of Dictatorship and Democracy.* Boston: Beacon Press, 1966.

Myrdal, Gunnar. "The 'Soft State' in Underdeveloped Countries." In Paul Streeten (ed.), *Unfashionable Economics: Essays in Honor of Lord Balogh.* London: Weidenfeld and Nicolson, 1970.

Newfarmer, Richard (ed.). *Profits, Progress, and Poverty: Case Studies of International Industries in Latin America.* Notre Dame, Ind.: University of Notre Dame Press, 1985.

North, Douglass. *Structure and Change in Economic History.* New York: W. W. Norton, 1981.

O'Connor, James. *The Fiscal Crisis of the State.* New York: St. Martin's Press, 1973.

O'Donnell, Guillermo. *Modernization and Bureaucratic-Authoritarianism.* Berkeley, Calif.: Institute of International Studies, University of California, 1973.

Offe, Claus. "Structural Problems of the Capitalist State." In K. von Beyme (ed.), *German Political Studies,* Vol. 1. London: Sage, 1974.

Offe, Claus, and Volker Ronge. "Theses on the Theory of the State." *New German Critique* (1975).

Olson, Mancur. *The Rise and Decline of Nations.* New Haven, Conn.: Yale University Press, 1982.

Ortiz, Guillermo, and Carlos Noriega. "Investment and Growth in Latin America." Washington, D.C.: International Monetary Fund, 1988.

Pack, Howard. "Industrialization and Trade." In Hollis B. Chenery and T. N. Srinivasan (eds.), *Handbook of Development Economics,* Vol. 1. Amsterdam: North-Holland, 1988.

Piore, Michael J., and Charles F. Sabel. *The Second Industrial Divide: Possibilities for Prosperity.* New York: Basic Books, 1984.

Prebisch, Raul. "Commercial Policy in the Underdeveloped Countries," *American Economic Review,* 49 (1959): 257–69.

Prebisch, Raul. *The Economic Development of Latin America and Its Principal Problems.* Lake Success, N.Y.: United Nations Department of Social Affairs, 1950.

Schultz, T. Paul. "Education Investment and Returns." In Hollis B. Chenery and T. N. Srinivasan (eds.), *Handbook of Development Economics,* Vol. 1. Amsterdam: North-Holland, 1988.

Schumpeter, Josef A. *The Theory of Economic Development.* Cambridge, Mass.: Harvard University Press, 1934.

Scitovsky, Tibor. "Two Concepts of External Economies." *Journal of Political Economy,* 62 (1954): pp. 143–51.

Shapiro, Helen. "State Intervention and Industrialization: The Origins of the Brazilian Automobile Industry." Ph.D. dissertation. New Haven, Conn.: Department of Economics, Yale University, 1988.

Singer, Hans. "The Distribution of Gains between Investing and Borrowing Countries." *American Economic Review,* 40 (1950): 473–485.

Srinivasan, T. N. "Neoclassical Political Economy: The State and Economic Development." New Haven, Conn.: Economic Growth Center, Yale University, 1985.

Taylor, Lance. "Gap Disequilibria: Inflation, Investment, Saving, and Foreign Exchange." Cambridge, Mass.: Department of Economics, Massachusetts Institute of Technology, 1989.

Taylor, Lance. *Varieties of Stabilization Experience.* Oxford: Clarendon Press, 1988.

Taylor, Lance. "Economic Openness: Problems to Century's End." Helsinki: WIDER, 1987.

Toye, John. *Dilemmas of Development.* Oxford: Basil Blackwell, 1987.

Watkins, Melville H. "A Staple Theory of Economic Growth." *Canadian Journal of Economics and Political Science* 29 (1963): 141–58.

Weffort, Francisco, *O Populismo na Politica Brasileira* (Rio de Janeiro: Paz e Terra, 1978).

Wilson, C. H. "Trade, Society, and the State." *Cambridge Economic History of Europe: Part IV.* Cambridge: Cambridge University Press, 1967.

Young, Allyn. "Increasing Returns and Economic Progress." *Economic Journal,* 38 (1928): 527–42.

CHAPTER 22

CAN THE REST OF ASIA EMULATE THE NICS?

Clive Hamilton

Australian National University

The high growth rates of the East Asian newly industrialised countries (NICs)—Taiwan, South Korea, Singapore, and Hong Kong—have made the economic performances of many other countries, including advanced ones, appear poor by comparison. Sustained real growth rates of 8 or 9 percent have expanded the limits of the possible well beyond the expectations of the 1950s and 1960s. Never before had countries been transformed so quickly from poor, underdeveloped economies into middle-income, industrial economies. The question naturally arises as to whether other countries can emulate the NICs, or, to pose the question quite differently, whether other countries are likely to adopt the strategies of South Korea and Taiwan in particular. Posing the question in these two ways raises a fundamental issue that will underlie the present discussion, that of whether economic success is principally due to the actions of governments in finding and applying the right policies.

This article focuses on four countries of Southeast Asia—Indonesia, the Philippines, Malaysia, and Thailand—and four countries of South Asia—Nepal, Bangladesh, Pakistan, and India—and discusses their prospects for industrial growth over the next twenty years. While it is possible to analyse current conditions and growth prospects, history is notoriously unpredictable, forever throwing up combinations of circumstances that no one can forsee. The present stage of Philippine history is an excellent example of this difficulty.

It needs to be asked at the outset what it is about the NICs that others want to emulate. The most remarkable aspect of the NICs' performance is their sustained high real growth rates of GDP (see Table 22-1). It is necessary to distinguish fast growth from

Reprinted with permission from *The Third World Quarterly,* 87, 4 1987: 1225–1256.

TABLE 22-1
COMPARING SIZES AND GROWTH RATES

	Gross domestic product $bn		Annual growth rate of GDP 1973–84	GDP per capita $ 1984	Annual growth rate of GNP per capita 1965–84	Share of GDI in GDP 1984
	1965	1984				
South Korea	3	83	7.2	2110	6.6	29
Taiwan	3	57	8.5[a]	2794[b]	6.7[c]	21[d]
Hong Kong	2	30	9.1	6330	6.2	24
Singapore	1	18	8.2	7260	7.8	47
Indonesia	4	80	6.8	540	4.9	21
Philippines	6	33	4.8	660	2.6	18
Malaysia	3	29	7.3	1980	4.5	31
Thailand	4	42	6.8	860	4.2	23
Nepal	1	2	3.1	160	0.2	19
Bangladesh	4	12	5.0	130	0.6	16
Pakistan	5	28	5.6	380	2.5	17
India	46	162	4.1	260	1.6	24

[a]1971–85.
[b]National income per capita.
[c]1966–85 GDP per capita.
[d]Share of gross capital formation.
Source: World Bank, *World Development Report 1986,* Washington D.C.; Taiwan, *Statistical Yearbook 1986,* Taipei.

the more general concept of development, although the two are clearly related. "Development" is taken here to mean the general improvement in human living conditions, including access to more consumption goods, better health care, greater job security, and better working hours and conditions. There are various quantitative indicators of these which are commonly used—per capita income and its distribution, the level of employment, life expectancy, and so on. These indicators of development do not cover the broader social changes that characterise the process. We will ignore development and concentrate on growth, although development does not necessarily follow growth.

Growth itself does not tell us anything about the process through which it occurs. Many forms of economic change involve fast growth. The dominant force behind rapid growth in the countries with which we are concerned here can be defined as the accumulation of industrial capital involving the expansion of investment in productive activity.

Accumulation of industrial capital can occur in various forms. The ownership of capital can be in domestic or foreign hands; the markets served by industrial firms may be at home or abroad; ownership may be private or public. We are concerned here with capitalist development, that is, the accumulation of capital in private hands. Some countries may have more state or collective enterprises than others, but in the NICs which are being emulated and the countries which are attempting to emulate them, it is private capital that is the principal dynamic force behind economic growth. As will become apparent in the discussion below, growth and development in socialist countries require a different mode of analysis.

It should also be stated at the outset that we are not arguing that industry is the only source of growth. The agricultural, mining, and service sectors are also of central importance. But the developed countries and the NICs have, uniformly, become advanced through the development of industry.[1] Other sectors, especially services and mining, may come to be the most dynamic sectors, but it is industry that leads most countries from underdeveloped to developed status.

What is it about industry that gives it this special status? Three factors can be identified. Firstly, industry takes a leading role partly because of its technological character, in particular its amenability to the investment of capital (mechanisation) and its proneness to technical advance. Secondly, as income rises, consumption preferences shift to industrial products. Thirdly and most importantly, industry has proven to be the principal bearer of capitalist social relations. Capitalism—the relationship between private ownership of the means of production and wage labour—has been and remains the central dynamic force for accumulation, the expansion of the means of production.

The question of the prospects for growth in Asia may be expressed in this form: What are the prospects for the rapid and sustained accumulation of industrial capital? The conditions which permit sustained accumulation are both economic and political. First international economic conditions will be considered, then internal economic conditions and, finally, the amenability of domestic power structures to accumulation.

Notice first, however, that considering the prospects for growth and development in Asia, or in the Third World generally, implies that the conditions facing each country are shared. This inevitably puts a great deal of stress on the importance of international economic conditions in determining the rate of growth. International economic conditions may be very important, especially for a small country, but they may also be irrelevant if the internal conditions are not conducive to growth. These include the internal political conditions, which vary enormously and are particular to each country's history.

Moreover, the question of emulating the NICs often implicitly assumes that the starting position of the rest of Asia is that of the NICs in the 1950s or early 1960s. In fact, circumstances have changed dramatically. Internationally, world markets are much tighter; there is increased competition between less developed countries. National economies have also changed very substantially; indicators of structural change in our sample of countries are included in Table 22-2.

INTERNATIONAL FACTORS

The foremost common factor influencing the growth prospects of developing countries is the growth of the world economy. The growth of markets for exports depends on the general buoyancy of the world economy and changes in levels of protection aimed at products from developing countries. With the rapid growth in world trade over the last

TABLE 22-2
CHANGES IN ECONOMIC STRUCTURE

	Share of agriculture in GDP		Share of industry in GDP		Growth rate of industry	Labour force in agriculture (percent)
	1965	1984	1965	1984	1973–84	1980
South Korea	38	14	25	40	10.9	36
Taiwan	24	6	30	46	10.5[a]	20
Hong Kong	2	1	40	22	8.0	2
Singapore	3	1	24	39	8.6	2
Indonesia	59	26	12	40	8.3	57
Philippines	26	25	28	34	5.3	52
Malaysia	30	21	24	35	8.7	42
Thailand	35	20	23	28	8.7	70
Nepal	65	56	11	12	—	93
Bangladesh	53	48	11	12	7.6	75
Pakistan	40	24	20	29	7.6	55
India	47	35	22	27	4.4	70

[a]1971–85.
   Source: World Bank, World Development Report 1986, Washington D.C.; Taiwan, Statistical Yearbook 1986, Taipei.

twenty-five years, the potential trading opportunities for South and Southeast Asia are greater than they were for the NICs in the early 1960s. Continued growth of South–South trade and the opening of the People's Republic of China to imports provide further opportunities.

While recent increases in protection by some industrial countries have been most detrimental to labour-intensive exports from developing countries, this protectionism is unlikely to be extended, given the political dominance of free trade ideology, and may be wound back. Nevertheless, the region is now crowded with NICs, near-NICs, and aspiring-NICs so that the competition for markets between exporters has become intense. This is reflected in the attempts by various countries in the region to attract foreign export-producing capital by means of ever more tempting subsidies.

The World Bank[2] predicts a growth rate of per capita GDP in developing countries of between 2.0 and 3.9 percent for the decade 1985–95, with exports growing at a rate of between 3.2 and 7.1 percent. The influence of the growth of the world economy on each country will clearly depend on its degree of integration into world markets. An indication of the degree of integration of our selected countries is the share of exports in GDP which appears in column 1 of Table 22-3. According to World Bank projections, middle-income oil importers such as Thailand will perform particularly well, especially if they are exporters of manufactures, whereas oil exporters such as Indonesia and Malaysia will find it more difficult in an era of lower oil prices. Low-income Asian countries—including those in South Asia—have quite good prospects despite, or perhaps because of, their low dependence on the world

TABLE 22-3
FEATURES OF THE TRADE REGIME

	Share of exports in GDP 1984	Growth rate of exports 1973–84	Shares in 1983 Exports of			Commodity concentration[b] 1985
			Fuels, minerals, etc.	Other primary	Other	
South Korea	37	15.1	3	6	91	26
Taiwan	57	14.4[a]	2	8	90	11
Hong Kong	107	12.9	2	6	92	—
Singapore	—	7.1	31	13	56	32
Indonesia	23	1.4	80	12	8	64[c]
Philippines	21	5.6	13	36	51	14
Malaysia	56	7.5	35	43	22	45[c]
Thailand	24	10.4	6	62	32	26
Nepal	11	—	5	43	52	20
Bangladesh	8	2.9	4	35	61	66
Pakistan	11	7.4	2	34	64	36[c]
India	6	3.3	18	29	53	—

[a]1971–85.
[b]Percentage contribution of three major commodities or items in total merchandise exports.
[c]1984.
Source: World Bank, *World Development Report 1986,* Washington D.C.; Taiwan, *Statistical Yearbook 1986,* Taipei; Column 6—Asian Development Bank, *Key Indicators of Developing Member Countries of ADB,* July 1986.

economy. However, it is difficult to see good prospects for the stagnant economies of Nepal and Bangladesh which are barely managing to grow in per capita terms (see column 5 of Table 22-1).

Those countries which have a high dependence on exports of commodities are likely to have difficulty with the volatility that this dependence imparts to their economies. Sustained growth is based on sustained investment and the latter requires a degree of stability and certainty about the future. Indonesia, Malaysia, and Bangladesh are more likely to suffer (see column 6 of Table 22-3), although Bangladesh is not heavily dependent on exports. It is not possible to predict changes in prices of primary commodities on world markets.

A few other features of the world economy have changed substantially since the early 1960s when the NICs entered their periods of rapid industrialisation. Firstly, there is much greater international trade in technology. It is now technically easier to set up factories and to introduce new production processes than it was twenty-five years ago, so that the logistical difficulties of establishing a new industry are much reduced. On the other hand, access to some of the more sophisticated technology is much more expensive. Secondly, the growth of international banking now provides much easier access to credit for financing industrial investments. This will be discussed in more detail in the next section, but it is worth noting here that the greater availability of finance is, like technology, offset by its much greater cost.

DOMESTIC ECONOMIC CONDITIONS

Within each country various economic factors contribute to or detract from the overall rate of growth. These factors can be roughly divided into those which contribute to the availability of savings and those which influence the productiveness or efficiency of potential investments. They are not sufficient in themselves to ensure high levels of productive and self-sustaining investment; several political conditions, to be discussed in the next section, are required to ensure that high savings are transformed into productive investments, but the savings and investment criteria can be thought of as necessary conditions.

The principal factors which ensure the availability of savings to investors are a high domestic savings rate, the absence of serious foreign drains on domestic resources through debt burdens, the associated access to foreign credit, and financial institutions sufficiently developed to permit savers and industrial investors to come together. This last factor should not be overemphasised, however, because while the existence of sound institutions can encourage additional savings, in the absence of official institutions, informal lending in kerb markets will always spring up to satisfy the needs of at least some savers and investors. For example, South Korea has long been held up as an example of the problems of financial disintermediation, but in practice, flourishing kerb markets have satisfied most commercial needs.

Some indicators of these principal factors appear in Table 22-4. The savings rates for the NICs in columns 1 and 2 indicate the levels required for sustained growth. The Southeast Asian countries more or less satisfy this domestic savings condition, but among the countries of South Asia only India has been able to attain a savings rate of 20 percent. A high level of foreign debt may be indicative of the confidence international lenders have in the growth prospects of the country concerned; more often, high levels of debt have not been covered by a compensatory expansion of productive capacity. In these circumstances, the significance of accumulated debt lies in the drain it represents on resources for potential investment. When export revenues fail to grow the debt provides a very serious strain on the economy. Debt-service ratios for 1984 are recorded in the fourth column of Table 22-4. Note that these ratios refer to long-term debt only, so that in practice a substantially greater proportion of annual export revenue is being spent on debt servicing. Those countries that have substantial debts and are unlikely to be able to expand export revenues rapidly, such as the Philippines, Indonesia, Thailand, and Pakistan, are likely to experience problems. The credit ratings of column 5 are indicative of the ease with which each country will be able to obtain foreign loans. The Philippines among the Southeast Asian countries will have difficulties, and only India among the South Asian countries will have easy access to foreign funds.

Since the mid-1970s a great literature has burgeoned on the growth-inhibiting effects of financial repression. Too much has been made of this; both South Korea and Taiwan maintained very fast growth for years while their financial systems were severely repressed by tight government control. Informal markets are impossible to suppress, although the high interest rates they charge can deter potentially productive investments, especially by small farmers. This is why governments committed to both

TABLE 22-4
FACTORS CONTRIBUTING TO THE AVAILABILITY OF SAVINGS

	Domestic savings rate		Long-term debt service in 1984 as percentage of		Credit rating[f] 1987	M2/GDP 1983
	1970–81	1982–84	GNP	Exports		
South Korea	24	27	6.6	15.8	59.9	38
Taiwan	32	24	—	—	74.5	56[g]
Hong Kong	28[a]	26	—	—	69.3	110[h]
Singapore	29	42	—	—	74.8	73
Indonesia	20	20	5.5	19.0	45.5	21
Philippines	25	20	4.5	17.9	22.1	25
Malaysia	25	29	—	—	57.0	61
Thailand	21	20	5.4	21.5	53.6	48
Nepal	15[b]	9	0.4	3.4	—	29
Bangladesh	9[c]	1	1.3	14.2	19.2	26
Pakistan	13[d]	6	2.8	27.1	30.4	44
India	20[e]	22	1.1	13.8	50.6	42

[a]Savings exclude net current transfers from abroad; elsewhere these are included.
[b]1976–81.
[c]1973–81.
[d]1972–81.
[e]1970–79.
[f]Country credit ratings provided by leading international banks.
[g]1977.
[h]1980.
Source: Columns 1 & 2—World Bank, *World Tables* 3rd edition, Washington D.C.; World Bank, *World Development Reports 1984–86,* Washington D.C.; Taiwan, *Statistics Yearbook 1986,* Taipei. Columns 3 & 4—World Bank, *World Development Report 1986.* Column 5—*Institutional Investor,* March 1987. Column 6—IMF, *International Financial Statistics 1985.*

high growth and financial regulation always need to provide public loans at low rates to industrial and other ventures. In column 6 of Table 22-4 we record the ratio of M2 (money and quasi-money) to GDP which provides a rough indication of levels of financial development. It is apparent that only Indonesia and the Philippines among the Southeast Asian countries may run into problems in supplying private savings to investors, while the ratios of Nepal and Bangladesh, though low, are probably adequate for their stages of development.

The conditions that are required to translate a high volume of savings into a high volume of productive investment are in large measure political and will be discussed in the next section. For the present it is important to attempt to get some idea of how productive these investments might be. It is very difficult to determine this in advance even for a single project, but there are some features of the economic environment which are prima facie conducive to greater productiveness of invested resources. One of these is the quality of the workforce. Some indicators of the quality of the workforce for the eight countries under study are provided in Table 22-5. Note that there is a strong relationship between income levels on the one hand and school enrollments and literacy rates on the other. While causation clearly runs more strongly from

TABLE 22-5
FACTORS CONTRIBUTING TO THE PRODUCTIVENESS OF INVESTMENTS

	Secondary school enrollments as percentage of age group 1983	Literacy rate 1980	Population growth rate 1980–2000	Annual growth rate of real wages in manu-facturing in the 1970s	Average monthly salaries of industrial workers US$ 1978
South Korea	89	96	1.4	9.0	312
Taiwan	56[a]	90	1.3[b]	7.2	165
Hong Kong	68	90	1.2	2.4	254
Singapore	69	84	1.0	6.5	198
Indonesia	37	62	1.9	—	130
Philippines	63	83	2.2	−6.6	75
Malaysia	49	60	2.1	1.4	150
Thailand	29	86	1.7	5.9	126
Nepal	22	19	2.6	—	—
Bangladesh	19	26	2.4	1.4	—
Pakistan	16	24	2.6	4.2	—
India	34	36	1.9	2.0	—

[a]Estimate only.
[b]1985 growth rate only.
Source: Column 1—World Bank, *World Development Report 1986;* Taiwan, *Statistical Yearbook 1986.* Column 2—ADB, *Key Indicators 1986.* Column 3—as for column 1. Column 4—ESCAP, *Economic and Social Survey of Asia and the Pacific 1985,* table I.29 (the years of coverage vary; see the source for details); Taiwan, *Statistical Yearbook 1986.* Column 5—Limqueco (1983, p. 291).

income levels to educational levels, countries which start out with higher-quality workforces will, ceteris paribus, have an advantage. India and the Philippines stand out from their groups in this regard.

Notice also that investment in improving the quality of the workforce overall is undermined by rapid population growth (column 3 of Table 22-5). Nepal, Bangladesh, and Pakistan will find it difficult to raise the quality of labour, while high educational levels in the Philippines will be eroded if population continues to grow at the present rate.

A further dimension of the workforce environment of investments is the level of application of labour, including the number of hours worked. Comparative data on this is patchy.[3] The degree of control by management over the labour force depends on both political factors such as repression of trade unions and economic factors such as the level of unemployment and alternative sources of income. Data on these are notoriously unreliable, but it would seem that most of the countries in question provide conditions amenable to stern control over industrial labour, with possible exceptions being provided by the Philippines, Malaysia, and India where trade union movements are relatively strong.

Some of these factors are expressed in the labour costs which industry faces but not always in a direct way. It may be that countries with stern control over labour have higher levels and growth rates of wages. Nevertheless, other things being equal, lower labour costs are important for the productiveness of investments principally in the case of traded goods. Once again reliable comparative data are scarce, particularly as wage rates within a country are not uniformly high or low but vary between markets for different types of labour. However, one can determine in general whether a country's wage levels are appropriate for its level of development and for a given level of reliance on international trade. High wage growth in Pakistan and Thailand may present difficulties, while falling real wages in the Philippines would be favourable to further industrial growth.

A second set of factors influencing the potential productiveness of investments relates to the appropriateness of the technology employed and the efficiency with which machinery and equipment are used. These are management decisions and reflect the quality of management of industrial enterprises. The determinants of the quality of management are probably more difficult to isolate and quantify than the determinants of the quality of labour, but this factor can be of crucial importance. Long experience in a commercial environment is undoubtedly important; industrialists in Korea and Taiwan could draw on their experience in the industries that grew up in the period of Japanese occupation. Exposure to the management practices of foreign companies can help in principle, but many countries have complained of the unwillingness of foreign companies to pass on their managerial skills. Within our group of countries, India and Pakistan, with longer histories of industrial production, have a natural advantage, while the *bumiputra* policies of Malaysia are likely to expand rapidly the cadre of effective managers. Indonesia, per contra, lacks a broad, high-quality management base and will take many years to acquire it.

A further significant factor in creating a favourable economic environment for investments is the development of physical infrastructure. A rough indication of the infrastructural development effort is contained in columns 1 and 2 of Table 22-6. Among the Southeast Asian countries, Indonesia and Malaysia appear to spend much more of their GDP on economic services than the Philippines and Thailand, while among the South Asian countries, India lags well behind the others possibly because of its relatively well-developed base. In the case of Nepal, and less so Bangladesh, geological instability and the very underdeveloped infrastructural base necessitate the channelling of a great proportion of government spending into building basic transport and power systems.

High levels of military expenditure can be a serious drain on resources which would otherwise be available for productive investments. Indications of levels of military spending appear in the third column of Table 22-6. In Southeast Asia, the Thai military extract a high price for staying out of government, while in South Asia tension between Pakistan and India imposes serious burdens on their economies.

A final key factor affecting the general efficiency of investments is the influence which tariffs, subsidies, and other measures that affect relative prices have upon resource allocation. Inefficient tariffs, for instance, can direct investments into areas of production which will not be internationally competitive and will therefore require continued protection. On the other hand, judicious use of tariffs can permit the establishment of new industries which may form the backbone of sustained development.

TABLE 22-6
FACTORS CONTRIBUTING TO THE PRODUCTIVENESS
OF INVESTMENTS

	Share of government expenditure in GDP 1984	Proportion of government spending on economic services 1972–1984	Share of defiance in central government expenditure 1983
South Korea	17	24	32
Taiwan	14	20	—
Hong Kong	15	22	—
Singapore	34	18	19
Indonesia	23	62[b]	12
Philippines	11	36	14
Malaysia	35	26	—
Thailand	18	19	20
Nepal	19	52	5[e]
Bangladesh	14	51[c]	—
Pakistan	25[a]	32[d]	35
India	15	24[d]	20

[a]1983.
[b]1975–84.
[c]1973–84.
[d]1975–80.
[e]1982.
Source: Column 1—ADB, *Key Indicators 1986.* Column 2-ADB, *Key Indicators 1986;* World Bank, *World Tables,* 3rd edition. Column 3—World Bank, *World Development Report 1986.*

The Korean government and Taiwanese authorities were unhesitating in their use of protection to foster local industry. Despite the recent, ideologically motivated clamour for liberalisation, no valid general statement about the merits or demerits of protection as such can be made.

The focus of this article has been on factors which directly influence industrial development rather than the agricultural sector. In fact, sustained urban industrial growth needs to be preceded or accompanied by a transformation of traditional agrarian social structures and production techniques. If this does not occur, the rural sector will impose an intolerable drain on industrial production, on account of:

1 The failure of the farming majority to provide a market for manufactured consumer goods. Even under export-oriented industrialisation, the bulk of demand for industrial output remains domestic;

2 Continuing high agricultural terms of trade resulting in high food prices and thus high wages in the cities;

3 The obligation for governments to divert substantial resources into agriculture without significant productivity increases resulting;

4 The burden of the traditional social relationships rooted in agricultural systems which work against the dynamic social instability that is characteristic of periods of rapid economic change.

Agriculture will provide a sympathetic environment for rapid industrial development if it has been shaken out of its fixed ways and is amenable to penetration by new relationships and technologies. Taiwan and Korea started out after the Second World War with a natural advantage in this regard. Japanese colonialism had thoroughly transformed traditional agrarian social relations and revolutionised methods of agricultural production, the former especially in Korea and the latter especially in Taiwan.[4] Land reform in the 1950s grew out of the rural turmoil left by the Japanese and took the process of agricultural transformation further. Not only did land reform destroy the rural power base of the landlord classes, but owner-cultivation was a means of improving agricultural productivity when combined with sympathetic state policies.

Elsewhere, the development of capitalism in agriculture has been a powerful force in destroying old social relations and the dead weight of custom, as well as providing a means for rapid improvement in productivity. Of the three principal forms of agricultural production relations—landlord-tenant, owner-cultivator, and capitalist—the first has tended to be associated with rural stagnation and political opposition to industrialisation policies, while the last, capitalism, has tended in recent times to be a dynamic force for growth. However, the relevance of the forms of agricultural production relations for industrial development lies not so much in the form or forms which dominate agriculture but in the *transition* from one form to another or others. It is the process of change itself that has been seen to be historically important.

It should be made clear that the sorts of agrarian revolutions we are talking about generally leave a large part of the rural population pauperised and starving for long periods, perhaps several decades. They are the casualties of social and economic transition; capitalist growth generally entails the impoverishment for long periods of large sections of the population.

In Southeast Asia, the Malaysian system of large plantations combined with small cash-crop farming has provided the necessary level of unsettlement in the rural sector. Less than half of Malaysian farmers own land,[5] and wage labour is very prevalent. While share-cropping is also widespread, capitalist farming is the dynamic mode. Indications of the prevalence of tenancy and the development of capitalist agriculture elsewhere can be found in Table 22-6. It is worth noting that tenancy is not nearly as widespread in South and Southeast Asia as it was in Northeast Asia (Japan, Korea, Taiwan) before the Second World War.[6] On the one hand, this frees South and Southeast Asia from some of the restraints on generalised growth and development imposed by traditional landlord-based agriculture; on the other hand, these countries are less able to benefit from the liberating effects of the overthrow of these traditional systems.

In India and Indonesia tenancy is relatively uncommon while wage-labour in agriculture is widespread. In Indonesia over recent decades, tenancy has been declining while wage labour has been growing, especially in Java. The technology of the Green Revolution and associated state policies, particularly in India, have strengthened the tendency towards capitalist farming. In India this was given an initial impetus by land

TABLE 22-7
CHARACTERISTICS OF AGRICULTURE

	Percentage of holdings wholly owned[a]	Percentage of farms hiring in labour[a]	Growth rate of agriculture 1972–85	Fertiliser consumption per hectare 1983
South Korea	—	—	7.7[b]	3311
Taiwan	—	—	1.5	—
Hong Kong	—	—	—	—
Singapore	—	—	-2.6[b]	7833
Indonesia	74	70	4.0[c]	745
Philippines	58	24	3.8	320
Malaysia	—	—	4.7	1115
Thailand	85[g]	29	4.5[d]	240
Nepal	—	—	1.7[e]	137
Bangladesh	58	45	1.7[f]	596
Pakistan	42	37	3.0	586
India	92	89	2.4[c]	394

[a]Figures are for the years, in order of appearance in the table, 1973, 1971, 1978, 1977, 1972, and 1970–71.
[b]1981–85.
[c]1972–84.
[d]1973–85.
[e]1976–85.
[f]1979–1985.
[g]*South*, September 1986 reports that in some areas 40 percent of farmers were renting all or part of their land.
Source: Columns 1 and 2—Booth and Sundrum (1985), tables 6.6 and 1.7. Column 3—ADB, *Key Indicators 1986.* Column 4—World Bank, *World Development Report 1986.*

reforms in the 1950s. In Thailand, tenancy is fairly uncommon but so is agricultural wage-labour, which suggests a predominance of family farms of sufficient size to provide a living. This helps explain the low level of fertiliser application in Thailand (see column 4 of Table 22-7). However, wage labour in agriculture has been rising rapidly since the early seventies,[7] suggesting significant change in traditional systems.

In the Philippines, the figures misleadingly indicate a relatively low level of use of wage-labour and a predominance of owner-cultivation. The capitalist plantation sector is more important than the figures suggest. The degree of landlessness and the prevalence of wage-labour have been rising in recent years. The instability of the agricultural sector in recent times, apart from the political difficulties it creates, is likely to stimulate the industrialisation process. Land reform, if it is significant, is likely to raise levels of output, reinvigorate the rural economy, and weaken the power of big landowners who resist the policies and changes necessary for rapid industrial growth. However, significant land reform in the Philippines is very unlikely.

In Bangladesh and Pakistan the use of wage-labour is common and so is tenancy. The situation is similar in Nepal. However, Bangladesh and Pakistan have experienced rises in landlessness (about a third of households were landless in Bangladesh in 1977) and a concomitant rise in the use of wage labour. In Pakistan particularly there has been a significant trend towards tenant evictions and a shift in power to middle-level farmers.[8] In Bangladesh and Nepal the patterns of farm ownership and production are settled and rigid and will not lend themselves easily to the upheavals that inevitably accompany industrial transformation. Where possible, the introduction of Green Revolution technology can help to transform these old patterns, though at the expense of the landless and owners of miniature farms. This has been true in Pakistan where capitalist farming has been replacing tenancy since the 1960s.

DOMESTIC POLITICAL CONDITIONS

The availability of adequate savings and opportunities for productive investment do not ensure that productive investments will actually occur. The transition from adequate savings to productive investment depends on political conditions broadly conceived. It has been argued that growth means that circumstances are favourable for the accumulation of industrial capital. These circumstances are complex products of diverse historical processes and generally involve the absence of political dominance by classes which derive wealth from unproductive, or zero-sum, activities. In order to encourage growth, political power must be in the hands of people at least sympathetic towards industrial development and perhaps under the influence of "growth coalitions"[9] made up of a nascent class of industrialists, technocrats committed to "modernisation," a "progressive" military, and possibly foreign capital. A growth coalition may ride on the back of popular political movements motivated by nationalism or by revolt against old exploitative relationships.

There are various sources of wealth accumulation which limit the scope for industrial accumulation and which lie at the root of low growth and underdevelopment. The traditionally most widespread form of holding wealth in underdeveloped countries is land ownership, and in many countries, as we will see, this remains the source of economic and political power of the ruling elites. It is important to distinguish landlords who derive income from renting out land to tenants, and capitalist farmers who employ wage-labour and gain income from the sale of agricultural products.

The second principal form of unproductive wealth accumulation lies in merchant activities. Commercial or merchant capital derives profit from trade, including international trade, without adding value to goods. Revenue is often derived through some sort of monopoly position and the ability to engage in speculation. While wholesale and retail activities are essential to industrial production and are in these circumstances productive, these services can contribute to overall economic growth only up to a point, a point beyond which they result only in redistribution. Another source of wealth often closely associated with commercial capital is financial capital, which often appears as informal lending and borrowing in both urban and rural areas. While financial capital may, like commercial capital, be subordinated to the needs of industrial capital, the dangers are that usury will become more attractive than productive investment and that the indebtedness of industrial firms may lead to asset stripping by creditors.

A third form of zero-sum activity covers a range of activities that might be summed up as profiteering and corruption, and includes profiteering from government contracts and aid monies. In some countries this form of wealth accumulation is extremely well developed and dominates the business activities of the urban propertied classes especially. It may result in the syphoning-off for consumption purposes of the bulk of the resources available for investment.

The fourth major form of unproductive wealth is represented by foreign capital flows. This may take the form of monies being deposited abroad by local wealthy elites, or it may be in the form of profit-taking by transnational corporations operating within one's borders. It is quite possible for outflows of funds overseas to diminish dramatically the resources available for productive investments at home, just as it is possible for capital inflows to add to domestic productive investments.

The last important drain on potentially productive resources is the state. Bloated, inefficient bureaucracies can soak up huge amounts of revenue, while military spending to maintain unstable or unpopular regimes can absorb vital development resources.

The distinction between productive and unproductive investments corresponds to the distinction between social and private profitability. An investment is socially profitable if it mobilises national resources in a way that expands national output. Such a project may also be privately profitable, but an investment which is privately profitable may not necessarily generate social profits. Private profits in such circumstances result from redistribution rather than efficient resource mobilisation and these investments are unproductive.

The importance of each of the above forms of asset accumulation is that they give control over potentially productive resources to groups which are likely to invest them in unproductive activities such as land ownership for rental purposes, usury, commodity speculation, extravagant consumption, military expansion, and overseas bank accounts. One of the essential thrusts of economic policymaking in the NICs, especially Taiwan and South Korea, was to limit severely, and in some cases to eliminate, opportunities for zero-sum activities. Landlordism was abolished, corruption was largely eliminated, speculation and usury were controlled, and foreign exchange flows were wholly regulated.

The difficulty all of this raises for the prospects of growth is that nascent industrial capital generally lacks the political as well as the economic power to impose on the economy and society the conditions it needs for rapid accumulation. One historically proven method is for industrial capital to accumulate gradually—in favourable economic conditions—until it can gain political power through economic strength. This was the case in Britain. If there is entrenched resistance from the old ruling class the supremacy of industrial capital may be attained through violent revolutions which sweep away the old social forces, such as in France, the USA, and most recently perhaps the Philippines.

In the Third World today, to achieve political power or at least to gain significant power over policy, industrial capital needs an ally. Sometimes, it seeks such an ally in military regimes, which may appear committed to economic development, to breaking the power of the landlords and promoting business. South Korea and Taiwan may seem to provide examples of this though detailed analysis of these situations reveals greater complexity.[10] Often, however, military regimes are aligned with reactionary social forces, especially landlords (such as in Latin America) or they may be wholly committed to their own enrichment and military adventure.

Sometimes, foreign powers see some advantage in encouraging development in their colonies or spheres of influence. They then give support to burgeoning business interests to ensure that they gain political power. This was the case in Singapore, for example.

Workers and peasants may align themselves with business classes under a nationalist banner in order to expel a common foreign enemy or a landlord-dominated or corrupt regime. These sorts of alliances sometimes back-fire on the bourgeois classes since the suitability of political conditions to capitalist hegemony may also make a country suitable for a revolution from below. In addition to the lower classes, intermediate classes including powerful bureaucracies, the police and the petty bourgeoisie, as well as professionals, may be brought together in the cause of nationalism.

The essential political condition for capitalist industrial growth was defined above as the absence of the political dominance of classes which derive wealth from unproductive activities or which are otherwise hostile to industrial development. This implies that the state should be free from the overwhelming, if not the total, influence of these classes—landlords, speculators, money-lenders, the military, and foreign interests inimical to industrial development.

It would be a mistake, however, to believe that the dominance of the state directly by industrial capital will bring about ideal conditions for industrial accumulation. The business class collectively may need protection from itself. Unconstrained, it may well create economic conditions which are comfortable for existing businesses but inimical to continued growth, for example and in particular, through protection from foreign competition. The transition from import-substituting industrialisation to a more open industrial economy needs to occur at a point where domestic business is strong enough to withstand international competition but not so well established as to be able to protect itself indefinitely.[11] Businesses need to be allowed to fail in order for the economy to continue to be efficient. This defines a further political condition necessary for sustained accumulation: economic policy needs to be aimed at economic growth through private accumulation rather than at simply protecting private capital. That is, it is necessary to have a state that is capable of taking hard decisions which are contrary to the interests of sections of the business class.

These carry with them a further implied political condition, namely that the state is both sufficiently strong and sufficiently independent from particular class interests to implement policies that will promote accumulation at the expense of other interests. Four of the most important of these sorts of policies are land reform, suppression of corruption, regulation of finance capital, and the control of labour. State power may be democratically or undemocratically based.

The next task is to apply these general statements to the particular histories and class structures of the eight countries selected for study. The purpose is to look very briefly at the social parameters that determine whether industrial capital can become the dynamic economic force within each country. In such brief reviews many of the subtleties are lost.

Indonesia

In Indonesia, the landlord class, such as it is, has not in recent times held the position of political authority that it has in countries like Malaysia and the Philippines. On the other hand, the Chinese who have dominated business in Indonesia have not been powerful enough in the face of ethnic and class hostilities to form political organisations to dominate the state. Some years after the fall of Sukarno in 1965, a very powerful bureaucratic-military elite emerged and remains the source of political power today.

The political power of the military-bureaucratic elite has been translated into economic power, so that powerful military or ex-military families now form the main focus of wealth accumulation in Indonesia. This wealth accumulation, however, is not based directly on productive activities, but takes the form of "tributes" extracted from the productive and unproductive activities of others. The dominant sources of government wealth have been oil sales, foreign investments, and foreign aid and the spending of this revenue has been the making of fortunes for favoured businessmen and others connected to the government. Generals and important military families take a share of most foreign ventures permitted to operate in the country, and the government allocates lucrative contracts and franchises to favoured families including, and especially, the family of Suharto. Nevertheless, a substantial portion of oil revenues in the boom years did go into building infrastructure and agricultural improvement.

The scale of corruption is unusual: it is so deep-rooted in the present political structure that it almost forms a mode of economic reproduction of its own. But even corruption needs to be based on some form of productive activity, and these are the businesses run by foreign and local, mostly Chinese, companies. The military-bureaucratic elite has largely stayed out of managing and furthering productive activities, relying on its partnership with these business groups. Moreover, this relationship and the continued viability of the regime has required that from time to time the more extreme abuses of political power be controlled, as in the case of the reform of the customs service in 1985.

While corruption has imposed a massive burden on the economy, by the end of the boom years of the 1970s a substantial class of domestic capitalists had emerged,[12] or rather, had been established, since its expansion had been very much a product of the economic activities of the state. This capitalist class has limited political power and is not so much the ally of the state as its prisoner. While the economy was flushed with oil revenue, the government could afford to be serious about building an industrial economy based on indigenous capital accumulation. The drastic decline in oil revenues has demonstrated that the state's commitment to growth and development is constrained. To pursue industrialisation, Indonesia would now need seriously to attack corruption and to expose much of domestic business to the cold winds of international competition as the economy can ill afford to featherbed domestic industry. The close ties between senior members of the government and some key business interests make this unlikely.

The economic self-interest of the ruling group will prevent it from ending the corruption and protection of local business that would be necessary for sustained growth.

If we compare the present Indonesian military regime with that of South Korea in the 1950s and 1960s, the striking difference is how little the South Korean officers became directly involved in business and how ruthless they were in suppressing corruption. Both regimes were strong enough to take the necessary measures, but only the South Koreans have been willing to take them.

Philippines

Under Marcos in the Philippines, the principal sources of wealth for the ruling classes were rents and profits from land ownership, including the sugar and coconut plantations, and the profits to be had from corruption, speculation, and government favour. Some of the foreign loans accumulated in the Marcos era were used to finance property deals and to expand personal bank accounts (especially of political friends and relations of the President) rather than to finance productive enterprise. While the ruling class has since the 1950s diversified into industry and commerce, the foundations of the wealth and power of many families remain in the provinces. The Aquino family falls into this category. Nevertheless, within the propertied classes a new group has emerged whose interests are tied directly to industrial accumulation.

The downfall of the Marcos regime was a product, as much as anything else, of the disaffection of major segments of the business class whose interests were being seriously harmed by the economic decline brought on by government mismanagement. But the bourgeois revolution of 1986 was directed much more against the close associates of the former President than at the old oligarchy itself.

The old oligarchy remains very much in place (as do many of the cronies) although there is no doubt that, for the time being, many forms of zero-sum activity associated with the Marcos regime are now more difficult. Rapid industrial development now depends on whether the new government has the political will to weaken drastically the power of the old landed oligarchy while maintaining an independence from the new business class. While land reform is a real possibility, it is going to be neither far-reaching nor confiscatory, so that the mass of workers and peasants will have to pay off the loans made to compensate the landowners. Nor will there be moves to turn landowners into industrial-capitalists, a scheme which had some success in South Korea, Taiwan, and Japan.[13]

Under present conditions, the political power of the old oligarchy, backed by powerful sections of the military, is too strong to permit the unleashing of industrial progress. The government remains heavily under the influence of classes whose interests lie other than in rapid industrial expansion, and is not in a position to take the harsh measures necessary for industrialisation to become the principal economic force.

Malaysia

In Malaysia, plantation wealth was mostly in the hands of foreign companies until taken over by the state in the 1970s. This means that the powerful landlord class that industrial capital has had to contend with elsewhere has been less influential. Nevertheless, landed interests are a significant force within the United Malay National

Organisation (UMNO), the dominant political party. The political influence of the landlords is partly neutralised, however, by that of the Malay peasantry, whose welfare is important to the political leadership.

The traditional centres of economic power in Malaysia have been the foreign, especially British, companies based on the plantations, and Chinese businesses engaged in commerce and some industrial processing. While there is no clearly dominant political class, the state has weakened the power of these groups firstly by acquiring ownership of the largest parts of the plantation, mining, and banking sectors, and secondly by giving preference to ethnic Malays over Chinese in encouraging new ventures. The New Economic Policy (NEP) set out explicitly to create a class of Malay capitalists, not so much in place of but complementary to the Chinese businesses. The strategy of state acquisitions followed by divestment to Malays (in the 1990s) could be quite successful. Certainly in South Korea, the government had success in creating a class of indigenous capitalists by handing over state property formerly owned by the Japanese.

Industrial growth will depend largely on the ability of the state to limit zero-sum activities. This may prove difficult. While heavily involved in the economy, the government is firmly committed to seeing private capital as the motor of industrial development. On the other hand, the governing class's commitment to growth is tempered by its need to keep various class interests satisfied, including those of the Malay working and peasant classes. At present the state is required to respond to strong demands from various segments of society and relies to some extent on broad support. This makes it difficult to take severe measures which will cause some to suffer. In the years ahead, the state will become increasingly dominated by the class of wealthy Malays it is now creating. The scope for corruption and nepotism—which is already significant in the NEP—will expand and industrial growth will be more difficult. Nor is there a politically powerful, cohesive, technocratic bureaucracy, as in Thailand, which can act as a counter to sectional interests.

The military is not politically important, but any dramatic decline in economic fortunes, as occurred for instance in the Philippines, could precipitate military involvement in politics. The economic structure of the country—with its very heavy reliance on exports of few primary commodities—makes it prone to this. The danger in Malaysia is not a lack of allies for the industrial bourgeoisie, but a lack of a countervailing force to restrain it.

Thailand

Thailand is unusual in that there is not a wealthy class of landowners with the political power to match its counterparts in other countries. The centre of economic power in Thailand lies with large business groupings some of which are centred on banking. This financial-industrial bourgeoisie continues to be family-based although in recent years attempts have been made to encourage public incorporation. The banks do not simply control the formal financial market but extend their influence through ownership of industrial and commercial enterprises. This business class is a postwar phenomenon stimulated further by the Vietnam War and US aid, much as the Korean War was important in giving prominence to business interests in South Korea.

Although by no means as thoroughly as in South Korea, successive Thai governments have attempted to eliminate the less socially desirable forms of wealth accumulation including corruption and the suppression of informal money markets. For instance, the government engineered the collapse of the wealthy chit funds. Nevertheless, foreign loans have been pumped into unproductive investments such as urban property development and, in particular, military spending.

The political power of the finance-based bourgeoisie does not match its economic power. Political power is held by generally pro-business parties backed by sections of the military and middle classes, in addition to the bureaucracy which has provided administrative stability at a time of rapid changes in political leadership. On the one hand, this means that the government is reluctant to make any move that will upset the military leadership. On the other hand, the military is professional in the sense that it confines itself to military and political affairs rather than taking on commercial and speculative and corrupt economic ventures, as in some countries of the region. This is connected to the parliamentary form of political power in Thailand.

While a system of corruption and patronage dominated leading circles in the 1950s and 1960s, the emergence of the industrial bourgeoisie and professional classes, including the influential technocrats in government, has ensured that economic growth and development have become dominant government objectives. The independence of the state from particular economic interests, apart from the military and bureaucracy whose interests are not primarily economic, has enabled it to take some of the difficult decisions that are necessary for industrial growth. However, the relatively pluralistic nature of state power weakens the ability of government to unbalance economic power relations as industrialisation commonly requires.

Nepal

In Nepal, the wealth of the dominant classes comes first of all from land ownership. While not as widespread as in other countries, tenancy and sharecropping operate at a sufficiently broad level to provide large incomes to local elite families. As in the Philippines, provincial wealth forms the basis of political power in the capital. In addition to landed wealth, there is a powerful class of merchants who dominate the foreign trade on which the economy wholly depends.

Political power is wielded principally by the royal family and the nobility, with the Palace Secretariat being the senior partner in an "alliance" with the official parliamentary government. Economic and political power coalesce in an alliance of the landlord and commercial classes with the ruling nobility; indeed, individuals generally are members of more than one of these groups. Landlords are often engaged in commerce. The royal family has a stake in most of the largest commercial activities including the airline, hotels, and trading companies. Foreign aid, which in comparative terms is very great, also provides a major source of income for the dominant classes.

The principal sources of wealth accumulation, then, are land ownership, foreign trade, and local businesses based on tourism and foreign aid. There is no significant industrial capitalist class and only minor industrial output of jute goods, cement, and iron products. Industrial expansion is severely constrained by the stranglehold on the economy held by Indian manufacturers and trading houses, and a reluctance by Nepalese commercial interests to jeopardise their own trading revenues by encouraging possibly independent domestic producers. On the other hand, there is emerging an increasingly influential cadre of "modern" bureaucrats mostly with overseas education who, despite being drawn predominantly from the ruling classes, have a stronger commitment to economic development. These technocrats are in a better position to understand the precarious future of the present structure, but are not powerful.

While the state may be strong enough to take measures to create an industrial bourgeoisie, it shows little willingness to do so since it serves so assiduously the interest of the aristocratic landowning and commercial classes. Land reform, which would be only a very first step in breaking the power of the land-based oligarchy and expanding agricultural productivity, is not on the agenda. There is no significant class of capitalist farmers that could spearhead moves for rural transformation. Nepal's extraordinary level of dependence on foreign powers—India for trade, and aid donors for revenue, military support and basic infrastructure—also works against major economic reform.

Bangladesh

In Bangladesh, despite legislative attacks on the landlord-tenant relationship there has been no widespread development of capitalist agriculture. Landlords remain the dominant economic class in the countryside, especially in the north and west of the country. While landownership is the principal form of wealth, the limited prospects for productive accumulation have led rural wealth into a variety of unproductive activities in addition to further land purchases and sharecropping. These include usury and mortgages on land, petty commodity trading, and conspicuous consumption.

The industrial-commercial classes are very weak in Bangladesh. The political power of the landlord and business classes was seriously weakened after separation from West Pakistan in 1971 since these classes were closely associated with West Pakistani dominance of East Bengal. With the taint of collaboration, these interests could have little influence in nationalist political parties. Some redistribution of land occurred after independence but the landlord class, while shaken, retained its economic power under the rule of the Awami League.

The industrial-commerical capitalist class suffered through large-scale expropriations. The state took over banking, insurance, transport, and large industries, mostly owned by non-Bengalis, but big Bengali-owned companies were nationalised too. The "socialism" of the Awami League weighed most heavily on the class of industrial-commercial capitalists. The shift to a policy of economic liberalisation after 1975 has, however, included some serious attempts to revive private investment through incentives and disinvestment by the state. The Ershad government is particularly keen to promote manufacturing and has pursued policies reminiscent of early South Korea and Taiwan. Growth of manufacturing has been at the reasonable annual rate of about 4 percent since the late 1970s, but by starting at such a low base and with a high population growth rate, significant progress will be slow.

While the industrial capitalist class in Bangladesh remains small, its lack of political influence on a government that is nevertheless seriously committed to promoting industry is potentially conducive to industrial growth. However, the repression dealt out by the present regime is a reflection of its weak position rather than its strength. While political parties wrangle over the transition to civilian rule, the military remains the basis of political power. In these circumstances, it is likely that the centre of wealth accumulation in Bangladesh will remain land ownership, usury, and the profits from foreign aid.

Pakistan

In Pakistan, land reform has failed to bring about significant transfers of land to the poorest farm workers. Nevertheless, the various attempts at land reform in the 1970s reflect the conflict in the countryside between landlords, tenants, and a newly emergent class of capitalist farmers responding to the Green Revolution. While this conflict found expression in the populist Bhutto years in attempts at land reform, the Zia regime since 1977 had seen the dominance of a military-bureaucratic apparatus that had been largely independent of particular sections of the propertied classes both rural and urban yet not sufficiently strong to override them. The regime had, however, continued to encourage the spread of capitalist farming.

The principal sources of wealth accumulation are in agriculture—both in land ownership and through capitalist production—and industry-commerce, with a strengthening class of manufacturing capitalists particularly in food processing and textiles. These manufacturers received a serious blow with partition of the country in 1971, as not only were their assets in East Pakistan seized but the lucrative flow of export revenues, from jute products especially, was cut off. However, industrial-commercial capital had received important support from the Zia regime through disinvestment in public enterprises and tax reductions. This class has not acquired sufficient size and economic power for it to become a major political influence on the government, but it is viewed sympathetically by the new technocrats in the bureaucracy.

In addition to these relatively productive sources of wealth, many fortunes have been made and reproduced through illegal and speculative activities, some connected with the war in Afghanistan, the spoils of which are the objects of conspicuous consumption. The prevalence of illegal activities and the degree of violence on the streets are indicative of the current regime's lack of control over the country. Despite the large commitment of resources to the military, the state is not strong. The government has difficulty maintaining civil order and cannot wholly suppress organised political opposition.

The military-turned-civilian regime draws some support from right-wing, urban petty bourgeois elements and claims the allegiance of Islamic fundamentalists. However, the loyalty of these groups is by no means uncritical. The Zia regime had also alienated big landlords, particularly in provinces other than Punjab, so that its social foundations appear quite unstable. This is compounded by serious regional conflicts which destabilise the whole country. US support has been very important in propping up the military and funding the rapid growth rates of recent years.

India

The economically dominant classes in India today are the industrial and commercial capitalists and wealthy capitalist farmers. A sizeable industrial bourgeoisie grew up in the period of import-substituting industrialisation in the 1950s and 1960s, although many industrial and commercial sectors are controlled by state enterprises. Capitalist farmers now dominate the countryside with the decline of landlordism under the pressures of land reform and the Green Revolution. This locates the predominant forms of wealth accumulation in industrial and commercial as well as agricultural production. In the absence of the more prominent forms of zero-sum activity found in other countries, these factors would suggest that India has good prospects for rapid industrial advance. However, this is not the case.

Political power is shared principally by industrial-commercial capital and wealthy capitalist farmers in conjunction with a class of bureaucrats which administers government and government enterprise. This is an uneasy alliance since there are serious structural conflicts between them. Note, however, that capitalist farmers tend to wield their political power in state governments, where most agricultural policy is made, rather than centrally. They come into conflict with industrial capital over matters such as the agriculture-industry terms of trade. Bureaucrats see their role as one of regulating and constraining industrial-commercial capital in particular. In practice, industrial-commercial capital is not strong enough to dominate state policy but it is strong enough to avoid most of the impact of the bureaucracy's regulatory measures.

This power-sharing arrangement, operating within parliamentary democratic forms, means that the state is not sufficiently powerful and independent to enforce the difficult measures that rapid industrial development requires. While the principal sources of wealth accumulation outside agriculture are in private and public industrial and commercial enterprises, neither of these is very efficient. Public enterprises generally do not generate a reinvestible surplus and thereby impose a drain on the economy. This is partly because they provide subsidised inputs, including finance, to private businesses. Private businesses are not rapid accumulators on the whole because they have been able to protect themselves from the competitive forces that would make them more efficient.

If the private sector were more dynamic and productive it would make sense, in terms of developing a more powerful class of industrial capitalists, to hand over public enterprises to private business as in South Korea and Taiwan. The important factor is not the *level* of state intervention and control but the degree of effectiveness it is permitted. South Korea and India have similar levels of state participation in national economies. The difference is that in South Korea, government intervention is used to discipline private businesses, whereas in India government economic management is not insulated from particular sectional interests and serves to cosset domestic industry rather than forcing it to be efficient. As long as the government accurately reflects the interests of the dominant classes, the hard decisions necessary for rapid industrialisation will not be taken. The recent liberalisations are unlikely to have a significant impact on this situation.

CONCLUSIONS

One of the important analytical points to emerge from this study is the error of "policy voluntarism." It is correct to conceive of the problem of growth in capitalist societies as one of choosing the correct set of government policies. Economic (and other) policies arise out of particular social conditions. This is a trite statement, but it is extraordinary to find large numbers of economists who make policy prescriptions that are doomed to failure from the beginning because they are not consistent with the pattern of class dominance. The fundamental thrust towards industrial growth and development grows out of the impersonal and largely uncontrollable social forces that make up history. Within these constraints economic policies can make a difference, sometimes an important difference, and as hinted in the country case studies above, the state can help *to create* the classes that will carry out industrialisation. But this leaves us with the questions of the *sort* of state that will be interested in such acts of creation, why they are interested, and whether they can be successful. In this light it is little wonder that the simple-minded World Bank formula of "get the prices right" has more often than not foundered on the rock of hostile class interests.

The error of policy voluntarism is allied with another error of received economic opinion of the World Bank variety, that of the negative influence on growth of government involvement in the economy. The simple data of Table 22-6, column 1 and a wealth of further evidence demonstrate that economic growth is not necessarily inhibited by government involvement. We have previously pointed to the case of South Korea where the extent of government ownership and regulation at detailed levels of the economy have been used to maximise the efficient growth of the economy. It is not the quantity of government intervention and planning that matters but its quality. In the successful NICs the quality has been consistently high while the quantity has varied considerably. The quality of government intervention and planning is less a product of the educational levels of government officials than of the independence of these officials and their political masters from sectional influences. Corruption, nepotism, undue outside influence, the lack of an overall vision and motivation, bureaucratic parochialism, officiousness, and political weakness all contribute to low-quality planning.

The present study has had two purposes. The first has been to lay down an analytical framework for making sensible assessments of the growth prospects of nations. The second has been to apply this framework to the eight selected countries. A summary of the arguments for each country can be found in Table 22-8, where each factor is denoted favourable (F) or unfavourable (U) in its likely impact on future growth. An overall assessment of future prospects on a scale of 1 to 5, from "poor" to "good," appears for each country at the foot of the table.

Both Indonesia and the Philippines have poor overall growth prospects, principally because of the economic and political dominance of classes which derive wealth from unproductive activities and the structural unwillingness of their governments to attack these classes. The growth prospects of Nepal are poor for similar reasons, although there the problem is compounded by the relative absence of opportunities for productive investments.

In Bangladesh, while faced with economic difficulties similar to Nepal's, including the unsympathetic character of agriculture, the prospects are a little better in so far as the state is more independent of the interests of unproductive classes. India has fewer of the political advantages of Bangladesh but has improved chances due to high availability of

TABLE 22-8
SUMMARY OF ECONOMIC AND POLITICAL CONDITIONS

	Indonesia	Philippines	Malaysia	Thailand	Nepal	Bangladesh	Pakistan	India
1. State of world economy	U	—	U	F	—	U	F	F
2. Availability of savings								
Domestic savings rate	F	F	F	F	U	U	U	F
Access to foreign loans	F	U	F	—	U	—	U	F
Financial intermediation	U	U	F	F	F	F	F	F
3. Productiveness of investments								
Quality of workforce	—	F	F	—	U	U	U	F
Control of workforce	F	U	U	F	F	F	F	U
Labour costs	U	F	U	U	F	F	U	F
Quality of management	U	U	F	—	U	U	F	F
Infrastructure	F	U	F	U	U	—	F	—
4. Sympathy of agriculture	F	F	F	F	U	U	F	F
5. Political conditions								
Dominance of unproductive classes	U	F	F	F	U	F	F	F
Independence of state	U	U	F	F	U	U	F	U
Strength of state	F	U	U	F	F	U	U	U
Proven commitment to growth	U	U	U	U	U	F	U	U
Overall growth prospects	2	1	4	5	1	2	3	3

Note: U = unfavourable; F = favourable; 1 = poor; 3 = doubtful; 5 = good.

savings and productive investment opportunities, and an agricultural system that is more amenable to the rapid structural changes that industrialisation brings about.

Pakistan has overall prospects similar to India's but for different reasons. Agriculture is sympathetic to industrial development, and recent industrial and infrastructural growth provide a foundation for future growth. While the government is relatively independent of wealthy interests it does not have firm control over civil order and economic policy. As a result, sufficient savings to finance industrial expansion are likely to be increasingly difficult to obtain.

Malaysia is rated as having better prospects. It has a political system that is relatively independent of the influence of unproductive classes, although there remains doubt over whether the government is sufficiently strong to take the steps necessary to restrain the emergent Malay capitalist class. The agricultural system has the required flexibility but the degree of control over labour is questionable.

Thailand appears to have the best prospects of the eight countries surveyed, with a strong political structure and a demonstrated willingness to make hard decisions. There remains some danger that finance capital may, in times of difficulty, withdraw from industrial investments, particularly since there is some doubt about available investment opportunities. While the flexibility of agriculture and current debt problems raise further doubts, the quality of Thai planning should see it through.

NOTES

1 Clive Hamilton, "Price Formation and Class Relations in the Development Process," *Journal of Contemporary Asia,* 17, 1, (1987) pp. 2–18.
2 World Bank, *World Development Report 1986,* Washington, D.C. 1986.
3 ILO, *Yearbook of Labour Statistics,* Geneva 1985.
4 Clive Hamilton, "Capitalist Industrialisation in East Asia's Four Little Tigers," *Journal of Contemporary Asia,* 13, 1 (1983).
5 F. Halim, "Rural Labour Force and Industrial Conflict in West Malaysia," *Journal of Contemporary Asia,* 11, 3 (1981).
6 Anne Booth and R. M. Sundrum, *Labour Absorption in Agriculture* (Oxford: Oxford University Press, 1986).
7 Ibid.
8 Ibid.
9 J. A. C. Mackie, "Economic Growth in the ASEAN Region: The Political Underpinnings," paper prepared for the Industrialisation Workshop, NCDS, Australian National University, Canberra ACT.
10 Hamilton, "Capitalist Industrialisation," op. cit.
11 Mackie, "Economic Growth," op. cit.
12 Richard Robison, *Indonesia: The Rise of Capital* (Sydney: Allen and Unwin, 1986).
13 Hamilton, "Capitalist Industrialisation," op. cit.

CHAPTER 23

THE PACIFIC BASIN
AND LATIN AMERICA

Dae Won Chol

UN Economic Commission for Latin America and the Caribbean

I. INTRODUCTION

There are three ways of approaching the subject of the simultaneous globalization and regionalization processes now taking place in the world economy. The first is to study the dynamics of economic relations among all three of the traditional geographic economic centres—the United States, the European Economic Community (EEC) and Japan—in order to determine what the main trends and most significant variables are. The second is to examine each of these centres separately, analysing the underlying phenomena within each of these economies as a means of understanding their internal dynamics. And the third is to analyse how the current processes differ from the operational patterns of the preceding economic system by, for example, making a distinction (within the overall internationalization process of the postwar period) between the globalization process now under way, which gathered steam in the second half of the 1980s, and the transnationalization process that marked the three preceding decades.

None of these three approaches affords a true picture of world economic events, however, because in each case their tools of analysis take into consideration only the three main traditional actors in the sphere of international trade (United States, EEC, Japan), thus overlooking a fourth actor that has burst upon the scene. During the 1980s the world witnessed the emergence in Asia of a new wellspring of growth composed of the newly industrializing economies (NIES) of Asia and the Association of South-East Asian Nations (ASEAN). The former group includes Hong Kong, the Republic of Korea, Singapore and Taiwan, while the latter includes the Philippines, Indonesia, Malaysia and Thailand.[1]

From *CEPAL Review,* 49 (April, 1993).

Thus, until the start of the 1980s the world's market economy system could accurately be described as a triad. Today, however, the two above-mentioned groups of Asian economies have begun to play such a crucial role in international economic relations that any thorough examination of globalization and regionalization processes at the world level must incorporate them into the discussion.

The objectives of this article are to determine, first, how we should interpret the emergence of the Asian NIEs and the ASEAN countries (the most recent NIEs) within the context of the new world economic order; second, what factors have contributed to the economic vitality of these groups within the context of the new Asian economic order; third, what new economic patterns or matrices have taken shape in the relations between these groups and the Latin American countries in terms of foreign direct investment (FDI) and the promotion of foreign trade; and, finally, what conclusions can be drawn from these analyses as regards economic cooperation between the Asian-Pacific countries (especially the NIEs) and Latin America within the new setting created by the globalization process in the Pacific Basin.[2]

II. THE PACIFIC BASIN IN THE NEW WORLD ECONOMIC ORDER

1. Three International Modalities for Changing Production Patterns: the Asian-Pacific, European-Atlantic and Latin American models

Within the framework of the ongoing globalization process, a new kind of specialization began to take shape in the production sector at the world level starting in the second half of the 1980s. In order to gain a clearer picture of this new global division of labour and how it is influencing the different international patterns of technical/-industrial development, it will be helpful to outline the above three modalities of changing production patterns on the basis of the changes seen in the corresponding industrial structures over the past two decades, with special emphasis on the period 1985–1992 and the approach taken by the 1991 UNIDO study.[3]

The Asian-Pacific modality, involving changes—due to an increase in value added—in production patterns at the three-digit level of the International Standard Industrial Classification (ISIC) in Japan, the Asian NIEs and the ASEAN countries, is notable for the rapid growth of the electrical and non-electrical machinery, chemical and plastic products industries, and, in particular, the electronics industry, which is a key factor in the third industrial revolution. This pattern is evident in almost all the Asian-Pacific countries, from Japan to the NIEs and from the ASEAN countries to China and India (UNIDO, 1992). If we plot this pattern on a graph, we end up with a shape that looks very much like a spaceship (see Figure 23-1).

The second, or European-Atlantic, modality corresponds to the United States, Canada and Europe; the changes in these areas' production patterns are characterized by the rapid growth of the plastics industry, followed by chemicals, non-ferrous metals, and paper and printing. The less intensive development of the electronics industry distinguishes this modality from the Asian-Pacific model (see Figure 23-2).

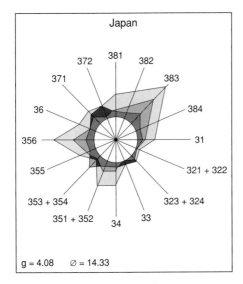

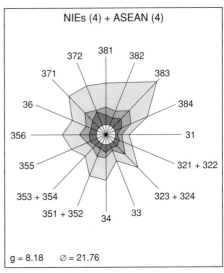

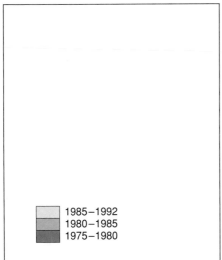

g = Annual GDP growth rate
(1975–1992 average)

∅ = Index of changes in production patterns
(1975–1992 average)

ISIC code	Industries
31	Food products
321, 322	Textiles
323, 324	Hides and skins
33	Wood and furniture
34	Paper and printing
351, 352	Chemicals
355	Rubber products
356	Plastic products
36	Nonmetallic products
371	Iron and steel
372	Nonferrous metals
381	Metal products
382	Nonelectrical machinery
383	Electrical machinery
384	Transport equipment

FIGURE 23-1
JAPAN, NEWLY INDUSTRIALIZING ASIAN ECONOMIES (ASIAN NIEs) AND MEMBERS
OF THE ASSOCIATION OF SOUTH-EAST ASIAN NATIONS (ASEAN): CHANGING
PRODUCTION PATTERNS, 1975–1992.
(Index of value added (1975 = 100), at constant 1980 prices) (*Source:* Adapted from United
Nations Industrial Development Organizations (UNIDO), *Industry and Development: Global Report,*
Vienna, 1991.)

The third modality of changing production patterns, which corresponds to Latin
America, involves a type of development based on non-ferrous metals and petroleum
and petroleum products; in other words, it is still based on raw materials. Since the
1980s many countries in the region have been overhauling their industrial structures by
means of privatizations and the liberalization of their trade and financial markets. Since

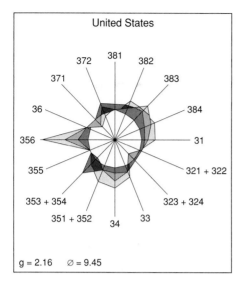

United States

g = 2.16   ∅ = 9.45

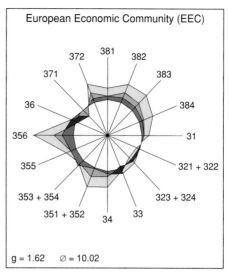

European Economic Community (EEC)

g = 1.62   ∅ = 10.02

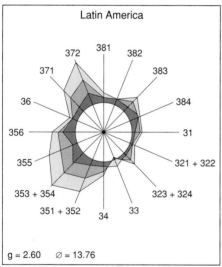

Latin America

g = 2.60   ∅ = 13.76

g = Annual GDP growth rate
(1975–1992 average)

∅ = Index of changes in production patterns
(1975–1992 average)

ISIC code	Industries
31	Food products
321, 322	Textiles
323, 324	Hides and skins
33	Wood and furniture
34	Paper and printing
351, 352	Chemicals
355	Rubber products
356	Plastic products
36	Nonmetallic products
371	Iron and steel
372	Nonferrous metals
381	Metal products
382	Nonelectrical machinery
383	Electrical machinery
384	Transport equipment

FIGURE 23-2
UNITED STATES, EUROPE AND LATIN AMERICA: CHANGING PRODUCTION PATTERNS,
1975–1992.
(Index of value added (1975 = 100), at constant 1980 prices) (*Source:* Adapted from United
Nations Industrial Development Organization (UNIDO), *Industry and Development: Global Report,*
Vienna, 1991.)

this industrial restructuring is seen primarily in terms of an intensification of industrialization (of the type associated with the second industrial revolution), it would be more
accurate to describe this process as a new modality for changing production patterns
based on the progressive absorption of technological innovations (chiefly in the fields of
micro-electronics, information sciences, biotechnology and new materials) correspond-

ing to the third industrial revolution. The main difference between "industrial restructuring" and the "realignment of technical/industrial systems" is that whereas the former involves a change in the industrial structure based on the use of the internal combustion engine and heavy machinery, with petroleum products as the main energy source, the latter is based on intensive use of micro-electronics and takes advantage of computerized memory storage capabilities to incorporate knowledge as a basic input.

If the transformation of production patterns is seen as an industrialization process involving the ongoing replacement of technologies having constant returns to scale with technologies that generate increasing returns (Murphy, Schleifer and Vishny, 1989), then it follows that the realignment of technical/industrial systems is preferable to industrial restructuring.

In view of the foregoing, efforts to change Latin America's production patterns in the 1990s will stand a greater chance of success if the changes are envisaged within the framework of an economic globalization process in which the third industrial revolution is playing a leading role. In addition to incorporating the above-mentioned elements, this "future-oriented" development strategy has a geo-economic connotation which suggests that the linchpin for this realignment of technical/industrial systems is to be found in the economic buoyancy of the Asian-Pacific region.

Since manufacturing has been assigned a central role in the effort to change production patterns, there should be a close correlation between GDP growth, the value added by manufacturing, and employment in the manufacturing sector. If we draw a comparison between Latin America, on the one hand, and the Asian NIEs and ASEAN countries as a group, on the other, we find that in the 1980s GDP growth fluctuated around 7%-8% for the Asian group and between 2% and 4% for Latin America. During that same decade, the value added by the manufacturing sector increased by between 7% and 14% for the Asian group, while for Latin America the figures ranged from −1% to 4%. Meanwhile, the growth rate for employment in the manufacturing sector fell sharply in Latin America and ended up with an average of less than 2%, whereas the Asian countries' average for the period 1985–1992 was nearly 4%. These figures reflect sharp differences between the two groups' development patterns; the pattern of the South-east Asian countries is primarily based on the value added to manufactures, which is not the case in Latin America.

In short, these three modalities of changing production patterns did not lead to similar rates of economic growth in the 1980s. Although it is safe to assume that Latin America's performance was influenced by its financial crisis, the real problem was that the development of the production system stagnated during the 1980s; unless the 1990s bring a turnaround in this trend, both the region's economic development and its chances of establishing a new position for itself in the sphere of international trade may be at risk.

2. The Growth of Intra-Pacific, Intra-Asian and Intra-Industry Trade

The end of the 1980s marked a profound change in the international economic order. In addition to the wave of political and economic reform that engulfed the former

Soviet Union, Eastern Europe and Germany, the economic bloc envisioned in Western Europe's plans to form a single market (Europe 92) began to take shape, steps were taken to create a North American free trade area, and the Enterprise for the Americas was unveiled. Another significant event was the emergence of South-east Asia as the new growth leader. The trend towards the consolidation of the Asian-Pacific region as a new hub of international trade on a par with that of the Atlantic heralds the birth of a new technical and economic centre of production in Asia. In fact, as the end of the twentieth century approaches, all indications are that, regardless of the form taken by the new international economic order, South-east Asia is likely to become one of its leading players.

The rapid growth of the Asian NIES' and ASEAN countries' trade has occurred thanks to the internal technical/industrial realignments carried out by each of these economies and to a development style based on increasing linkages between intra-industry trade and intraregional investment. In other words, the productive momentum generated by their internal industrialization drive has strengthened the economies of this region through multilateral trade in manufactures and investments in the realignment of their technical/industrial complexes, which have also been complemented by outward-looking initiatives.

On the new economic map of the Asian-Pacific region, there are three main focal points: Japan, the NIES and ASEAN. The economic growth of the ASEAN nations in recent years has outstripped that of the NIES, and its multiplier effect will be felt to an increasing extent in bordering countries such as Vietnam, Cambodia and Burma (Myanmar). Meanwhile, China is laying the groundwork for an effort to carry over the model it has set up along its coast into the inland areas of the country, which holds one-fifth of the world's population and has extraordinary economic potential. Along with China, India too is making an effort to join in the "flight of the wild geese", headed by Japan and followed by the Asian NIES and the ASEAN countries.

Thus, the industrialization process appears to follow a linear sequence of different yet mutually complementary stages of technological and industrial development, all of which seem to be leading in the same direction (Chen, 1989). For example, the "lead goose" is Japan, with its highly knowledge- and technology-intensive industries; it is followed by the NIES, whose industries are semi-intensive in knowledge and technology, and the ASEAN countries have also joined the flock, with their labour-intensive and semi-technology-intensive industries.

In order to arrive at an understanding of the movements, correlations and linkages within and among these three centres, it is useful to bear in mind the following phenomena: i) the ascendancy of intra-Pacific trade over intra-Atlantic trade; ii) the expansion of intraregional trade in the Asian-Pacific region; and iii) the intensification of intra-industry trade.

The United States' trade links with the Asian-Pacific region are growing stronger while its ties with Europe are, in relative terms, growing weaker. In the 1970s and 1980s, total United States trade with Europe grew at an average rate of 12% per year, while its trade with the Asian-Pacific region expanded by 18% annually; as a result, total intra-Pacific trade amounted to over US$300 billion per year, which was half as much again as the value of intra-Atlantic trade (US$200 billion).

The increase in Asia's intraregional trade is evidenced by the growing share of total Asian-Pacific exports accounted for by intraregional trade, which rose from 34% in 1986 to 45% in 1990 (GATT, 1992). This marks a departure from the trend of the early 1980s, when North America was the largest market for Asian-Pacific exports.

The expanding role of intraregional trade in Asia's total trade is illustrated even more clearly by the figures on intraregional imports, which had come to represent 50% of the total by 1989. Moreover, during the second half of the 1980s NIE imports from the Asian-Pacific region climbed from 61% to 66%. Intra-NIE imports also rose, from 7% to 14%, while imports from China jumped from 5% to 11%. It is also noteworthy that exports of manufactures from the ASEAN countries to the Asian NIEs increased by a factor of 70 between the early 1970s and the late 1980s, while their share of exports rose from 10% to 20%.

Horizontal intra-industry trade has been a significant component of intraregional trade. In terms of overall trends in exports of manufactures, Europe's and the United States' shares have shrunk while that of the Asian-Pacific region has burgeoned (Fukasaku, 1992). NIE exports of manufactures increased by a factor of 35 and those of ASEAN by a factor of 32 between the start of the 1970s and the end of the 1980s. The expansion of imports of manufactures was greater in the NIEs, which registered a 21-fold increase during the period in question. For example, in 1987 the Asian NIEs imported twice as much as Japan did (6% versus 3% of world imports of manufactured products). At the same time, however, the NIEs as a group were the second largest exporter of manufactures to ASEAN, with their 26% market share being surpassed only by Japan's 30%. China was also a net exporter of manufactures to the NIEs (Nohara and Kagami, 1991).

Between 1980 and 1990, the percentage of manufactures in total NIE and ASEAN exports and imports expanded substantially, which underscores their tendency to move towards an intra-industry-based trade/production pattern. In the case of the NIEs, for instance, manufactures made up over 90% of their total exports in 1990. The figure was much lower for the ASEAN member countries, but it still averaged around 50% for that year; in the space of a single decade, the Philippines, Malaysia and Thailand doubled the percentage of manufactures in their total exports, while Indonesia registered almost a tenfold increase.

The percentage of total imports accounted for by manufactures also expanded in both groups of countries, rising on average from about 55% to 70% in the NIEs and from approximately 60% to around 70% of total imports in the ASEAN countries between 1980 and 1990.

An analysis of the composition of both groups' exports of manufactures during the 1980s brings to light various changes: i) human-capital- and technology-intensive industries increased their share of such exports; ii) industries making intensive use of unskilled labour and natural resources saw their share decline (in Thailand and Malaysia, in particular, the role of natural resources was significantly reduced); and iii) the share of manufactured exports accounted for by natural resource-based industries tended to shrink in the NIEs, but these industries still play a major role in the ASEAN countries, even though their share also decreased during the period in question.

In terms of the Grubel-Lloyd intra-industry trade index[4] for manufactures in the Asian-Pacific region, all the countries exhibited sizeable increases during the 1980s. Among the NIEs, Hong Kong and Singapore registered values of 75% and 72%, respectively, while the figures for the Republic of Korea and Taiwan were both slightly over 40% in 1989. The ASEAN countries saw their shares expand considerably, with the shares of the Philippines and Thailand nearly doubling. The largest increase was recorded by Malaysia, whose index jumped from slightly over 30% in 1979 to 55% in 1989, putting the country in third place among all the Asian-Pacific economies.

Table 23-1 provides an overview of trends in the Asian-Pacific countries' intra-industry trade with their main trading partners for manufactures. As may be seen from the table, particularly high indexes have been recorded for the intra-industry trade of the various individual NIEs with the NIEs as a group (around 30%-40%), of the Republic of Korea and Taiwan with Japan, and of the ASEAN countries (especially Malaysia, at over 50%) with the United States. The largest intra-industry traders in the Pacific Basin (including Japan, the United States and Canada) are the Asian NIEs, with an (unweighted) average of almost 30%. They are followed by the United States and Canada. Europe and Japan are farther back in the ranking, with shares of 22% and 17%, respectively. China, for its part, has already garnered a 14% share of the Asian-Pacific economies' intra-industry trade.

In summary, strong manufacturing trade links have been established not only between the Asian NIEs and Japan, among the NIEs themselves, between the NIEs and the ASEAN, and within ASEAN, but also between the NIEs, ASEAN and the United States. This suggests that, along with the open-ended regionalization of the Asian-Pacific area, we may witness a stronger trend towards the globalization of trade in the Pacific Basin, in which the United States would play a pivotal role. Given the Latin American region's strong ties with the United States, this trend could have an increasing influence on Latin America's integration strategy as regards the Pacific Basin.

3. The New International Economic Order and the Role of the New NIE/ASEAN Hub: from a "Triad" to a "Quartet"

An examination of the present foreign trade structure, with its three traditional economic hubs (Japan, United States and Europe) and its new, fourth, centre (NIE/ASEAN), reveals that the NIEs are becoming increasingly influential with regard to the dynamism of the new international economic order.

This phenomenon is attested to in a study by the secretariat of the General Agreement on Tariffs and Trade (GATT, 1992) which found that a radical change had taken place in the ranking of the top merchandise exporters during the period 1980–1990. In 1979, Hong Kong was in 27th place, Taiwan was in 22nd place, the Republic of Korea in 29th, and Singapore was the 32nd largest exporter. One decade later, all of these economies were in the top 20 (Hong Kong was in 11th place, Taiwan in 12th, the Republic of Korea in 13th and Singapore in 18th place); the same trend was also observed among importers for that period.

Furthermore, the average growth rate recorded for NIE foreign trade in the period 1986–1989 was above the average for Asia as a whole (22%, not including Japan) as

TABLE 23-1

ASIAN-PACIFIC REGION: INDEX OF INTRA-INDUSTRY TRADE IN MANUFACTURES BETWEEN ASIAN-PACIFIC ECONOMIES AND THEIR MAIN TRADING PARTNERS

Asian-Pacific economies	Japan	Australia and New Zealand	NIEs[a]	ASEAN[b]	China	United States and Canada	OECD countries
Hong Kong	21.9	21.6	42.0	31.0	47.7	24.5	35.2
Singapore	21.3	31.2	43.2	57.2	19.2	43.8	37.8
Malaysia	22.2	19.3	46.0	43.5	11.2	53.3	27.9
Republic of Korea	36.0	9.0	32.9	19.8	-	24.7	20.2
Taiwan	31.8	9.7	29.0	16.3	-	19.6	25.7
New Zealand	4.8	57.3	10.4	13.5	1.7	22.2	13.9
Thailand	10.6	15.1	32.1	20.9	20.2	32.3	19.6
Japan	-	7.2	27.0	11.4	14.5	26.7	34.1
Australia	6.7	51.0	16.2	12.4	3.8	18.1	14.1
Philippines	10.6	14.2	15.5	23.2	9.1	28.7	13.4
Indonesia	5.8	7.5	12.9	21.2	1.9	4.1	4.8
Unweighted average	17.2	22.1	27.9	24.6	14.4	27.1	22.4

[a]Newly industrializing Asian economies.
[b]Association of South-East Asian Nations.
Source: K. Fukasaku, Economic Regionalization and Intra-Industry Trade: Pacific-Asian Perspectives, OECD Technical Papers, No. 53, Paris, Organization for Economic Cooperation and Development (OECD), 1992.

well as the world average (14%), since the NIE figures for that period were over 26% for imports and 23% for exports. In other words, the rate of increase in NIE foreign trade during that period was nearly twice as high as the growth rate of world trade.

These trends and changes entail a realignment of traditional trade links. Until recently, the United States was unquestionably the largest market for NIE exports. Now, however, the Asian-Pacific market (Japan, the NIES, ASEAN and China) is becoming increasingly important, and intra-NIE trade has surpassed trade between the NIEs and Japan. In fact, with a growth rate of 36%, intra-NIE trade was the fastest-growing component of NIE exports between 1986 and 1989, since the rate of increase of NIE exports to Japan was 31%, exports to ASEAN countries rose by 30% and sales to the United States increased by 14%.

Trade relations between the NIEs and ASEAN have been remarkably buoyant compared with the relations between these groups and the three traditional centres of world trade, and this means that we need to make some changes in the way we have traditionally talked about the world trade structure, since the incorporation of another actor into the new international economic order may very well alter its future course of development.

As may be seen in Table 23-2, in 1988 the total value of NIE and ASEAN exports to the United States (US$83 billion) was nearly the same as the value of Europe's exports to that country (US$84 billion) and quite close to that of Japan's exports to the United States (US$90 billion) as well. It is also interesting to note that the value of United States exports to the Asian NIEs was quite similar to the value of its exports to Japan. In other words, the NIEs are as large a market for the United States as Japan is.

As regards the value of exports to Japan, NIE/ASEAN exports together exceeded those of the United States and were double the level of European exports. NIE exports to the Japanese market constitute an extraordinary case in that they exceeded the value of total European exports to Japan, while United States exports to that country were only 1.5 times as great as those of the NIEs. Meanwhile, Japan's exports to the NIEs were

TABLE 23-2
THE NEW "QUARTET" IN INTERNATIONAL TRADE (UNITED STATES, JAPAN, EUROPE AND NIEs + ASEAN):[a] MERCHANDISE TRADE, 1988
(Billions of Dollars)

Source/destination	NIEs + ASEAN	United States	Europe	Japan	Total exports
NIES + ASEAN	-	83	40	44	167
United States	42	-	70	38	150
Europe	30	84	-	20	134
Japan	63	90	45	-	198
Total imports	135	257	155	102	649

[a]Newly industrializing Asian Economies (Asian NIEs) plus the member countries of the Association of South-East Asian Nations (ASEAN).
Source: Original calculations based on figures provided in the Japanese Foreign Trade Yearbook, 1990, in *Nikkei Economic Daily,* 1991.

worth more than its exports to Europe, and the total value of Japanese exports to the NIES and ASEAN was almost 1.5 times the value of its sales to Europe.

The economic vitality of the Asian countries as a group (the NIES, the ASEAN countries and Japan) is also reflected in the figures for Asia's exports to the United States, since these amount to twice the value of Europe's exports to that market, which indicates that intra-Pacific trade is outperforming intra-Atlantic trade. Moreover, the combined value of NIE and ASEAN exports to the European market is almost on a par with Japanese exports to Europe. In fact, when all these Asian nations' exports are taken together, their total value surpasses that of United States exports to the European market.

As a corollary to the factors discussed above, it may be said that, in addition to constituting a model of rapid economic growth, the NIES and ASEAN have also come to be a vigorous centre of economic growth in Asia. We therefore need to analyse the new global economic situation in terms of a quartet (United States, Europe, Japan and the NIES plus ASEAN) of leading actors rather than of the conventional triad (United States, Europe and Japan). South-east Asia must now be regarded as another player whose importance will increasingly depend on the NIES' participation in the technological and economic circuit that links Japan, the NIES, ASEAN and China.

III. THE FACTORS UNDERLYING THE ECONOMIC BUOYANCY OF THE ASIAN-PACIFIC REGION

1. Foreign Direct Investment (FDI) In the Asian-Pacific Region: Trends and Prospects

An examination of the new Asian economic order is the best way to gain a clear picture of the globalization process taking place in the market-economy system, since its epicentre is located in the Asian-Pacific region. This analysis reveals that such constructs as R. Vernon's product cycle theory and the Heckscher-Ohlin theorem are no longer valid. Owing to the emergence of a new and more complex global division of labour based on increasing horizontal integration, FDI is not motivated only by comparative advantages, but also by new chains or circuits of value-adding activities in which global corporate strategies play a very important role.

In terms of the new Asian economic order, the year 1986 was a turning point in a variety of ways: i) in response to the 1985 Plaza Agreement, Japan took advantage of the edge it has over the United States and Europe in the high-technology microelectronics sector (Makino, 1991), employing such mechanisms as the diversification of its production system, mergers and acquisitions, and other "new forms of FDI" (Oman, 1984) to intensify the globalization of its economy in an effort to become more competitive; ii) starting in that same year, the NIES managed to attain the largest trade surplus in the region, which enabled them to become a major foreign investor; and iii) the ASEAN countries achieved the undisputed status of "new NIES" by marking up economic growth rates that have outpaced even those of the NIES themselves.

Behind this Asian economic buoyancy lies a new intraregional trend in FDI. It will be recalled that the first surge in FDI from the NIES coincided with the second boom in Japanese FDI. The chain of events underlying these developments was as follows: the Plaza Agreement of 1985 led to a revaluation of the Japanese yen which immediately gave the NIES a greater competitive edge in the world market, and the surplus achieved by these economies during the second half of the 1980s was transferred to the ASEAN countries in the form of FDI. It should be emphasized that, despite the correlation between the two above-mentioned upswings in FDI, Japan channeled its investments primarily to the tertiary sector, whereas the NIES directed their investments chiefly to the manufacturing sector (especially in the ASEAN countries and Latin America).[5]

Contributory factors in the second Japanese FDI boom, which followed on the heels of the Plaza Agreement, included: i) exchange-rate adjustments, particularly the sharp rise in the yen against the United States dollar; ii) trade disputes between Japan, the United States and the European Economic Community (EEC); and iii) wage hikes, labour shortages and the series of financial deregulation measures associated with the internationalization of the banking system. As a result of all these changes, Japanese FDI grew at a record rate in 1986–1990: indeed, over 70% of the total stock (US$227 billion) of Japanese FDI was built up during those five years. Even though the United States and Europe took in over two-thirds of the annual flows of such investment, during the period in question Japanese FDI accounted for 65% of total FDI in the NIES, 45% in the ASEAN countries and 90% in China.

One of the most notable events which occurred in respect of FDI during the 1980s was the NIES' emergence as one of the largest investors in the Asian-Pacific region and as a potentially major investor in other regions. During the 1980s, the stock of Taiwanese FDI in Malaysia skyrocketed by a factor of 250, to US$2.3 billion. This sum is equivalent to 35% of the total FDI flow to Malaysia in 1990, and is far more than Japan's FDI in that country. Thailand, for its part, received approximately US$500 million in FDI from the NIES in 1989, which was about 30% of its FDI total. In 1989, the largest investments in China came from Hong Kong and Macao, which together invested US$2.3 billion. At the same time, the NIES are now taking those of their labour-intensive industries that generate less value added and relocating them in developing countries, while they are bringing over more science- and technology-intensive industries from the developed countries.

In analysing the linkages between FDI and foreign trade, it is important to note the influential role which the mounting inflow of such investment to the Asian-Pacific region has played in the expansion of that region's foreign trade. Initially, FDI generates a flow of capital goods from source countries to recipient countries. Parent companies provide their subsidiaries with parts and components for assembly, and the subsidiaries then send the semi-finished goods for final processing in a third country or for the last stages of their assembly in the source country. The spatial globalization of production entails a relocation of production activities via FDI such that national borders cease to represent an obstacle and bilateral or trilateral trade flows are set in motion.

The Asian-Pacific region's relative importance as a new FDI source and destination has changed substantially. NIE transnationals have played an unprecedented role in bringing this change about by beginning to make foreign investments both in the Asian-Pacific region itself and in other developing and developed nations. The countries' efforts to set up a framework for investors were complemented by the creation of regional, bilateral and international instruments designed to provide guarantees for transnational investors in this region. In addition, in rapidly growing economies such as the NIES and the ASEAN countries, international agreements are being negotiated more swiftly in order to protect their investments in other countries of the region and in the rest of the world. At the regional level, ASEAN has emerged as an important vehicle for the coordination of investment policy and joint programmes aimed at boosting FDI flows. The ASEAN countries have also agreed to standardize their investment policies so as to reduce the competition among member countries through, *inter alia,* the liberalization of trade within ASEAN under the provisions of trade preference agreements; semi-public ASEAN manufacturing enterprises; the South-East Asian Association for Regional Cooperation; cooperation in the field of human resources development, and an industrial master plan.[6]

The recent increase in the volume of FDI in the Asian-Pacific region reflects not only local comparative advantages but also the global strategies of transnational corporations headquartered in developed countries (especially Japan) which call for the establishment of subsidiaries in the region to supply both local and foreign markets within the context of a process of progressive globalization. In order to gain a clearer notion of the relationship between FDI and trade in that context, an analysis of Japanese investments in the Asian Pacific will be helpful.

As regards local manufacturing supply, the subsidiaries of Japanese transnationals in the NIES and ASEAN countries make about 50% of their purchases on the local market. Local suppliers' market share in the ASEAN countries is growing remarkably fast; indeed, 90% of all precision instruments and 65% of all electrical machinery, iron and steel, and transport equipment are supplied by local producers. These figures attest to the growing "import-substituting endogenization"[7] of the ASEAN nations, which is speeding up the Asian-Pacific region's progress towards self-sufficiency (Nohara and Kagami, 1991).

Although FDI flows amount to no more than 10% of gross domestic capital formation, in most of the countries the economic contribution made by transnational corporations, as measured by such indicators as stock ownership and sales, is the source of much of their industrial activity: in the late 1980s it accounted for over 50% of such activity in Hong Kong, Thailand and the Philippines, and for more than 40% of total Taiwanese exports of electronic equipment in 1986. Furthermore, especially in countries with generous endowments of natural resources, subsidiaries of transnational corporations are very large employers in the primary sector. In Fiji, for example, such subsidiaries provide three-quarters of all the jobs in the mining sector, and in Hong Kong they provide half of all the jobs in the electrical equipment industry, as well as half of the total value added by the manufacturing sector and exports. In Singapore, they account for 50% of all sales and a considerably larger percentage of exports, value added and employment; they are particularly active in the electrical equipment and petrochemicals industries. In fact, for these industries, transnationals account for over 45% of the total in all the indicators except export levels in the majority of Asian-Pacific countries (CTC, 1991).

The predominance of FDI in the electrical equipment industry[8] is one of the basic characteristics of the realignment of technical/industrial systems in most of the Asian-Pacific countries. Within this sector, transnational corporations have invested in everything from component assembly to manufacturing activities having the greatest technological content. It appears that FDI in the NIES is increasingly moving towards more complex manufacturing activities, such as the production of motor vehicles (Republic of Korea) and electrical equipment (Hong Kong, Taiwan and the Republic of Korea).

2. The Realignment of Technical/Industrial Systems in the Asian-Pacific Region

The vigorous growth of trade and financial activity in the Asian-Pacific region has been achieved through the creation of new competitive advantages, which, in turn, have led to changes in production patterns and, consequently, in trade patterns. As the lead country moves on to new products containing more value added and more technological inputs, it makes up for its traditional products' loss of competitiveness by shifting their production base to countries where production costs are lower; these countries then substitute these products for their imports and later go on to become net exporters. The source country, for its part, becomes a net importer of these products again and moves on to create new products for export (Hugues, 1989; ESCAP, 1991).

Within about 10 years' time, this process will enable most of the Asian-Pacific nations, and particularly the ASEAN countries and China, either to compete with Japan on an equal footing or to gain a competitive edge over it in almost all the export product lines of importance today. Meanwhile, Japan will have moved on to the production of new items containing a still larger proportion of technological and human-capital inputs.

According to data compiled by UNIDO (1991), at existing price levels the NIES already manufacture articles that are more competitive than those produced by Japan in most of the electronics industry's product lines. Even China has an edge over Japan in the production of radio receivers, and the fans produced by Malaysia and Thailand out-compete those made in Japan. What is more, it is projected that within the next three years Malaysia will become more competitive than Japan in various lines of electronic products. The NIES (chiefly the Republic of Korea) will also gain an advantage over that country in various types of machinery and electronics, including individual semiconductors. In sum, the current trend towards "catching up" with more technically and industrially complex forms of production will probably enable most of the NIES to take Japan's place in various industries within the machinery and electronics sectors, while Malaysia, Thailand and China will move into the position left open by the NIES.

In view of these phenomena, it is important that we re-interpret the dual role of the NIES in the Asian-Pacific region. As we said earlier, the NIES promote FDI from developed countries in high-technology sectors, while at the same time investing heavily in the ASEAN countries. Over the past 40 years the production of labour-intensive goods has shifted from Japan to the NIES, from the NIES to ASEAN, and from ASEAN to China, and in the near future these activities are likely to move on to Indochina (especially Vietnam) and southern Asia.

Because of this process, the countries' comparative advantages are constantly changing, thereby rendering invalid approaches that define economic integration solely in terms of cross-sectoral complementarity. What is happening in South-east

Asia demonstrates the increasing importance of intra-industry complementarity in economic integration processes.

Bearing these changes in mind, in the following chapter we will undertake an analysis of the economic relations between the Asian NIEs and Latin America. In the course of this examination, we will seek to identify the complementary aspects of the relationship between integration into trade flows and the integration of production in the Pacific Basin.

IV. THE NEW ECONOMIC RELATIONS BETWEEN THE NIES AND LATIN AMERICA

Latin America's economic relations with the NIEs have an impact in three areas: the growth of trade, potential technological cooperation and new direct investments in production.

1. The Expansion of Trade between the NIES and Latin America in the 1980s

Trade relations between Latin America and the NIEs changed significantly in the 1980s. Even during the economic crisis, trade between these two regions exhibited an unusual, and relatively unilateral, intensity (see Table 23-3): while Latin America expanded its trade with these economies more than with any other world region, the NIEs were increasing their trade with other markets (e.g., ASEAN). Total trade between Latin America and the NIEs in 1990 was three times as great as it had been at the start of the 1980s in terms of value. The member countries of the Latin American Integration Association (ALADI) accounted for the bulk of total Latin American-NIE trade in terms of value, although total NIE trade with the Central American Common Market (CACM) also exhibited an upward trend.

The Republic of Korea has undoubtedly played the largest role in Latin American-NIE trade relations: in the 1980s total trade between the CACM and the Republic of Korea soared by over 500% and Republic of Korea-ALADI trade by 350%. This means that the value of merchandise trade between Latin America and the Republic of Korea jumped from US$600 million to US$2.8 billion during the decade. Strong upturns were also seen in trade between Latin America and Taiwan (200%), Singapore (150%) and Hong Kong (130%).

Latin American imports from the Asian NIEs doubled during the 1980s. The reasons for this increase included: i) the international competitiveness of NIE manufactures, which apparently motivated Latin America to turn away from its traditional sources of imports in favour of new industrial zones with more competitive prices, and ii) the NIEs' drive to expand their share of world export markets during the 1980s by opening up new markets for their products, including that of Latin America.

Traditionally, Latin American imports from the NIEs have been manufactures, whereas most of its exports to the NIEs have been natural resource-based goods. Since the continuation of this situation perpetuates an existing form of cross-sectoral complementarity, it follows that this type of trade will tend to widen the technological gap that separates Latin America from the Asian NIEs.

TABLE 23-3
NEWLY INDUSTRIALIZING ASIAN ECONOMIES (ASIAN NIEs) AND LATIN AMERICA.[a] MERCHANDISE TRADE, 1980 AND 1990
(Percentage Variation and Millions of Dollars)

		Exports to ALADI & CACM			Imports from ALADI & CACM			Total trade (exports + imports)		
		1980	1990	Variation (%)	1980	1990	Variation (%)	1980	1990	Variation (%)
Republic of Korea	ALADI	274.2	1 093.2	298.6	320.3	1 562.3	387.7	594.5	2 655.5	346.6
	CACM	21.2	126.4	496.2	2.9	25.8	789.6	24.1	152.2	531.5
	Total	295.4	1 219.4	312.8	323.3	1 588.1	391.3	618.6	2 807.7	353.8
Taiwan	ALADI	458.0	754.7	64.7	190.8	1 281.5	571.6	648.8	2 036.2	213.8
	CACM	30.1	98.0	25.5	19.5	8.1	-41.5	49.6	106.1	113.8
	Total	488.1	852.7	74.6	210.3	1 289.6	7 513.2	698.4	2 142.3	206.7
Singapore	ALADI	237.3	273.0	-	118.8	605.8	409.9	356.1	878.8	146.7
	CACM	-	12.5	-	-	8.7	-	-	21.2	-
	Total	237.3	285.5	20.3	118.8	614.5	417.2	356.1	900.0	152.7
Hong Kong	ALADI	263.9	265.6	0.6	111.9	609.6	444.7	375.8	875.2	132.8
	CACM	8.8	30.7	248.8	3.2	2.7	-84.3	12.0	33.4	178.3
	Total	272.7	296.3	8.6	115.1	612.3	431.9	387.8	908.6	134.2
NIEs (total)	ALADI	1 233.4	2 386.5	93.4	741.8	4 059.2	447.2	1 975.2	6 445.7	226.3
	CACM	60.1	267.6	345.2	25.6	45.3	76.9	85.7	312.9	265.1
	Total	1 293.5	2 654.1	105.1	767.4	4 104.5	434.8	2 060.9	6 758.6	227.9

[a]Latin American Integration Association (ALADI) and Central American Common Market (CACM).
Source: International Commodity Trade Data Base (COMTRADE) and others.

The value of total Latin American exports to the Asian NIEs increased more than fivefold between 1980 and 1990, the largest buyers of Latin American exports during this period being the Republic of Korea (a fivefold increase in value) and Taiwan (with a sixfold increase).

Thanks to this trend, Latin America's 1980 trade deficits with all these economies had been transformed into large surpluses by 1990. A product-by-product analysis of NIE-Latin America trade flows for the period 1980–1990 brings to light several features. First, NIE exports to the Latin American region became considerably more diversified in most cases (the Republic of Korea was the exception, since its exports exhibited a marked degree of specialization), as did Latin American exports to the NIEs (except for those sold to the Taiwanese market). Second, the type of trade taking place between Latin America and the Asian NIEs changed during the decade from an intra-sectoral flow of commodity trade in combination with inter-sectoral trade[9] to a type of trade marked by greater inter-industry complementarity.[10] The sizeable increase during the 1980s in inter-industry trade between Latin America and South-east Asia (including Japan, the NIEs and ASEAN) appears to herald the emergence of a new and different production/trade pattern whose potential should be explored.[11]

It is of interest to note that (primarily vertical) intra-industry trade accounted for a larger share of total trade between the two regions than it did in the trade flows for the period 1986–1990 between Latin America and the United States, between Latin America and Europe and among the Latin American countries themselves.

The trend towards more intra-industry trade between Latin America and South-east Asia may be illustrated by comparing their manufacturing industries' shares of total exports. For example, if we use the Grubel-Lloyd index, we see that in the period 1980–1988, the manufacturing sectors of three Latin American countries considerably increased their shares of intra-industry trade with South-east Asian countries: Chile's index jumped from 0% to 21%; Mexico's rose from 1% to 16% and Colombia's from 4% to 24%. In these Latin American countries, the relative importance of South-east Asia in intra-industry trade within the manufacturing sector is between 15 and 20 times greater than that of Europe (ECLAC, 1991).

This would seem to point to a budding opportunity for increased economic cooperation between South-east Asia and Latin America, especially with regard to the establishment of intra-industry trade links and of new reciprocal ties between their economies. To make such cooperation a reality, however, Latin America will have to meet the challenge of actually changing its production patterns in order to increase its exports' value added through systematic efforts to promote the development of endogenous scientific and technological capabilities and cooperative links in this field while at the same time modifying its institutional structures to promote Asian investment in the manufacturing sector. The dynamism of trade between the NIEs and Latin America provides us with a suitable environment for exploring these possibilities.

2.   The Potential for Cooperation in the Field of Technology

Unlike the United States and post-1992 Europe, the Asian-Pacific region encompasses a broad spectrum of highly diverse countries, some of which are in situations similar to those of some Latin American countries. This raises the possibility of integrating some aspects of production through greater intra-industry trade between Latin America and Asian-Pacific countries or groups; for example, such trade could be increased with Japan, as the world's main source of technological innovations, particularly in high-technology products; with the NIEs, which are increasingly concentrating on products requiring intensive use of high technology and of human and physical capital; with ASEAN, which is primarily an exporter of natural resource-based and labour-intensive goods; and with China, which had one of the highest growth rates in the world during the 1980s and is an increasingly competitive exporter of manufactures involving abundant inputs of low-cost labour.

Latin America could attain greater integration of production, both vertical and horizontal, with any one of these countries or groups of countries.[12] Indeed, in terms of the new strategy for changing Latin America's production patterns, the Asian-Pacific region could be the area that offers the greatest potential for economic cooperation in the 1990s; in order to develop that potential, however, we will have to set aside our traditional view of Latin America's comparative advantages in favour of a new concept based on dynamic, competitive advantages.

In the present process of reorganization of the global economic order, such an increase in integration will be possible only if the countries move up to more advanced technical/industrial levels. Since the Asian-Pacific region is where this process is taking place most rapidly today, Latin America's integration with that region is essential, especially in view of the impact that the realignment of technological systems is likely to have on the world economy in the near future.

3. Trends in Asian NIE Foreign Direct Investment in Latin America

During the second half of the 1980s, foreign direct investment by the Asian NIEs (particularly the Republic of Korea and Taiwan) in Latin America was stimulated by: i) the NIEs' incorporation into the Generalized System of Preferences (GSP) of the United States; ii) their labour force's rising wages; iii) the revaluation of their currencies; iv) their labour-intensive industries' declining ability to compete against ASEAN and China; v) the need to diversify their production base in line with the globalization process; vi) the growing protectionism of developed countries, which pressured Korean and Taiwanese exporters to relocate their production bases so that they could re-export to the North American market; and vii) the need to adapt swiftly to technological change, which led to a rapid recycling of the types of technologies that require less capital.

Circumstances in Latin America that have helped to attract direct investment from the NIEs include: i) the region's inexpensive labour; ii) its geographic proximity to the United States re-export market; iii) the hemispheric integration process called for by the Bush Administration's Enterprise for the Americas initiative, the incentives offered under the Caribbean Basin Initiative and the GSP; iv) the tax incentives available to enterprises in the region's export processing zones; v) the ready local supply of raw materials; vi) access to the region's internal market potential; vii) the growing stability of Latin American democracies; viii) a greater receptiveness to the technologies of the Asian NIEs, whose direct investments are concentrated in the manufacturing sector; and ix) the growing openness of the capital market and the introduction of legal modifications that have made the regulations pertaining to FDI more flexible.

Let us now see what factors could draw a greater volume of FDI to Latin America in the next few years. The first wave of NIE investment in Central America—much of which came from the Republic of Korea and Taiwan—took place under the terms of the incentives provided by the Caribbean Basin Initiative (CBI); in fact, almost all the resulting production activities re-exported their goods to the United States market. There are two constraints, however, that will have an increasing effect on this first wave of investment: from an internal standpoint, NIE investment is overconcentrated in one industry (textiles and wearing apparel), while from an external angle, Central American exports are limited by United States quotas. This means that if greater concentration in the textiles and clothing industry does not lead to increased re-exports to the United States, then NIE investors will have only two options: to diversify their production base, relocating it in countries eligible for CBI incentives that are not subject to quotas; or to diversify their activities to include other product lines for which incentives are provided under the Generalized System of Preferences. The recent increase in Korean FDI in Honduras is a clear example of the first option; for examples of the second, we might look to the diversification of FDI into other manufacturing activities, such as the electrical equipment/electronics industry. In this last regard, there is one variable—the Latin American countries' free trade agreements with the United States—that is having a greater impact than expected on the inflow of NIE investment to Latin America, as is illustrated by the massive flow of Korean investment recently received by Mexico.

If Latin America can manage to attract more NIE investment to its manufacturing sector—i.e., to attract a "second wave" of NIE investment and channel it into industries that are not only labour-intensive but also technology-intensive—this could lead to a realignment of the region's technological systems, given the greater technological content that products would then have and the speed with which technologies are recycled by the Asian NIEs. This means that what Latin America needs to do is to see to it that this first wave of NIE investment in the textiles industry is followed by a second wave of FDI into other, more technology-intensive, manufacturing activities. It would seem that, in a sense, Latin America's chances of successfully changing its production patterns may increasingly depend on whether or not it joins in the process of economic renewal now taking place in the Asian Pacific. The grounds for such a statement include the fact that the NIEs will be the world's most important new source of FDI during the 1990s (since their investments are concentrated in the manufacturing sector, are technology-intensive and are recycled rapidly) and the observation that, in order for Latin America to change its production patterns, it will need to undertake a more comprehensive realignment of its technological systems as it enters into the third industrial revolution.

It may therefore be assumed that during the 1990s the framework for the region's new form of integration into the world market will be shaped by the lead "quartet"

(United States, the EEC, Japan and the NIEs + ASEAN) and that the framework for the integration of its production activities will have to be based on the realignment of technological systems now under way in the NIEs and the ASEAN countries—a realignment which is having a direct impact on the effort to change Latin America's production patterns.

If a general trend towards a reduction of trade barriers within the framework of GATT occurred, then an increase in trade would be possible, especially in view of the following factors: the NIEs' recent move towards trade liberalization and the important potential of this market, which has not yet been fully explored; the fact that the NIEs have a higher import coefficient than such developed countries as the United States and Japan; and the increase in complementarity to be expected as progress is made towards more complete vertical (inter-sectoral) and horizontal (intra-sectoral) integration of production.

V. FROM TRADE INTEGRATION TO A NEW TYPE OF INTEGRATION OF PRODUCTION IN THE PACIFIC BASIN

Up to the early 1980s it was commonly believed, first, that Latin America's trade with South-east Asia would grow less rapidly than its trade with developed countries owing to competition from Southeast Asian countries that are rich in natural resources (e.g., Thailand, Malaysia and Indonesia) and, second, that greater economic cooperation between these two regions was therefore not feasible.

Events in ASEAN during the final years of the 1980s proved, however, that the growth of commerce is increasingly determined by trends in intra-industry trade. Although it is true that until the early 1980s the inter-sectoral complementarity between Japan and the NIEs, on one side, and ASEAN, on the other, was the linchpin of vertical integration in the Asian-Pacific region, from the mid-1980s onward intra-sectoral complementarity has come to play an increasingly important role in that region's horizontal integration. As was said earlier, the expansion seen during that period in intra-industry trade flows between the NIEs and ASEAN was the result of the former's investments in the latter's manufacturing sector.

These events have direct implications for the effort to change Latin America's production patterns. After all, less than a decade ago, conditions in many countries of the Asian-Pacific region were less conducive to a transformation of production patterns than in many Latin American countries. Today, however, these Asian countries' economic development outlook is radically different: Malaysia is the world's largest producer of semiconductors; Thailand has become a paradigm of development by virtue of its ability to combine the growth of natural resource-based industries with the development of its electronics industry and has taken up the leadership position in ASEAN; Indonesia boosted the percentage of manufactures in its total exports from under 5% in 1980 to nearly 40% in 1990; the Philippines is regaining its political stability and hopes to find its way on to the Asian economic growth path with the help of a mounting inflow of FDI; and China's "sleeping giant" economy is beginning to wake up. All these Asian countries except the Philippines grew at an average pace of between 7% and 10% per year in the 1980s. Furthermore, the fact that the Philippines was an exception to this rule suggests that geographic proximity is not always a decisive factor in gaining access to a process of rapid economic growth.

The common denominator for all these Asian economies that grew so rapidly between 1979 and 1989 is that they carved out a position for their economies in the world market by creating new competitive advantages rather than by relying on the traditional sort of comparative advantages. It may be supposed that the changes to be made in Latin America's production patterns should incorporate this same sort of "upward and onward" approach which is so characteristic of the technology of the third industrial revolution.

An analysis of the Asian experience suggests some guidelines for such an effort. First, the change in the ASEAN export mix brought about by its shift from the primary to the manufacturing sector was associated not only with FDI from Japan and the United States, but also with a greater flow of FDI from the NIEs. There may thus be reason to believe that the increased flow of NIE investment into Latin America, which has been directed primarily to its manufacturing sector, may help to expand Latin America's intra-industry trade with South-east Asia. A considerable increase in such trade has already been seen in, for example, Mexico, Colombia and Chile.

In this era of economic globalization, an increase in investment prompts an increase in trade flows. In the case of the NIEs, because of their need to raise the technological content of their products in order to remain competitive, the recycling of technology is carried out in countries having lower production costs. Thanks to this relocation, the ASEAN countries were blessed with the lion's share of NIE-source FDI during the second half of the 1980s. The data for 1991, however, indicate that FDI in the ASEAN countries is now growing more slowly, which the experts attribute to shortcomings in their infrastructure, rising costs (chiefly wages) and over-investment, i.e., a level of investment that exceeds these countries' production capacity and is thus fueling inflation. This demonstrates that although geographic proximity, along with ethnic identify, is still important—as is commonly asserted in connection with the Chinese "diasporas" in Hong Kong, Singapore and Malaysia—it is not the only determinant. Today, NIE investment tends to flow to whatever country in the world offers the best competitive opportunities in production and trade. Latin America is no exception, as is demonstrated by the fact that the Republic of Korea's investments in the region more than doubled during the second half of the 1980s.

NIE-source FDI differs from other types of FDI in the following ways: first, the pace at which it recycles technology is among the fastest in the world—owing to the double "push" it gets from the NIEs' efforts to catch up with Japan while the ASEAN countries try to catch up with them—and encompasses everything from labour-intensive to technology- and human capital-intensive technologies; second, as a consequence of the above, this FDI is made on the "cutting edge" of competition between Japan's highest-technology activities and the ASEAN countries' greater capacity for technological endogenization (Ernst and O'Connor, 1992); and third, both the trajectory of strategic change in NIE technological and industrial development and the way in which it is being accomplished suggest what the future course of development of technology-intensive products is likely to be and serve as a frame of reference for developing countries such as those of ASEAN and Latin America as they take decisions regarding the positioning of their technical and industrial activities within the world economy. There is no question but that the ASEAN countries benefited from this strategic frame of reference during the 1980s, as may be inferred from Malaysia's policy of "looking eastward" (Onn, 1989), which has sparked imitative measures in Indochina (especially Vietnam) and in the islands of the Pacific (Alagh, 1989; Choo and Ali, 1989; Schlosstein, 1991).

Moreover, as we have been saying throughout this article, the liberalization of Asian-Pacific trade is spreading from the export processing sector to other activities and is coupled with the deregulation of commodity prices, wages, interest rates and exchange rates. Consequently, production bases could expand, in a geographic sense, throughout the region. And this, with the support of increased investment in the Asian-Pacific region, has swelled intraregional (from Japan and the NIEs) and interregional (with the United States) trade flows based on competitive advantages. Thus, in considering the possibility of the linkage of the Latin American economies under the terms of the Enterprise for the Americas initiative (and the North American free trade area), we must also consider the possible linkages entailed by regional and hemispheric integration, *vis-à-vis* integration within the framework of the Pacific Basin.

For example, Japan/ASEAN and NIE/ASEAN, NIE/China and United States/ASEAN production linkages with the North American market hint at new types of production relations between, for instance, the NIEs and Latin America (at present such a relationship exists only with Central America) and ASEAN and Latin America. So long as Japan does not act as a substitutive recipient of the products generated by the above-mentioned production linkages, the North American market will continue to be of vital importance for exports of manufactures. Under these circumstances, the global extension of the production chain from South-east Asia to Latin America could be a feasible option in view of the Latin American region's proximity to the main market for such exports, the United States.

On the other hand, if an inward-looking regional Asian economic bloc were to be formed—such as the East Asian Economic Caucus (EAEC) proposed by Prime Minister Mahattir of Malaysia in 1990, which would include Japan, the NIEs, ASEAN, China, Myanmar and Vietnam but would exclude the United States, Canada, Australia and New Zealand—it could inhibit Latin America's participation in the integration of the Pacific Basin. Fortunately, in view of the characteristics of the Asian-Pacific production and trade structure within the context of the Pacific Basin, many Asian countries are opposed to this introverted type of regionalization. In other words, since the United States is—at least for the time being—[13] an irreplaceable economic linchpin for intra-Pacific integration, this means that if Asian regionalization is carried far enough, it will inevitably lead to fuller globalization of the Pacific Basin. This became evident at the Asia-Pacific Economic Cooperation Council meeting in Seoul in 1991, when China, Taiwan and Hong Kong joined this group, previously made up of the United States, Canada, Japan, the Republic of Korea, Singapore, the ASEAN countries, Brunei, New Zealand and Australia (making a total of 15 participants). Clearly, the possibility of Latin America's incorporation will be one of the tasks of the 1990s.

In summary, within the framework of intra-Pacific cooperation, Latin America has two options: it can join the group of Pacific Basin countries by means of inter-sectoral specialization, or it can achieve integration through the intensification of intra-industry trade with the Asian countries. All the indications are that it would be "easier" for Latin America to accomplish this through inter-sectoral economic cooperation. However, if broader variables are taken into consideration—such as the globalization process, the third industrial revolution, the realignment of technical/industrial systems, and the "catching up" path to integration, then intra-industry integration appears to be the best option. This task must be accomplished in order for the region to change its production patterns (ECLAC, 1992); in other words, the success of Latin America's economic development effort will increasingly depend upon the new economic configuration emerging in the Pacific Basin, which is the epicentre of the economic globalization process and of the realignment of technical/industrial systems at the world level.

NOTES

1 Singapore and Brunei are also permanent members of ASEAN. For the purposes of this study, however, Singapore is grouped with the Asian NIEs and Brunei is not considered, since its economy is too small to have any major influence on the performance of ASEAN.

2 For our purposes here, the Asian-Pacific region includes Japan, the NIEs, the ASEAN countries, China, Australia and New Zealand, while the Pacific Basin includes the above plus the United States, Canada and Latin America.

3 In the UNIDO study, the value θ for changing production patterns is defined as:

$$\text{Cos } \theta = \frac{\Sigma_i(t) \cdot {}_i(t-1)}{\sqrt{[\Sigma_i(t)^2] \cdot [\Sigma_i(t-1)^2]}}$$

where $_i(t)$ is the share of the total value of the manufacturing aggregate in year t that is accounted for by activity $_i$. The value θ is interpreted as the angle between two vectors $_i(t-1)$ and $_i(t)$, measured in degrees. Thus, the maximum theoretical value is 90 degrees (see UNIDO, 1991).

4 The Grubel-Lloyd index is expressed as follows:

$$I_{gl} = \frac{\Sigma_i\Sigma_j\Sigma_k[(X_{ijk} + M_{ijk}) \cdot (X_{ijk} - M_{ijk})]}{\Sigma_i\Sigma_j\Sigma_k[X_{ijk} + M_{ijk}]} \cdot (100)$$

where X_{ijk} denotes exports of product $_i$ by country $_j$ to country $_k$ and M_{ijk} represents imports of product $_i$ by country $_j$ from country $_k$. The greater the extent of intra-industry trade, the closer I_{gl} will be to I (Grubel and Lloyd, 1975).

5 As is generally known, there have been two booms in Japanese FDI: one between 1969 and 1972, and the other between 1985 and 1989. The first upturn had three causes: i) the revaluation of the yen following the collapse of the Bretton Woods system in 1971; ii) the Japanese Government's deregulation of FDI; and iii) the 15% annual increase in Japanese wage levels during the early 1970s. These three factors explain why there was such a large outflow of Japanese investment during the 1969–1972 period. Most of this investment went to developing countries, since investors were seeking locations with low labour costs, and within such countries, the bulk of investment funds went to labour-intensive industries such as textiles and electrical machinery.

6 On the subject of regional cooperation in the Asian-Pacific area, see ESCAP, 1991, chap. IX, pp. 331–369. See also CTC, 1991.

7 In using the term "import-substituting endogenization" we are seeking to emphasize the distinctive traits of the industrialization process now under way in the ASEAN countries. Their original model has been the experience of the NIEs, which were able to generate an "endogenous core of technical progress" oriented towards exports of manufactures. Even though this concept does not depart from the fundamental concepts of import-substituting industrialization, the two modalities do differ in terms of the processes resulting from their actual implementation in, for example, South-east Asia and Latin America.

8 On the subject of FDI in the electronics sector in Malaysia and Thailand, see Lim and Fong, 1991.

9 Except in the case of Hong Kong, which at the start of the 1980s maintained a vertical intra-industry trade link with ALADI (ALADI exported ships and boats while Hong Kong exported watches and clocks).

10 The exception here was commerce between Singapore and ALADI, which as of 1990 involved three types of trade: intra-sectoral trade in primary products (mainly semi-finished goods), inter-sectoral trade, and vertical inter-industry trade (Singapore supplies colour television sets and ALADI provides photographic film, plates and paper).

11 We do not feel that the results of this new pattern will affect our hypothesis regarding the relationship between Latin America and the NIEs.

12 This statement is based on the following line of reasoning. When intra-industry trade predominates, the reallocation of resources takes place chiefly among the companies in the same industry, rather than between different companies in different industries; it follows that, all other factors being equal, an intra-industry adjustment will therefore be less costly than an inter-industry adjustment. Moreover, the changes in income distribution brought about by the liberalization of trade will be less dramatic if the industrial adjustment is based primarily on intra-industrial, rather than inter-industrial, specialization (Fukasaku, 1992).

13 As noted in the introduction to this article, Japan is already one of Latin America's largest markets. What we are suggesting here, however, is that in the new global economic order that is taking shape as we approach the year 2000, the United States will continue to play a predominant role in the globalization of the Pacific Basin.

BIBLIOGRAPHY

Alagh, Yoginder K. (1989): The newly industrializing economies and the developing Asian and Pacific region: a view from South Asia, *Asian Development Review,* vol. 7, No. 2, Manila, Asian Development Bank (ADB).

Chen, Edward K. Y. (1989): Trade policy in Asia, Seiji Naya (ed.), *Lessons in Development: a Comparative Study of Asia and Latin America,* Washington, D.C., International Center of Economic Growth (ICEG).

Choo, Hakchung and Ifzal Ali (1989): The newly industrializing economies and Asian development: issues and options, *Asian Development Review,* vol. 7, No. 2, Manila, ADB.

CTC (United Nations Centre on Transnational Corporations) (1991): *World Investment Directory,* vol. 1, New York.

ECLAC (Economic Commission for Latin America and the Caribbean) (1991): *Latin American Trade and Growth: Some Unanswered Questions* (LC/R.1027), Santiago, Chile, Statistics and Projections Division.

────── (1992): *Social Equity and Changing Production Patterns: an Integrated Approach* (LC/G.1701 (Ses.24/3)), Santiago, Chile.

Ernst, Dieter and David O'Connor (1992): *Competing in Electronics Industry: the Experience of Newly Industrializing Economies,* Paris, Organization for Economic Co-operation and Development (OECD), Development Centre.

ESCAP (Economic and Social Commission for Asia and the Pacific) (1991): *Industrial Restructuring in Asia and the Pacific. In Particular with a View to Strengthening Regional Co-operation,* Bangkok, United Nations, March.

Fukasaku, Kiichiro (1992): *Economic Regionalization and Intra-Industry Trade: Pacific-Asian Perspectives. Technical papers, No. 53,* Paris, OECD.

GATT (General Agreement on Tariffs and Trade) (1992). *International Trade 90-91,* vols. I and II, Geneva.

Grubel, Herbert and P.J. Lloyd (1975): *Intraindustry Trade: The Theory and Measurement of International Trade in Differentiated Products,* London, Macmillan.

Hugues, Helen (1989): Catching up: The Asian newly industrializing economies in the 1990s, *Asian Development Review,* vol. 7, No. 2, Manila, ADB.

Lim, Linda Y.C. and Pang Eng Fong (1991): *Foreign Direct Investment and Industrialization in Malaysia, Singapore, Taiwan and Thailand,* Paris, OECD, Development Centre.

Makino, Noboru (1991): Jejo unoen young won ha da *(The Eternity of the Manufacturing Sector: The New Industrial Society vs the Post-Industrial Society),* original Japanese text translated into Korean by Son Se Il, Ed. Chung Kye Institute.

Murphy, Kevin M., André Schleifer and Robert Vishny (1989): Industrialization and the big push, *Journal of Political Economy,* vol. 97, No. 5, Chicago, IL, The University of Chicago.

Nohara, Takashi and Mitsuhiro Kagami (1991): *Development of Asian-Pacific trade and its implications for NAFTA,* document presented at the Seminar on the Free Trade Agreement between Mexico, the United States and Canada and its Possible Effects on the Pacific Basin, 25-27 November, Mexico City, El Colegio de México.

Oman, Charles (1984): *New Forms of International Investment in Developing Countries. The National Perspective.* Paris, OECD, Development Centre, October.

Onn, Fong Chan (1989): Malaysia: in pursuit of newly industrializing economy status, *Asian Development Review,* vol. 7, No. 2, Manila, ADB.

Schlosstein, Steven (1991): *Asia's New Little Dragons: the Dynamic Emergence of Indonesia, Thailand and Malaysia,* Chicago, IL, Contemporary Books.

UNIDO (United Nations Industrial Development Organization) (1989): *Industry and Development: Global Report 1988/89,* Vienna.

────── (1990): *Industry and Development: Global Report 1989/90,* Vienna.

────── (1991): *Industry and Development: Global Report 1990/91,* Vienna.

────── (1992): *Industry and Development: Global Report 1991/92,* Vienna.

CHAPTER **24**

GLOBAL FEMINIZATION
THROUGH FLEXIBLE
LABOR

Guy Standing

International Labor Organization, Geneva

1. INTRODUCTION

The 1980s might be labeled the decade of labor deregulation. It has also marked a
renewed surge of feminization of labor activity. For reasons to be considered, the types
of work, labor relations, income, and insecurity associated with "women's work" have
been spreading, resulting not only in a notable rise in female labor force participation,
but in a fall in men's employment, as well as a transformation—or feminization—of
many jobs traditionally held by men. It is no coincidence that this shifting pattern has
been closely related to an erosion of labor regulations. There has been *explicit* deregulation, whereby formal regulations have been eroded or abandoned by legislative
means, and *implicit* deregulation, whereby remaining regulations have been made less
effective through inadequate implementation or systematic bypassing.

To elaborate on this thesis, it is necessary to trace the emergence of the supply-side
politico-economic agenda that has dominated policy making in most of the world in
the 1980s. This agenda, it will be argued, has led to a series of changes in women's
economic roles, increasing their use as workers but weakening their income and
employment security in both low-income industrializing and industrialized countries.
By focusing on the global spread of flexible labor practices and the supply-side "structural adjustment" development strategy, it will be argued that existing policies—and
the data on which they are based—are inadequate, and that specific alternatives offer
far more hope of benefiting working women and men in the coming decade.

Reprinted with permission from *World Development,* 17, 7 (1989), pp. 1077–1098, Elsevier Science Ltd,
Pergamon Imprint, Oxford, England.

2. LABOR IMPLICATIONS OF SUPPLY-SIDE ECONOMICS: THE CULT OF INSECURITY

For most of the twentieth century, and particularly after 1945, the dominant develop-ment model can be described as "social adjustment," with a redistributive welfare state as the long-term objective. It was to be achieved through a diverse array of labor rights, protective legislation, and other forms of security, and a larger role for the pub-lic sector in economic and social policy. In the 1970s that model ran into trouble, first losing its legitimacy and then being displaced from intellectual hegemony by the early 1980s.[1]

In considering the changing economic situation and its effects on women, six developments have been critical. First, whereas previously trade took place between countries or regions with similar costs (or labor rights) and was a fairly small per-centage of most countries' Gross National Product (GNP), in the 1970s the global economy became far more open to internationally competitive trade, as various low-income countries became producers of exports and potential exports. A second factor was that by the late 1970s sustained Keynesian demand management had become associated with rising inflation, and internationally had contributed to excessively rapid lending. The result was indebtedness, as deflationary policies were adopted in the industrialized countries in the mid- and late-1970s. A third related factor was that the welfare state became perceived by some as "crowding out" productive invest-ment and by others as ineffectual in redistributing the benefits of growth. A fourth factor was what some have called technological stalemate, whereby labor-saving innovations became more predominant than product innovations, which led to a more intense search for cheap-labor forms of production. The subsequent "technological revolution," associated with microelectronics and satellites, was a fifth eroding fac-tor, since it gave rise to more managerial options and to more intensive international competition, partly because the new technology was so internationally mobile. Finally, the growth of open unemployment accompanying these developments weak-ened workers' bargaining power and put welfare states under tremendous pressure.

Although one could quibble with these stylized facts, essentially they combined to give intellectual and political legitimacy to an ideology of supply-side economics, where market mechanisms and cost competitiveness were given overwhelming emphasis. This crystallized in a global strategy of "structural adjustment and stabiliza-tion," and has been linked to radical changes in labor relations in most parts of the world economy.

This argument does some injustice to nuance in the interest of brevity. But in essence, the supply-side model entails a global strategy of growth based on open economies, with trade liberalization as vital and export-led growth as the only viable development strategy. As such, cost competitiveness is elevated to utmost significance, and from that, labor market regulations become "rigidities," which raise costs and thus harm living standards and employment. An irony is that in the 1980s many of the pre-vious objectives of economic growth, notably a whole set of labor and social rights, became perceived increasingly as costs and rigidities.

A few key features of the supply-side agenda are worth noting. The goal of "rolling back the State" means focusing on rewarding merit and combining fiscal reform with a minimalist rather than "redistributive" welfare state; poverty alleviation and universal social security are no longer priority issues. A consequence of increasing "selectivity" or "targeting" has been that fewer people are entitled to state benefits in industrialized countries. This has given a boost to "additional worker" effects (pushing more women into the labor market), the informal or "black economy," and precarious forms of working, since those without rights to benefits have been obliged to find whatever income-earning work they can. It is scarcely an exaggeration to say that the leaders have become the led; international competition from low-income countries where labor costs and labor rights are least developed has been instrumental in weakening the rights and benefits of those in the lower end of the labor market of many industrialized economies.[2] In effect, within labor markets income security has been eroded, and economically and socially vulnerable groups have been most likely to suffer.

The supply-side economic model rejects neocorporatist State planning and incomes policy, whereas faith in market mechanisms is absolute. One consequence is that the strength of "insiders" in the labor market has also been eroded, notably unionized (male) wage workers. That in turn has strengthened the pressure for labor market deregulation, weakening both employment security legislation and customary practices preserving job security. In country after country, including many developing countries, governments have taken steps to make it easier for employers to dismiss workers or reduce the size of their labor force, as, for example, in the Philippines, where legislation is planned to remove most enterprises from coverage by various labor laws. By such means, they have encouraged a more flexible approach to job structures, making it easier to alter job boundaries and the technical division of labor. This has reduced the job "rights" of existing employees and allowed greater resort to so-called external labor markets. Because the employment, income, and job security of insiders has weakened, employers have been able to substitute lower-cost labor. In many cases, job flexibility also reduces the premiums that employers usually attach to workers' employment continuity and on-the-job experience.

A further aspect of supply-side economics concerns income security directly. Governments have been urged to remove or weaken minimum wage legislation and institutional safeguards, on the grounds that such wages reduce employment. One might question the logic of that argument, but among the likely consequences of a weakening of protective machinery is a growth of very low-wage employment, consisting of jobs paying "individual" rather than "family" wages. Research shows that when low-wage jobs spread, it is women whose employment in them increases. Even in many developing countries where minimum wage legislation was only weakly enforced, it at least set standards and had demonstration effects. Deregulation sanctions and encourages bad practices.

An aspect of the supply-side agenda has been the stabilization and structural adjustment policy packages urged on many developing countries by the International Monetary Fund (IMF), the World Bank, and other international and national donor agencies, largely in the wake of the debt crisis. To assess what is happening and likely to happen to women in the labor market, we must appreciate what this orthodox strategy involves.

First, overwhelming emphasis is put on trade liberalization and the need to orient production to export-led industrialization. This entails cutting subsidies to domestic "nontradeable" production, often including staple food items (with such effects as lengthening women's working day). It has meant macroeconomic deflation to reduce domestic consumption or living standards, so as to shift resources to export industries, again often having adverse effects on low-income women who produce basic consumer goods. The supply-side agenda has meant a focus on cost-cutting international competitiveness, in practice implying a strenuous search for ways of lowering unit labor costs, which of course means that firms will find ways of employing workers prepared or forced to take low-wage jobs. Finally, it has also meant a spread of new production techniques, usually as part of the search for least-cost methods. This, no doubt, has increased the scope for more refined technical divisions of labor. Thus, for such conventional supply-side reasons as improved efficiency and renewed growth, governments have been pressed to remove labor market regulations, cut the public sector, and privatize public enterprises and services, all of which in one way or another have eroded employment security and led to a reduction of employment.

In the context of this global supply-side perspective, corporate management strategy has evolved in clear directions in the past decade. Stimulated by high unemployment, by new technology, by more aggressive international competition (notably from Japan and the newly industrialized countries), by deregulation and the erosion of union strength, and by the desire to overcome the uncertainty induced by the international economic instability, enterprises everywhere are devising means of reducing the fixed costs of labor. There is a global trend to reduced reliance on full-time wage and salary workers earning fixed wages and various fringe benefits. Companies and public sector enterprises in both developed and developing economies are increasingly resorting to casual or temporary workers, to part-timers, to subcontracting, and to contract workers. In the process, they further erode employment and income security.

Particularly in industrialized countries there has been a shift in these directions and from direct to indirect forms of employment, including subcontracting from larger to smaller units of production, "networking," and a revival of homeworking and other forms of outwork. But these trends have also been occurring in industrializing economies, where until recently it had been presumed that the long-term trend of industrial development would involve a shift from unregulated, informal labor to secure, regular employment. The global pursuit of flexible low-cost labor has encouraged industrial enterprises everywhere to reduce their fixed wage labor force, make payment systems more flexible, and use more contract workers, temporary labor, and out-sourcing through use of homeworking or subcontracting to small informal enterprises that are not covered by labor or other regulations and that bear the risks and uncertainty of fluctuating business. That is the context in which to assess the changing labor market position of both men and women in many parts of the world.

At the same time, industrial enterprises have been introducing modern technologies that have been associated with changing skill and job structures. The debate over the "de-skilling" or upgrading effects of modern technology is unresolved, but the evidence seems to support two pertinent trends. The use of craft skills learned via apprenticeships and prolonged on-the-job learning has declined; such crafts have traditionally been dominated by male "labor aristocracies." Second, there is a trend toward skill polarization, consisting of an elite of technically skilled, high-status specialist workers possessing higher-level institutional qualifications, coupled with a larger mass of technically semi-skilled production and subsidiary workers requiring minor training typically imparted through "modules of employable skill," that is, by short-term courses of a few weeks or even by on-the-job learning. This polarization places greater reliance on external than on internal labor markets, since more workers are in "static" rather than "progressive" jobs involving little or no prospect of upward mobility, or firm-specific returns to on-the-job continuity. This, of course, weakens one reason traditionally given for discrimination against women: that women have a higher probability of labor turnover. If there were less benefit from on-the-job learning and experience, this presumption would not matter, even if true. Indeed, for many monotonous jobs high turnover may have a positive benefit for employers, since maximum efficiency may be reached after only a few months, thereafter plateauing or declining. This is one reason for resorting to temporary employees, for job-rotating, or for collapsing job classifications into more broadly based job clusters such that workers can be shifted from one set of tasks to another from time to time. But this represents a growth of job insecurity to accompany the income and employment insecurity that have marked the growth of more flexible labor markets.

3. GLOBAL FEMINIZATION?

In the 1960s, economists commonly argued that the growth of the modern sector in developing countries contributed to the marginalization of women as workers.[3] But the distinction between "modern" and "traditional" or "formal" and "informal" sectors has become much less clear, if it ever was clear. In various respects, trends discussed in the preceding section represent widespread informalization of labor in most sectors. This may well explain the absolute and relative growth in the use of female labor around the world and a "feminization" of many jobs and activities traditionally dominated by men. Although the concepts and measurements of labor force participation are notorious, the international data strongly suggest that women's participation has been rising while male equivalent participation has been falling (see Tables 24-1 and 24-2).

First, outward-oriented development strategies, based on export-led industrialization, have brought a rapid growth of low-wage female employment. Indeed, no country has successfully industrialized or pursued this development strategy without relying on a huge expansion of female labor. And in export processing zones of many industrializing countries it is not uncommon for three-quarters of all workers to be women.

The reasons are well known. Much of the assembling and production line work is semi-skilled and low paid; young women, particularly in the newly industrialized countries (NICs) in Asia, have been socially and economically oppressed for so long that they have low "aspiration wages" and low "efficiency wages."[4] They are prepared to work for low wages for long work weeks, normally without agitating to join unions, and when their productivity declines after a few years of youthful diligence they are replaced by new cohorts.

Typically, in countries that have pursued the export-led industrialization strategy recommended as part of structural adjustment programs, the female labor force partic-

TABLE 24-1
VARIATIONS IN ADULT[a] MALE AND FEMALE ACTIVITY RATES IN THE 1980s

	Men, rose		Men, fell		Men, no change	
	Developing	Developed	Developing	Developed	Developing	Developed
Women, rose	Barbados Chile Egypt Guam Jamaica Peru Senegal Thailand 22%[c]	Canada South Africa 10%	Algeria (−) [b]Costa Rica (−) Ecuador (−) Israel (−) Korea, Rep. (0) Kuwait (+) Netherlands Antilles (0) Singapore (+) Trinidad and Tobago (0) 25%	Australia (0) Finland (−) France (0) Fed. Rep. of Germany (0) Greece (+) Italy (+) Japan (0) Netherlands (+) Norway (+) Portugal (−) Spain (+) United States (+) 60%	Honduras Indonesia Mauritius Pakistan Puerto Rico Seychelles Sri Lanka Venezuela 22%	Austria Denmark New Zealand Sweden 20%
Women, fell	Cameroon (−) Argentina (+) 6%	0	Haiti 3%	0	0	0
Women, no change	Bolivia Panama Philippines 8%	Iceland 5%	Bahrain Guatemala 6%	Ireland 5%	Hong Kong Syrian Arab Rep. Zambia 8%	0

[a] Age coverage is 15–64 except as follows: 15–49: Cameroon (1985), Syrian Arab Republic (1984); 15–59: Costa Rica, Panama, Seychelles (1985), Sri Lanka (1981), Thailand, Zambia; 16–59: Guam; 16–64: Puerto Rico, Norway, Spain, Sweden; 18–64: Israel (1980); 20–59: Algeria (1980), Finland (1980), Italy, Jamaica, South Africa.
[b] Symbols in parentheses indicate net direction of change, male and female combined: (+) Net increase; (−) Net decrease; (0) Zero net change.
[c] Percentage of countries in the category.
Source: ILO, Yearbook of Labor Statistics (various years).

TABLE 24-2
VARIATIONS IN ACTIVITY RATES[a] (PERSONS 15–64), 1980s BY PERCENTAGE
OF COUNTRIES WITH EACH TYPE OF CHANGE, TOTAL AND BY SEX

Population	Type of change	Developing countries	Developed countries
Women	Increased	69	90
	Decreased	8	0
	No change	22	10
	Total	99	100
Men	Increased	36	15
	Decreased	33	65
	No change	31	20
	Total	100	100
Total	Increased	61	65
	Decreased	22	15
	Compensated[b]	8	20
	No change	8	0
	Total	99	100

[a]For national definitions of activity rates and labor force participation, refer to the ILO *Yearbook of Labor Statistics*. For a critique of the relevance of this concept in developing countries, see Standing (1981). Figures have been rounded.
[b]Activity rates of men and women changed in the opposite directions, involving a fall in male and a rise in female activity rates, so that they approximately offset each other.

ipation rate is high and has risen. In such countries the female share of nonagricultural employment has grown (see Tables 24-3 and 24-4). And it is likely that the female share of production worker employment is also relatively high and rising. The available figures generally bear this out, even though in some countries, particularly in Latin America, the relationship may have been weakened by the debt-induced recession (see Table 24-5).

These limited data are still inconclusive, although they scarcely support Boserup's thesis that with industrial development women would be pushed out of production work. In support of an alternative thesis that trade liberalization and export-led industrialization tend to increase female employment, it has been observed that the female proportion of productive wage workers rose in all countries that had set up large Export Processing Zones—the Dominican Republic, El Salvador, Honduras, Hong Kong, Republic of Korea, Malaysia, Mexico, the Philippines, Puerto Rico, Singapore, Sri Lanka, and Thailand.[5] Productive employment, of course, covers only direct wage earners, and there is growing evidence that, for reasons discussed in the previous section, much of the employment connected with export industries, as well as others, is indirect if not concealed altogether. A very good example comes from a study in Mexico that should be replicated in many more countries. This study showed that production was organized through a complex process of subcontracting, with the labor-intensive, lower-paid, more informal activities being put out to women workers, many of whom were not recorded in the workforce.[6] This is a classic instance of "modern" production relying on

TABLE 24-3

PERCENTAGE SHARE OF WOMEN IN NONAGRICULTURAL EMPLOYMENT,[a] 1975–87

Country	Source[b]	1975	1980	1985	1986	1987
Africa						
Botswana[c]	(3)	19	24	30	31	n.a.
Egypt[d]	(1)	10	11	16	n.a.	n.a.
Gambia[e]	(3)	10	12	15	15	n.a.
Kenya	(3)	n.a.	17	20	21	21
Malawi	(3)	7	9	16	14	n.a.
Mauritius	(3)	20	26	35	36	36
Niger[c]	(2)	4	4	7	7	n.a.
Swaziland	(3)	22	26	31	31	n.a.
Tanzania[d]	(3)	12	17	17	n.a.	n.a.
Zimbabwe	(3)	13	13	16	n.a.	n.a.
Latin America and the Caribbean						
Barbados[c,f]	(1)	42	43	44	45	45
Bermuda	(3)	n.a.	43	46	47	47
Brazil[c,f]	(1)	33	35	38	39	n.a.
Chile	(1)	n.a.	34	36	36	35
Colombia	(1)	37	39	38	39	40
Costa Rica	(1)	n.a.	30	34	34	35
Cuba	(3)	n.a.	36	41	41	n.a.
Haiti	(4)	66	71	n.a.	n.a.	n.a.
Jamaica	(1)	46	48	48	48	n.a.
Netherlands Antilles[g]	(4)	35	n.a.	37	37	n.a.
Panama[e]	(1)	38	39	40	40	40
Paraguay	(4)	39	35	n.a.	n.a.	n.a.
Peru	(1)	n.a.	n.a.	n.a.	n.a.	40
Puerto Rico	(1)	35	38	39	40	40
Trinidad and Tobago	(1)	28	31	34	34	34
Venezuela	(1)	32	32	32	32	32
Asia and the Pacific						
Bahrain[e,h]	(4)	n.a.	10	11	n.a.	n.a.
Cyprus[c]	(4)	30	33	35	35	36
Hong Kong	(3)	40	39	40	40	41
India	(3)	10	11	12	12	n.a.
Indonesia[c]	(1)	37	34	37	39	n.a.
Israel	(1)	33	37	39	39	40
Jordan[d]	(3)	14	17	23	n.a.	n.a.
Korea, Rep.	(1)	33	35	38	38	39
Malaysia	(1)	n.a.	30	33	34	n.a.
Philippines	(1)	47	46	48	48	47
Singapore	(1)	30	35	36	38	38
Sri Lanka	(3)	18	18	25	28	n.a.
Syrian Arab Rep.[d,e]	(1)	8	9	9	n.a.	n.a.
Thailand	(1)	42	42	44	44	n.a.

[a]Coverage refers to total employed except as follows: Employees—Botswana, Gambia, Kenya, Mauritius, Niger, Swaziland, Tanzania, Zimbabwe, Cuba, India, Jordan, Sri Lanka; All persons engaged—Malawi, Bermuda, Hong Kong. Figures have been rounded.

[b](1) Labor force survey; (2) Social insurance statistics; (3) Establishment surveys; (4) Official estimates.

[c–h]Figures were not available for the years specified, and those of the closest years were given as follows: [c]1975 = 1976; [d]1985 = 1984; [e]1980 = 1979; [f]1980 = 1981; [g]1975 = 1977; [h]1985 = 1982.

Source: ILO, *Yearbook of Labor Statistics* (various years).

TABLE 24-4
PERCENTAGE[a] OF WOMEN AMONG MANUFACTURING EMPLOYEES, DEVELOPING
COUNTRIES, 1975–87

Country	Source[b]	1975	1980	1985	1986	1987
Africa						
Botswana	(3)	n.a.	17	27	24	n.a.
Kenya	(3)	n.a.	9	10	10	10
Mauritius	(3)	49	56	62	59	57
Swaziland	(3)	16	26	27	31	n.a.
Tanzania	(3)	10	9	n.a.	n.a.	n.a.
Zimbabwe	(3)	8	7	7	n.a.	n.a.
Latin America						
Costa Rica	(1)	n.a.	27	30	30	31[c]
Cuba	(3)	n.a.	26	31	31[d]	n.a.
Mexico	(2)	n.a.	21	25	26	n.a.
Panama	(1)	25	n.a.	24	26	n.a.
Puerto Rico	(3)	48	48	49	48	48
Venezeula	(3)	21	24	n.a.	n.a.	n.a.
Asia and the Pacific						
China	(4)	n.a.	40	40	41	41
Hong Kong	(3)	52	50	50	50	50
India	(3)	9	10	10	9	9
Jordan	(3)	12	10	n.a.	n.a.	n.a.
Korea, Rep.	(3)	n.a.	45	42	42	n.a.
Singapore	(1)	41	47	46	47	48
Sri Lanka	(3)	32	31	39	45	n.a.
Thailand	(1)	41	42	45	45	n.a.

[a]Figures have been rounded.
[b](1) Labor force survey; (2) Social insurance statistics; (3) Establishment surveys; (4) Official estimates.
[c]Prior to 1987: including mining.
[d]Prior to 1986: including water.
Source: ILO, *Yearbook of Labor Statistics* (various years).

what is depicted as "premodern," or informal, labor relations. The pressure to avoid overhead and other indirect labor costs in the quest for competitiveness has surely accentuated such tendencies.

Other aspects of the structural adjustment strategy have also affected women's employment. Consider three: the pursuit of lower wages (and greater wage differentials and wage flexibility), labor market deregulation, and the cutback of the public sector, through either general public expenditure contractions or privatization.

Not only do women workers receive lower wages in general, but they are more prepared to work for lower "aspiration wages" for well-known reasons. The erosion of minimum wage legislation, or of its implementation, and the sanctioning of a general lowering of wages are likely in themselves to lead to a substitution of women for men, partly because men are less willing to work for sub-family wage rates and partly because they would be expected to respond to lower wages by reducing their "effort

TABLE 24-5

PROPORTION OF WOMEN AMONG PRODUCTION WORKERS (ALL STATUSES[a])
(Percentage, 1970s and Most Recent)

Country	Source[b]			Country	Source[b]		
Africa				Belize	C	1970	1980
Botswana	C	1981	1984–85		C	10	13
	LFSS	7	23	Costa Rica	C	1973	1987
Cameroon	C	1976	1982		HS	12	20
	OE	12	8	Chile	C	1970	1986
Egypt	LFSS	1975	1984		LFSS	12	15
	LFSS	2	6	Dominican	C	1970	1981
Ghana	C	1970	1984	Republic	C	22	14
	C	35	45	Ecuador	C 10%	1974	1982
Morocco	C 10%	1971	1982		C	15	12
	C 5%	16	23	El Salvador	C	1971	1980
Mauritius	C	1972	1983		HS	19	24
	C	6	21	Guatemala	C	1973	1981
Seychelles	C	1971	1981		C	14	12
	OE	10	15	Guyana	LFSS	1977	1980
South	Cs	1970	1985		C	15	9
Africa	C	7	13	Haiti	C	1971	1982
Tunisia	C	1975	1980		Cs	43	32
	LFSS	24	22	Jamaica	LFSS	1976	1986
					LFSS	26	23
Latin America and the Caribbean				Mexico	C	1970	1980
Bahamas	HS	1970	1980		C	24	17
	C	11	12	Panama	C	1970	1986
Barbados	HS	1977	1987		LFSS	11	12
	LFSS	22	26	Paraguay	C 10%	1972	1982
					C	28	18

[a]Includes conventional categories: own-account workers, employees, employers, and unpaid family workers. Figures have been rounded.

[b]C = Census; C . . . % = Census: sample tabulation, size specified; Cs = Census: sample tabulation, size not specified; HS = Household survey; LFSS = Labor force sample survey; OE = Official estimates.

Source: ILO, Yearbook of Labor Statistics (various years).

bargain." So, employers are inclined to hire women more readily. While the promotion of female employment may be desirable, this is surely not the way to achieve it.

As for labor market deregulation, it has affected the economic position of women in various ways. Consider the principle of "equal pay for equal work." As of late 1988, 108 countries had ratified the International Labor Organization's (ILO's) Equal Remuneration Convention No. 100. Among those that have not ratified it are a disproportionate number of countries that are pursuing an export-led industrialization strategy, especially those with large export processing zones: Hong Kong, the Republic of Korea, Malaysia, Mauritius, Singapore, Sri Lanka, and Thailand. Other countries, like India, have different legal minimum wages for men and women in certain industries, on the official presumption that women do the less arduous work, which is far from the case. Besides such loopholes in official regulations, any informalization of labor

TABLE 24-5
PROPORTION OF WOMEN AMONG PRODUCTION WORKERS (ALL STATUSES[a])
(Percentage, 1970s and Most Recent) *(continued)*

Country	Source[b]			Country	Source[b]		
Peru	C	1972	1981	Korea, Dem.	C 10%	1970	1976
	C	14	11	People's Rep.	LFSS	24	30
Puerto Rico	LFSS	1975	1988	Korea, Rep.	C	1975	1987
	LESS	20	24		LFSS	28	31
St.-Pierre and	C	1974	1982	Malaysia	C	1970	1980
Miquelon	C	7	5		C	17	22
Trinidad and Tobago	LFSS	1978	1986	Nepal	C	1971	1976
	LFSS	13	12		HS	9	21
Uruguay	C 12%	1975	1985	Philippines	C	1970	1987
	C	20	18		HS	33	22
Venezuela	C 25%	1971	1987	Singapore	C	1970	1987
	HS	10	10		LFSS	19	29
Virgin Islands	Cs	1970	1980	Sri Lanka	C	1971	1981
(United Kingdom)	C	2	5		C	15	13
Asia and the Pacific				Syrian Arab Republic	LFSS	1970	1984
Bahrain	C	1971	1981		LFSS	5	4
	C	0	1	Thailand	LFSS	1970	1980
Bangladesh	C	1974	1984		LFSS	29	30
	C	5	17	Oceania			
Brunei	C	1971	1981	Cook Islands	C	1976	1981
	C	3	4		C	22	15
Hong Kong	Cs	1976	1986	Fiji	C	1976	1986
	C	37	33		C	4	10
India	C	1971	1981	French Polynesia	C	1977	1983
	C	12	13		C	8	17
Indonesia	C	1971	1985	Samoa	C	1976	1981
	HS	27	26		C	6	9
Israel	Cs	1972	1987	Tonga	C	1976	1986
	LFSS	12	13		C	5	13
Jordan	OE	1976	1979				
	C	3	1				

relations can be expected to undermine whatever protective effect regulations might have on equal wages. Accordingly, more labor market flexibility implies implicit deregulation, and could be expected to lead to a widening of sexual earnings inequality. The available data, for what they are worth, suggest a more complex story. While the sex differential is relatively great in economies pursuing export-led industrialization, the differential shows signs of narrowing in Korea, unlike other NICs (see Table 24-6). Not too much should be read into those figures, since money earnings are only part of total compensation; a loss of entitlement to fringe benefits is most closely associated with labor flexibilization.

It is often claimed that regulations designed to protect women workers generously contribute to discrimination against them by employers. This has been reported from countries where, for example, maternity leave benefits are paid mainly or wholly by the

TABLE 24-6
FEMALE EARNINGS AS A PERCENTAGE OF MALE EARNINGS IN MANUFACTURING (Selected Developing Countries)[a]

Country	1975	1976	1977	1978	1979	1980	1981	1982	1983	1984	1985	1986	1987
Africa													
Egypt	68	75	63	92									
Kenya	66	77	56	54	70	63	59	76	80	77	76	73	63
Tanzania		79	88	82	82	79	78						
Swaziland	71	66	78	71	83	81	82	81	61	55	72	73	
Latin America													
El Salvador	90	86	81	82	79	81	86	89	77	84	82		
Netherlands Antilles							51	66	65	67	68	64	
Asia													
Burma	89	82	103	87	89	86	89	91	92	94	99	86	
Cyprus	47	49	50	48	50	50	54	56	55	56	56	56	58
Hong Kong								78	79	81	79	78	76
Jordan				54	60	58	64						
Korea, Rep.	47	49	45	44	44	45	45	45	46	47	47	49	50
Singapore						62	62	63	64	65	63	56	58
Sri Lanka						81	87	82	71	69	72	78	71

[a]Blank spaces indicate no available data. Figures have been rounded.
Source: ILO, Yearbook of Labor Statistics (various years).

employer[7]; the problem is apparently less acute in countries in which the benefits are funded through worker and employer contributions to the social security system.[8] Nevertheless, informalization of employment reduces labor costs in that respect and means that fewer women workers receive such benefits. Legislation targeted at relatively large industrial enterprises stipulating that they must provide crèches has also been cited as deterring the recruitment of women wage workers.[9] Once again, explicit and implicit deregulation may mean more employment of women, but on less favorable terms. Mothers of young children are left to find alternative—and probably costly or inadequate—child care arrangements. Or they may take informal, low-income work that can be combined with childrearing, or drop out of the labor force altogether. In effect, labor deregulation of this kind means transferring labor costs from the firm, or even the State, to the individual workers, most of whom are in the poorer strata of society.

In various countries regulations have long existed to limit the working time of women workers or to prohibit night work, as stipulated by ILO Convention No. 89 of 1948. These regulations have been criticized by supply-side and structural adjustment theorists on the grounds that they reduce employment of the "protected" groups. It is interesting that 62 countries have ratified the Night Work (Women) Convention, but whereas 26 of those did so in the 1950s and 22 did so in the 1960s, only 10 ratified in the 1970s and only 4 in the 1980s; five have denounced it in the past eight years. With the spread of shift work, often done by women, governments have not only moved away from such regulations, but have failed to implement those that exist or have granted exemptions to various industries, often those operating in export zones, as in Malaysia, Mauritius, and Pakistan.[10]

The shift away from large centralized workforces toward more decentralized, flexible systems implies less emphasis on those behavioral characteristics that traditionally have been cited as justification for discrimination against the recruitment of women, such as women's alleged higher absenteeism and labor turnover.[11] Indeed, in the desire to avoid overhead and other nonwage labor costs, the decentralization—including putting out, contract labor, and subcontracting to subsidiary enterprises—typically puts more pressure on workers to cut their labor supply "price." We should, therefore, give more attention to the mechanisms of control that force workers to labor with high intensity for miserably low incomes, an issue discussed more fully in the next section.

What about the implications for skill formation? Both deregulation and "flexibilization" have accelerated the erosion of notions of vocational skill and of job security (traditionally defended by demarcation rules). Within many industries, skill polarization favors the feminization of employment. Traditionally, sexual inequality *within* the labor market has been perpetuated through sexual segregation in entry to specific jobs, covering both the level of recruitment and subsequent promotion. However, if a growing proportion of all "jobs" have no promotion potential—that is, are "static" rather than "progressive"—then one mechanism intensifying sexual inequality is reduced.[12] Moreover, the well-known "overcrowding" explanation of low female earnings—due to women being crowded into a smaller number of sex-typed jobs—may well lose force if the jobs being whittled away are predominantly "male jobs." Of course, this might be offset if male workers proceeded to bump out women from other slots or took the major share of the new jobs. However, the latter seems unlikely to happen.

Although much less so in Latin America than in other regions, not only do the data suggest that women are being substituted widely for men in various occupational categories, including manufacturing and production work in countries as diverse as Ghana, Swaziland, Bangladesh, and Costa Rica (see Tables 24-4 and 24-5), but there are good reasons to suppose that substitution will continue as a long-term trend.

This is further supported by a remarkable change between the 1970s and 1980s. In the earlier decade, women's unemployment rates rose relative to men's in many more countries than where the reverse occurred. In the 1980s, in the vast majority of both industrialized and developing countries, female unemployment declined relative to male, so that in a substantial number their open unemployment rate became lower than the male equivalent. This marked a tremendous shift.[13]

Some observers attribute substitution to growing labor force attachment of women, some to improvements in schooling or access to training, some even to the beneficent effects of antidiscrimination legislation. But it has almost certainly more to do with the feminization of labor, a desire to have a more disposable (or flexible) labor force, with lower fixed costs, and so on. In other words, for women there will be *less* problem of job entry. As so often, among developing countries the Republic of Korea has been at the forefront of change in this respect; there, 24 of the 30 jobs formerly barred to women have been recently opened to them.

This decrowding process extends to both manual and nonmanual employment. Traditionally, women have comprised a comparatively large proportion of all professional and technical workers in developing countries, largely because of their prominence in professions such as teaching and nursing. Traditionally, with development the growing professions were in industry, where in most parts of the world women have been underrepresented. However, it seems to be a global trend that enterprises have been restructuring to erode middle management, following an era when this category had mushroomed almost everywhere. Now, many middle-management functions are being delegated either to clerical workers, most of whom are women (except in some South Asian countries), or to production workers. Whether one interprets the trend as one of upgrading or reskilling or simply intensifying clerical work, the long-term trend is likely to be a further substitution of women for men. It would be a mistake to think this trend has relevance only for industrialized countries such as the United States. It is further reason for believing that the importance of sexual segregation per se in perpetuating sexual inequality in the labor market will decline. Policy attention should be focused elsewhere.

Before turning to that issue, it is worth reiterating that for manual production jobs, technological and organizational changes have tended to create a jobs polarization, with an elite of technicians (or "crafticians") in specialist jobs coexisting with a growing mass of semiskilled flexi-workers and a dwindling number of jobs for technically unskilled workers. This may increase female industrial employment—because semi-skilled, static jobs are reserved largely for women—but the disappearance of low-wage jobs at the bottom may hit the most vulnerable groups of all; impoverished, uneducated women are left to "crowd" into those jobs, pushing down their wages even further. As a remedial policy, it may be too late or impractical to stress basic education for such women. Basic education may be part of the long-term policy answer, but for currently uneducated women forced to compete for the low-paying, unskilled jobs in industry, minimum wage and other forms of protective regulations and/or strong trade unions representing their interests are surely essential. Those who wish to see such regulations dismantled need to offer some more viable alternative.

In the more flexible labor markets envisaged for the 1990s, the attendant insecurities will be intensified by a web of dependency relations. Decentralized or individualized relationships between workers and employers, or between workers and impersonal enterprises or middle-men, give much greater scope to exploitative and oppressive forms of control, including debt bondage, outright coercion, and casual beck-and-call labor relations. This is where policy will have to focus.

Along with deregulated and decentralized labor in industry, a key theme of the orthodox structural adjustment strategy is "privatization." This has severe implications for women. Not only are women's wages and employment conditions better on average in the public sector than in the private, but wage differentials between men and women are smaller in the public sector.[14] There is *prima facie* reason to suppose, therefore, that women's wages will fall absolutely and relatively by virtue of cutbacks in the public sector or as a result of privatization. But the extent of decline will vary. The tendency will be relatively less likely where there is a so-called policy of cutting public expenditure with a human face, so that smaller cuts are made in social programs like health and education, sectors where women public employees are concentrated.

A complicating aspect in assessing the impact of privatization and public expenditure cuts is that the incidence of redundancy may hit women disproportionately hard, especially where they make up a relatively large proportion of less secure, nontenured posts or marginal positions. Careful study of this phenomenon is still required, since we do not know which groups suffer relatively from the direct effect.[15] However, it is interesting to note that the scanty data available do indicate that in many developing and industrialized countries, women not only have accounted for a greater share of public sector than private sector employment—with notable exceptions, such as India—but their share of public employment has, if anything, grown in recent years (see Table 24-7).

The indirect effects are even harder to unravel. In countries where men have predominated in the public sector, as in most of Africa, they will make up the great majority of redundant workers. Will those men drive women out of small businesses or those few private-sector wage jobs that women have obtained? Ex-public-sector workers often have received large redundancy payments with which they could acquire petty capital and drive out existing businesses, many of which are dominated by women.[16] This tendency may be compounded by the contacts men gained from their long presence in the public sector.

In short, women have good reason to fear the marginalization effects of privatization, at least in Africa. But this is not all. Falling public employment may, as in Peru, lead to more women entering the low-income labor market as "additional workers" because of higher male and female unemployment.[17] If they enter an already crowded sector, one can predict that average incomes will decline, along with the security of participating in such activities.

TABLE 24-7
FEMALE SHARE OF PUBLIC SERVICE EMPLOYMENT,[a] SELECTED DEVELOPING COUNTRIES (Percent)[b]

Country	1975	1976	1977	1978	1979	1980	1981	1982	1983	1984	1985	1986	1987
Africa													
Benin			13				15						
Botswana			19			20		35	37		36		
Burkina Faso	16									20		38	
Burundi							41						
Ethiopia								20		22		23	
Kenya	18	18	19	19	18	18	19						
Malawi							12	12	11	12	12		
Morocco									29	28	28	29	
Nigeria			11	11	11	13							
Rwanda									32		33		
Swaziland			27	27	26		25	31	30	32	33	34	
Latin America and the Caribbean													
Barbados							43	45	42				
Bolivia					24	24	24	24		24			
Brazil							23						
Cuba	30	31	30	30	31	33	33	37					
Jamaica					48	50	48	48	38	39	39		
Panama				46	47			41	43	43	43	45	
Trinidad and Tobago								32				34	
Venezuela					41	41	42	43		43	44	45	46

Asia and the Pacific

Country											
Bahrain											
Cyprus	20	28	29	30	31	32	32	32	32	31	33
Hong Kong	21	21	22	24	23	25	28	28	28	33	29
India						10			11		
Indonesia			23	23	23	24	27	27	29	29	30
Kuwait							31	31	34		35
Qatar					11	12	19	21	20		
Syrian Arab Republic						20			24		

Source: Bahrain: Statistical Abstract, 1985; Barbados: "Labour Force Report," 1975–83; Belize: "1980–81 Population Census of the Commonwealth Caribbean"; Benin: "Revue de Statistique et de Legislation du Travail," July 1984; Bolivia: "Anuario de Estadisticas del Trabajo,: 1982; Botswana: "Statistical Bulletin," regular publication; 1977: Employment Survey 1982; Brazil: "Anuario Estatistico do Brasil," regular publication, 1986, government reply; Burkina Faso: "Annuaire Statistique du Burkina Faso," October 1984; Burundi: Government reply, ILO. General Report, JCPS, 3rd Session, 1983; Cuba: "Anuario Estadistico de Cuba," 1986; Cyprus: 1977–82, "Statistical Abstract," 1985 and 1986; 1983–86; "Labour Statistics Bulletin," December 1986; Ethiopia: Government reply; Hong Kong: "Hong Kong Monthly Digest of Statistics," regular publication; India: "Pocket Book of Labour Statistics," regular publication, data supplied to ILO, government reply; Indonesia: Statistical Yearbook of Indonesia, regular publication; Jamaica: "The Labour Force," regular publication; Kenya: "Statistical Abstract," regular publication; Kuwait: Government reply; Malawi: "Reported Employment and Earnings Annual Report," regular publication; Mali: ILO research data; Mexico: "Encuesta Continua Sobre Ocupacion, 2nd Semester 1978"; Montserrat: "9th Statistical Digest," 1984; Morocco: "Annuaire Statistique du Maroc," regular publication; Nigeria: Digest of Statistics, regular publication; Pacific Islands: "Quarterly Bulletin of Statistics," 1980; Panama: "Situacion Social; Estadisticas del Trabajo," regular publication; Paraguay: "Encuesta de Hogares por Muestra: Mano de Obra," 1977; Peru: "Censos Nacionales de Poblacion y de Vivienda," July 1984; Qatar: "Annual Statistical Abstract," regular publication; Reunion: "Economie de la Reunion, Panorama," 1987; Rwanda: Government reply; Swaziland: "Employment and Wages," regular publication; Syrian Arab Rep.: "Statistical Abstract," regular publication; Trinidad and Tobago: "Quarterly Economic Report," regular publication; Venezuela: "Encuesta de Hogares por Muestreo," regular publication.

[a] Public service employment in the total public sector except: Central government—Burundi, Ethiopia, Mali, Rwanda, Kuwait, Bahrain; Government—Botswana, Morocco, Mexico, Trinidad & Tobago; Federal government—Nigeria; Public administration—Brazil.

[b] Blank spaces indicate no available data. Figures have been rounded.

TABLE 24-8
SHARE OF WOMEN IN SELF-EMPLOYMENT (NONAGRICULTURAL SECTORS) IN SELECTED DEVELOPING COUNTRIES
(Percentage, 1970s and Most Recent)[a]

Country	Source[b]			Country	Source[b]		
Africa				**Asia and the Pacific**			
Ghana	C	1970	1984	Bangladesh	C	1974	1984
	C	73	77		C	3	8
Seychelles	C	1971	1981	Hong Kong	Cs	1976	1986
	OE	23	19		C	16	20
				India	C	1971	1981
Latin America and the Caribbean					C	9	8
Costa Rica	C	1973	1987	Indonesia[c]	C	1971	1985
	HS	13	27		HS	24	41
Chile	C	1970	1986	Korea, Dem.	C	1970	1976
	LFSS	28	28	People's Rep.	LFSS	25	39
Dominican Republic	C	1970	1981	Korea, Rep.	C	1975	1987
	C	23	27		LFSS	29	35
Ecuador	C	1974	1982	Kuwait	C	1975	1985
	C	25	22		C	1	1
El Salvador	C	1971	1980	Nepal	C	1971	1976
	HS	48	65		HS	13	31
Guatemala	C	1973	1981	Singapore	C	1970	1987
	C	29	25		LFSS	13	19
Mexico	C	1970	1980	Sri Lanka	C	1971	1981
	C	28	33		C	12	9
Peru	C	1972	1981	Thailand	LFSS	1970	1980
	C	31	29		LFSS	40	44
Puerto Rico	LFSS	1975	1988	United Arab	C	1975	1980
	LFSS	16	15	Emirates	C	1	1
Venezuela	C	1971	1987	**Oceania**			
	HS	17	23	Fiji	C	1976	1986
					C	15	23
				French Polynesia	C	1977	1983
					C	31	33
				Samoa	C	1976	1981
					C	30	27

[a]Figures have been rounded.
[b]C = Census; Cs = Census: sample tabulation, size not specified; HS = Household survey; LFSS = Labor force sample survey; OE = Official estimates.
[c]Includes agriculture.
Source: ILO, *Yearbook of Labor Statistics* (various years).

Finally, stabilization and adjustment strategies have involved deflation of aggregate demand, leading to higher unemployment and more widespread resort to informal survival responses among the poor, particularly in urban areas. Women have long been concentrated in such activities, both as petty traders or "pre-entrepreneurs" and as dependent workers, whether in familial enterprises or as wage workers. In eras of stagnation and recession, these activities will normally become more precarious, and the vulnerable groups will be hit hardest. However, in many countries women are well entrenched in self-employment and in small-scale production and trade. Indeed, although there is little time-series information available, the data suggest that in most countries for which such statistics are available, women have comprised a growing proportion of the self-employed (see Table 24-8). Whatever else the data might suggest, they do not indicate that women have been squeezed out of own-account activities by recent economic developments. What such activities include, and conceal, is quite another matter, and may represent a deterioration in the labor market position of women in general. Unfortunately, the data are rather unhelpful in this regard, which brings us to a crucial issue for the further understanding of what is happening to women in developing countries, and thus, what policies donors and planners should consider for the near future.

4. DATA PRIORITIES

Much has been made of the "invisibility" of women workers in conventional labor force statistics. It is time that we concentrated on the distortions provided by the available data on women's labor activity. This issue is particularly acute in the context of what appears to be a growing diversity of forms of labor relations.

The basic starting point is that the conventional "work status" classification (used tentatively earlier) is grossly deficient. Too many types of labor relations are compressed into the four statuses: own-account, employer, unpaid family worker, and wage worker. To understand the mechanisms of labor force participation, data are needed on different forms of *control.*

While we cannot go into details here, seven critical aspects of control are insufficiently covered by conventional labor statistics. The first is *control over self,* over one's own labor power; bonded laborers or serfs have no control over their choice of activity, and as we know many women are extremely vulnerable in this respect in many parts of the world. Second, there is *control over labor time.* Many women have no choice over whether they work the number of hours that would suit their particular needs and, as in typical export processing zones, have to accept 60 hour workweeks, drop out of the workforce, or lose a disproportionate part of their income for failing to fulfill the required quota.[18] The number of workers who are in such onerous situations, where, for example, a flexible payment system means that they would forfeit their bonus share of income for failing to work the full, long workweek, is unknown.

Third, there is *control over means of production,* such as land, tools, and spaces in which to work. Women usually have little or no control in that respect, and may have to rent machines or have their labor status determined by others such as middlemen who own equipment. Although some attention has been paid to women's lack of control over means of production and its consequences for incomes and work activity, the full range of control mechanisms should receive far more attention, for they have adverse consequences for equity, efficiency, and economic growth.

Fourth, there is *control over raw materials,* inputs purposely transformed into output. Many women, in particular, are exploited by monopolist merchants or manufacturers who charge them excessive amounts for their material so that their net income is much less than it may appear from piece payments.

Fifth, there is *control over output.* If a woman carpet maker were allowed or enabled to sell her wares herself, she could often do far better than when she is forced to accept payment for it from relatives, a merchant, or a manufacturer. No decent study of working women should leave out this dimension of the production process.

Sixth, there is *control over proceeds of output.* This usually means control over the income derived from work. Crude earnings data can be far more misleading indices of net disposable income for some groups than for others. In many situations, women workers receive very little net disposable incomes for themselves or for their immediate needs because relatives or intermediaries deduct large parts of it. Thus, if a woman receives only 20 percent of the income from her work because some intermediary takes the remainder, her welfare would scarcely be improved by policy assistance focused on raising her gross income (through training, for instance), since most of her poverty would be "structural." It is for such reasons that policy makers should focus far more on the multiple mechanisms of control.

Seventh, there is *control over labor reproduction.* This too is critical, and refers to the ability to develop and maintain the woman's own "skills" and work capacity. As such, it is not the same as control over one's labor power. In the case of labor reproduction, the concern is primarily with workers' capacity and with education and training. Many impoverished women have so little control over their working lives that their working *capacity* is debilitated by what they are forced to do. They may seem to earn a reasonable income today, but it is earned only by loss of future earning capacity. Although ample anecdotal evidence on this process exists, far more analytical and policy attention should be focused on this aspect of work.[19] That aside, control over labor reproduction concerns the skill development potential of specific activities. Most workers—and the vast majority of women, in particular—are trapped in work activities in which they have no possibility of developing skills. The controls and constraints may consist of the type of work or external mechanisms. In some places, for example, social norms dictate that to remain in the social structure women do the gathering and weeding, sewing, dairying, and animal husbandry; they have no access to other skills. How are such behavioral patterns reproduced? Although the social pressures are crucial, efforts should be made to identify the direct mechanisms. More statistical information is needed on such forms of control.

In sum, if more relevant policies are to be developed and if international donors are to increase their effectiveness, then analyses and data gathering should concentrate not just on the relative "invisibility" of working women, but also on the distortions of conventional data in other, even more crucial respects. Access to and control over means of production are often cited as vital for raising the autonomy and real living standards of women. This is surely correct, but should not lead to neglect of other aspects of the production and distribution process, where access and control are equally important.

5. LABOR VULNERABILITY

If there is an international feminization of labor relations, is there a corresponding growth of vulnerability, precariousness, and insecurity? The notion of vulnerability is complex, and it may be useful to proceed by recognizing that specific groups are vulnerable by sector, by social stratification, and by labor status.[20]

Women are, first, vulnerable to income and employment insecurity by virtue of the *sector* of their involvement, and their relative disadvantage varies by sector. In most low-income countries women in agriculture and rural areas generally are the most desperately affected, particularly on plantations. Outside agriculture, as the data reviewed earlier showed, women comprise a disproportionately large number of employees of small-scale enterprises, precisely where vulnerability to bankruptcy and chronic impoverishment are usually greatest. Often women in those units are unpaid or severely underpaid, a problem made worse by implicit and explicit labor deregulation of small-scale businesses; sex-related income differentials tend to be much greater in small units, perhaps because larger enterprises are affected by formal regulations and social exposure that lessen wage discrimination. This suggests that efforts to promote small-scale enterprises—often in preference to large concerns—are likely to worsen women's economic vulnerability unless countervailing measures are implemented.

Women have been extensively employed by multinational export-oriented enterprises, often in export processing zones. Critics have been vociferous in highlighting the adverse consequences, although other observers point out that conditions are often much worse for women not employed by such multinationals. Anybody who has been into, say, modern electronics factories in Southeast Asia, has to recognize the force of the latter argument. Nevertheless, one must also recognize the forms of vulnerability to which women workers are exposed in such enterprises. First, they are employed largely in semiskilled, static jobs with little or no chance to develop skills or aptitudes that they could use subsequently. They are then vulnerable to a loss of vital social skills and working capacity, because they must work excessively long workweeks and often face exposure to health-sapping working conditions. This problem has been compounded by the overwhelming preference of employers for young single women who are expected and encouraged to leave their jobs after a few years or when they marry. Compared to other workers, their employability declines fairly quickly, making them vulnerable to aging earlier than most people. Have policy makers really addressed the question: what then?

Such industries are also vulnerable to international trade fluctuations and to productive investment and disinvestment decisions taken in another part of the globe. Enterprises may have to lay off production workers with little warning—one more reason that they prefer women.[21]

The other major sectoral dimension is the public-private sector one, since as noted earlier, women workers fare relatively better in public sector enterprises. If privatization schemes are to proceed, international agencies and others must be persuaded to introduce measures that protect the incomes and employment conditions of women workers affected by the change. Too few privatization initiatives have paid attention to the vulnerability of the workers who lose the relative security of public sector employment.

Finally, there are those sectors in which women are vulnerable to "invisibility." In most parts of the world women represent large proportions of the workforce in agricultural small-holdings, in family farms or businesses, and in petty trade, all of which tend to be inadequately recorded or recognized when policies are being devised or reformed. Perhaps in international and national policy debates this invisibility problem is less than used to be the case. But everyone should be wary about the issue becoming passé, for adequate solutions have not yet been found to the conceptual and statistical problems.

Women are also peculiarly vulnerable by virtue of their *social status,* besides their systematic oppression in most cultures of the world. Social stratification takes many forms, some of which relate to "life-cycle" events, some to other stratifying social influences. One common stratifying influence is migrant status. Women make up a majority of migrants in many developing countries, and many of them travel alone in search of work. Too often this aspect has been neglected in women's studies or in donor programs. Women migrants and, most of all, women labor circulants are acutely vulnerable. They tend to gain entry to labor markets only by taking the most precarious jobs and have little prospect of upward mobility. The plight of such women is desperate. In India, for example, it has been widely reported that hard-pressed rural families send wives and daughters to cities to support them through prostitution.[22] And in Thailand thousands of young village girls flock to Bangkok to work as prostitutes until their "charms fade," often in notorious conditions.[23] Other young women enter urban labor markets through domestic employment, for little pay, often unknown to any labor authority or conveniently overlooked. Far more attention should be given to the mechanisms of control used in the migration process and to the kinds of policies that could ameliorate the vulnerability of what are, typically, ill-educated teenagers.

Two other dimensions of social vulnerability deserve even more emphasis than they have received in recent years. Many women, probably the vast majority, are vulnerable to poverty and labor market marginalization by virtue of their dependency status in families. Others, however, are primarily or wholly responsible for their household income and subsistence. They tend to be among the poorest of the poor. In Costa Rica, for example, although only 16 percent of urban households were recorded as being headed by women, more than 37 percent of indigent (the poorest) urban households were female headed.[24] In the Sudan, a quarter of all low-income households were headed by women, half of whom were over 50.[25] In Calcutta, the poorer the household, the more likely it was to be dependent on female earners. Across the world the story is essentially the same: single mothers, widows, and migrant women dependent on their own resources are the most vulnerable of all, not only to poverty, but to exploitation and labor marginalization.

Finally, workers are vulnerable by virtue of their *labor status.* Earlier sections of this paper have depicted the international feminization of labor as closely associated with growing labor flexibility, by which secure, protected well-paid wage employment is once again being displaced by other labor relations. One can predict that when enough data have been generated on these issues, the two trends will be shown to be linked closely. As it is, women are most vulnerable to insecure labor status employment. For instance, they are more likely to be hired as marginal, casual wage workers. In some countries, the introduction, strengthening, or enforcement of minimum wage regulations has led to the substitution of women casual workers for male permanent workers. In Zimbabwe, for example, underpayment persisted through a conversion of permanent to casual, contract or piece-rate workers, since they were not covered by the regulations; this was most likely to happen in small-scale enterprises.[26]

In India, women are also concentrated in casual wage labor, and relatively high female unemployment has been attributed in part to women being able to obtain only short-term casual jobs. Elsewhere, women wage workers are more often than men classified in that peculiar category, "permanent casuals," and thereby unable to acquire legal entitlement to benefits or statutory forms of protection.

Beyond recognized wage labor, evidence is mounting that women are increasingly utilized as "outworkers." Particularly with respect to this heterogeneous category one needs to focus on the diverse mechanisms of control and exploitation (bearing in mind that "control" and "exploitation" are not synonymous). Valuable research projects are in progress on "putting out" industries and other forms of outwork. But so far, few effective strategies to enhance the status and living standards of such workers have been implemented.

Of course, many "self-employed" women are far from the image that the term conventionally implies. At the very least, statistically, own-account workers should be separated from contract or piece-rate outworkers, whose net earnings tend to be minimal, and even negative in slack periods or in periods of illness or family mishaps. These contract workers are the most "flexible" labor force of all, bearing a large share of the risk of business fluctuations. In many countries, the international recession in the 1980s and the adoption of stabilization and structural adjustment policies led enterprises to shift from direct wage employment to such forms of labor.[27] As noted earlier, the renewed growth of such indirect, flexible labor will necessitate a considerable policy reformulation in the near future if the previous international trend toward social protection is to be revived.

6. CONCLUSION

It would be pretentious to pose a full policy and research agenda on the basis of this brief overview. Nevertheless, some leading questions do suggest themselves. First, if the era of labor flexibility persists, will women and men be pushed far more into labor statuses in which they face multiple forms of control? To answer that question, we need to review critically the type of statistics that are collected, and consider alternative concepts that could identify potential points of policy intervention. Second, to what extent are earnings or income data valid measures of women's net disposable income, that is, the cash or other income that they could use for their own needs? Taking account of deductions by intermediaries, including relatives, it is likely that a large and growing proportion of women workers receive much lower net incomes than the scanty data on earnings suggest. Third, whither labor regulations in labor markets characterized by informality and flexible work statuses? If regulations on, for instance, wages, safety, and maternity leave are being eroded or bypassed, how could workers organize to obtain socially desirable benefits, and how could governments assist? Fourth, the same questions arise with respect to social security, especially bearing in mind that even in many industrialized economies a dwindling proportion of women actually are entitled to existing social security.

Fifth, whither antidiscriminatory legislation? Discrimination is a particularly insidious process; even if one form of discrimination is partially tackled, other forms are likely to grow, which is why it needs to be attacked on many fronts at once. It is possible that the sexual segregation of jobs is becoming *relatively* less important, and that career paths and differential access to fringe benefits and bonus payments is becoming relatively more critical.[28]

Sixth, has too much attention been devoted to schooling and training as the avenue to higher incomes, labor market security, and mobility? Besides the likelihood that most forms of labor market inequalities are structural, it is possible that in recruiting for a wide range of jobs, screening devices other than formal schooling are becoming more important, while prior vocational training is scarcely needed for access to most jobs. This is because a more developed technical division of labor and growing emphasis on semiskilled labor must surely diminish the relevance of vocational training. Of course we should not dismiss automatically the need for training policies, but "training" should be put in its proper context—a minor component of any strategy to improve women's economic and labor market status.

Seventh, how could unions protect women in the more flexible labor markets of the 1990s? Unless communal unionism develops in place of craft or industrial unions, protection of vulnerable groups will be partial at best and easily circumvented. Male-dominated trade unions must fully incorporate women and struggle for "women's issues" at least as strongly as for others; otherwise their collective strength will continue to dissipate.

Finally, when will donor agencies and national policy makers turn to that most neglected of groups, older women? Already a majority of the elderly (aged 55 or older) are in developing countries. Their marginalization in almost all respects is a somber specter, too often resulting in premature death, thereby concealing the seriousness of the process. With urbanization and industrialization, kinship support networks are being eroded, yet very few women workers have pension rights; nor do women have employment security or access to retraining or labor market assistance in times of recession or structural adjustment. If this paper made just one plea, it would be that international agencies should devote more resources to assisting older women workers, the growing number who will soon be in that category, and those pushed out of the labor force prematurely—the easily ignored "potential" workers in their 50s and 60s. Given today's flexible, insecure labor processes, and weakened social support systems, the needs of older women have never been greater.

These eight sets of issues are by no means exhaustive, but they do suggest some reordering of priorities. Although women may be gaining economically in some crude senses of that term, the crucial point is that feminization in the sense used here represents pervasive insecurity. Traditionally, women have been relegated predominantly to more precarious and low-income forms of economic activity. The fear now is that their increased economic role reflects a spread of those forms to many more spheres. That is scarcely what should be meant by progress.

NOTES

1 Standing (1988).
2 That is not an argument for cutting exports from industrializing economies, as some might claim.

3 Boserup (1983).

4 The "aspiration wage" is the level at which a person would be prepared to accept employment; the "efficiency wage" is the wage level at which a worker would work with optimum efficiency once in employment. Many people fail to make this distinction.

5 Anker and Hein (1986), p. 95.

6 Beneria and Roldan (1987).

7 For example, di Domenico (1983); Date-Bah (1986).

8 See, for example, Scott (1986).

9 International Center for Research on Women (1980).

10 See, for example, Dror (1984), p. 709.

11 Anker and Hein (1985).

12 Standing (1981).

13 An important caveat here is that the data do not include observations for many African countries. For those which have observations, the trend is in the same direction as that in other regions.

14 See, for example, Papola (1986). During the past decade of adjustment, private-public sector wage differentials have apparently narrowed or disappeared in many countries, particularly for "educated labor."

15 An official US study found that women were disproportionately affected by job cuts in the privatization of federal agency programs. Rein (1985), p. 132.

16 Collier (1988).

17 Scott (1986), especially p. 357.

18 See, for example, Fuentes and Ehrenreich (1983), p. 23.

19 See Standing (1981), chap. 4, for one review of evidence on this issue.

20 A more detailed discussion of these dimensions is presented in Standing (1987).

21 Lim (1985), p. 30. This was a joint UNCTC/ILO study.

22 Pandhe (1976), p. 52.

23 Phongpaichit (1982).

24 Pollack (1989).

25 ILO (1976), p. 70.

26 Shopo and Moyo (1986).

27 See, for example, Penouil and Lachaud (1986), pp. 37–38.

28 Relatively more attention should be paid to the factors that cause women to shift from male-dominated to female-dominated jobs rather than to those that cause initial sex segregation. See, for example, Jacobs (1983).

REFERENCES

Anker, R., and C. Hein. "Why Third-World Urban Employers Usually Prefer Men." *International Labour Review* 124, no. 1 (January–February 1985): 73–90.

Anker, R., and C. Hein, eds. *Sex Inequalities in Urban Employment in the Third World* (London: Macmillan, 1986).

Beneria, L., and M. Roldan. *The Crossroads of Class and Gender: Industrial Homework, Subcontracting and Household Dynamics in Mexico City* (Chicago: University of Chicago Press, 1987).

Boserup, E. *Women's Role in Economic Development* (New York: St. Martin's Press, 1970).

Collier, P. "African Public Sector Retrenchment: An Analytical Survey." WEP Labour Market Analysis Working Paper no. 27 (Geneva: ILO, November 1988).

Date-Bah, E. "Sex Segregation and Discrimination in Accra-Tema: Causes and Consequences." In R. Anker and C. Hein, eds., *Sex Inequalities in Urban Employment in the Third World* (London: Macmillan, 1986), chap. 6, pp. 235–276.

Deshpande, L. K. "Flexibility in the Bombay Labour Market." WEP Labour Market Analysis Working Paper no. 24 (Geneva: ILO, August 1988).

di Domenico, C. M. "Male and Female Factory Workers in Ibadan." In C. Oppong, ed., *Male and Female in West Africa* (London: George, Allen and Unwin, 1983).

Dror, D. M. "Aspects of Labour Law and Relations in Selected Export Processing Zones." *International Labour Review* (November–December, 1984): 709.

Fuentes, A., and B. Ehrenreich. *Women in the Global Factory* (New York: Institute for New Communications, South End Press, 1983).

International Centre for Research on Women. *Keeping Women Out: A Structural Analysis of Women's Employment in Developing Countries* (Washington: USAID, 1980).

International Labour Organisation. *Growth, Employment and Equity: A Comprehensive Strategy for the Sudan.* (Geneva: ILO, 1976).

Jacobs, J. "The Sex Segregation of Occupations and the Career Patterns of Women" (Harvard University, Ph.D. dissertation, May 1983).

Lim, L. *Women Workers in Multinational Enterprises in Developing Countries* (Geneva: ILO, 1985).

Pandhe, M. K., ed. *Bonded Labour in India* (Calcutta: Indian School of Social Sciences, 1976).

Papola, T. S. "Women Workers in the Formal Sector of Lucknow, India." In R. Anker and C. Hein, eds., *Sex Inequalities in Urban Employment in the Third World* (London: Macmillan, 1986), chap. 4, pp. 171–212.

Penouil, M., and J. P. Lachaud. "Le Secteur Informal et la Marché du Travail en Afrique Noire Francophone." World Employment Programme, Working Paper no. 37 (Geneva: ILO, 1986).

Phongpaichit, P. *From Peasant Girls to Bangkok Masseuse* (Geneva: ILO, 1982).

Pollack, M. "Urban Poverty and the Labour Market in Costa Rica." In G. B. Rogers, ed., *Urban Poverty in the Labour Market Access* (Geneva: ILO, 1989).

Rein, M. "Women in the Social Welfare Labor Market" (Berlin: Wissenschaftezentrum, Discussion papers 85–18, 1985).

Scott, A. M. "Economic Development and Urban Women's Work: The Case of Lima, Peru." In R. Anker and C. Hein, eds., *Sex Inequalities in Urban Employment in the Third World* (London: Macmillan, 1986), chap. 8, pp. 313–365.

Shopo, J., and S. Moyo. "Vulnerable Segments of the Labour Market in Zimbabwe" (ILO-SATEP, May 1986, mimeo.).

Standing, G. *Labour Force Participation and Development* (Geneva: ILO, 2d ed., 1981).

Standing, G. "A Labour Status Approach to Labour Statistics." World Employment Programme Working Paper no. 139 (Geneva: ILO, August 1983).

Standing, G. "Vulnerable Groups in Labour Processes." WEP Labour Market Analysis Working Paper no. 13 (Geneva: ILO, May 1987).

Standing, G. "European Unemployment, Insecurity and Flexibility: A Social Dividend Solution." WEP Labour Market Analysis Working Paper no. 3 (Geneva, ILO, July 1988).

CHAPTER **25**

PRIVATIZATION AND SOCIAL WELFARE

Robert Devlin

UN Economic Commission for Latin America and the Caribbean

I INTRODUCTION

The crisis of 1982—the worst in the region since the 1930s—detonated a process of radical economic policy change throughout Latin America. It also proved to be relatively unresponsive to traditional conjunctural stabilization and adjustment policies.[1] Moreover, its magnitude and protracted nature dealt a fatal blow to the dominant economic strategy in the region, which had been typically characterized by an emphasis on inward-looking import substitution and ample direct State intervention.[2] What emerged to take its place, gradually at first, but with ever greater intensity as the decade proceeded, was a new paradigm inspired by the traditional liberal market principles that were especially fashionable in some industrialized countries during the 1980s. Thus, the policy focus of most Latin American countries broadened so that adjustment and stabilization efforts included major neoconservative-oriented structural changes focusing on internal and external liberalization and deregulation and the promotion of a subsidiary role for the State in the domestic economy. One of the cornerstones of the new approach (baptised the Washington Consensus) is the privatization of public enterprises.[3]

This paper provides an overview of the privatization processes pursued in the region, and focuses on some socioeconomic dimensions of the process which have not been given much attention to date. The first section discusses the magnitude of the privatization processes in Latin America. In the next section, an analysis is made of some of the apparent motives behind the countries' decision to privatize. The third section focuses on one objective which has sometimes been too easily traded off in privatiza-

From *CEPAL Review*, #49 (April 1993).

tion processes—social equity—and suggests ways in which the net social benefits of the process could be enhanced. The last section presents some conclusions.

The subject of privatization in developing countries raises a vast number of potential issues which become still more complex when examined in the fast-moving context of individual countries. For this reason the overview is relatively general in its focus and selective in its content. It also should be mentioned that the comments made concentrate on divestiture, which so far has been the most prevalent privatization technique in the region.

II THE MAGNITUDE OF PRIVATIZATION PROCESSES

Public enterprises (PEs) have typically had a high profile in the economic activity of the region. Ironically, however, consistent and comprehensive data on the region's PEs are hard to come by. Their importance can nevertheless be illustrated by reference to a few countries. For instance, just before the crisis the value added by PEs as a percentage of GDP was about 5% in Brazil, 14% in Chile, 8% in Mexico and 30% in Venezuela. Likewise, the region's PEs were major investors in fixed capital, with their activity in this area often equivalent to a quarter or more of total gross investment (Table 25-1). Each country's story as regards the origin of its PEs is different, but in practically all cases there is a combination of factors related, among other things, to the deliberate promotion of investment and development, nationalization measures deriving from unexpected political or financial events, the support of macroeconomic stabilization objectives, and employment and distributional considerations.[4]

TABLE 25-1
LATIN AMERICA: SELECTED INDICATORS OF THE PARTICIPATION OF PUBLIC ENTERPRISES BEFORE THE 1982 CRISIS

	Value added as % GDP	Fixed investment as % of gross investment (1980)	Participation in domestic credit (1978)	Employment (% of total) (1980)
Argentina	4.6[a]	15.4	...	3.1
Brazil	4.7[b]	25.8[c]	11.2	3.0[d]
Chile	14.2[e]	15.8	...	20.4[c]
Colombia	2.6[a]	12.7	...	...
Costa Rica	...	23.2	12.8	...
Ecuador	...	21.1	...	...
Guatemala	1.1[a]	13.3[f]	...	...
Honduras	...	14.6[g]	...	...
Mexico	8.2[e]	23.1	18.9	...
Paraguay	3.1[a]	6.5[f]	...	...
Peru	...	10.4	26.4	...
Uruguay	...	18.3[f]	...	...
Venezuela	30.9[e]	35.7	1.6	...

Source: Nair and Felippides (1988); Floyd, Gray and Short (1984).
[a]1978–80 (factor cost). [b]1982 (market prices). [c]1981. [d]1982. [e]1980 (market prices). [f]1978–80. [g]1978–1979.

Data for a considerable number of the countries in the region indicate that just before the crisis the overall financial performance of the region's PEs was almost uniformly associated with heavy financing requirements (Table 25-2). The picture improves markedly for a few countries when the PEs' balances are adjusted for transfers between the firms and central government. Nevertheless, it is noteworthy that even after that adjustment important pre-crisis financing requirements were registered for the PEs of Argentina, Brazil, Colombia, Costa Rica, Ecuador (non-oil) and Mexico (non-oil).

During the crisis years PEs confronted a very complex operational environment as central governments tried to stabilize domestic prices and reduce the public sector's financing requirements. The serious fiscal problems induced adjustments in the region's PEs and a reduction of their demands for financing: between 1981–1982 and 1986–1987 the countries with initial deficits either lowered their negative balances or converted them into surpluses and, with the exception of Venezuela, those with initial surpluses increased their positive balances. Excluding Venezuela and the oil-producing PEs of Mexico and Ecuador, the total improvement in the PE balances of the countries

TABLE 25-2

LATIN AMERICA: SAVINGS AND DEFICITS OF PUBLIC ENTERPRISES, 1980–1981 AND 1986–1987[a]

(Percentages of GDP)

Country	D 1980–1981 (1)	D 1986–1987 (2)	D* 1980–1981 (3)	D* 1986–1987 (4)	DH (5)	Absolute variation in D* (6)=(4)-(3)
Argentina	-3.39	0.59	-4.92	-2.75	-3.21	2.17
Bolivia	0.10	-2.90	3.65	7.95	7.70	4.30
Brazil	-1.69	0.10	-3.10	-2.10	-4.22	1.00
Chile[b]	-1.33	0.78	5.47	10.33	11.93	4.86
Colombia	-2.00	-1.41	-3.16	0.08	-0.21	3.24
Costa Rica	-2.37	0.97	-1.55	3.46	4.11	5.01
Ecuador	-0.63	-1.77	4.60	4.09	4.46	-0.51
(Non-oil-exporters)	(-1.60)	(-0.55)	(-1.92)	(-0.67)	(-1.44)	(1.25)
Mexico	-1.30	0.25	1.49	4.62	3.53	3.13
(Non-oil-exporters)	(-1.57)	(-0.26)	(-6.22)	(-4.97)	(-5.77)	(1.25)
Uruguay	0.26	0.10	2.69	3.14	3.00	0.45
Venezuela	-2.33	-2.62	11.08	5.16	-0.05	-5.92
Total[c]	-1.48	-0.74	1.20	2.63	1.68	1.43
Subtotal[d]	-1.14	-0.32	-0.80	1.22	0.90	2.02

Source: ECLAC, Economic Development Division.
[a]The symbols used in this table are the following:
D = Total income less total expenditure.
D* = D – T (T = net transfers to central government, as registered in its accounts).
DH = D* plus difference in net capital account between 1980–1981 and 1986–1987.
[b]For the period 1986–1987, the values used were those for 1985, which is the last year for which figures are available.
[c]Simple average, excluding Chile.
[d]Simple average, excluding Chile, Venezuela and the petroleum enterprises of Ecuador and Mexico.

listed in Table 25-2 was equivalent to 2% of GDP. It should be noted, however, that while significant, the improved financial balance nevertheless had an artificial component because it included the effects of sharp and unsustainable cutbacks in investment activity. This is seen in column DH of Table 25-2, which calculates financial balances on the basis of pre-crisis investment levels.

Expenditure cutbacks and adjustments in scales of charges were initially the most important instruments for reforming the financial performance of PEs. However, sooner or later almost all of the countries in the region began to opt for more drastic reforms involving outright divestiture or liquidation of their PEs.[5] The scope of most of these privatization programmes has been extremely ambitious, including in almost all the cases major public services. The countries with the greatest experience in this respect are Chile and Mexico, followed by Argentina, Venezuela and Brazil.

Chile was the region's pioneer in privatization. In the period 1975–1982 the military government "reprivatized" more than 200 firms (mostly in the tradeable goods and finance sectors, and worth more than US$1.2 billion in total) which had been nationalized or operationally taken over in the special circumstances of the controversial policies of the previous democratic government. Many of these reprivatized firms fell back into the government's hands in 1982–1983 as a consequence of a gigantic systemic collapse of the Chilean economy (Ffrench-Davis, 1982), but they were quickly transferred back to the private sector in 1984–1985 (Sáez, 1991; Hachette and Lüders, 1992). Soon afterwards, in 1985, the military government announced the beginning of the privatization of many of the country's large traditional PEs, which had hitherto been considered untouchable. Between 1985 and 1989 thirty public enterprises—producing both tradeable goods and major public services—were divested in whole or in part, generating income equivalent to US$1.3 billion (Tables 25-3 and 25-4). At its peak in 1987–1988 the income from privatization operations was equivalent, on average, to 2% of GDP and 7% of current revenues of the consolidated public sector. At the end of 1989 there were 45 public enterprises in the country, compared to more than 200 in 1974 and 75 in 1970 (Sáez, 1991). These remaining PEs included the giant copper firm CO-DELCO, petroleum refining, and water and sanitation facilities.

In 1990, Chile's new democratic government slowed the pace and altered the content of the privatization programme: control of only a limited number of small public firms would be sold to the private sector, while a few other PEs would sell minority share packages. The government also planned to allow private participation in new public infrastructure projects, especially those sponsored by the public water and sewerage companies. In 1991 a small State shipping firm was sold and a minority share package in the Iquique free trade zone was offered on the local stock market.

Mexico followed Chile in the pioneering of privatization in the region. The De la Madrid government initiated the process in 1983 and it was intensified in 1989 by the new Salinas de Gortari administration. The reform policy caused the number of public firms to decline from 1155 in 1982 to 280 in 1990 (Secretaría de Hacienda y Crédito Público, n.d.). About a third of this reduction was due to outright sale and the rest to liquidations, mergers and transfers to local authorities (Ruprah, 1992a; Tandon, 1992). The process initially focused on relatively small tradeable goods firms, but the size of the firms increased with time (Aeroméxico; Mexicana de

TABLE 25-3

LATIN AMERICA: VALUE OF PRIVATIZATION OPERATIONS IN SIX COUNTRIES,[a] 1983–1991

Year	Amount[b]	GDP[c] (%)	Fiscal income[d] (%)
	Mexico		
1983	40	—	—
1984	5	—	—
1985	115	0.1[e]	0.4
1986	100	0.1	0.4
1987	170	0.1	0.4
1988	520	0.3	1.2
1989	730	0.4	1.6
1990	3 205	1.3	5.2
1991	10 550	3.8	12.7
	Chile		
1983	—	—	—
1984	—	—	—
1985	10	0.1	0.3
1986	230	1.4	4.0
1987	310	1.7	5.6
1988	560	2.5	8.1
1989	235	0.9	3.0
1990	—	—	—
1991	—	—	—
	Argentina		
1983–1989 (no privatization operations were effected)			
1990	2 105[f]	3.4	19.2
1991	2 901[f]	4.5	21.2
	Brazil		
1983–1990 (no privatization operations were effected)			
1991	1 700[g]	0.4	1.6
	Venezuela		
1983–1990 (no privatization operations were effected)			
1991	2 300	4.5	15.0
	Colombia		
1983–1988 (no privatization operations were effected)			
1989	50	—	—
1990	75	—	—
1991	690	0.2	—

Source: Calculated on the basis of data from Gerchunoff and Castro (1992); Hachette and Lüders (1992); Ruprah (1992a); National Economic and Social Development Bank (BNDES), Brazil; Fondo de Inversiones de Venezuela; and ECLAC, Economic Development Division.

[a] Refers to value of sales and not necessarily to cash flow.

[b] Millions of dollars.

[c] Equivalent in dollars.

[d] Current income of the non-financial public sector.

[e] Equivalent in pesos.

[f] Includes foreign public debt paper valued at secondary market rates. Also includes original terms for the sale of Aerolineas Argentinas, which were modified in 1992.

[g] Payment was almost exclusively in domestic debt paper.

TABLE 25-4

LATIN AMERICA: SECTORAL DISTRIBUTION OF PRIVATIZATION, ON THE BASIS OF
DIVESTITURE OPERATIONS, 1989–1991
(Percentages)

Sectors	Argentina	Mexico	Brazil	Venezuela	Chile	Colombia
Agriculture	—	2	—	—	—	—
Air transportation	14	3	3	6	—	—
Banking	—	52	—	5	—	3
Electricity	—	—	—	—	—	—
Manufacturing	2	10	95	—	—	72
Mining	27	—	—	—	—	—
Surface transport	5	—	2	2	—	25
Telecommunications	53	33	—	87	—	—
Others	—	—	—	—	—	—
Total	100	100	100	100	—	100

Source: Latin Finance (1991 and 1992) and ECLAC, Economic Development Division.

Aviación) and the programme eventually included major public services, of which
TELMEX is the most important. Road networks and commercial banks are also subject
to privatization.

The total value of sales of PEs over the period 1983–1991 was more than US$15
billion, 90% of this being concentrated in 1990–1991 (Table 25-3). This concentration
reflects the large size of the firms privatized in this period and the greater importance
of outright sales relative to earlier years: the value of the sales in this latter period was
huge, averaging the equivalent of 2.5% of GDP and 9% of current fiscal revenue.
Unless the petroleum and electricity sectors become subject to privatization (the Constitution currently deems them to be strategic), it would appear that the Mexican
process of divestiture could soon wind down.

Argentina began its programme in late 1989 under the new Menem government. In
1990–1991 seventeen publicly-owned firms involved in the production of tradeable
goods, including oil, and major public services were wholly or partially privatized;
moreover, the most heavily trafficked highways were transformed into private concessions with rights to charge tolls. The value of sales of PEs in the period reached US$5
billion, equivalent on average to 4% of GDP and 20% of current fiscal revenue (Table
25-3).[6] The Argentine scheme is probably one of the most ambitious in all Latin America, since the government plans to privatize all its remaining PEs and many public services during 1992–1993.

Brazil began to privatize under the Collor de Mello administration in October 1991.
Four firms were sold during that year for a value of US$1.7 billion, equivalent to about
0.4% of GDP and 1.6% of current fiscal income.[7] The government initially identified 55
firms for privatization, all of them engaged in the production of tradeable goods. It is
expected that the new government of Itamar Franco will introduce some modifications
in the programme.[8]

Venezuela has about 370 State entities in a very wide array of sectors (Fondo de Inversiones de Venezuela, 1992); moreover, some of the firms are mixed capital ventures with foreigners. The government began a privatization process in late 1990 with a small bank. Then 7 firms producing tradeable goods and major public services were sold in 1991. The sales produced US$2.3 billion, equivalent to more than 4% of GDP and 15% of fiscal revenue. Twenty-nine more firms in tradeable goods sectors and tourism services were scheduled to be sold in 1992. The original list, however, is rapidly expanding as 43 additional firms are being prepared for privatization, including the Caracas water supply company (Fondo de Inversiones de Venezuela, 1992). Nevertheless, the pace of the country's privatizations stagnated in the second half of 1992, due to events reflecting serious political instability.

Most other countries in the region are much less advanced in the privatization process than those mentioned above. However, by 1992 virtually every government in the region, except Cuba, had announced a major privatization programme and most had at least begun some minor sales of public firms.

III WHY ARE THE COUNTRIES PRIVATIZING?

In the theoretical framework of Jones, Tandon and Vogelsang (1990), a country should privatize public enterprises if this will bring about a positive net change in social welfare. This occurs when the social value of the privatized firm, plus the net social value of the public sector's receipts from its sale, is greater than the social value of the firm under public ownership.[9]

Of course few governments have had the time or inclination to make a complicated cost-benefit analysis in every case: they have typically relied on a more general and intuitive approach. Nevertheless, even in a more informal framework the number of factors potentially supporting privatization are often perceived to be so large that it is not surprising that so many governments have decided to initiate privatization programmes without more ado. Indeed, the scope of privatizations is becoming so massive that most governments seem in practice to be mimicking the strategy of Mexico's Salinas government: with respect to individual PEs the Mexican authorities changed the initial ministerial question from the De la Madrid administration's "Should we privatize?" to "Why shouldn't we privatize?". This reformulated question has been behind the accelerated pace of privatization measures in that country (Ruprah, 1992a).

Below, I shall try to outline some of the major factors that seem to be explicitly or implicitly propelling the privatization processes in the region. The list is by no means exhaustive, but rather reflects those factors, or arguments, which I perceive to be of broad influence in the decision to privatize. The weights for each one, of course, differ among the countries.

It is also important to note that the analysis does not include detailed evaluation of the validity of the arguments involved. Such a task is beyond the scope of this article, in view of the very specific nature of many aspects of privatization, the difficulty of isolating many of the relevant causal factors, the as yet limited experience of the privatized enterprises, and the almost metaeconomic nature of some of the most enthusiastic arguments put forward in favour of divestiture.

1. Structural Factors

a) Ideology   As mentioned above, there has been an ideological shift in the region that lays stress on private sector initiative. The central idea is the "subsidiary State", i.e., in the commercial sphere the public sector should be limited to essential activities that the private sector cannot or will not perform. The new focus has won growing theoretical support (summarized nicely by Killick, 1989) and has been further encouraged by the political success of England's ambitious privatization programme during the Thatcher government. The interpretation can be subtle and selective, but it can also be more emphatic and quantitative, picturing government failure as nearly always worse than private market failure: hence the advocacy of drastic reduction of the size of the State in absolute terms, irrespective of the theoretical merits of public intervention. The benefits of the new strategy purport to be greater efficiency through the freeing-up of market forces and greater equity and social participation through the democratization of capital (Hanke, 1987).

The new ideology can be observed in virtually all the governments of the region, though it has not always been a first, or even second, order consideration in the decision to privatize. It was, however, clearly the main motivation of the Chilean privatization process of 1985–1989 (Hachette and Lüders, 1992), carried out as part of a programme proposed by the military government's ideologically hard-line "Chicago boys". Mexico's programme also had ideology as a first-order consideration. In that country, the emergence of a new young generation of U.S.-educated government bureaucrats, less emotionally linked to the Statist tradition that followed the Mexican Revolution, brought with it the perception that the State-dominated economy needed fundamental rebalancing (Ruprah, 1992a). The tone of Mexico's reform has been subtle and selective, however, with the government emphasizing that the State would redeploy its efforts to the social sector (Khanna, 1992).

b) Internal Efficiency   Experience in the region suggests that the public sector often has difficulty playing the dual role of principal and agent. It is generally accepted that the principal-agent problem can be more difficult when ownership is dispersed, due to the limited access to information and the free-rider problem. Hirschman (1970) argued that the principal has two options in this respect: to defend his interests ("voice") or to retreat ("exit"); moreover, in the situation in question the exercise of "voice" to demand greater efficiency involves high costs, while a large part of the potential benefits of effective "voice" are bestowed on third parties. It is because of this that "exit" is often the preferred response; indeed, it reflects an old Wall Street dictum: "If you don't like the management, then sell your stock".

This traditional problem of the relationship between principals and agents could be considered potentially much more serious for a public enterprise, because in this case the dispersion of ownership is extreme: the public sector is permeated by society at large. In this environment the principal's potential objectives cover the entire spectrum of interests that can be effectively voiced by that society. However, as the use of voice and the monitoring of performance have high costs, voice will likely be exercised only by those groups which perceive enough benefits to pay the costs that are needed for that effective voice. Since the benefits of greater efficiency in a public firm are dispersed very widely throughout society, the exercise of voice for this objective can be neutralized by the stronger voices of groups with objectives that will bring them more tangible and concentrated benefits.

This intensified principal-agent problem of public firms is by no means an insurmountable obstacle, however, as is demonstrated by a number of countries with a tradition of efficient public enterprise management. Indeed, there is evidence that what really matters for efficient firm management is market structure rather than ownership *per se* (Vickers and Yarrow, 1988). Nevertheless, it could be plausibly argued that, other things being equal, the social cost (effort) of exercising voice on behalf of efficiency is relatively less for the principals of a privatized firm than for those of a public enterprise.

Exit (privatization) and the reallocation, or reduction, of the State's net worth could therefore be proposed as an attractive and less costly option for the achievement of greater efficiency. In effect, the privatization of PEs creates substantially more concentrated ownership, which in turn narrows the principal's potential objectives and enhances his power to monitor the performance of management and labour. In sum, it is assumed that the voice of profit maximization will face fewer competing voices (and hence lower monitoring costs) when the firm is in private hands.

Where monopoly power is involved, efficiency in the allocation of resources will require some type of public regulation of the privatized firm. However, since public monitoring must now take place "outside" the firm itself, there will be a rise in the public cost of gathering the relevant information needed for effective regulation. Nevertheless, a decision to privatize must mean that the new public costs of external regulation are perceived to be less than the sum of the public costs that must be assumed if the State is to effectively play the triple role of principal, agent and public regulator of an enterprise. At least theoretically, privatization creates a more transparent division of labour, which makes for potentially better accountability: to put this simply, the private principals and agents must only pursue some mode of profit maximization, while public regulators must only pursue efficiency in resource allocation. Meanwhile, the State can reallocate its receipts from privatization to other activities with returns that are socially high, but privately too low to attract private capital, or else the receipts can be allocated to the reduction of public debt. Roughly speaking, in either case the government's net worth remains constant (assuming no undervaluation of the firm sold). Alternatively, the State can retreat and reduce its net worth, by using the privatization receipts to finance current public outlays.

All of the governments of the region have appealed to efficiency to justify the privatization of their firms. It is generally accepted that most PEs have traditionally confronted a proliferation of conflicting public objectives, such as investment, acting as conduits for foreign savings, charging low prices to aid the poor or to support stabilization efforts, creating demand for the products of domestic capital goods industries, regional development strategies, distributing political largesse of different types, etc. Some of these objectives were consistent with development, while others were not, but clearly the institutional arrangement was often inefficient, as a single instrument (the PE) was invariably used to accomplish multiple, and often conflicting, social objectives.

In practice, efficiency criteria seem to have been an especially important motivating factor in countries like Argentina, Peru and Venezuela, which have had notoriously inefficient PEs and government apparatus that has been judged too weak to effect the reforms needed to raise the voice of efficiency. In other words, authorities have seen "exit" (in the form of privatization) as the only viable option for overcoming the principal/agent problem. On the other hand, the efficiency factor may have been less of a driving force in a few countries with strong government apparatus and the potential ability to reform PEs, or those where the PEs' performance was already at least acceptable in general terms. The best example is Chile, where the military government had the power and demonstrated capacity to reform enterprises: aided by an extremely authoritarian setting, the authorities effectively created greater concentration of ownership in PEs—thus lowering the costs and raising the benefits of exercising the voice of efficiency—even though the principal remained nominally public. As a consequence, Chilean PEs were generally relatively efficient and financially viable well before the decision to privatize them.[10]

c) **Changes in Sectors Considered to Be "Strategic"** Since the decision of almost all the countries in the region to dramatically and rapidly liberalize trade (ECLAC, 1992a), governments have assumed that deregulated markets are now contestable and that foreign competition will cause the number of domestic monopolies and oligopolies in the tradeable goods sectors to decline markedly. In effect, regulation of rents by market forces in principle reduces the need for direct regulation via public ownership.

Many authorities are of the opinion that changing technology and innovative administrative techniques have eroded, or at least called into question, the presence of natural monopolies in many public services. Indeed, some technical support has emerged in favour of: i) depackaging certain major domestic public services, as has occurred in the Chilean and Argentine electricity sectors; ii) dividing former monopolies into duopolies, as in the case of the Argentine telephone system (this makes possible, at least in principle, external public regulation via "yardstick competition" between the two firms);[11] and iii) building and managing public infrastructure through regulated private concessions, as in the case of the Argentine and Mexican road networks. These technical developments, coupled with deregulation and the formation of contestable markets, have reduced the perceived need for PEs.

Monopolistic and oligopolistic control of internationally tradeable goods (including technologies), as well as the dominant position of the U.S. economy, has been sharply reduced by the great expansion of the world economy since the war. In effect, Latin American countries objectively face a more competitive world economy and a more complex geopolitical matrix than they did in the inter-war period and in the 1950s and 1960s. The active participation of European firms, including those from Spain, in the privatization processes of Argentina, Chile, Mexico and Venezuela,[12] as well as that of privatized Chilean companies in the divestiture processes of Argentina and Peru, bear witness to the dispersion of international economic power. In these circumstances it could be argued that there is less need for a strong countervailing force in the form of State ownership of productive enterprises.

d) Repositioned Private Sectors   One of the factors giving rise to the public entrepreneur was the immaturity of domestic private sectors and markets. After the considerable post-war growth and integration of Latin America with world economies and cultures, there is now a feeling in the region that the domestic private sectors have matured to the point where they are capable of successfully operating in many sectors formerly dominated by PEs.

Recent developments in the world economy have also strengthened the apparent attractiveness of transferring property to the private sector. The State's debt crisis, plus its forced absorption of private sector debts,[13] have combined to help make the latter a superior player in world capital markets. There is also some perception that more competitive world markets have also shifted advantage to the private sector because of its capacity for quickly accessing and adapting changing technology and forming alliances with foreign partners. These developments have caused governments to seek opportunities for realigning their public investment portfolios.

e) The Perceived Need to Project Consistency   In the context of a transition to a model which gives priority to private capital, an important State presence—even an efficient one—in economic sectors that are attractive to local entrepreneurs can create a degree of conflict and uncertainty which may ultimately lead to a decision to privatize. For instance, when the State maintains a commercial presence in a sector that has been largely privatized, it could be a disincentive for private investment there, because of the private firms' fear that they will not be able to effectively compete with the State entity, which potentially can receive favours from public policies. On the other hand, the value of the public sector's patrimony in the sector can also effectively deteriorate if the government withholds new investments in order to avoid being accused of squeezing out private initiative. In these circumstances political pressures can eventually develop to a point where even potentially useful State firms are sacrificed in order to preserve or promote the new consensus about the division of labour between the public and private sectors.[14]

2. Conjunctural Factors

a) Political Credibility   Governments have often used privatization measures as a signal of their commitment to the new ideological model, thereby attempting to improve the expectations of domestic and international economic agents. While this motive is widespread in the region, it has been especially important for newly-elected governments which have become committed (by conviction or circumstances) to a neoconservative economic strategy, but which have initially lacked the ideological credentials of the Washington Consensus and/or have encountered difficulties in pushing forward reforms on other fronts.

Credibility was a factor of prime importance in the emergence of Argentina's first round of privatizations in 1989/1990. Assuming power in the middle of an economic crisis, the government's surprise announcement of the privatization of ENTel and Aerolíneas Argentinas was motivated in part by the need to transform a formerly populist image and stabilize the expectations of the economic agents.[15] Credibility also seems to have been a first-order consideration in the Collor de Mello government's decision to privatize in Brazil; in effect, it did indeed produce some concrete forward movement in a troubled economic setting that had not been receptive to across-the-board reforms. Credibility also appears to have had a lot of weight in the privatization operations of the newly-elected governments in Venezuela and Peru, which also assumed power in the midst of severe economic crises. In the first-named government, it was part of a programme that erased an initially populist image, and in the latter it helped to give definition to a new political party that had lacked a clear image when it assumed power.

b) Fiscal Crisis and Stabilization   The sale of State assets can temporarily close macroeconomically destabilizing fiscal gaps. The sale itself creates an immediate financial transfer to the government, while it also affects future fiscal flows. If a firm was losing money, an annual negative fiscal transfer could be converted into positive flow of tax revenue, assuming private ownership is profitable. If the public firm was already profitable, the net future flow depends on the tradeoff between taxes and dividends of the public firm and taxes paid by the privatized firm.

The privatization option becomes tempting when possibilities for reducing fiscal expenditure have been exhausted; when the government is unable or unwilling to raise revenue through increased tax collection, or when non-inflationary sources of public finance have become exhausted. In these circumstances there is the option of capitalizing the potential future receipts of a public enterprise through its privatization. This might be termed a "Pan Am" effect, as financial distress induces the sale of potentially profitable assets to finance expenditures which cannot be compressed without threatening the short-term viability of the entity in question.

A fiscal deficit which generates serious inflation and balance of payments problems is obviously a socially costly phenomenon: the situation can inhibit reforms, bring unwanted conditionality from the IMF, paralyze investment and growth, and have regressive distributional effects. Hence, every peso of additional revenue today, employed to close the fiscal gap, could have a very high social rate of return. Moreover, in a situation of severe macroeconomic disequilibria and recession, a peso of fiscal revenue will usually have a higher shadow price than a peso of private consumption or investment.

In these circumstances, an increase in tax collection could be an attractive option, especially if the taxes involved are not regressive in character. However, in an open, highly deregulated economy with an economic recession and a weak political and institutional setting, greater tax collection—especially of a progressive type—could be very difficult to effect. Indeed, in today's fragile political settings, an increased tax burden can intensify capital flight and deepen the recession, with negative net consequences for fiscal income and stabilization. A more assertive tax policy will also frequently be accused of sending the wrong signals to the private sector; after all, the strategy that is fashionable today views most taxes as distortionary and welfare-reducing (Atkinson and Stiglitz, 1980).[16]

Privatization is clearly an expedient way to bypass the above dilemma. But using the privatization receipts to finance expenditure is analogous to borrowing. Thus, when used to finance current outlays, privatization reduces the public sector's net worth; moreover, this strategy only postpones rather than eliminates the need for further fiscal adjustment in the form of increased taxes or cutbacks in expenditure (Hemming and Mansoor, 1988).

The desire to finance fiscal deficits has been an important consideration in decisions to initiate privatization. Since money is fungible, it is difficult to isolate the use made of receipts derived from divestiture. Nevertheless, the existence of global fiscal deficits during periods of privatization is indicative of financing via divestiture, and moreover, deficits on current fiscal balances hint of some financing of current expenditures, inducing a direct loss of public sector net worth.[17] Using these assumptions, privatization appears to have been used as a financing instrument in Chile in 1985–1986, in Argentina in 1989–91, and in Mexico in 1983–1990 (Table 25-5).[18] Also, the global surpluses registered in Mexico and Venezuela in 1991 would have been deficits without privatization receipts. As for the implicit financing of current outlays, this appears to have occurred in Argentina and Mexico up until 1991. More specific tracking of income and outlays in the case of Chile (Marcel, 1989) led to the conclusion that 50% of the Chilean privatization receipts in 1985–1986 went to finance current outlays, thus reducing the public sector's net worth. Finally it should be mentioned that a primary motive for the recent privatization operations in Venezuela and Peru has been the desire to relax severe fiscal constraints.

TABLE 25-5
LATIN AMERICA: FISCAL BALANCES FOR FIVE COUNTRIES[a]
(Percentages of GDP)

	1983	1984	1985	1986	1987	1988	1989	1990	1991
Chile									
Current savings	-0.5	0.3	3.6	4.8	5.3	8.0	7.0	5.6	5.5
Total balance	-3.5	-4.6	-2.9	-2.0	2.6	3.9	5.5	1.5	1.7
Mexico									
Current savings	-2.8	-2.1	-3.4	-9.9	-12.2	-9.8	-5.7	-2.0	0.8
Total balance	-8.1	-7.1	-8.0	-14.5	-14.4	-9.7	-5.1	-2.9	3.4
Argentina									
Current savings	—	—	-1.9	-0.5	-1.7	-3.5	-1.6	-2.9	-1.6
Total balance	—	—	-5.4	-4.1	-6.7	-8.6	-4.8	-5.1	-2.2
Brazil									
Current savings	-1.4	-2.8	-8.1	-7.1	-6.1	-12.6	-20.1	-10.1	-10.0
Total balance	—	—	—	—	—	—	—	—	—
Venezuela									
Current savings	—	—	—	—	8.1	4.0	10.4	12.6	10.7
Total balance	—	—	—	—	-4.4	-8.6	-1.1	0.2	1.2

Source: ECLAC, *Economic Survey of Latin America and the Caribbean,* various numbers and Centre for Economic and Social Development Studies (CEDES), Buenos Aires.
[a]Consolidated public sector.

As a fiscal situation stabilizes, a country has more opportunities to use privatization receipts to finance reductions of public debt and to promote an overall improvement of net worth. In late 1990 Mexico began to earmark privatization receipts for a special fund, and a considerable amount of these resources has apparently been channelled to debt reduction: domestic public debt was reduced by US$7 billion in 1991 and by US$5 billion in the first quarter of 1992. Moreover, in 1992 the government quietly effected buybacks of US$7 billion of public foreign commercial bank debt (equivalent to nearly 10% of the total public foreign debt) through the use of privatization receipts. It is estimated that total public debt, which in 1986 was equivalent to about 80% of GDP, was 29% of GDP by the end of 1992.[19] Debt reduction became an important use for Chile's privatization receipts beginning in 1987 (Hachette and Lüders, 1992). The receipts from Argentina's initial round of privatization operations (1989/90) involved direct reduction of foreign debt, as a considerable part of the payment was made in promissory notes bought on the secondary market.[20] Much of the country's receipts in the second round of privatization initially went to finance general expenditure, but with a fiscal surplus in 1992 more funds were being earmarked for reduction of public debt.

It is usually not easy to determine whether privatization has acted as a direct substitute for taxation. However, in Chile it is very likely that privatization financed the military government's fiscal reforms of 1984 and 1988, which sharply lowered direct and indirect taxes.[21]

c) Investment Constraints on Public Enterprises The fiscal crisis during the 1980s was seen as a serious obstacle to new investment in public firms and social infrastructure. As noted earlier, when the crisis broke, it was an easy matter to postpone the investments of PEs, and this was in fact done, in order to improve short-term financial balances (Table 25-2). Even profitable public firms became prisoners of the central government's financial crisis. As the decade progressed, the investment lag became intolerable, especially in public services with a higher degree of visibility. As the public sector's debt problem persisted, privatization came to be perceived as a way to ease the public enterprises' growing investment bottleneck. In effect, through privatization a public firm could escape the central government's fiscal restraint and thus have more freedom to invest. Moreover, the receipts from the privatization could potentially allow the State to reinvigorate public social investment, or reduce debt. The investment bottleneck has almost always been used as one of the arguments for privatization, even in countries like Chile where many PEs were relatively efficient and profitable. As mentioned above, Mexico has laid special stress on the need to sell PEs in order to strengthen social investment.

d) Catalytic Effects When an economy is in a deep recession, the public sector is traditionally expected to act in countercyclical fashion and stimulate activity through expansive monetary and/or fiscal policy. However, excessively procyclical public policies in Latin America were a major cause of the crisis; hence, when the crisis hit the region there were few degrees of freedom for stimulative public action. Moreover, the new paradigm in the region discouraged public activism. In these circumstances privatization could be interpreted as an unconventional form of economic "pump priming".

A severe crisis, coupled with the uncertainty generated by a shift to a new economic model and radically different domestic relative prices, can cause the private sector to initially boycott its own domestic economy, by refusing to repatriate flight capital and by withholding taxes and investment. This obviously aggravates the fiscal problem and also is not a very healthy situation for a strategy in which the private sector is supposed to be the primary engine of economic growth. Privatization seems to have been viewed as a last resort to "stir the pot" and break the stalemate. As mentioned above, privatization can generate extraordinary receipts for the government which help it to close the fiscal gap. While fiscal balancing through privatization can be only a temporary strategy, it does buy time until more permanent financing can be found. Moreover, since the domestic private sector will purchase State assets by repatriating capital and foreign participants will bring their own dollars, a significant part of the privatization receipts should be in foreign exchange. This will have the double-barreled impact of closing the fiscal gap and anchoring the exchange rate, both of which can be conducive to short-term price stabilization and better expectations.

It is also perceived that privatization can raise the private sector's disposition to save and invest. This is because it is usually less risky to buy existing firms than to invest in a start-up operation. Moreover, public firms often provide greater and more accurate information than can be found in other sectors of the economy. Another consideration is that many PEs, but especially those that provide public services in monopolistic or quasi-monopolistic markets, are inherently attractive low-risk and cash-rich operations in which shareholders can more easily appropriate a significant part of any efficiency gains. Finally, in a crisis environment the investment activity of highly visible privatized firms—even if not additive—could conceivably create positive externalities and help turn around the private sector's expectations.

Privatizations can also broaden and deepen moribund stock markets, give rise to windfall profits (especially when the firms involved are undervalued), and generate new wealth and more optimistic expectations. This, coupled with the externalities of reinvigorated privatized firms and relaxed external constraints, can contribute to a recovery in the rate of domestic economic activity. More growth, in turn, will naturally boost fiscal revenue and also provide a better environment for fiscal reforms; consequently, privatization receipts can be gradually replaced with more stable sources of revenue.

Isolating and measuring all the catalytic effects of privatization operations is clearly an impossible task. Nevertheless, there are some judgements which point to probable catalytic effects of privatization. For instance, the World Bank has judged that the massive return of flight capital and influx of foreign portfolio investment in Mexico in 1989–1991 is largely a derivative of that country's privatization programme (Tandon, 1992). Mexico's stock market, one of the fastest growing in the world, has been stimulated by the privatization of PEs, particularly that of Telmex, which accounts for more than a quarter of the market's index (Ruprah, 1990a). Indeed, it has been commented that recent stock market developments have given rise to a whole new set of entrepreneurs.[22] The investment activity of privatized firms, for example in the telecommunications, air transport and finance sectors, has also generated much publicity and international interest, perhaps contributing to the growing optimism in that country (Ruprah, 1990a and 1992b). Likewise, the second selloff of the residual shares of Argentina's ENTel also stimulated a boom in that country's stock market (Gerchunoff and Castro, 1992).

In Chile, Hachette and Lüders (1992) controversially attribute several catalytic effects to the second round of privatizations in that country, pointing to the fact that during that period, private savings and investment levels, although relatively low, rose quite sharply. According to these authors, this may have reflected the higher marginal rate of return on investment in privatized firms. The privatization process is also judged to have broadened, deepened and stimulated the stock market, creating a dynamic new source of private wealth in Chile.

e) Pacifying Foreign Creditors Privatization processes are strongly "encouraged" by the international financial community. A programme of this type could therefore enhance external economic relations, especially with the IMF, the World Bank and commercial lenders.

This consideration was probably important in Argentina's decision to initiate privatization in 1989, when there was a perceived need to pacify the commercial banks. In early 1988 the country had fallen into a moratorium, which was relaxed only marginally in 1989 by the initiation of partial debt service payments. A stoppage of payments traditionally raises tensions with foreign creditors, and indeed in early 1989 the banks were becoming more aggressive in their dealings with countries in a moratorium, as manifested by Citibank's "set-off" of some official deposits of Ecuador, another country which was limiting its debt service payments just like Argentina (Altimir and Devlin, 1992).

A privatization programme like Argentina's, which makes foreign debt paper an eligible means of payment, creates attractive options for the banks, especially the big lenders making up the Advisory Committees that are in charge of debt renegotiations. On the one hand, the banks gain by the rise in the secondary market price resulting from the increased demand for debt paper (in the case of Argentina, that price rose by some 50% during the finalization of the first round of privatizations). In these circumstances, banks can sell off their bad loans at a smaller loss and also gain commissions if they are contracted to secure paper for third parties interested in participating in the privatizations. On the other hand, a bank can avoid a loss on its own loan portfolio by capitalizing it through the purchase of a PE. It is no surprise, therefore, that some very large banks on Argentina's Advisory Committee were attracted by the sale of ENTel, and ultimately two of the country's major lenders, Citibank and Morgan Guaranty, actually bought major share holdings in the newly privatized company (Gerchunoff and Castro, 1992).

IV IMPROVING THE SOCIAL BENEFITS OF PRIVATIZATION

Latin America had a very difficult ten years of structural adjustment and stabilization efforts in the 1980s, coupled with delicate transitions to democracy. Substantial progress has been made on all fronts. Indeed, in the early 1990s cautious optimism has arisen about the region's future prospects: Chile seems to have fully turned the corner towards economic recovery,[23] Mexico could be following a similar path, and a number of other countries are to different degrees consolidating their adjustment and transformation processes (ECLAC, 1991). The slow recovery from the crisis of 1982 has been socially very costly, however, as there are signs that income distribution and social equity have deteriorated sharply in many of the countries, most of which were already noted for their serious inequalities of income and opportunities (ECLAC, 1992a).

The deteriorated social matrix can be judged worrisome not only on normative grounds, but also in more concrete respects. On the one hand, the sustainability of the recovery will require social stability, and this in turn requires improvements in social equity. On the other, many dimensions of social equity are functional—indeed vital— to the construction of the modern institutional and human capital needed to transform the region's economies into truly internationally competitive enterprises (ECLAC, 1990 and 1992a). The recent serious political problems in Venezuela, Haiti, Brazil and Peru have focused international attention on the social plight of the region and contributed to a surge in international concern about the effects of adjustment on social equity. The new focus certainly vindicates some analytical pioneers who argued a number of years ago that adjustment policies needed a more human face (Cornia, Jolly and Stewart, 1988).

The region's privatization processes are an integral part of the adjustment efforts. However, evaluating the effects of privatization is difficult because of, among other things, the large number of tradeoffs that must be considered, the excessively broad nature of the relevant counterfactuals, and the difficulty in accounting for the externalities that many attribute to the process. But even more importantly, the privatization experience in developing countries is still relatively immature, even for pioneers like Chile; hence it will be a number of years before we really know all the resulting social benefits—and costs—of the region's decision to privatize.

Notwithstanding the above, the World Bank (Galal *et. al.,* 1992) has attempted to grapple with some of these difficult problems. In a study of nine divestiture (privatization) operations in three developing countries, it found that eight of them improved global welfare. Thus, to its own question "did divestiture make the world a better place or not?", the Bank answers with a "resounding yes".

Needless to say, studies such as that carried out by the Bank involve numerous subjective judgements which many reasonable people could disagree with. But one conclusion can be drawn from the study without much debate: whatever the social gains from the region's divestitures have been and will be, they can undoubtedly be improved upon in future exercises.

In effect, divestiture processes have been conditioned by multiple objectives but, as has often been the case in questions of adjustment, social equity has not always carried much weight. This is unfortunate, because the tradeoff between social equity and other objectives can be relatively small, and indeed important complementarities would seem to exist. There are many ways that social equity can be enhanced in privatization exercises. While space is too limited for a comprehensive review, five key areas worth consideration are outlined below.

1. Transparency

Transparency improves social welfare because it reduces possibilities for corruption, collusion and the misuse of inside information, all of which permit privileged gains from the sale of public assets. It can also be complementary with many other objectives. Since transparency opens the process to more public scrutiny, errors can be checked more easily and fairer evaluations can be made as to whether the government's stated objectives—regarding the privatization process as well as its end product—are being reasonably fulfilled. The closer results are to objectives, the more likely it is that privatization will have a "happy ending" for the firms, the government, and the general public, which in turn reduces the risk of policy backlash. Transparency also enhances the efficiency of the "learning by doing" process which is an inevitable part of any government's privatization programme. An enhanced flow of information will obviously also contribute to overall market efficiency and price maximization.

Transparency can also enhance the government's credibility and have catalytic effects, especially when past governments have had a reputation for corruption or cronyism. It is also consistent with the objective of democratization and broader participation in economic matters and in society more generally.

Of course, transparency trades off with the speed of the privatization process. This could be an important consideration, since some analysts have given top priority to this latter objective; as one highly regarded economist once commented: "privatization should be implemented with less concern about the correct way to do it and more emphasis on getting it done quickly" (Woodrow Wilson Center, 1991). However, most of the objectives that commonly drive privatization processes are not necessarily enhanced by speed; indeed many of them, such as productive and allocative efficiency, credibility, government revenue, catalytic effects, etc., to say nothing of social equity, can be seriously compromised by a hasty privatization process.

Most governments in the region have confronted very heavy external, and sometimes internal, pressure to greatly accelerate their privatization processes. It is encouraging that some have been able to resist such pressures, while at the same time proceeding in a deliberate fashion with their objective of privatizing PEs.

The conflicting pressures that governments face are captured in the remarks of a person who was formerly in charge of privatization efforts in Brazil, a country with one of the more transparent programmes: ". . . one can always choose urgency, make bad shareholder decisions, leave significant debts pending, reduce the minimum price, etc. These, however, are not good recipes for a successful privatization programme. Indeed, they are detrimental to the principles of openness and transparency, as well as to the public wealth (represented by the assets being sold off). We chose to go about things carefully. Right from the start, we knew that this would result in us having to pay a political price: the ever alert critics, those who are not committed to openness, and even analysts who have good will, yet suffer from academic ingenuousness, would condemn the supposed sluggishness of the process. I do not have the slightest doubt, however, that we made the correct choice" (Marco Modiano, 1992).

While more transparency may be feasible, there is at least one area where the tradeoffs can be exceptionally great: fiscal urgency (earlier termed the "Pan Am" effect). Social welfare demands that a country with a highly destabilizing fiscal gap must close it as soon as possible, and a rapid privatization process could conceivably be the only way to do that. However, experience has shown that rapid processes can be prone to very serious errors (Hachette and Lüders, 1992; Gerchunoff and Castro, 1992); indeed, emerging problems such as corruption, undervaluation, etc. could conceivably neutralize the positive effects of financing the fiscal gap. But the mentioned tradeoff is nevertheless very real and is frequently a challenge for the region's policy makers.

In the face of fiscal urgency, one possible alternative to a rapid privatization process is a non-confrontational moratorium on foreign debt payments. However this is a tricky strategy in which only a few countries have been successful (Altimir and Devlin, 1992). A better public solution would be to strengthen the resource base of the World Bank, IMF and IDB, for this would enable the multilateral organizations to provide more direct compensatory budgetary support to governments formally committed to extensive privatization processes. As is true with the adjustment problem in general, adequate compensatory financing will allow a borrower to design a more deliberate, transparent, efficient and socially equitable privatization programme. This should also be of interest to the multilateral lenders, because more efficient and equitable programmes will clearly enhance their borrowers' creditworthiness.

What actions could improve transparency? The potential list is long, but a few key policies can be mentioned:

i) Information   Reserved documentation should be the exception rather than the rule. While a limited amount of reserved information may be justified during negotiations for the sale of PEs, the public should have easy access to all the information after the transaction is completed, including the preparations for the sale of the firm (debt absorption, labour relations, capital restructuring, etc.), reports on its valuation and on the preselection and selection processes, administrative and promotional costs, and details of the buyers and their financing of the purchase.

ii) Subsidies   If sales require subsidies, these should not be hidden in preferential prices and credit terms. Rather, subsidies should be awarded in such a way that they are explicit and easily accountable to the public (e.g., rebates which must be applied for *after* the firm has been purchased at an unsubsidized price). This is an important consideration because a double standard has tended to emerge during the period of privatizations: proponents of structural adjustment rankle at hidden subsidies in the social area but turn a blind eye to subsidies hidden in underpriced asset sales and below-market credit terms.

iii) Earmarking of Sale Receipts   These should be deposited in a special account (Mexico has done this). While earmarking is often frowned upon in public finance, it is justified here by the extraordinary nature of the income.

iv) Ex-post Evaluation   An independent official technical agency (as opposed to a merely formal legal entity) should be responsible for ex-post evaluations of individual privatization operations, on the basis of *ex-ante* agreed criteria formulated jointly by the Congress and the Executive branch.

v) Rules on Disclosure   Privatized firms should sometimes be subject to certain special disclosure rules which facilitate access to the types of information needed for effective *ex-post* evaluation of the results of privatization.

vi) Conflicts of Interest   An explicit code of conduct should be adopted for government officials and subcontracted technicians involved in the decision to privatize and the process itself. For instance, central government employees involved in privatization operations could be prohibited from working in privatized firms for a given period, e.g., five years. Also, such government employees (including executives of the firms to be privatized) could be prohibited from owning shares in privatized enterprises for a stipulated period.

2. Price Maximization

It must be remembered that the government's revenues are a key determinant in the welfare gains from privatization (Jones, Tandon and Vogelsang, 1990). Thus, when public assets are for sale, prices must be maximized as much as possible. Price maximization is important because it eliminates hidden subsidies for privileged buyers and keeps public wealth in the public domain where it can be used for consensual public purposes. Unfortunately there is some evidence that privatization processes suffer from a tendency to seriously underprice the State's assets (Vickers and Yarrow, 1988; Seth, 1989; Marcel, 1989; Errázuriz and Weinstein, 1986; Herrera, 1991; Gerchunoff and Coloma, 1992). Another possible indicator of underpricing can be indirectly inferred from the aforementioned World Bank study (Galal *et. al.,* 1992): of the total of four countries studied, only in Malaysia—a very cautious privatizer—was the government consistently a bigger winner in the privatization operations than the new private shareholders.

The price maximization strategy is conditioned by some important tradeoffs between these and other factors, as mentioned further on. Some central considerations for maximization are presented below.

i) When selling a firm, the price does not depend on its value to the public sector, but rather its alternative value as private property. Thus, the point of reference for price maximization should be an estimate of the firm's value to the private sector. This will usually be higher than the value of the firm for the public sector, due to efficiency differentials, synergies, opportunities for diversification, etc.

ii) The following sequence should be followed as far as possible: privatization should come near the end of the adjustment process, that is to say, after liberalization, correction of relative prices, settling down of interest rates to their long-term values, introduction of legal frameworks governing property, labour and market behaviour, and after economic recovery has already begun. In this way, the real value of the firm will be more apparent, private sector risk premiums will be less distorted, and the privatized firm itself will be more likely to be successful. Privatization should initially focus as much as possible on the tradeable goods sector—where learning by doing can have lower costs—and only later progress to any big public service firms which may be earmarked for privatization.[24] Saving enterprises in the non-tradeables sector for the later stages is also useful because their sale will thus coincide with a period when exchange rates are probably appreciating with respect to the levels registered during periods of adjustment and thereby raising the relative value of the types of services they produce.

iii) Public firms, but especially large ones, should be restructured before sale, introducing reforms that are reasonably feasible and that enhance efficiency and profitability (Martín del Campo and Winkler, 1992). This will make the value of the firm more visible to the private sector and also raise the bargaining power of the seller, because it is easier to hold out for a higher price when a firm is commercially viable. Even when no reforms of the PEs are feasible, official valuation exercises should not necessarily be based on the firm's value "as is", since at least some of the private sector's reforms can be easily anticipated. Moreover, "normal" market discount rates should be used when valuing firms. In this way, the costs of undertaking a sale when private discount rates are distorted and unusually high become clear to the public. This approach moreover could raise political pressure for more optimal preparation, sequencing and pricing of sales.

iv) Firms should be sold to the highest bidder, minimizing as much as possible considerations that go beyond objective efficiency. Efforts should be made to attract as many bidders as possible: sometimes this may point to the desirability of encouraging foreign participation by such means as placement of shares on international stock and American Depository Receipt (ADR) markets. Sales on preferential terms should be avoided: as mentioned earlier, if subsidies are deemed necessary, they should be given directly and explicitly, separately from the sale transaction itself.

v) Since fixing the correct price is often a process of trial and error, there can be an advantage in selling shares in small packages that are timed to avoid market saturation and capture the best price. Beginning a privatization operation with the sale of a controlling package has been shown to maximize receipts in a number of cases; in effect, the transfer of control to a good operator, and/or favourable evolution of the economy, can raise the value of the firm and allow the government to share in the gains through a latter contingent sale of its residual share holdings.[25] Mexico's pursuit of this strategy was rather clever: it involved prior restructuring of TELMEX's capital so that voting control could be had for as little as 21% of the company's total shares; this raised the number of financially eligible bidders and later helped maximize the price of the government's contingent selloff of residual shares.

vi) Payment should be demanded in cash. Payment in debt paper has several disadvantages. First, it erodes transparency, since it is hard to determine the real value of the debt instrument. Second, payment in foreign debt can narrow the competitive base of bidding, since some potential bidders will not have easy access to the secondary market, while others (especially banks) will have exceptionally good access. Third, if reduction of foreign debt is an important goal, it would seem more efficient to follow Mexico's example: accept only cash sales and use the receipts to negotiate a concerted Brady deal and/or discreetly withdraw debt paper from the secondary market in such a way that it puts minimum pressure on prices. Fourth, as far as pacifying banks irritated by arrears is concerned, the need to do so on a grand scale may be exaggerated, as the banks have shown only limited ability to retaliate beyond the starting of a manageable brush fire (Altimir and Devlin, 1992).

vii) The State can retain a special "golden" share in a privatized firm, designed to entitle it to share in profits if, in the future, the yield of the enterprise exceeds some mutually agreed level. The "golden" share is a contingency formula which obliges both parties to share in the risk of privatization. This could be a useful strategy when a PE must be sold in adverse market conditions. This option could initially depress the sale price, but it would at the same time enhance the probability of a happy ending for the firm and recovery of the property's value for the State at a later date.

As already mentioned, price maximization must trade off with other objectives. However, once again the tradeoffs do not always have to be large and indeed one can find complementarities.

There can obviously be a serious tradeoff between price and efficiency. The highest bidder is not always the most efficient operator (in a dynamic sense, which includes the operator's propensity to invest). Moreover, a higher price will be fetched for a firm with effective monopoly power than for one facing effective competition or external regulation. In sum, it is reasonable to condition price by dynamic internal and allocative efficiency criteria, since efficiency is the other major missing ingredient in Latin America's needed economic transformation (ECLAC, 1992a).

Price is often sacrificed for a specially targeted distribution of shares. Two prevalent target groups have been small investors (popular capitalism) and workers (labour capitalism). The former are ostensibly targeted to democratize capitalism and improve the efficiency of markets. The latter are targeted ostensibly to enhance productivity.

Popular capitalism, at least as sometimes practiced in the region,[26] raises legitimate questions about whether the implicit price subsidy is, socially speaking, really worth it. First, unless there is a virtual giveaway of the public firm to every citizen, there is reason to suspect that in a poor developing country the so-called popular capitalism will not be so popular.[27]

Second, one of the technical justifications for promoting popular capitalism—discouraging market-efficient takeover threats—is weakened when the main motive for share participation is not risk-adjusted future returns but rather exploitation of an easy and almost guaranteed rent.[28] On the one hand, the rent seekers have less incentive to be well-informed shareholders, making them prone to herd behaviour and exit.[29] On the other, uninformed and dispersed shareholders create favourable conditions for the emergence of an organized group that may take entrenched control of the firm; moreover, the group may well pay a price that is lower than if control had been sold by open bid at the time of privatization.[30] It should also be mentioned that the debate over whether concentrated or dispersed ownership is more effective for international competitiveness is by no means resolved (especially in the context of a developing country) (Akyuz, 1992; Welch, 1992), thus making popular capitalism something of an act of faith.

Third, if monetary incentives are deemed necessary to promote capitalist values (of course there may be better ways), it is more transparent and equitable to sell the shares at the highest possible price and offer the possibility of applying for clearly identifiable rebates that make the subsidy explicit and accountable to the general public. Of course, none of these considerations apply if popular capitalism is really a ploy to gain political or ideological advantages; in that case, the hidden subsidy may be a quite effective, albeit cynical, tool.[31]

Privatization operations have often transferred shares to the firm's workers on preferential terms. Chile probably has the region's most extensive experience in this area, but the strategy has appeared on a lesser scale in most other countries as well.[32] The technical logic behind labour capitalism would seem to make most sense only if the workers gain a large enough block of shares to hold and sustain representation on the board of directors of the privatized firm. But in this case, since workers possess "inside" information about the firm, there would obviously be little reason to subsidize the price of their shares and credit. On the other hand, if workers receive subsidized shares without board representation, they could conceivably suffer in the medium term as short-term capital gains could erode a trade union's discipline and effectiveness as a collective bargaining tool.[33]

The preferential distribution of shares to workers in the region has usually not been large enough to give them sustained representation on the board of directors. In reality, the underlying motive of the offer usually seems to have been the reduction of labour's resistance to privatization: a strategy which has tended to work quite well. However, if the main purpose of a subsidized share distribution is to co-opt workers, a more efficient alternative might be to simply link the privatization to the establishment of a profit-sharing arrangement for them, thereby reserving the sale of shares for the highest bidders. This approach could improve the net sale proceeds for the State, as it avoids the lower sale price deriving from the subsidy given on the shares distributed to workers and the uncertainty that prospective shareholders might feel regarding the future role of workers in the management of the firm. Moreover, a profit-sharing programme could have larger spread effects in the local economy than a special subsidized sale of shares to workers of certain public enterprises. In effect, it establishes a precedent that other private firms can more plausibly be encouraged to imitate, which in turn opens up prospects of institutionalizing profit-sharing for all workers in the productive sector of the economy. Finally, as an incentive to productivity, profit-sharing for risk-shy workers may be better than a gratuitous distribution of shares because it avoids the problems of worker morale that can arise from unfavourable fluctuations in the region's still thin and volatile domestic stock markets.

The objective of price maximization could also conceivably trade off with a subsidy for capitalists, designed to serve as a catalyst for private sector investment and growth. While this particular tradeoff finds some support in certain technical circles, the awarding of rents to a select group of domestic capitalists in order to stimulate the overall economy's animal spirits is certainly a controversial hypothesis that is difficult to test. If subsidies are deemed necessary it is clearly more efficient and equitable to grant them directly in the form of a tax credit or other publicly accountable instrument. In any event, the externalities derived from hidden subsidies in a privatization operation are probably exaggerated and far less important than those emerging from sound overall public macro-economic and social reform programmes (which can be aided by a share price maximization strategy), astute international bargaining and fortuitous exogenous events.[34]

A price maximization strategy should also be compatible with the objective of projecting political credibility. Once again, a conflict could arise most easily in cases of great fiscal urgency. This is yet another reason why greater transitory direct compensatory budgetary support should be forthcoming from the international financial agencies.

3. Assignment of Privatization Receipts to a Social Development Trust Fund

If there were absolutely no alternative role for the State, the outcome of a privatization process would be a proportionate shrinking of the public sector. However, even if one were to make the extreme assumption that there is no future direct role for the State in productive activities,[35] there would still be a serious need to strengthen public goods in the social area. Indeed, after ten years of regressive adjustment in the region, most would concede that the social sector (including public infrastructure) is one area where the State should focus its future efforts. While in some instances support for social development could be provided by imaginative private initiatives, there is often no satisfactory alternative to public action.

In the social area it is not always easy to distinguish conceptually between current and capital outlays. Nevertheless, from an accounting standpoint, recurrent social expenditure has suffered most during the crisis, and in relative terms it is here that financial support is most urgently needed in the years ahead (ECLAC, 1992c). Thus, in addition to earmarking privatization receipts for a special account, it might be helpful to further earmark all, or at least a significant part, of the income for a national social development trust fund. This type of policy would establish a permanent and flexible base for increased social expenditure on either the current or capital account.[36] Of course, earmarking might be hard to accomplish when there is a general situation of fiscal urgency, but on the other hand, if authorities were legally required to earmark their extraordinary income for social expenditure, this could serve as a political tool to focus attention on other ways to balance budgets, e.g., tax reforms, cuts in excessive military expenditures, or more aggressive debt renegotiation strategies.

4. Fair Compensation for PE Employees

As an alternative to a strategy of layoffs followed by new hiring, greater efforts could be made to exploit possibilities of retraining and redeploying labour within the firm. Shares with representation on the board of directors, or profit-sharing, could be exchanged for concessions on wages. When systematic layoffs are necessary in privatization programmes, indemnification is simply not enough.[37] Cash payments can easily be squandered; hence, the workers affected need counselling, retraining, relocation assistance and follow-up monitoring of their reintegration into the market. Since redundant employment in State firms is a "public problem", it would seem appropriate to finance retraining, counselling and indemnifications with special solidarity taxes or soft loans from international development banks, which incidentally have historically been major creditors of many PEs.[38]

5. Effective Regulation

From the standpoint of social welfare, a key assumption of successful privatization is that firms can be regulated externally by the public sector as well as or better than when they were under direct public ownership. However, the transfer of ownership creates new types of problems that must be surmounted.

It is often argued that liberalization of trade is sufficient to regulate tradeable goods sectors and ensure reasonable internal efficiency. However, this may be only partly true in a developing country, as there will be lags and remaining obstacles to price competition on account of, among other things, the small size of many markets, which creates price inelasticities; the upfront costs of establishing distribution networks; exclusive dealership arrangements; collusion; and the considerable transport costs in South America. Thus there will be a need for new domestic institutional and legal structures to promote desirable levels of competition and to control arbitrary pricing strategies, especially in the case of durable goods (technical norms for quality and consumer safety are, of course, also desirable).

As far as large public service firms are concerned, the usual strategy up to now has been to transfer public monopolies into private hands. This is not necessarily a bad decision; in spite of recent arguments which have undermined the strength of the traditional natural monopoly concept, in some sectors there is still legitimate room to debate the effects of deconcentration on allocative efficiency. In effect, a developing country may not want to assume the risk of experimenting with the breaking-up of integrated public service systems.

Notwithstanding the above, the new regulatory frameworks which have emerged in the region's privatization of public service sectors often allow for new entrants, which introduces the assumption of an immediate or future contestable market. However, when the dominant operator in the market is very large, it, rather than the potential new entrant, is the real threat to the market, so that in many cases the practical relevance of contestability as a serious regulatory factor is suspect (Vickers and Yarrow, 1988). Thus, even if a market is contestable in principle, effective direct price/quality regulation of the new privatized industries by public authorities is of paramount importance for allocative efficiency and social equity.

The region's regulatory challenge is a major one, especially in public services. First, effectively regulating powerful monopolies is inherently a difficult and sometimes conflictive task which can test the mettle of even the most zealous regulators and sophisticated government administrations.[39] Second, the speed with which regulatory systems have emerged in Latin America suggests that flaws are likely to be discovered in them after privatization, and when these are serious, countries will have to find ways to correct them without disrupting investment or the stock markets, where privatized public service firms usually carry much weight. Third, regulatory systems must also be flexible in face of the fast changing technological developments in some public service sectors. Fourth, regulators may also have to be international diplomats, as many new owners of public service firms are foreign enterprises and many of the latter are owned by foreign governments.

The signs are that the region's regulatory capacity is lagging far behind the speed of its privatization processes. The problem is not so much the lack of formal systems— they are often quite sophisticated and imaginative, as in the case of the Chilean electricity sector (Banlot, 1993)—but rather that they are emerging with little or no track record and apparently weak or non-existent enforcement systems.[40] The problem is aggravated by the fact that, in order to attract buyers and finance their investment commitments, scales of charges were often subjected to prior adjustments which were extremely generous to the privatized firms.[41]

When regulatory frameworks are permissive, this could mean that the authorities have decided to trade off the improved internal efficiency of a privatized firm against a potential deterioration in allocative efficiency, wagering implicitly that the loss of static allocative efficiency and social equity will be more than compensated by the catalytic effects of the enhanced profitability of capital in the privatized sector. Unfortunately, from the standpoint of equity this could be another version of the "trickledown" approach to development that tended to dominate thinking in the 1980s. Moreover, it assumes that the tradeable goods sector can prosper even with potentially significant distortions in the relative prices of important domestic public services.

Key ingredients for success in regulation include the following:

i) Regulatory systems should be set up well before the privatization of a public service firm (Paredes, 1992) so that a track record can be established and some of the worst operational problems can possibly be ironed out while the firm is still State property. At the very least, it would be wise to avoid the simultaneous privatization of several public service sectors which still have "virgin" regulatory systems.

ii) Regulatory systems should be based on straightforward, impersonal rules that are clearly defined, technically consistent with the administrative skills of the country's prospective regulators, and comprehensible not only to shareholders and management, but also to consumers; sophisticated regulatory systems which may offer a great deal of theoretical satisfaction may in practice create more regulatory problems than solutions.

iii) Regulatory systems in developing countries must be designed to take into account dynamic and not just static efficiency.

iv) Regulatory bodies should be independent public entities whose board appointments should be staggered so as not to coincide with political cycles.

v) Regulatory personnel should be technically qualified, very well paid relative to the industry that is being regulated, and prohibited from working in the regulated industry for a specified period after their appointments are terminated.

vi) The regulatory board should have fluid channels of communication with its relevant industry, but at the same time it should always have the last word on regulatory decisions.

vii) A special legal framework should be established to settle disputes between firms and the regulators.

viii) The regulator must have a clear, practical, and increasingly severe set of sanctions at its disposal in case of a firm's non-compliance.

ix) Reviews of the regulatory framework for public service sectors should be spread out over an extended period so as to avoid the bunching of review sessions; in this way potential disputes could be less damaging to overall economic confidence.[42]

It is often overlooked that an essential public service can never be fully privatized, because the operator of last resort will always be the public sector. To avoid the moral hazard that could affect private owners, the State should probably consider regulating privatized firms more comprehensively than is traditionally the case, including their debt accumulation, dividend policy, diversification and investment. An alternative would be to forego more comprehensive regulation but charge the privatized firm a risk premium for "public insurance" covering the contingent costs of State intervention should the firm enter into a critical operating condition. The moral hazard problem could be more volatile in regulatory frameworks that copy England's RPI-X formula,[43] because unexpected shocks arising from bad management decisions and/or exogenous factors cannot be passed on to prices. Finding commercially viable ways to control moral hazard is admittedly a difficult task. However, ignoring the problem could mean seriously underestimating the costs of privatization.

Finally, it could be argued that effective regulation will lower the sale price of PEs, compared with firms granted extensive market power. But perhaps the tradeoff is not all that large, since astute purchasers will surely discount the effects of excessively permissive regulatory frameworks that will very likely be subject to serious adjustments at a later date.

V CONCLUSIONS

Privatization is now a fact of life in Latin America. Most of the countries' programmes are very ambitious, and there is little sign of the trend slowing down before a large part of the region's PEs have been divested. The theoretical and practical benefits of divestiture in a developing country would seem to be strongest in most conventional tradeable goods sectors, where liberalized markets can be counted on to autonomously perform a large part of the regulatory function (hopefully complemented by antimonopoly laws and consumer protection norms). In contrast, they are more problematical in sectors involving capital-dense public services, or those which have large externalities for macroeconomic management; in these cases, the impact of divestiture on social welfare will be immediately linked to the ability of governments to administratively regulate the privatized firms on a continuous and effective basis.

Clearly, the poorer a country and the more unsophisticated its public administration, the greater the need for caution in the decision to divest large public service firms.[44] In any event, only time will tell the degree to which the actual process and end product of divestiture improves social welfare. Whatever the benefits to be had from privatization, however, they can be improved upon if more attention is given to the objective of social equity.

We have focused proposals on five key areas that can raise the social benefits of privatization: greater transparency; more systematic efforts to maximize the sale price; fair compensation for displaced workers; the earmarking of sale receipts for social development, and effective public regulation.

Of course, social equity must trade off with other objectives. However, the tradeoffs with many of the commonly stated objectives of privatization do not necessarily entail major sacrifices in terms of equity, for many complementarities would seem to exist. In fact, the most threatening tradeoff seems to be fiscal urgency. Thus, it would be helpful if multilateral organizations strengthened, or at least front-loaded, their budgetary support for developing countries willing to initiate a careful and socially equitable divestiture programme. This can be justified on grounds which these organizations readily understand: improved creditworthiness of their borrowers.

In sum, reform of public enterprises through privatization is necessarily a complicated task that must balance real tradeoffs. However, the prime factors in deciding on privatization should be social equity and dynamic efficiency, and these considerations should be traded off for other objectives only reluctantly and in ways which make not only the benefits but also the social costs of the decision explicit to the public. Late-comers in privatization can clearly learn lessons from more advanced programmes on how to improve the net social benefits of the process. Nevertheless, even the best privatization schemes will probably leave some problems that will have to be mopped up by later governments. In view of this, privatization should be seen not so much as an "event" but rather as a "process" in which one can expect that the divestiture of PEs will produce the need for other reforms, especially in the regulatory area. The success of governments in managing this latter transition will also be an important determinant of the net social benefits of privatization.

NOTES

1 Apart from the sheer magnitude of the crisis and the fragility of the new democratic political regimes, the slow response was also undoubtedly related to the very serious shortcomings in the construction of multilateral conditionality and the official management of the debt problem, which tended to underfinance the adjustment process. See Devlin (1989), Ramos (1992), Killick *et al.* (1984) and Ground (1984).
2 But the financial crisis was also a setback for the monetary approach to the balance of payments and for proponents of "self-regulated" credit markets. See Ramos (1986), Ffrench-Davis (1982) and Devlin (1989).
3 There is a whole range of privatization techniques, of which divestiture—total or partial transfer of State-owned enterprises to the private sector—is only one. For a discussion of this, see ECLAC (1992b).
4 For an excellent history of public enterprises in Chile see Ortega (1989).
5 From here on, the term "PEs" will be used broadly to include public entities that are not necessarily formally classified as enterprises.
6 About US\$1.1 billion of the total amount represents the market value of foreign debt paper which was used as a means of payment in several transactions.
7 Almost all the sales were paid for in the form of domestic debt instruments.
8 It is already known that the new government plans to modify some aspects of the privatization programme, in particular by drastically lowering the amount of debt paper that can be used as a means of payment.
9 In other words, the government should sell the firm if $V_{sp} + (\alpha_g - \alpha_p)Z > V_{sg}$, where V_{sp} is the social value of the firm under private ownership; V_{sg} is the social value of the firm under public ownership; Z is the sale price, and α_g and α_p are the shadow prices of the public and private sector income, respectively. Naturally, the social value of the firm under public or private ownership will be assessed in the light of a wide range of indicators of the net benefits for society. See Jones, Tandon and Vogelsang (1990).
10 Moreover, many of the remaining instances of inefficiency were imposed by the military government's ideological preferences, which induced explicitly restrictive policies on the expansion of PE activity. For instance, the public telephone company was not allowed to diversify into new services: new investment was limited; profits were siphoned off to the central government budget, and the capacity to borrow was very restricted. This firm was also seriously hurt by the 1982/1983 economic collapse, induced in part by the government's macroeconomic policy (Castillo, 1991).
11 For a discussion of yardstick competition, see Vickers and Yarrow (1988).
12 Ironically, some of the European firms like Telefónica, Iberia and France Telcom are public enterprises.

13 During the external debt renegotiations creditors frequently required the public sector to absorb the private sector's debts with foreign banks. This was a highly arbitrary policy with no real economic justification (Devlin, 1989).

14 This problem seems to be emerging in Chile, especially in the electric power sector, where private and public firms compete in a sometimes conflictive setting. There has been a dispute between a State power generation firm and privatized power generation companies over investment in a thermal plant in Northern Chile.

15 Prior to being voted into power, the Peronist Party had opposed a partial privatization of ENTel which had been proposed earlier by the Alfonsín government (Gerchunoff and Castro, 1992).

16 This latter argument would seem to be almost irrelevant for Latin America, which already confronts huge disequilibria and distortions due to the crisis. Indeed, in such a "third best" world, it is difficult to assert that direct taxes will be distortionary.

17 It has been argued that privatizations are analogous to emitting bonds and therefore should be a "below the line" item in the fiscal accounts. Governments, however, tend to put privatization receipts above the line, thus causing the published accounts to understate deficits or overstate surpluses (Mansoor, 1988).

18 There was an overall deficit in Brazil in 1991, but that country's privatization operations were paid for almost entirely in domestic public debt instruments. The Argentine privatizations of 1989/1990 were also paid for to a large extent with foreign public debt instruments.

19 According to the Minister of Finance of Mexico, as quoted in *Latin American Weekly Economic Report* (1992a).

20 The privatization of ENTel and Aerolíneas Argentinas generated only US$300 million of cash for assets valued at US$1,500 million. This was due in part to the government's decision to receive payment in foreign bank debt, the nominal sum of which was US$7 billion (Gerchunoff and Castro, 1992). The retirement of the debt had little effect on fiscal cash flow because the government was in a moratorium (Altimir and Devlin, 1992).

21 Some have characterized these reforms as regressive (Marfan, 1984).

22 See Moffett, 1992.

23 Standard & Poor have just given Chile a BBB investment rating.

24 Mexico, but especially Chile in the period 1985–89, followed this sequence (Martín del Campo and Winkler, 1992). Brazil has so far also been broadly following this path.

25 This strategy has worked in Argentina and Mexico (Gerchunoff and Castro, 1992; Ruprah, 1990a).

26 A number of countries in the region have engaged in preferential distributions, but Chile has clearly been the main practitioner of this strategy. During the military regime preferential sales to the general public and public sector workers (including the Armed Forces) created some 120,000 popular capitalists (Sáez, 1991).

27 Our examination of the home addresses of 46,000 popular capitalists in one of the largest Chilean privatization operations (the sale of the ENDESA electricity firm) suggests that it is extremely likely that there was disproportionate participation by upper income groups. This conclusion is based on the distribution of popular capitalists in the different municipalities of Santiago, a highly socially-stratified city with 40% of the country's population. About 45% of the shares sold to the popular capitalists (at a preferential price and with subsidized credit) were purchased by residents of this city. Of that amount, slightly more than 50% were bought by residents of four municipalities where nearly 70% of the households are in the top two income distribution deciles.

(The primary data on popular capitalism came from CORFO, while data on income distribution were provided by Arturo León, of ECLAC's Statistics and Projections Division).

28 Regarding the preferential sales of ENDESA shares, the official brochure distributed to public employees stressed that "the offer involves no cost to the workers" (CORFO, 1988).

29 There are signs of erosion of the small shareholders' base in Chile's privatized firms; for example, ENDESA's small shareholders declined by 11% between 1989 and 1991.

30 In 1989, the holding company ENERSIS was set up and gained control of ENDESA with 12% of the company's total shares. The price paid was quite attractive, since share prices were relatively depressed at the time of the purchase. See Sáez, 1991.

31 In Chile, the authorities also viewed popular capitalism as a way to discourage renationalization (Hachette and Lüders, 1992) and perhaps gain an advantage in the upcoming 1989 plebiscite. Popular capitalism in England also apparently had political objectives (Vickers and Yarrow, 1988).

32 In Chile at least 15 privatization operations offered shares to workers on preferential terms. Although the amounts of shares varied, the general pattern was that a few small firms (e.g., subsidiaries of ENDESA) were sold entirely to workers, while employees of large privatized firms were given small blocks of shares ranging from 6–10%. Major exceptions were CAP, where workers secured more than 30% of the shares in a highly controversial transaction (Errázuriz, Fortunati and Bustamante, 1989), IANSA (21%), and LAN Chile (15%). In a few privatization operations workers joined together of their own initiative to borrow resources in financial markets and purchase additional shares. However, even in cases where workers nominally gained a large block of shares it is difficult to ascertain to what degree they participated in decision-making, because shares often came to be managed by investment trusts. In Mexico, workers have also occasionally participated in sales: for example, they were sold 4% of TELMEX, in the country's largest privatization operation. In the case of Aeroméxico, the pilots' union secured 35% of the firm (Ruprah, 1992b). In Argentina, 10% of a privatized firm's shares are frequently earmarked for workers.

33 My thanks are due to Hernán Gutiérrez for this latter observation.

34 Privatization operations do not seem to have been the decisive factors in economic recoveries. In Mexico, the decisive factor appears to have been the announcement of the North American Free Trade Zone, coupled with a coherent and tough adjustment/stabilization programme (of which privatization was a part). In Chile, the recovery was underway before privatization began. This, coupled with a depreciating exchange rate, could be the principal reason behind rising private savings and investment. Recovery in Venezuela, for its part, was set off by the favourable effects of the Gulf War on the petroleum sector, coupled with a draconian adjustment programme.

35 Of course, in practice, there probably is a future role for State enterprises due to the infant industry argument, considerations about strategic macroeconomic management, regulatory requirements for firm-level information in oligopolistic public service sectors; public choice, etc. Indeed, as Lahera (1992) has commented, there should be a flexible conceptualization of State participation in the economy. If the State's entrance into economic activity is easy and its exit difficult, there are probabilities of eventual inefficiencies and rents. On the other hand, if entrance is impossible and exit easy, the activity of the State will not always be compatible with development.

36 My thanks are due to Martine Guerguil for sharing with me her idea about a trust fund.

37 Information on the fate of workers is an area of analysis that needs much more attention. Mexico's latter rounds of privatization operations were characterized by the official objective of avoiding layoffs; for instance, in the privatization of TELMEX, with 49,000 workers, there were no dismissals. This was due in part to the workers' acceptance of changes in labour contracts and the government's decision to establish a retraining facility within the firm for employees displaced by new technology. On the other hand, the peaceful tone of industrial relations was also influenced by demonstration effects: in 1988, as a prelude to privatizing Aeroméxico, the government confronted a striking union by suddenly declaring the firm bankrupt. The workforce dropped overnight from 12,000 employees to less than 4,000 (Ruprah, 1992b). Moreover, Mexican unions claim that 100,000 workers have lost their jobs either through direct privatization or through rationalization of State agencies (*Latin American Weekly Report,* 1992b). In Chile, privatization operations were not generally associated with massive layoffs; indeed employment in many firms expanded. However, the workforce of public enterprises had already been drastically reduced in earlier public enterprise reforms; by 1986 the labour force in major public enterprises was 40% less than it had been in 1974 (Sáez, 1991). In Argentina, although there has been a layoff of workers as part of the preparation for the privatization of a steel complex, the general strategy has been to cancel labour contracts and let workers renegotiate them with the privatized firms. The outcome of this process should be studied in order to ascertain how workers have fared in their new contractual limbo.

38 The World Bank has financed indemnification payments in some countries.

39 This has been shown by the experience with companies like British Telecom, British Gas, etc. (*The Economist,* 1992).

40 For the cases of Mexico and Argentina see Ruprah (1990a and 1992b) and Gerchunoff and Castro (1992), respectively. The Chilean systems have a track record, since they were first established in the early 1980s; even so, there has been much confusion in the interpretation and enforcement of the different systems.

41 See Gerchunoff and Castro (1992) and Ruprah (1990a). In Chile, rates underwent severe adjustment well before privatization. It should be mentioned that the investment constraint argument in respect of privatization is weakened when the main source of finance for new investment is government-authorized increases in the scales of charges.

42 Long periods between review sessions could, however, create the need for very large adjustments. An alternative worth considering is a continuous review process which induces mini-adjustments, much like a crawling peg exchange rate system.

43 This formula means that regulated prices rise on average by less than the rate of domestic inflation (the Retail Price Index—RPI). This is supposed to be an incentive for innovation and cost reduction. However, there may be little room to absorb shocks such as a failed project, debt refinancing problems, etc. The telecommunications sectors in Argentina and Mexico will be regulated by variants of the RPI-X formula. In the case of Argentina, however, there are adjustments for adverse movements of the exchange rate. See Gerchunoff and Castro (1992) and Ruprah (1990a).

44 Other alternatives might be explored, such as performance contracts for public firms or payment of fees to an experienced private operator who undertakes to pursue publicly outlined objectives.

BIBLIOGRAPHY

Altimir, Oscar and Robert Devlin: (1992), Una reseña de la moratoria de la deuda en América Latina, in Oscar Altimir and Robert Devlin (eds.), *Moratoria de la deuda en*

América Latina: experiencia de los países, Mexico City, Fondo de Cultura Económica.

Akyuz, Yilmaz (1992): Financial Reform and the Development Process, Geneva, United Nations Conference on Trade and Development (UNCTAD).

Atkinson, Anthony and Stiglitz, Joseph (1980): *Lectures on Public Economics,* New York, McGraw-Hill.

Banlot, Vivianne (1993): La regulación del sector eléctrico: la experiencia chilena, in Oscar Muñoz (ed.), *Más allá que las privatizaciones: hacia el estado regulador,* Santiago, Chile, Ediciones CIEPLAN.

Castillo, Mario (1991): Privatizaciones de empresas públicas en Chile: el caso del sector de telecommunicaciones, Santiago, Chile, ECLAC, *mimeo.*

CORFO (Corporación de Fomento) (1988): *Ponga su futuro en acción,* Santiago, Chile.

Cornia, Giovanni Andrea, Richard Jolly and Frances Stewart (1988): *Adjustment with a Human Face,* vols. I-II, Oxford, Clarendon Press.

Devlin, Robert (1989), *Debt and Crisis in Latin America: The Supply Side of the Story,* Princeton, NJ, Princeton University Press.

ECLAC (1990), *Changing Production Patterns with Social Equity,* Santiago, Chile, United Nations publication, Sales No. E.90.II.G.6

――― (1991), *Preliminary Overview of the Latin American and Caribbean Economy, 1991* (LC/G.1696), Santiago, Chile.

――― (1992a), *Equity and Changing Production Patterns: an Integrated Approach* (LC/G.1701 (SES.24/3), Santiago, Chile.

――― (1992b), *La reestructuración de empresas: el caso de los puertos de América Latina y el Caribe,* "Cuadernos de la CEPAL" series, No. 68, Santiago, Chile. United Nations publication, Sales No. S.92.II.G.9.

――― (1992c), *Education and knowledge: Basic pillars of changing production patterns with social equity* (LC/G.1702 (SES. 24/4) Rev.1), Santiago, Chile.

Errázuriz, Enrique, Rodolfo Fortunati and Cristián Bustamante (1989): *Huachipato,* Santiago, Chile, Academia de Humanismo Cristiano, Programa de Economía del Trabajo (PET).

Errázuriz, Enrique and Jacqueline Weinstein (1986): *Capitalismo popular y privatización de empresas públicas,* Santiago, Chile, Academia de Humanismo Cristiano, Programa de Economía del Trabajo (PET), Working Paper No 53.

Ffrench-Davis, Ricardo (1982): El experimento monetarista en Chile: una síntesis crítica, *Colección Estudios CIEPLAN,* No 9, Santiago, Chile, Corporación de Investigaciones Económicas para América Latina (CIEPLAN), December.

Floyd, Robert, Clive Gray and R. Short (1984): *Public Enterprises in Mixed Economies,* Washington, D.C., International Monetary Fund (IMF).

Fondo de Inversiones de Venezuela (1992): *Política de privatizaciones y reestructuración,* Caracas, June.

Galal, Ahmed, Leroy Jones, Pankaj Tandon and Ingo Vogelsang (1992): Synthesis of cases and policy summary, paper presented at the Conference on the Welfare Consequences of Selling Public Enterprises, Washington, D.C., World Bank, 11-12 June, *mimeo.*

Gemines (1989): *Analisis de la coyuntura económica,* Santiago, Chile, August.

Gerchunoff, Pablo and Lilian Castro (1992), La racionalidad macroeconómica de las privatizaciones: El caso argentino, paper presented at the Regional Seminar on Reforms of Public Policy, ECLAC, Santiago, Chile, 3–5 August, *mimeo.*

Gerchunoff, Pablo and Germán Coloma (1992): Privatizaciones y reforma regulatoria en la Argentina, paper presented at the Regional Seminar on Reforms of Public Policy, ECLAC, Santiago, Chile, 3–5 August, *mimeo.*

Ground, Richard Lynn (1984): Orthodox adjustment programmes in Latin America: A critical look at the policies of the International Monetary Fund, *CEPAL Review,* No 23, Santiago, Chile, ECLAC, August. United Nations publication, Sales No. E.84.II.G.4.

Hachette, Dominique and Rolf Lüders (1992): *La privatización en Chile,* San Francisco, ICS Press.

Hanke, Steve (1987): "Introduction" in Steve Hanke (ed.), *Privatization and Development,* San Francisco, ICS Press.

Hemming, Richard and Ali Mansoor (1988): *Privatization and Public Enterprises,* Occasional Paper No. 56, Washington, D.C., IMF.

Herrera, Alejandra (1991): *Privatización de los servicios de telecommunicaciones: El caso argentino,* New York, Columbia Business School, August.

Hirschman, Albert (1970): *Exit, Voice and Loyalty,* Cambridge, MA, Harvard University Press.

Jones, Leroy, Pankaj Tandon and Ingo Vogelsang (1990): *Selling Public Enterprises,* Cambridge, MA, MIT Press.

Khanna, Vikram (1992): Mexico's economic resurgence highlighted at World Bank conference, *IMF Survey,* Washington, D.C., IMF, 25 May.

Killick, Tony (1989): *A Reaction Too Far,* London, Overseas Development Institute.

Killick, Tony, Graham Bird, Jennifer Sharpley and Mary Sutton (1984): The IMF: Case for a change in emphasis, in Richard Feinberg and Valeriana Kallab (eds.), *Adjustment Crisis in the Third World,* New Brunswick, Transaction Books.

Lahera, Eugenio (1992): Un sector público con entrada y salida, *El Diario,* Santiago, Chile, 29 April.

Latin American Weekly Economic Report (1992a): Aspe announces big debt mop-up, London, 18 June 1992.

———— (1992b): Counting the cost of privatization, London, 13 August.

Latin Finance (1991): Privatization in Latin America, Florida, USA, March.

———— (1992): Privatization in Latin America, Florida, USA, March.

Mansoor, Ali (1988): *The Budgetary Impact of Privatization,* Washington, D.C., IMF.

Marcel, Mario (1989): *La privatización de empresas públicas en Chile 1985–1988,* Notas Técnicas, No. 125, Santiago, Chile, CIEPLAN.

Marco Modiano, Eduardo (1992): Statement delivered at the Seminar on the Politics and Economics of Public Revenues and Expenditures, sponsored by the World Bank and Ministry of Economic Affairs, Brasilia, 10–12 June.

Marfán, Manuel (1984): Una evaluación de la nueva reforma tributaria, *Colección Estudios* CIEPLAN, No 13, Santiago, Chile, CIEPLAN, June.

Martín del Campo, Antonio and Donald Winkler (1992): State-owned enterprise reform in Latin America, *CEPAL Review,* No. 46, April.

Moffett, Matt (1992): Mexico's bull market lifts new generation into the wealthy elite, *Wall Street Journal,* 6 May.

Ortega, Luís (1989) (ed.): CORFO: *50 años de realizaciones, 1939–1989,* Santiago, Chile, University of Santiago, Department of History.

Paredes, Ricardo (1993): Privatización y regulación: lecciones de la experiencia chilena, in Oscar Muñoz (ed.), *Más allá que las privatizaciones: hacia el estado regulador,* Santiago, Chile, Ediciones CIEPLAN.

Nair, Govindan and Anastasios Filippides (1988): *How Much Do State-Owned Enterprises Contribute to Public Sector Deficits in Developing Countries—And Why?,* Washington, D.C., World Bank, Working Paper No. 45, December.

Ramos, Joseph (1986): *Neo-Conservative Economics in the Southern Cone of Latin America, 1973–1983,* Baltimore, Johns Hopkins Press.

——— (1992): Equilibrios macroeconómicos y desarrollo, in Osvaldo Sunkel (ed.), *El desarrollo desde dentro,* Mexico City, Fondo de Cultura Económica.

Ruprah, Inder (1990a): *Privatization: Case Study Teléfonos de México,* Mexico City, *mimeo.*

——— (1990b): *Privatization: Case Study Compañía Mexicana de Aviación,* Mexico City, CIDE, *mimeo.*

——— (1992a): *Divestiture and reform of public enterprises: the Mexican case,* Mexico City, *mimeo.*

——— (1992b): *Aeromexico,* Mexico City, *mimeo.*

Sáez, Raúl (1991): *An overview of privatization in Chile: the episodes, the results and the lessons,* Santiago, Chile, *mimeo.*

Secretaría de Hacienda y Crédito Público (n.d.): *El proceso de enajenación de entidades paraestatales,* Mexico City.

Seth, R. (1989): Distributional issues in privatization, *Federal Reserve Bank of New York Quarterly Review,* Vol. 14, No. 2, Summer.

Tandon, Pankaj (1992): *Mexico,* Vol. 1, paper presented at the Conference on the Welfare Consequences of Selling Public Enterprises, Washington, D.C., World Bank, 11–12 June.

The Economist (1992) Off with the lot, 15 August.

Valenzuela Silva, Mario (1989): Reprivatización y capitalismo popular en Chile, *Estudios Públicos,* No 33, Santiago, Chile, Centro de Estudios Públicos (CEP), Summer.

Vickers, John and George Yarrow (1988): *Privatization: An Economic Analysis,* Cambridge, MA, MIT Press.

Welch, John (1992): *The New Finance of Latin America: Financial Flows, Markets, and Institutions in the 1990s,* Dallas, Federal Reserve Bank of Dallas.

West, Peter (1991): Latin America's return to the private international capital market, *CEPAL Review,* No. 44 (LC/G.1667-P), Santiago, Chile, August.

Williamson, John (1990): *The Process of Policy Reform in Latin America,* Washington, D.C., Institute for International Economics.

Woodrow Wilson Center (1991): *Noticias,* Spring.

THE HUMAN DIMENSION
OF DEVELOPMENT

True development is a process which increases human welfare, both in the short and the long runs. However, it also implies social change, either encouraging it or accepting its inevitability, while attempting to ensure that its effect on human welfare is positive.

Both human welfare and social change are quite complex and multidimensional in their own right, complicating efforts to understand, measure, encourage, or assess them. Attempting to deal with the two together, under the rubric of development, compounds the difficulty. The earlier parts of the book have dealt with many of the issues of development. We now must focus specifically on the prime objective of development, the welfare of the human beings involved in the process of social change.

You should recall that in the aggregate the past forty years have witnessed dramatic improvements in most measures of human welfare (for example, life expectancy, literacy, infant mortality, and access to food and other goods). However, such measures may mask other less favorable elements of the process, such as the continuation of underdevelopment in certain geographic areas or among certain groups. Social change may also result in the dislocation and disruption of existing systems which may threaten the welfare of those involved, at least in the short run.

The article by Denis Goulet and Charles K. Wilber neatly captures the ambiguities and difficulties of social change. They note that there have been more than a few cases in which a generation has been sacrificed for the bright promise of future development. And there have been other cases in which the basic values of peoples have been cavalierly disregarded in the quest for development—they have been denied "cognitive respect." Today we must add one other situation in which human welfare is not respected; that is, the reaction to social change that results in efforts to turn back the

465

clock to a time of imagined tranquility and greatness. The near genocide in Bosnia and in Rwanda are the clearest contemporary examples of this chilling form of "antidevelopment."

However simply to resist the social change implied by development is to overlook and accept the very real costs of *under*development. Goulet and Wilber point out that 1.4 million more African infants die every year than would die if the infant mortality rate equaled that of the developed countries. They are victims of underdevelopment; respect for human welfare demands confronting this situation. Similarly, certain cultural practices of underdevelopment are objectionable on broad human grounds beyond simple ethnocentrism, for example, use of infanticide for population control or disfiguration of females as a means of social control. At a minimum, development can provide the opportunity to deal with the underlying issues and can encourage different behavior, while retaining cognitive respect. Goulet and Wilber conclude that the costs of underdevelopment outweigh the costs of development. So development and social change should be accepted and reaction rejected. At the same time decision makers must attempt to minimize social costs and to find broad standards of acceptability. In that way we may eventually reach an equilibrium at a higher level of development, after more than 500 years of change.

Tony Beck provides a dramatic case study of the costs of underdevelopment in detailing the basic survival strategies of the poorest members of a West Bengal village in India. His findings correspond with those of most studies on the poorest of the poor: They are generally landless or have few if any assets; are often in debt, illiterate, isolated, and ill; and are most often in female-headed households. They are resourceful and will migrate, take on debts, or sell assets to keep themselves and their families in existence. If necessary to survive they will change their eating patterns, use common property, and provide each other mutual support. Despite these efforts, their life of poverty and underdevelopment remains precarious. Beck suggests that development policy must find ways to work in the power gaps in villages to provide better choices for the poorest of the village, always listening to their own description of their needs. Social change and development is a complex process, but its potential benefits to the poor are substantial.

The article by Ariel Dorfman on the Matacos people of "the impenetrable" scrub forest of Argentina deals more directly with how the process of social change affects a people attempting to maintain their traditional way of life. Political and economic pressures from Argentina, beginning around 1879 and including murder and theft, destroyed the traditional way of life. As a result the Matacos seemed "headed for a dead end" of extinction as their situation deteriorated year after year. With the help of outsiders many of the Matacos have attempted to engage social change and development on their own terms. This has forced dramatic adjustments. They have moved toward sedentary occupations of farming, fishing, and lumbering with some success, though their dependency on outside resources has grown. And the process has changed their understanding of themselves as they have begun to lose their own symbols and traditions, despite the "cognitive respect" they have been afforded. Dorfman's conclusion about the effect of social change is ambiguous, although there is no turning back.

The costs of both development and underdevelopment are borne most heavily by women. They are overrepresented among the poorest, and as change comes, especially in rural areas, their burden often grows because they are required to take on additional tasks in the home as well as in production. These observations were made most persuasively by Ester Boserup (1970), and recently updated by Irene Tinker (1990).

Maria de Los Angeles Crummett's article provides an overview of how both underdevelopment and development have affected women's migration patterns in Latin America. The stagnation in traditional agriculture often drove women from the rural areas to the cities for better income opportunities which they shared with the family that remained behind. Similarly, increased opportunities for employment in the maquila industry drew young women from the rural areas and inserted them into a very different social and economic life. And, just as with the Matacos, the results have been quite ambiguous. But underdevelopment left few alternatives.

Boserup's work spawned a new field of inquiry, now called women in development (WID). Kandiyoti's article provides an overview of the WID work and catalogues the effect of development processes on women in rural areas. It complements Standing's treatment in Part Five of women in manufacturing employment. Kandiyoti is critical of the work that has been done to date, however, because it is technocratic and unclear about assumptions, claims, and goals. Her own assessment is that the problems and the effects of different policies vary greatly with geography; for example, 87 percent of African women in the labor force are in agricultural production, compared with only 14 percent in Latin America. In addition, most assistance to women is stopgap and does not deal with the structures that affect their well-being. This leads to contradictory policy prescriptions. For example, WID policy in Africa emphasizes basic human needs, while national agricultural policy emphasizes market-based strategies, even though the latter may be detrimental to satisfying women's basic needs. The implication is that women must take charge of the development process rather than allowing technicians from donor agencies to guide it. So again the issue of social change and human welfare is complex.

The final article by Peter Gall describes an attempt to deal with these complexities and to measure, at a national level, human welfare/human development, and to suggest the factors that generate the differential national experiences of human development. A human development index was created, based on measures of life expectancy, literacy, and purchasing power. The resulting ranking of countries showed that some countries with low incomes do better in human development terms than countries whose incomes are higher. There are a number of suggestions of factors which generate these differences. The article closes by examining the drag of military expenditures on human development and exploring the contribution of freedom to human development.

This article brings us full circle to Goulet and Wilber. Both development and underdevelopment have their costs. The challenge is to understand and accept this "tragic" nature of development, while attempting to find approaches that lie in the middle ground and improve human welfare while maintaining cognitive respect. The task is to develop a substantive basis of improvements in human welfare to justify that "bias toward hope" that must accompany development efforts.

REFERENCES

Boserup, Ester. *Women's Role in Economic Development.* New York: St. Martin's Press, 1970.

Tinker, Irene, ed. *Persistent Inequalities: Women and World Development.* New York: Oxford University Press, 1990.

CHAPTER 26

THE HUMAN DILEMMA
OF DEVELOPMENT

Denis Goulet and Charles K. Wilber

University of Notre Dame

Some argue that, because economic development exacts tremendous social costs, it should be undertaken slowly, only with great deliberation, so as to minimize social disruption. In this light, the orthodox agenda of *rapid* economic growth as the surest route to the elimination of poverty is seriously questioned. The strategy of implementing major economic structural reforms designed to increase output in agriculture and industry is judged against the high price of social change which accompanies rapid development.

Although social change, especially when associated with industrialization, has always entailed a high price, the price of *not* developing is also very high. Historian E. H. Carr notes that "the cost of conservation falls just as heavily on the underprivileged as the cost of innovation on those who are deprived of their privileges."[1] Underdevelopment's high costs include chronic disease, hunger, famine, premature death, and degradation of the human spirit generation after generation. Thus is a painful dilemma posed for development agents conscious of the high social costs of sudden structural changes, yet dedicated to reducing underdevelopment's miseries as rapidly as possible.

THE HIGH SOCIAL COSTS OF DEVELOPMENT

Few writers are more insightful than the sociologist Peter Berger in exposing the high social price of development. The title of Berger's landmark book, *Pyramids of Sacrifice: Political Ethics and Social Change,* is an apt metaphor: The Great Pyramid at Cholula, Mexico, testifies in stone to what Berger calls "the relation among theory,

Prepared for this publication.

sweat and blood."[2] The pyramid was built as an altar of sacrifice, and the theory legitimizing its construction was brutally simple: "If the gods were not regularly fed with human blood, the universe would fall apart."[3] Although the Aztecs bear the stigma of being history's chief executioners at Cholula, Berger concludes that later generations of leaders everywhere—politicians, military commanders, planners, and revolutionaries, abetted by social theorists—continue to immolate innocent, and usually silent, victims in needless sacrifices to insatiable gods.

Berger views development (in both its capitalist and socialist incarnations) and revolution as contemporary Molochs who devour the living flesh of millions, all in the name of a "better life" for *future* generations. One thinks here of Sartre's play *Dirty Hands* in which Hugo asks: "What is the use of struggling for the liberation of men if we despise them to the point of brainwashing them?" The conversation between Hugo and Hoederer is revealing:

> "If we don't love men, we can't struggle on their behalf."
> "I am not interested in what men are but in what they are capable of becoming."
> "I, on the contrary, love them for what they are. With all their sloppiness and filth, with all their vices. I love their voices, their warm hands . . . the worried look on their faces and the desperate combat they wage."

Pyramids of Sacrifice needs to be read as a *cri de coeur* against the perpetration of monstrous cruelties—and their legitimization by intellectuals—on living generations of men, women, and children in myriad lands. The criminals are the hosts of planners, social theorists, and change agents who purport to speak *for* the people. Tragedy is compounded by their assumption that their own perception of reality is more correct than that of the masses. Berger denounces that special blend of arrogance and benevolence which too many development enthusiasts and revolutionaries share with missionaries of old, the transformational zeal which denies to poor people that "cognitive respect" of their own perceptions of reality which is theirs as a basic right.

If any aspiration may be said to be universal, across lines of cultural space and individual personality, it is this: Every person and society wants to be treated by others as a being of worth, for its own sake and on its own terms, regardless of its utility or attractiveness to others. Therefore, Berger is right in demanding that planners, revolutionaries, and social scientists show "cognitive respect" for all populations. He himself deserves "cognitive respect" for defending this view against the mainstream of experts who glibly decree the superiority of their own diagnosis of oppression and misery and thereafter proceed to prescribe "appropriate" remedies: economic growth, or revolution and socialist transformation. The stakes are high and in no way can be reduced to the risk of a series of laboratory experiments. Experts who touch people's lives irresponsibly may damage them beyond repair.

Such warnings will remain necessary so long as development keeps confronting societies in distress with a cruel choice between bread and dignity. The facile slogan states that bread can be had with dignity; the harsh reality, however, is that dignity must often be sacrificed to obtain bread, or that the very aspiration after greater dignity becomes distorted as a quest for more bread. *Pyramids* pungently reminds us of two truths: (1) "Not by bread alone does man live," and (2) upon closer examination even the bread may be a stone!

No ethical issue is so resistant to easy answers as that of generations sacrificed now in exchange for the possibility of future development. This agonizing question leads many close to despair. Here one evokes two additional works which closely parallel Berger's own: Barrington Moore's *Reflections on the Causes of Human Misery* and Robert Heilbroner's *An Inquiry into the Human Prospect.*[4] All three authors end their foray into the history of social change on a note of rational pessimism tempered by an appeal to the transrational duty of not despairing. Uniformly they conclude that as much human suffering results from trying to "improve mankind" as from cynically exploiting it; therefore, they tend toward a "hands off history" stance to minimize suffering.

Thus Berger's brief against sacrificing present generations to prepare a better future for their children should be read as one instance of a more generalized disaffection among Western believers in progress. All facile optimism must now be rejected, every easy belief in the necessarily upward movement of history as well as the very imagery of improvement and evolutionary (or revolutionary) emancipation of the human race. Nevertheless, it would be puerile to react by swinging to the other side of the pendulum, since any serious view of history grasps the irreducibly *tragic* nature of social change.

One senses that Berger has grown discouraged over the inability of social science, development theory, or revolutionary action to deliver its promised "cargo" at a tolerable human cost. But it is an initial mistake ever to suppose that genuine development can be gained, fully or even in part, at "tolerable" human costs. Therefore, Berger should conclude not by saying "avoid social change (developmental growth and revolution) like the plague." Rather he should say: "Let us engage in an unending struggle against present structural injustices (with their train of alienation, misery, underdevelopment, worship of material well-being, etc.) so as to construct history while we bear witness to transcendence."

Although Berger is right in denying that revolution or development can be ethically pursued at *any* price, he is wrong in omitting the third element in the argument: Doing nothing also makes intolerable exactions in sacrificed generations. Writing before the 1964 military coup, Brazilian economist Celso Furtado described the enormous sacrifices paid by generations of his country people living in conditions of "underdevelopment": unnecessary deaths, continued abuse of the poor by privileged classes, constant frustration in efforts to improve their lot. Small wonder, he adds, that

> the masses in the underdeveloped countries have not generally put the same high valuation on individual liberty that we do. Since they have not had access to the better things of life, they obviously cannot grasp the full meaning of the supposed dilemma between liberty and quick development. . . . The liberty enjoyed by the minority in our society is paid for by a delay in general economic development; hence [it] is at the expense of the welfare of the great majority. . . . Very few of us have sufficient awareness of these deeply inhuman characteristics of underdevelopment. When we do become fully aware, we understand why the masses are prepared for any sacrifice in order to overcome it. If the price of liberty for the few had to be poverty of the many, we can be quite certain that the probability of preserving freedom would be practically nil.[5]

Furtado's words remind us that most men and women live in conditions far below those objectively demanded by human dignity. Thus, throughout history generations have always been "sacrificed." Why, then, should Berger condemn in absolute terms the prolongation of certain generational sacrifices a little longer while the progressive emancipation of a populace is being wrought? The point is this: although Berger correctly laments the high sacrifices demanded in the names of development and revolution, he wrongly ignores the equally high costs required by the stance of "keeping things as they are."

THE HUMAN COSTS OF UNDERDEVELOPMENT

Table 26-1 presents two indicators of the human costs of underdevelopment. To illustrate, of 12 million children born each year in sub-Saharan Africa, approximately 1.5 million die before they reach their first birthday. If these countries had the infant mortality rate of the industrialized market economy countries, the mortality of infants would be approximately 0.1 million. This means that because of underdevelopment 1.4 million infants die *each year* in sub-Saharan Africa alone.

The "mathematics of suffering" may be morbid, but it does lend perspective to the human costs of economic *underdevelopment.* Economist Franklyn Holzman faces the problem of human costs squarely; his consideration of the problem is worth quoting at length.

> Let us now turn to the case of the nation caught in the "Malthusian trap," nations in which: (1) there has been no increase in the standard of living for centuries—perhaps there has even been a decline, (2) increases in output lead to a corresponding fall in the death rate so that no change in the standard of living occurs, i.e., those who live remain

TABLE 26-1
THE HUMAN COSTS OF UNDERDEVELOPMENT

Countries grouped by national income per capita	Infant morality rate per thousand live births	Life expectancy at birth in years
Low-income countries		
(less than $400)		
Sub-Saharan Africa only	129	48
All except China and India	114	52
China and India only	59	63
Low-middle-income countries		
($400 to $1,700)	83	58
Upper-middle-income countries		
($1,700 to $7,500)	56	65
Industrial market economies	9	76
East European nonmarket economies	19	68

Source: The World Bank, *World Development Report 1986* (New York: Oxford University Press, 1986), pp. 180–81, 232–35.

at subsistence, (3) the death rate is so high relative to the death rate in nations which have experienced secular economic progress that it is fair to say the inability to escape the "Malthusian trap" is responsible for the (premature) death of most of those born, and finally (4) escape from the "trap" requires a rate of investment so high that increases in productivity outrun increases in population. With such nations the case for a high rate of investment for a long period of time (one which enables the nation to escape the "trap") becomes much easier to justify and value judgments easier to make. The essential distinction between this case and that of the progressive economy is that loss of life can no longer be considered an "absolute," i.e., an infinite disutility. It was reasonable to consider it in this way in a progressive economy because loss of life is not comparable by any measure, with other changes in the level of individual welfare. In the case of the "Malthusian trap" nation, however, one is put in the position of having to compare losses of life between periods. That is to say, failure to attempt to escape the "trap" may be considered equivalent to condemning to death, needlessly, members of future generations. Under these circumstances, loss of life would seem to become a legitimate and measurable datum of the system. The question facing the planner is: shall we raise the rate of investment in the present to a point high enough to escape the "trap" even though this will involve a rise in the death rate of the present generation if we know that it will increase the life expectancy and raise the standard of living of countless future generations? No matter what his decision, the planner faced with such a question is responsible for imposing the death sentence on someone. When life and death are compared on this plane, escape from the trap might well seem to be the superior alternative since by simple addition it becomes obvious that more lives would be saved than lost in the process.[6]

Most of the world's populations live in conditions of poverty which are difficult for the affluent West to understand. And the effect of these conditions on the dignity of individuals, the degradation of their very being, cannot be measured.[7] One must, accordingly, contrast this urgent reality of poverty with the allegedly high social costs of development efforts to end poverty. The human cost of economic development has doubtless been very high in the past, but it does not necessarily follow that these costs are an inescapable part of all industrialization or agricultural modernization processes.

There exist several reasons why industrialization is not a painless process. First, there is the need in many countries for radical changes in social structure which often can be brought about only by a social revolution of greater or lesser violence. The old order fights to maintain its dominance while the new order defends itself against counterrevolutionary menaces. And the period of revolution is not restricted to the time of open civil war, but perdures until the inhibiting features of the old social structure are eradicated.

A second reason, closely allied to the first, is the need to develop new social institutions and to socialize people into new habits and values. Peasants must be transformed into factory workers by teaching them new kinds of discipline. People must be convinced that new ways of doing things can be good and beneficial, usually a difficult endeavor. Luddites rose up and smashed the new textile machinery during the British Industrial Revolution, and later Russian peasants tried to sabotage the kolkhoz as an institution. The type of labor discipline required in an industrial society is alien to the habits of a preindustrial society, and it is no easy thing to convince people of the need for new habits and discipline by persuasion alone. Not that the need for discipline and change is not understood, but usually what is understood is not willed ardently enough. Consequently, the passage from one set of habits and values to another is difficult, and often requires some resort to compulsion. This compulsion took the form of the *explicit coercion* of the state police power to expedite the movement from individual to collective farms and to enforce factory discipline in the Soviet Union of the 1930s. In capitalist countries the *implicit coercion* of the market mechanism, under which most must sell their labor where and when they can, transferred labor from rural to urban areas and imposed discipline through the threat of starvation and unemployment.

A third reason why industrialization is painful is the need to increase the rate of capital accumulation, a process which involves widening the margin between consumption and total output. Notwithstanding the prevalence of low consumption levels in underdeveloped countries, these levels cannot be raised substantially in development's early stages. According to Gunnar Myrdal, "Often it is argued that [the] more human approach is what distinguished economic development under democratic conditions from what would take place under a Communist regime—in my opinion a rather dangerous assertion if, realistically, living standards will have to be kept low in order to allow development."[8] The need to limit consumption in favor of capital accumulation can cause a rise in social discontent. The poorer classes will feel that after fighting for the recent revolution, and/or reforms, they are entitled to its fruits. The middle classes and upper classes will resent the curtailment of their former privileges and "luxury" consumption. To keep this unrest from upsetting the development plans or from leading to counterrevolution a powerful government policy of coercion may sometimes be needed. But coercion, as it enables capital to be accumulated, also increases the social cost of doing so. Clearly, development is no smooth evolutionary process of change. On the contrary, says Gerschenkron: ". . . the happy picture of a quiet industrial revolution proceeding without undue stir and thrust has been . . . seldom reproduced in historical reality."[9] The changes needed to initiate economic development are more likely to resemble a gigantic social and political earthquake.

TOWARD A MIDDLE GROUND

On balance, the *human costs* attendant upon capitalist and communist development are probably lower than the *human costs* attaching to continued underdevelopment. And it is particular historical circumstances, rather than the development process itself, which seem to account for the major share of these human costs. The task facing development agents thus becomes one of finding ways to minimize inevitable social costs accompanying economic development efforts and to agree upon standards for evaluating the acceptability of these costs relative to the potential benefits of the process.

Seeking refuge in some predetermined ideological position does not solve the problem, for as Richard Ohmann points out:

> A man who subscribes to a moral or social ideology runs the risk that someone will put it into practice and thereby burden it with a wretched freight of human error and venality. The guillotine becomes an argument against libertarianism, juvenile gang wars an argument against permissive parenthood, the carpetbaggers an argument against eman-

cipation. When this happens, the ideologist may recant; or he may save his ideology by disowning the malpractice as irrelevant perversion. A third response is possible: to accept *la guillotine* along with *la liberté;* but in a man of good will, this requires a strong stomach and a certain obstinacy.[10]

No response seems fully adequate to the problem. Quite possibly no adequate answer exists inasmuch as all relevant normal moral standards in this matter are so ambiguous. Nevertheless, the problem can be understood more clearly by a brief discussion of two factors affecting moral judgments.

The first factor is that "objective conditions control the environment in which behavior takes place."[11] One obvious example of this is a state of war. Restrictions of civil liberties, for example, are usually judged more acceptable in wartime than in time of peace. In Donald Bowles' cryptic phrase, ". . . the death of a political enemy on a battlefield is approved, the domestic execution of a political prisoner is disapproved."[12] A program of economic development is akin to a war on poverty. As such it is likewise an objective condition. Under these conditions, policies to restrict luxury goods consumption, to mobilize underemployed labor for projects such as reforestation, and to control population movements from rural to urban areas could be judged differently than if they were pursued during "peacetime."

Secondly, one must advert to the "ideology affecting the norms by which man evaluates such behavior."[13] In the example just cited, a state of war is an objective condition, while the historical tradition and system of beliefs which shape people's attitudes about civil liberties comprise the ideology or value system. Obviously these two factors interact. The objective conditions can alter the ideological commitments. Even under roughly similar objective conditions, value systems can yield diverse judgments as to the moral status of identical actions. For example, when Nicaragua abrogates democratic procedures it is condemned by some and excused by others. When South Africa, Taiwan, and South Korea do the same the response is reversed by the two groups.

In addition, of course, different value systems will judge the same actions or behavior differently. Raising the price of a good to take advantage of a temporary scarcity in its supply would have been condemned as a sin by Medieval Catholicism; in a capitalist society it would be considered good business practice.

The above discussion highlights the complexity of the problem of evaluating the social costs of economic development. Humanity seems to be faced with a dilemma. On one hand, the failure to overcome underdevelopment *allows* untold human suffering to continue. On the other hand, the process of overcoming these human costs through speeding up development will most likely *generate* some new ones; and the faster the old human costs are overcome the more severe the new. Also, there is the danger that the centralized power needed to generate rapid development will be used, as with Stalin, to consolidate personal power and establish totalitarianism.

Peter Berger issues the challenge that "We must seek solutions to our problems that accept *neither* hunger *nor* terror."[14] But this need not necessarily invalidate the difficult goals of pursuing authentic development and genuine revolution. And by definition neither authentic development nor genuine revolution makes absolutes of success. The qualified pursuit of both is an urgent duty because prevailing structures of underdevelopment perpetuate both hunger and terror.

NOTES

1 E. H. Carr, *What Is History?* (New York: Alfred A. Knopf, 1962), p. 102.
2 Peter L. Berger, *Pyramids of Sacrifice: Political Ethics and Social Change* (New York: Basic Books, 1974), p. 5.
3 Ibid.
4 See Barrington Moore, *Reflections on the Causes of Human Misery* (Boston: Beacon Press, 1972) and Robert Heilbroner, *An Inquiry into the Human Prospect* (New York: Norton, 1974).
5 Celso Furtado, "Brazil: What Kind of Revolution?" in Laura Randall, ed., *Economic Development, Evolution or Revolution* (Boston: D.C. Heath, 1964).
6 Franklyn Holzman, "Consumer Sovereignty and the Rate of Economic Development," *Economia Internazionale,* 11, 2 (1956): 15–16.
7 For illuminating views on the effect of poverty on the human spirit see Carolina Maria de Jesus, *Child of the Dark* (New York: E. P. Dutton, 1962), and Oscar Lewis, *The Children of Sanchez* (New York: Random House, 1961).
8 Gunnar Myrdal, *An International Economy* (New York: Harper & Brothers, 1956), p. 164.
9 Alexander Gerschenkron, *Economic Backwardness in Historical Perspective* (New York: Praeger, 1965), p. 213.
10 Richard Ohmann, "GBS on the U.S.S.R." *The Commonweal* (July 24, 1964), p. 519.
11 Karl de Schweinitz, "Economic Growth, Coercion, and Freedom," *World Politics,* 9, 2 (January 1957): 168.
12 W. Donald Bowles, "Soviet Russia as a Model for Underdeveloped Areas," *World Politics,* 14, 3 (April 1962): p. 502.
13 De Schweinitz, op. cit., p. 168.
14 Berger, op. cit., p. xii.

CHAPTER 27

SURVIVAL STRATEGIES AND POWER AMONGST THE POOREST IN A WEST BENGAL VILLAGE

Tony Beck

University of British Columbia

INTRODUCTION

Recent attention to rural indigenous technical knowledge and farming systems in South Asia and Africa has concentrated mainly on agricultural technology and small farmers; and a growing literature on the causes of and responses to famine has focused on events which drastically affect large populations. Less interest has been shown in the landless and in "everyday forms of poor people's survival."

Survival strategies means the activities of poor people in times of stress which they see as crucial for the continued running of their household. This focus concentrates on their own priorities, and points to activities mainly outside the "formal economy." In this article it does not include organised and spontaneous violent and nonviolent resistance by the poor.[1] In West Bengal and no doubt in India generally, exploitative and oppressive village social structure is the main cause of poverty. For the outsider the problem is not only to document this, but to decide what action to take. Power relations cannot be ignored, but neither in many cases can they be dealt with directly. Those who advocate or examine radical alternatives at village level should be aware of the moral problems of doing so as outsiders.[2] The boundaries of empirical research on rural poverty by outsiders are perhaps marked by areas of organisation and cooperation by the poor. A practical focus, as in this article, can be to look for "gaps" or "soft areas" in the village power structure (Chambers 1983, pp. 157–63)—areas already used by the poor, that can bring benefits to them by exploiting the present system, and which, strengthened in the long term, could change the balance and structure of power.

From *IDS Bulletin,* 20, 2 (1989), pp. 23–33. Copyright © Institute of Development Studies, Sussex.

Theoretically, concentrating on poor people's priorities is an adaptation of the idea of people's history developed by British Marxist historians such as Thompson, Hill, Samuel, and others.[3] This involves giving a "worm's eye" or "people's" view of the world, and a respect for and political sympathy with the poor as makers of their own histories.

This approach may have two possible effects. First, it can challenge a dominant view of the poor—that they are passive, irresponsible, or conservative, and its political corollary, that poor people are there to be planned for.[4] Challenging these views may change how plans are made, or even make it acceptable to propose that poor people can make their own plans. Second, this approach has policy implications, in particular how poor people's own strategies can be built upon and improved. In a different geographical context, Richards (1985, 1986) and Watts (1983) argued for backing and improving small farmer's indigenous agricultural strategies. Little has been written on the priorities perceived by poor rural landless people, on how they organise their lives, and how their more informal activities could be supported. To throw light on these questions, this article presents research findings from a village in West Bengal and explores their policy implications.

THE VILLAGE, "MENTAL-METRICISM," AND WHO THE POOREST ARE

The Case Study Village

Although only 40 km from Calcutta (or three hours by public transport) Fonogram village[5] in north 24 Parganas District remains relatively isolated. Local transport is limited, the main forms being foot and bicycle. There is a small town two and a half kilometers away which holds a twice weekly market. Most villagers do not often have the time to go further afield.

Fonogram is a Muslim village of 140 households and a population of about 830. It is mainly agricultural, "aman" being the year's main rice crop, harvested in October/November. West Bengal as a whole has a net sown area of roughly 13.6 mn acres and a rural population in the early 1980s of around 40 mn with about one-third of an acre available per person (the second lowest land-person ratio in India, next to Kerala) (Bandepadhyay 1983). Net sown area for Fonogram is about 162 acres (according to the Census of India for 1971), so its population density is even higher than the all West Bengal figure. An estimated one-third of households in Fonogram are operationally landless, and strategies for survival should be seen in the context of both scarcity and unequal holding of land.

Interviews were carried out with 22 respondent households in the winters of 1986/87 and 1987/88. In both these years the main part of the "aman" crop was destroyed by flooding, which meant little work for those usually employed as agricultural labourers, damage to several of the respondents' houses, and a period of general austerity (although the market price of rice, the main staple, did not increase noticeably in either year). In 1986/87 interviews were held as to how respondents were coping after the flood. A questionnaire designed from these interviews was used in 1987/88 concentrating on survival, and the villagers' views on social, economic, and political aspects of village life. Quantitative methods were seen to be inadequate for analysing the villagers' replies. My own findings have, therefore, been placed in the wider context of literature on poverty and survival to draw out their representativeness.

Of the 22 households, seven were female headed (all widows) and two respondents were widowers; in all, I spoke to 12 women, three men, and seven families (husband, wife, their parents and/or their grown up children). Twenty of the households were operationally landless (five without homestead land). Employment patterns of respondents were irregular, but the primary occupations of the main household earners were as follows: ten agricultural labourers, three labourers on lorries, three sharecroppers, three factory workers, one maid, one hawker, and one marginal farmer.

Mental-Metricism

Sen (1983) and Kynch and Sen (1983) have pointed out some analytical difficulties in development and poverty measurement studies based on respondents' perceptions, particularly that these may differ markedly from a more objectively measurable "reality." Sen has suggested focusing instead on "capabilities" or macro-level indicators of ill- or well-being, such as long-term mortality or literacy rates. This is part of a wider debate about the quality of poverty and whether or not it has an absolute or relative core (see Sen 1983 vs. Townsend 1985).

To concentrate solely on statistical analysis of macro-level data (or indeed similar analysis of micro-level data), however, ignores the paradigmatic basis of collection and use of such data—that it is based, in the Indian context, on a particular, dominant view of the poor and a political ideology that sees the poor as passive and dependent— a kind of statistical cannon fodder; and it is also to ignore the causes of poverty. Equally, such statistical analysis of macro- (or micro-) level data on literacy and mortality rates, for example, overlooks the "informal economy" in which the poor operate, which is crucial to their survival, and through which they conduct a large part of their affairs. It is useful and balanced to look for ways to combine macro- and micro-level statistical analysis with poor people's own perceptions and for ways in which these complement each other.

If village studies concerned with poor people's views are to be representative rather than idiosyncratic, there is a need for comparative material from which to generalise. As statistical analysis of data receives its legitimacy from its supposed accuracy, so village studies will become more credible as representative (or not) if comparable studies show similar findings (or not). Those few articles that I have come across on survival strategies in South Asia all comment on a lack of comparative material.[6] However, widespread evidence of, for example, enforced changes in consumption by the poor in times of food shortage, or of share-rearing of livestock by poor families, now suggests that these priorities and actions of the poor should be taken into account when policy is being considered.

Who Are The Poorest?

Drawing on recent work by Chambers (1988, pp. 17–18) and Lipton (1983a,b,c and 1985) on the "characteristics" of the poorest, and other sources including my field work, it is possible to suggest, in an eastern South Asian context, how the poorest act and which households they are in. They are likely:

1 To be exploited in terms of receipt of wages or credit, and to be in debt;

2 To be flexible in terms of coping, using a variety of strategies and able to work at a number of jobs (see Van Schendel 1986; p. 44; Jiggins 1986; p. 11; Caldwell 1986, pp. 682,691; Cain 1977, p. 209);

3 To be resilient and active in areas concerned with the running of the household (see below);

4 To be part of an informal village support network with other poor families (see below);

5 To be illiterate, but to want to educate their children;

6 To be landless or to have a small amount of unproductive land (see Lipton 1985), and to be irregularly employed;

7 To have relatively few assets or exchange entitlements (Lipton 1985; Sen 1982);

8 To be in clinical danger of undernutrition, and to spend at least 80 percent of their income without achieving 80 percent of minimum nutritional requirements (Lipton 1983a);

9 To have illness or have had recent illness in the household, and to be physically weak;

10 To be isolated in locational terms, and in terms of village power (Chambers 1983, pp. 111–14);

11 To be female headed (Gulati 81, p. 170; Mencher 1985, p. 364; Begum 1985, p. 231), and/or have large, young families (Lipton 1983c);

12 Not to belong to any political party (see below); and,

13 To spend substantial household time on common property resource activities (Jodha 1986).

Many of the poorest households are therefore likely to be landless labourer households with a female, physically weak, or often ill main earner, and/or several young children. This is a rough checklist which could be added to, and is dependent on regional variations, but the more of these indicators there are located in a household, the greater chance that this household is among the poorest. A single statistical indicator of poverty cannot expect to capture the depth and variety of the lifestyle of the poorest at village level,[7] nor can a concentration on the formal village economy; and policy is liable to be misdirected if based solely on such indicators.

STRATEGIES FOR SURVIVAL, AND POWER

Some survival strategies, such as taking debts, selling assets, and migration, are relatively well recognised. Others identified during the fieldwork are less so, and will be presented here: use of common property resources (CPRs); changes in eating and food preparation; share-rearing of livestock; and mutual support networks. All these are mainly undertaken by women and children, and challenge the dominant view that the poor are passive. While extreme crises such as famine are met by sequences of sur-

vival strategies (Corbett 1988), everyday survival strategies vary in relative importance at different times. They also interlink, but can for the time being be described
separately.

Use of Common Property Resources

Strategies using CPRs includes gleaning, collection of fuel, and collection of wild
foodstuffs.

Gleaning   Gleaning in Fonogram had been restricted by two bad agricultural
years due to flooding, and also by those who owned the fields. However, 17 out of
22 respondents reported gleaning whenever there was time, and that this was an
activity carried out mainly by children. In the remaining five households there were
either no children, or respondents were out all day at work. Estimates of the amounts
gathered ranged from "a handful," to 12 kg an acre, to 5 kg for a good day, to 25 kg
a season. This can be compared to the amount of government aid received after the
two floods—most respondents reported receiving 2–3 kg of wheat each year from the
government.[8]

Collection of Fuel   All respondents who could gathered twigs, branches, leaves,
and cow dung. This collection was seasonal, mainly in the winter and summer, but not
in the rainy season, as then no leaves fall and no-one pastures their livestock—a seasonal problem for the poorest not often noted. Most respondents did not quantify in
their own minds the time spent on gathering fuel, but a common remark was that one
person working for a morning (three to four hours) could collect enough to last for two
days. For the most part where there are children in the household, they do the gathering.[9] Most of the households' fuel requirements were met in this way, although all
respondents said that the availability of CPR fuels had steadily decreased over time
because of pressure on resources.

Jodha (1975, p. 1620, fn. 14), Caldwell (1986, p. 683), Dasgupta (1987, pp. 106–7),
and Howes and Jabbar (1986) provide comparative South Asian material on the importance of gathered fuel to poor households, and Jodha (1986, pp. 1174–75) has estimated that poor households in 21 districts of seven states in dry tropical western and
southern India, meet 66–84 percent of their fuel requirements from CPR activities, a
finding that is mirrored in Fonogram village.

Gathering of Wild Foods   Almost all the respondents gather and eat wild foods,
and gathering is done whenever and wherever possible and necessary—a point
stressed by all respondents. Reported wild plants gathered were "shojina pata" (horse
radish), "kolmi pata" (an "edible aquatic plant"), "neem pata" (margosa), "kochu" (an
"esculent edible root"), "dumur" (fig), "pather pata" (jute leaves), and "helingsha" (a
kind of watercress). Crow (1984, p. 1756), Greenough (1982, p. 231), Currey (1981,
p. 128), and Rahaman (1981, p. 137) all report consumption of "kochu" by poor families in famine conditions in Bengal and Bangladesh. These wild foods cannot be consumed too often or they will cause health problems.

Children also gather fruits such as plums, tamarind, and mango, and Sengupta (1978, p. 9) describes "landless families living on jackfruit or mango in Malda and Coochbehar (West Bengal)." All this again suggests the inadequacy of the use of income or outlay to measure poverty.[10]

Jodha (1986) estimates that poor households spend 10–20 percent of their time on CPR activities, generating 15–25 days of work per household every three weeks in this way. Given this cumulative importance of CPRs, it might be worth questioning Lipton's assertion (1983a, p. 48) that "Hungry Indians are poor, and attempts to solve their food problems by (e.g.) persuading them to gather and cook more wild food and vegetable tops tends to neglect collection and cooking costs." It seems poor, hungry people are already active in this area, and do not need to be persuaded to gather.

Changes in Eating and Food Preparation

Changing patterns of eating and food preparation are less well known as a coping strategy than gathering. Spending by the poorest in Fonogram is irregular ("whenever money or a loan is available we get food" as one respondent put it), and so are their eating patterns.

"The stomach won't understand unless it gets rice" one respondent told me. But when ordinary rice is not available, several other substitutes are. Respondents reported eating "khud"—broken rice grains, about 25 grams of which come out of 1 kg of sieved rice, and which are sold only in the village, usually by better-off families. "Khud" costs about two-thirds of the price of the cheapest market rice. This can be fried with oil and salt and alleviates hunger. They also reported drinking the water left over after rice had been boiled in it ("bhater fan"), which is usually given to livestock, and eating parts of chaff left after threshing. Greenough (1982, p. 233) also notes the consumption of rice water during the 1943 Bengal famine.

Certain foods fill the stomach better than others. Several respondents said that they ate "par routi" (leavened bread) and then drank a lot of water to fill the stomach, or "gola routi" (flour mixed with water and fried like an omelette), which was considered more filling than "chapati." "Fatter" varieties of rice were preferred, as they were considered to give more energy; those doing manual work thought that they needed a fatter grain than "babus" (gentlemen) who wear wristwatches and trousers and sit in offices all day, and who prefer thinner varieties. Salt tea is also commonly taken, as sugar or molasses is too expensive, as is "pan" as an appetite suppressant.

A common response to the question of eating patterns after the two floods was: "we made one meal stretch into two," "we ate one day and fasted the next," or "we ate once a day and got by like that." Jodha (1975, p. 1620, fn. 15, 1978, pp. A38–9), Caldwell (1986, p. 688) and Van Schendel (1986, p. 43) all report regulation of consumption as a strategy for dealing with food shortage. Sleeping and fasting when no work was available, was quite common. Lipton (1983a, pp. 32–3) and Dirks (1980, p. 23) consider the nutritional side of this strategy, and Hartmann and Boyce (1983, p. 172) and Harari and García-Bouza (1982, p. 35) also give examples for Bangladesh and India.

Eight of the 22 respondents in Fonogram said that if they received a little more money they would save it for the next day rather than use it immediately to buy food.

There is some evidence to suggest that poor people do plan for the long-term future by regulating consumption of food to protect assets. A connection between "voluntary" cuts in consumption and protection of assets may partly explain the finding of a longitudinal study over five years in four districts of the Kosi hill area of Nepal (Nabarro, Cassels et al. 1987) that land sales decreased but nutritional status did not improve. If poor households do protect assets by resorting to cuts in consumption, and where, as in Eastern India, there is discrimination against females (Harriss 1986), policies and programs to provide assets for the poor may perversely mean that women get less within the household.

Cuts in consumption are an enforced part of the lifestyle of the poorest. Within the narrow confines in which they found themselves, respondents had developed an expertise in food management. There were, however, several stories about irresponsible spending by some of the poorest households, and there is no reason to suppose that irresponsibility in spending is a characteristic solely of the rich.

One respondent, a widow with four young children and irregular income, when asked how she remained healthy on what seemed an inadequate diet, vividly described the different ways in which rich and poor people eat. She mimicked how rich persons would have five or six dishes of different foods in front of them and would take a little from each, turning up their noses at most of the dishes as being too spicy or too sweet, and therefore ending up eating only a small quantity; whereas poor persons would eat the whole of whatever was put in front of them, whatever the quality or quantity. This was a reminder that it is not only the rich who have views about how and what poor people eat.

Share-Rearing of Livestock

Twenty of the respondent households had some livestock, the two exceptions being unable to keep any as they had no courtyard to their houses. Of these 20, seven were share-rearing livestock and five others had share-reared in the previous five years. One other household wanted to share-rear but could not because of unavailability of animals. Five mentioned difficulty in getting animals.

The system is known locally as "poussani," which means to rear. The most common arrangement is that a household will raise a female goat, cow, duck, or chicken given to them by another, usually richer, household. After the animal has given birth twice, the first born and the mother are returned to the owner, and the rearer keeps the second born. In the case of a male animal, the proceeds after sale are divided equally between owner and rearer.

Livestock can be vitally important in sustaining poor households during periods of crisis (see Chambers 1983, pp. 129–30 for examples), but share-rearing and its importance to the poor have tended to be overlooked by researchers. Yet this system was operating in Bengal in the 1930s and 1940s, as Cooper (1984, p. 80) comments: "The landlord ensured that the sharecropper was provided with the means of production without actually bearing the costs of raising the livestock, even increasing his own stock."[11]

Share-rearing, in various forms, is common throughout South Asia today, and elsewhere.[12] Jodha (1986, pp. 1180, fn. 10) refers to how large farmers share-rear out of the poor, throughout seven states of western and southern India:

> Though varying in its extent, the practice of "salvaging" unproductive animals was observed in practically all the study areas. Large farmers gave their unproductive animals to the poor for maintenance as it was clearly costly to maintain them . . . When such animals became productive they were returned to the large farmer and net additions to the value of such animals (after becoming productive) were shared by the two parties. Depending on the type of animal . . . the terms and conditions governing this practice differed from region to region. In areas like Gujarat and Rajasthan such herding was an important source of income for the rural poor.

And Blaikie et al. (1979, p. 64) comment on share-rearing in West Central Nepal, noting that in several locations visited all the breeding of oxen was undertaken on this basis by labouring and artisan households. Bearing in mind that share-rearing potentially benefits both owner and rearer, it is perhaps not surprising that it is so widespread.

Mutual Support Networks and Power

Power relations in the village from the poor person's perspective would seem to be central in understanding the problem of poverty, but this perspective is usually avoided in favour of others less controversial. As Breman (1985, p. 34) has observed:

> In India there is a great scarcity of literature in which those living in the lowest echelons of society themselves speak out. For South Gujarat the region towards which my research has been directed for more than two decades now, I do not know of a single publication in which exploitation and repression is reported on the basis of experience from within.

I now proceed to deal with power relations with an awareness of the paradox involved in such research—that these relations are central to village life, but an area around which the researcher can only skirt.

Discussions were held with the respondents on the reasons for their poverty, how it feels to be poor, the characteristics of rich and poor people, whether the poor help each other or are helped by the rich, whether the rich cheat the poor, why the poorest do not get organised, and the importance of self-respect. Respondents themselves made the division into rich and poor—"gherastao" and "gorib." (For a similar definition of village differentiation based on poorer villagers' views, see Van Schendel, 1981, 90.)

None of the respondents belonged to a political party, and only one was familiar with government laws on sharecropping or homestead rights. In a wider, more formal sense, therefore, respondents could be considered apolitical. But their lack of involvement in formal politics did not mean that they did not hold strong "political" ideas about what was happening in their village.

As to how most respondents viewed their poverty, most replied in this manner: "Do you think I like being poor—don't you think I'm unhappy being poor?" Poverty also meant a loss of respect which was worse than hunger; apart from three who differed, all other respondents did not hesitate in saying that for them respect was more important than food, and that "without respect food won't go into the stomach." If this feeling is widespread among the poor in India, then planners' and academics' exclusive interest in income and nutrition is inadequate for understanding poverty.

When asked whose fault ("doash") it was that they were poor, all 22 respondents saw their poverty in terms of a similar apolitical causality—either they had lost their land or other assets, or were unable to work, or had not inherited any property, or they said that the population was increasing whereas land was not, or blamed the weather, or bad luck. As one woman put it: "We are poor because we have no land and my husband can't work . . . We had six 'bighas' of land before and plough cows and my husband could work five years back." Not one of the respondents thought their poverty was the fault of the rich in the village.

At the same time, respondents had definite ideas about the characteristics of the rich (and it should be remembered that it is Fonogram's poorest villagers' views that are presented here). Two respondents thought rich people helped poor ones, but the rest were adamant that they received no help ("shahajo") from the rich. About this, there was almost unanimous animosity. As one elderly widow put it:

> Rich people don't mix with the poor at all—even if we were dying and called them they wouldn't come. J. is going by motorcycle, A. by lorry and H. by cycle. I'm going by foot, shoeless. In the rainy season the rich eat well, but we have to eat fig leaves and get sick.

And a young landless labourer said more vividly: "Rich people are drinking poor people's blood, talking to them but not giving them anything."

Almost all agreed that rich people cheated poor people by giving too low wages, by making them work too hard, or giving too low prices for land or other assets. But no respondents made a causal connection between their own poverty and others' wealth. As another landless labourer said: "It's my own fault we are poor, not the fault of rich people."[13] However, the poor did not stop at insulting the rich. One newly wealthy family in particular, as well as other rich families, was the subject of theft and attack. Theft of pump sets and power lines were also common in the three years after 1985, when electricity had been introduced into the area. No-one familiar with the long history of "peasant" protest in Bengal will be surprised at the use of these "weapons of the weak."

Equally, almost all respondents thought that poor people helped and did not cheat each other. This help consisted mainly of small loans of either money, rice, or other edibles. This was despite the fact that there had been some disputes between the respondent households and between household members over relatively large loans and other serious matters such as "theft" of land.[14] While loans between poor households were considered as help, loans from rich to poor were not: everything depended on the attitude of the lender. K. Jansen (1986, pp. 19 and 25; table 5) has also commented on the importance of intrafamily loans in six villages in Noakhali District of Bangladesh, where such loans make up 32 percent of total village lending and were mainly used for household subsistence purposes.

One of the questions asked of respondents was why poor people did not cooperate with each other. The example was given of forming a buying cooperative which would cut prices at the local market, as buying could then be done in bulk. The most common reply was that there was no unity among the poor, that they all got money at different times, and that those who received money first would try to buy the best quality goods.

While the rich were powerful, the poor were too jealous of each other to work together. The word jealousy or envy ("hingsha") was used several times. As one landless labourer said: "The poor work together sometimes when farming. But they can't work together usually because of lack of resources. They can't go shopping together because some people go later and some earlier."

Although adequate resources may be necessary if poor people are to cooperate rather than compete, it did seem as if there was a strong tradition of mutual support amongst the poorest in the village, based on the informal system of loans, and that they were also united in their animosity towards the rich, an animosity that was often strongly voiced.

There is an extensive literature on mutual support systems among the rural poor. Caldwell (1986, p. 694) points out from his work in Karnataka "the importance of marriage networks as a central mechanism in the insurance system against disaster," and Jiggins (1986, p. 16) notes: "One feature which stands out is the resilience of female household networks to seasonal stress and calamity; far from being among the most vulnerable, more critical study of the advantages of their organisational and economic flexibility may show that they are the 'survivors'."

Other recent evidence (see Van Schendel 1986, pp. 48–9; Howes and Jabbar 1986, p. 25; and Dasgupta 1987, p. 114 for South Asian material; and see also fn. 15) suggests that Lipton's assertion (1983a, p. 66), may be open to question: "Traditional rural compensations, the institutions of mutual help, were often exaggerated, and anyway are under pressure from both population growth and economic modernisation."

Respondents in Fonogram reported going from house to house asking for "khud" and "bhater fan" as well as for building materials. But the main kind of loans between poorest households was in the form of small amounts of money or foodstuff, which all respondents mentioned giving or taking. Other forms of mutual support were looking after children or livestock. There is a complicated system of exchange, borrowing, receiving, and giving in Fonogram village. But a distinction is made between a "loan" between poor people which is an expression of support, friendship, and solidarity, and a loan begged from either another poor person or someone better-off, which involves a subordinate relationship.

Policies to Support Poor People's Strategies

What scope is there for policies to support these strategies of the poor? This can only be answered in context. Other strategies such as migration and sale of assets may be more the concern of men, but those discussed here focus mainly on the home and women and children's labour. Various factors affect these strategies. The cultural environment is one determinant of consumption patterns (K. Jansen 1986), and also of whether or not poor women go outside the house to work. Strategies are perhaps more likely to vary by gender and ability than by age. The political setting in which they find themselves will, obviously, also influence the actions of the poorest. Mechanisation may affect strategies such as gleaning (Scott 1985, pp. 118–19). Environmental factors will also affect how the poorest people survive; those living in an area with a high person/land ratio and scarce CPRs may have strategies very different from those living in the low person/land area described by Richards (Richards 1985). There are also overt and covert political strategies, with which the student of English agrarian history is familiar—trade union activity, "spontaneous" violence, or breaking of agricultural machinery. Individual and community strategies for survival may also differ. Given this variety of possible actions by poorest people, perhaps the most useful way of analysing survival strategies would be to identify those most likely to be supported by NGOs or governments, and to consider how poor people's efforts and those of outsiders can be linked.

Any consideration of policy in eastern South Asia has to take into account a high degree of centralisation of planning, a male-dominated and inefficient bureaucracy, and an overburdening of extension and village-level workers (for the latter, see NIRD 1985, pp. 80–81, 286–91). Scarcity of land and CPRs are also major constricting elements for policy, as are the competing interests of landless labourers, sharecroppers, and marginal farmers. Also, the strategies of the poorest described here, because they are part of an informal, and sometimes invisible, economy, may not be as amenable to government support as are those more informal agricultural activities carried out by small farmers and described by Richards and Watts. The possibility of "reformist" outsider policy should be viewed in the light of these constraining contexts.

Use of CPRs and Famine Foods

Use of CPRs is a thorny policy area. Changes in policy priorities towards an interest in CPRs can be seen in a recent World Bank publication which deals briefly with how rural households try to cope with transitory food insecurity (World Bank 1986, p. 26):

> In extreme cases in India, Ethiopia and Bangladesh, the starving eat a drought resistant legume, known as kessari dal, even though it can lead to paralysis. Since poor families draw on these famine foods in times of need, more research is needed to identify all sources of such foods, to understand fully how they are used, to determine what can be done to ensure their availability during periods of stress, and to develop a nontoxic variety of kessari dal or a processing method that will eliminate the toxic effect.

Indigenous methods of detoxification available for other plants (see Corkhill 1949; p. 7; Bhandari 1974, p. 77; and Leakey 1986; p. 38) suggest that it may be possible to develop such detoxification processes using village knowledge. A shift in research priorities towards "famine foods," as suggested, would surely benefit the poorest who are the main users of such foods.

Share-Rearing of Livestock

The system of share-rearing livestock described above raises questions about the Government of India's central poverty alleviation program, the Integrated Rural Development Programme (IRDP), which provides subsidy and loans to the poor to enable them to buy assets—often livestock. Problems with IRDP include leakages away from intended beneficiaries, unavailability of good quality livestock at reasonable prices, and lack of green and dry fodder (Rath 1985; Singh 1985, p. 335; Seabright 1987).

IRDP is based on top-down planning approaches—a scheme is devised, beneficiaries identified, and loans and subsidies given. At the same time the indigenous share-rearing method of loaning livestock that is widespread throughout South Asia has been ignored by planners, who may not even be aware of its existence. As share-rearing can benefit both (richer) loaner and (poor) borrower, it presents a "gap" where reformist policy can feasibly build upon strategies used by the poor. Most respondents in Fonogram village said that it had become increasingly difficult to find livestock to share-rear. If this scarcity is widespread (and the demand for livestock for the IRDP may be one cause of scarcity), incentives may be necessary to persuade livestock owners to lend—perhaps in the form of loans to the rearer to buy good quality feed. Backing up and improving this indigenous method might help reduce the problem of too few good quality livestock, and market "imperfections" that have meant IRDP recipients purchasing overpriced, poor quality animals.

Mutual Support Networks

To move to mutual support networks, various commentators have suggested agricultural cooperative development as the next step forward for the Communist Government of West Bengal. But little attention seems to have been given to either agricultural labour union activity or more informal kinds of poor people's organisation and cooperation. Yet BRAC has shown in Bangladesh (Chen 1983) that it is possible to organise groups of poor landless women, using their skills for productive work, as long as the groups are homogeneous, and there is an economic incentive for the women to participate. While the poorest may "exploit" each other (partly because they have no other choice than to do so), it does seem that there is a strong existing indigenous system of cooperation among the poorest, based partially on an animosity towards the rich, that could act as a basis for the formation of groups to receive loans. Yet Government intervention in this area has up until now been at best unpromising.[16]

Policy in General

In the case of policy in general, much depends on the view the policy maker takes of the poor person. This is particularly relevant in the case of nutrition and poor people's preferences in food. Rich people's interest in what poor people eat is nothing new. Attempts to control the diet of the poor for political reasons date back, in Britain, at least until the late eighteenth century (Hammond and Hammond 1948; p. 119). Historically, little research on nutrition has looked at the preferences of poor people and how these might be included in nutrition policy, nor the political consequences of conducting nutritional studies. One of the major debates about poverty in India—on the level of nutrition and income necessary for a poor person to survive—has followed this historical pattern. This debate has focused almost exclusively on "scientific" and statistical estimates, and various participants have performed various forms of statistical acrobatics to support their argument. Practically no-one has asked poor people how much they think they need to eat, or attempted to measure this against "scientific" estimates. Yet poor people's preferences might be vitally important in deciding on the type and quality of food to be dispensed in times of emergency, or through ration shops. This form of "intellectual colonialism"—viewing the poor as those to be measured, weighed and planned for, rather than as people who make choices and decisions—needs to be challenged by empirical research which accepts that the poor have a voice.

CONCLUSION

This article has attempted to show that the poorest people, especially women and children, rather than being passive or apolitical, are active in their household survival strategies. While, in a South Asian context, the poorest live in an oppressive social system, which partly defines their actions, they also exploit that system for their own benefit. Measures to support and improve their present strategies may be of more use to them than externally imposed schemes (which include intermediate technology such as solar power or biogas), the benefits of which are likely to be appropriated by those at village level who have more power.

Although more comparative empirical evidence is needed to argue against the dominant paradigm that the poor are passive or followers, there is also a need for outside researchers to be aware that their solutions to poverty are likely to be marginal to its main causes. Equally, those who have never been active in cooperatives or trade unions should perhaps be wary of advising poor women and men to join or form such organisations. While poor people may want political support and sympathy, they may not want advice. So it may be that research concerned with the rural poor should be less about identifying their characteristics and giving advice, and more about listening to and presenting poor people's views. As one poor woman in Mymensingh District, Bangladesh, told someone who suggested she cook more green leafy vegetables (McCarthy 1984, p. 55):

> Don't worry about what I feed my family. You just give me some money and I will take care of it. You don't have to assume that I don't know what to feed my family. The problem is that I happen to be poor, and if you can't do anything about that then get out of here. Don't waste my time.

NOTES

1 For the moral and social difficulties of dealing with power at Indian village level, see Breman (1985).
2 This is meant with reference to empirical research, and not other more historical or academic forms of research.
3 For a similar use of such theory, on a much broader historical scale, see Watts (1983). For use of this theory in relation to Bengal, see Van Schendel and Faraizi (1984), and to Madras 1876–78, Arnold (1984). My focus here is on people rather than history.
4 For a further discussion of the political connection between ideology, planning, and the characteristics of the poor, see Beck (1988).
5 A pseudonym.
6 There is, however, a large survival literature from the Second World War, much of it by labour camp prisoners—Eugenia Ginzburg, Bruno Bettelheim, and Primo Levi, for example—and inhabitants of cities under siege, such as Olga Friedenberg and Vera

Ibner on Leningrad. Interesting parallels could be drawn between strategies used by (intellectual) survivors and those used by the rural poor in South Asia today.

7 The inadequacies of statistical measurement of poverty are discussed at further length in Beck (1988).

8 Sengupta (1978, p. 7) has described Santal children collecting grain from rat holes and other kinds of gathering in Birbhum district of West Bengal. For Bangladesh, see also Siddiqui (1982, p. 358) for gleaning, Cain (1977, pp. 204, 209) who refers to children opening rat holes and gleaning, and Begum (1985, p. 235) for regional differences in gleaning practices.

9 Children also collect snails to feed to poultry. Date palm leaves are left on the side of ponds with most of the leaf submerged, and the snails crawl onto the leaves. Other livestock fodder is also gathered, as are various household materials, and livestock are taken regularly to graze on fallow land.

10 Most of the comparative literature on gathering wild foods deals with famine situations rather than periods of regular stress. For a list of famine foods in Nigeria, see Watts (1983, pp. 432–33) and for a more detailed discussion in Ethiopia, Rahmato (1988, pp. 8–10). For a review of other literature see Longhurst (1986; p. 32), and for a general discussion, Leakey (1986).

11 Sunil Sengupta has told me that "poussani" was operating several generations before the 1940s.

12 For references to share-rearing (technically known as agistment) in villages in Bangladesh see Howes and Jabbar (1986, pp. 24–25), Hartmann and Boyce (1983, p. 163), Westergaard (1983, pp. 52–57), Chen (1983, pp. 3, 148, 163), Siddiqui (1983, p. 357), Van Schendel (1981, pp. 90, 112, 167, 172, 331 fn. 7), and E. Jansen (1986, p. 44). For India, as well as Jodha see Epstein et al. (1983, p. 121), Bose (1984, pp. 100, 104), and Dasgupta (1987, p. 110). Paul Seabright has told me the system also operates in Tamil Nadu. For West Africa see White [1986, p. 24 (Niger)], and Chambers et al., eds. [1981, p. 86 (Mali)], and for Ethiopia, Rahmato (1988, p. 16). In Botswana, the system is known as "mafisa." Andrew Turton has told me that it operates widely in Northern Thailand, Jon Rigg has referred me to agistment in the highlands of Papua New Guinea and pointed out that government "buffalo banks" using agistment system are common in Thailand, and David Nabarro has told me that the system is found throughout Nepal.

13 Arens and Van Beurden make a similar point about "class consciousness" in Bangladesh (1977, p. 77). For different views see BRAC (1979) and Epstein et al. (1983, p. 127). See also Van Schendel (1981, p. 92).

14 A subject not discussed here is intrafamily sale of assets and land leading to greater intrafamily differentiation, which may be common in West Bengal. Poverty and violence are closely interlinked, and there were many examples of intrafamily violence in Fonogram.

15 See also Longhurst for Northern Nigeria (1986, p. 30), Toulmin for Mali (1986, p. 66), and Rahmato for Ethiopia (1988, p. 7). Dirks (1980, p. 113) has suggested that such networks will break down in times of extreme stress. Splitting of families is also common. Lest these strategies be thought exclusive to the Third World, see McKee (1987, p. 113) on households with unemployed males in present day Britain. "Neighbours were variously described as providing help with household goods, furniture, childminding or children's clothes. Women's networks were often the key to these exchanges."

16 For the failure of such groups to take off under the government's Development of Women and Children in Rural Areas programme in Bankura and Purulia districts of West Bengal, see Ghatak (1985), who attributes failure mainly to inefficient administration.

REFERENCES

Arens, J., and J. Van Beurden. *Jhagrapur: Poor Peasants and Women in Bangladesh.* Arens and Van Beurden. Amsterdam (distributed by Third World Publications), 1977.

Arnold, D. "Famine in Peasant Consciousness and Peasant Action in Madras 1876–8." In R. Guha (ed.), *Subaltern Studies,* 3, Oxford University Press, 1984.

Bandopadhyay, N. *Evaluation of Land Reform Measures in West Bengal: A Report.* Calcutta: Center for Studies in Social Sciences, 1983.

Beck, T. "Beyond Enumeration: Survival of the Poorest and Poverty Measurement in India." Paper given at IDS. London: Sussex, and the Institute of Commonwealth Studies, 1988.

Begum, S. "Women and Technology in Rice Processing in Bangladesh." In *Women in Rice Farming,* IRRI/Gower, 1985.

Bhandari, M. M. "Famine Foods in the Rajasthan Desert." *Economic Botany,* 28, 1 (1974).

Blaikie, P. M. et al. *The Struggle for Basic Needs in Nepal.* Paris: OECD, 1979.

Bose, P. K. *Classes in a Rural Society: A Sociological Study.* Calcutta: Ajanta, 1984.

BRAC. *Peasant Perceptions: Famine.* Dhaka: Bangladesh Rural Advancement Committee, 66 Mohakhali C.A., 12, 1979.

Breman, J. "Between Accumulation and Immiseration: The Partiality of Field Work in Rural India." *Journal of Peasant Studies,* 13, 1 (1985).

Cain, M. T. "The Economic Activities of Children in a Village in Bangladesh." *Population and Development Review,* 3, 3 (1977).

Caldwell, J. et al. "Periodic High Risk as a Cause of Fertility Decline in a Rural Environment: Survival Strategies in the 1980–83 South Indian Drought." *Economic Development and Cultural Change,* 34, 4 (1986).

Chambers, R. *Rural Development: Putting the Last First.* Longman, 1983.

———. "Poverty in India: Concepts, Research and Reality." *Discussion Paper* 241 Sussex: IDS, January 1988.

——— et al. (eds.). *Seasonal Dimensions to Rural Poverty.* London: Frances Pinter, 1981.

Chen M. *A Quiet Revolution: Women in Transition in Rural Bangladesh.* Salenkman, 1983.

Cooper, A. "Sharecropping and Sharecropper Struggles in Bengal, 1930–50." Ph.D. diss. University of Sussex, 1984.

Corbett, J. "Famine and Household Coping Strategies." *World Development,* 16, 9 (1988): 1099–112.

Corkhill, N. C. "Dietary Change in a Sudan Village Following Locust Visitation." *Africa,* 19, 1 (1949).

Crow, B. "Warning of Famine in Bangladesh." *Economic and Political Weekly* (EPW), no. 40, October 6, 1984.

Currey, B. "The Famine Syndrome: Its Definition for Relief and Rehabilitation." In John R. W. Robson (ed.), *Famine, Its Causes, Effects and Management.* Gordon and Breach, 1981.

Dasgupta, M. "Informal Security Mechanisms and Population Retention in Rural India." *Economic Development and Cultural Change,* 36, 1 (1987).

Dirks, R. "Social Responses during Severe Food Shortages and Famine." *Current Anthropology,* 21, 1 (1980).

Epstein, T. S. et al. *Basic Needs Viewed from Above and Below: The Case of Karnataka State.* India, Paris: OECD, 1983.

Ghatak, M. "Development of Women and Children's Rural Areas of Bankura and Purulia Districts: An Evaluation." Calcutta: CRESSIDA (Mimeo), 1985.

Greenough, P. *Prosperity and Misery in Modern Bengal.* Delhi: OUP, 1982.

Gulati, L. *Profiles in Female Poverty.* Delhi: Hindustan Publishing Corporation (India), 1981.

Hammond, J., and B. Hammond (1st ed. 1912). *The Village Labourer.* Guild Books, 1948.

Harari, D., and Jorge García-Bouza. *Social Conflict and Development: Basic Needs and Survival Strategies in Four National Settings.* Paris: OECD, 1982.

Harriss, B. "The Intrafamily Distribution of Hunger in South Asia." Paper given at the Institute of Commonwealth Studies postgraduate seminar series, October 1986.

Hartmann, B., and J. K. Boyce. *A Quiet Violence: View from a Bangladesh Village.* London: Zed Press, 1983.

Howes, M., and M. A. Jabbar. "Rural Fuel Shortages in Bangladesh: The Evidence from Four Villages." *Discussion Paper* 213, Sussex: IDS, 1986.

IDS, "Seasonality and Poverty." *IDS Bulletin,* 17, 3 (July 1986).

Jansen, E. *Rural Bangladesh: Competition for Scarce Resources.* Norwegian University Press (distr. OUP), 1986.

Jansen, K. 1986. "Survival Strategies of the Rural Poor in Bangladesh." Centre for Development Research, Copenhagen (Mimeo).

Jiggins, J. "Women and Seasonality: Coping with Crisis and Calamity." In IDS, op. cit., 1986.

Jodha, N. S. "Famine and Famine Policies: Some Empirical Evidence." *EPW,* no. 41, October 11, 1975.

———. "Effectiveness of Farmers' Adjustments to Risk." *ERW,* Review of Agriculture no. 26, June 1978.

———. "Common Property Resources and Rural Poor in Dry Regions of India." *EPW* no. 27, July 5, 1986.

Kynch, J., and A. K. Sen. "Indian Women: Well-Being and Survival." *Cambridge Journal of Economics,* 7, 3/4 (1983).

Leakey, C. "Biomass, Man and Seasonality in the Tropics." In IDS, op. cit., 1986.

Lipton, M. "Poverty, Undernutrition and Hunger." *World Bank Staff Working Paper,* no. 597. Washington D.C.: World Bank, 1983a.

———. "Labour and Poverty." *WBSWP,* no. 616. Washington D.C.: World Bank, 1983b.

———. "Demography and Poverty." *WBSWP,* no. 623. Washington D.C.: World Bank, 1983c.

———. "Land Assets and Rural Poverty." *WBSWP,* no. 744. Washington D.C.: World Bank, 1985.

Longhurst, R. "Household Food Strategies in Response to Seasonality and Famine." In IDS, op. cit., 1986.

McCarthy, F. "The Target Group: Women in Rural Bangladesh." In E. J. Clay and B. B. Schaffer (eds.), *Room for Manoeuvre: An Exploration of Public Policy in Agricultural and Rural Development.* Gower, 1984.

McKee, L. "Households during Unemployment: The Resourcefulness of the Unemployed." In J. Brannen and G. Wilson (eds.), *Give and Take in Families: Studies in Resource Distribution.* Allen and Unwin, 1987.

Mencher, J. "Landless Women Agricultural Labourers in India: Some Observations for Tamil Nadu, Kerala and West Bengal." In *Women in Rice Farming,* IRRI, Gower, 1985.

Nabarro, D., C. Cassels, et al., "The Impact of Integrated Rural Developments: The Kosi Hill Area Rural Development Programme, East Nepal." Department of International Community Health, Liverpool School of Tropical Medicine, October 1987.

NIRD. "Administrative Arrangements for Rural Development: Proceedings of the National Workshop held at the National Institute for Rural Development (Hyderabad)." Government of India Publications, 1985.

Rahaman, M. M. "The Causes and Effects of Famine in the Rural Population." In John R. K. Robson (ed.), *Famine: Its Causes and Management,* Gordon and Breach, 1981.

Rahmato, Dessalegn. *Peasant Survival Strategies.* Geneva: International Institute for Relief and Development, Food for the Hungry International, 1988.

Rath, N. "Garibi Hatao: Can IRDP do it?" *EPW,* no. 6. February 2, 1985.

Richards, P. *Indigenous Agricultural Revolution,* Hutchinson, 1985.

———. *Coping with Hunger,* Allen and Unwin, 1986.

Scott, J. *Weapons of the Weak: Everyday Forms of Peasant Resistance.* New Haven, Conn.: Yale University Press, 1985.

Seabright, P. "Identifying Investment Opportunities for the Poor, Evidence from the Livestock Market in South India." Cambridge: Department of Economics (Mimeo), 1987.

Sen, A. K. *Poverty and Famines.* Oxford: Clarendon Press, 1982.

———. "Poor, Relatively Speaking." *Oxford Economic Papers,* 35 (1983).

Sengupta, S. (with M. G. Ghosh). "State Intervention in the Vulnerable Food Economy of India and the Problem of the Rural Poor." Paper for workshop on problems of public distribution of foodgrains in Eastern India, March 7–9, 1978. (Mimeo)

Siddiqui, K. "The Political Economy of Rural Poverty in Bangladesh." Dhaka: National Institute of Local Government, 1982.

Singh, K. "Eradicating Rural Poverty: Lessons of IRDP Experience." In NIRD, op. cit., 1985.

Toulmin, C. "Access to Food, Dry Season Strategies and Household Size amongst the Bambara of Central Mali." In IDS, op. cit., 1986.

Townsend, P. "A Sociological Approach to the Measurement of Poverty—A Rejoinder to Professor Amartya Sen." *Oxford Economic Papers,* 37 (1985).

Van Schendel, W. "Peasant Mobility: The Odds of Life in Rural Bangladesh." Assen: Van Gorcum, 1981.

———. "Self Rescue and Survival: The Rural Poor in Bangladesh." *Journal of South Asian Studies,* 9, 1 (1986).

———, and Faraizi, A. H. *Rural Labourers in Bengal 1880–1980,* Comparative Asian Studies Programme, Rotterdam: Erasmus University, 1984.

Watts, M. *Silent Violence: Food, Famine and Peasantry in Northern Nigeria,* University of California Press, 1983.

Westergaard, K. *Pauperization and Rural Women in Bangladesh: A Case Study,* BARD, Comilla, 1983.

White, C. "Food Shortages and Seasonality in WoDaaBe Communities in Niger." In IDS, op. cit., 1986.

Whitehead, A. "Women's Solidarity—and Divisions Among Women." *IDS Bulletin,* 15, 1 (1984).

World Bank. *Poverty and Hunger: Issues and Options for Food Security in Developing Countries.* Washington D.C.: World Bank, 1986.

CHAPTER **28**

INTO ANOTHER JUNGLE: THE FINAL JOURNEY OF THE MATACOS?

Ariel Dorfman

As a child, one of my friends thought the Matacos were some sort of animal. He had been brought up on a sugar mill in the province of Tucumán, Argentina, where at night the adults would tell stories. One story dealt with something called Matacos, which were hunted down by the hundreds in the jungles of the Gran Chaco forest. He remembered, above all, an evening when a guest of his father related how Matacos had been picked off one by one by soldiers from the back of a moving train. This confirmed his impression that the victims were monkeys or other wild beasts.

That idea persisted until several years later. One morning he went out into the yard and saw his grandmother standing in front of two small, bronze-faced children, an impassive brother and sister. With a pair of large scissors, she began to shear off their black, dirty hair. "These Matacos," she announced, "are full of lice. This is the only way to get rid of them."

It was only then that my friend realized that the Matacos were Indians.

• • • • • •

There is a vast region in the Argentine province of Chaco, some two million hectares of dry scrub forest, known as El Impenetrable. I found nobody who could fix the date when the phrase first came into use, but everybody agrees that it describes no ordinary jungle. A thick, intertwined bramble of vegetation stretches densely for miles, with an occasional solitary tree jutting above the low bush, to form a suffocating wall of thickets you can neither enter without a guide nor leave alive were that guide to abandon you.

From *Grassroots Development,* 12, 2 (1988), pp. 2–15.

But it is not the forest alone that isolates the zone. The land cannot absorb all the water that flows into it. Water from the sky during months of rain. Water swelling from rivers that are fed by the remote Andes when they thaw, rivers overflowing their boundaries and changing course unpredictably. For days, often weeks, the roads are cut off—they can be navigated for miles as if they were narrow lakes. Afterward, withering months of dry heat, even of drought, will come, but that does not matter—the local people know that soon enough they will have more water than they know what to do with.

Most people would find such a place, alternating between swamp and arid scrubland, not only impenetrable but, frankly, uninhabitable. What to others is inhospitable and menacing is to the remaining Matacos—15,000 of the extant 23,000 are concentrated in this area—a last refuge and, perhaps, a last opportunity to survive.

It is here, on the northern frontier of El Impenetrable, bordering the brown, muddy currents of the tumultuous Bermejo River, that the village of El Sauzalito lies. It is here that a remarkable experiment is being carried out to try to save a people from extinction.

· · · · · ·

In 1879, at the exact moment when the Indians in the United States were being massacred by superior firepower, Julio Roca, then Argentina's minister of war and soon to be its president, defined a new strategy toward the Indians who still controlled vast territories of the republic. "It is necessary," he said, perhaps thinking of the newly invented Remington rifle, "to directly search out the Indian's hiding place and make him submit or expel him." The resulting offensive against the Indians of the Pampas was known as *La Campaña del Desierto* (the Campaign of the Desert), and it all but exterminated the nomadic warriors who roamed the rich, fertile plains that were needed for grazing cattle and raising wheat. At the same time, though with less resources and urgency, the Gran Chaco (called the Green Desert) was conquered, and the remaining tribes of Indians were pushed back. This culminated, finally, in the expedition to the river Pilcomayo in 1912 and the massacre that was probably at the source of those stories my friend once heard around the bonfire in Tucumán.

The Matacos have their own version of what happened. Andrés Segundo is a 54-year-old Mataco who learned how to write 40 years ago. One of the first things he wrote down was his grandparents' memory of that expedition against his people, a recollection repeated today by his own children and grandchildren. He reads from his notebooks, and because his words are difficult to follow, I try to understand better by focusing on the print. Though the words are Spanish, the small, scrubby letters look almost indecipherable. As his fingers trace the hieroglyphics across the page, his voice is slurred, repetitive, incantatory.

> We did not know where those soldiers came from or why. They found where the aborigines [the Matacos never use the words "Indians" or "natives" to refer to themselves] lived and came with rifles, with bullets, beating people up. The Matacos went into the *monte* [the bush]. There was one woman with a child. She was hurt. She threw the child away. That is what my grandfather told me. They hunted the aborigine as if he was a tiger. . . . We were not harming anyone. We lived from the land, gathering the things that belonged to nobody. I do not know why the soldiers came.

The reason is, in fact, quite simple. They came because by then Argentina was producing goods for export to foreign markets—and a lot of Indian land was there for the taking. "The settlers would come," Manuel Fernández, another Mataco chronicler, told me, "and ask for permission to clear land or settle down. They might give the tribe a cow." The Indians interpreted this as a gesture of gratitude. The settlers understood that they had bought the land. To the Matacos, that was absurd: How could you sell the land? The Army arbitrated the disputes.

Their territory began to dwindle—but even so, the Matacos were not to be left alone on what remained. The Argentine economy needed not only their land—but their bodies as well.

Andrés Segundo has also recorded this event. His uncle told him of the day that a stranger arrived. He had been sent by the owner of a remote sugar mill in search of field hands to cut cane. The long journey that followed is recorded on yellowing scraps of paper—how they walked for a month, whole families, until they reached the train. Andrés Segundo tells the tale in a monotone, almost without emotion, as if these catastrophes were natural and not manmade. It rained along the route, it seems (I write "it seems" because the details are blurred, as if it were still raining and there were mud on the words themselves). The little ones cried from the cold. A terrible wind swept down, trees fell, people were killed.

That was to be the first, but not the last, trip. Trapped in a system of debt bondage, increasingly dependent on manufactured goods, the Matacos kept returning to the sugar plantations (cotton would come later). Part of the year they were seasonal workers, hiring out for low wages and cheap merchandise; the rest of the time they hunted and fished, and ate fruits and berries.

But even this divided, miserable life was endangered. By the 1960s, fewer workers were being hired—the era of mechanization had set in. (On the plane back from the Northeast, I happened to sit next to a major Argentine cotton exporter. Texas Instrument in hand, he calculated, for my benefit—punching plus and minus buttons, doling out percentages—how mechanization had made the migrants increasingly obsolete.)

The Matacos found themselves in a precarious situation. The monte was eroding, animal species were disappearing, the ecological equilibrium of the region had been fractured, wages were insufficient. ("There was no work," Andrés Segundo explained, "but we had to eat anyway.") Along with malnutrition, diseases like tuberculosis, Chagas, and parasitosis became prevalent. Infant mortality rose.

As the 1970s began, the future looked still bleaker for the Matacos. They had survived natural floods and disasters for centuries, but they could not withstand the manmade flood of modern civilization. Like so many other contemporary tribes of aborigines, the Matacos seemed bound for extinction.

· · · · · ·

There was no road to El Sauzalito 12 years ago. Had you been able to get there, you would have found a scattering of thatched huts in the middle of a clearing overgrown with weeds. Remove the steel machetes, some clothing, a couple of bottles and tin cans, and you might have thought you were visiting the Stone Age.

Today El Sauzalito is connected by a dirt road to Castelli, 200 miles away, and by radio to the outside world. In the center of the town is a plaza, with benches, planted flowers, gravel pathways. Nearby is a bungalow where the elected mayor and aldermen meet, along with an office for the justice of the peace and a civil registrar. A hospital, a grade school, and a high school have been built. Most, though not all, of the inhabitants live in brick houses. And there is electricity.

More important, instead of losing population, El Sauzalito is growing. Couples are marrying, children are being born. I met several young men who had left to log trees but were now returning home for good. The movement is centripetal, not centrifugal as before.

Just a few miles away, you can still find small settlements that remind you of El Sauzalito's recent past: sparse collections of huts barely differentiated from the surrounding monte. But the real distance is not measured in miles. To transform El Sauzalito, thousands of hours of energy have been expended by the Matacos, and resources have poured in from the outside. If the resources were to dry up, if the Matacos were to sink into apathy, this new version of El Sauzalito would probably slip back in time, slip away into the waiting overgrowth, and once again begin to die.

· · · · · ·

At the beginning of this century, a doctor by the name of Maradona wrote a book, *Através de la Selva* (Crossing the Jungle), in which he narrates his visits to various Indian communities of the Gran Chaco. "The Indian," he writes of the Mataco, "speaks softly and is even gentle in the way he treats you, but his savage, suspicious, and egoistic nature quickly prevails." On other pages, he mentions their criminal personality, their readiness to destroy. Other adjectives he uses are "indolent," "decadent," "ridiculous," "sanguinary."

The Argentine Constitution, of course, uses none of these words to describe the Indian. But by mandating that the Indian be converted to Catholicism as a way of guaranteeing peace (Article 67, Item 15), it legally affirms the inferiority of native civilization and culture and denies Indians the right to their own beliefs. It is not surprising, therefore, that a 1978 decree put the undersecretary for Indian affairs also in charge of the welfare of minors, the elderly, and the handicapped.*

Indians are lumped together with those who are not adults, with those who have already lived out their usefulness and are waiting for death.

· · · · · ·

When Diego Soneira arrived in El Sauzalito in 1973 as the representative of the Instituto del Aborigen, a sort of Bureau of Indian Affairs, he had already spent several years working in the area and was convinced that only a dramatic alteration in their way of life could save the Matacos. They had been, until then, constantly on the move, either as nomads in the jungle or as migrants on the plantations. Neither form of subsistence offered any guarantee of stability. What the Matacos needed was to become

---

Editor's note: Since this article was written, new legislation was passed in 1987 that calls for sweeping reforms in the treatment of Indians in Argentina.

the legal owners of their own land so they would never again be expelled from it. But this meant they had to till that land and become sedentary.

This was not going to be easy. Though they had learned something about growing subsistence crops from the outreaches of the Incan empire many centuries ago and later picked up a bit more from the whites, the Matacos were primarily hunter-gatherers. What had taken the human race many thousands of years, the Matacos would have to achieve in a generation.

Soneira, however, was not the kind of bureaucrat who comes to visit the poor or the Indians armed with theories and suggestions that others must enact and then leaves for a comfortable home. He knew that if this change were to have any chance of success, it would have to be carried out by the Matacos themselves and could not be imposed from the outside. And he knew this meant accompanying the Matacos, living as they did. A former priest who lost none of his missionary zeal when he gave up the priesthood, Soneira arrived in El Sauzalito to stay. Six other white people—experts in health, agriculture, education—joined him, among them his new wife, Nene, and her mother, Clemencia Sarmiento, known to one and all from then on as Mami.

Of course, the Matacos were suspicious. They had no way of knowing that Diego was different from the other white men who had brought ambitious proposals and then went away richer than when they arrived and certainly better off than the Indians who they left behind. In their first meeting with Soneira—which has assumed a sort of legendary, almost foundational status in the memory of El Sauzalito and is now narrated in a confused tangle of versions—eight Matacos were ready to cooperate; 150 others opposed his presence. (Each Mataco I spoke to included himself among the eight.) What *is* clear is that, in spite of a majority who wanted to refuse them entry, the group managed, after hours of discussion during a deluge, to pitch three tents in the middle of the bush, in the exact spot where the central plaza now proudly stands. As the days slipped by, Soneira and his companions gradually won the confidence of the Matacos, though he would be expelled twice from the town when they did not receive everything they wanted. Soneira eventually created the Asociación Promotores Chaco, which brought in outsiders to help the Matacos develop agricultural projects. Today, there are 40 *promotores* throughout El Impenetrable.

To focus only on the outside advisors, however, is unfair to the many Matacos who had concluded on their own that they were heading for a dead end. Without these Matacos, Soneira's plans would never have worked.

Ernesto Reynoso, for one, the *cacique,* or chieftain of the Matacos, had watched his people's situation deteriorate year by year. Like Soneira, he had come to believe that land ownership was the best hope for the Matacos. Nobody had elected Reynoso to his post; no other candidate wanted the job. While he may tend to exaggerate his own role ("I made this place; I am the *tata,* the big father of this place; I am the authority here"), all agree that he *was* indispensable. Over the years, he was to prove himself a wily advocate: tirelessly pestering authorities to exact promises of aid, then knocking on doors to hold them to those promises. A stubborn rock of a man, he knew that if aid were to be continued, his people would have to show results. Behind him and beside him, therefore, stand many other Matacos. His pride in what has been accomplished is their pride. "These are the machines that did everything," he says, lifting up his arms. "And these legs, they did the walking. Everything you see—the plaza, the hospital, the fields—we made it all."

His great-grandfather did not know a word of Spanish. He lived off the honey and the iguana and the fish. With machete, pickax, and shovel, his grandfather helped to build the railroad from Formosa to Salta. His father was a *bracero* on the plantations. Reynoso himself began to pick cotton when he was five years old. His wife died on one of those month-long treks to the cotton fields.

"Someday," he told me, "we will have Mataco doctors. Who knows? Perhaps someday my grandchild will pilot a plane."

• • • • • •

But the confluence of these two streams—the whites devoted to the Matacos and the Matacos' faith in themselves—might have been insufficient if another sort of downpour had not taken place. In 1975, the Argentine military overthrew the government of Isabel Perón.

How ironic that this event would help the Matacos, who when they vote at all, tend to vote Peronist. The military government, as history has shown, was not overly interested in helping those who lived on the margins of society. Obsessed with security, however, they worried that the Gran Chaco was so underdeveloped and isolated that it would be vulnerable to foreign attacks. And the very notion that something "internal" could also be "impenetrable" was an insult to the geopolitical, macho pride of the military.

The armed forces therefore supplied an enormous quantity of resources to the region, most quite useless. In the middle of the jungle, for instance, in an area with few natives, a small concrete town was built from scratch, replete with telephone lines, satellite-dish television, and air-conditioned buildings staffed by government employees with nothing to do all day but wait for the next showcase visit.

But in El Sauzalito, funds could be used for plans that were already under way. Thus when the governor of the province came for a visit and noted that a great deal had already been accomplished with little outside support, he offered Diego Soneira the post of mayor, or *intendente*. Though the military government's national policy ran directly counter to his own democratic ideals, Soneira saw the chance to further develop the area, pay the promotores' salaries, and channel municipal money into essential infrastructure.

As Soneira reports it, he told the governor that there were two ways to approach the development of El Impenetrable. One alternative was to see it as an enormous enterprise. "In that case," he said, "your purpose is to make money, and you exploit things to produce an immediate benefit. Or you can see a vast school here. This means that, like any form of education, you will run a deficit in the short run, with the benefits coming many years from now. I am not an entrepreneur. If you want me and my people to work here, we must be allowed to make this place into a school that will give the Indians a chance to learn how to live on their own and not be condemned to live off welfare forever."

The governor, surprisingly, agreed.

• • • • • •

It was inevitable that someday the vast school of and for the Matacos would run into trouble because this effort is made up of two separate, and one might almost say contradictory, learning processes. The first, which has had priority until now, is to modernize the Mataco economy, allowing its members to cope with an overwhelming foreign civilization that technologically and organizationally is far more powerful than theirs. The second, which was only implicit and thus far has found no institutional expression or funding, is to help the Matacos save their identity and sustain what makes them unique as they become integrated into a world whose rules they did not make.

The problem is that to become modern and have an economic base of their own, the Matacos must break their traditional patterns of social organization. For hunter-gatherers, Nature is the provider: The future depends on reading the natural world carefully, not on the systematic planning of one's work. You collect enough to last for a brief period, and when that stock has been depleted, you go out and get more. Such a culture does not conceive of the idea, for example, that a crop can be ruined if you leave the fields for a week, that there are such things as capitalization, or credit to be repaid. The future is really not in one's hands. "This may happen," the Matacos told me. "And then again, perhaps it may not."

Nor are the Matacos accustomed to fulfilling collective obligations. Formerly in their community, each family could leave without permission. Decisions were not made by a majority and imposed upon a minority. This is a perfectly logical structure if the renewable forest is always there—but it invites disaster if the earth must be worked, tractors allocated, seed and fertilizer distributed, if survival depends on taming Nature through mutual cooperation.

The Matacos have been relatively successful in this venture. This is evident in the number of buildings and facilities, in the increased standard of living, in the many hectares (still insufficient) now under irrigation, in the crops exported and the timber sold, and above all, in their capacity to organize. They control and regulate their own economic activities through the Asociación Comunitaria, with a subcommission for each industry—agriculture, lumber, tree-felling, repair work, and soon, fishing. The association allows the Matacos to plan their work, distribute the benefits, do the accounting, discuss and solve their difficulties.

The promotores, to be sure, are still on hand with suggestions, expertise, techniques—as an unavoidable bridge to a confusing outside world—and they may remain until a new generation is educated. Yet, the Matacos are obviously weaving their uncertain way to relative autonomy.

Achieving this first educational objective, however, has forced the Matacos to deal with the second, which has been perpetually postponed. The promotores did not initiate this experiment as a way to painlessly ingest one more aboriginal tribe into the stomach of the twentieth century. The idea was that the Matacos should modernize without losing their values and perspectives, their own culture.

The difficult question, of course, is the same one that is heard in many other places in the Third World: "Can it be done?"

• • • • • •

The day I arrived in El Sauzalito, a little Mataco girl had just died. She was the sixteenth child to die in the last four months.

A few hours later, I met the doctor who at the time was supposedly in charge of the community's health. I had heard vague stories about him—a man who turned away the sick if they called outside the regular schedule, a man who did not visit the other communities, a man who supposedly had said that the only way to make an Indian work was to fire a couple of shots at him. But even those stories did not prepare me for the person who swaggered through the door. He began by verbally abusing the whole experiment: It was, he said—his eyes protruding from a thin, bony face—"a total failure." Instead of advancing, the Matacos were going backwards. He branded the recent decision to plant cotton as ludicrous and stated that what was needed was a *criollo* landowner to establish some order. Finally, he turned around, crouched slightly, and using his buttocks as a metaphor, wiped them with his hand to show how worthless he considered everything.

"Why are you here then?" I asked.

His answer chilled me. "I am not human," he said. Perhaps he meant "humanitarian"—but the word he may have used mistakenly suited his manner quite well. "I didn't come here to save anybody, but for my own benefit. I'm almost 60. If I had retired as an ordinary doctor, I would be a beggar. That's why I agreed to come to this place. So I could retire with the pension of a hospital director."

I would not mention the doctor except that he personifies, in my opinion, two undeniable facts about the Mataco condition: First, many outsiders come to such places not to help those who live there but to help themselves. Second, and perhaps more significantly, the Matacos had been trying to get the doctor replaced ever since he arrived three years earlier. They had received repeated assurances that he would soon depart, but there he sat, symbol of all the things—far too many things—that the Matacos do not control and yet are essential to their well-being. The Matacos can do little about the world economic crisis or that of the Argentine economy—even though these crises mean that their products fetch lower prices, that inflation eats up their benefits, and that subsidies and services become even scarcer.

The apparent hostility and complexity of the outside world creates among the Matacos an added dependency on the external buffers that protect and benefit them. Without the promotores or outside aid, the Matacos could not have begun their journey toward autonomy; but now they tend to think of those factors as permanent. With some embarrassment, wherever I went, I had to submit to a long litany of needs and petitions and complaints, as if each person were demanding that I solve his problems.

This is not, of course, unique to the Matacos. The dilemmas of paternalism and dependency are present in most development projects. It is not my purpose to explore here how those problems can be overcome. What does matter at this point is to note that if all power—both evil and good—seems to come from outside, then the Matacos' sense of self-worth is weakened. Everything they learn tells them that the road to autonomy, the road to success, passes through the abrogation and eradication of their past identity.

· · · · · ·

The anthropologist Edward Spier, in his classic study of the Yaqui Indians, coined the phrase "enduring peoples" to designate those human groups who have "experienced incorporation into nation-states, and have existed within or outlasted nation-states." He examines "the Cataláns and Basques of Spain; the Welsh and the Irish, formerly of Great Britain; the Cherokees, the Hopis, and the Senecas of the United States; the lowland Mayas of Mexico; and finally, the Jews of many different states."

In all of these cases, he finds that a people will persist—despite drastic changes in genetic constitution, place of residence, language, customs, and beliefs—if they continue to hold a common identity, that is, a stock of symbols and experiences that allow them to have a common understanding of the world and of their relationship to other cultures. Peoples who are unable to maintain the consciousness of their ethnicity are unable to remember their past collectively or use it to interpret the present and will probably be absorbed.

Can the Matacos endure?

Do they have within their culture the resilience and flexibility to go through the rites of modernization without disintegrating as an independent cultural entity?

There is at this point no way of telling for sure. What I saw and heard was not overly encouraging.

In 1944, the Matacos were converted to Christianity by missionaries of the Anglican Church. For the first time, the Indians received some elementary education, health care, and protection from the incursions of the army and the white settlers who would often kill a Mataco or two for fun. But the Indians were also taught to forget their own legends and stories, to feel ashamed of their past, and to stop dancing and singing their traditional music.

I asked the Matacos I met to tell me stories and myths from their past. They either pretended not to understand my question or told me they could not remember. When I repeated several legends or described beliefs about the dead and their spirits—things I had read in collections edited by foreign anthropologists—people nodded, agreeing that these were stories they knew. They did not, however, admit to telling their own children these tales, to sharing that body of sacred law that contains moral guidance and the threads of communal identity. Some promotores told me that something similar happens with songs and dances: The Matacos sing hymns at church, but the old instruments and melodies are being put aside and forgotten.

The only Mataco I met who was prepared to recount and discuss the old myths was—strange as it may seem—Ernesto Avendaño, the Anglican pastor of El Sauzalito. Perhaps he was sure enough of the divine origins of his own beliefs to be able to admit knowing those stories. He explained, in any case, that they were mere superstitions and were no longer necessary to his people. The songs, he added, were learned as apprenticeship to witchcraft, but all that was a thing of the past.

Since this rejecting attitude is the basic belief of most Matacos—or at least what they profess to believe—the situation is delicate for the promotores. Patricio Doyle, a former Catholic priest who has focused on the cultural future of the Matacos, does not want to interfere with their religious beliefs or their forms of worship. But he does want to discover what remains of their values, skills, and legends, what the Matacos can build on as they become part of the Western world and the Argentine nation.

He is now working on a *revistita,* a small magazine in Mataco and Spanish that will belong to the community itself and serve as a vehicle for amplifying the multiple voice of the Matacos. He hopes the Matacos will begin to express their present problems as well as what belongs to their past and their collective memory.

He has also managed to persuade two experts in the development of art and recreation among marginal groups to come from Buenos Aires and work with the local people.

And yet Patricio Doyle, who has spent many years among the Matacos, does not speak their language. Nor, for that matter, does any other promotor, not even Diego Soneira. Nor do any of the white children. Some words are understood, some conversations can be followed vaguely, but not one of the people who have come to help the Matacos survive as a cultural entity is fluent in their language. No matter how they have tried, they have been unable to learn it or even find Matacos who will teach them.

I heard the language often during my stay. Once, I remember, I was at a meeting that Mario Pisano, a promotor, held with the residents of nearby Vizacheral to discuss future fishing activity. After some words had been exchanged in Spanish, one of the men suddenly switched to Mataco, and the rest soon joined in with a flowing antiphony. Before one person had ended, another had begun, as if speaking to himself and yet to all of them, as if somebody inside were listening, murmuring very low— only ears accustomed to the bush could distinguish each sound—and on it went, a honied, intertwining superimposition of voices, until they stopped. They had reached some sort of conclusion, one and all of them, and Spanish was once again the language to be used. I felt, during these moments, as if they were defending their last refuge on earth, those thickets of syllables that only they could understand.

It almost seems as if the Matacos are unwilling to teach the promotores their language. Once you give strangers your language, it is as if you have given them your jungle, your land, your trees. It is in the language, after all, that places and birds, animals and customs are named and invoked.

Perhaps I had caught a glimpse of the real Impenetrable—the language, the one place in the world that belongs only to the Matacos.

• • • • • •

The Matacos have beautiful legends.

Like those of all peoples, they narrate the origins of the universe, the reason why there are men and women, how the animals appeared, why it rains and why honey exists, the struggles of heroes and the voyages of tricksters.

Some of their legends seem to be recent because they exhibit a considerable awareness of white, dominant people.

In one of these, the Matacos explain why they are so few and other tribes so populous. According to this tale, the different races and nations crawled out from underground through a hole dug by an armadillo. All the men and women of each race were able to escape and populate the earth. But when the Matacos' turn came, only a few appeared before a pregnant Mataco woman got stuck in the hole and was unable to move. And so, many Matacos remain unborn.

Another legend says Christians and Matacos resided together long ago in one house "where everything could be found." Everything that was good—the axes, tools, horses, cattle, beautiful clothes for women—was taken by the ancestors of the Christians, and the Matacos were left with only clay pots, dogs, and "other inferior things."

The clay pot, which the Matacos make with great skill and elegance, is the protagonist of another short tale. It began to compete with the iron pot, saying that it could cook as well and as quickly over fire. But the iron pot won, and so the pot made of earth cracked, and was thrown away.

The Matacos have beautiful legends, but they feel defeated. A people will survive only if they are able to take pride in their own culture.

· · · · · ·

Between 1821 and 1982, almost 6.4 million immigrants came to Argentina. In 1895, immigrants made up 25.5 percent of the population, and by 1914, this figure had risen to 30 percent, the highest proportion in the world.

No statistics record how many Matacos there once were. So we cannot know what proportion is now left.

· · · · · ·

Some 420 miles south of El Sauzalito is the city of Resistencia, the capital of the province of Chaco.

In the central plaza of Resistencia—christened with that name because it triumphantly *resisted* the assaults of the savages—there is a statue. It is the copy of a statue I have seen often in art and history books and whose original I once contemplated in Rome itself. It was given to the city of Resistencia by the resident Italian-Argentine community, and it portrays the twins Romulus and Remus suckling a she-wolf.

That is how Rome saw its origins, as if there had been no previous tribes on its peninsula, no previous inhabitants. And the immigrants who came to the Argentine northeast saw themselves opening supposedly virgin territory just like the Romans did: each of them a Romulus, each a Remus coming to establish tiny empires in a foreign land.

There is no statue in Resistencia to the ancestors of Andrés Segundo or Ernesto Reynoso.

There is no statue of their ancestors anywhere.

· · · · · ·

By a strange coincidence I heard Rome mentioned the first morning I arrived in El Sauzalito. Although the reference had nothing to do with immigration, it may have had something to do with empires.

I asked Patricio Doyle why he had left Buenos Aires, what he was doing in this remote place.

"Christ was not born in Rome," Doyle answered. "He was born in Bethlehem. Who knows what will be born in this faraway land and radiate, by example, elsewhere?"

· · · · · ·

Most of the Matacos I spoke with seemed unaware of their purported transcendence or of the cultural crossroads they have come to.

I hesitated before writing down the previous sentence. I really cannot be certain that it is true.

The problem is that I was barely able to communicate with the Matacos during my brief stay. We talked, of course, extensively. Yet there was, except for one occasion, no deep contact—no moment when two people come together and know they are sharing something, that there is some understanding. I lacked their language, and they used mine without eloquence, though often with great dignity. Their Spanish, moreover, besides not being their native tongue, is the language of those who dominate them, and they must have supposed that what I would write about them might be essential for future aid or grants. They were careful, therefore, of what they said. Nor did it help that I lacked an interpreter: Translations at least pretend that there is some equality in the interchange. And there was the incredible reserve and intractability of the women, with whom I was never able to speak at all and whose importance in the conservation and transmission of an oral, autochthonous culture cannot be overstated.

I was not frustrated by this lack of connection. I interpreted it as a sign that the Matacos had secret paths in their forests to which I had no access, treasures they would not yield easily. I was glad they had something hidden—and only hoped that behind their silence, or the words that are like silence, there are strengths upon which they can build as their experiment continues. As they become more self-assured, they should be able to engage in an ever more significant dialogue with the outside world.

But there was, as I suggested, one exception. His name is Ramón Navarrete. As the *primer consejal,* or deputy mayor, of the *municipio,* he had attained the highest political and administrative post a Mataco ever held. I had tried to speak to him on several occasions, and he was always busy. Only on my last day in El Sauzalito—as the afternoon turned into what I can only describe as a green-hot evening—were we able to talk.

When democracy and elections returned to Argentina in 1983, Diego Soneira decided to step down as intendente. The concentration of so much power in his hands had allowed the community to take gigantic steps forward, but it had also created confusion and seemed a bit artificial. It was time, Soneira believed, for the people themselves to administer their own institutions, to be less sheltered from the outside world. They had to learn not to look to him for all the answers. Though the Matacos constituted a large majority of the population, they did not propose one of their own as mayor, preferring a criollo who was sympathetic to them and had administrative experience. They did, however, elect three *consejales,* or aldermen, and Navarrete is one of them. He is not a leader, as is Ernesto Reynoso, but he is—of all the Matacos—the one who best understands how language and Argentine society work. He is the closest example to an "intellectual" that I found in the Mataco community.

Like intellectuals everywhere, Navarrete is anguished. He must cope with burdens he only vaguely comprehends—budgets, sick leaves, papers in triplicate, the wonders of modern-day bureaucracy—and at the same time respond to the increasing demands of Matacos who believe the municipio exists to provide jobs and food.

To live between two worlds, where tradition and newness constantly mingle and conflict, is after all one of the primary experiences of modernity in the Third World. It is as if, he said, he had given me a quick lesson in Mataco and then sent me into the bush to fend for myself. Would I easily survive?

Navarrete has become an explorer, the Mataco who has ventured farthest into what Mami calls "the white jungle," the jungle of civilization where people play according to different rules, where newcomers can easily get lost among other swamps and traps that await and tempt them.

· · · · · ·

Navarrete learned Spanish from an Anglican missionary when he was seven years old; but it was only when he reached his first year of high school and studied grammar—many years later as an adult—that he realized Mataco, just like Spanish, must have certain rules and categories. Since then he has been studying his own language, trying to discover its inner laws.

This is not a detached intellectual pursuit. Navarrete has seen tribes in Salta who no longer speak their original tongue. He feels that each time an old man dies, a universe of words and stories dies with him. So Navarrete plans to teach the language to the Mataco children, as part of their curriculum. He is also interested in helping the promotores learn the language. He patiently explained several words I wanted to learn, but in spite of his excellent Spanish, our attempts often broke down at a loss for the proper usage.

He has not, however, been able to teach Mataco at school, although the law specifically recommends bilingual education. A previous school director let him work, but the next administrator opposed his presence there, saying he was unqualified. (Who, though, is qualified to certify teachers of Mataco?)

Navarrete's problem is symptomatic. If the Matacos are to become self-sufficient, the school must prepare the children for the future while the parents are learning in the fields and the offices—and this must be done in a way that shows respect for their culture. Instead, the Mataco children feel unwelcome in school. The dropout rate is outrageously high.

One of Navarrete's older daughters, now 18, had to repeat first grade three times and finally decided to stop wasting her time. It is true that in those times, she and the rest of the family had to periodically migrate to pick cotton. Now things seem better. Several Matacos have graduated from high school—and now work in the Asociación Comunitaria. They are essential to Patricio Doyle's plan to publish the revistita. Navarrete's nine-year-old daughter has already completed three years of elementary school without repeating a grade and will herself enter high school in just a few years.

What would he like her to be?

"A lawyer," he says. "What we most need are lawyers who can defend our interests."

Navarrete is anguished and open and doubtful. He is trying to build bridges over rivers that keep changing course.

He is the only Mataco who did not ask me for anything.

· · · · · ·

I spent several days in El Sauzalito without meeting Diego Soneira. It turned out he was in the faraway village of El Espinillo, some 200 miles across El Impenetrable. I went to see him on my last day in the region.

I found him trying to put a lumbermill into operation. It had been erected a couple of years before, but the contractor had done everything wrong, and the mill had never worked. In a casual conversation with regional authorities, Soneira had mentioned what a pity such economic potential was being wasted, when the machinery could be repaired. He had been invited to try. What white technicians had failed to accomplish, or even propose, Soneira was going to do with Matacos. They had, after all, been operating a successful lumbermill for years.

If I needed a symbol of how far the Matacos have come, this was it. Instead of receiving help, Mataco operators, carpenters, and electricians were giving it to others, spreading their knowledge across El Impenetrable. And the others, in this case, were Toba Indians, rivals of the Matacos for centuries. In fact, some Matacos in El Sauzalito—who one promotor playfully calls *los rezongones,* or complainers—had told me before I left that Diego should be home with them, that he did not care for them anymore.

Meanwhile, Diego would have liked nothing better than to be back in El Sauzalito. He had brought his wife and his seven children with him because the job was supposed to be over in a few days. Then several machine parts that he needed to complete the job were delayed, and the authorities also failed to give him some unspecified aid they had promised. A few days had turned into a week. The nine Soneiras, plus the five Mataco technicians, were sleeping in an abandoned brick house, cooking over an open fire in the patio. They were without running water and were assaulted each evening—at exactly five past eight—by the most venomous, stubborn, hostile mosquitoes they had ever encountered. (And these people know an awful lot about mosquitoes.) The mosquitoes were so terrible, in fact, that they forced the Soneiras to seek refuge each evening in the sweltering heat of their sleeping quarters—and managed to infiltrate the premises anyway, if one were to believe the blood-stained walls.

And yet, the Soneiras were all cheerful, and Diego was calm, confident, tireless. Perhaps it was better to have seen him here, as if he were on another adventure, starting from scratch in a relatively strange place. It may be that in this way I was able to catch a glimpse of what the man must have been like when he arrived in El Sauzalito so many years ago. There was no doubting his strength or his magnetism.

He watched me watch him and finally smiled and said: "I know what you are going to ask me. Everybody always asks me the same thing. You want to know why I came here, why I stay here?"

It was as if he had read my mind. So I asked him something different when we finally sat down. I asked him two questions. How long did he think this experiment would last? When would he know if he had been successful?

He said he did not know the answer to the first question, but he may have responded to it in answering the second.

"I'll be successful when I'm not needed anymore," Diego said.

And then he went off, 150 miles of dirt road away, to search for the missing spare parts.

• • • • • •

One day in El Sauzalito, under the burning noon sun, I ventured a little into the monte.

I did not go alone. My idea was to be guided by a Mataco. I wanted to experience what it would be like to be submerged in a habitat where he was the master, where his sense of smell, his ears that notice the slightest twitch of a leaf, his extraordinary eyesight and foresight would make him my superior. I wanted to be in a place where all my knowledge and skill would be useless, where his culture reigned and mine was out of place. I wanted, in a way, to experience what the Matacos must feel every day as they confront white, Western civilization: to be at a loss, displaced, defenseless.

I was not in El Sauzalito long enough to take such a trip, nor had I built up enough confidence with a Mataco so he might take me along on one of the frequent hunting expeditions.

I settled for an artificial second best. Mami called two young Matacos—8 and 11 years old, respectively—to guide me toward a still-wild area near the Río Bermejo, where the town ends.

I was not sure if they understood just what it was that I wanted, but they moved with me toward the river, and for a while I convinced myself that I was on the verge of the desired experience. They glided barefoot through a labyrinth of undergrowth, moving through the thickets, scaring flocks of pale-blue butterflies, somehow able to find their way in that tangled vegetation.

If it were not for these boys, I thought to myself, I would be lost. It was a game I was playing with myself, of course. I knew that the town was nearby and that I was in no real danger of losing my way. As if to answer me, there was suddenly a noise in the bushes and I sensed something big lurching toward us. But no wild beast emerged. It was merely a pig, one of the few remaining from a failed livestock experiment. It snorted across our path. I wondered what the two Mataco kids thought of this expedition. But they would not answer any of my questions—just a nod of their heads once in a while, a pause to look back to see if I was following.

After we reached the river, they decided to come back by another route, and they got lost. Several times we reached a wedge of canes and weeds and vines that would not let us pass. We had to backtrack. And then, again, a few more yards and the need to start over. Finally, they made their way to the river, retraced their steps to a familiar path, and managed to get me safely home.

What is the meaning of this experience?

Should I emphasize the boys' surefooted, fleeting movements at the beginning of the excursion, proving how Mataco children are still acquainted with the jungle and will somehow continue in the traditions of their forefathers? Or is the second stage more significant, when they lost their sense of direction and the bushes seemed alien to them as they would not have been to their ancestors when they were children?

Or was there no significance whatsoever in that brief exploration? Was not their conduct distorted by my very presence, their need to please me, their need to interpret my rather sophisticated and enigmatic desires?

I cannot tell. I would have to be a Mataco.

I would have to be a Mataco to know exactly where the two boys are going.

CHAPTER 29

THE "WOMEN'S MOVEMENT"

María de los Angeles Crummett

Volumes of literature spanning the social sciences have scrutinized the causes and consequences of the massive migration of rural Latin Americans to their region's exploding towns and cities. Amidst all this analysis, however, very little attention has been paid to female migrants.

This omission is striking, since census data indicate that in Latin America more women than men migrate to the cities—about 100 women for every 85 men. Why do women predominate in this great movement?

One obvious reason, of course, is the greater demand for female labor in cities. During the first phases of Latin American urbanization and industrialization, for example, more job opportunities existed for women than men in domestic service, street vending, and such labor-intensive industries as textiles and food processing.

Yet women's migration can't be fully explained unless their living and working conditions in the countryside are also examined, and here several other factors come into play.

A STATE OF CRISIS

Most important, Latin American agriculture is in a state of crisis. For decades, the farm sector has endured negative growth rates, falling prices for basic grains, and heightened food dependency. In many countries, agriculture's decline began in the postwar period. Technical, financial and human resources were diverted from the rural sector to spur industrialization in the urban sector. At the same time, large-scale com-

From *CERES* (FAO) 24 #5, pp. 22–25.

mercial production for export grew at the expense of traditional peasant agriculture. For the *minifundistas* or the smallholding sector of the peasantry, which includes 50 to 90 per cent of producers, agriculture's drive toward modernization intensified rural poverty, landlessness and migration to the cities.

These transformations throughout the Latin American countryside profoundly altered peasant women's roles within agriculture. The fact that women post the highest rates of migration suggest they are most adversely affected by changes in agriculture.

The commercialization of agriculture across Latin America has, for example, reduced demand for a permanent labor force, substituting for it temporary, seasonal laborers. Farm mechanization, in particular, has resulted in fewer permanent job opportunities, and on the whole women workers have been disproportionately displaced from the permanent work force.

Women are first to be displaced by technological innovations because men are relatively more privileged in terms of access to such essential resources as education, agricultural information and training, and credit. Women are simply more easily bumped from tasks that can be mechanized or taken over by wage labor, and they increasingly end up working in agriculture only on a temporary basis, during peak seasons—often in the most labor-intensive, poorest-paid tasks.

Studies also show that, where commercialization of agriculture has resulted in a decrease in the number of small, family holdings, women are further marginalized in agricultural production. On subsistence or below-subsistence minifundios, they tend to work more in secondary or less important income-generating activities than in actual farm production. These trends have been noted in Chile, Brazil, Peru and other countries. With the relative weight of the agricultural sector and the rate of wage employment in agriculture declining steadily, rural women are left without employment opportunities in farming. Evidently, this is an important reason for the predominance of women in the rural-urban migrant stream.

Compounding the problem of declining job opportunities for women in rural areas is the unequal distribution of land resources on the family farm itself, which works against female children. Older daughters in rural regions, for instance, are responsible for numerous tasks within the household, including care of younger siblings and helping with domestic chores. Additionally, they take part in a variety of economically productive activities on the family farm. However, once younger sisters are able to take over some of these jobs, older daughters are expected to marry or encouraged to seek wage work, often by migration to cities.

Among poor peasant and landless households, the shortage of land often makes migration the only option available to women. Sons are also expected to find paid work; yet in contrast to the encouragement of daughters to leave, sons are discouraged from leaving. Overall, their economic opportunities in the rural sector are greater than women's, not only because of greater local opportunities in paid labor but because in most cases land rights are passed to sons.

STRONG INDUCEMENTS

Certainly, demographic pressures on the land coupled with a growing dependence on wage income form a strong inducement for working-age children of both sexes to migrate. Carmen Diana Deere's study of northern Peru's highland Cajamarca Province, *Household and class relations,* indicates that during the 1960s pressure on the land was sufficiently acute to drive significant numbers of peasants into migrating either permanently or temporarily from the province. Sons and daughters confronted different situations. From the age of 12 or 13, sons were involved with their fathers in local wage work. By the time a young man reached 15 or 16, he was migrating with his father on a temporary basis to the northern coast.

A young woman had fewer possibilities for local employment while very young, but could capture the wage of an adult woman (as a domestic servant in the city) at a younger age than could a young man. By the time a girl turned 16, she would have migrated permanently to the capital, Lima, to work as a domestic.

In Oaxaca, Mexico, the need for cash income among the poor peasantry has also led to the expulsion of working-age children, but rural-urban migrants are overwhelmingly young, single girls. In *Economía campesina, unidad doméstica, y migración,* Kate Young hypothesizes that in the 1940s, '50s and '60s increasing poverty within the peasant community led to the expulsion of daughters, rather than sons, for two main reasons.

First, farm production in Oaxaca is dominated by men. Second, and more important, many of the economic activities of women and their daughters—making food and clothing and preparing products for sale locally—were being undermined by more efficiently produced manufactured goods. Thus, when economic pressure forced peasant households to send family members out to seek wage work, young single girls, the majority under 20, were the first to leave.

The 1970s, however, saw a diversification of the migration pattern in Oaxaca. Greater economic pressure on the poor to acquire cash income and increased opportunities for wealthier households led to a situation where people of all ages were leaving. Nevertheless, most migrants were young, between the ages of 10 and 29, and more were female than male. So, though over time more and more household members from different classes were drawn into migration, young women of the poor peasantry continued to be the most vulnerable to migratory pressures.

The migration of daughters and other family members to cities plays a critical role in the economic maintenance of rural households. On one hand, family expenditures on food, clothing and other items are reduced as one or more members migrate. On the other, peasant households are able to survive as units of production, thanks in part to the money sent by migrant children. Remittances are used to purchase farm animals or agricultural inputs, to pay off debts, or—among the poorest peasant families—to cover daily living expenses.

NEGATIVE EFFECTS

Yet migration of working-age children can also have negative effects on rural households, by transferring workloads from the young to the old and increasing the labor burden of the women and children who remain behind. Deere's study shows women of the poor peasantry assume greater responsibility for agricultural production—an activity previously dominated by men—as sons and male heads of households leave in search of wage work elsewhere.

In addition to greater workloads in agriculture, studies by Deere, Young and others find that the expulsion of daughters from smallholder households increases many mothers' household chores. The care of younger children, traditionally a responsibility of older daughters, is added to the mothers' already heavy workloads. A number of other tasks in which daughters participate, such as food preparation, animal care, and fuel and water collecting, also become the mothers' charge. The time taken by the added burdens imposed by migration of older daughters also hinders women's participation in other non-farm economic activities, especially petty trade.

This author's own fieldwork in Aguascalientes, Mexico, provides another example of the impact on women of rural-urban migration.

In Aguascalientes the commercialization of agriculture, beginning in the 1940s, eroded the economic viability of smallholder rain-fed agriculture and provoked an increase in the number of landless agricultural wage workers. A major consequence of this process was an outflow of rural inhabitants. Between 1940 and 1960, the migrant stream was composed largely of young single women from poor peasant and landless laborer households, migrating to the cities. In the 1960s, however, young men constituted a far greater percentage (60 per cent) of the migrant population. This change reflects the effects of mechanization within irrigated areas of the state, which reduced the demand for agricultural workers.

The erosion of women's productive activities in the rural areas and the demand for female labor in the cities explain the early tendency for women to dominate the migrant stream. The sharp decrease in female migration after 1960 appears to be a result of increasing opportunities for women in both rural and urban areas in the state. Most important, the growth of the textile and garment industries in the city of Aguascalientes in the 1960s increased the demand for a permanent female labor force. These industries also flourished in numerous rural communities and employed a predominantly young and female work force. The textile and garment industries in turn promoted the growth of *maquila doméstica,* or piecework manufacture of women's and children's clothing in the home—an activity exclusively employing women.

INTERNATIONAL MIGRATION

The 1980s witnessed a resurgence of female migration from the rural communities of Aguascalientes. In contrast to earlier migration patterns, however, women were migrating almost exclusively to urban communities in the United States.

Women's increasing involvement in international migration—a trend present in numerous sending communities throughout rural Mexico—can be traced to changes in local employment and income opportunities for both men and women, wrought in large part by Mexico's devastating economic crisis of the 1980s. These changes are nowhere more evident than in the guava-growing region of Calvillo, where the landless and poor peasantry earn the bulk of their wage income from seasonal labor in the guava orchards, piecework in the home, and temporary migration to the United States.

Throughout the 1970s and '80s, these three activities—guava, *maquila* and migration—provided rural households in Calvillo an important measure of economic and social stability. Male heads of households and older sons worked in the guava fields during the harvest period and during the off-season headed north across the U.S.-Mexican border in search of farm or service-sector work. Remittances provided many households the economic wherewithal to purchase an array of consumer durables (TVs, stereos, pickup trucks), to cover education and health expenses, and to make investments on the land or in their physical living conditions.

Maquila employed adult women, and all female children from the age of seven or eight worked as unpaid family laborers. During the period of male migration to the United States, piecework became the primary if not the sole source of household income. Even though home work is very poorly remunerated, the availability of year-round work in *maquila* meant day-to-day expenses were being met in the interim before remittances arrived. Moreover, the nature of *maquila,* paid work in the home, enabled child care and other household tasks to be performed alongside wage work.

Among smallholder households, the combination of temporary male migration to the United States and women's paid work in the home enabled families to continue cultivating the land, as well as to retain their land rights. Most important, migration and *maquila* permitted nearly all landed and landless households to remain in Calvillo, where their families had lived for generations.

By the early 1990s, the three most important income-earning activities in Calvillo had undergone dramatic transformations. Guava production, once a major purveyor of temporary seasonal employment in the region, floundered under the Mexican government's efforts to privatize agriculture. The removal of price supports for key agricultural inputs (electricity for irrigation, fertilizers, machinery), for instance, sharply increased production costs for guava producers. Many growers went bankrupt while others attempted to remain competitive by taking entire groves out of production or introducing labor-saving equipment into the production process. These changes, among others, cut labor demand by more than half.

With wage work in guava scarce and employment outside of agriculture limited, male migration to the United States increased dramatically. Yet, unlike the migrant pattern established earlier where both fathers and sons migrated for several months of the year to the United States and then returned to Calvillo for the guava harvest, the current group of male migrants is comprised overwhelmingly of young single men who remain in the United States for long periods, averaging up to five years.

The dominance of sons in the contemporary migrant pool has had major implications for sending households. Family members report that remittances from sons are more sporadic and less substantial than remittances from male household heads. Moreover, sons remitting considerable sums of money often have their earnings earmarked for specific personal expenditures such as a wedding, or home construction. Families also maintain that because of poor job opportunities in Calvillo (and a booming market for immigrant labor in the United States), sons have little incentive to return home. Consequently, ties to family and relatives in Calvillo have weakened over the years; several interviewees reported they had lost contact altogether with their sons in the United States.

The changes in intensity and composition of the migrant population in turn altered the traditional role played by women's earnings from *maquila,* namely, to tide families over in the interim before remittances arrived. As remittances became a less reliable source of household income, women attempted to maximize earnings by increasing the total number of hours family members devoted to piecework and, if economically feasible, to purchase or rent an industrial sewing machine, thereby increasing productivity. Households with sewing machines were also able to take advantage of one of the better paid jobs in *maquila:* embroidered collars for women's dresses. By the beginning of the 1990s, however, women engaged in *maquila* complained they were barely able to make ends meet.

RECESSION'S EFFECTS

The economy-wide recession of the 1980s fundamentally restructured the textile and garment industries in Aguascalientes. By the end of the decade more than 40 per cent of the firms in these industries had been foreclosed or merged with larger establishments. The concentration of production in the hands of larger, more technologically efficient firms meant fewer workers both in and outside the factory. Consequently, rural home workers receive far less work than in previous years and most of the available work consists of *deshilados,* or hand-stitching of designs on women's and children's blouses—the most labor-intensive and worst-paid task in the industry.

Intermittent and poorly remunerated work in *maquila* has made it virtually impossible for women to meet basic food, clothing and housing needs on *maquila* earnings alone. To maintain household income many rural women have attempted to diversify income sources. Most activities, however, are low-paying, highly irregular informal sector occupations such as street vending, selling animal stocks or marketing small surpluses produced by landed households. Children, particularly older daughters, have also helped their mothers meet the family's need for cash. Yet in spite of women's (and children's) increased contribution to household income, lower returns to female labor mean many households don't achieve minimum levels of well-being.

Faced with a long-term slump in *maquila,* few alternative or viable off-farm jobs, and a sharp drop in remittance income, growing numbers of rural women have opted to follow the well-established migration trajectory of their male kin. In a number of cases, women have moved with their families or joined migrant husbands in the United States. The largest contingent of female migrants, however, consists of daughters in their early to mid-20s. Like their male counterparts, these young women migrate in search of work and remain in the United States for years at a time. Although single daughters are more likely than sons to remit money to their parents in Calvillo, their remittances are relatively low.

The mass exodus of people, especially young people, from Calvillo in the decade of the 1980s has all but transformed rural life. First, the sheer volume of migration—"Even the dogs want to go north" is how one woman described the situation—has had a visible impact on Calvillo's demographic structure. The increased incidence of female migration in addition to already high and growing rates of male migration has left entire communities with few young people of working age.

Second, the shift from temporary, circular migration to permanent settlement in the United States has taken its toll on smallholder agriculture. Although production on the land does not represent an important source of income for poor peasant households, subsistence cultivation continues to be a chief source of food for Calvillo's rural poor. Yet when women are left behind because of the migration of husbands and older children (90 per cent of smallholder households in Calvillo have sent at least one migrant), women experience great difficulty juggling domestic chores, wage work and the numerous agricultural tasks performed by other family members prior to migration. Not only are women disadvantaged by overwork, but they also lack access to public and private institutions granting credit, technical assistance and other agricultural services. In some cases, remittances have enabled women to hire laborers to work the land. In most cases, however, women have found it necessary to abandon agricultural production altogether.

Finally, the migration of children of both sexes has increased tensions within the family unit. The prolonged absence of male migrants in conjunction with irregular and insufficient remittance income, for example, has led to an increase in *de facto* and *de jure* female-headed households. Not infrequently, women abandoned for long periods of time take up residence with other women, particularly their mothers or married daughters. In addition, women migrating to join spouses in the United States often leave their young children behind with grandparents. Both situations have augmented women's domestic burdens and severely strained already meagre household budgets.

In Calvillo, then, structural economic changes including the privatization of guava production, dwindling remittances, and the virtual collapse of *maquila* work, have encouraged, if not forced, women to migrate. As in the case of male migration, female movement has resulted in a number of positive changes for the women involved: it offers women the chance to improve their standard of living and the opportunity to break out of traditionally restrictive roles in the countryside.

DOWNWARD SPIRAL

From the standpoint of the rural family and community, however, the most recent wave of female migration is problematic. Most serious is the fact that international labor migration, once a primary means to ensure rural households' economic viability, no longer forms part of a family strategy for survival or upward mobility. In this context, female migration is not another strategy to diversify household income sources, but rather a response to households' downward economic spiral.

Better job opportunities for rural women in areas like Calvillo, especially in local non-agricultural employment, will no doubt lower female migration. Yet, unless rural development schemes address the constellation of economic and social forces affecting both women and men in the contemporary Latin American countryside, female participation in U.S.-bound migration is likely to continue. Barring fundamental changes in agriculture and other rural economic activities, women's economic opportunities may rest more and more in the cities, and on the other side of the border.

CHAPTER 30

WOMEN AND RURAL DEVELOPMENT POLICIES: THE CHANGING AGENDA

Deniz Kandiyoti

Richmond College, Surrey, England

INTRODUCTION

Policy interest in rural woman started manifesting itself in the early 1970s at a time when widespread disenchantment was being felt with the effects of current development policies on the agrarian sectors of most Third World countries. These policies had, broadly speaking, resulted in stagnating levels of food production, nutritional decline, and a destructuring of rural communities, fueling massive rural to urban migration. Concern over absolute poverty, and levels of rural and urban unemployment and underemployment, increasingly started appearing on the policy agenda. As the emphasis shifted from "modernization" to the provision of the poorest people's basic needs (food, shelter, health, etc.) distributional issues came to the fore, although initially the effects of gender inequality did not receive separate attention above and beyond those of class membership. In time, and especially after the UN Decade for Women started in 1975, a growing body of research under the broad rubric of women in development (WID), started documenting the counterproductive effects of ignoring rural women's contributions and their special needs from the point of view of both agricultural productivity and the overall welfare of rural families.[1] Thus, policy proposals related to rural women became intimately linked to an ongoing assessment of strategies of rural development.

Studies on women in development have made several important contributions. They have expedited the demise of modernization or "trickle-down" theories of development by illustrating how modernization has had demonstrably different effects not

Reprinted with permission from *Development and Change,* 21 (1990), pp. 5–22, by permission of Sage Publications Ltd.

only on different rural strata but on men and women, often contributing to a deterioration of conditions and increased workloads for the latter.[2] They have brought women into a previously genderless (and hence myopic) consideration of the links between subsistence and peasant production and the capitalist sector in less developed countries, and questioned the nature of the relation of unpaid family labour to wage labour both in more advanced economies and the Third World. They have addressed the methodological and conceptual biases in accounting for women's work (Agarwal, 1989; Beneria, 1981; Dixon, 1982). Finally, numerous case studies have alerted us to the fact that rural development policies will not have their intended effect, or might even produce unintended negative outcomes, if the role and position of women in rural households is not explicitly taken into account.

As things stand now, an apparent consensus seems to have been generated by this accumulation of both fact and polemic such that organizations with finalities as diverse as those of the World Bank, different UN and government agencies, private foundations, and feminist groups are clamouring to relieve rural women of their drudgery, to increase their control over resources, and to equip them with credit, know-how, and appropriate technologies.

A certain style of advocacy has developed over the years which is quite technocratic in general tone and which maintains that assisting rural women—far from being a frivolous, if benevolent, exercise—is, on the contrary, certain to pay dividends in terms of "development." Thus the case for explicit support of rural women's activities is often presented as a basic-rights issue which also makes good economic or "development" sense. Part of the rationale behind this style of presentation has been that it is so hard to "sell" the idea of assisting women to governments, bureaucracies, and other male-dominated agencies, especially when they have dire problems and other priorities, that only hard-headed fact and proof that the goals of assisting women and promoting development are totally congruent with one another could have any impact at all. The result has been that the possible contradictions contained in policy proposals emanating from different, though often implicit, assumptions about both women and development are often glossed over, and are becoming much harder to identify.

The aim of this paper is to review and evaluate some of the most commonly held assumptions about the desirability of making rural women the target of direct policy measures, the goals that are sought in doing so, and the means advocated to achieve these goals. In so doing, I will attempt to show how mainstream WID research has closely followed, reflected, and responded to changing international priorities in matters of development assistance, but has seldom clarified its basic premises or spelt out the political implications of its stated objectives.

ASSUMPTIONS

The instrumentality of policy interventions aimed at rural women is generally clearly spelt out. Some of the concrete areas in which such interventions are expected to produce beneficial results are population control, health delivery, food production, nutrition, and the alleviation of absolute poverty through expanded opportunities for "income-generation." Most policy papers tend to stress the intrinsic congruence between the goals of greater equity for women and increased productivity. Their thinking is based on a set of commonly held assumptions, some of which have been well substantiated and documented and others less so. These may be summarized as follows:

1 Women are de facto food producers and active participants in the agrarian sectors of the Third World.

2 Some of the main constraints on women's productivity are related to the labour time involved in their daily household maintenance tasks.

3 A reduction or freeing of labour time from household tasks implies its possible diversion to income-generating activities.

4 Women's access to income is more likely to pay welfare dividends for the community at large (especially for children) than men's incomes.

5 Women's productivity and potential for income-generation may be raised with minimal capital outlays.

The first assumption is generally documented through extensive material from sub-Saharan Africa, where women's involvement in food production is highest and where food shortage is worst. It is a fact that African women's farming activities take place on an ever-shrinking resource base, with extremely primitive technology and with severely stretched time resources. However, at a more global level, the extent of women's involvement in subsistence production is a function of the nature of local farming systems, access to resources, and the degree of overall commoditization of the agrarian sector. There are therefore important regional disparities in women's participation in agricultural production, ranging from a high 87 percent of the female labour force in low-income African countries to a low 14 percent in Latin America (ILO/INSTRAW, 1985).

The agrarian sectors of many regions of the Third World have become commoditized to the extent that subsistence farming can account only for an absolutely minimal fraction of a household's needs. In many parts of Asia and Latin America the women of landless or near-landless households are forced to rely on wage earnings from varied and intermittent sources. This is to some extent reflected in policies directed at rural women: those relating to Africa frequently stress the need to assist subsistence farming, whereas in Asia the accent is on employment creation programs and expanded opportunities for wage-work.

Women's type and level of involvement in agricultural activities is consistently mediated by rural households' access to productive resources. These activities may range from postharvest processing and care of livestock with relatively little involvement in fieldwork for women from relatively wealthy landed families, to greater participation in or actual "feminization" of fieldwork in smallholder or near-landless households, especially in areas of selective male outmigration, to exclusive reliance on wage-work for women from landless households. Since both the intensity and modality of women's cultivation and crop-related activities depend on their location in rural stratification, the type of assistance they could benefit from not only varies, but may introduce important divergences of interest among women from different strata. Although project-level documents generally acknowledge these differences, broader policy statements on assistance to rural women tend to identify them in a more amorphous manner and single them out as a disadvantaged and vulnerable group who shoulder the burden of feeding and maintaining families, frequently without any form of outside support.

In this respect there are significant regional variations in sex-selectivity of outmigration from rural areas with important consequences for women. In Africa, selective male outmigration has resulted in a high proportion of female-headed rural households, whereas in Latin America women's higher rates of migration have resulted both in their greater representation in the urban service sector and in increases in urban-based, female-headed households. In Asia sex ratios in outmigration have tended to be more balanced, and there is a lower overall incidence of female-headed households. However, whether they are primarily responsible for ensuring the survival of their families or not, women's daily household maintenance tasks are uniformly singled out among the factors setting a limit to their labour productivity and income-earning ability.

The second assumption is clearly documented through a satisfactory number of time–budget studies indicating that tasks such as water fetching, fuel collection, food processing and preparation can account for the better part of an adult woman's extremely long working day. Allocating resources to better sanitation, easy access to water points, cheap sources of fuel, improved means of porterage and transportation can thus have immediately beneficial effects on women's daily workloads (Carr, 1978). The introduction of labour- and time-saving appropriate technologies for laborious operations such as food processing may be somewhat more problematic in that it may have different consequences for different classes of rural women: an alleviation in the workload of women from landed households, and a loss of livelihood for landless women who receive wages for such processing operations performed for other households (Whitehead, 1985). However, it must be kept in mind that proposals to upgrade women's daily maintenance tasks ultimately aim at increasing their labour productivity, which brings us to the third assumption, namely that women's freed time may be diverted towards income-generating activities.

These activities consist either in upgrading the areas in which women are already involved (through the provision of improved techniques and tools for cultivation, access to farm credit, extension services, etc.), or in the creation of new sources of livelihood through rural-based cottage industries from fruit canning and soap making to textiles and brick making, depending on local skills and resources. A certain amount of training and education, as well as the creation of organizations to facilitate credit and marketing outlets (such as women producers' cooperatives) are advocated as realistic objectives. What is striking about many of the proposals for women's projects is that they seem to be relatively oblivious of similar rural development projects geared to men, and the lessons learned from their shortcomings. This, I will argue, is because the criteria for success for women's projects are much less stringent, and because they do not have exactly the same aims as projects geared to male farmers. I will return to this point in the course of the discussion of the fifth assumption, namely that significant improvements can be achieved with very meagre resources.

An important rationale behind increasing women's direct control over resources in general, and cash in particular, stems from the assumption that women are more likely to use these resources to further the immediate welfare of their families, especially the nutrition and health of their children. Certainly some of the available data tends to suggest that increases in male incomes do not automatically translate themselves into improved nutritional levels for the family as a whole, and that consumer durables and leisure activities may divert considerable income from the household budget (Hanger and Moris, 1973; Palmer, 1977; Young, 1978). This is even more true of women with migrant husbands receiving only intermittent support, and totally true of female-headed households who have no other support. Even though this position may be seen as a realistic recognition of a de facto situation, it nonetheless inscribes itself in the more general current tendency to accept women as the "responsible" reproducers assisted by public agencies, thus extending the ideology of the "good mother" to the field of legislation and assistance. While this tendency has been the subject of extensive commentary in the case of the welfare states of industrialized countries,[3] the parallels to be drawn with international aid assistance to Third World women have not yet appeared on the agenda. In Third World countries where no safety net is provided by local welfare states, and in regions where male responsibility for dependants is at least normatively present, women themselves may be likely to put up fierce resistance to measures by-passing the male household head, even though they may in practice contrive ways of increasing their own control over household income. There is very little recognition given to the fact that interventions to increase women's direct control over income are likely to have different consequences for different categories of women, depending on their age, class, and marital status.

Finally, an assumption that is never really fully spelt out, but quite persistently present, is that the goal of assisting rural women can be realistically achieved with relatively modest capital outlays, mainly through a better use of local resources, the provision of training and credit facilities, as well as reasonably priced, easy-to-maintain appropriate technologies. This is reflected in the kinds of projects that involve women. A recent report describes them as having

> suffered by being scattered, small and peripheral to the main thrust of planning processes, programmes and projects. Different agencies (international and national) have financed a plethora of small projects in various sectors with little coordination nor concern for sustained financial viability, capacity to grow and expand or replicability (Sen and Grown, 1987, p. 82).

This brings us back to a point alluded to earlier, namely that different, less stringent criteria are applied to projects for women. It might be worth looking at some of the reasons for this state of affairs before proceeding further.

First, in the case of women any increment in productivity, however modest, may easily be seen as a major advance over labour time totally taken up with daily maintenance tasks. The question, of course, remains as to whether women will have any degree of autonomy over the way they dispose of their labour, or whether they will become better and more efficiently integrated into processes deepening the subordination of small peasant producers. A very crude analogy could be made here between attitudes to male subsistence farming and women's household maintenance tasks at very different phases of accumulation. Subsistence farming received a great deal of negative attention from the colonial state in so far as it held back land and labour from commercial crops and effectively acted as a barrier to the expansion of cash cropping. Women's involvement in "nonproductive" tasks is now acting as a brake on a dangerously stagnating subsistence sector which has deteriorated to the point of not being able to reproduce itself, as is plainly the case in Africa. A frankly negative assessment of the growth of WID research in Africa suggests that women have now been identified as a problem for state and international agencies because, among other things, "They have persistently sought to manipulate alternative, parallel markets for their produce and resisted efforts by different social forces—including husbands—to labour without any foreseeable return" (Mbilinyi, 1984, p. 290). From this perspective, WID projects may be seen as attempts at tighter control and more efficient monitoring of women's activities. However, whereas men's priorities did not necessarily coincide with those of colonial governments, which often had to resort to coercive measures of labour control, there is a greater degree of congruence between women's need to reduce household drudgery and increase their income, and official interest in a more productive and efficient rural economy. Women should certainly take full advantage of this interest, whilst not losing sight of the broader picture and of the fact that projects to assist them might have different final objectives, depending on the donor agencies and the local bureaucracies administering them.

Secondly, one rapidly becomes aware of the fact that the ultimate aim of aid to rural women is to promote greater self-sufficiency rather than development in the sense of expansion and qualitative change. The subsistence production of rural women and women's poverty is now attracting attention because a growing number of Third World countries have become net importers of foodstuffs, and uncontrollable migration to urban centres in search of jobs is creating severe problems with politically unsettling implications.

Assistance to rural women often appears as part of a series of stop-gap measures to tackle some of the most visible outcomes of underdevelopment, such as hunger and malnutrition. It seems highly improbable, however, that such assistance can have lasting benefits unless it is accompanied by sweeping changes in land distribution, pricing, and credit policies; in short, an onslaught on the mechanisms that reproduce and intensify inequalities within the agrarian sector. This is an area where current trends are not necessarily conducive to optimism, not least because of the contradictory objectives which different policy choices may represent.

To give but one example on food production in sub-Saharan Africa, the Lagos Plan, the Berg Report, and the policies of the Reagan government seemed to be at odds with one another. The Lagos Plan, endorsed by governments in the region, advocated greater self-reliance in food; the Berg Report (accepted by the World Bank) argued for accelerated export production supplemented by food aid, whereas the Reagan administration cut back aid substantially, with the exception of a few countries deemed strategic to US interests. Given the external debt links of most underdeveloped countries, the likelihood that their agrarian sectors will be subject to tight monitoring by supranational agencies, such as the IMF, is extremely high. So far, most efforts towards increasing the productivity of peasant production and the real incomes of rural producers (in supervised credit schemes, smallholder projects, and other "peasant" packages) have been accompanied by an intensification of labour within the household which has primarily affected women's workloads. The unremunerated labour of women, as well as their wage-earning potential, will thus continue to represent an important economic resource for a whole series of beneficiaries, from household heads to governments. Arguments to the effect that households are not egalitarian institutions, and that some projects work to the detriment of women's and children's welfare, will be weighed against countervailing policy objectives, such as the need to maintain, protect, or even recreate a smallholder sector or other family-based forms of livelihood, as a means of increasing productivity or tempering rapid processes of differentiation among the peasantry.

There is a sense in which policy documents on assistance to rural women and broader rural development policies almost seem to emanate from different universes. The former still use the language of "basic needs," whereas the latter distinguish themselves by a strong market orientation. It is important to reflect on the meaning of this disjunction. Is it the case that they emanate from totally different sections within the international planning community? Is there some sort of division of labour, whereby women-directed policies unwittingly come to represent the "welfare" arm of monetarist policies? Or is there some other combination of factors, including the creation of a new conventional wisdom in the area of development assistance?

One policy analysis paper draws our attention to the shift from an earlier equity-oriented approach in matters of assistance to women, which stressed the widening gender gap created by development policies, to a poverty-oriented approach, which documents the importance of raising the productivity and income of poor women as a more general growth and poverty-alleviation strategy. This shift is explained as follows:

> In the face of economic theorists' and policymakers' lack of interest, the equity approach to research on women has evolved into an alternative approach that links women's issues to poverty and tries to quantify the positive effects that may result from incorporating women's concerns into economic development programs (Buvinic, 1983, p. 16).

This lack of interest, however, begs the question, and can be better interpreted in the context of yet another shift in priorities in response to the global economic trends of the 1980s. The hardships provoked by recession and the implementation of severe stabilization measures, and the grossly unequal distributive effects of structural adjustment packages are now accepted as an established fact. The accent is on crisis management and on "buffering" some of the worst excesses in human suffering terms of current international economic policies (Cornia et al., 1987).

Behind the rather bland and uniform sounding recommendations to equip and empower poor Third World women, there may lie a wide range of frankly contradictory objectives from simply making women more efficient managers of poverty, to using their claims and organizations as a political vehicle for far-reaching redistributive measures, both within and across nations.[4] With very few exceptions, policy documents on WID effectively avoid and obscure these troublesome issues by presenting assistance to women as a technical rather than a political issue.

GOALS AND MEANS

The evidence of increasing levels of female poverty and its implications for community welfare has, as pointed out earlier, been instrumental in promoting a wide-ranging reassessment of rural women's access to resources: access to land and water, to agricultural inputs, credits and services, to education, training, and extension, and to institutions and organizations. Ensuring an increase in women's rights of appropriation over resources and over their own labour has been declared a priority to be furthered through the following measures:

1 The protection of women's existing sources of livelihood.

2 The elimination of discriminatory legislation in the ownership and control of productive assets.

3 The promotion of equitable access to agricultural inputs, credit, extension services, and education.

4 The support of extra-household forms of organization of women's labour.

5 The encouragement of an increased capacity for political empowerment and organization.

An area to which development planners are invited to show special sensitivity concerns changes which actually result in the loss of women's control over earnings which were traditionally theirs. There are numerous examples of such loss of income in agriculture, food processing, manufacture, and trading (see Petritsch, 1981). One of the best-documented instances is the case of the introduction of Japanese rice-hullers in Indonesia, depriving poor women of one of their few sources of wage-work (Cain, 1981). The same applies to Bangladesh, where there is concern over the informal diffusion of custom-husking which decreases the need for hand-pounding performed by poor women. In this case the divergence in the interests of women who are wage-workers with no alternative income-generating opportunities and those who are family labourers is quite apparent.

However, even in cases where technological innovation has less class-specific results, important policy dilemmas are involved. It seems short-sighted to adopt protectionist attitudes vis-à-vis women's traditional activities and to bemoan their loss if they involve obsolete technologies and very low productivity. The real challenge would seem to lie in ensuring that the upgrading or modernization of certain areas of activity either do not result in losses for women or can be compensated for by the creation of viable local alternatives. It has so far been the case that the reorganized or modernized activities which were previously considered as women's work are redefined as male tasks, so that an actual change in personnel takes place. For instance, commercial rice milling in Bangladesh is a male occupation, and modern dairies in India have male employees, whereas traditional milk producers were women. Although innovation may in some cases produce a lower overall demand for labour, serious attempts should be made to ensure that women continue to retain control over organizationally and technologically more sophisticated versions of their farming, processing, marketing, and handicraft activities. This goal is especially hard to achieve, not only because women lack training, skills, capital, and mobility, but also because they may come up against opposition from other factional interest groups. There have been instances where women's interests were so clearly at variance with those of officials that resistance took the form of organized protest, as in the case of the Chipko movement in India, where women's interest in access to forests and forest products became part of a broader environmental conservation drive (Sharma, 1984). It seems clear that women's ability to organize and become mobilized to safeguard their livelihood is critical to the success of such policies, though such mobilization is greatly hampered, both by divergences in the interests of women of different class, caste, or ethnic membership and the low overall level of women's political participation.

The elimination of legislation barring women from access to productive assets (in terms of inheritance, ownership, and control of property) is also a clear priority. Although land reforms can improve the access of the poor, including women, to land rights, their effects on women have been shown to be quite variable depending on definitions of beneficiary status, their ability to accommodate women's customary land-use rights where they exist, and their success in integrating women into mass organizations (such as co-operatives) as full members (Deere, 1984; Tadesse, 1982; Brain, 1976; von Werlhof, 1983; Palmer, 1985). On the whole, piecemeal legal measures, especially if they are confined to title ownership only, will have a limited impact unless they are backed up by a whole package of measures covering every phase of the production process including marketing.

Separate attention has been given to women's access to agricultural inputs, credit and services, extension and education, and all have been found inadequate (see UNESCO, 1964, 1973; Ashby, 1981; Staudt, 1975/6; Berger and De Lancey, 1984; Lycette, 1984). Access to the above, and especially to favourable credit and marketing terms, are problematic for all economically and politically disadvantaged groups. In the case of rural women these problems are compounded by the fact that their recognition as legal adults has yet to be established in many places, that official sources discriminate against them, that they lack the ties of clientship and patronage which male farmers often mobilize to establish their solvency, and are required to operate in a world from which they have in many places been totally excluded. Since aid donors are well aware that local power structures will not give way and be modified to accommodate poor women's needs, the creation of special projects, programs, and funds appears to be the only way of circumventing their constraining effects. This gives rise to the frequently voiced complaint that women's projects remain marginal to the mainstream of development efforts, which is of course perfectly true, but does not in itself lead to a clear analysis of exactly what would be involved for things to be otherwise.

Another issue of concern in modifying rural women's "productive package" is what happens to their domestic responsibilities. Attempts to increase rural women's productivity in the absence of parallel efforts to reduce their reproductive work merely result either in intolerable workloads, or in a redistribution of such tasks among women of different age groups within the same household, e.g., school-age daughters withdrawn from school in order to keep house and take care of siblings. Croll's (1981) review of socialist policies in the Soviet Union, China, Cuba, and Tanzania shows that despite an explicit commitment to increase rural women's productivity, the resources allocated to alleviate women's reproductive and domestic load are inadequate and have actually declined, due to the cost of substituting services (such as crèches, nurseries, and public dining rooms) for women's unremunerated labour. Policy documents calling for the improvement of rural women's productivity in the Third World rarely make any direct reference to this problem, except in connection to appropriate technologies for heating, cooking, water and fuel collection, and food processing.

In fact, on closer inspection it appears that what is being called for is not simply an increase in women's labour productivity but an intensification and elaboration of their mothering and nurturing roles as well. For instance, the so-called participatory strategies for health delivery are predicated upon women's willingness as mothers to adopt, administer and ultimately finance the GOBI "technologies" which have a decisive impact on child survival—growth monitoring, oral rehydration therapy, breastfeeding and improved weaning practices, and immunization. Given the increasingly restricted availability of public funds in the health sector, the onus is on women to extend their traditional responsibilities as the feeders and healers of their families to include the provision of basic health care, although it is candidly acknowledged that this will make new demands on their time and financial resources (Leslie et al., 1986).

One of the persistent obstacles to increasing women's rights of appropriation over the resources they generate is seen to reside in the maintenance of production and exchange relations within the household. At least, this forms part of the reasoning behind the advocacy for extra- or supra-familial institutions to organize rural women's productive activities. A strong case is made for instance for separate women's organizations such as women-only cooperatives, which are justified on several grounds: building on already existing female networks or modes of cooperation, avoiding confrontation with cultural patterns which oppose the mixing of unrelated men and women, and, finally avoiding a submergence of women's interests and loss of leadership to men. Organizational strategies which bring women together in collective work groups are also seen as a means of circumventing male control over resources by making it possible for women to sell goods and services directly (Dixon, 1981).

In principle, one might expect benefits from extra-household organizations in terms of increased productivity, greater control over one's labour time, and possibly enhanced bargaining power in the domestic situation. However, little detailed attention is paid to the crucial factors which could make these benefits materialize—or fail to do so. Clearly this would depend on the one hand on the nature of the work, the regularity, security, and amount of income earned and on the nature of domestic arrangements, including different modes of resource allocation within households and broader cultural expectations on the other. For some women, the fact that they become more exploitable in market terms, since they are typically organized in small-scale, low-capital, and essentially vulnerable enterprises, may not be immediately compensated by gains in their domestic status. This may be especially true in areas where the cultural disparagement of women's nondomestic work is strongest.

Since it is hard to hope for significant advances in rural women's rights of appropriation over resources and access to services without a certain measure of political empowerment, the final and most intractable question concerns their potential for organization and participation in political pressure groups. WID literature is very mixed on this issue. It ranges from a set of technocratic prescriptions operating in what appears to be a political vacuum, to a limited recognition of the political dimension of the interventions proposed. Typically, the issue of women's movements, their possible conflicts with other factional interests, and their potential for alliances with other forms of struggle are not squarely confronted. There is, on the other hand, a growing body of scholarship documenting instances of women's collective action and their increasing participation in popular protest movements (Jelin, 1987). A noteworthy feature of such movements concerns the "politicization" of women's daily struggles around issues of primary relevance to their lives—from food prices and the general cost of living, through the lack of social services to the disappearance of their children at the hands of repressive regimes. Strategies for rural women's empowerment ultimately cannot avoid the complicated set of issues posed by women's grass-roots movements and the challenges they may represent.

In conclusion, project and policy proposals for rural women as they appear in WID research frequently suffer from several shortcomings. They tend to ignore, deemphasize, or conceal the broader development context in which women-specific projects are inscribed, and thus make it more difficult to discern who the ultimate beneficiaries of women's projects will be. Even though there is a strong suggestion that women's projects, unlike packages for male farmers, are more likely to benefit the whole community, and especially its more helpless members such as children, the welfarist tone of this body of policy does not accord well with the pervasive concern over instituting more efficient forms of labour control over peasant producers, where the household as a production unit is still the cheapest way to obtain the labour of an entire family. Little acknowledgement is given to the fact that increasing women's productivity has to be matched with substantial, as opposed to cosmetic, relief from reproductive tasks, especially if this relief involves costly alternatives such as better infrastructure and overall sanitation. Finally, there is considerable ambiguity over the broader redistributional issues that assisting poor rural women raises. It is frequently unclear whether rural women will be better equipped to simply make do with what they already have, or whether genuinely new resources will be allocated to them. Most importantly, the political implications of such allocations are seldom spelt out. Ultimately, this ambiguity can only be resolved not by examining women's projects, which are surprisingly uniform in both tone and content, but with reference to the broader policies and goals of the agencies and policy-making bodies concerned.

NOTES

1 The following represent a few typical examples of a much broader literature: Palmer, 1977; IDS, 1978; Abdullah and Zeidenstein, 1982; Dauber and Cain, 1981; D'Onofrio-Flores and Pfafflin, 1982; Lewis, 1981.

2 This reassessment was initiated by the pioneering work of Ester Boserup, although divergences developed in the identification of both the causes of women's subordination in the Third World and the means to achieve change. See Boserup, 1970; Beneria and Sen, 1981. For critiques of development policies also see Rogers, 1980; Ahmed, 1980; Chaney and Schmink, 1976.

3 For reviews of this question in West European and Scandinavian welfare states see Sassoon, 1987, and for the United States see Brown, 1981.

4 For instance, two texts covering very similar ground but with important differences in emphasis are Sen and Grown, 1987 and Joekes, 1987. The former is much more forth-

right about spelling out a political project centred around poor Third World women's claims.

REFERENCES

Abdullah, T. A., and Zeidenstein, S. A. *Village Women of Bangladesh: Prospects for Change.* Oxford: Pergamon Press, 1982.

Agarwal, B. "Work Participation of Rural Women in the Third World: Some Data and Conceptual Biases." In K. Young, ed., *Serving Two Masters,* pp. 1–26. New Delhi: Allied Publishers, 1989.

Ahmed, Z. "The Plight of Rural Women: Alternatives for Action." *International Labour Review,* 119, 4 (1980): 425–38.

Ashby, J. "New Models for Agricultural Research and Extension: The Need to Integrate Women." In B. Lewis, ed., 1981, pp. 144–238.

Beneria, L. "Conceptualising the Labour Force: The Underestimation of Women's Economic Activities." In N. Nelson, ed., *African Women in the Development Process,* pp. 279–98. London: Frank Cass, 1981.

Beneria, L., and Sen, G. "Accumulation, Reproduction and Women's Role in Economic Development: Boserup Revisited." *Signs,* 7, 2 (1981): 10–28.

Berger, M., and De Lancey, W. *Bridging the Gender Gap in Agricultural Extension.* Report prepared for USAID, Office of Women in Development, Washington, DC: ICRW, 1984.

Boserup, E. *Women's Role in Economic Development.* London: George Allen & Unwin, 1970.

Brain, T. L. "Less than Second Class: Women in Rural Settlement Schemes in Tanzania." In N. Hafkin, and E. G. Bay, eds., *Women in Africa: Studies in Social and Economic Change,* pp. 265–82. Stanford, Calif.: Stanford University Press, 1976.

Brown, C. "Mothers and Fathers and Children: From Private to Public Patriarchy." In L. Sargent, ed., *Women and Revolution,* pp. 239–67. London: Pluto Press, 1981.

Buvinic, M. "Women's Issues in Third World Poverty: A Policy Analysis." In M. Buvinic, M. A. Lycette, and W. P. McGreevey, eds., *Women and Poverty in the Third World,* pp. 14–33. Baltimore, Md.: Johns Hopkins University Press, 1983.

Cain, M. "Java, Indonesia: The Introduction of Rice Processing Technology." In R. Dauber, and M. Cain, eds., 1981, pp. 127–38.

Carr, M. *Appropriate Technology for African Women.* United Nations Economic Commission for Africa, 1978.

Chaney, E., and Schmink, M. "Women and Modernization: Access to Tools." In J. Nash and H. Safa, eds., *Sex and Class in Latin America,* pp. 160–82. New York: Praeger, 1976.

Cornia, G. A., Jolly, R. and Stewart, F., eds. *Adjustment with a Human Face: Protecting the Vulnerable and Promoting Growth.* Oxford: Clarendon Press, 1987.

Croll, E. J. "Women in Rural Production and Reproduction in the Soviet Union, China, Cuba and Tanzania: Socialist Development Experiences." *Signs,* 7, 2, (1981): 375–99.

Dauber, R., and Cain, M. L., eds. *Women and Technological Change in Developing Countries.* Boulder, Colo.: Westview Press, 1981.

Deere, C. D. "Rural Women and Agrarian Reform in Peru, Chile and Cuba." In *Women on the Move: Contemporary Changes in Family and Society,* pp. 57–81. Paris: UNESCO, 1984.

Dixon, R. B. "Jobs for Women in Rural Industry and Services." In B. Lewis, ed., 1981, pp. 271–328.

Dixon, R. B. "Women in Agriculture: Counting the Labour Force in Developing Countries." *Population and Development Review,* 18 (1982): 539–66.

D'Onofrio-Flores, P. M., and Pfafflin, S. M. *Scientific-Technological Change and the Role of Women in Development.* Boulder, Colo.: Westview Press, 1982.

Hanger, J., and Moris, J. "Women and the Household Economy." In R. Chambers, and J. Moris, eds., *Mwea: An Irrigated Rice Settlement in Kenya,* pp. 209–44. Munich: Weltform Verlag, 1973.

IDS. "Women and Green Revolutions." Paper presented at the Conference on "Continuing Subordination of Women in the Development Process," Institute of Development Studies, Sussex, 1978.

ILO/INSTRAW. *Women in Economic Activity: A Global Statistical Survey (1950–2000).* Geneva and Santo Domingo: ILO/INSTRAW, 1985.

Jelin, E., ed. *Ciudadania e Identidad: Las Mujeres en los Movimientos Sociales Latino-Americanos.* Geneva: UNRISD, 1987.

Joekes, S. *Women in the World Economy.* Geneva and New York: INSTRAW and Oxford University Press, 1987.

Leslie, J., Lycette, M., and Buvunic, M. "Weathering Economic Crises: The Crucial Role of Women in Health." Report prepared for USAID, Office of Women in Development. Washington, DC: ICRW, 1986.

Lewis, B., ed. *Invisible Farmers: Women and the Crisis in Agriculture.* USAID, Office of Women in Development. Washington, DC: ICRW, 1981.

Lycette, M. A. "Improving Women's Access to Credit in the Third World." Report prepared for USAID, Office of Women in Development. Washington, DC: ICRW, 1984.

Mbilinyi, M. "Research Priorities in Women Studies in Eastern Africa." *Women's Studies International Forum,* 7, 4 (1984): 289–300.

Palmer, I. "Rural Women and the Basic Needs Approach to Development." *International Labour Review,* 115, 1 (1977): 97–107.

Palmer, I. *The Impact of Agrarian Reform on Women.* Women's Roles and Gender Differences in Development, monograph No. 6. West Hartford, Conn.: Kumarian Press, 1985.

Petritsch, M. "The Impact of Industrialization on Women's Traditional Fields of Economic Activity in Developing Countries." UNIDO Seminar on the Role of Women in the Development of Industrial Branches Traditionally Employing Female Labour, Sofia, Bulgaria, October 15–18, 1981.

Rogers, B. *The Domestication of Women: Discrimination in Developing Societies.* London: Kogan Page, 1980.

Sassoon, A. S., ed. *Women and the State.* London: Hutchinson, 1987.

Sen, G., and Grown, C. *Development, Crisis and Alternative Visions: Third World Women's Perspectives.* New York: Monthly Review Press, 1987.

Sharma, K. "Women in Struggle: A Case Study of the Chipko Movement." *Samya Shakti: A Journal of Women's Studies,* 1, 2 (1984): 55–62.

Staudt, K. A. "Women Farmers and Inequities in Agricultural Services." *Rural Africana,* 29 (Winter 1975/6).

Tadesse, Z. "The Impact of Land Reform on Women: The Case of Ethiopia." In L. Beneria, ed., *Women and Development: The Sexual Division of Labour in Rural Societies,* pp. 203–22. New York: Praeger, 1982.

UNESCO. *Access of Girls and Women to Education in Rural Areas.* Paris: UNESCO, 1964.

UNESCO. *Study in the Equality of Access of Girls and Women to Education in the Context of Rural Development.* Paris: UNESCO, 1973.

von Werlof, C. "New Agricultural Cooperatives on the Basis of Sexual Polarisation Induced by the State." *Boletin de Estudios Latin Americanos y del Caribe,* 35 (1983): 39–50 (Amsterdam: CEDLA).

Whitehead, A. "Effects of Technological Change on Rural Women: A Review of Analysis and Concepts." In A. Ahmed, ed., *Technology and Rural Women: Conceptual and Empirical Issues,* pp. 27–64. London: George Allen & Unwin for the ILO World Employment Programme, 1985.

Young, K. "Modes of Appropriation and the Sexual Division of Labour: A Case Study of Oaxa, Mexico." In A. Kuhn and A. M. Wolpe, eds., *Feminism and Materialism,* pp. 124–54. London: Routledge & Kegan Paul, 1978.

CHAPTER **31**

WHAT REALLY MATTERS— HUMAN DEVELOPMENT

Peter Gall

For years, economists, politicians, and development planners have measured average per capita income to chart year-to-year progress or decline within a country. As a result, a great deal of national development activity was focused on economic growth, often neglecting the human dimension of development. What was needed was a new way to measure development—human development—and a new strategy to meet human needs.

Now there *is* a way to measure human development. A team of leading scholars has created a new Human Development Index (HDI) for the United Nations Development Programme (UNDP). *Human Development Report (1990),* to be published annually for UNDP, quantifies the human condition and ranks countries by their success in meeting human needs. It also examines why some countries lag behind and recommends concrete steps to move countries forward. The result is a fresh and uncompromising look at how people's lives are enriched or impoverished throughout the world, in rich countries and poor. (See Table 31-1.)

Even countries of low per capita gross national product (GNP) may rank high on the Human Development Index—that is, their people live relatively long lives, are mostly literate, and generate enough purchasing power to rise above poverty. On the other hand countries with high per capita GNP may still have low rates of human development. The difference lies in the way national leaders set their priorities and allocate government funds, and in the degree of freedom that citizens enjoy to act on their choices and influence their own lives.

From *World Development (UNDP),* 3, 3, pp. 4–12.

Japan comes out with the highest HDI ranking. For the most recent years for which data is available (1987 for life expectancy and income, 1985 for literacy), average life expectancy in Japan was 78 years. Adult literacy was 99 percent. The average real income level, adjusted to reflect purchasing power, was US$13,135 (lower than in nine other developed countries).

At the other end of the spectrum is Niger, with life expectancy of 45 years, literacy of 14 percent, and average adjusted real income of $452. Among poorer countries, the highest human development ranking goes to Costa Rica, which has no standing army, boasts a life expectancy of 75 years, a literacy rate of 93 percent, and average adjusted real income of $3,760.

The report zeroes in on several key questions. Does a government care more about economic development alone or about health care and education as well? Does it spend the money it controls more on armaments or on teachers? Are women just toilers in the fields or do they share in the wealth and responsibilities of a nation?

The answers tell a lot about a country. Brazil's per capita income grew over 6 percent a year in the 1970s so that the country is now considered "upper middle-income," but the distribution of that income is "among the worst in the world," says the Report. Brazil's childhood mortality rate is almost twice that of Sri Lanka, a country with one-fifth the per capita income.

Twenty-five developing countries spend more on the military than on education and health. There are eight times more soldiers in the developing countries than physicians. On the other hand, Costa Rica targeted literacy for action, and particularly women's education, so that female literacy rose from 17 percent in 1960 to 65 percent in 1980. Educating the women helped speed the decline in mortality of infants and children under five.

The book, which is being published commercially by Oxford University Press, is bound to stir controversy. Not only does it name countries that it feels have ignored human development opportunities, it recommends that international donors attach "benign conditions" as strings to development assistance, such as lower military spending or channeling more money to schools or public health.

Developing countries' military spending on arms holds a particular place of shame in the book, which discloses that annual military costs represented nearly 160 million man-years of income, three times the equivalent military burden of industrialized countries. "Obviously, the poverty of the people of the developing world has been no barrier to the affluence of their armies," the Report concludes.

The book makes two major contributions to development. The first is the creation of the triple-component Human Development Index itself. The authors selected *life expectancy* as one component not only for its own value, but because it speaks to health care delivery and the ability of people to live long enough to achieve goals. *Literacy* not only helps people to get and keep jobs, but to understand their surroundings and culture. *Purchasing power*—per capita income adjusted to account for national differences in exchange rates, tariffs, and tradable goods—demonstrates the relative ability to buy commodities and meet basic needs. The Report also recommends policy options for UNDP's own field officers, for leaders in both industrialized and develop-

TABLE 31-1

	Low human development index				Medium human development index				High human development index		
		Human dev. index	GNP per capita rank 1987			Human dev. index	GNP per capita rank 1987			Human dev. index	GNP per capita rank 1987
1	Niger	.116	20	45	Egypt	.501	49	85	Malaysia	.800	80
2	Mali	.143	15	46	Lao People's Dem. Rep.	.506	9	86	Colombia	.801	72
3	Burkina Faso	.150	13	47	Gabon	.525	93	87	Jamaica	.824	62
4	Sierra Leone	.150	27	48	Oman	.535	104	88	Kuwait	.839	122
5	Chad	.157	4	49	Bolivia	.548	44	89	Venezuela	.861	95
6	Guinea	.162	31	50	Myanmar	.561	11	90	Romania	.863	84
7	Somalia	.200	23	51	Honduras	.563	53	91	Mexico	.876	81
8	Mauritania	.208	40	52	Zimbabwe	.576	45	92	Cuba	.877	66
9	Afghanistan	.212	17	53	Lesotho	.580	35	93	Panama	.883	88
10	Benin	.224	28	54	Indonesia	.591	41	94	Trinidad and Tobago	.885	100
11	Burundi	.235	18	55	Guatemala	.592	63	95	Portugal	.899	94
12	Bhutan	.236	3	56	Viet Nam	.608	16	96	Singapore	.899	110
13	Mozambique	.239	10	57	Algeria	.609	91	97	Korea, Rep. of	.903	92
14	Malawi	.250	7	58	Botswana	.646	69	98	Poland	.910	83
15	Sudan	.255	32	59	El Salvador	.651	56	99	Argentina	.910	89
16	Central African Rep.	.258	29	60	Tunisia	.657	70	100	Yugoslavia	.913	90
17	Nepal	.273	8	61	Iran, Islamic Rep. of	.660	97	101	Hungary	.915	87
18	Senegal	.274	43	62	Syrian Arab Rep.	.691	79	102	Uruguay	.916	86
19	Ethiopia	.282	1	63	Dominican Rep.	.699	51	103	Costa Rica	.916	97
20	Zaire	.294	5	64	Saudi Arabia	.702	107	104	Bulgaria	.918	99
21	Rwanda	.304	26	65	Philippines	.714	46	105	USSR	.920	101
22	Angola	.304	58	66	China	.716	22	106	Czechoslovakia	.931	102

Rank	Country	Value	No.
23	Bangladesh	.318	6
24	Nigeria	.322	38
25	Yemen Arab Rep.	.328	47
26	Liberia	.333	42
27	Togo	.337	24
28	Uganda	.354	21
29	Haiti	.356	34
30	Ghana	.360	37
31	Yemen, PDB	.368	39
32	Cote d'Ivoire	.393	52
33	Congo	.395	59
34	Namibia	.404	60
35	Tanzania, U. Rep. of	.413	12
36	Pakistan	.423	33
37	India	.439	25
38	Madagascar	.440	14
39	Papua New Guinea	.471	50
40	Kampuchea	.471	2
41	Cameroon	.474	64
42	Kenya	.481	30
43	Zambia	.481	19
44	Morocco	.489	48

Rank	Country	Value	No.
67	Libyan Arab Jamahiriya	.719	103
68	South Africa	.731	82
69	Lebanon	.735	78
70	Mongolia	.737	57
71	Nicaragua	.743	54
72	Turkey	.751	71
73	Jordan	.752	76
74	Peru	.753	74
75	Ecuador	.758	68
76	Iraq	.759	96
77	United Arab Emirates	.782	127
78	Thailand	.783	55
79	Paraguay	.784	65
80	Brazil	.784	85
81	Mauritius	.788	75
82	Korea, Dem. Rep. of	.789	67
83	Sri Lanka	.789	38
84	Albania	.790	61

Rank	Country	Value	No.
107	Chile	.931	73
108	Hong Kong	.936	111
109	Greece	.949	98
110	German Dem. Rep.	.953	115
111	Israel	.957	108
112	USA	.961	129
113	Austria	.961	118
114	Ireland	.961	106
115	Spain	.965	105
116	Belgium	.966	116
117	Italy	.966	112
118	New Zealand	.966	109
119	Germany, Fed. Rep. of	.967	120
120	Finland	.967	121
121	United Kingdom	.970	113
122	Denmark	.971	123
123	France	.974	119
124	Australia	.978	114
125	Norway	.983	128
126	Canada	.983	124
127	Netherlands	.984	117
128	Switzerland	.986	130
129	Sweden	.987	125
130	Japan	.996	126

ing countries, for nongovernmental organizations, and for academics who both study and help shape development policies.

One of the keys to enlarging human development lies in deciding how to allocate scarce resources—between expensive hospitals and primary health care, between urban and rural services, between subsidies to powerful groups such as wealthy landowners and weaker groups such as the absolute poor and the homeless. "Such a restructuring of budget priorities will require tremendous political courage," warns the Report.

As a guide for governments and all those involved with development issues, the study yielded a number of conclusions and policy messages. Among them:

• Removing the immense backlog of human deprivation remains the challenge for the 1990s. It is true that developing countries have made very significant progress towards human development in the last three decades. Life expectancy rose from 46 years in 1960 to 62 years in 1987. The under-five mortality rate was halved. Adult literacy rose from a rate of 43 percent to 60 percent. But there are still more than a billion people in absolute poverty, 800 million who go hungry every day, and 14 million children who die each year before their fifth birthday.

• Average measures of progress in human development conceal immense disparities within developing countries, between urban and rural areas, between men and women, between rich and poor. Rural areas have half the access to health services and safe drinking water that urban areas have. High-income groups often preempt many of the social service benefits.

• Respectable levels of human development are possible even at fairly modest levels of income, or as the Report says: "Life does not begin at $11,000, the average per capita income in the industrialized world." Chile, Costa Rica, Jamaica, Sri Lanka, Tanzania, and Thailand do far better in human development than in raising incomes, "showing that they have directed more of their economic resources towards human progress."

• Social subsidies are absolutely necessary for poorer income groups. "Simply stated, economic growth seldom trickles down to the masses." Although not too costly—generally less than 3 percent of GNP—subsidies establish a safety net. When removed without an alternative net, as in Morocco and China during recent periods of high growth, "the ensuing political and social disturbance has cost far more than the subsidies themselves."

• Technical cooperation must be restructured if it is to help build human capabilities in developing countries. Instead of development budgets going to the salaries and travel of foreign experts, much more must go to help train national personnel and build institutions that can take on the burden of human development and become self-sufficient. "The yardstick for measuring the success of technical assistance programmes," says the Report, "must be the speed with which they phase themselves out." Also, nongovernmental organizations, or NGOs, must be used much more to help people help themselves. The reason: "NGOs are generally small, flexible, and cost-effective."

• A significant reduction in population growth rates is essential for improvements in human development levels. The share of developing countries in world population is expected to grow from 75 percent in 1980 to 84 percent by 2025. The growth, above all in Africa and South Asia, reflects an "urgent need to strengthen programmes of family planning, fertility reduction and maternal and child health care." And if population growth continues while access to international assistance lags and trade outlets continue to shrink in the industrial countries, "the compulsion to migrate in search of better economic opportunities will be overwhelming—a sobering thought for the 1990s."

• Sustainable development strategies mean more than the protection of natural resources and the physical environment. Any form of debt—financial debt, the debt of human neglect, or the debt of environmental degradation—is like borrowing from future generations. Sustainable development should aim at limiting all these debts.

The book concedes shortcomings in the first Human Development Index. There is not enough data, for example, to pinpoint income distribution in all countries studied. Nor is there an accepted way to measure personal freedom. But the first Report does address the issue of freedom, and lists 15 developing countries which have achieved relatively high levels of human development within a reasonably democratic political and social framework. These countries are Costa Rica, Uruguay, Trinidad and Tobago, Mexico, Venezuela, Jamaica, Colombia, Malaysia, Sri Lanka, Thailand, Turkey, Tunisia, Mauritius, Botswana, and Zimbabwe.

In any concerted international effort to improve human development, says the Report, "priority must go to Africa." Even if the international community earmarks an overwhelming share of resources for Africa and patiently helps to rebuild African economies and societies as the Report urges, it will take Africa "at least 25 years to strengthen its human potential, its national institutions and the momentum of its growth."

Africa is the hardest region of the world in which to live. It has the lowest life expectancy, the highest infant mortality rates, and the lowest literacy rates—and women's literacy is only 61 percent that of men. Average per capita income in Africa fell by 25 percent during the 1980s. To be poor in Africa is to command little in the way of resources and to have little power to change things. To be a poor woman in Africa is to have still less of either.

The Report specifically calls for changing laws to provide women equal access to incomes, employment opportunities, credit, and technology, and to offer women far more education and health care, particularly maternal health care. Funds should be directed to safety nets for the poor, such as nutritional support programs in health clinics and school feeding programs. To boost the flow of resources to rural areas, more decisions must be made locally and not by central governments. "Such decentralization of decision-making," says the Report, "may be one of the most important ways of reducing rural-urban income gaps."

While most of the Report concentrates on the developing world, the rich, industrialized nations come in for attention, too, as examples of development which often goes astray. In the United States, the number of homeless people has risen tremendously in the past five years, and in the United Kingdom income gaps widened during the 1980s, leading to deepened poverty.

It is the element of freedom, which is immeasurable, that the Report calls "the most vital component of human development strategies." People must be free to actively participate in setting development priorities, formulating policies, implementing projects, and choosing who shall run their country so that social goals "do not become mechanical devices in the hands of paternalistic governments."

ANNEX 1: STRUCTURAL ADJUSTMENT—THE HUMANE APPROACH

In developing countries, structural adjustment programs often receive a mixed welcome. Many leaders understand the need to balance budgets, to cut public spending, and to free market forces in order to get their economies on track. But they are also aware of the negative consequences, including rising unemployment, declining wages, and cuts in spending on social services that often accompanied the adjustment programs of the 1980s.

The challenge is to balance budgets without unbalancing human lives, and some countries have found ways to adjust with less pain than most. Chile undertook massive public works programs, at one time employing as much as 13 percent of the work force. In Botswana, needy infants and children were monitored carefully, and supplied with food and other support as necessary.

One of the countries that coped best was Zimbabwe. Not long after its independence in 1980, Zimbabwe suffered a series of economic shocks which required adjustment. Some measures taken were orthodox, such as restraining credit growth, reducing subsidies, devaluing the currency, and raising interest rates. But the government also took steps that were unusual, restraining dividend payouts, continuing import controls, and adopting a more expansionary economic policy than most such packages approved by the International Monetary Fund.

Indeed, for much of the 1980s Zimbabwe adjusted on its own because it failed to reach agreement with the IMF. At the same time, it continued to protect Zimbabwe's most vulnerable groups.

• Loans were channeled to low-income farmers, whose share of credit from the Agricultural Finance Corporation more than doubled from 17 percent in 1983 to 35 percent in 1986. Those loans and other marketing reforms nearly quadrupled low-income farmers' share of marketed maize and cotton from 10 percent to 38 percent.

• Spending on health and education rose from 22 percent of total government spending in 1980 to 27 percent in 1984, while allocations for defence and administration dropped from 44 percent to 28 percent. Spending on primary education rose from 38 percent to 58 percent of the education budget. More money went to preventive health care during those years as well.

• Special food programs provided drought relief and a supplementary feeding program for undernourished children. More than 250,000 children received food supplements at the peak of the drought in 1984.

Because of these conscious policy decisions, the economic costs of adjustment did not become human costs. The infant mortality rate continued to decline, primary school enrollment rose sharply, and malnutrition did not rise despite the drought.

ANNEX 2: WHERE DOES THE MONEY GO—TO SOLDIERS OR TEACHERS?

Money that could be used for human development often goes to military budgets instead, even in the poorest countries. Military expenditures in developing countries have multiplied by seven times over the last 25 years to almost $200 billion, compared with a doubling by the industrialized countries. Three-quarters of the global arms trade today takes place in developing countries.

In the industrialized countries there are, on average, 105 soldiers for every 100 teachers, suggesting greater support for war than wisdom. In developing countries, there are on average only 68 percent as many soldiers as teachers. But as with any indicator, averages can disguise enormous disparities. Costa Rica has no standing army, while Ethiopia, which is engaged in a bitter civil war, has almost five times the number of soldiers as teachers.

The *Human Development Report 1990* has produced a statistical table (Table 31-2) reflecting some of the highest and lowest ratios of soldiers to teachers.

ANNEX 3: WHAT VALUE FREEDOM?

The Report puts a higher value on human development achievements in countries with a reasonable degree of democracy and a lower value on those with authoritarian governments. "Human freedom is vital for human development," says the Report. "People

TABLE 31-2

	Armed forces as percentage of teachers
High soldier-teacher ratio	
Ethiopia	494
Iraq	428
Oman	275
Chad	233
Democratic Yemen	200
Pakistan	154
Low soldier-teacher ratio	
Costa Rica	0
Mauritius	10
Côte d'Ivoire	13
Ghana	14
Jamaica	20
Brazil	24

must be free to exercise their choices in properly functioning markets, and they must have a decisive voice in shaping their political future."

The Report's authors intend to fashion a quantitative measure of freedom, to be included in a future index. Until then, it has listed 15 top countries whose high human development levels have been achieved "within a reasonably democratic political and social framework" (see Table 31-3).

TABLE 31-3

FIFTEEN COUNTRIES WITH RELATIVELY DEMOCRATIC HUMAN DEVELOPMENT

	HDI rank, 1–130[a]
Latin America, Caribbean	
Costa Rica	103
Uruguay	102
Trinidad and Tobago	94
Mexico	91
Venezuela	89
Jamaica	87
Colombia	86
Asia	
Malaysia	85
Sri Lanka	83
Thailand	78
Middle East, North Africa	
Turkey	72
Tunisia	60
Sub-Saharan Africa	
Mauritius	81
Botswana	58
Zimbabwe	52

[a]Of the 130 countries ranked, ranks 1–44 were listed as being of "low" human development, 45–84 of "medium," and 85–130 of "high" human development.

PART SEVEN

WHAT IS TO BE DONE?

The readings in the book have covered the many elements of the political economy of development and underdevelopment, ranging from methodology and history to the specific questions of industry's and agriculture's roles in the development process. Part Six centered these concerns squarely in their fundamental context: the human element of development and underdevelopment.

Social change is occurring and will continue, and conscious effort to guide it in a positive direction can benefit the human beings involved. There can be honest disagreements on the relative roles of the market, government, and international organizations; however, only the most ideologically blind would deny the need to guide the course of events in a positive direction. Since development became a goal after World War II, we have learned a great deal about the process and have amassed lessons, both positive and negative. Nonetheless, the task remains daunting. The purpose of this part is to suggest the directions that must be taken to overcome the loss of development momentum during the 1980s, while avoiding the false paths that have been taken in the past.

The greatest task perhaps may be beyond the scope of this book. In his assessment of development economics, Albert Hirschman (1983) suggested that the major failure of development economists was their loss of hope for the very possibility of development. They had retreated to narrow technical issues or abandoned the field entirely. Hirschman exemplifies an alternative, for he has retained his "bias for hope," based on his experience with the development process and his clear sense that social change cannot be avoided. So one key task for those interested in or working in the field of development is to accept social change and the possibility that it can be for the better. With that accomplished, the articles in this part can help us envision "what is to be done."

Denis Goulet, in a classic article, provides a vision of what true development would be, a world of justice, and new forms of behavior that reflect liberation from oppression. His vision is utopian, perhaps, but can there be hope without some such utopian vision of a better world? Can development become a hinge word in that effort and can development/liberation become truly a victory cry for all human beings? A number of the examples given by Goulet seem outdated, given events of the past twenty-five years. However, his perspective must remain as a challenge to all who would aid human development.

Paulo Freire's classic article focuses on those who have borne the costs of underdevelopment—the oppressed—and on the fundamental change in their lives and attitudes that any true process of development/liberation requires. He points to the difficulties involved: the fear of freedom, the tendency to paternalism, the tendency of the oppressed to become oppressors, and their desire to be like the oppressors. Freire expresses the hope that social change can incorporate a pedagogical dimension and that "cointentional" education can unmask the dimensions of oppression and counter its sustaining myths. Such a process can lead to true development and liberation.

Inga Thorsson and the United Nations call our attention to one of the clearest examples of "antidevelopment," arms and military expenditures. They point out that "the arms race and underdevelopment are not two problems; they are one. They must be solved together, or neither will ever be solved." Both must be linked to the issue of security, realizing that security can be better provided through development than through military expenditures. The points made in the article have taken on a new dimension with the cooling of the Cold War; but their importance is emphasized by the stubborn resistance to efforts to reduce arms expenditures. Even the intelligence apparatus of the United States, estimated to absorb $28 billion in annual expenditures, has not diminished, despite the disappearance of the Soviet Union, which was its reason for being. Thorsson's points bear repeating since there is no evidence that changing international conditions will free up world resources for development efforts. The Iraqi invasion of Kuwait and the subsequent armed reaction indicate that one result may simply be an intensification of conflict in Third World areas. The ability and willingness of the Haitian military to oppress its own citizens and of the Somali warlords to try to expand their geographic control again show the downside to Third World military expenditures. Thus it is important to assess military expenditures from the perspective of their effect on development.

These visions of liberation, development, and antidevelopment lead into an examination of the steps that can be taken to foster development/liberation. The remaining articles provide a variety of approaches to this central problem. They grow integrally out of the earlier parts of the book and show how those analyses can guide us in dealing positively with the problem of development.

One of the key changes in recent years in the structure of the world economy is the increased interest in regional integration, be it in Central Asia or in the Western hemisphere. The article by Gert Rosenthal explores the reasons for this increased interest and its likely evolution. In part this interest grows from the successful experience of Europe, in part it is a logical extrapolation of the movement to liberalization. In either case, regional integration efforts directly contradict the movement to ethnic and tribal conflict and national disintegration that is occurring in other areas. At their best they can deal with the central issues of human development, such as environmental protection and workers' rights; at their worst they can simply provide the elite of a country another means of aggrandizement. In any case, their importance at the present time indicates that they must be considered for their possible effect on development.

John Cartwright's article shows how the continuing debt problem can be linked with issues of sustainable development to move both toward a more desirable outcome. He points out that the difficulties of the 1980s have led to an intensification of the exploitation of natural resources as a means of satisfying debt obligations. The cost of these steps is high and argues for the intrinsic value of conservation. Experience has shown that one favorable element in the continuing debt overhang is the possibility, realized in a number of cases, of using those blocked resources to further conservation efforts. While such steps will not *solve* either problem, they can fundamentally alter the situation in particular circumstances.

Norman MacIsaac and Abu N. M. Wahid's description of the Grameen Bank in Bangladesh returns the focus to the people of the South. The Grameen Bank has been one of the most successful "grassroots development" efforts, providing small loans to the poorest, to those who struggle for survival, as in Beck's East Bengal. Access to even this small resource has opened entirely new avenues for these Bangladeshis, and their responsiveness and responsibility are impressive. A high proportion of the beneficiaries are women, which means that the benefits will extend to their families as well. The experience of the Grameen Bank indicates that carefully developed programs, growing out of the needs of the poor, can confront the structures of poverty and stimulate a process of true human development.

This leads into the final article of this part, by Keith Griffin and John Knight, on the elements of "human development." They use Sen's idea of capabilities and entitlements and see much of the challenge of development as the mobilization of underutilized human resources. Their survey of performance on measures of capabilities—life expectancy, infant mortality, and education access—reiterates the important advances that development has brought. But the decade of the 1980s, with slower growth, higher unemployment, and a widespread government fiscal crisis, has endangered these gains and made further gains contingent on careful thinking and policy development. They emphasize three aspects that policymakers must take into account. First, policy should encourage the development of human capabilities through mobilizing local resources as well as through traditional human capital formation efforts in health, education, and sanitation. Second, the link between human development and the distribution of income, wealth, and power should be taken into account, with policies designed to ensure improved distribution. Finally, while the alleviation of poverty is an ethical imperative, it is also functional for increasing long-run growth performance in countries. So resources spent on the military would be better used in alleviating poverty, and government restrictions on grassroots and private activity should be reduced. Their conclusion is that human development is not only essential, it is also possible.

That is the proper note on which to end the book. It embodies the bias toward hope that guides development and developmentalists. The problems remain daunting, and development/liberation is neither easy nor guaranteed. Mistakes have been made in the past, and different mistakes will be made in the future. On the other hand, there have been notable successes and much has been learned from the experience of the past forty years. Our hope is that the 1990s can see a rekindling of interest in development and of the willingness to confront the challenges inherent in commitment to true human development.

REFERENCES

Hirschman, Albert O. "The Rise and Decline of Development Economics." In his *Essays in Trespassing: Economics to Politics and Beyond.* Cambridge: Cambridge University Press, 1981.
World Bank. *World Development Report, 1990.* Oxford: Oxford University Press, 1990.

CHAPTER 32

"DEVELOPMENT" . . . OR LIBERATION?

Denis Goulet

University of Notre Dame

Latin Americans in growing numbers now denounce the lexicon of development experts as fraudulent. To illustrate, Gustavo Gutierrez, a Peruvian theologian and social activist, concludes that "the term development conveys a pejorative connotation . . . (and) is gradually being replaced by the term liberation . . . there will be a true development for Latin America only through liberation from the domination by capitalist countries. That implies, of course, a showdown with their natural allies: our natural oligarchies."[1]

Gutierrez is a major spokesman for "theology of liberation." Numerous seminars and conferences have already been held on the theme in Colombia, Mexico, Uruguay, Argentina, and elsewhere. For Gutierrez—as for Gustavo Perez, René Garcia, Rubem Alves, Juan Segundo, Camilo Moncada, Emilio Castro,[2] and others—"liberation" expresses better than "development" the real aspirations of their people for more human living conditions. Gutierrez does not attempt to review all the changes in the definition of development since the Marshall Plan was launched in 1947. This task has already been performed by others.[3] Instead he focuses his critical gaze on three perspectives with one of which most experts in "developed" countries identify.

THREE VIEWS OF DEVELOPMENT

For many economists development is synonymous with economic growth measured in aggregate terms. A country is developed, they hold, when it can sustain, by its own

Reprinted from the *International Development Review,* 13, 3 (September 1971), by permission of the publisher. Copyright © 1971 by the Society for International Development.

efforts and after having first reached a per capita GNP (Gross National Product) level of $500 (for some observers) or $1000 (for others), an annual rate of growth ranging from 5% to 7%. According to these criteria, certain countries are highly developed, while those on the lowest rungs of the ladder are either underdeveloped or undeveloped. Similar comparisons can also be established between different regions and sectors within a single economy. Although this view is generally repudiated today, it still retains some vestigial influence, thanks to the impact of works like Walt Rostow's *The Stages of Economic Growth* and to the dominant role still played by economists in planning. Even when they give lip-service to other dimensions in development, many economists continue to subordinate all noneconomic factors to the practical requirements of their growth models.

The second outlook, far more prevalent today, was summarized at the start of the United Nations' First Development Decade in U Thant's phrase, "development = economic growth + social change." The trouble with this formula is that it either says too much or says too little since not any kind of growth will do, nor any kind of change.

Most social scientists adopt some variant of this conception as their own working definition of development; it is broad enough to embrace a variety of change processes emphasizing economic, social, cultural, or political factors. Nearly always, however, social scientists subordinate value judgments about human goals to the achievement of economic growth, to the creation of new social divisions of labor, to the quest for modern institutions, or to the spread of attitudes deemed compatible with efficient production. The last point is well illustrated by those who affirm that "modernity" is not the presence of factories, but the presence of a certain viewpoint on factories.

Behind an array of theories and special vocabularies, however, lingers the common assumption that "developed" societies ought to serve as models for others. Some observers, eager to minimize culture bias, reject the notion that all societies *ought* to follow patterns set by others. Nevertheless, they assert that modern patterns are inevitable, given the demonstration effects and technological penetration of modern societies throughout the world.

A third stream of development thinkers stresses ethical values. This group has always constituted, in some respects, a heretical minority. Its position centers on qualitative improvement in all societies, and in all groups and individuals within societies. Although all men must surely have enough goods in order to be more human, they say, development itself is simply a means to the human ascent. This perspective, at times called "the French school," is linked to such names as economist François Perroux, social planner Louis Lebret, theorist Jacques Austruy, and practicing politicians like Robert Buron and André Phillip. According to these men and their disciples, social change should be seen in the broadest possible historical context, within which all of humanity is viewed as receiving a summons to assume its own destiny. Their ideas have influenced United Nations agencies in some measure, but they have made their greatest inroads in religious writings on development: papal encyclicals, documents issued by the World Council of Churches and the Pontifical Commission on Justice and Peace, pastoral letters drafted by bishops in several countries. The single geographical area where the French school has achieved considerable penetration is Latin America.

This is why the conclusion reached by Gutierrez is particularly significant. According to Gutierrez, the French school, because of its historicity and its insistence on norms for social goals, is the least objectionable of the three perspectives he criticizes. Nevertheless, he argues, the realities barely hinted at by the French are better expressed by the term "liberation" than by "development." By using the latter term the French school does not dramatize its discontinuities with the other perspectives sharply enough. Worse still, its spokesmen employ such notions as foreign aid, technical cooperation, development planning, and modernization in ways which remain ambiguous at best. Consequently, in the eyes of many Latin Americans "development" has a pejorative connotation: it does not get to the roots of the problem and leads to frustration. Moreover, "development" does not evoke asymmetrical power relations operative in the world or the inability of evolutionary change models to lead, in many countries, to the desired objectives. Therefore, says Gutierrez, it is better to speak of liberation, a term which directly suggests domination, vulnerability in the face of world market forces, weak bargaining positions, the need for basic social changes domestically and for freer foreign policies.

THE LANGUAGE OF LIBERATION

To substitute for "development" the term "liberation" is to engage in what Brazilian educator Paulo Freire calls "cultural action for freedom."[4] Liberation implies the suppression of elitism by a populace which assumes control over its own change processes. Development, on the other hand, although frequently used to describe various change processes, stresses the benefits said to result from them: material prosperity, higher production and expanded consumption, better housing or medical services, wider educational opportunities and employment mobility, and so on. This emphasis, however, errs on two counts. First, it uncritically supports change strategies which value efficiency above all else, even if efficiency must be gained by vesting decisions in the hands of elites—trained managers, skilled technicians, high-level "manpower." A second failing, analyzed by Harvard historian Barrington Moore in *Social Origins of Dictatorship and Democracy,* is the dismissal of violence as unconstructive and the refusal to condemn the violence attendant upon legal change patterns.

Not theologians alone, but social scientists, planners, educators, and some political leaders in Latin America prefer the terminology of liberation to that of development. They unmask the hidden value assumptions of the conventional wisdom and replace them with a deliberate stress on self-development as opposed to aid, foreign investment, and technical assistance. Since I have written a detailed critique of the Pearson, Peterson, Jackson, and other development reports elsewhere,[5] there is no need to repeat here what is there said regarding the value assumptions and critical omissions of these reports. What is germane to the present discussion is the confirmation given these criticisms by Third World spokesmen in UNCTAD (United Nations Conference on Trade and Development) and GATT (General Agreement on Tariffs and Trade) meetings.[6] Not surprisingly, more and more leaders from underdeveloped areas are coming to regard "development" as the lexicon of palliatives. Their recourse to the vocabulary of liberation is a vigorous measure of self-defense, aimed at overcoming the structural vulnerability which denies them control over the economic, political, and cultural forces which impinge upon their societies. Even to speak of liberation, before achieving it, is a first conquest of cultural autonomy. Ultimately what is sought is to alter relationships between director and directed societies, between privileged elites and the populace at large within all societies. Ever more people are coming to understand that "to be underdeveloped" is to be relegated to a subordinate position in history, to be given the role of adjusting to, not of initiating, technological processes.

The language of liberation is being nurtured in societies where a new critical consciousness is being formed. For these societies, the models of genuine development are not those billed by U.S. aid agencies as success stories—South Korea, Greece, Taiwan, and Iran. Industrialization and economic growth have no doubt taken place in these lands, but no basic changes have occurred in class relationships and the distribution of wealth and power; the larger social system remains structurally exploitative. Moreover, economic gains have been won under the tutelage of repressive political regimes. Finally, as one European has observed, "U.S. aid seems to work best in countries which are lackeys of American foreign policy."

Revolutionary Latin Americans reject this kind of development. They look instead to China, Cuba, and Tanzania as examples of success. In China, mass starvation has been abolished and a feudal social system overthrown. Elitism in rulers is systematically uprooted whenever it reappears, and technological gains are subordinated to the cultural creation of a new man capable of autonomy. Cuba, notwithstanding its economic mistakes, freely admitted, has overcome its servile dependence on the United States and asserts itself increasingly in the face of the Soviet Union, upon whom it still relies heavily for financial, technical, and military assistance. Moreover, Cuba has abolished illiteracy in sensational fashion, decentralized investment, and reduced the gap in living conditions between the countryside and the cities. And Tanzania is admired because it rejects mass-consumption as a model for society, practices self-reliance in its educational system (choosing to grant prestige to agricultural skills rather than to purely scientific ones geared to large-scale engineering projects); accepts foreign aid only when the overall impact of the projects financed will not create a new elite class within the nation itself, and in general subordinates economic gains to the creation of new African values founded on ancient communitarian practices.

For liberationists, therefore, success is not measured simply by the quantity of benefits gained, but above all by the way in which change processes take place. Visible benefits are no doubt sought, but the decisive test of success is that, in obtaining them, a society will have fostered greater popular autonomy in a nonelitist mode, social creativity instead of imitation, and control over forces of change instead of mere adjustment to them. The crucial question is: Will "underdeveloped" societies become mere consumers of technological civilization or agents of their own transformation? *At stake, therefore, is something more than a war over words; the battle lines are drawn between two conflicting interpretations of historical reality, two competing principles of social organization.* The first values efficiency and social control above all else, the second social justice and the creation of a new man.

Western development scholars are prone to question the validity of the new vocabulary of liberation. As trained social scientists, they doubt its analytical power, explanatory value, and predictive capacities. Yet their scepticism is misplaced inasmuch as empirical social science has itself proved unable to describe reality, let alone to help men change it in acceptable ways. Of late, however, a salutory modesty has begun to take hold of social scientists. Gunnar Myrdal (in *Asian Drama*) confesses the error of his early days as an "expert" on development, and challenges (in *Objectivity in Social Research*) the assumptions behind all value-free theories and research methods. More forcefully still, Alvin Gouldner, in *The Coming Crisis of Western Sociology,* argues the case for a new Utopian, value-centered radical sociology for the future. And economist Egbert de Vries[7] reaches the conclusion that no significant breakthroughs in development theory have been achieved in the last decade. Western development scholars, therefore, themselves lost in deep epistemological quagmire, are ill-advised to scorn the new theories.

One finds in truth great explanatory power, analytical merit, and predictive value in the writings of Latin American social scientists on development, dependence, and domination.[8] The new liberation vocabulary is valid, even empirically, because it lays bare structures of dependence and domination at all levels. Reaching behind the neutral "descriptive" words of developmental wisdom, it unmasks the intolerably high human cost to Latin Americans of economic development, social modernization, political institution-building, and cultural westernization. The reality described by these writings is the pervasive impotence of vulnerable societies in the face of the impersonal stimuli which impinge upon them. Furthermore, their vocabulary enjoys high prescriptive value because it shows this powerlessness to be reversible: if domination is a human state of affairs caused and perpetuated by men, it can be overthrown by men. Finally, the highly charged political language of liberation has great predictive value to the extent that it can mobilize collective energies around a value which is the motor of all successful social revolutions—HOPE. Liberated hope is not the cold rational calculus of probability à la Herman Kahn or Henry Kissinger, but a daring calculus of *possibility* which reverses the past, shatters the present, and creates a new future.

"DEVELOPMENT" AS A HINGE WORD

In spite of its absolute superiority, however, the language of liberation remains, for many people in the "developed" world, tactically unmanageable. The historical connotations of the word sometimes lead them to resist mobilization around its theme, especially if these people are not themselves oppressors, but inert beneficiaries of impersonal oppressive systems. A second category of people may also find it difficult to respond, namely those insurgent professionals who can subvert "the system" only by mastering its tools and serving as a fifth column in alliance with revolutionary groups on the outside. Understandably, these persons will need to continue using the currently available "professional" terminology. It is considerations such as these which lie behind the question: Can "development" serve a useful hinge role in mobilization? The answer is affirmative if one agrees with political scientist Harvey Wheeler that

> . . . we don't possess a *revolutionary* social science to serve the utopian needs of the revolution. And those learned enough to create it are divorced from the activists who must prepare the way for the new utopianism. . . . Somehow, the radical activists and the radical scientists—the utopians—must come together.[9]

Desired changes within "developed" societies can ensue only in the wake of concerted (and much unconcerted) action emanating from a variety of change agents. There can be no objection on principle, therefore, to granting tentative validity to "development" as a hinge word.

For the benefit of those who have not yet been weaned from the sweet milk of palliative incrementalism,[10] "development" needs to be redefined, demystified, and thrust into the arena of moral debate. If critically used as a hinge word, it may open up new perspectives and render the leap into "liberation" possible for many people. Nevertheless, only from the third perspective on development summarized above can one find a suitable platform whence to make this leap of faith. The reason is that, of the three viewpoints, only this ethical, value-laden, humanist approach is rooted in history, and not in abstract theory. Before the language of liberation can sound convincing to the categories of people I have described, it must be shown that "development," as normally understood, alienates even its beneficiaries in compulsive consumption, technological determinisms of various sorts, ecological pathology, and warlike policies. Worst of all, it makes those who benefit from development the structural accomplices of the underdevelopment of others. Surely this cannot be what authentic development is. As one reflects on its goals, he discovers that development, viewed as a human project, signifies total liberation. Such liberation aims at freeing men from nature's servitudes, from economic backwardness and oppressive technological institutions, from unjust class structures and political exploiters, from cultural and psychic alienation— in short, from all of life's inhuman agencies.

A new language, able to shatter imprisoning reality, must be born from the clash between vocabularies nurtured in different soils. The first will gestate in a Third World matrix and express the emerging consciousness of those who refuse to be objects, and declare their intent to become subjects, of history. The keys to this vocabulary are the conquest of autonomy and the will to create a new future. At the opposite pole, out of "developed" societies, must arise a subversive redefinition of development itself. Its function will be to destroy the First World's uncritical faith in the universal goodness of its notions of progress, achievement, social harmony, democracy, and modernization. Confrontation between the two is required because neither "development" alone nor "liberation" alone fully transcends both cultural domination and purely negative responses to oppression. Moreover, both terms can be used by symbol manipulators to mystify reality or rationalize palliative change strategies.

Nevertheless, it is clear that competing terminologies of development and liberation are not equally subject to distortion. On the scales of human justice, the interests which they express do not balance each other out. There is indeed, as Camus writes, universal meaning in the rebel's refusal to be treated as something less than a man. And as Marx put it, the oppressed masses are the latent historical carriers of universal human values. The battle to free men is not comparable to the struggle to maintain or expand privilege. Consequently, every trace of elitism and cultural manipulation must be purged from the development vocabulary and replaced with the symbols of liberation. Even then history will not give men any respite; rather, it will propel them into asking: Liberation for what? Ancient teleological questions reappear, concerning the good life, the good society, and men's final purposes. That they should keep arising is no sign of the weakness of men's words, but merely a clue to the grandeur of their historical task. That task is to strive endlessly to outstrip not only alienating material conditions but all particular images of the ideal society as well.

Intellectuals who discuss revolution and violence often utter irresponsible words which place bullets in other people's guns. As they debate development and liberation, the danger they face is less dramatic but no less destructive in the long run. For most of them resort to persuasive political definitions, thereby preempting all the intellectual ground upon which descriptive and evocative definitions might find their place. Such habits render genuine liberation impossible since true cultural emancipation admits of no sloganism, no sectarianism, no simplism. Revolutionary consciousness is critical of self no less than of others; and it brooks no verbal cheating even to achieve ideological gains. In final analysis, any liberation vocabulary must do two things. The first is to unmask the alienations disguised by the development lexicon: the alienation of the many in misery, of the few in irresponsible abundance. The second is to transform itself from the rallying cry of victims alone into the victory chant of all men as they empower themselves to enter history with no nostalgia for prehistory.

Success proves difficult because men have never fully learned the lesson implied in a statement by the Indian mystic Rabindranath Tagore that, ultimately, only those values can be truly human which can be truly universal.

NOTES

1 Gustavo Gutierrez Merino, "Notes for a Theology of Liberation," *Theological Studies,* 31, 2 (June 1970): 243–61.

2 The writings of these men are found largely in papers circulated by documentary services such as LADOC (Latin American Bureau, U.S. Catholic Conference), ISAL (Iglesia y Sociedad en América Latina), and the Theology of Liberation Symposium (in Spanish), Bogota.

3 Cf. the excellent work by Jacques Freyssinet, *Le Concept de Sous-Dévelopment,* Mouton, 1966. A brief review of the different meanings attached to the word "development" can be found in Denis Goulet, "That Third World," *The Center Magazine,* I, 6 (September 1968): 47–55.

4 Cf. Paulo Freire, *Cultural Action for Freedom,* Harvard Educational Review and Center for the Study of Development and Social Change, Monograph No. 1, 1970. One may also consult the same author's *Pedagogy of the Oppressed,* Herder and Herder, 1970.

5 Cf. Denis Goulet and Michael Hudson, *The Myth of Aid: The Hidden Agenda of the Development Reports,* IDOC Books, 1970. This work contains two essays, one by Goulet entitled "Domesticating the Third World," and a second by Hudson on "The Political Economy of Foreign Aid."

6 On this cf., e.g., Guy F. Erb, "The Second Session of UNCTAD," *Journal of the World Trade Law,* 2, 3 (May–June 1968): 346–59. For a Latin American view, see the document entitled, "The Latin American Consensus of Viña del Mar," dated May 17, 1969.

7 Egbert de Vries, "A Review of Literature on Development Theory," *International Development Review,* 10, 1 (March 1968): 43–49.

8 Cf., e.g., such works as F. Cardoso and E. Falleto, *Dependencia y Desarrollo en América Latina,* Santiago, 1967; Theotonio dos Santos, *El Nuevo caracter de la dependencia,* Santiago, 1968; Celso Furtado, *Dialéctica Do Desenvolvimento,* Rio de

Janeiro, 1964; numerous essays by Alberto Guerreiro Ramos (a Brazilian now teaching at UCLA), et al.

9 Harvey Wheeler, "The Limits of Confrontation Politics," *The Center Magazine,* 3, 4 (July 1970): 39.

10 The difference between palliative and creative incrementalism is explained in Denis Goulet, *Is Gradualism Dead?,* Council on Religion and International Affairs, 1970.

CHAPTER 33

PEDAGOGY OF THE OPPRESSED

Paulo Freire

While the problem of humanization has always, from an axiological point of view, been man's central problem, it now takes on the character of an inescapable concern.[1] Concern for humanization leads at once to the recognition of dehumanization, not only as an ontological possibility but as an historical reality. And as man perceives the extent of dehumanization, he asks himself if humanization is a viable possibility. Within history, in concrete, objective contexts, both humanization and dehumanization are possibilities for man as an uncompleted being conscious of his incompletion.

But while both humanization and dehumanization are real alternatives, only the first is man's vocation. This vocation is constantly negated, yet it is affirmed by that very negation. It is thwarted by injustice, exploitation, oppression, and the violence of the oppressors; it is affirmed by the yearning of the oppressed for freedom and justice, and by their struggle to recover their lost humanity.

Dehumanization, which marks not only those whose humanity has been stolen, but also (though in a different way) those who have stolen it, is a *distortion* of the vocation of becoming more fully human. This distortion occurs within history but it is not an historical vocation. Indeed, to admit of dehumanization as an historical vocation would lead either to cynicism or to total despair. The struggle for humanization, for the emancipation of labor, for the overcoming of alienation, for the affirmation of men as persons would be meaningless. This struggle is possible only because dehumanization, although a concrete historical fact, is *not* a given destiny but the result of an unjust order that engenders violence in the oppressors, which in turn dehumanizes the oppressed.

Reprinted from the author's *Pedagogy of the Oppressed,* translated by Myra Bergman Ramos (New York: Herder and Herder, 1970), pp. 29–56, by permission of the author and The Seabury Press. Copyright © 1970 by Paulo Freire.

Because it is a distortion of being more fully human, sooner or later being less human leads the oppressed to struggle against those who made them so. In order for this struggle to have meaning, the oppressed must not, in seeking to regain their humanity (which is a way to create it), become in turn oppressors of the oppressors, but rather restorers of the humanity of both.

This, then, is the great humanistic and historical task of the oppressed: to liberate themselves and their oppressors as well. The oppressors, who oppress, exploit, and rape by virtue of their power, cannot find in this power the strength to liberate either the oppressed or themselves. Only power that springs from the weakness of the oppressed will be sufficiently strong to free both. Any attempt to "soften" the power of the oppressor in deference to the weakness of the oppressed almost always manifests itself in the form of false generosity; indeed, the attempt never goes beyond this. In order to have the continued opportunity to express their "generosity," the oppressors must perpetuate injustice as well. An unjust social order is the permanent fount of this "generosity," which is nourished by death, despair, and poverty. This is why the dispensers of false generosity become desperate at the slightest threat to its source.

True generosity consists precisely in fighting to destroy the causes which nourish false charity. False charity constrains the fearful and subdued, the "rejects of life," to extend their trembling hands. True generosity lies in striving so that these hands—whether of individuals or entire peoples—need be extended less and less in supplication, so that more and more they become human hands which work and, working, transform the world.

This lesson and this apprenticeship must come, however, from the oppressed themselves and from those who are truly solidary with them. As individuals or as peoples, by fighting for the restoration of their humanity they will be attempting the restoration of true generosity. Who are better prepared than the oppressed to understand the terrible significance of an oppressive society? Who suffer the effects of oppression more than the oppressed? Who can better understand the necessity of liberation? They will not gain this liberation by chance but through the praxis of their quest for it, through their recognition of the necessity to fight for it. And this fight, because of the purpose given it by the oppressed, will actually constitute an act of love opposing the lovelessness which lies at the heart of the oppressors' violence, lovelessness even when clothed in false generosity.

But almost always, during the initial stage of the struggle, the oppressed, instead of striving for liberation, tend themselves to become oppressors, or "sub-oppressors." The very structure of their thought has been conditioned by the contradictions of the concrete, existential situation by which they were shaped. Their ideal is to be men; but for them, to be men is to be oppressors. This is their model of humanity. This phenomenon derives from the fact that the oppressed, at a certain moment of their existential experience, adopt an attitude of "adhesion" to the oppressor. Under these circumstances they cannot "consider" him sufficiently clearly to objectivize him—to discover him "outside" themselves. This does not necessarily mean that the oppressed are unaware that they are downtrodden. But their perception of themselves as oppressed is impaired by their submersion in the reality of oppression. At this level, their perception of themselves as opposites of the oppressor does not yet signify engagement in a struggle to overcome the contradiction,[2] the one pole aspires not to liberation, but to identification with its opposite pole.

In this situation the oppressed do not see the "new man" as the man to be born from the resolution of this contradiction, as oppression gives way to liberation. For them, the new man is themselves become oppressors. Their vision of the new man is individualistic; because of their identification with the oppressor, they have no consciousness of themselves as persons or as members of an oppressed class. It is not to become free men that they want agrarian reform, but in order to acquire land and thus become landowners—or, more precisely, bosses over other workers. It is a rare peasant who, once "promoted" to overseer, does not become more of a tyrant toward his former comrades than the owner himself. This is because the context of the peasant's situation, that is, oppression, remains unchanged. In this example, the overseer, in order to make sure of his job, must be as tough as the owner—and more so. Thus is illustrated our previous assertion that during the initial stage of their struggle the oppressed find in the oppressor their model of "manhood."

Even revolution, which transforms a concrete situation of oppression by establishing the process of liberation, must confront this phenomenon. Many of the oppressed who directly or indirectly participate in revolution intend—conditioned by the myths of the old order—to make it their private revolution. The shadow of their former oppressor is still cast over them.

The "fear of freedom" which afflicts the oppressed,[3] a fear which may equally well lead them to desire the role of oppressor or bind them to the role of oppressed, should be examined. One of the basic elements of the relationship between oppressor and oppressed is *prescription*. Every prescription represents the imposition of one man's choice upon another, transforming the consciousness of the man prescribed to into one that conforms with the prescriber's consciousness. Thus, the behavior of the oppressed is a prescribed behavior, following as it does the guidelines of the oppressor.

The oppressed, having internalized the image of the oppressor and adopted his guidelines, are fearful of freedom. Freedom would require them to eject this image and replace it with autonomy and responsibility. Freedom is acquired by conquest, not by gift. It must be pursued constantly and responsibly. Freedom is not an ideal located outside of man; nor is it an idea which becomes myth. It is rather the indispensable condition for the quest for human completion.

To surmount the situation of oppression, men must first critically recognize its causes, so that through transforming action they can create a new situation, one which makes possible the pursuit of a fuller humanity. But the struggle to be more fully human has already begun in the authentic struggle to transform the situation. Although the situation of oppression is a dehumanized and dehumanizing totality affecting both the oppressors and those whom they oppress, it is the latter who must, from their stifled humanity, wage for both the struggle for a fuller humanity; the oppressor, who is himself dehumanized because he dehumanizes others, is unable to lead this struggle.

However, the oppressed, who have adapted to the structure of domination in which they are immersed, and have become resigned to it, are inhibited from waging the struggle for freedom so long as they feel incapable of running the risks it requires. Moreover, their struggle for freedom threatens not only the oppressor, but also their own oppressed comrades who are fearful of still greater repression. When they discover within themselves the yearning to be free, they perceive that this yearning can be transformed into reality only when the same yearning is aroused in their comrades. But while dominated by the fear of freedom they refuse to appeal to others, or to listen to the appeals of others, or even to the appeals of their own conscience. They prefer gregariousness to authentic comradeship; they prefer the security of conformity with their state of unfreedom to the creative communion produced by freedom and even the very pursuit of freedom.

The oppressed suffer from the duality which has established itself in their innermost being. They discover that without freedom they cannot exist authentically. Yet, although they desire authentic existence, they fear it. They are at one and the same time themselves and the oppressor whose consciousness they have internalized. The conflict lies in the choice between being wholly themselves or being divided; between ejecting the oppressor within or not ejecting him; between human solidarity or alienation; between following prescriptions or having choices; between being spectators or actors; between acting or having the illusion of acting through the action of the oppressors; between speaking out or being silent, castrated in their power to create and re-create, in their power to transform the world. This is the tragic dilemma of the oppressed which their education must take into account.

[This paper] will present some aspects of what the writer has termed the pedagogy of the oppressed, a pedagogy which must be forged *with,* not *for,* the oppressed (whether individuals or peoples) in the incessant struggle to regain their humanity. This pedagogy makes oppression and its causes objects of reflection by the oppressed, and from that reflection will come their necessary engagement in the struggle for their liberation. And in the struggle this pedagogy will be made and remade.

The central problem is this: How can the oppressed, as divided, unauthentic beings, participate in developing the pedagogy of their liberation? Only as they discover themselves to be "hosts" of the oppressor can they contribute to the midwifery of their liberating pedagogy. As long as they live in the duality in which *to be* is *to be like,* and *to be like* is *to be like the oppressor,* this contribution is impossible. The pedagogy of the oppressed is an instrument for their critical discovery that both they and their oppressors are manifestations of dehumanization.

Liberation is thus a childbirth, and a painful one. The man who emerges is a new man, viable only as the oppressor-oppressed contradiction is superseded by the humanization of all men. Or to put it another way, the solution of this contradiction is born in the labor which brings into the world this new man: no longer oppressor nor no longer oppressed, but man in the process of achieving freedom.

This solution cannot be achieved in idealistic terms. In order for the oppressed to be able to wage the struggle for their liberation, they must perceive the reality of oppression not as a closed world from which there is no exit, but as a limiting situation which they can transform. This perception is a necessary but not a sufficient condition for liberation; it must become the motivating force for liberating action. Nor does the discovery by the oppressed that they exist in dialectical relationship to the oppressor, as his antithesis—that without them the oppressor could not exist[4]—in itself constitute liberation. The oppressed can overcome the contradiction in which they are caught only when this perception enlists them in the struggle to free themselves.

The same is true with respect to the individual oppressor as a person. Discovering himself to be an oppressor may cause considerable anguish, but it does not necessarily lead to solidarity with the oppressed. Rationalizing his guilt through paternalistic treatment of the oppressed, all the while holding them fast in a position of dependence, will not do. Solidarity requires that one enter into the situation of those with whom one is solidary; it is a radical posture. If what characterizes the oppressed is their subordination to the consciousness of the master, as Hegel affirms,[5] true solidarity with the oppressed means fighting at their side to transform the objective reality which has made them these "beings for another." The oppressor is solidary with the oppressed only when he stops regarding the oppressed as an abstract category and sees them as persons who have been unjustly dealt with, deprived of their voice, cheated in the sale of their labor—when he stops making pious, sentimental, and individualistic gestures and risks an act of love. True solidarity is found only in the plenitude of this act of love, in its existentiality, in its praxis. To affirm that men are persons and as persons should be free, and yet to do nothing tangible to make this affirmation a reality is a farce.

Since it is in a concrete situation that the oppressor-oppressed contradiction is established, the resolution of this contradiction must be *objectively* verifiable. Hence, the radical requirement—both for the man who discovers himself to be an oppressor and for the oppressed—that the concrete situation which begets oppression must be transformed.

To present this radical demand for the objective transformation of reality, to combat subjectivist immobility which would divert the recognition of oppression into patient waiting for oppression to disappear by itself, is not to dismiss the role of subjectivity in the struggle to change structures. On the contrary, one cannot conceive of objectivity without subjectivity. Neither can exist without the other, nor can they be dichotomized. The separation of objectivity from subjectivity, the denial of the latter when analyzing reality or acting upon it, is objectivism. On the other hand, the denial of objectivity in analysis or action, resulting in a subjectivism which leads to solipsistic positions, denies action itself by denying objective reality. Neither objectivism nor subjectivism, nor yet psychologism is propounded here, but rather subjectivity and objectivity in constant dialectical relationship.

To deny the importance of subjectivity in the process of transforming the world and history is naïve and simplistic. It is to admit the impossible: a world without men. This objectivistic position is as ingenuous as that of subjectivism, which postulates men without a world. World and men do not exist apart from each other, they exist in constant interaction. Marx does not espouse such a dichotomy, nor does any other critical, realistic thinker. What Marx criticized and scientifically destroyed was not subjectivity, but subjectivism and psychologism. Just as objective social reality exists not by chance, but as the product of human action, so it is not transformed by chance. If men produce social reality (which in the "inversion of the praxis" turns back upon them and conditions them), then transforming that reality is an historical task, a task for men.

Reality which becomes oppressive results in the contradistinction of men as oppressors and oppressed. The latter, whose task it is to struggle for their liberation together with those who show true solidarity, must acquire a critical awareness of oppression through the praxis of this struggle. One of the gravest obstacles to the achievement of liberation is that oppressive reality absorbs those within it and thereby acts to submerge men's consciousness. Functionally, oppression is domesticating. To no longer be prey to its force, one must emerge from it and turn upon it. This can be done only by means of the praxis: reflection and action upon the world in order to transform it.

Making "real oppression more oppressive still by adding to it the realization of oppression" corresponds to the dialectical relation between the subjective and the objective. Only in this interdependence is an authentic praxis possible, without which it is impossible to resolve the oppressor-oppressed contradiction. To achieve this goal, the oppressed must confront reality critically, simultaneously objectifying and acting upon that reality. A mere perception of reality not followed by this critical intervention will not lead to a transformation of objective reality—precisely because it is not a true perception. This is the case of a purely subjectivist perception by someone who forsakes objective reality and creates a false substitute.

A different type of false perception occurs when a change in objective reality would threaten the individual or class interests of the perceiver. In the first instance, there is no critical intervention in reality because that reality is fictitious; there is none in the second instance because intervention would contradict the class interests of the perceiver. In the latter case the tendency of the perceiver is to behave "neurotically." The fact exists; but both the fact and what may result from it may be prejudicial to him. Thus it becomes necessary, not precisely to deny the fact, but to "see it differently." This rationalization as a defense mechanism coincides in the end with subjectivism. A fact which is not denied but whose truths are rationalized loses its objective base. It ceases to be concrete and becomes a myth created in defense of the class of the perceiver.

Herein lies one of the reasons for the prohibitions and the difficulties . . . designed to dissuade the people from critical intervention in reality. The oppressor knows full well that this intervention would not be to his interest. What *is* to his interest is for the people to continue in a state of submersion, impotent in the face of oppressive reality. . . . "To explain to the masses their own action" is to clarify and illuminate that action, both regarding its relationship of the objective facts by which it was prompted, and regarding its purposes. The more the people unveil this challenging reality which is to be the object of their transforming action, the more critically they enter that reality. In this way they are "consciously activating the subsequent development of their experiences." There would be no human action if there were no objective reality, no world to be the "not I" of man and to challenge him; just as there would be no human action if man were not a "project," if he were not able to transcend himself, to perceive his reality and understand it in order to transform it.

In dialectical thought, word and action are intimately interdependent. But action is human only when it is not merely an occupation but also a preoccupation, that is, when it is not dichotomized from reflection. Reflection, which is essential to action, is implicit in Lukács' requirement of "explaining to the masses their own action," just as it is implicit in the purpose he attributes to this explanation: that of "consciously activating the subsequent development of experience."

For us, however, the requirement is seen not in terms of explaining to, but rather dialoguing with the people about their actions. In any event, no reality transforms itself,[6] and the duty which Lukács ascribes to the revolutionary party of "explaining to the masses their own action" coincides with our affirmation of the need for the critical intervention of the people in reality through the praxis. The pedagogy of the oppressed, which is the pedagogy of men engaged in the fight for their own liberation, has its roots here. And those who recognize, or begin to recognize, themselves as oppressed must be among the developers of this pedagogy. No pedagogy which is truly liberating can remain distant from the oppressed by treating them as unfortunates and by presenting for their emulation models from among the oppressors. The oppressed must be their own example in the struggle for their redemption.

The pedagogy of the oppressed, animated by authentic, humanist (not humanitarian) generosity, presents itself as a pedagogy of man. Pedagogy which begins with the egoistic interests of the oppressors (an egoism cloaked in the false generosity of paternalism) and makes of the oppressed the objects of its humanitarianism, itself maintains and embodies oppression. It is an instrument of dehumanization. This is why, as we affirmed earlier, the pedagogy of the oppressed cannot be developed or practiced by the oppressors. It would be a contradiction in terms if the oppressors not only defended but actually implemented a liberating education. . . .

The pedagogy of the oppressed, as a humanist and libertarian pedagogy, has two distinct stages. In the first, the oppressed unveil the world of oppression and through the praxis commit themselves to its transformation. In the second stage, in which the reality of oppression has already been transformed, this pedagogy ceases to belong to the oppressed and becomes a pedagogy of all men in the process of permanent liberation. In both stages, it is always through action in depth that the culture of domination is culturally confronted.[7] In the first stage this confrontation occurs through the change in the way the oppressed perceive the world of oppression; in the second stage, through the expulsion of the myths created and developed in the old order, which like specters haunt the new structure emerging from the revolutionary transformation.

The pedagogy of the first stage must deal with the problem of the oppressed consciousness and the oppressor consciousness, the problem of men who oppress and men who suffer oppression. It must take into account their behavior, their view of the world, and their ethics. A particular problem is the duality of the oppressed: they are contradictory, divided beings, shaped by and existing in a concrete situation of oppression and violence.

Any situation in which "A" objectively exploits "B" or hinders his pursuit of self-affirmation as a responsible person is one of oppression. Such a situation in itself constitutes violence, even when sweetened by false generosity, because it interferes with man's ontological and historical vocation to be more fully human. With the establishment of a relationship of oppression, violence has *already* begun. Never in history has violence been initiated by the oppressed. How could they be the initiators, if they themselves are the result of violence? How could they be the sponsors of something whose objective inauguration called forth their existence as oppressed? There would be no oppressed had there been no prior situation of violence to establish their subjugation.

Violence is initiated by those who oppress, who exploit, who fail to recognize others as persons—not by those who are oppressed, exploited, and unrecognized. It is not the unloved who initiate disaffection, but those who cannot love because they love only themselves. It is not the helpless, subject to terror, who initiate terror, but the violent, who with their power create the concrete situation which begets the "rejects of life." It is not the tyrannized who initiate despotism, but the tyrants. It is not the despised who initiate hatred, but those who despise. It is not those whose humanity is denied them who negate man, but those who denied that humanity (thus negating their own as well). Force is used not by those who have become weak under the preponderance of the strong, but by the strong who have emasculated them.

For the oppressors, however, it is always the oppressed (whom they obviously never call "the oppressed" but—depending on whether they are fellow countrymen or not—"those people" or "the blind and envious masses" or "savages" or "natives" or "subversives") who are disaffected, who are "violent," "barbaric," "wicked," or "ferocious" when they react to the violence of the oppressors.

Yet it is—paradoxical though it may seem—precisely in the response of the oppressed to the violence of their oppressors that a gesture of love may be found. Consciously or unconsciously, the act of rebellion by the oppressed (an act which is always, or nearly always, as violent as the initial violence of the oppressors) can initiate love. Whereas the violence of the oppressors prevents the oppressed from being fully human, the response of the latter to this violence is grounded in the desire to pursue the right to be human. As the oppressors dehumanize others and violate their rights, they themselves also become dehumanized. As the oppressed, fighting to be human, take away the oppressors' power to dominate and suppress, they restore to the oppressors the humanity they had lost in the exercise of oppression.

It is only the oppressed who, by freeing themselves, can free their oppressors. The latter, as an oppressive class, can free neither others nor themselves. It is therefore essential that the oppressed wage the struggle to resolve the contradiction in which they are caught; and the contradiction will be resolved by the appearance of the new man: neither oppressor nor oppressed, but man in the process of liberation. If the goal of the oppressed is to become fully human, they will not achieve their goal by merely reversing the terms of the contradiction, by simply changing poles.

This may seem simplistic; it is not. Resolution of the oppressor-oppressed contradiction indeed implies the disappearance of the oppressors as a dominant class. However, the restraints imposed by the former oppressed on their oppressors, so that the latter cannot reassume their former position, do not constitute *oppression.* An act is oppressive only when it prevents men from being more fully human. Accordingly, these necessary restraints do not *in themselves* signify that yesterday's oppressed have become today's oppressors. Acts which prevent the restoration of the oppressive regime cannot be compared with those which create and maintain it, cannot be compared with those by which a few men deny the majority their right to be human.

However, the moment the new regime hardens into a dominating "bureaucracy"[8] the humanist dimension of the struggle is lost and it is no longer possible to speak of liberation. Hence our insistence that the authentic solution of the oppressor-oppressed contradiction does not lie in a mere reversal of position, in moving from one pole to the other. Nor does it lie in the replacement of the former oppressors with new ones who continue to subjugate the oppressed—all in the name of their liberation.

But even when the contradiction is resolved authentically by a new situation established by the liberated laborers, the former oppressors do not feel liberated. On the contrary, they genuinely consider themselves to be oppressed. Conditioned by the experience of oppressing others, any situation other than their former seems to them like oppression. Formerly, they could eat, dress, wear shoes, be educated, travel, and hear Beethoven; while millions did not eat, had no clothes or shoes, neither studied nor traveled, much less listened to Beethoven. Any restriction on this way of life, in the name of the rights of the community, appears to the former oppressors as a profound violation of their individual rights—although they had no respect for the millions who suffered and died of hunger, pain, sorrow, and despair. For the oppressors, "human beings" refer only to themselves; other people are "things." For the oppressors, there exists only one right: their right to live in peace, over against the right, not always even recognized, but simply conceded, of the oppressed to survival. And they make this concession only because the existence of the oppressed is necessary to their own existence.

This behavior, this way of understanding the world and men (which necessarily makes the oppressors resist the installation of a new regime) is explained by their experience as a dominant class. Once a situation of violence and oppression has been established, it engenders an entire way of life and behavior for those caught up in it—oppressors and oppressed alike. Both are submerged in this situation, and both bear the marks of oppression. Analysis of existential situations of oppression reveals that their inception lay in an act of violence—initiated by those with power. This violence, as a process, is perpetuated from generation to generation of oppressors, who become its heirs and are shaped in its climate. This climate creates in the oppressor a strongly possessive consciousness—possessive of the world and of men. Apart from direct, concrete, material possession of the world and of men, the oppressor consciousness could not understand itself—could not even exist. Fromm said of this consciousness that, without such possession, "it would lose contact with the world." The oppressor consciousness tends to transform everything surrounding it into an object of its domination. The earth, property, production, the creations of men, men themselves, time—everything is reduced to the status of objects at its disposal.

In their unrestrained eagerness to possess, the oppressors develop the conviction that it is possible for them to transform everything into objects of their purchasing power; hence their strictly materialistic concept of existence. Money is the measure of all things, and profit the primary goal. For the oppressors, what is worthwhile is to have more—always more—even at the cost of the oppressed having less or having nothing. For them, *to be* is *to have* and to be the class of the "haves."

As beneficiaries of a situation of oppression, the oppressors cannot perceive that if *having* is a condition of *being,* it is a necessary condition for all men. This is why their generosity is false. Humanity is a "thing," and they possess it as an exclusive right, as inherited property. To the oppressor consciousness, the humanization of the "others," of the people, appears not as the pursuit of full humanity, but as subversion.

The oppressors do not perceive their monopoly on *having more* as a privilege which dehumanizes others and themselves. They cannot see that, in the egoistic pursuit of *having* as a possessing class, they suffocate in their own possessions and no longer *are;* they merely *have.* For them, *having more* is an inalienable right, a right they acquired through their own "effort," with their "courage to take risks." If others do not have more, it is because they are incompetent and lazy, and worst of all is their unjustifiable ingratitude towards the "generous gestures" of the dominant class. Precisely because they are "ungrateful" and "envious," the oppressed are regarded as potential enemies who must be watched.

It could not be otherwise. If the humanization of the oppressed signifies subversion, so also does their freedom; hence the necessity for constant control. And the more the oppressors control the oppressed, the more they change them into apparently inanimate "things." This tendency of the oppressor consciousness to "in-animate" everything and everyone it encounters, in its eagerness to possess, unquestionably corresponds with a tendency to sadism.

> The pleasure in complete domination over another person (or other animate creature) is the very essence of the sadistic drive. Another way of formulating the same thought is to say that the aim of sadism is to transform a man into a thing, something animate into something inanimate, since by complete and absolute control the living loses one essential quality of life—freedom.[9]

Sadistic love is a perverted love—a love of death, not of life. One of the characteristics of the oppressor consciousness and its necrophilic view of the world is thus sadism. As the oppressor consciousness, in order to dominate, tries to deter the drive to search, the restlessness, and the creative power which characterize life, it kills life. More and more, the oppressors are using science and technology as unquestionably powerful instruments for their purpose: the maintenance of the oppressive order through manipulation and repression.[10] The oppressed, as objects, as "things," have no purposes except those their oppressors prescribe for them.

Given the preceding context, another issue of indubitable importance arises: the fact that certain members of the oppressor class join the oppressed in their struggle for liberation, thus moving from one pole of the contradiction to the other. Theirs is a fundamental role, and has been so throughout the history of this struggle. It happens, however, that as they cease to be exploiters or indifferent spectators or simply the heirs of exploitation and move to the side of the exploited, they almost always bring with them the marks of their origin: their prejudices and their deformations, which include a lack of confidence in the people's ability to think, to want, and to know. Accordingly, these adherents to the people's cause constantly run the risk of falling into a type of generosity as malefic as that of the oppressors. The generosity of the oppressors is nourished by an unjust order, which must be maintained in order to justify that generosity. Our converts, on the other hand, truly desire to transform the unjust order; but because of their background they believe that they must be the executors of the transformation. They talk about the people, but they do not trust them; and trusting the people is the indispensable precondition for revolutionary change. A real humanist can be identified more by his trust in the people, which engages him in their struggle, than by a thousand actions in their favor without that trust.

Those who authentically commit themselves to the people must reexamine themselves constantly. This conversion is so radical as not to allow of ambiguous behavior. To affirm this commitment but to consider oneself the proprietor of revolutionary wisdom—which must then be given to (or imposed on) the people—is to retain the old ways. The man who proclaims devotion to the cause of liberation yet is unable to enter into *communion* with the people, whom he continues to regard as totally ignorant, is grievously self-deceived. The convert who approaches the people but feels alarm at each step they take, each doubt they express, and each suggestion they offer, and attempts to impose his "status," remains nostalgic toward his origins.

Conversion to the people requires a profound rebirth. Those who undergo it must take on a new form of existence; they can no longer remain as they were. Only through comradeship with the oppressed can the converts understand their characteristic ways of living and behaving, which in diverse moments reflect the structure of domination. One of these characteristics is the previously mentioned existential duality of the oppressed, who are at the same time themselves and the oppressor whose image they have internalized. Accordingly, until they concretely "discover" their oppressor and in turn their own consciousness, they nearly always express fatalistic attitudes toward their situation.

> The peasant begins to get courage to overcome his dependence when he realizes that he is dependent. Until then, he goes along with the boss and says "What can I do? I'm only a peasant."[11]

When superficially analyzed, this fatalism is sometimes interpreted as a docility that is a trait of national character. Fatalism in the guise of docility is the fruit of an historical and sociological situation, not an essential characteristic of a people's behavior. It almost always is related to the power of destiny or fate or fortune—inevitable forces—or to a distorted view of God. Under the sway of magic and myth, the oppressed (especially the peasants, who are almost submerged in nature)[12] see their suffering, the fruit of exploitation, as the will of God—as if God were the creator of this "organized disorder."

Submerged in reality, the oppressed cannot perceive clearly the "order" which serves the interests of the oppressors whose image they have internalized. Chafing under the restrictions of this order, they often manifest a type of horizontal violence, striking out at their own comrades for the pettiest reasons.

> The colonized man will first manifest this aggressiveness which has been deposited in his bones against his own people. This is the period when the niggers beat each other up, and the police and magistrates do not know which way to turn when faced with the astonishing waves of crime in North Africa. . . . While the settler or the policeman has the right the livelong day to strike the native, to insult him and to make him crawl to them, you will see the native reaching for his knife at the slightest hostile or aggressive glance cast on him by another native; for the last resort of the native is to defend his personality vis-à-vis his brother.[13]

It is possible that in this behavior they are once more manifesting their duality. Because the oppressor exists within their oppressed comrades, when they attack those comrades they are indirectly attacking the oppressor as well.

On the other hand, at a certain point in their existential experience the oppressed feel an irresistible attraction toward the oppressor and his way of life. Sharing this way of life becomes an overpowering aspiration. In their alienation, the oppressed want at any cost to resemble the oppressor, to imitate him, to follow him. This phenomenon is especially prevalent in the middle-class oppressed, who yearn to be equal to the "eminent" men of the upper class. Albert Memmi, in an exceptional analysis of the "colonized mentality," refers to the contempt he felt toward the colonizer, mixed with "passionate" attraction toward him.

> How could the colonizer look after his workers while periodically gunning down a crowd of colonized? How could the colonized deny himself so cruelly yet make such excessive demands? How could he hate the colonizers and yet admire them so passionately? (I too felt this admiration in spite of myself.)[14]

Self-depreciation is another characteristic of the oppressed, which derives from their internalization of the opinion the oppressors hold of them. So often do they hear that they are good for nothing, know nothing, and are incapable of learning anything—that they are sick, lazy, and unproductive—that in the end they become convinced of their own unfitness.

> The peasant feels inferior to the boss because the boss seems to be the only one who knows things and is able to run things.[15]

They call themselves ignorant and say the "professor" is the one who has knowledge and to whom they should listen. The criteria of knowledge imposed upon them are the conventional ones. "Why don't you," said a peasant participating in a culture circle, "explain the pictures first? That way it'll take less time and won't give us a headache."

Almost never do they realize that they, too, "know things" they have learned in their relations with the world and with other men. Given the circumstances which have produced their duality, it is only natural that they distrust themselves.

Not infrequently, peasants in educational projects begin to discuss a generative theme in a lively manner, then stop suddenly and say to the educator: "Excuse us, we ought to keep quiet and let you talk. You are the one who knows, we don't know anything." They often insist that there is no difference between them and the animals; when they do admit a difference, it favors the animals. "They are freer than we are."

It is striking, however, to observe how this self-depreciation changes with the first changes in the situation of oppression. I heard a peasant leader say in an *asentamiento*[16] meeting, "They used to say we were unproductive because we were lazy and drunkards. All lies. Now that we are respected as men, we're going to show everyone that we were never drunkards or lazy. We were exploited!"

As long as their ambiguity persists, the oppressed are reluctant to resist, and totally lack confidence in themselves. They have a diffuse, magical belief in the invulnerability and power of the oppressor.[17] The magical force of the landowner's power holds particular sway in the rural areas. A sociologist friend of mine tells of a group of armed peasants in a Latin American country who recently took over a latifundium. For tactical reasons, they planned to hold the landowner as a hostage. But not one peasant had the courage to guard him; his very presence was terrifying. It is also possible that the act of opposing the boss provoked guilt feelings. In truth, the boss was "inside" them.

The oppressed must see examples of the vulnerability of the oppressor so that a contrary conviction can begin to grow within them. Until this occurs, they will continue disheartened, fearful, and beaten.[18] As long as the oppressed remain unaware of the causes of their condition, they fatalistically "accept" their exploitation. Further, they are apt to react in a passive and alienated manner when confronted with the necessity to struggle for their freedom and self-affirmation. Little by little, however, they tend to try out forms of rebellious action. In working toward liberation, one must neither lose sight of this passivity nor overlook the moment of awakening.

Within their unauthentic view of the world and of themselves, the oppressed feel like "things" owned by the oppressor. For the latter, *to be* is *to have,* almost always at the expense of those who have nothing. For the oppressed, at a certain point in their existential experience, *to be* is not to resemble the oppressor, but *to be under* him, to depend on him. Accordingly, the oppressed are emotionally dependent.

> The peasant is a dependent. He can't say what he wants. Before he discovers his dependence, he suffers. He lets off steam at home, where he shouts at his children, beats them, and despairs. He complains about his wife and thinks everything is dreadful. He doesn't let off steam with the boss because he thinks the boss is a superior being. Lots of times, the peasant gives vent to his sorrows by drinking.[19]

This total emotional dependence can lead the oppressed to what Fromm calls necrophilic behavior: the destruction of life—their own or that of their oppressed fellows.

It is only when the oppressed find the oppressor out and become involved in the organized struggle for their liberation that they begin to believe in themselves. This discovery cannot be purely intellectual but must involve action; nor can it be limited to mere activism, but must include serious reflection: only then will it be a praxis.

Critical and liberating dialogue, which presupposes action, must be carried on with the oppressed at whatever the stage of their struggle for liberation.[20] The content of that dialogue can and should vary in accordance with historical conditions and the level at which the oppressed perceive reality. But to substitute monologue, slogans, and communiqués for dialogue is to attempt to liberate the oppressed with the instruments of domestication. Attempting to liberate the oppressed without their reflective participation in the act of liberation is to treat them as objects which must be saved from a burning building; it is to lead them into the populist pitfall and transform them into masses which can be manipulated.

At all stages of their liberation, the oppressed must see themselves as men engaged in the ontological and historical vocation of becoming more fully human. Reflection and action become imperative when one does not erroneously attempt to dichotomize the content of humanity from its historical forms.

The insistence that the oppressed engage in reflection on their concrete situation is not a call to armchair revolution. On the contrary, reflection—true reflection—leads to action. On the other hand, when the situation calls for action, that action will constitute an authentic praxis only if its consequences become the object of critical reflection. In this sense, the praxis is the new *raison d'être* of the oppressed; and the revolution, which inaugurates the historical moment of this *raison d'être,* is not viable apart from their concomitant conscious involvement. Otherwise, action is pure activism.

To achieve this praxis, however, it is necessary to trust in the oppressed and in their ability to reason. Whoever lacks this trust will fail to initiate (or will abandon) dialogue, reflection, and communication, and will fall into using slogans, communiqués, monologues, and instructions. Superficial conversions to the cause of liberation carry this danger.

Political action on the side of the oppressed must be pedagogical action in the authentic sense of the word, and, therefore, action *with* the oppressed. Those who work for liberation must not take advantage of the emotional dependence of the oppressed—dependence that is the fruit of the concrete situation of domination which surrounds them and which engendered their unauthentic view of the world. Using their dependence to create still greater dependence is an oppressor tactic.

Libertarian action must recognize this dependence as a weak point and must attempt through reflection and action to transform it into independence. However, not even the best-intentioned leadership can bestow independence as a gift. The liberation of the oppressed is a liberation of men, not things. Accordingly, while no one liberates himself by his own efforts alone, neither is he liberated by others. Liberation, a human phenomenon, cannot be achieved by semihumans. Any attempt to treat men as semi-humans only dehumanizes them. When men are already dehumanized, due to the oppression they suffer, the process of their liberation must not employ the methods of dehumanization.

The correct method for a revolutionary leadership to employ in the task of libera-tion is, therefore, *not* "libertarian propaganda." Nor can the leadership merely "implant" in the oppressed a belief in freedom, thus thinking to win their trust. The correct method lies in dialogue. The conviction of the oppressed that they must fight for their liberation is not a gift bestowed by the revolutionary leadership, but the result of their own *conscientização.**

The revolutionary leaders must realize that their own conviction of the necessity for struggle (an indispensable dimension of revolutionary wisdom) was not given to them by anyone else—if it is authentic. This conviction cannot be packaged and sold; it is reached, rather, by means of a totality of reflection and action. Only the leaders' own involvement in reality, within an historical situation, led them to criticize this situation and to wish to change it.

Likewise, the oppressed (who do not commit themselves to the struggle unless they are convinced, and who, if they do not make such a commitment, withhold the indis-pensable conditions for this struggle) must reach this conviction as Subjects, not as Objects. They also must intervene critically in the situation which surrounds them and whose mark they bear; propaganda cannot achieve this. While the conviction of the necessity for struggle (without which the struggle is unfeasible) is indispensable to the revolutionary leadership (indeed, it was this conviction which constituted that leader-ship), it is also necessary for the oppressed. It is necessary, that is, unless one intends

---

*Editor's note: The term *conscientização* refers to learning to perceive social, political, and economic contradictions, and to take action against the oppressive elements of reality.

to carry out the transformation *for* the oppressed rather than *with* them. It is my belief that only the latter form of transformation is valid.

The object in presenting these considerations is to defend the eminently pedagogical character of the revolution. The revolutionary leaders of every epoch who have affirmed that the oppressed must accept the struggle for their liberation—an obvious point—have also thereby implicitly recognized the pedagogical aspect of this struggle. Many of these leaders, however (perhaps due to natural and understandable biases against pedagogy), have ended up using the "educational" methods employed by the oppressor. They deny pedagogical action in the liberation process, but they use propaganda to convince.

It is essential for the oppressed to realize that when they accept the struggle for humanization they also accept, from that moment, their total responsibility for the struggle. They must realize that they are fighting not merely for freedom from hunger, but for

> . . . freedom to create and to construct, to wonder and to venture. Such freedom requires that the individual be active and responsible, not a slave or a well-fed cog in the machine. . . . It is not enough that men are not slaves; if social conditions further the existence of automatons, the result will not be love of life, but love of death.[21]

The oppressed, who have been shaped by the death-affirming climate of oppression, must find through their struggle the way to life-affirming humanization, which does not lie *simply* in having more to eat (although it does involve having more to eat and cannot fail to include this aspect). The oppressed have been destroyed precisely because their situation has reduced them to things. In order to regain their humanity they must cease to be things and fight as men. This is a radical requirement. They cannot enter the struggle as objects in order *later* to become men.

The struggle begins with men's recognition that they have been destroyed. Propaganda, management, manipulation—all arms of domination—cannot be the instruments of their rehumanization. The only effective instrument is a humanizing pedagogy in which the revolutionary leadership establishes a permanent relationship of dialogue with the oppressed. In a humanizing pedagogy the method ceases to be an instrument by which the teachers (in this instance, the revolutionary leadership) can manipulate the students (in this instance, the oppressed), because it expresses the consciousness of the students themselves.

> The method is, in fact, the external form of consciousness manifest in acts, which takes on the fundamental property of consciousness—its intentionality. The essence of consciousness is being with the world, and this behavior is permanent and unavoidable. Accordingly, consciousness is in essence a "way towards" something apart from itself, outside itself, which surrounds it and which it apprehends by means of its ideational capacity. Consciousness is thus by definition a method, in the most general sense of the word.[22]

A revolutionary leadership must accordingly practice *cointentional* education. Teachers and students (leadership and people), cointent on reality, are both Subjects, not only in the task of unveiling that reality, and thereby coming to know it critically, but in the task of re-creating that knowledge. As they attain this knowledge of reality through common reflection and action, they discover themselves as its permanent re-creators. In this way, the presence of the oppressed in the struggle for their liberation will be what it should be: not pseudoparticipation, but committed involvement.

NOTES

1 The current movements of rebellion, especially those of youth, while they necessarily reflect the peculiarities of their respective settings, manifest in their essence this preoc-cupation with man and men as beings in the world and with the world—preoccupation with *what* and *how* they are "being." As they place consumer civilization in judgment, denounce bureaucracies of all types, demand the transformation of the universities (changing the rigid nature of the teacher-student relationship and placing that relation-ship within the context of reality), propose the transformation of reality itself so that universities can be renewed, attack old orders and established institutions in the attempt to affirm men as the Subjects of decision, all these movements reflect the style of our age, which is more anthropological than anthropocentric.

2 As used throughout this paper, the term "contradiction" denotes the dialectical conflict between opposing social forces.—Translator's note.

3 This fear of freedom is also to be found in the oppressors, though, obviously, in a dif-ferent form. The oppressed are afraid to embrace freedom; the oppressors are afraid of losing the "freedom" to oppress.

4 See Georg Hegel, *The Phenomenology of Mind* (New York, 1967), pp. 236–37.

5 Analyzing the dialectical relationship between the consciousness of the master and the consciousness of the oppressed, Hegel states: "The one is independent, and its essential nature is to be for itself; the other is dependent, and its essence is life or existence for another. The former is the Master, or Lord, the latter the Bondsman." Ibid., p. 234.

6 "The materialist doctrine that men are products of circumstances and upbringing, and that, therefore, changed men are products of other circumstances and changed upbring-ing, forgets that it is men that change circumstances and that the educator himself needs educating." Karl Marx and Friedrich Engels, *Selected Works* (New York, 1968), p. 28.

7 This appears to be the fundamental aspect of Mao's Cultural Revolution.

8 This rigidity should not be identified with restraints that must be imposed on the former oppressors so they cannot restore the oppressive order. Rather, it refers to the revolu-tion which becomes stagnant and turns against the people, using the old repressive, bureaucratic State apparatus (which should have been drastically suppressed, as Marx so often emphasized).

9 Eric Fromm, *The Heart of Man* (New York, 1966), p. 32.

10 Regarding the "dominant forms of social control," see Herbert Marcuse, *One-Dimensional Man* (Boston, 1964) and *Eros and Civilization* (Boston, 1955).

11 Words of a peasant during an interview with the author.

12 See Candido Mendes, *Memento dos vivos—A Esquerda católica no Brasil* (Rio, 1966).

13 Frantz Fanon, *The Wretched of the Earth* (New York, 1968), p. 52.

14 *The Colonizer and the Colonized* (Boston, 1967), p. x.

15 Words of a peasant during an interview with the author.

16 *Asentamiento* refers to a production unit of the Chilean agrarian reform experiment.—Translator's note.

17 "The peasant has an almost instinctive fear of the boss." Interview with a peasant.

18 See Regis Debray, *Revolution in the Revolution?* (New York, 1967).

19 Interview with a peasant.

20 Not in the open, of course; that would only provoke the fury of the oppressor and lead to still greater repression.

21 Fromm, op. cit., pp. 52–53.

22 Alvaro Vieira Pinto, from a work in preparation on the philosophy of science. I consider the quoted portion of great importance for the understanding of a problem-posing pedagogy and wish to thank Professor Vieira Pinto for permission to cite his work prior to publication.

CHAPTER 34

THE ARMS RACE
AND DEVELOPMENT:
A COMPETITIVE
RELATIONSHIP

Inga Thorsson

Formerly Undersecretary of State for Disarmament Sweden

THE SECRETARY-GENERAL'S REPORT ON DISARMAMENT AND DEVELOPMENT

In the Final Document of the 1978 Special Session on Disarmament, the General Assembly requested the Secretary-General, with the assistance of a group of experts, to prepare a study on the relationship between disarmament and development. An Expert Group was appointed and, under the able leadership of Inga Thorsson, held ten meetings between 1978 and 1981. The Expert Group was aided in its work by forty research reports which it was able to commission.

The Report of the Secretary-General on the "Study of the Relationship Between Disarmament and Development" was issued on October 5, 1981. The Secretary-General described the study as "an important attempt by the international community to thoroughly investigate the proposition that a balanced and generally acceptable pattern of economic and social development is inextricably related to disarmament". He continued, "The clear and widely shared understanding of this relationship may provide a basis for the formulation of practical measures by Governments that would both promote disarmament and further development". . . . We have presented here excerpts from Inga Thorsson's presentation of the Report in the 2nd Committee of the General Assembly.

Common sense alone tells us that military preparations are an economic burden. The arms race and development are to be viewed in a competitive relationship, particularly in terms of resources. Or to put it another way: the arms race and underdevelopment

Reprinted from *Development*, 1 (1982), pp. 12–15, 20, the quarterly journal of the Society for International Development.

are not two problems; they are one. They must be solved together, or neither will ever be solved.

It is a historical fact that governments have, over the past 30 years, spent vast resources on armaments, resources which—on grounds of morality, on grounds of equal human justice, on grounds of enlightened self-interest—ought to have been directed to ending world poverty and building for human and material development. In this way world armaments are among the causes of poverty and underdevelopment.

The 1972 U.N. study on this same theme concluded that disarmament and development "stand fundamentally apart." Taking their point of departure, this statement is still true. Ten years ago and, as duties of the industrialized countries went, development was simply equated with development assistance. But since then, the development discussion has been broadened to involve basic structural changes in all societies, within states and among states, including more equitable distribution of income, access to the means of production and greater participation by all groups in decision making, and progress towards the establishment of a New International Economic Order.

In the present study we have introduced a new conceptual framework, defined in a dynamic triangular interrelation between disarmament, development, and security. We have taken a broader approach to the problem of security. In our era, national security can no longer be equated with military might. Even less can international security, i.e., security *for all,* do so. Also, we demonstrate that threats to security may be made and aggravated in many ways, including those that go far beyond purely military threats. It was recognized by the first Special Session on Disarmament that the arms race itself has become a threat to the security of nations. Thus, disarmament, particularly nuclear disarmament, would directly enhance security, and, therefore, prospects for development.

National security is not a goal in itself. Its ultimate purpose must be to secure the independence and sovereignty of the national state, the freedom of its citizens—freedom and the means to develop economically, socially, and culturally, which defines exactly what we mean by "development." In today's world this can never be achieved by any state at the expense of others. In a world of interdependence, only through global, or international, security will it be possible to reach the objective of national security for the ultimate goal of freedom, well-being, and human dignity for people throughout the world.

Today there is an array of intensifying nonmilitary threats which aggravate the security problems of states. Such nonmilitary threats can be described as:

• Widespread reductions in prospects for economic growth;
• Existing or impending ecological stresses, resource scarcities—notably in the field of energy and certain nonrenewable raw materials—and a growing world population. Today's stresses and constraints may translate into tomorrow's economic stresses and political conflicts;
• The morally unacceptable and politically hazardous polarization of wealth and poverty.

The appalling dimensions of poverty, the destruction of the environment, the accelerating race for arms, and the resulting global economic malaise are largely problems of our own making. The Group states that it is well within our collective capabilities and within the earth's carrying capacity to provide for basic needs for the world's entire population, and to make progress towards a more equitable economic order, at a pace politically acceptable to all. The Group reaffirms that the arms race is incompatible with the objectives of a New International Economic Order. Of course, also in the future, economic growth is possible even with a continuing arms race, but it would be relatively slow, and very unevenly distributed both among and within regions of the world. We show, on the other hand, that a cooperative management of interdependence can be in the economic and security interests of all states. But the adoption or rather the evolution of such an outlook is quite improbable if the arms race continues.

It is imperative that nonmilitary challenges to security are treated as nonmilitary. If this is not recognized, if states fail to accept and persevere in tackling these challenges through voluntary measures and cooperation, there is a grave risk that the situation will deteriorate to the point of crisis where, even with a low probability of success, the use of military force could be seen as a way to produce results sufficiently quickly. This is far from being a remote possibility. In recent time there has been a marked and increasing tendency in international relations actually to use or threaten to use military force in response to nonmilitary challenges, not only to "security," but also to the secure supply of goods and the well-being of the nations which face these challenges.

The study has documented that at least 50 million people are directly or indirectly engaged in military activities world-wide. This figure includes, *inter alia,* an estimated 500,000 qualified scientists and engineers engaged in research and development for military purposes.

Military research and development remains by far the largest single objective of scientific enquiry and technological development. Approximately 20 percent of the world's qualified scientists and engineers were engaged in military work at a cost of around 35,000 million dollars in 1980, or approximately one-quarter of all expenditure on research and development. Virtually all this R and D takes place in the industrialized countries, 85 percent in the USA and the USSR alone. Adding France and Britain would push this share above 90 percent.

It stands to reason that even a modest reallocation to development objectives of the current capacity for military R and D could be expected to produce dramatic results in fields like resource conservation and the promotion of new patterns of development, better adapted to meeting the basic needs of ordinary people. This is, *inter alia* evident from the fact, which is also among our findings, that, on an average, a military product requires 20 times as much R and D resources as a civilian product.

The 1972 report on the subject identified more than 70 possible alternative uses. Our present investigations suggest, in more elaborated and detailed ways, for instance, that production workers in the military sector could quite easily transfer their skills to the development, production, and installation of solar energy devices. Environment, housing, and urban renewal are other areas likely to gain from the possible rechanneling of military R and D. New transport systems, particularly in urban areas, are sorely needed and have long been regarded as a major civilian alternative for the high technology industries in the military sector.

In purely financial terms, world-wide military expenditures by 1981 exceed, as we all know, the astounding level of 520,000 million dollars, representing 6 percent of world output. Member States certainly realize that this amount is roughly equivalent to the value of all investible capital in all developing countries combined.

The effect on the economic and social spheres in our societies of the arms race extend far beyond the fact that 5 to 6 percent of the world's resources are not available to help satisfy socially productive needs. The very fact that these resources are spent on armaments accentuates the inefficient allocation of the remaining 94 to 95 percent, within and between nations. Three fundamental characteristics of the arms race reinforce this disallocation: *first,* the sheer magnitude of the volume of resources; *second,* the composition of expenditure, most particularly the stress on R and D, affecting investment and productivity in the civilian sector; and *third,* the fact that this massive effort has now been sustained for over 30 years.

As an illustration of the contribution which can be made by disarmament measures, even limited, to world development, one study submitted to the Group projects global economic prospects under three types of hypothetical scenarios, viz., a continued arms race, an accelerated arms race, and modest disarmament measures involving the release of some resources for reallocation to the developing countries. Utilizing the United Nations input-output model of world economy it is calculated that an acceleration of the arms race would adversely affect global economic well-being in all but one of the regions of the world. A wealth of numerical data is presented in chapter III of the report. I will here highlight some general results. Besides the negative impact on per capita consumption, an accelerated arms race will also result in a decline of the world's stock of capital, reduce the value of nonmilitary exports, and entail reductions in industrial employment in the poorest regions of the world.

In contrast, a scenario of even modest disarmament measures is shown to yield higher per capita consumption for different regions and in addition bring about a higher world GDP, a larger capital stock, a general increase in the agricultural output, to mention only a few of the obvious economic gains. Besides these global economic gains, a scenario of modest disarmament would also yield significant benefits for the poorest regions of the world. This conclusion is by itself of considerable significance when it is remembered that in many cases, increases in military outlays by industrial countries have been accompanied by a decline in their aid transfers, despite the repeated request for the fulfilment of the UN targets for official development assistance and despite the fact that existing volumes of assistance are grossly inadequate to meet the basic aid requirements for the poorer countries. The report shows that even a minor part of savings from modest disarmament has the potential of dramatically enhancing present levels of assistance.

We can make similar calculations for the past. For instance, if half the funds spent on armaments throughout the world from 1970 to 1975 had instead been invested in the civilian sector, it has been calculated[1] that annual output at the end of that period would have been 200,000 million dollars higher than it actually was—a figure in excess of the aggregate GNP of Southern Asia and the mid-African regions. And mark well, this growth would most likely have been achieved without any extra demand for investible resources.

Military outlays fall by definition into the category of consumption and not investment. As a consequence, steadily high or increasing military outlays tend to depress economic growth. This effect may be direct through displacement of investment, and indirect through constraints on productivity.

A study conducted in the late 1960s by Emile Benoit is much cited as showing that military outlays do not have negative effects on economic growth for developing countries. In reality Benoit's own conclusion was more modest.[2] He said:

> Thus we have been unable to establish whether the net growth effects of defence expenditures have been positive or not. On the basis of all the evidence we suspect that it has been positive for the countries in our sample, and at past levels of defence burden, but we have not been able to prove this.

This suspected positive relationship of Benoit's has been contested as spurious, since it was simultaneously correlated with other important socioeconomic factors in the economies of those developing countries, particularly a high net inflow of foreign assistance. Based on today's level of research, it can now be confidently refuted. In our study we do recognize that the availability of unutilized and underutilized resources in developing countries may produce short-term results, suggesting a parallelism between high rates of growth and significant military spending, a situation which is, by the way, frequently associated with foreign dependence. In the long run, however, the totality of the socioeconomic consequences of sizeable military outlays outweighs any immediate economic spinoffs into the civilian sector.

On the basis of the present report, and the research commissioned for it, we can confidently conclude that military budgets are deadened expenditures in all kinds of economies, be they market, centrally planned, or mixed; be they industrialized or developing. Military expenditures do *not* foster growth. Through their inflationary effects—thoroughly analysed in the study—and the general economic and political malaise to which they contribute, military spending *inhibits* the capital investment required for development. Through the drain on the most valuable research talents and funds, it *restrains* productivity gains and *distorts* growth in science and technology. The military sector is not a great provider of jobs. On the contrary it is shown that military spending is one of the least efficient kinds of public spending. It drains away funds that could relieve poverty and distress. The very nature of military spending heightens tensions, reduces security, and underpins the system which makes even more arms necessary.

This study has in my view strengthened the economic and social case for the disarmament-development relationship by identifying military spending as an impediment to economic growth and social development and the arms race as an obstacle to the establishment of a New International Economic Order.

The Group has indicated the political and economic potentials of rationally imperative alternatives in suggesting that policies aimed at implementing the disarmament-development relationship are likely to broaden the base of East-West détente and put the North-South dialogue in a mutually advantageous frame of reference.

Its report should not be considered an individual project. I should like to express a hope for an effective follow-up process, to the benefit, first of all, of the billions of human beings inhabiting this world of ours.

NOTES

1 United Nations Disarmament Fact Sheet, no. 9, "Cost of the Arms Race," 1979.
2 Emile Benoit, *Defence and Economic Growth in Developing Countries* (Lexington, Mass.: Lexington Books, 1973), p. 4.

APPENDIX

[The following are the recommendations from the report of the group of experts on disarmament and development.]

On the basis of its findings and conclusions, implicit in this entire report and more explicitly summarized above, the Group makes the following recommendations:

1 That all Governments, but particularly those of the major military Powers, should prepare assessments of the nature and magnitude of the short- and long-term economic and social costs attributable to their military preparations so that their general public be informed of them.

2 That Governments urgently undertake studies to identify and to publicize the benefits that would be derived from the reallocation of military resources in a balanced and verifiable manner, to address economic and social problems at the national level and to contribute towards reducing the gap in income that currently divides the industrialized nations from the developing world and establishing a new international economic order.

3 A fuller and more systematic compilation and dissemination by Governments of data on the military use of human and material resources and military transfers.

4 That the disarmament-development perspective elaborated in this report be incorporated in a concrete and practical way in the ongoing activities of the United Nations system.

5 That Governments create the necessary prerequisites, including preparations and, where appropriate, planning, to facilitate the conversion of resources freed by disarmament measures to civilian purposes, especially to meet urgent economic and social needs, in particular, in the developing countries.

6 That Governments consider making the results of experiences and preparations in their respective countries available by submitting reports from time to time to the General Assembly on possible solutions to conversion problems.

7 That further consideration be given to establishing an international disarmament fund for development and that the administrative and technical modalities of such a fund be further investigated by the United Nations with due regard to the capabilities of the agencies and institutions currently responsible for the international transfer of resources.

8 That the Secretary-General take appropriate action, through the existing inter-agency consultative mechanism of the Administrative Committee on Coordination, to foster and coordinate the incorporation of the disarmament and development perspective in the programmes and activities of the United Nations system.

9 That the Department of Public Information and other relevant United Nations organs and agencies, while continuing to emphasize the danger of war—particularly nuclear war—should give increased emphasis in their disarmament-related public information and education activities to the social and economic consequences of the arms race and to the corresponding benefits of disarmament.

CHAPTER **35**

REGIONAL INTEGRATION
IN THE 1990s

Gert Rosenthal

UN Economic Commission for Latin America and the Caribbean

I INTRODUCTION

As a consequence of the protracted crisis of the 1980s and of changes in the international scene, in recent years Latin America and the Caribbean have exhibited a steadily
increasing response capacity. Governments and civil societies have sought out new
ways of adapting to changing circumstances and of responding to the numerous challenges they face. One of the many manifestations of this adaptation process is a
renewed interest in the potentials of intraregional cooperation. In contrast to the
atmosphere that surrounded the conclusion of formal economic integration agreements
in the 1980s, lately the region has witnessed the proliferation of quite different sorts of
arrangements, arrangements that display a high degree of heterogeneity in terms of
both their modalities and their geographic configurations.

Indeed, numerous trade preference arrangements have been made, in most cases as
part of the limited-scope agreements provided for under the terms of the 1980 Treaty
of Montevideo; attempts have been mounted to establish free trade areas (without necessarily adopting a common tariff); and efforts have been made to form customs
unions (free trade areas combined with a common tariff) or common markets (customs
unions involving some degree of macroeconomic-policy coordination, especially with
respect to foreign exchange matters, taxes and interest rates). For the first time ever,
extending the coverage of free trade agreements to encompass the entire hemisphere
has become a possibility; on a selective basis, the free trade agreement among Mexico,
Canada and the United States which is now awaiting ratification and, on a more gen-

From *Cepal Review,* 50 (August, 1993).

eral level, the Enterprise for the Americas, announced in mid-1990 by the United States Government, both point in this direction.

II REAWAKENED INTEREST IN INTEGRATION

What accounts for this resurgence of interest in integration when, just a few years ago, the subject had virtually disappeared from the Governments' agenda of priorities? The continued development of the European Community and the formation of a free trade area between Canada and the United States have certainly helped to legitimize agreements aimed at establishing trade-preference groupings. In addition, the laborious, slow-moving progress of the multilateral negotiations being held within the framework of the General Agreement on Tariffs and Trade (GATT) has prompted many Governments to work towards the same objectives by means of partial-scope agreements with like-minded countries. In order to reconcile such initiatives with GATT, article 24 of the Treaty is usually cited, since this provision permits the establishment of trade groups among countries which grant each other reciprocal trade preferences without requiring that they necessarily be extended to the rest of the countries.

In Latin America and the Caribbean, a number of additional factors have helped to further enhance the legitimacy which the idea of integration as such has acquired at the international level. Some of these factors have arisen in response to the possibility of extending the free trade area existing between the United States and Canada to Mexico and, eventually, to other countries in the region. Others are discrete phenomena. Examples of the latter include the gradual convergence of the economic models being applied, the growing political affinity to be observed among democratically-elected civilian governments, a decrease in the potential costs of trade diversion thanks to an increasing degree of trade liberalization in almost all the countries of the region and, in general, a priori assessments of the situation which indicate that the potential benefits of such agreements will far outweigh their possible costs.

III INTERNATIONAL POSITIONING AND INTEGRATION COMMITMENTS

It is also helpful to examine recent integration commitments within the broader context of the determined efforts being made by all the Governments of the region to improve their countries' positions within the international economy. This has been their response to the increasing globalization of the economy and to the shortcomings of the industrialization strategy followed by many countries in the past. In recent years, government action has been directed towards enhancing the international competitiveness of the goods and services that each country has to offer.

In the mid-1980s, intraregional trade agreements did not play a major role in the countries' efforts to improve their international positions; on the contrary, some experts maintain that they were leading in quite the opposite direction. This was because, first of all, the idea had taken firm hold that such agreements served the purposes of import-substituting industrialization but were of no help in an export drive; in some cases it even came to be believed that they actually hindered progress towards greater international competitiveness. Secondly, the Latin American and Caribbean regional market was smaller than that of the major economies of the Organization for Economic Cooperation and Development (OECD) and exhibited slow or zero growth. In the eyes of many Governments, the best course of action was therefore to concentrate on gaining access to large, fast-growing markets.

This view began to change for the reasons mentioned earlier and, above all, because enough information had become available to show that integration commitments among a given group of countries are not necessarily incompatible with the establishment of a more open and more transparent international economy. Thus, in recent years the idea has begun to gain acceptance, in both academic and government circles, that an open international economy free of artificial barriers to a free flow of trade in goods and services does not necessarily exclude the possibility of integration commitments and, in fact, that such arrangements may even contribute to the achievement of that goal.

This is indeed plausible. From a conceptual viewpoint, integration commitments can contribute to the accomplishment of the main tasks on the regional development agenda. This statement is based on a number of well-known arguments, including the potential contribution of expanded markets to an increase in efficiency (as a result of economies of scale and the elimination or reduction of monopolistic rents) and to technical progress and innovation, as well as their effect on investment levels. Moreover, an implicit part of this reasoning is the assumption that the potential costs of trade diversion will tend to decrease markedly in the presence of widespread trade liberalization.

It is also true, however, that intraregional agreements and any future arrangements of a hemispheric scope need to be designed in such a way as to be conducive to the achievement of an international economy free of protectionism and of barriers to trade in goods and services. At the same time, we must be cognizant of the risk that the formation of economic blocs of developed countries may lead to a fragmented world in which trade flows freely within these groups but is subject to a greater degree of regulation between one bloc and another.

It is important to note that Latin American and Caribbean integration is justified—albeit for different reasons—in both cases, i.e., whether the formation of large groupings of developed countries helps facilitate the establishment of an integrated world economy or whether it contributes to the fragmentation of that economy. In the first case, integration would contribute to the achievement of the objective pursued by all the Governments of the region in the Uruguay Round; in the second case, at least it would place the region within one of the groups making up that fragmented international economy. From a regional standpoint, integration also offers a way of diversifying risk in an international economy that is rife with uncertainty.

IV MAIN FEATURES OF THE NEW INTEGRATION COMMITMENTS

If we are to describe existing integration schemes, we must first know what type of integration we are dealing with. The initiatives taken in the developed world have been exceedingly varied in nature. For example, the characteristics of the European Community's broad-ranging accords, which are leading it towards the formation of a regionwide economy, are a far cry from the types of commitments made by Canada, the United States and Mexico in the North American Free Trade Agreement. In East Asia, where no formal integration agreements have been concluded, trade liberalization and geographic proximity are none the less contributing to a steady increase in reciprocal trade, which is, moreover, being augmented by reciprocal investment. In this instance, geographic proximity and lower transaction costs are creating implicit preferences among the countries of that region and are thus facilitating the formation of another bloc of interdependent countries.

Along the same lines, the Latin American and Caribbean region of today abounds in agreements of widely differing characteristics and contents. At the risk of oversimplification, we may identify at least four types of trade-preference arrangements which can be defined in terms of the degree of commitment made among the countries concerned. The simplest category includes agreements for the reduction of tariffs on a given list of products, which are thus accorded preferential treatment *vis-à-vis* similar products coming from other countries. This type of bilateral or multilateral agreement does not involve any significant degree of economic policy coordination.

The second type of agreement calls for a more comprehensive form of tariff reduction, and in this case the corresponding negotiations therefore focus on the lists of exceptions rather than on the products to be subject to liberalization measures. The result is the creation of a free trade area that does not set up a common level of protection in respect of non-member countries. In such cases it is possible that products from the rest of the world may be brought into the country with the higher tariffs via an indirect route by taking advantage of the lower tariffs of the other member countries of the free trade area; to this end, the products in question are first exported to the lower-tariff member countries and are then reexported to another country under the provisions of the free trade agreement. The conventional method of blocking this indirect flow of imports from the rest of the world is to establish rules of origin for products included in the free trade regime; under such rules, a given level of processing or a specified percentage of national content is required.

The third category of agreements are those that not only set up a free trade area but also add to it a common tariff in order to forestall the relative price distortions that can be caused by tariff-generated cost differences. The advisability of setting up a common external tariff for the members of an integration scheme—which is the main difference between a customs union and a free trade area—will depend on the characteristics of the countries involved. Assuming that their levels are low, common tariffs would be more justified for countries having a large volume of reciprocal trade and similar economic structures. Under these circumstances, the application of differentiated tariffs to the various products would create unequal levels of effective protection for each party and would set the stage for charges of unfair trade practices and the establishment of trade restrictions, as well as encouraging contraband trade.

In the fourth category of agreements, a free trade area and common tariff are coupled with a programme of macroeconomic policy coordination. The aim of such a programme is to avert distortions in relative prices caused by cost differences attributable to the exchange rate, export subsidies, rates of taxation or interest rates.

V SOME REQUIREMENTS

The foregoing suggests that the level of commitment which any given group of countries will be prepared to make will depend on how economically interdependent they are, how similar their approaches to macroeconomic and policy management are, how complementary their economic structures and stages of development are, how much they trust each other, and many other factors. The economic ramifications of each type of arrangement in terms of potential costs and benefits will vary from one situation to another.

This underscores the complexity of the many arrangements currently existing in the region and raises the question as to whether it would be wise to seek an eventual convergence of all these schemes or whether it would be better to permit the emergence of a range of different types of agreements reflecting the different types of situations which do, in fact, exist in the region. The second option would appear to be more realistic, at least for the foreseeable future, although it would be advisable to promote the adoption of some common standards regarding the application of mechanisms and instruments in order to pave the way for any subsequent bid to expand the geographic scope of existing agreements.

What is true for Latin America as a whole is not necessarily valid for subregional processes which have already generated a high degree of economic interdependence, however. The fact, for example, that some countries in Central America seem to want to move forward more rapidly than others could at some point jeopardize the consolidation of their subregional integration process. There is, then, a limit to the feasibility of allowing many different agreements to coexist within a single subregional process. This limit is reached when commitments which some countries wish to make will adversely affect the commitments already made by all the countries participating in a given subregional integration process.

VI TRADE MECHANISMS AND INSTRUMENTS

With respect to mechanisms and instruments, if the economic subregions being formed are to be in keeping with the principle of multilateralism, some requirements regarding the content of bilateral and subregional agreements will have to be met; in essence, this means that the regulations and standards established by such agreements need to be in accordance with the provisions of GATT, to which the vast majority of the countries in the region have adhered.

Integration arrangements' common denominator is that they seek to reduce tariffs with a view to the formation of a free trade area. The agreements signed in recent years tend to cover a wide range of products, and negotiations have therefore centred around the lists of exceptions rather than the lists of products to be subject to liberalization measures. Furthermore, the areas of activity or products placed on those lists of exceptions are usually limited to those regarded as "sensitive", such as the automobile industry in Mexico or grain crops in many countries.

Tariff preferences are usually granted on the basis of a tariff reduction timetable which, starting from the maximum tariff rates in effect, gradually leads to full trade liberalization (a zero tariff rate) among the parties concerned. These agreements should also include precisely defined rules of origin to facilitate customs operations and prevent indirect importation, as well as setting up transparent, nondiscriminatory, permanent safeguards and clear, flexible procedures for settling trade disputes. Such agreements are usually accompanied by commitments regarding the gradual elimination of non-tariff trade barriers and other subjects on the GATT agenda, such as trade in services and standardized regulations in the area of intellectual property.

If such agreements are limited to the creation of a free trade area, and if they also give rise to large-volume reciprocal trade flows, there will be a tendency to broaden their scope in order to prevent price differences attributable to disparate conditions in the various signatory countries—tariffs, export subsidies, tax rates, interest rates— from heightening relative price distortions and influencing decisions regarding the location of new production activities designed to supply this expanded market.

This is why the parties to an agreement aimed at promoting trade, investment and cooperation may feel it is necessary to establish a common tariff and align some of their macroeconomic policies (MERCOSUR, the Central American Common Market, the Caribbean Community, the Andean Group). However, although such measures will help to align conditions in the member countries, they will also result in a greater subordination of domestic policy to these integration commitments.

By the same token, some of these accords provide for plans to phase out export subsidies and discriminatory taxes, the elimination of transport-related barriers to foreign trade, and the adoption of agreements regarding services and investment. In the case of the North American Free Trade Agreement concluded by Mexico, Canada and the United States, a marked emphasis on agreements concerning intellectual property, environmental protection and workers' rights is also to be observed.

This does not mean, however, that as the commitments made by the countries are fulfilled, this process will inevitably give rise to new and deeper commitments. Indeed, the experiences of the 1960s suggest that it may be unfounded to take a linear view of integration commitments as leading to greater and greater levels of interdependence.

It should also be noted that agreements regarding tariff levels are sometimes supplemented by other measures—e.g., in the area of government purchasing—which tend to give preference to the acquisition of goods and services from other signatory countries.

VII OTHER INTEGRATION MECHANISMS

As stated earlier, today there is a widespread tendency to regard the pooling of markets as the pivotal element in integration agreements. This frequently prompts charges that excessive importance is being attributed to trade arrangements at the expense of other potential benefits of integration. The first factor to be borne in mind in this regard is that the primary purpose of these arrangements is not to increase trade as much as it is to stimulate production and boost productivity.

Secondly, trade arrangements do not preclude the promotion of other more specific cooperation initiatives; in fact, they may help bolster such efforts. For example, joint projects aimed at improving infrastructure and transport services, electrical power generation and distribution systems, technological research and human resources development, especially in highly specialized fields, can obviously benefit all parties concerned.

Moreover, the implementation of integration agreements will be furthered by the adoption of specific, ongoing programmes to promote trade and investment. In recent years meetings of entrepreneurs and employers, dissemination activities and development agencies have all helped to promote co-investment and to step up trade among various countries of the region. An effort should also be made to encourage intra-Latin American investment, which could become an important vehicle for technological innovation regardless of the types of formal agreements concluded by groups of countries.

VIII HEMISPHERE-WIDE AGREEMENTS

No analysis of contemporary integration agreements can fail to mention a subject that would have been completely unthinkable just 10 years ago: the incorporation of Latin American countries into a free trade area with highly developed countries or, in other words, into an arrangement of reciprocal concessions. What makes it possible even to entertain this possibility, from the standpoint of the Latin American countries, is that unilateral processes of trade liberalization have reached such a point that national producers are now faced with competition from the most efficient of international producers regardless of whether formal integration agreements are in place or not.

In other words, by way of example, it was probably more traumatic for Mexican industry to make the transition from the unbounded tariff protection it enjoyed in the mid-1980s (such as was afforded by import permit requirements) to its present moderate levels of protection (tariff rates of about 10%, on average) than it will be for it to move from the present situation to the zero tariff rate that is to apply to imports from the United States and Canada. In return, Mexican producers will have more secure access to those countries' markets and will have the opportunity to join in new production activities that will be set up to supply this larger shared market.

Of course there will also be risks. Many activities—on both sides of the border—will succumb to the increased competition, and the Governments may find that they have less manoeuvering room in their management of macroeconomic policy. But in an imperfect world, and in view of the protectionist winds that are blowing in many parts of the world, the possibility of joining in a free trade area with the United States and Canada would seem to be an attractive option for many Latin American countries, especially in an international setting that does not afford an abundance of opportunities. This is all the more so in view of the fact that the act of signing integration agreements with the United States and Canada will not necessarily prevent the region from expanding its commercial and financial ties with other centres of growth in the international economy.

As we said at the outset, the United States' sudden interest in signing agreements to set up a free trade area with its neighbours has had a profound impact on intra-Latin American integration schemes. Moreover, the instruments provided for under the North American Free Trade Agreement (NAFTA) are essentially the same as those being applied under the terms of subregional integration agreements in Latin America. Hence the need to continue to explore regional integration and hemispheric integration as two facets of the same subject.

IX   THE PROBLEM OF THE LESS DEVELOPED COUNTRIES

The greatest obstacle to integration during the 1960s and 1970s was probably the poorest countries' opposition to the planned distribution of the presumed costs and benefits of integration. Today, however, to our astonishment, we see that these same countries are willing to undertake commitments for integration with such highly industrialized countries as the United States and Canada. This is one of the many consequences of the wave of trade liberalization that has washed over the world. In fact, even the doctrine of non-reciprocal preferences for the poorest countries has begun to give way to the principle of reciprocity in such agreements. In this respect, the nature of the problem posed by the less developed or smaller countries has changed radically in recent years.

None the less, we should not allow ourselves to be carried away by this new trend, since common sense still tells us that, due to diseconomies of scale and shortcomings in the areas of organizational capacity and financial soundness, many firms in the region are not in a position to compete with their United States counterparts. At the very least, one would hope that longer transition periods would be provided for firms in the less developed countries to gear up to face this new type of competition, and perhaps more flexible rules regarding value added (origin). In addition, integration initiatives should not only promote trade liberalization but should also serve to create conditions conducive to a broad-ranging dissemination of technologies by means of such measures as the enactment of flexible legislation in the area of intellectual property, the establishment of information networks, the mobilization of skilled human resources and the promotion of foreign investment.

X   CONCLUSIONS

A great many conclusions can be drawn from the above discussion. Perhaps the main one is that, just as economic integration played a functional role in the import-substitution model of decades past, it can also do so in the contemporary model for enhanced competitiveness in the international market. It may even be that the potential benefits of integration are greater than those suggested by a static analysis of trade creation and diversion, since the impact of these broader arenas for economic activity in terms of innovation and improved resource allocation—at the company level and within the overall system to which those firms belong—will surely contribute to an increase in productivity and efficiency.

Secondly, recent intra-Latin American (and, some day, intra-hemispheric) integration pacts are compatible with the stated objective of virtually all the countries of the region of improving their position within the international economy. For the most part, these agreements abide by the spirit and letter of GATT while seeking to raise the level of competitiveness and promote market diversification in order to reduce the risk represented by total reliance on the demand of OECD countries. Indeed, these agreements can be viewed as a sign of the fact that the countries are exercising their right to choose options which will enable them to develop their potentials in an uncertain and fiercely competitive international economy. None of the agreements signed to date is being pursued "at the expense of" another grouping but rather as a means of making progress, in the company of a group of similar countries, towards the achievement of the major objectives of the multilateral negotiations being conducted within the framework of GATT (the Uruguay Round).

A third conclusion concerns the present way in which the countries are approaching their integration commitments. What is different is not the agreements' means of implementation, but rather the context in which they are being applied. In other words, as the globalization of the economy proceeds, tariff preferences as well as rules of origin and safeguards are taking on a very different meaning from what they signified in a situation marked by high levels of tariff protection. On the one hand, the costs of trade diversion are now much lower than they used to be; on the other, the substantial reduction in tariff levels already carried out in the region makes tariff preferences less important than before, while bilateral agreements regarding other trade policy tools—safeguards, anti-dumping measures and rules of origin, as well as sectoral arrangements—may hinder trade rather than promoting it.

Fourthly, existing integration agreements in the region are notable for their diversity, inasmuch as they range from relatively simple agreements involving few formal requirements (superficial integration) all the way to initiatives calling for the formation of an advanced form of economic union (comprehensive integration). This makes it difficult to envision the configuration of a regionwide free trade area in the foreseeable future; instead, it would seem wise to encourage the conclusion of a number of different agreements whose contents would vary according to the relevant parties' degree of similarity and as the circumstances of each country grouping would appear to dictate.

This having been said, a fifth conclusion is that there is a limit to how many agreements there can be, since, under certain circumstances, different agreements could conflict with one another. What is happening at the present time in Central America is an example: no country in that subregion can enter into negotiations on its own regarding tariff concessions with an outside country because this would infringe upon the common Central American tariff. In these cases, the procedure is for the member countries of a given group that have a greater commitment to integration to negotiate agreements with third-party countries on a joint basis. The interests of eventual convergence would also be served, at least in some cases, if integration groups agreed to abide by common rules and procedures.

A sixth observation is that, in situations where the countries engage in a considerable volume of reciprocal trade, have similar production structures and are geographic neighbours, there will be a strong tendency to complement a free trade area or a system of trade preferences with a common tariff in order to ward off distortions in resource allocation and to avoid encouraging contraband trade. In such situations, it is also important to align the countries' macroeconomic policies, since marked differences in exchange rates or regulations, interest rates or taxation levels can produce as much distortion as differences in tariff levels can. This undoubtedly introduces a greater degree of complexity into the administration of integration agreements.

A seventh conclusion is that trade preferences can and should be complemented by other joint measures to resolve shared problems in a wide range of areas, including the development of infrastructure, technological research, marketing, finance and training.

Finally, we can see that Latin America is currently going through a period of innovation in respect of integration-oriented institutional arrangements. It would seem that the Governments prefer to work with existing mechanisms rather than establishing common institutions. Accordingly, some processes are being guided by intergovernmental commissions while others receive support from ad hoc secretariats. There is apparently some resistance to delegating authority to intergovernmental or supranational agencies. Private enterprise has also gained in importance as a leading actor in the integration process, both through investment in neighbouring (or more distant) countries and in its role as a vector of technology.

CHAPTER 36

CONSERVING NATURE, DECREASING DEBT

John Cartwright

University of Western Ontario

Two crises haunt the Third World today: the debt burden and environmental degradation. The debts arising from the borrowing which took place in the 1970s in order to
produce economic growth, and which failed to cover its costs have brought to Third
World countries a legacy of run-down infrastructure and reduced social services, a situation compounded by the insistence of Western lenders that they curtail expenses still
further in order to keep paying. At the same time, and in part because of these pressures, many Third World countries are rapidly running down their stock of natural
resources—forests, fisheries, minerals, and grazing lands—with the result that they
suffer frequent droughts and floods, erosion, landslides, and other "natural" disasters,
and face the loss of a patrimony which could provide their future generations
indefinitely with a comfortable and secure means of living.

While there are no simple or easy solutions to either of these crises, the industrialised countries are beginning to realise that Third World environmental degradation
will adversely affect their own long-term well-being, and that they should therefore be
contributing to Third World environmental protection or restoration out of self-interest. Herein lies an opportunity for the Third World to achieve a measure of debt relief,
while protecting key natural ecosystems and moving towards more environmentally
sustainable modes of economic activity. This article will focus on one widely discussed approach: the reduction of debts owed to Western lenders in exchange for the
conservation of natural ecosystems.

Reprinted from *Third World Quarterly,* 11, 2 (April 1989), pp. 114–27.

THE ECONOMIC CRISIS: WHAT DOES IT INVOLVE?

Few observers really believe that the Third World can repay the debt, of over one trillion dollars, that it owes to Western private lenders, governments and international institutions; certainly the banks, which have quietly written off substantial portions of their overseas loans and sold others at heavy discounts, do not seem to consider repayment to be possible. A combination of the ability of modern technology to create substitutes for most of the Third World's raw materials, the increase in value added through processing, protectionist barriers against Third World manufactures, and high US interest rates aimed to cushion the devaluation of the dollar make it almost inconceivable that heavily indebted Third World countries could pay off their debts on terms anywhere near as stringent as those currently imposed upon them. These factors are clearly beyond the Third World's control, and thus in a morally just world these countries might well be forgiven their debts. However, in our present world it is unlikely that Western bankers and governments will drop all their claims for repayment, no matter how severe the cost to debtor countries in terms of health and educational facilities, communications, environmental protection, and even human lives,[1] although one can argue that the Third World countries were sold a bill of goods in the 1970s by Western bankers anxious to recycle "petrodollars" and by development "experts," who now insist that the Third World pay the price for their bad advice.

At the same time, the exploitation of natural resources is intensified in order to finance interest repayments on the debt. Much of this "resource development" is carried out by foreign-owned businesses, although some of the benefits go to a rather limited number of nationals. Almost always it is a "once-off" activity, whether it be creating a nickel mine in the Dominican Republic or logging a virgin forest in Indonesia, and because to a large extent it is a forced sale, countries are not realising as much gain from liquidating their capital as they might under less urgent circumstances.

NATURAL ECOSYSTEMS IN THE THIRD WORLD: WHAT IS BEING LOST?

The destruction of natural ecosystems through agriculture, urbanisation, and resource extraction has always been a facet of human progress. However, until this century it generally took place against a background of substantial blocks of natural areas which remained intact. What is new in the present situation is that all the areas comprising major ecosystems may be destroyed within the next fifty years, and this would result in costs even higher than those imposed by, for example, dumping toxic wastes into the ground or the oceans.

I use the term "natural ecosystems" here to refer to those ecosystems not significantly altered by human intervention. Such human activity as does occur (such as gathering nuts or fruit, collecting building materials, or hunting game) does not result in substantial changes in the ecosystem. Any ecosystem, of course, is undergoing constant change, but on a biological time-scale measured in centuries or millenia: a plant develops a poison such as caffeine or nicotine to ward off attacks by insect predators, an insect species develops an enzyme which can dispose of this poison and thus allows it to eat the plant. Out of these processes of adaptation come countless substances which we have found beneficial. "Conservation" involves maintaining a sufficient amount of each natural ecosystem so that these processes of evolution can continue undisturbed. Conservation also entails using those parts of the world that we do alter in ways that will allow future generations to continue to use them. In short, conservation is about foreclosing the fewest possible options for future generations.

Among the natural ecosystems being destroyed today through logging, clearing for agriculture, pollution and drainage, tropical moist forests (or "rainforests") are the most significant. These forests contain at least half the species of living organisms on our planet, as well as the greatest quantity of living material, or biomass, per unit of space. Estimates by Norman Myers on the basis of data from the early 1980s suggest that just under 200,000 km^2 a year were being destroyed or grossly disrupted[2]; more recent data suggest that the rate of destruction has increased sharply, with Brazilian Amazonia alone losing 125,000 km^2 in both 1987 and 1988.[3] Even at the slower rate, all the world's remaining eight million km^2 of tropical forest would have disappeared by the year 2035 at the latest, and lowland forests, which are most accessible for logging, would be gone much sooner.

The most obvious costs of this destruction are borne by the people who rely on the forests for their homes and livelihoods; and the world economy loses products such as rubber, Brazil nuts, and rattan. Loss of large blocks of forest means a 50 percent reduction in rainfall around and within them. The montane forests hold soil and water, thus providing year-round water supplies, and protection against landslides and the silting of hydro-electric and irrigation dams. These services are considered to be "free," but there is a substantial economic cost if any of them are taken away. For example, in Honduras the unit cost of providing drinking water for the capital from a protected forest source was calculated at 0.04 the cost of providing water from a deforested watershed.[4]

But the more serious consequences of losing these forests will not arise until well into the future, and are payable by people far removed from the scene of destruction. In order to cope with the diverse predators and pathogens that could destroy them, tropical plants protect themselves by means of an astounding range of genetic adaptations. Substances such as curare, the Amazonian hunters' poison now widely used in surgery as a relaxant, and vincristine, derived from the rosy periwinkle of Madagascar and which has vastly improved the survival chances of children suffering from leukemia, are widely known examples of the pharmaceutical drugs which have already been discovered in this cauldron of life. There are potentially hundreds, if not thousands of such substances in the tropical forests—if we can find them before they are wiped out.[5] Similarly, there is an immense potential range of industrial substances, from petrol substitutes to gums and rubbers to canes and edible oils.[6] With the developments of modern biotechnology, the possibility of incorporating genes that provide resistance to plant diseases (which, of course, are also constantly evolving ways to overcome the plants' resistance) has greatly increased; but the genetic material is needed in order to accomplish these "miracles." This particular cost of the destruction of tropical rainforest will be borne, therefore, by future generations throughout the world in the form of more costly or less diversified foods and industrial materials, as well as illnesses and deaths that might have been prevented. Since the wealthier and more technologically advanced countries of the North would be the first to benefit from this genetic pool, they should be prepared to pay for its survival.

A further cost of tropical deforestation may be a change in global weather patterns and climate, extending to the major food-growing zones of the northern hemisphere. One source of change could be the increased albedo (reflection of the sun's energy from the Earth's surface) as forest is transformed into cropland or pasture; this could lead to a weakening of the tropical heat engine which affects air circulation patterns as far north as the mid-latitudes of Canada and the Soviet Union, and in particular to decreased rainfall in the world's major grain belts.[7] But the albedo effect is minor compared to the potential problems arising from the "greenhouse effect": carbon dioxide and other gases trap increased amounts of the sun's energy in the atmosphere, with the resulting increase in world temperatures probably producing inland droughts and rising sea levels, as well as other unpredictable effects. The replacement of tropical forests by the much lower biomass of farm crops and secondary growth has been estimated to release at least two billion tonnes of carbon (in the form of carbon dioxide) into the atmosphere each year, and while this is less than the five billion tonnes released world-wide each year by the burning of fossil fuels, it still approximately equals the 2.3 billion tonnes net annual increase of atmospheric carbon that has been measured.[8] In other words, bringing a total halt to tropical forest destruction (or halving the consumption of fossil fuels) would be enough to reduce the total output of carbon dioxide to a level that could be absorbed by the earth's "carbon sinks."

There are, in short, strong motivations of self-interest that ought to lead the Western industrial states to support effective conservation measures. Even at that supremely self-satisfied gathering of major Western political leaders, the 1988 economic summit in Toronto, Chancellor Helmut Kohl of Germany proposed that they ought to reward developing countries that protected their forests by forgiving some of their debts,[9] although there was no mention of this proposal in the final communiqué by all the leaders.

But while protection of tropical ecosystems may be of interest to the North, which already has largely devastated its own natural ecosystems, what do Third World countries stand to gain? On the face of it, there would seem to be a great deal of logic in the "conventional wisdom" that these ecosystems contain the main resources they possess, such as timber, hydroelectric power, fertile land for agriculture, and so on, and that they should follow the same path as the already rich nations by exploiting these resources on a once-off basis to build up their wealth, which they could then gradually channel into other more industrial activities.

There are several good reasons why the protection of these ecosystems would be more beneficial to Third World countries than their destruction. First, the noneconomic benefits of conservation are significant to many indigenous peoples, who find sacred or spiritual qualities in their natural surroundings. Although these people generally hold only marginal political power within their states, their desire to conserve these areas will continue to gain more and more support, even if for more aesthetic and recreational reasons, from an increasingly numerous and prosperous urban middle class, as one can already see happening in such newly industrialising countries as Malaysia. Nigel Collar has argued persuasively that to wipe out these ecosystems and the species in them is to curtail the freedom of individuals, by denying them the opportunity to enjoy the existence of such species in the future[10]; and on a more materialistic level, a loss of ecosystems cuts down future options for all human activities, economic as well as social.

Second, while volcanic and floodplain soils are capable of sustaining agriculture for centuries, the majority of tropical soils are not. Most forest clearing in Amazonia and in Africa can provide only a few years of cleared-land farming before the farmers are forced to move on. Sustainable farming in single locations involves getting farmers to adopt often labour-intensive methods, such as the "matengo pit" system of alternating pits to catch water and heaped-up soil in order to grow plants on dry hillsides,[11] or the "chinampas" system of agroforestry in tropical moist forests,[12] whose benefits may not be apparent until there is no new land to clear.

Finally, the economic argument that exploiting one's natural resources to the full will provide the wealth to finance more technological development depends on some rather shaky assumptions. First, it assumes that somewhere there are the raw materials available to support this industrialisation, and in particular, adequate food supplies that a country can import. Second, it assumes either that the country will be able to sell its industrial products on world markets, or else that it has a big enough domestic market to absorb the increasing range of products from its industrialisation. Third, it assumes that the money it can get from its present exploitation of natural resources is in fact sufficient to finance this industrialisation.

The case for conservation, then, involves both the positive arguments that it offers long-term sustainable economic benefits and a range of noneconomic benefits; and a negative one—that the alternative to exploiting one's natural ecosystems on a one-shot basis in order to build up financing for more advanced technological development is a mirage. The struggle to protect natural ecosystems continues to be an uphill battle, which leads to the question: who benefits from their destruction, and in what ways?

THE POLITICS OF CONSERVATION: THE LOCAL ARENA

A clear answer is suggested by examining who benefits from such ecologically destructive "development" activities such as the current logging practices in Southeast Asia and Africa, and the clearing of forest for settlement and ranching projects in Brazil. In logging, while some local people are employed to fell and haul logs, the bulk of the money goes to the timber concessionaires and their overseas backers; and since raw logs are still shipped overseas, much of the final value, added through processing, goes to Japanese and other overseas industries.[13] In Brazil, poor settlers in Amazonia have cleared their patch of land, discovered in two or three years that it would not yield a living, sold to large-scale speculators and moved on to try elsewhere, conveniently taking the pressure for land reform off their regions of origin. In short, the major benefits from development activities tend to go to an already affluent group and to companies from the industrialised states. Some poorer citizens may improve their situation, such as the Javanese resettled as a result of Indonesia's transmigration scheme, but for many settlers the gains are only short-term and the local inhabitants are almost invariably left worse off by the destruction of their homeland.

Many of these activities give the appearance of benefiting the poor and the landless, but it is an illusion.

Even when they are not benefiting in financial terms from the exploitation of natural ecosystems, the privileged sectors of society are generally very much aware that the alternative to allowing the poor to exploit these areas is to permit major land reforms. It is therefore only to be expected that their willingness to support the conservation of these areas will generally be limited. Add to this the fact that they can benefit as *compradors* in the logging, mining, and other exploitative activities undertaken by foreign companies, and one sees a very potent source of opposition to any large-scale conservation effort.[14]

Beyond these economic pressures favouring the quick exploitation of natural resources, Third World political leaders generally share with their counterparts in the North the view that natural ecosystems simply represent "free" resources to be exploited as expeditiously as possible, and that the best measure of well-being for a people is the extent to which it can transform these resources into material goods for consumption without limit. Few leaders yet seem ready to accept the view of the Prime Minister of Norway, Harlem Brundtland, or President Oscar Arias of Costa Rica, that "growth" and "conservation" need not be conflicting goals, but can indeed be complementary ones.[15] Third World leaders, whether popularly based or self-appointed, tend to face less domestic pressure than their Northern counterparts to consider environmental alternatives because their environmental movements generally are relatively weaker; they also are under stronger pressure to achieve economic development because of population growth, demands for land, and desire for more material wealth, in addition to the demands of their creditors.

Unfortunately, those who benefit from the protection of natural areas such as parks or reserves are not necessarily those who lose out under development schemes. I have already noted that one important long-term benefit of conserving Third World natural ecosystems—the preservation of a diversity of genetic resources—will probably be most fully exploited by the more technologically advanced societies. Also, both scientific researchers and tourists visiting reserves and parks are likely to come from the more affluent countries (although we should note that the results of some of this research will trickle down to the local population). Within the country which is setting aside protected areas, the people most likely to visit are the members of the middle class, a pattern already clearly established in India and to a lesser extent in Latin America. The services provided for visitors have generally been organised by large outside operators, although there are a few parks where local people manage the concessions, as in Amboseli Park, Kenya.[16] The local inhabitants, in fact, have all too frequently been pushed aside or ignored when a reserve has been established, with the result that the reserve begins to resemble an armed fortress fending off the outside world.[17] Alternatively, where the central government operates the facilities, collects entrance fees, and generally takes any revenue arising from conservation activities, little monetary benefit comes back to either the park or the local people.

A reserve existing in a sea of local hostility is not likely to survive for long, especially if the central government wishes to gain popularity among the local populace. There is another biological reason for involving the local people in the maintenance of reserves. Few countries can set aside the blocks of 1,000 km^2 that many biologists consider desirable for the long-term survival of an ecosystem as complex as a tropical rainforest.[18] This does not necessarily mean that there will be massive impoverishment of the biota if primary forests are reduced to a series of smaller fragments; a number of studies[19] suggest that a modest primary forest core surrounded by a larger buffer which provides suitable habitat for larger or more sparsely distributed species should probably not lose too many species, provided that the buffer zone is only utilised in relatively low-impact ways (such as controlled hunting and selective logging). Such an arrangement is being tested in Bolivia's Beni World Biosphere Reserve, and also in the Korup Park in Cameroon. This approach of allowing the local human inhabitants to carry out a range of monitored activities within a protected area offers two key benefits: it expands the area in which a natural ecosystem can continue to function, with all that this implies for the maintenance of species and genetic diversity; and it does not threaten the lifestyles of the local inhabitants.

CONSERVATION: THE INTERNATIONAL DIMENSION

Even if a national political leader were willing to confront both his own national business class and powerful foreign corporations by seeking to protect key portions of ecosystems, he would have other problems to overcome. The most pressing problem would be debt relief: how could the money be found to meet the annual interest payments? This is where the debt crisis has temporarily opened a "window of opportunity" for some conservation measures. While such measures can only make a small dent in the total debt problem (even Rubinoff's grand scheme of compensation for a world-wide system of tropical forest reserves involved only some $3 billion a year, less than one-fiftieth of the total annual debt service bill),[20] they do offer a mutually face-saving compromise on the debt issue, while providing a substantial benefit in terms of conservation. Some purists will object that since the debts themselves were illegitimately foisted on the Third World, any action which legitimates them ought to be repudiated (just as hard-liners among the banking fraternity dismiss any action which appears to "forgive" debtors), but it seems to me unrealistic to expect that creditor governments and private institutions will ever accept a total repudiation of these debts, and thus it would be sensible to seek a myriad of modest actions that could be undertaken relatively quickly, and that could contribute to an overall reduction of the debt burden.

Among conservation nongovernmental organisations (NGOs) in the West, "debt-for-conservation" swaps have attracted wide attention. The sale by creditor banks of debts at a discount in the secondary market has allowed Western conservation NGOs to buy up some of the debts, and then arrange to write off the debt in exchange for the debtor country putting some local currency (and effort) into conservation. Three widely publicised agreements were reached in 1987. In Bolivia, the government had created the Beni Biological Reserve of 134,000 hectares in 1982, but lacked the funds to develop and safeguard it effectively. Seeking the resources to make the reserve effective, a US foundation, Conservation International, in 1987 acquired a Bolivian debt of $650,000, discounted to $100,000, from a Swiss bank. Conservation International then cancelled the $650,000 debt, and in exchange the Bolivian government set up a zone of 1.4 million hectares around the reserve and a $250,000 endowment, to be managed by a Bolivian foundation, and asked Conservation International to advise on the management of the reserve for the next five years. Steps are currently under way to draw up a management plan which will involve the local people in the buffer zone around the reserve.[21] In Costa Rica and Ecuador somewhat different arrangements were made with World Wildlife Fund-US and the Nature Conservancy. These NGOs acquired debts at a heavy discount, and cancelled them in return for long-term local currency bonds issued by the governments concerned, in order to finance conservation activities. In each of these cases, the specific scheme arose out of a broad commitment by the national government to protect the area concerned, and the implementation arrangements are under the control of a locally based foundation: this has so far succeeded in deflecting the charge that foreigners are forcing the country to do what they want. Other similar arrangements are under negotiation, aided by a US Internal Revenue Service ruling which allows US banks to claim as a tax deduction the value given by the debtor country in its own currency to the conservation NGO for the debt instrument, even though it had sold the instrument to the NGO for a good deal less.[22]

Limited in scope though they are, these arrangements have enabled governments to protect critical areas to which they might not otherwise have been able to allocate resources. The fact that such areas have been operated through national conservation foundations and have been fitted within the context of overall government conservation objectives has reduced the perception that foreigners are dictating the government's priorities.[23] Unlike debt-for-equity swaps, they do not give ownership of a country's resources to a foreign entity. However, it remains to be seen whether such schemes could be worked in a situation where powerful business interests or other government departments have different goals, such as, for example, Peru's Manu Park or parts of Sumatra or Irian Jaya in Indonesia. It is also cause for concern that so far the emphasis has been on the immediate task of setting aside and protecting specific areas; yet if these areas are to avoid biological isolation and continual encroachment, the people living around them must be provided with access to alternative land, fuelwood, and other resources. This could be achieved through some kind of sustainable agroforestry on lands already altered by human activity, but would be both costly and time-consuming.

Private arrangements between NGOs and Third World countries make only a very small impact on the two problems of ecosystem destruction and debt payments. For example, the Costa Rican scheme involves some $5.4 million of debt, and the country has put a limit of $50 million on all such schemes whereas it owes a total of $4 billion. As far as conservation is concerned, the total need is equally beyond the capabilities of the private NGOs. To protect only 10 percent of the world's tropical forests would involve creating some 800 reserves of 1,000 km^2 each, and even if such blocks could be found, the countries concerned might plausibly argue that selling the timber in one such reserve could earn them $5-10 billion.[24]

The financing for conservation on a scale that will match these potential earnings and thus protect viable portions of the tropical world's natural ecosystems will have to come through schemes either backed by or financed directly by governments. The use of debt swaps here raises a number of much greater difficulties, beginning with the willingness of Western governments to fund such actions (which will require a major lobbying effort by their NGOs). The World Bank and the International Monetary Fund (IMF) say that they are at present precluded by their charters from "forgiving" debts through such arrangements, although lobbying is under way in the USA and elsewhere to change these rules.

From a Third World perspective, the fact that Western governments have the power to exert greater pressure on them than that of Western NGOs means that the danger of their priorities being set by outsiders is increased. To be sure, this is already being done on a far larger scale through the IMF, but this hardly justifies accepting what could easily be seen as yet another form of neocolonialism. Then too, there is the question of whether Western governments would try to pass off debt-for-conservation swaps as an alternative to more fundamental changes in the international economy, or use them to justify curtailing aid programs, in which case there would be no new money coming into the Third World.

Third World NGOs also have further justifiable concerns: whether the government in question would in fact involve local people in any conservation arrangements, and more broadly, who within the country would reap what kind of benefits from the deal; what type of control the government might be able to exercise over the activities of the NGO as part of its monitoring of the arrangements; and whether the government would use this revenue to justify cutting back other funding for conservation programs. There is also considerable concern that massive plans worked out by Western and Third World governments acting in concert are likely to be aimed at further exploitation of natural areas rather than at their protection. The major example of such a scheme, the Tropical Forest Action Plan (backed by the World Bank) is sufficiently ambiguous in its goals to have led the NGOs concerned to believe that it will simply commercialise forests in ways that reduce poor peoples' access to them, and turn primary forests into plantations.[25]

Finally, for both governments and NGOs there is the moral question underlying any attempt at long-term conservation while short-run needs remain unfulfilled. As one Latin American conservationist explained: "The banks are asking us to put aside land for the future, while people are dying of hunger and ill health." The only answer to this, he suggested, was to ensure that conservation was carried out in ways that did provide benefits for people, and to make clear to people the nature of these benefits.[26]

Despite these cautions, Third World countries concerned about their long-term self-interest would do well to examine such arrangements with institutions from the North, both private NGOs and also government agencies. The value of biological reserves—particularly tropical rainforests—can only increase as our need for, and our ability to use, genetic materials grows. There is a sharpening awareness, among the public and even among politicians in the West, of the importance of these genetic reservoirs as well as of the potential climatic impact resulting from the destruction of tropical forests. Such awareness gives Third World states an opportunity to obtain wealth from these areas without necessarily cutting them down and selling them to the industrialised states. Provided that they also bargain for the financing to establish alternative ways of living on the land for their people, Third World states *can* have their forests and live off them too, for a price a good deal lower than they will have to pay once they have exhausted them by present methods of exploitation.

It can be objected that debt swaps of any sort tacitly grant the legitimacy of the Third World's debts, and therefore should be totally shunned. I suggested above that such a view is unrealistic, and in any case, even if there were some eventual possibility of achieving a full repudiation of these debts, the threat to natural ecosystems is severe enough that action needs to be taken even at the cost of principles. (I could draw a parallel here to the readiness of African front-line states to buy food from South Africa when faced with famine.)

Many people in both the North and the South now recognise that the contribution of tropical ecosystems to the welfare of mankind is so great that everyone ought to contribute to their survival. With sufficient prodding from their own NGOs, Third World governments can press for financial support, in order to help them to protect major ecosystems from further damage; and they can certainly expect support in this demand from Northern NGOs. Since most states can be moved to act when their own well-being is threatened, the present situation provides a promising opportunity for Third World governments to seek an improvement on both their environmental and economic front.

NOTES

1 Even such an apolitical body as UNICEF has charged that the deaths of at least 500,000 children in 1988 could be attributed to the cuts in health care forced by countries' struggles to pay their foreign debt charges. *Globe and Mail* (Toronto), December 21, 1988.

2 N. Myers, "Tropical Deforestation and a Mega-extinction Spasm," in M. Soulé, ed., *Conservation Biology: The Science of Scarcity and Diversity* (Sunderland, Mass.: Sinauer Associates, 1986), p. 399. See also N. Guppy, "Tropical Deforestation: A Global View," *Foreign Affairs,* 2, 4 (Spring 1984): 929.

3 *Guardian Weekly* (London) October 30, 1988.

4 C. Queseda Mateo, "La Tigra National Park: A Source of Concern," *IUCN Bulletin,* 18, 10–12 (October-December 1987): 14.

5 See N. Myers, *The Primary Source: Tropical Forests and Our Future* (New York: W. W. Norton, 1985), pp. 210–23.

6 Ibid. pp. 226–59.

7 For differing views in this debate, see C. Sagan et al., "Anthropogenic Albedo Changes and the Earth's Climate," *Science,* 206 (1979): 1363–68, and G. L. Potter et al., "Albedo Change by Man: Test of Climatic Effects," *Nature,* 291, (7, May 1981): 47–49.

8 G. M. Woodwell, "The Carbon Dioxide Question," *Scientific American,* 238, 1 (January 1978): 37.

9 *Globe and Mail* (Toronto) June 20, 1988.

10 N. J. Collar, "Species Are a Measure of Man's Freedom: Reflections after Writing a Red Data Book on African Birds," *Oryx,* 20 (1986): 18.

11 R. Dumont and M. F. Mottin, *Stranglehold on Africa* (London: André Deutsch, 1983), p. 151.

12 J. D. Nations and D. I. Komer, "Central America's Tropical Rainforests: Positive Steps for Survival," *Ambio,* 12, 5 (1983): 232–38.

13 Data in a detailed study of Malaysia's industry indicate that more than three-quarters of the sawlogs are exported unprocessed. See R. Kumar, *The Forest Resources of*

Malaysia, (Singapore: Oxford University Press, 1986), pp. 91, 100. He also notes that while it contributes more than 5 percent of GDP, the forest industry employs less than 3 percent of the labour force, and most of that is in saw-milling and other processing activities (pp. 9, 154).

14 The conflicts in Brazil between Indians, rubber tappers, and others who depend upon or live in the Amazonian forest, and the large ranchers who wish to clear it, are a case in point. See, for example, *International Wildlife,* (July–August 1988): 24–28. In fairness, we should note that a few large companies, such as the Brazilian mining company CVRD and the Sabah Foundation in Malaysia, have done excellent conservation work—but they are exceptional.

15 For Gro Brundtland's views, see H. Brundtland, *Our Common Future* (New York: Oxford University Press, 1987) (hereafter *Brundtland Report*).

16 D. Western, "Amboseli National Park: Enlisting Landowners to Conserve Migratory Wildlife," *Ambio,* 11 (1982): 302–308.

17 For examples from Africa, see D. Turton, "The Mursi and National Park Development," and R. H. V. Bell, "Conservation with a Human Face: Conflict and Reconciliation in African Land Use Planning," both in D. Anderson & R. Grove, eds., *Conservation in Africa* (Cambridge: Cambridge University Press, 1987); also S. Oldfield, ed., *Buffer Zone Management in Tropical Moist Forests: Case Studies and Guidelines* (Gland, Switzerland: IUCN Tropical Forest Programme, 1988), p. 16.

18 I. Rubinoff, "A Strategy for Preserving Tropical Rainforests," *Ambio,* 12, 5 (1983): 255–58.

19 For example, A. D. Johns, "Selective Logging and Wildlife Conservation in Tropical Rainforest: Problems and Recommendations," *Biological Conservation,* 31 (1985): 355–75.

20 I. Rubinoff, "A Strategy for Preserving Tropical Rainforests," 257–58.

21 For details of this and other debt swaps, see B. Bramble, "How Debt Can Be Swapped for Trees," Washington D.C.: US National Wildlife Federation, unpublished paper, May 1988; and for a more general examination, see her "The Debt Crisis: The Opportunities," *Ecologist,* 17, 4–5 (1987): 192–99.

22 US Internal Revenue Service, *Advance Ruling* 87–124, November 12, 1987.

23 Various Latin American delegates at the International Union for the Conservation of Nature General Assembly in Costa Rica, February 1988, told me that there was surprisingly little objection in their countries to the debt-for-nature swap approach; a few intellectuals thought Latin Americans should be undertaking these measures themselves without outside help, but there was little objection to the idea of conserving these areas.

24 For example, the Danum Valley reserve of the Sabah Foundation contains an estimated $750 million worth of timber in its 9,300 hectares, or about $8 million per km^2, a figure in line with other Asian dipterocarp forests. African primary forests would be worth about the same, while Amazonian ones would be worth somewhat less.

25 The TFAP is described in *Tropical Forests: A Call for Action,* 3 volumes, Washington, D.C.: World Resources Institute, 1985. For critiques, see especially V. Shiva, "Forestry Myths and the World Bank: A Critical Review of *Tropical Forests: A Call for Action,*" *Ecologist,* 17, 4–5 (July–November 1987): 142–49; M. Renner, "A Critical Review of *Tropical Forests: A Call for Action,*" ibid. p. 150; and various letters in ibid. 18, 1 (1988): 35–40.

26 Eric Cardich Briceño of Peru, at IUCN General Assembly, San José, Costa Rica, February 3, 1988.

CHAPTER 37

THE GRAMEEN BANK: ITS INSTITUTIONAL LESSONS FOR RURAL FINANCING

Norman MacIsaac and Abu N. M. Wahid

Tennessee State University

INTRODUCTION

Formal financial institutions have long neglected the functionally landless poor.[1] About 50 percent of the Bangladeshi population who own less than one-half acre of cultivatable land are functionally landless. The rural poor have been bypassed due to their lack of collateral, under the pretext that they are high-risk clients. It is assumed that, given their extreme poverty, the landless would use this credit injudiciously for short-term consumption and be unable to repay their debts.

Formal credit, though used extensively as an instrument of agricultural development, has largely excluded the landless rural peasants who need it so badly; they comprise the majority of the rural population and are the most disenfranchised of people of Bangladesh. This neglect of the rural landless in Bangladesh is consequential in light of the growing number of landless in this country, and the inability of agriculture to absorb these landless peasants into the labor force. In 1951 the landless numbered eight million; then, years later, there were fifteen million; and in 1993 they are over fifty million. This mass of landless peasants has been growing so rapidly that, even if agricultural growth were to meet the government's most optimistic targets, employment in this sector would still be insufficient to meet the employment needs of the rural landless.[2] In fact, it is estimated that 75 percent of the rural population cannot find full employment in agriculture.[3] It is therefore abundantly clear that rural nonfarm employment must be created if Bangladesh is to absorb its youthful and growing population into the labor force.[4] With a clear understanding of this

Reprinted with permission from Abu Wahid, ed. *The Grameen Bank: Poverty Relief in Bangladesh.* Boulder, Colo: Westview Press, 1993: pp. 181–207.

proposition, Grameen Bank began its operation in Bangladesh as a formal financial institution on October 2, 1983.

This chapter is directed to highlight the special characteristics of the Grameen Bank and its institutional lessons for rural financing. The next section gives a vivid description of the Grameen Bank, its innovative approach and operations. The third section describes the institution-building process of the Grameen Bank. The last section of this chapter focuses on the lessons of the Grameen Bank experiences for theory and practice of rural financing.

SPECIAL CHARACTERISTICS OF THE GRAMEEN BANK

The Grameen Bank took a fundamentally new approach to the problem of lack of access to credit for the poor. Unlike previous efforts to improve access, the Grameen Bank was founded on the rejection of traditional assumptions about banking. Muhammad Yunus, the founder of the Grameen Bank, recognized the failure of earlier efforts to reform the banking system and initiated the Grameen Bank Project as a totally new institution in response to hitherto unmet needs. In 1978 he wrote:

> What the situation calls for is not more of the same, but creating a completely new type of bank suited to the rural environment. Although under the pressure of circumstances many new things have been granted onto the main body, these granted-on features have not modified the basic character of the banking operation.[5]

Yunus claimed that banking was an "institution for the rich designed to make the rich richer, and to keep the poor out."[6] Institutionalized banking in Bangladesh practiced systematic discrimination on the basis of gender, social status, and illiteracy.

In a talk addressed to a Toronto audience in 1988, Yunus described the Grameen Bank model as an attempt to take traditional banking, which was "standing on its head," and turn it right side up. The result was the Grameen Bank model, designed to meet the needs of the rural landless poor. Some of the basic traits of this model are listed below.

Targeting the Landless

The Grameen Bank targets the functionally landless poor, a group it defines as those rural dwellers who own no more than one-half acre of land or assets valued not more than one acre of land. By targeting homogeneous groups of poor rural landless peasants, the bank can rely on a degree of solidarity between borrowers that would not be possible between disadvantaged and landowning individuals. This is especially important in the context of the power structure of rural Bangladesh.

Group Lending

The bank uses the group lending approach to reduce the risk of nonpayment. Although loans are disbursed on an individual basis, the group is very important in that it provides both collective support and peer pressure.

Unlike collateral-based lending operations, the bank does not base loan eligibility primarily on the banker's assessment of the financial feasibility of projects proposed for funding by the bank. Rather, the group itself acts as a mechanism for the determination of creditworthiness. Because all members of the group must maintain a good credit rating to remain eligible for new loans, group members watch over and support each other in their economic endeavor. They share an interest in ensuring that other group members invest in feasible and productive undertakings.

Income-Generating Activities

Borrowers contract loans for activities with which they are already familiar such as paddy husking, cattle fattening, milch cow raising, shopkeeping, traditional cottage industries, rickshaw pulling, bicycle repair, trading or other activities. These activities seldom require special training, and they generate a regular income for the borrower. The Grameen Bank extends loans to members involved in literally hundreds of different income-generating activities.

Small Regular Payments

The Grameen Bank lends funds ranging from $100 to $300, averaging about $80 per person, repayable within one year. Borrowers, whom the bank refers to as members, pay back the principal, in addition to interest and other charges, on a weekly basis.[7] The regularity and smallness of payments reduces the burden of the debt for the loan recipient and allows the bank assistant to spot repayment problems early. Because the bank members use loan funds to generate regular income, weekly loan payments are derived from the additional earnings.

Commercial Interest Rates

The Grameen Bank lends funds at 16% per annum, and since January 1992, at a rate of 20% per annum. While this is equal to or greater than rates charged by the national commercial banks, it is far more affordable than rates charged by the moneylenders.

Savings, Group and Emergency Funds

The weekly installment by each member includes the payment on the principal, 16 percent interest, plus three other components which constitute the group's savings and insurance fund.

First, each borrower must contribute to an Emergency Fund or emergency insurance plan. According to the mode of operation up until January 1992, each loan recipient would pay an additional sum of money equal to 25% of the interest charged, or four percent of the principal. This amount would go to the Emergency Fund, from which members could withdraw up to 50% of their contribution, or Tk 2,500, whichever is less, with the approval of the group and the bank, in case of death, default or disability.

According to changes in effect as of January 1992, the Emergency Fund will function as an insurance policy administered by the bank. Under the new arrangement, the borrower will pay an "insurance" charge which varies according to the size of the loan (For instance, Tk 5 for Tk 2000 loan; Tk 10 for Tk 3000 loan; Tk 15 for Tk 4000 loan, etc.). The bank will offer the same services as before, but will manage the fund as an insurance policy rather than a group fund for emergency purposes.

Second, a sum equal to 5 percent of the principal goes into the Group Fund. In addition, every member must contribute 1 taka every week to this fund. The Group Fund is a collective savings account and receives an annual rate of interest of 8.5 percent. The group members may decide, on a consensual basis, if and when they wish to extract money from this fund. Money from the Group Fund is usually lent out to group members interest free. This fund allows individuals access to money in times of sickness or social ceremony without need to revert to the informal credit market.

Contact with the Poor

Direct and continual contact with the poor is one of the keys to the bank assistants' understanding of, and compassion for, the poor. The motto is "Take the bank to the borrowers, not the borrowers to the bank." Weekly visits permit the bank workers to maintain regular contact with the villagers to monitor their progress and obtain feedback on the success or shortcomings of their ventures. Even more significantly, because no transactions take place in an office, the bank meets the poor on their own turf, thereby reducing feelings of "contractual inferiority."[8] The close contact with borrowers increases the bank assistants' ability to determine the creditworthiness and needs of the client population.

Openness of Bank Transactions

Contrary to traditional banking, which is based on the privacy of financial information concerning the borrower, at the Grameen Bank all discussion and transactions take place in the presence of other members. This encourages openness and honesty, and helps discourage exaggerations and misinformation. Each group member shares an interest in ensuring the success of the group, and thus has a stake in making sure others will be able to repay their loans.

Decentralization

The Grameen Bank project began operating in different districts early in its development. This exposed the project, at the earliest stages, to a variety of regional conditions and constraints. Decentralization enabled the project to develop in response to a wider variety of problems and to discern which of these were applicable nationwide and which could be traced to largely regional circumstances. The early geographic dispersion also created an atmosphere of "healthy competition" between branches, and developed an early foundation of competent independent managers.[9]

Staff Training

The quality of bank staff has been one of the keys to the bank's success. Bank assistants must go through a six-month training course before they are posted. This course includes five months of field work and three weeks of in-class study during which the trainees examine subjects varying from record-keeping to group dynamics.

After only two days of lectures at the Training Institute in Dhaka, the bank sends the trainees to the villages where the real learning takes place. During the first two months, each trainee must write detailed case studies of two borrowers, one male and one female. There are two rules to follow when doing the case studies. First, the trainee must record the description of the loan recipient's situation exactly as described by the bank member. Thus the trainee must refrain from all interpretation of the peasant's version, regardless of the bank trainee's personal judgment of the facts. Secondly, the trainee must meet with the borrower to do the case study at the convenience of the borrower himself/herself. This exercise teaches trainees about rural life, poverty, and how the poor perceive the bank. It also teaches them to listen.

Minimalist Approach

In contrast to the "integrated" approach, which offers a complete package of inputs and activities including training, market support and other services, the Grameen Bank concentrates initially on credit alone.

Judith Tendler's study of the Ford Foundation LEIG (Livelihood, Employment, Income Generation) program concluded that the most successful programs were "minimalistic," that is, they concentrated either on a specific trade or subsector, or on the delivery of one single input such as credit.

According to Tendler, the minimalist approach succeeds because of the following reasons: first, specific narrowly-focused programs are easier to manage and evaluate. They run less risk of spreading scarce resources such as managerial and technical capabilities too thinly. By contrast, integrated approaches inevitably carry higher unit costs of lending and demand greater organizational sophistication.

Second, because of the higher costs and encumbrances, integrated programs seldom succeed in reaching large numbers of small borrowers. Programs which limit their own scope of activities are easier to replicate than integrated approaches which consist of a "package" tailored to a specific situation. Tendler found that those programs which concentrate on supplying one "missing component" had the highest rate of "success."

Muhammad Yunus has referred to the Grameen Bank approach as "anti-training." According to him, the Grameen Bank differs fundamentally from other microenterprises support programs which offer training and credit simultaneously. The Grameen Bank, by contrast, believes that borrowers already possess relevant skills to use credit productively without formal training, and thus concentrates first on credit to finance activities with which borrowers are already familiar.

Nevertheless, using the term "minimalist" to describe the Grameen Bank approach may be misleading. The Grameen Bank is not "minimalist" in the sense that it focuses exclusively on credit. Over the years, Grameen Bank has developed a number of other credit and noncredit activities to meet client needs not directly related to group lending activities.

Studies, Innovation, Development and Experimentation (SIDE)

This is a division of the Grameen Bank which undertakes studies, identifies, and supports technological innovations. It disseminates these new technologies to borrowers and runs developmental and experimental projects testing new larger-scale technologies in various sectors of the economy. By 1989, loans for SIDE initiatives accounted for Tk 265.15 million, or 8 percent of total disbursement that year. Most SIDE initiatives in 1989 were for "experimental projects" owned and operated by the bank itself.

Housing Loans Program

This program is designed to extend low-interest loans for the purchase of durable, flood-resistant housing for the poor. Housing loans accounted for 11 percent of loan disbursements in 1988 and 1989.[10]

The Sixteen Decisions

The Grameen Bank adopted the Sixteen Decisions list in a national workshop in March 1984. The Sixteen Decisions is a broad program covered by economics, social, political, and sanitation experts of rural life. The Grameen Bank members are required to abide by these Sixteen Decisions as a de facto constitution.[11] The outstanding characteristic of the bank is not that it focuses on one single element, but rather that it began with credit and gradually increased the number of services offered as the bank grew. The Grameen Bank approach is thus characterized by an institution-building process which begins with credit and gradually adds on other client services.

Adaptation to Local Power Structure

Grameen Bank microlending activities have been successful in averting major confrontation with the elite because the borrowers' microactivities do not pose a fundamental and consistent threat to the vested interests of the rural power structure. This is not to say that the Grameen Bank has not met with resistance. While certain groups, such as pump mill owners or traders, have benefitted economically as a result of the bank's intervention, other groups have been affected negatively. For example, rural power elite like some Union Parishad leaders, and well-off farmers affected by the rise in agricultural wages, have often expressed their displeasure with the impact of Grameen Bank activities.

However, the rural rich have little interest in undermining the bank's activities as long as there is nothing to gain from the subversion itself.

. . . the richest and the most influential section of the rural rich in Bangladesh (which has extensive links with the urban rich) . . . does not appear to have much interest in destroying Grameen Bank's efforts.[12]

That is, rural elite have not sought to systematically subvert Grameen Bank microlending activities because it is not in their interest to do so,[13] at least as long as Grameen Bank members confine themselves to relatively small-scale, low-technology activities. The bank's experiment in "collective enterprise," however, demonstrates how larger-scale economic activities using more productive technologies are confronted with much greater interference by rural elite.

Special Services

In addition to the above-mentioned characteristics, the Grameen Bank started some special services for its members. They include the following:

1 A *Special Savings Account* was begun by some centers to finance the construction of a center house where members hold meetings and set up a school center. The construction of center schools began in 1980, and by 1986 there were over 2000 schools in operation.

2 The *Children's Welfare Fund* is a fund used by borrowers to contribute to the education of their children. The fund covers operational expenses such as books, supplies, and the teacher's salary.

3 A *Seed Distribution Program* is designed to encourage borrowers to cultivate vegetables around their homestead for consumption or sale. Through this program, hundreds of thousands of bank members purchase seeds through their bank assistant and grow their own vegetables.

THE INSTITUTION-BUILDING PROCESS

The Current Programs

While the Grameen Bank Model itself has received considerable attention, it is important to underline that this structure was not just "well designed." Rather, this design is the product of a particular process of institutional development.

The Grameen Bank is not the result of makeshift reforms, but rather of an incessant process of institution-building in response to the demands of the political, social and economic environment of rural Bangladesh. Indeed, the institutional innovations that make the Grameen Bank unique are not necessarily, in themselves, impressive. As Jayanta Kumar Ray writes: "These innovations . . . have no breathtaking novelty. Rather they are obvious remedies to obvious deficiencies.[14]

The innovations within the bank are the result of a structure and an attitude conducive to innovation in response to the perceived structure in Bangladesh, which has showed resistance to "practices they perceive as not being consonant with good banking principles,[15] the Grameen Bank has succeeded in creating a structure conducive to innovation.

The Grameen Bank began, not as a design "made in Washington," but as an informal research project. The project began so modestly that it was only a year or two after it began that the label "action-research project" was adopted. The project began, not with an elaborate logical framework analysis, but with a list of some 42 landless persons living in the vicinity who needed a small amount of credit to bypass traders who were usurping the fruits of their labor.

Despite the small scale of the project, however, its director took no shortcuts around the existing bureaucracy. Rather than lending from his own money, Muhammad Yunus undertook a negotiating process with the bank. After initially being laughed out of the bank manager's office, it took Yunus some six months to obtain 10 loans, totaling less than $200.

Unlike so many projects that are designed as experiments under special conditions, the Grameen Bank Project developed facing the true constraints of the socioeconomic, financial and political environment. In the process, it had to deal with conditions of massive poverty, the rural power structure, cultural values and resistance from the banking institution.

> Many action research projects which are designed to develop and test new techniques and institutions are conducted under a variety of "special project" conditions. . . . In a sense they are social laboratories and, like science laboratories and experiment stations, they develop "solutions" which are successful under specific and often non-replicable conditions.[16]

The Grameen Bank evolved as it did because it grew in reaction to, rather than in spite of, prevailing conditions in rural Bangladesh. For example, the bank developed its staff training program as a response to the failure of the Bangladeshi education system to impart to students an understanding of the reality of rural poverty in Bangladesh. To fill the gap left by the formal education system, the training process teaches recruits to view poverty from the village perspective.

Unlike so many experimental projects which seek to "test" new ideas, the Grameen Bank began without external inputs such as foreign expertise, technology, or formal sponsorship from the Bangladeshi government. The Grameen Bank Project led a daily struggle at the grassroots level, dealing with the banks, government and rural elite to gain acceptance and develop a program in tune with the prevailing environment of rural Bangladesh.

The Future Scenario

The Grameen Bank has expanded rapidly yet steadily since it began as an experimental project fifteen years ago (see Figure 37-1). In the latest phase of expansion, Phase III, the bank is expected to grow at a rate of 125 branches per year from 1989 to 1992. By the end of Phase III, the Grameen Bank will have one million clients, 200,000 groups, and 37,642 centers. It will be operating in an estimated 80 percent of the districts of Bangladesh. Phase IV (1992–95) will bring the total number of Grameen Bank members to 1.5 million. This expansion of bank activities will lead to several major organizational challenges in the 1990s.

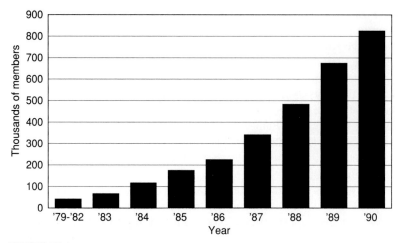

FIGURE 37-1
GRAMEEN BANK: INCREASE IN MEMBERSHIP 1979–90.
*Data for 1990 is estimated. Sources: *Grameen Bank Annual Reports* from 1987 to
1989 (Dhaka: Grameen Bank, 1988, 1989, 1990); prior to 1987, data from M. Yunus,
"Grameen Bank: Operation and Organization" in *Microenterprises in Developing
Countries,* edited by Jacob Levitsky (London: Intermediate Technology Publications,
1989).

MAINTAINING PERFORMANCE
IN A GROWING BUREAUCRACY

Numerous studies are critical of the bank's ability to maintain the efficacy of its operations despite rapid expansion. Dharam Gahi, for example, wrote that " . . . it is only
to be expected that with the passage of time and expansion in size of the project, there
might well be a decline in the enthusiasm and dedication of staff and some deterioration in the overall quality of the project, especially with respect to its nearly perfect
record in loan repayment.[17] Pradumna Rana writes that, if the Grameen Bank expands
to cover a large area, "the results may fall short of those achieved so far with close
supervision."[18]

As a single financial institution in an undisciplined and corrupt financial environment, some question the extent to which the bank can continue to function as an
exception to the rule. According to Braverman and Guasch, it is not at all unusual for
collateral-free credit programs to sustain high repayment rates in the short run. However, high repayment rates are seldom sustained in the long run.[19] According to Harry
W. Blair, although a rural development program may succeed in preventing elite from
perverting the program in the short term and as long as the scale of operations remains
small, "on a larger scale and over the longer run, unfortunately, it appears impossible
to prevent the perversion of rural development programs by local elite.[20]

The Grameen Bank has hitherto been able to resist "perversion" despite expansion
by developing a number of institutional mechanisms. For example, to avoid nepotism,
male workers never work in their home area, and all bank assistants are rotated so they

serve a different set of ten villages every year. Moreover, to accommodate this increasingly large and decentralized institution, an "early warning system" has been developed. The bank's Management Information System is designed to analyze data and identify "danger signals" such as rapid increase or fall in the number of loans, or a decline in loan recovery in a given branch or area. As the bank continues to grow, it is increasingly dependent on such mechanisms to maintain performance.

Financial Sustainability and Dependence on Donor Funding

A 1988 study by Mahabub Hossain[21] found that operating costs rose considerably in the 1980s. The study concluded that the Grameen Bank is incapable of covering the cost of lending without outside support.

The Grameen Bank is presently dependent on subsidized funding to ensure its financial survival. In 1987 the cost of administration and refinancing for loan activities was Tk 114.8 million. Yet the bank generated only Tk 65.1 million in income from loan operations.

While the bank claims to be "making a profit," it does so only by borrowing from international agencies at concessional rates of interest,[22] in excess of the financial needs of its clients. By reinvesting these funds, it obtains handsome rates of interest. The bank calls revenues generated in this manner "other operations." These revenues have increased steadily since 1983 and now account for a significant portion of the bank's income. Profits received from "other operations" have made it possible for the bank to show overall profit, but in fact the bank is not yet a viable profitable institution on its own because the bank's operating expenses are relatively larger than its operating income.

While a large portion of these high operating costs are due to expansion, Hossain's study found that even "mature" branches were not able to recover the cost of lending. In branches which had been operating for two years, the average cost of operation was still too high to make the bank's lending activities self-sustaining.

However, Muhammad Yunus argues that Hossain's analysis fails to consider the age structure of the branches. First, the Grameen Bank director claims that Hossain overestimated costs: Yunus claims that branches do not reach a minimum level after two years (as Hossain assumed in his study). Rather, it takes three or more years for lending costs to reach a minimum.

Second, Muhammad Yunus claims that, in June of 1990, 152 of the bank's 700 or so branches were operating at a cost of 6 percent or less of the total loan amount. He thus remains confident that financial sustainability is attainable once expansion has stopped.

Furthermore, the Bank has recently changed its interest rate charges to increase financial sustainability. Under the changes introduced in January 1992, the interest rate increased to 20% on regular loans and 8% for housing loans. In addition, the Emergency Fund contribution of 25% of the interest charge will be replaced with a small surcharge. For instance, under the previous system, the borrower would normally contribute over Tk 80 to the Emergency Fund for a Tk 4000 loan. As of January 1992, the borrower will pay a surcharge (Tk 15) for that same loan. For this fee, the Bank will guarantee similar services to those offered under the Emergency Fund arrangement.

These changes not only increase the Bank's financial sustainability, they do so without imposing important increases in the cost of borrowing. The 4% increase in interest rate charges is offset by eliminating the mandatory 4% contribution to the Emergency Fund. The new surcharge on Emergency Fund services, on the other hand, amounts to an increase in borrowing costs of less than one percent. In short, this is an interesting change because it increases the bank's financial sustainability, while imposing only a very small change in costs incurred by the borrower. Bank officials assure this new system will not change the services available to the borrower.

Notwithstanding, in addition to its effort to ensure financial sustainability, the bank must also maintain the incentive for loan repayment. In fact, the two goals go hand in hand. If average loan size does not increase at a rate equal to or greater than inflation rate, then administrative costs will rise as a percentage of the total loan fund. Moreover, if the average loan size is not growing, and if recipients are not continually improving their living conditions and embarking upon new activities, then incentive to repay loans may weaken and repayment rates may fall. Consequently, the financial sustainability question is closely tied to responding to the needs of a "mature" bank clientele.

Responding to the Needs of a "Mature" Clientele

The bank members must be prepared for the technological challenges of the 1990s. Not only must Grameen Bank members move into more productive areas to continue increasing their income, they must also be prepared to compete with technological improvements in sectors in which they are presently involved.

> The reason for caution emanates from the fact that in the foreseeable future, the situation may not persist in the face of increasing competition from substitutes produced in the modern sector, unless measures are taken to improve the techniques of production and quality of goods.[23]

To deal with these constraints, the SIDE initiative will play an increasingly important role in the Grameen Bank in the 1990s.

The bank has yet to demonstrate its ability to cost-efficiently integrate borrowers into larger-scale activities using more advanced technology. While "experimental projects" like Joysagar Fish Farm, Chokoria Shrimp Farm, and Deep Tube Well projects have reportedly made good progress, the failure of "collective enterprises" is not encouraging. Donors have expressed concern that the Grameen Bank's involvement in "experimental projects" will divert energy, time and resources away from the relatively successful microlending operations. In response to these concerns, the bank maintains financing for microlending and experimentation separate.

Adjusting to Slowing Expansion

Ever since it began, the Grameen Bank has expanded at an astounding rate. This has created many new posts and has allowed plenty of room for advancement and promotion. With the massive expansion for the period 1989–92, the prospects for promotion and increased involvement in the bank never cease to increase. But what will happen when the boom is over? These bank assistants and bank managers are highly educated. The former have at least secondary school education and the latter are required to hold a postgraduate degree. Bank assistants work long hours in a rural setting.

> A new recruit may be initially shocked to find that weekly holidays—for half of the day on Thursday, and the full day on Friday—do not mean much in practice. [. . .] A new entrant to the Grameen Bank may ruefully discover that it is not enough to work for at least twelve hours a day.[24]

In sum, states Ray, the Grameen Bank puts bank assistants through "staggering tests of diligence and patience—unthinkable in a normal state agency."[25] Given the demands placed on the Grameen Bank assistants, it is only natural to question their continued willingness to endure such harsh working conditions if opportunities for advancement are reduced. As Atiur Rahman pointed out in a study prepared for the Canadian International Development Agency, "Already tensions are building up among the lower tiers of bank workers."[26]

LESSONS FOR RURAL FINANCIAL THEORY AND REPLICATION

The Grameen Bank has thus far extended hundreds of thousands of loans to the rural poor at the same rate of interest as the nationalized commercial banks and succeeded in attaining a repayment rate of over 98 percent, compared to about 30 to 40 percent for agricultural loans in Bangladesh.[27] Given the present emphasis on interest rate reform in rural financial markets, the Grameen Bank's performance is significant because this bank is the product of institutional innovation, not interest rate policy.

Despite the impact of the Grameen Bank on the accessibility of credit for the poor, the Rural Financial Market (RFM) approach, centered on interest rate reform rather than institutional elements, is now recognized as the dominant analytical approach in the study of rural credit. This perspective on rural financial markets, which has influenced agencies including the World Bank and USAID, focuses on interest rates as the "Most important element in improving rural financial market performance."[28]

The RFM school of thought emphasizes the need to establish interest rates which reflect the scarcity of capital. Cheap credit, it is argued, creates distortions, and thus undermines rural development. Subsidization creates excess demand for credit, which leads to credit rationing. This skews credit allocation in favor of rural elite and investment in technology appropriate to large-scale farms, and too often for nonproductive purposes. In addition, low interest rates impact negatively upon the ability of financial institutions to generate savings deposits. In short, low interest rates frustrate the mobilization of domestic resources for technological advancement and distort the allocation of scarce financial resources.

The case of the Grameen Bank stands in support of the view that, while the RFM model is a useful tool for the analysis of rural financial markets, it explains only one set of variables constraining the accessibility of credit for the poor. Interest rate reforms may be necessary to ensure institutional financial viability and to improve the allocation of scarce resources towards productive investment. However, these reforms are insufficient to improve the access of the poor to formal credit at reasonable prices. As the Grameen Bank demonstrates, building financial institutions which can increase access for the poor requires more than simple adjustments in interest rates.

The Grameen Bank provides support to the call by Braverman and Guasch for more study of institutions and institutional environments as key elements in understanding financial markets and their role in the development process. To date, economists have largely overlooked institutional factors:

> Following the decline in attention to the "institutional school," modern economics literature has largely overlooked the analysis of institutions, institutional change, and reform mechanisms in general, treating them as exogenous elements seldom analyzed with any rigor.[29]

The Grameen Bank should serve as an example of the importance of institutional development in increasing the accessibility of credit for the poor.

NOTES

1 Malcolm Lyall Darling, *The Punjab Peasant in Prosperity and Debt,* Oxford, 1925.

2 World Bank, *Bangladesh: Promoting Higher Growth and Human Development* (Washington, DC: World Bank, 1987), p. 147.

3 Syed Sadeque, "The Rural Financial Market and Grameen Bank Project in Bangladesh: An Experiment in Involving Rural Poor Women in Institutional Credit Operations," *Savings and Development* 2 (1986): 181–195.

4 See R. Islam (ed.), *Strategies for Alleviating Poverty in Rural Asia* (Geneva: ILO, 1985), p. 119; see also: Joseph F. Stepanek, *Bangladesh: Equitable Growth?* (New York: Pergamon Press, 1979), p. 41.

5 M. Yunus (1978), *On Reaching the Poor,* Grameen Trust, Dhaka.

6 M. Yunus, Lecture hosted by the Calmeadow Charitable Foundation in Toronto (June, 1988).

7 In cases where weekly payments are not possible (seasonal activities, for example), the bank may accept token weekly payments during the period of low cash flow.

8 Social barriers constitute formidable, if not insurmountable, obstacles between the banks and the poor. When dealing with the traditional banking system, the poor fall victims to what A. Whitehead has described as "contractual inferiority": "illiterate, ill-clad [peasants] must plead their case with status-conscious officials." (A. Whitehead, "Effects of technological change on rural women: a review of analysis and concepts," in *Technology and Rural Women,* London: Intermediate Technology Publications, 1985). Contractual discrimination is an especially stringent constraint for poor rural women. First, a larger proportion of women tend to be illiterate. Second, Bangladeshi women are confined by "guardianship" (according to which, throughout her life, a Bengali woman is subordinate to her male guardian, commencing with her father, then her husband, then her son). In traditional banks, a woman may not apply for credit in the absence of her guardian.

9 Dr. Yunus describes the importance of geographical dispersion in the bank's expansion: "Grameen Bank: Organization and Operation," in *Microenterprises in Developing Countries,* ed. Jacob Levitsky (London: Intermediate Technology Publications, 1989.)

10 For further details on the Housing Loans Program, see Chapter 6.

11 For details, see Chapter 2.

12 J. K. Ray, *To Chase a Miracle* (Dhaka: University Press Ltd., 1987), p. 228.

13 In *To Chase a Miracle* (Dhaka: University Press, 1987), J. K. Ray writes, " . . . the ruling circle (including the rural rich) does not have much interest in destroying the Grameen Bank even though it may feel uncomfortable about the Grameen Bank's activities and try to obstruct some of these activities in some areas for some short periods." (p. 231)

14 J. K. Ray, op. cit., p. 221.

15 J. A. McGregor, "Credit and the Rural Poor: the Changing Policy Environment in Bangladesh," *Administration and Development,* Vol. 8, No. 4 (October–November 1988): 469.

16 S. Biggs, "Awkward but Common Themes in Agricultural Policy," in *Room for Manoeuvre: An Exploration of Public Policy in Agriculture and Rural Development,* eds. E. J. Clay and B. B. Schaffer (London: Heinemann Educational Books, 1984), p. 67.

17 D. Ghai, *An Evaluation of the Impact of Grameen Bank Project* (Rome: IFAD, 1984), p. 58.

18 Pradumna B. Rana, *Improving Resource Allocation Through Financial Development,* Bangladesh (Manila: ADB, 1986), p. 36.

19 Avishay Braverman and J. Luis Guasch, "Rural Credit Markets and Institutions in Developing Countries; Lessons for Policy Analysis from Practice and Modern Theory," *World Development,* Vol. 14, No. 10/11 (1986): 1256.

20 H. W. Blair, "Rural Development, Class Structure and Bureaucracy in Bangladesh," *World Development,* Vol. 6, No. 1 (January 1978), p. 75.

21 Mahabub Hossain (1988), *Credit for Alleviation of Rural Poverty: the Grameen Bank in Bangladesh,* International Food Policy Research Institute, Washington, DC, and Bangladesh Institute of Development Studies, Dhaka.

22 Although the Bangladesh Bank charges 8.5 percent on funds, the interest rates charged by IFAD and other donors are much lower. The Grameen Bank has managed to lower the cost of funds by increasing its borrowing from external donors, while decreasing the amount of funding obtained from the Bangladesh Bank. This change in sources of funding, in favor of concessional foreign loans and grants, led to a decrease in the average cost of funds from 5.8 percent in 1985 to 3.0 percent in 1987.

23 A. Rahman & S. Hossain, *Impact of Grameen Bank Operations on the Level, Composition and Distribution of Income and Expenditure of the Rural Poor* (Dhaka: BIDS, 1986), p. 53.

24 J. K. Ray, op. cit., p. 223.

25 Ibid., p. 223.

26 For details, see chapter 12.

27 Recovery rates of the Bangladesh Agricultural Bank have ranged from a high of 41 percent to a low of 14 percent between 1985 and 1989 (Source: *"Bangladesh Recent Economic Developments,"* (Washington, DC: IMF, 1989), p. 30.

28 Adams *et al, Undermining Rural Development with Cheap Credit* (Boulder: Westview Press, 1984), p. 6.

29 Braverman and Guasch, "Rural Credit Markets and Institutions in Developing Countries: Lessons for Policy Analysis from Practice and Modern Theory," *World Development* 10/11 (1986): 1263.

CHAPTER 38

HUMAN DEVELOPMENT: THE CASE FOR RENEWED EMPHASIS

Keith Griffin and John Knight

University of California at Riverside and Oxford University Institute
of Economics and Statistics

The process of economic development can be seen as a process of expanding the capabilities of people.[1] The ultimate focus of economic development is human development. That is, we are ultimately concerned with what people are capable of doing or being. Can they live long? Can they be well nourished? Can they escape avoidable illness? Can they obtain dignity and self-respect? Are they able to read and write and communicate and develop their minds?

According to this view, development is concerned with much more than expanding the supplies of commodities.[2] The enhancement of capabilities often requires changing technologies, institutions, and social values so that the creativity within human beings can be unblocked. This, in turn, results in economic growth, but growth of gross domestic product (GDP) is not the same thing as an expansion of capabilities. The two are, of course, linked but they are not identical.

Economic growth can be seen as a means to the end of enhancing people's capabilities. Yet, economists traditionally have concentrated on the production of goods and services and on its rate of growth. Increased physical output, in turn, has been assumed to give rise to greater economic welfare.

More recently, it is true, greater emphasis has been placed on the distribution of goods among people and on considerations of need and equity. The philosopher John Rawls defined deprivation in terms of the availability of "primary goods" or "things it is supposed a rational man wants whatever else he wants,"[3] and the International Labour Organisation attempted to translate the concept into operational terms with its

Reprinted from *Journal of Development Planning,* 19 (1989), pp. 9–40.

advocacy of "basic needs."[4] Basic needs, however, remains a goods-oriented view of development, whereas what is wanted is a view that puts people first.

This is the great merit of the human capabilities approach, pioneered by Amartya Sen.[5] The connection between goods and capabilities can readily be illustrated. A bicycle, for instance, is a good; by providing transport, it gives a person the capability of moving from one place to another. It is the concept of capabilities that comes closest to our notion of the standard of living and, more generally, to our notion of development. Goods may provide the basis for a high standard of living, but they are not in themselves constituents of it. A person's standard of living has some components that his money cannot buy. An illiterate person in poor health would not enjoy the same capabilities, and thus the same standard of living, as an otherwise identical person, not only because he would be likely to have a lower income but also because literacy and health directly affect capabilities.

Although there is some relationship between income per capita and human well-being, as the term is commonly understood, the statistical association is not close and divergences from the general tendency are at least as striking as the general tendency itself.[6] Human fulfilment is about whether people live or die, whether people eat well, are malnourished or starve, whether women lead healthy and tolerable lives or are burdened with annual childbearing, a high risk of maternal mortality, the certainty of lifelong drudgery, whether people can control their lives at work, whether their conditions of work are tough and unpleasant, whether people have access to work at all, whether people control their political lives, whether they have the education to be full members of society with some control over their destiny. These are all aspects of the standard of living—but only loosely included or not included at all in the measure of GNP per capita.

Any approach that puts people first must come to terms with the fact that in the Third World the average age of the population is low, although it is tending to rise slowly. In 1980 in the developing countries as a whole, 39.1 percent of the population were less than 15 years of age as compared to 23.1 percent in the developed countries. Conversely, only 4.0 percent of the population of the Third World is over 65 years, whereas in the developed countries 11.3 percent of the population is older than 65.[7] Thus, human development in the Third World is necessarily concerned in large part with enhancing the capabilities of the young.

It is natural to inquire whether economic growth during the past two decades has been accompanied by increased human capabilities. Certainly there has been growth: in no group of countries did per capita income fail to rise during the period 1965–1985 (see Table 38-1). Some groups of countries did much better than others, however. The developing countries as a whole grew faster than the industrial market economies (3.0 percent a year compared to 2.4 percent a year). But within the Third World there was a tendency for the poorest countries to fall relatively further behind the less poor. Thus, GNP per capita in the middle-income economies increased 3.0 percent a year, whereas in India the rate of growth of income per capita was 1.7 percent and in the "other low-income countries" only 0.4 percent. China, where GNP per capita increased 4.8 percent a year, was the great exception. Among the middle-income countries, East Asia

TABLE 38-1
GROWTH OF GNP PER CAPITA,
1965–1985
(Annual Percentage)

Low-income economies	2.9
China	4.8
India	1.7
Other low-income	0.4
Middle-income economies	3.0
Lower middle-income	2.6
Upper middle-income	3.3
High-income oil exporters	2.7
Industrial market economies	2.4

Source: World Bank, *World Development Report 1987* (Oxford, Oxford University Press, 1987).

did much better than Latin America. As shown below, human capabilities increased relatively most rapidly in both China and East Asia.

The general rise in average incomes could be a misleading guide to the income gains of the poor. In some countries, including large ones, the incidence of poverty remains high. This often is due in part to a high and even rising degree of inequality in the distribution of income. A large number of cross-sectional studies of countries have been undertaken and these have been used to provide support for the hypothesis of growing inequality.[8] Moreover, a number of studies of individual countries, based on time-series data, have shown that inequality was increased along with a rise in average incomes. Indeed, some authors have attempted to show that not only has inequality increased but that in some countries for quite long periods the absolute standard of living of some sections of the poor has declined.[9] It cannot be assumed, therefore, that the basic human capabilities have risen to the same extent as average incomes.

The debate today is not over whether inequality within countries has increased but whether increased inequality is inevitable. The balance of recent evidence suggests that the degree of inequality is not closely related to the level of income per capita, as was once thought, but to factors dependent upon the strategy of development that is followed. These factors include the distribution of productive assets (particularly land), the distribution of educational opportunities, the employment intensity of the development path, and the general policy stance of government. It is possible, therefore, for governments successfully to pursue distributive equity objectives as well as growth objectives. Similarly, governments have it within their power to promote the enhancement of human capabilities by means of their education, health, nutrition, participation, and other policies. Moreover, the twin objectives of distributive equity and human development will often involve the same policies.

Taking a long view, there is no doubt that the basic human capabilities have indeed increased in the third world. Perhaps the best indicator of this is the increase in life expectancy at birth since around 1950. In the poorest countries, life expectancy at mid-century was between 30 and 40 years; today it is at least 50 years in most countries and rises to 70 or more for females in such countries as China, Malaysia, Sri Lanka, Chile, and Argentina.

The data on infant mortality tell a similar story to that of life expectancy. There has been a long-run decline everywhere and in some countries the decline has been dramatic, with the rate falling by 50 percent or more. This is true in Latin America for Argentina, Chile, and Colombia and in Asia for China, Malaysia, the Philippines, and Sri Lanka. However, infant mortality rates remain very high, that is, above 100 per 1,000 infants less than one year old, in Bangladesh, Pakistan, the United Republic of Tanzania, and Côte d'Ivoire. As with life expectancy, there is only a weak correspondence between infant mortality rates and per capita incomes.

Data on life expectancy and infant mortality for the period 1965 to 1985 are included in Table 38-2. Figures 38-1 and 38-2 show similar movements since 1955, but by region, in life expectancy, and infant mortality, respectively. The long-run improvements in both indexes are apparent for all regions. However, as with income, averages may overstate somewhat the gains to the poor whose access to health services is marginal in many countries. There is considerable evidence that health delivery systems (oriented toward hospital-based, high-technology, specialized services) provide limited population coverage and contribute to an unequal distribution of health services.

TABLE 38-2
LIFE EXPECTANCY, INFANT MORTALITY, AND GNP PER CAPITA

	Life expectancy at birth (years)				Infant mortality (deaths per 1,000 aged under one year)		GNP per capita (US dollars)
	Male		Female				
	1965	1985	1965	1985	1965	1985	1985
Low-income countries	47	60	50	61	127	72	270
India	46	57	44	56	151	89	270
China	54	68	55	70	90	35	310
Other low-income	44	51	45	53	150	112	200
Middle-income countries	53	60	56	64	104	68	1 290
Lower middle-income	47	56	50	60	132	82	820
Upper middle-income	58	64	62	69	84	52	1 850
High-income oil exporters	48	61	51	65	115	61	9 800
Industrial market economies	68	73	74	79	23	9	11 810

Source: World Bank, *World Development Report 1987* (Oxford, Oxford University Press, 1987).

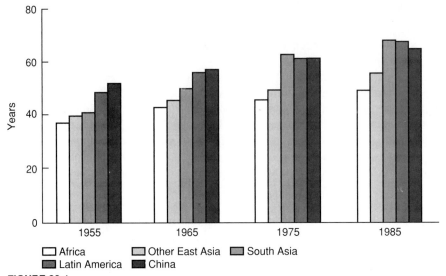

FIGURE 38-1
LIFE EXPECTANCY.

FIGURE 38-2
INFANT MORTALITY (DEATHS PER 1,000 LIVE BIRTHS).
Source: United Nations Secretariat.

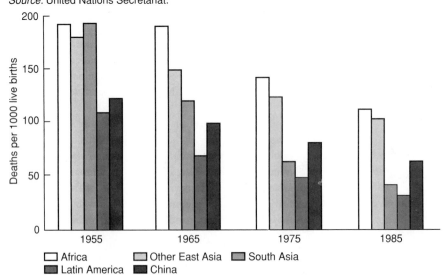

Turning now to primary education, it is evident that this is one of the great success stories of the Third World, at least in quantitative terms (see Table 38-3). It is less certain that there have been improvements in the quality of education. School enrollments have expanded rapidly in the past 20 years and in most countries primary education for boys is universal or nearly so. The position of girls is less good, but even so, in over half the countries more than 90 percent of girls attend primary school, although they are less likely than boys to complete their primary education. Less favourable treatment in educating young girls continues to be a problem, especially in Pakistan (where twice as many boys as girls attend school) but also in India, Bangladesh, Egypt, and Côte d'Ivoire. Although illiteracy rates still are more than 52 percent in Africa and South Asia, one can anticipate that they will continue to fall as the proportion of the population with a primary school education rises. None the less, the absolute number of illiterate persons will probably increase for years to come.

Secondary education has also grown rapidly, although often from a small base (see Table 38-3). Still, between one-third and two-thirds of the relevant age group attends a secondary school in most Third World countries, including the two largest, India and China. The third largest—Indonesia—has expanded its secondary school system rapidly and has overtaken the two Asian giants. Serious shortcomings remain in Pakistan and Bangladesh (where expansion of the system has been slow) and in sub-Saharan Africa (where, apart from the United Republic of Tanzania, expansion has been fast). Given the difficulties encountered in Asia and Africa at the time of independence, progress in secondary education has been remarkable.

Thus, the indicators suggest that there has been a long-term increase in human capabilities in the Third World. The growth not only in output but also in capabilities reflects the application by society of cumulative collective knowledge. Never before

TABLE 38-3
PRIMARY AND SECONDARY SCHOOL ENROLLMENT RATIOS
(Percentage of Age Group)

	Primary		Secondary	
	1965	1984	1965	1984
Low-income countries	74	97	21	32
India	74	90	27	34
China	89	118	24	37
Other low-income	44	70	9	23
Middle-income countries	85	104	22	47
Lower middle-income	75	103	16	40
Upper middle-income	96	105	29	56
High-income oil exporters	43	75	10	45
Industrial market economies	107	102	63	90

Source: World Bank, *World Development Report 1987* (Oxford, Oxford University Press, 1987).

has the stock of knowledge in the world increased so rapidly or been so widely disseminated as it has in the past 40 or 50 years. Nonetheless, world-wide access to science and technology is unequal. The diversity of the world's languages is a source of enrichment and cultural plurality and within many countries language is a unifying force. But within some countries linguistic heterogeneity is a source of disunity and conflict and between countries language can act as a barrier restricting access of hundreds of millions of people to world knowledge. Yet, the barriers are slowly being overcome, not least because language teaching has greatly increased the number of people who can speak more than one language.

Nationally and internationally there have been dramatic changes in the ways information and culture are transmitted. There was a time in human history when most education occurred within the family. Gradually, however, the transmission of knowledge became institutionalized, first within the church and other religious organizations and later within state schools and, to a lesser extent, private schools. More recently, superimposed on these inherited means of spreading knowledge, information, and cultural values, the mass media have become increasingly prominent. Both deliberately and unintentionally, in both formal and informal ways, the mass media now exercise an enormous influence over what people know, how people interpret and understand the world, and what values people adopt and act upon.

HUMAN DEVELOPMENT IN THE CURRENT ECONOMIC CONTEXT

We have seen that, viewed in long-term perspective, there has been remarkable progress in human development in the Third World. Recent short-term developments, however, have been unfavourable and in some countries a full-scale crisis has emerged. The most obvious sign of crisis is the dramatic slowing down in the rate of growth of per capita GDP between the last half of the 1970s and the present. The deceleration of growth occurred in all regions of the Third World (excluding China), and in every region, except South Asia and East Asia, average incomes fell markedly (see Table 38-4).

Parallel to the decline in growth rates has been a fall in the rate of growth of the productivity of labour. The phenomenon is widespread throughout Asia, Africa, and

TABLE 38-4
RATE OF GROWTH OF GDP PER CAPITA, 1976–1987
(Annual Percentage)

	1976–1980	1981–1985	1986	1987
Africa	1.9	−3.5	−4.9	−2.6
Latin America	2.8	−1.8	1.6	0.4
Western Asia	0.8	−3.9	−0.3	−3.9
South Asia and East Asia	4.1	2.9	3.2	2.7

Source: Department of International Economic and Social Affairs, United Nations Secretariat.

Latin America and, indeed, in Africa and Latin America, the average level of productivity declined, not just the rate of growth of productivity. During the period 1980–1985, the average productivity of labour declined 1.5 percent a year in Africa and 2.7 percent a year in Latin America.[10] This reflects the fact that in Africa and Latin America total output increased less rapidly than the size of the labour force, and in Latin America total output actually declined. A reduction in value added per employed worker is, of course, desirable in a period of recession in so far as it allows large numbers of people to continue to secure a livelihood rather than become openly unemployed. On the other hand, a fall in output per person-year inevitably puts downward pressure on the real wages and incomes of those who remain in employment and on the level of profits (and hence on investment and long-term growth of output and employment).

In practice, rates of urban unemployment in the major cities of Latin America tended to rise (see Table 38-5) and nonagricultural real wages in Africa and parts of Latin America tended to fall (see Table 38-6). In Latin America and the Caribbean the rate of open urban unemployment rose from 6.8 percent in 1970, to 7.1 percent in 1980, to an estimated 10.3 percent in 1986. In some countries, of course, unemployment rates were considerably higher than this, for example, in Colombia, Chile, Peru, and Venezuela.

In Chile, real industrial wages in 1986 were 7.9 percent lower than they had been in 1980. In Mexico, the fall was 33.9 percent and in Peru, 34.5 percent. The situation in parts of Africa was equally as bad. In Kenya, for example, real nonagricultural wages in 1985 were 22 percent lower than they had been in 1980, whereas in the United Republic of Tanzania in 1983 the fall was 40 percent.

Slow growth, declining productivity, rising unemployment, and falling real wages and average incomes have resulted in increased poverty and an acceleration in the number of hungry people in the world. According to the World Food Council, between 1970 and 1980, hunger grew by 15 million people, or an average of 1.5 million people a year. The first half of the 1980s added almost 40 million hungry people, or close to 8

TABLE 38-5
OPEN URBAN UNEMPLOYMENT, 1970–1986
(Percentage)

	1970	1980	1986
Argentina	4.9	2.9	5.2
Brazil	6.5	6.2	3.6
Chile	4.1	11.7	13.1
Colombia	10.6	9.7	13.8
Mexico	7.0	4.5	4.8
Peru	8.3	10.9	11.8
Venezuela	7.8	6.6	11.8

Source: International Labour Organisation, *Overview of the Employment Situation in the World* (Geneva, November 1987), table 9, p. 39.

TABLE 38-6
REAL WAGES IN NONAGRICULTURAL ACTIVITIES
(Index: 1980 = 100)

	Year	Index
Africa		
Kenya	1985	78
Malawi	1984	76
United Republic of Tanzania	1983	60
Zambia	1984	67
Zimbabwe	1984	89
Latin America[a]		
Argentina	1986	103.5
Brazil	1986	112.8
Chile	1986	91.9
Colombia	1986	116.5
Mexico	1986	66.1
Peru	1986	65.5
Venezuela	1985	104.6

[a]The data refer to wages in industry.
Source: International Labour Organisation, *Background Document,* High-level Meeting on Employment and Structural Adjustment, Geneva, November 1987, tables 9 and 10, pp. 28 and 32.

million per year—a fivefold increase in the average annual growth rate.[11] The absolute number of undernourished people increased in every region of the Third World, but only in Africa did the proportion of undernourished people rise, namely, from 29 percent in 1979–1981 to 32 percent in 1983–1985.[12] Changes in nutrition deficiency during the period 1971 to 1985, using data and standards from the Food and Agriculture Organization of the United Nations (FAO), are presented in Figure 38-3.

Problems of environmental, ecological, and political deterioration exacerbate the long-term economic problem in some parts of the Third World. In the Sahel, the Himalayas, and the Andes, economic progress is hampered by desertification or erosion, partly the result of climatic change and partly of population pressure. In other areas, deforestation is upsetting the ecological balance, to the detriment of poor people. In many developing countries, war and political instability exacerbate the poverty problem by withdrawing confidence in the currency, diverting scarce resources, destroying assets, disrupting assistance programmes and sapping incentives and motivation at family and community levels.

The world economy has evidently undergone a profound change in recent years. This change was not planned and in fact has been highly disorderly. World financial markets expanded rapidly for several years and then collapsed in October 1987; remedial measures have brought with them the threat of economic recession; exchange rates have been unstable and have moved in unpredictable ways. These changes have had disruptive consequences for economic progress and have inflicted severe damage on the real economies of many Third World countries.

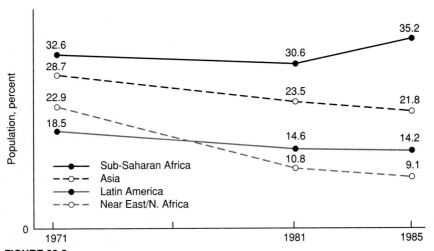

FIGURE 38-3
NUTRITION DEFICIENCY (CALORIE INTAKE BELOW 1.2 BMR THRESHOLD).
Source: Food and Agriculture Organization of the United Nations.

It is important to recognize that the current economic crisis is policy induced. It is not an arbitrary act of nature but a consequence of changes in economic philosophy and in government policies. The policies introduced during the past decade reflect both a revised view of the proper role of the State and changed governmental preferences as between inflation and a higher level of economic activity.

The debt crisis is yet another manifestation of massive world economic imbalances. By 1985 a number of Third World countries were deeply in debt to the international banking system and multilateral financial institutions. In absolute terms the largest Third World debtors were Brazil ($106.7 billion), Mexico ($97.4 billion), Argentina ($48.4 billion), the Republic of Korea ($48 billion), and Indonesia ($35.8 billion).[13] In per capita terms, however, a great many other countries have very large external borrowings and have been having enormous difficulties servicing their debts (see Table 38-7). In Mali, Senegal, Zambia, Bolivia, Côte d'Ivoire, and Chile, the per capita external debt is greater than the per capita income and in a number of other countries per capita external debt is more than half as large as per capita GNP. Already, several countries have had to suspend payments of interest on the debt and postpone repayment of capital.

The banks find themselves in the position of having to make greater provision in their balance sheets for bad debts, while extending additional loans to the Third World so that at least some of the interest can be repaid. The time may come when both creditors and debtors recognize that an orderly program of debt forgiveness would be to everyone's advantage. Meanwhile, the developing countries have become net suppliers of resources to the rich countries. In 1980 the capital-importing developing countries received a net transfer from the rest of the world of $39.4 billion, but by 1985 resources were flowing in the opposite direction and these developing countries transferred $31 billion to the rich countries.[14]

TABLE 38-7

PER CAPITA INCOME AND PER CAPITA EXTERNAL INDEBTEDNESS IN 25 COUNTRIES, 1985

(US Dollars)

	Per capita GNP	Per capita external debt
Ethiopia	110	44.2
Bangladesh	150	64.9
Mali	150	195.9
Niger	250	180.5
India	270	46.3
Kenya	290	206.8
United Republic of Tanzania	290	162.6
Senegal	370	271.8
Pakistan	380	132.0
Zambia	390	669.1
Bolivia	470	620.6
Indonesia	530	220.5
Philippines	580	478.7
Egypt	610	501.9
Côte d'Ivoire	660	836.2
Zimbabwe	680	255.1
Nigeria	800	184.0
Peru	1 010	735.9
Colombia	1 320	494.5
Chile	1 430	1,671.2
Brazil	1 640	787.1
Mexico	2 080	1,236.4
Argentina	2 130	1,588.3
Republic of Korea	2 150	1,854.3

Source: World Bank, World Development Report 1987 (Oxford, Oxford University Press, 1987).

Many governments have been forced by an outflow of resources to cut investment, reduce public expenditure, and impose a deflationary contraction on the economy. At the same time, in order to service at least part of the debt, attempts have been made to shift resources in favour of the export sectors. This process is described as structural adjustment. It also reflects the need for long-term development strategies that do not assume substantial resource inflows in the future.

Structural adjustment has forced governments to reveal their expenditure priorities and, unfortunately, many governments have shown that, in practice, human development receives very low priority. Indeed, in many countries, central government outlays on the social sectors have decreased relative to total government expenditure and in real per capita terms. Education and health have been particularly hard hit. In contrast, the proportion of central government expenditures on general public administration has risen between 1972 and 1985 from 36 to 39 percent in the low-income countries, from 24 to 36 percent in the lower middle-income countries, and from 18 to 32 percent in the upper middle-income countries. Some data for selected countries are presented in Table 38-8.

TABLE 38-8
CENTRAL GOVERNMENT EXPENDITURE ON EDUCATION AND HEALTH AS PERCENTAGE OF TOTAL GOVERNMENT EXPENDITURE

	Education		Health		Public administration	
	1972	1985	1972	1985	1972	1985
Low-income countries, e.g.:	13.2	7.6	4.9	3.7	36.2	39.1
Burkina Faso	20.6	16.9	8.2	5.5	37.6	37.9
Malawi	15.8	12.3	5.5	7.9	36.7	36.4
Zaire	15.2	0.8	2.3	1.8	56.1	86.2
Kenya	21.9	19.8	7.9	6.7	30.2	35.3
United Republic of Tanzania	17.3	7.2	7.2	4.9	22.6	48.6
Sri Lanka	13.0	6.4	6.4	3.6	37.7	66.2
Lower middle-income countries, e.g.:	16.4	13.8	5.2	3.8	24.0	36.1
Bolivia	31.3	12.2	6.2	1.5	31.2	70.2
Indonesia	7.4	11.3	1.4	2.5	41.2	33.9
Turkey	18.1	10.0	3.2	1.8	18.3	54.1
Tunisia	30.5	14.3	7.4	6.5	25.1	25.7
Chile	20.0	13.2	10.0	6.1	20.0	18.4
Upper middle-income countries, e.g.:	12.3	10.6	7.9	4.6	18.3	32.3
Brazil	8.3	3.2	6.7	7.6	18.3	38.0
Mexico	16.4	12.4	5.1	1.5	15.2	44.4
Argentina	20.0	9.5	0.0	1.8	20.0	21.3
Venezuela	18.6	17.7	11.7	7.6	24.8	31.1

Note: Public administration covers expenditure on the general administration of government not included in other categories of economic and social services. Especially in large countries, where lower levels of government have considerable autonomy and are responsible for many social services, central government expenditure on education and health may account for only a small fraction of the total.
Source: World Bank, *World Development Report 1987* (Oxford, Oxford University Press, 1987).

In each of the three groups of countries included in Table 38-8, central government expenditure on education and health in 1985 was proportionately lower than it was in 1972. In the low-income countries, for example, education accounted for 13.2 percent of central government expenditure in 1972 but only 7.6 percent in 1985; health accounted for 4.9 percent in 1972 but only 3.7 percent in 1985. Expenditure on defence, in contrast, actually rose, from 17.2 percent of government expenditure in 1972 to 18.6 percent in 1985. That is, in the latter year, expenditure on the military in the poorest countries of the world was nearly 65 percent higher than spending on education and health combined.

In the low-income countries the share of education in central government expenditure fell 42.4 percent between 1972 and 1985, whereas the share of health fell 20.4 percent. The pattern of cuts was reversed in the middle-income countries: in the lower middle-income countries the share of education declined 15.9 percent compared to a cut of 26.9 percent in health expenditure, and in the upper middle-income countries there were cuts in shares of 13.8 percent and 41.8 percent in education and health, respectively.

The share of education fell in six of the seven low-income countries selected for the table. Indeed, in Zaire, government expenditure on education virtually ceased. The situation regarding health expenditure was as bad or, considering the initial conditions, even worse. In most Third World countries, government expenditure on health services was low even in 1972. By 1985 the share of health in total public expenditure had fallen in each of the groups of countries and in almost all the countries listed.

Overall, then, the picture is not encouraging. There seems to be a clear bias within the political system towards a reduction of public expenditure on human development in times of distress. This possibly reflects underlying changes in currents of thought about the appropriate role of government, as mentioned earlier. This change in economic philosophy appears to have originated in the advanced industrial economies, particularly in the United States of America, the Federal Republic of Germany, and the United Kingdom of Great Britain and Northern Ireland, and to have spread from there to many developing countries. However, in addition to the change in currents of thought, the reduction in expenditure on human development appears to have been a short-run and, as we shall see, a short-sighted response to the series of crises in which governments found themselves. Given the need for structural adjustment, many governments considered it was easier or more expedient to reduce expenditure on human development than on other items in the central government's budget.

The situation, however, is not altogether bleak. Indeed, there has been continued improvement in countries that have been able to maintain economic growth and avoid the worst impact of the 1980s recession. The above average performance of the South Asian and East Asian countries of 2.7 percent GDP growth per capita per year during the period 1981–1985 was accompanied by continuing progress, and even some acceleration, in health and nutritional trends. Sectoral policies emphasizing the need for accelerating agricultural production in formerly food-importing countries and for expanding low-cost, wide-coverage programs in health, nutrition, and water supply have been important contributory factors.

Moreover, several countries in Africa, other parts of Asia, and Latin America have been able to sustain expenditure on human development even while implementing structural adjustment programs. For instance, targeted programs in the area of child health and nutrition throughout the 1970s and early 1980s enabled Chile to achieve a continuous decline in infant and child mortality despite serious economic fluctuations; an example of a successful sectoral program during adjustment was the drought relief program in Botswana, backed up by a comprehensive system of monitoring nutritional status.[15] Indonesia is one of the countries that managed to expand expenditure on education and health as a proportion of total government expenditure, from 8.8 percent in 1972 to 13.8 percent in 1985 (see Table 38-8).

There are policy choices to be made; there are a number of alternative responses open to governments. Even in times of economic crisis and reduced public resources, governments can make the following choices:

1 A reduction in the quantity of services provided, for example, by curtailing the volume of food distributed through public channels such as food-for-work programs or government-owned ration shops;

2 A deterioration in the quality of services provided, for example, by allowing teacher-pupil ratios to fall sharply or, because of foreign exchange shortages, by reducing expenditure on school textbooks;

3 Reducing inefficiency within the public services, for example, by eliminating the wasteful use of construction materials or by inviting suppliers to tender bids;

4 An improvement in targeting to favour the poor, for example, by switching health expenditure from large urban hospitals to rural clinics or by reallocating educational expenditure from university to primary education;

5 Greater cost recovery of publicly provided services, for example, by introducing tuition fees for university studies (combined with scholarships for the poor) or by charging for certain types of medical care.

In our view, the objectives of policy during periods of structural adjustment should be to safeguard human development programs whenever possible and, if curtailment of public expenditure is unavoidable, to ensure that the burdens of adjustment are borne by those most able to do so. In many Third World countries the opposite has occurred: human development programs have been savagely cut and the brunt of the adjustment has fallen on the poor. This has weakened long-run prospects for development, while increasing inequality and poverty. It would instead have been much better to restructure human development programs, to reduce inefficiency, to improve targeting and, where necessary, to maintain the existing level of services, to introduce discriminatory user charges. The case for this approach will be made at greater length below.

DEVELOPMENT OF HUMAN CAPABILITIES: SCOPE AND DEFINITIONS

The development of human capabilities should be seen not as an objective with a definitive end-point but as a process continuing in time without end. It is an approach to overall development that puts the well-being of people first and that regards human beings simultaneously as both means and ends of social and economic policy. It is not, of course, a formula that can be applied mechanically, but it does contain ingredients that distinguish it from commodity-centred approaches to development. It places considerable emphasis on local resource mobilization as a way of allowing people to develop their capabilities and on participation as an agent of constructive change.

In many Third World countries, government is highly centralized and authoritarian. The people often are relegated to the status of subjects and come to fear and distrust government. Particularly in rural areas, and above all among the poor, government officials are seen more as coercive than as persuasive agents. Thus, the relationship between the State and the majority of the people is not conducive to the mobilization of large numbers of people for development. At the very least, a strategy that gives priority to the development of human capabilities requires decentralized administration to the local level and administration at that level by officials who enjoy the confidence and support of the great majority of the population.

Beyond this is the need to organize the population so that it can participate in its own development. Participation, or the opportunity to participate if one wishes, is, of course, an end in itself, but participation also has a number of instrumental values that make it attractive to a process of human development. First, participation in representative community-based organizations can help to identify local priorities, to determine which needs are essential or basic and which are of secondary importance, and to define the content of development programs and projects so that they reflect accurately local needs, aspirations, and demands. Next, having identified priorities and designed the programs that incorporate them, participation in functional organizations (service cooperatives, land reform committees, irrigation societies, women's groups) can be used to mobilize support for national and local policies and programs and local projects. Lastly, participation can be used to reduce the cost of public services and investment projects by shifting responsibility from central and local government (where costs tend to be relatively high) to the grass-roots organizations (where costs tend to be low). In some cases, for example, it may be possible to organize the beneficiaries of an investment project and persuade them to contribute their labour voluntarily to help defray construction costs. In other cases some of the public services (clinics, nursery schools) can be organized, staffed, and run by local groups rather than by relatively highly paid civil servants brought in from outside. Thus, in an appropriate context, participation can flourish and in so doing contribute much to development.

The instrumental value of participation and human development is not limited to the economic sphere; they also are of value in other spheres of life. There is, for example, a political dimension to human development. If formal democracy is not to be an empty shell, then people must have an education and information so that all groups in society are aware of the issues facing the country and can participate effectively in the political process.

Human development is of intrinsic value too. In some respects the development of human capabilities is increasingly regarded as a right to which all people are entitled. This right, in many societies, includes the ability to read and write, access to basic health care, and freedom from starvation. In addition, certain aspects of human development are akin to consumption goods in the sense that they are sources of satisfaction or pleasure. Education is desired in part for its own sake; employment, too, provides direct satisfaction by giving a person the recognition of being engaged in something worth his while[16]; and a clean and healthy environment can be a source of aesthetic pleasure.

We are particularly concerned, however, with the ability of human development expenditure to increase the productive capacity of an economy and raise the level of material prosperity. There are several ways it can do this.[17] First, human development expenditure can raise the physical, mental, and cognitive skills of the population through education and training. Secondly, public policy that focuses on human development can assist in the efficient deployment and full utilization of knowledge and skills; it can increase entrepreneurial and managerial capabilities, and it can transform theoretical knowledge into applied technology through research and development programs. Thirdly, public policy can establish an institutional framework that enhances incentives, removes impediments to resource mobility and resource mobilization, and increases participation in decision-making, which, in turn, can help to improve economic efficiency.[18]

Many programs could be classified as human development programs, but in the discussion below we shall restrict consideration to three broad categories: education and training; health services, water supply and sanitation; and food security and nutrition policies. It must be stressed, however, that although these programs can be listed separately there are in fact a great many complementarities among them.

For example, a program of school meals, intended to improve the nutrition of young people, often leads to reduced school drop-out rates and hence to an increase in the quality of the education system. Similarly, reduced infant mortality rates combined with greater education for women and greater nonfarm employment opportunities for women are associated with lower fertility rates and a lower rate of increase of the population.[19] Women, indeed, play a key role in human development not only because they account for half or more of the total population but also because they have a major responsibility in most societies for ensuring adequate nutrition for the family, caring for the sick, and educating the young before they enter the formal education system. In addition, recent research has shown that the weight at birth and the subsequent development of young children are affected by the state of health of the mother during pregnancy. Hence, there is complementarity between the health of the mother and that of the child.

In most developing countries women have substantially less access to education, to jobs, to income, and to power than men. Women's levels of health and nutrition are often inferior to men's. Women generally account for the largest proportion of deprived people. The improvement of human capabilities requires in particular that the capabilities of women be improved. In some countries attitudes and customs will have to change; governments can play a role in this process, for example, through programs directed at women.

Employment, too, is complementary to many human development programs. Employment evidently requires and is dependent upon skills being present in the labour force. But employment also generates skills in a process of learning by doing and, conversely, lack of employment can easily lead to the loss of skills. Unemployment represents not only a loss of potential output in the present, but by destroying skills, it represents a loss of future output as well.

In countries where unemployment is high, perhaps because of the way structural adjustment policies have been implemented, there may be scope for the direct mobilization of labour on capital formation projects. Underutilized human resources in the form of unemployed labour can sometimes be transformed into investment which can help to sustain long-run economic growth. Labour-intensive construction projects can be used to expand irrigation facilities, to create reservoirs and sources of safe water, to provide dirt farm-to-market roads, to undertake field terracing, anti-erosion works, and tree planting projects, and to build schools, clinics, and community centres.[20] In principle, such programs have the capacity to mobilize local resources that might otherwise remain unused and thereby raise the level of output and the rate of growth. Moreover, if they are properly administered, they do this by creating sources of income, in the form of employment, for some of the poorest members of society and thereby lead to a redistribution of income in favour of those most in need. In this way the creation of employment can lead directly to an enhancement of human capabilities.

HUMAN CAPITAL FORMATION, PHYSICAL INVESTMENT, AND ECONOMIC GROWTH

Expenditures on improving human capabilities have the potential to yield a return to society no less than the return from physical capital formation. Take the example of education. The standard technique for determining priorities for educational expenditure is social rate of return analysis. Some broad conclusions can be drawn from the many studies on this question that have been conducted in developing countries (see Table 38-9). First, the private rate of return to all levels of education is normally extremely high, reflecting in part the government subsidization of education. These high private rates of return help to explain the strength of private demand and of political pressure for education, which in turn have contributed to its rapid expansion in recent decades. Secondly, the social rate of return to all levels of education, although consistently lower than the corresponding private return, is generally no less than average rates of return on fixed capital investments. Thus, despite the rapid expansion, there are many developing countries in which education is still under-provided. Thirdly, the estimated social rate of return is generally highest at the primary level and lowest at the tertiary level of education.

Such estimates have to be treated with caution. There is a limit to what one can learn about the social benefit of educational expansion from cross-section estimates of private earnings streams. The earnings differences between different educational levels may be attributable to various noncausal correlates of education, such as intelligence and determination, rather than, or in addition to, education itself. In so far as this is important, social rate of return estimates are biased upwards. On the other hand, there are various reasons why such estimates may understate the social value of education. They do not take into account the various "externalities" to which education can give rise, such as the potential effect of educated people on the productivity of those around them or on the health of their families. Nor do they take account of the power of edu-

TABLE 38-9
RETURNS TO INVESTMENT IN EDUCATION, BY REGION, TYPE, AND LEVEL

Number of countries reporting	Region	Social		
		Primary	Secondary	Tertiary
16	Africa	28	17	13
10	Asia	27	15	13
10	Latin America	26	18	16
45	Developing countries	24	15	13
15	Developed countries	—	11	9
Number of countries reporting	Region	Private		
		Primary	Secondary	Tertiary
16	Africa	43	26	32
10	Asia	31	15	18
10	Latin America	32	23	23
45	Developing countries	31	19	22
15	Developed countries	—	12	12

Source: World Bank, *Financing Education in Developing Countries. An Exploration of Policy Options* (Washington D.C., 1986), p. 7.

cation to enrich the lives and capabilities of people in ways other than by raising the production of goods and services. Moreover, a recognition that investment in human beings makes less use of scarce foreign exchange than does investment in machinery and equipment would similarly favour educational expenditures.

The social return to expansion of primary education depends largely on its effects on the productivity of peasant farmers. The evidence suggests that this in turn depends on whether farmers are operating in a traditional or a modernizing environment—one in which change is rapid. Education assists farmers to obtain and evaluate information about improved technology and new economic opportunities, and thus to innovate.[21] The level of education required depends on the levels of technology currently in use and potentially suitable.[22] Education being complementary to other inputs, its value cannot be assessed in isolation. It depends on the degree of access to credit, extension services, new seeds, and other inputs. The greatest impact on rural development can thus be made where education is part of a package of measures.

Perhaps because of the rapid expansion of education in many developing countries, the quality of education is frequently unsatisfactory. The same educational attainment may require more years of schooling in a developing than in a developed economy. In part, this reflects a lack of early environmental stimulation of children and the inadequacy of their health and nutrition. However, it also reflects the quality of teacher training and the strain on resources—often associated with rapid quantitative expansion—such as overcrowded classrooms, high pupil-teacher ratios, lack of textbooks, and ill-equipped facilities. In time of fiscal restriction, expenditure on physical inputs is squeezed more than salaries. In some countries there is also a problem of incentives.

If the priorities of pupils and their teachers are to perform well in examinations in order to secure good jobs, and if examinations test rote-learning, then repetition, memorization, and rigid book-learning are encouraged in the schools—the so-called diploma disease.[23] Empirical research has suggested that in Brazil the social rate of return on expenditure for improving the quality of primary schooling would exceed that for increasing its quantity.[24]

In a sense, governments, perceiving a choice between high-quality education for a few and low-quality education for many, have opted for the latter. Indeed, the decision may not have been a conscious one in that educational expansion has often proceeded uncontrolled, impelled along by political pressures. Yet, low educational quality is not inevitable.[25] In the first place, improvements in quality may be possible without raising costs, for example, through curricular and examination reform or less reliance on seniority rules in promotions. Secondly, some expenditures on qualitative improvements may yield high rates of return, for example, training courses in leadership and management for head teachers. Thirdly, the use of pupil fees for particular purposes such as additional textbooks and the involvement of parents and communities in supportive actions may harness the enthusiasm for educational improvements.

There has been a long-run improvement in the various indicators of health in the developing countries over the post-War period. Thus, for instance, the infant mortality rate for the developing countries as a whole fell from 180 per 1,000 in 1950–1955 to 137 in 1960–1965, to 104 in 1970–1975, and to 88 in 1980–1985.[26] However, there is a wide variety of experience, and the gains in many countries have been modest if seen in relation to the improvements that could have been made on the basis of existing knowledge of primary health care and basic nutrition. Progress since 1980 has been more limited. The available evidence suggests that the decline in infant mortality was halted and even reversed during the 1980s in many Latin American and African countries. Indicators of child malnutrition increased in African countries after 1980. By contrast, malnutrition and mortality continued to decline in the majority of South and East Asian countries.

At present, there are economically feasible solutions to most of the health and nutrition problems that afflict many millions of people in the poor countries. The basic ingredients of primary health care would include the following: a simple pregnancy management program; oral rehydration therapy to cure digestive tract infections and improved water supply, sanitation, and health education to prevent them; immunization against the six communicable diseases; and an essential drug program covering some 15–20 basic products.

The reduction of malnutrition is more difficult: people are hungry because they lack resources to grow enough food or to buy it. The fundamental solution to protein-energy malnutrition may thus require a redistribution of resources, but directed food subsidies and direct feeding schemes can assist. Recent improvements in food technology can help to overcome micronutrient deficiencies, for example, by fortifying the country's salt with iron or iodine.

Studies have shown that improvements in water supply can have dramatic effects on the incidence of diarrhoeal diseases. The cost of providing vaccine doses against six main vaccine-preventable diseases is about $1.20 per child. The per capita cost of

15 essential drugs needed at the village health post level is only some \$0.50–0.60 per year, and an episode of diarrhoea can be treated with oral rehydration salt available commercially at \$0.15–0.20. The costs of combating micronutrient deficiencies are low: vitamin A capsules cost \$0.10, the cost of iodizing salt is \$0.05, and iron fortification of salt or centrally processed grains costs \$0.05–0.09, all per person per year.[27]

The costs of providing primary health care are low, and yet provision is not as widespread as it could be. According to a World Health Organization (WHO) estimate, some three quarters of all health spending in the developing world is being used to provide expensive medical care for a relatively small urban minority.[28] Moreover, modern hospitals and costly medical technology absorb the great majority of health-related foreign aid to developing countries. There is a case for reallocating resources towards low-cost, high-impact primary health care measures.

Health expenditures of this sort can be justified not only by their effect on peoples' capabilities to enjoy life, but also by their effect on productivity. There is evidence that dietary energy improvements have an immediate effect on the performance of workers and that supplementation of micronutrients can have an even more dramatic effect on anaemic workers. Growth retardation at an early age, caused by dietary deficiency or infection, is a powerful mechanism for perpetuating the vicious circle of poverty, mal-nutrition, and stunting. Severe malnutrition of children under five leads to lifelong impairment of cognitive and physical performance. If children can be protected from these harmful effects, their long-run productivity and income could be greatly enhanced, and the resources required for their subsequent health care could be reduced. Moreover, the benefits need not stop there: primary health care lends itself to social mobilization and community participation in the design and delivery of pro-grams, and this is likely to result in communities being better organized, more self-reliant, and more vocal.

The creation of human resources is one thing; their effective utilization is another. It is important that there be the right environment and incentives for human resources to be used fully and productively. Their effective use requires that factor prices reflect their scarcities. The failure of markets to secure this outcome can result in economic inefficiency, associated with, for example, mismatch of supply and demand, unem-ployment of labour, and brain drain. A potential problem is that the free market out-come may well conflict with income distribution objectives of government. In that case, the better solution may be to pursue income distribution objectives by means of other instruments.

Human capabilities can be dormant, waiting to be tapped, lacking perhaps in organi-zational initiative. Sometimes these capabilities can be tapped through greater participa-tion of people at the grass-roots level. Obstacles may arise from gross inequalities in power, wealth, and incomes between different groups and classes in society. The lack of freedom of association and organization may constitute a barrier in some cases. There are also societies in which discriminatory practices based on gender, race, caste, reli-gion, status, etc. effectively preclude equal economic or social participation by some groups. Illiteracy, limited education and knowledge, lack of confidence, passivity, and so on also constitute barriers to participation of individuals and groups in society.

Some of these obstacles are more amenable to policy than others. The role of government has to be examined carefully. Experience suggests that local people will not be motivated if group activities are both controlled and taxed by government. Perhaps the effective role of government is to provide information and an organizational framework, to ensure that the incentives are right, and let the people do the rest.

HUMAN DEVELOPMENT AND THE DISTRIBUTION OF INCOME

It is widely believed that expenditure on human development programs either is distributionally neutral or else discriminates in favour of the poor. This view, however, is not generally correct. Concerning Asia and the Pacific, one study reports that

> Inequality in opportunities to benefit from human resources development is pervasive in the developing countries of the region. There is inequality between sexes, among regions within each country, between rural and urban areas and among persons in different economic and social groups.[29]

What is true of Asia and the Pacific is equally true of Africa and Latin America. The major beneficiaries of human development programs tend to be males, households living in the large urban areas, and people with middle or high incomes. Females, residents in the rural areas and those with relatively low incomes benefit proportionately less than others from the resources allocated to human development. This is due in part to "urban bias" in the provision of services, in part to a failure, for cultural and sociological reasons, of some of the intended beneficiaries to use the public services and facilities that are provided, but above all to a pattern of unequal subsidies among programs that effectively favours upper-income groups. The per capita subsidy of human development programs used disproportionately by the relatively better off (such as university education) tends to be much higher than the per capita subsidy of programs used largely by the poor (such as health clinics in rural areas). Consequently, the potential of expenditure on human development to reduce social rigidities, increase social mobility, and thereby ameliorate inequality remains large.

There is thus a need, particularly in times of structural adjustment, for governments to change the composition of their human development expenditure programs to ensure that, on balance, most of the benefits accrue to those in the lower half of the income distribution.[30] This can be done, for example, by switching resources from expenditure on urban hospitals to expenditure on primary health care (particularly in countries where hospitals account for 50–60 percent of government health funds), and by switching resources from university education to primary and secondary education (particularly since expenditure per university student often is 30–40 times greater than expenditure per primary school student).

In addition to a change in the composition of public expenditure, there may be a case in some countries for introducing user charges to help cover part of the cost of human development programs. If the tax system were optimal and progressive, and if the benefits of public expenditure programs were equitably distributed, the case against user charges would be quite strong and the case in favour of universal free education and health services would be attractive. But since tax systems in the developing countries often are in practice regressive, and since the benefits of many human development programs are reaped disproportionately by the better off, there may be an argument on grounds of equity for charging for services. In addition, where the alternative to imposing charges is to cut services, there may be an argument on grounds of long-term development for requiring users to cover at least part of the cost.

It is, of course, essential that if user charges are introduced they are designed in such a way that they do not add to the regressivity of the tax system. This can be done in several ways. First, user charges should be avoided as much as possible on services largely used by the poor, for example, primary education, primary health care, and public water points. Secondly, in the case of services and facilities used by both the poor and the rich, for example, secondary education, non-basic health services, and piped water, user charges should be selective, discriminating among users according to per capita income. Thirdly, full-cost charges should be imposed on services used largely by upper-income groups, for example, university education and sophisticated medical treatment available only to a few. But, fourthly, where full-cost charges are imposed, low-income groups should be entitled to scholarships (e.g., for university education) or exempted from the charge or subject to only a nominal charge. In this way, a system of user charges can actually be used to create a more egalitarian society.

No system of user charges, however, can counteract discrimination in access to services. This is something that requires positive intervention by the State. One of the clearest cases of discrimination is that against women. In some countries, namely, Bhutan, Nepal, India, and Pakistan, discrimination is so blatant that, contrary to the pattern everywhere else, the life expectancy of women is less than that of men. This reflects in part a lower regard for the health of female infants than for male infants. In education, too, there is great discrimination. On average, the illiteracy rate among females in the developing countries is 75 percent higher than among males, that is, 48.9 percent illiteracy among women as compared to 27.9 percent among men.[31] In primary school, women account for 44 percent of the pupils in the developing countries; in secondary schools, 39 percent; in tertiary education, 36 percent. In the least developed countries, the situation is even worse: women account for only 20 percent of those studying in tertiary education and 11 percent of the teaching staff in tertiary education.

In addition to discrimination based on sex, there is discrimination based on race (as in South Africa, Fiji, and Malaysia) and on religion (as in the Islamic Republic of Iran). Finally, there are specific problems associated with people of a particular age. In some countries the problem takes the form of child labour, that is, of some children entering the labour force, for example, in the carpet-making industry, before they have received primary and secondary education. In others it is reflected in a disproportionately high incidence of unemployment among the urban youth, a high incidence of long-term unemployment and consequently of unemployability among some sections of the young and, partly as a result of this, a sense of hopelessness accompanied by social disorders such as criminality and drug addiction.

The distribution of the benefits of human development programs among the social classes is slightly paradoxical. Most of the absolute benefits of public services in health, nutrition, education, housing, and transport accrue to the nonpoor, but even so, public subsidies and benefits in kind account for a higher proportion of the total income of the poor than of the nonpoor. Everything else being equal, therefore, a reduction in public expenditure is likely to fall most severely on the poor.

To avoid this, we have suggested that governments alter the composition of public expenditure and, possibly, introduce discriminatory user charges. In the next section we shall discuss the possibility of more accurate targeting of benefits in favour of the poor. It must be recognized and confronted squarely, however, that a redistribution of public resources in favour of the poor may in some circumstances be at the expense not of the rich but of the lower-middle classes. This could easily occur, for example, as a by-product of a switch of expenditure from urban to rural areas. Such a reallocation of resources might well be politically difficult to achieve, particularly if the urban population is more vociferous and better organized than the scattered rural population. In other words, the political economy of public expenditure cannot be ignored when designing human development programs—politics do impose constraints on policy makers—but at the same time it must be recognized that in many developing countries large sections of the poor have been denied an equitable share of the benefits of government programs.

HUMAN DEVELOPMENT AND THE ALLEVIATION OF POVERTY

There is a temporal dimension to the alleviation of poverty. It is important to know whether policies that alleviate poverty in the short term do so at the expense of long-term success. Sustained economic growth is crucial to reducing poverty in the long run. Among the decisive factors will be the rates at which resources such as physical and human capital accumulate and technical progress occurs, in relation to the growth of the population and labour force. The converse relationship may also be true, however. That is, immediate poverty alleviation may be good for growth. For instance, in so far as measures to enhance human capabilities through improved knowledge and health help people to escape from a vicious circle of poverty, they may make possible further, long-run improvements in their condition. The normal view that capital expenditures promote growth whereas current expenditures raise only current welfare need not hold for such measures.

While economic growth is not sufficient to ensure human development, sustained growth is likely to be central in the long run to policies intended to expand the capabilities of all people in the Third World. The austerity currently experienced in many parts of Latin America and Africa is likely, if continued for much longer, to be incompatible with the maintenance of democratic political processes and with the continuation of human development programs at acceptable levels. In Latin America, for example, the debt crisis has forced countries to undergo a massive contraction in aggregate demand, substantial depreciation of exchange rates, and often, after more than a decade of trade liberalization, a reimposition of nontariff barriers to trade and very high tariffs on imports. The result has been a decline in the real value of imports by more than 45 percent between 1980 and 1985 (as well as a fall in the real value of exports because of lower commodity prices). Employment, investment, and growth have all suffered severely. Unfortunately, the adjustment measures that have had to be adopted in many parts of Africa and West Asia have been even more deleterious. A revival of growth is essential in all three of these regions.

Nonetheless, it may be possible to adopt medium-term measures to contain poverty during the period of financial and economic crisis. One way to do this is to target the benefits of human development programs to favour the poor. Targeting presupposes, of course, that it is possible to identify the poor in general or those with specific needs, for example, for improved nutrition. This, in turn, requires that data be available and in a form that permits analysis in terms of relevant social categories, for example, by level of income, occupational group, social class, and age.

The difficulties and costs of accurate targeting should not be underestimated and in some cases it may be cheaper and more efficient to provide a universal service rather than attempt to discriminate in favour of particular groups. Moreover, there is a danger, indeed a virtual certainty, that every targeted program will fail to reach some of the intended beneficiaries while providing services to some unintended beneficiaries. A study of the Indian integrated rural development program, for example, showed that 20 percent of the actual beneficiaries had incomes above the poverty line and hence, in principle, were not eligible for participation in the scheme.[32]

Targeted programs that rely on the exercise of discretion by government officials are vulnerable to corruption and abuse. Programs targeted at people with an income below some arbitrary minimum or with food consumption below some arbitrary daily caloric minimum fall into this category. More likely to be successful are programs that rely on self-targeting or else are universally available within a restricted category. Examples of the latter include free lunches to all primary school children or rationed food supplies available only to inhabitants of rural areas. The chances of corruption in such cases are pretty low, but conversely the chances of providing benefits to many who are not poor are pretty high.

Self-selection of beneficiaries has great appeal because in principle it is possible to offer universal coverage while in practice designing the program in such a way that it is attractive primarily to those most in need of assistance. Food-for-work programs, for instance, can be open to all, yet it is obvious that they will appeal primarily to the unemployed from households where average food consumption and incomes are low. Similarly, it is possible to design a limited food rationing system to which everyone has access but which in practice favours the poor, the rest of the community voluntarily obtaining its supplies elsewhere.[33] The easiest way to do this is by concentrating on varieties of foodgrains and qualities of products that are of special interest to low-income groups and that are characterized by low or even negative income elasticities of demand.

The general point is that it may be possible to redesign human development programs, for example, by better targeting, to ensure that, particularly in times of increased hardship, a higher proportion of total benefits accrues to the poor. This general point can be extended by considering whether it is possible within a context of falling public expenditure to change the composition of public expenditure in order to give higher priority to reducing poverty. This, of course, raises the issue of the importance given by policy makers to human development as compared to the claims for spending by other government services.

Military expenditure can be used to illustrate the choices facing governments. In extreme cases, expenditure on defence is a multiple of expenditure on education and health. The data must be interpreted with caution as statistical conventions appear to vary from one country to another, but the figures may provide a rough indication of orders of magnitude (see Table 38-10). In the low-income countries as a whole, average expenditure on defence was 18.6 percent of total central government expenditure, whereas education and health combined accounted for 11.3 percent of government spending. In the lower middle-income countries the proportions were 14.2 and 17.6 percent respectively.[34]

Governments need to ask themselves whether reduced expenditure on the military would lead to reduced national security. In many cases, perhaps a majority, it is doubtful that it would. Governments should also consider whether slack and inefficiency in the armed services is greater than in other areas of public expenditure. Anecdotal evidence suggests that it often is. Similarly, defence procurement policies could be reconsidered: the market for military equipment is in general oligopolistically organized and hence not very competitive and the price mark-up on supplies is high. The scope for financial savings in the defence budget may be much greater than in other areas of public spending and, if so, it may be possible to release resources for human development programs without impairing a country's ability to defend itself.

Finally, it may be possible, particularly during a relatively short period of economic crisis, to use some of the resources allocated to the military services to support human resources, antipoverty, and public investment programs. It is common for the armed forces to be used to help the civilian population when natural catastrophes such as floods and earthquakes occur. The question being raised here is whether the armed forces could play a constructive role over a longer period when economic catastrophes occur. The manpower and construction equipment of the armed forces might be used to sustain public investment in infrastructure (roads, bridges) and to construct the physical facilities needed for human resource programs (rural clinics, primary schools). Equally, the training facilities of the armed forces could be used to train the civilian labour force in useful skills (electricians, mechanics). In this way, the conflict in priorities between military expenditure and human resource development could at least be reduced.

There may also be opportunities to reduce poverty by mobilizing slack local resources. The ease with which this can be done depends in part on the degree of grass-roots participation, a topic that was briefly discussed earlier. Particularly in the rural areas, and particularly during the off-peak seasons, the supply of labour is likely to be highly elastic and its opportunity cost low. If this labour is combined with technology of low capital intensity, it should be possible to generate substantial employment, raise the incomes of the working poor, and produce productive assets of lasting value. The organizational intensity of a strategy of local resource mobilization, however, is likely to be high. In effect, the mobilization of labour is used as a substitute for physical capital. But again, the cost of mobilizing slack local resources can be kept to a minimum if the local population already has been organized around institutions intended to promote their well-being.

TABLE 38-10
DEFENCE EXPENDITURE AS PERCENTAGE OF TOTAL CENTRAL GOVERNMENT
EXPENDITURE IN SELECTED COUNTRIES, 1972 AND 1985

	1972	1985
Low-income countries	17.2	18.6
Burkina Faso	11.5	18.2
Nepal	7.2	6.2
Malawi	3.1	5.7
Zaire	11.1	5.2
Burma	31.6	18.5
Kenya	6.0	12.9
United Republic of Tanzania	11.9	13.8
Ghana	7.9	7.5
Pakistan	39.9	32.3
Sri Lanka	3.1	2.6
Uganda	23.1	16.7
Lower-middle-income countries	15.7	14.2
Bolivia	18.8	5.4
Indonesia	18.6	12.9
Morocco	12.3	14.9
Philippines	10.9	11.9
Dominican Republic	8.5	8.4
Thailand	20.2	20.2
El Salvador	6.6	20.3
Paraguay	13.8	10.2
Turkey	15.5	10.9
Mauritius	0.8	0.8
Ecuador	15.7	11.3
Tunisia	4.9	7.9
Costa Rica	2.8	3.0
Chile	10.0	11.5
Upper-middle-income countries	14.4	9.7
Brazil	8.3	4.0
Uruguay	5.6	10.8
Yugoslavia	20.5	54.8
Mexico	4.2	2.7
Argentina	10.0	8.8
Republic of Korea	25.8	29.7
Venezuela	10.3	6.1
Israel	40.0	27.8
Oman	39.3	43.0
Singapore	35.3	20.1

Source: World Bank, *World Development Report 1987* (Oxford, Oxford University Press, 1987).

The capability of small-scale, locally based development to be self-sustaining is often underestimated. If resource mobilization is successful in raising rural incomes, experience shows that a significant proportion of the additional income may be ploughed back into investment, which then raises incomes further in the next period. In other words, marginal savings rates are potentially quite high even among very low-income households. Thus, human development programs based in rural areas should not be regarded as income transfers to the poor but as an efficient way of raising the incomes of the poor on a sustained basis.

In the urban areas, particularly in what is known as the informal sector, it may be possible to mobilize slack resources and release entrepreneurial initiative simply by removing government-imposed obstacles to progress. Quite often government policy towards the urban informal sector contains too few elements of inaction, restriction, and harassment.[35] The punitive demolition of squatter settlements merely destroys the housing of the poor; it does not result in better health or a more sanitary environment. Similarly, trade licensing systems create monopoly rents for license holders while discouraging investment in the informal sector. The effect of this is to harm the lower-income groups by reducing employment as well as the supply of goods and services originating in the informal sector which the poor consume. From Kenya to Peru,[36] the informal economy is usually thought of as a problem rather than as a reservoir of frustrated initiative and untapped talent and a way out of underdevelopment for many of the poor.

Yet, especially at a time when public expenditure is falling, and expenditure on human development is falling faster than average, a strong case can be made for removing laws and regulations that make it difficult for the poor to help themselves, to put a roof over their heads, to obtain a job, to establish a small shop or enterprise. If the ability of the State to help the poor in a time of economic crisis is declining, the least that can be done is to make certain that the State does not aggravate the problem of poverty or obstruct the efforts of low-income groups to improve their situation through their own exertions.

CONCLUSIONS

The peak of enthusiasm for "investment in human beings" occurred during the 1960s. Since the first oil crisis, the pendulum has swung in the other direction. The question has become: how to manage the economic crisis and return to economic growth? There is again a tendency to consider education, health, and social services as consumer goods—luxuries to be afforded in good times but not in bad. The pendulum has swung too far towards the neglect of human resource development.

Our object has been to provide a counterweight. When governments face a severe dilemma of having to choose between adjusting to short-term economic and fiscal constraints and pursuing long-run human resource goals, there is a danger that the former will dominate the latter. For instance, the costs of neglecting the former are more calculable, and more attributable, than the long-run costs to the development process of neglecting the latter. Nevertheless, the solution to the short-term problems of the present may contribute to a series of equally pressing short-run problems in the future.

We advocate that a broader view be taken of the development process than is normal—a view that encompasses not only the growth of national income per head and improvements in its distribution but also the enhancement of the capabilities of people to be and to do more things and to lead fuller lives. Education, health, and nutrition have an important role to play in helping people to develop their capabilities. The enhancement of human capabilities is both an end in itself and a means to higher production and income. There is evidence that the economic returns for expenditures on education and health can be high. There is thus a good case for protecting such expenditure against the fiscal squeeze that generally accompanies economic recession and structural adjustment programs.

Although the distributional effects of government taxation and expenditure are often regressive, with richer households receiving larger benefits, it is the poor who may suffer most from public expenditure cuts, in that the smaller absolute benefit to the poor is nevertheless a more important part of their income. The basic public services, such as primary education and basic health care, in particular need to be protected, for reasons both of efficiency and of equity. There is a case for greater targeting of subsidized public services on the poor, for example, by concentrating on poor rural areas and using self-selective schemes such as food-for-work. If it is naïve to expect that, in a period of curtailment, additional funds will be provided or that funds will be diverted from other activities, such as defence, for those activities that enhance human capabilities, then at least the basic services should continue to be generally provided free and, where it would not be a regressive move, selective cost recovery might be introduced to maintain and enlarge programs providing nonbasic services.

NOTES

1 Amartya Sen, "Development: Which Way Now?" *Economic Journal,* 93, 372 (December 1983): 755.
2 Amartya Sen, "Goods and People," in *Resources, Values and Development* (Oxford: Basil Blackwell, 1984), pp. 510 and 511.
3 John Rawls, *A Theory of Justice* (Cambridge: Harvard University Press, 1971), p. 92.
4 International Labour Organisation, *Employment, Growth and Basic Needs: A One-World Problem* (Geneva, 1976).
5 Amartya Sen, *Resources, Values and Development . . .,* pp. 315–16.
6 See Amartya Sen, "Public Action and the Quality of Life in Developing Countries," *Oxford Bulletin of Economics and Statistics,* 43, 4 (November 1981); and Keith Griffin, *Alternative Strategies for Economic Development* (London: Macmillan, 1988), chap. I.
7 World Bank, *World Development Report 1984* (Oxford: Oxford University Press, 1984), table 4.2, p. 67.
8 See, for example, Felix Paukert, "Income Distribution at Different Levels of Development: A Survey of Evidence," *International Labour Review,* CVIII, 2–3 (August–September 1973); and Montek S. Ahluwalia, "Inequality, Poverty and Development," *Journal of Development Economics,* 3, 3 (September 1976).
9 Keith Griffin and Azizur Rahman Khan, "Poverty in the World: Ugly Facts and Fancy Models," *World Development,* 6, 3 (March 1978); and Irma Adelman and Cynthia Taft Morris, *Economic Growth and Social Equity in Developing Countries* (Stanford: Stanford University Press, 1973).

10 International Labour Organisation, *Overview of the Employment Situation in the World* (Geneva, November 1987), p. 2.

11 World Food Council, *The Global State of Hunger and Malnutrition and the Impact of Economic Adjustment on Food and Hunger Problems* (April 1987), p. 3.

12 Ibid., table 1, p. 16.

13 World Bank, *World Development Report 1987* (Oxford, Oxford University Press, 1987), table 16, pp. 232–33.

14 United Nations Children's Fund, *Adjustment with a Human Face* (Oxford: Oxford University Press, 1987). The net transfer is calculated as the difference between loans, direct investments, and grants received and profit repatriation, interest, and capital repayments.

15 United Nations Children's Fund, *Adjustment with a Human Face . . .*, Vol. 1, pp. 289–94.

16 Amartya Sen, *Technology, Employment and Development* (Oxford: Clarendon Press, 1975), p. 5.

17 See Louis Emmerij, "The Human Factor in Development," *Human Development: The Neglected Dimension* (United Nations publication, Sales No. 86.III.B.2), p. 20.

18 For evidence that participation raises the return on physical capital and increases the productivity of labour, see Conrad Phillip Kottak, "When People Don't Come First: Some Sociological Lessons from Completed Projects" (Washington, D.C.: World Bank, 1985); and David C. Korten, "Community Organization for Rural Development: A Learning Process Approach," *Public Administration Review* (September–October 1980).

19 Robert Cassen, "Population and Development: A Survey," *World Development,* 4, 10–11 (1976): 788–96.

20 See J. Gaude and others, "Rural Development and Labour-Intensive Schemes: Impact Study of Some Pilot Programmes," *International Labour Review* (July–August 1987).

21 M. E. Lockhead, D. T. Jamison, and L. J. Lau, "Farmer Education and Farm Efficiency: A Survey," *Economic Development and Cultural Change,* 29 (1980). 37–76.

22 Daniel Cotlear, "The Effects of Education on Farm Productivity: A Case Study from Peru" (1987).

23 R. P. Dore, *The Diploma Disease, Education, Qualification and Development* (London: George Allen and Unwin, 1976).

24 Jere Behrman and Nancy Birdsall, "The Quality of Schooling: Quantity Alone May Be Misleading," *American Economic Review,* 73, 5 (1983): 928–46.

25 Jocelyn Dejong and John Oxenham, "The Quality of Education in Developing Countries" (1987).

26 *World Population Prospects. Estimates and Projections as Assessed in 1984* (United Nations publication, Sales No. E.86.XIII.3).

27 Figures from G. A. Cornia, "Investing in Human Resources: Health, Nutrition and Development for the 1990s" (November 1987).

28 Cited in Cornia, op. cit., p. 23.

29 *Economic and Social Survey of Asia and the Pacific 1986* (United Nations publication, Sales No. E.87.II.F.1), part two, p. 171.

30 See G. A. Cornia, "Social Policy Making During Adjustment," in Khadija Haq and Uner Kirdar, eds., *Human Development, Adjustment and Growth,* (Islamabad, North-South Round-table, 1987), pp. 85–88.

31 United Nations Educational, Scientific and Cultural Organization, Office of Statistics, *The Current Literacy Situation in the World* (Paris, May 1987), p. 4.

32 N. J. Kurian, "IRDP—How Relevant Is It?" (May 1987), p. 7.

33 See Keith Griffin and Jeffrey James, *The Transition to Egalitarian Development* (London: Macmillan, 1981), chap. 4.

34 World Bank, *World Development Report* 1987 . . .

35 International Labour Organisation, *Employment, Incomes and Equality: A Strategy for Increasing Productive Employment in Kenya* (Geneva, 1972), p. 226.

36 See Hernando de Soto, *El Otro Sendero: La Revolución Informal* (Lima: Editorial El Barranco, 1986). See also Victor Tokman, "The Informal Sector Today: A Policy Proposal." Paper presented to the Round-table in Managing Human Development, Budapest, September 6–9, 1987.

BIBLIOGRAPHY

**PART ONE / THEORY AND METHOD
IN ECONOMIC DEVELOPMENT**

Baldacchino, Godfrey. "Bursting the Bubble: The Pseudo-Development Strategies of Microstates." *Development and Change,* 24 (1993): 29–51.

Baran, Paul. "Economic Progress and Economic Surplus." *Science and Society,* 17, 4 (Fall 1953): 289–317.

Cebotarev, E. A. "Women, Human Rights and the Family in Development Theory and Practice." *Canadian Journal of Development Studies,* 9, 2 (1988): 187–200.

Chenery, Hollis, et al. *Redistribution with Growth: An Approach to Policy.* Oxford: Oxford University Press, 1974.

_____, and M. Syrquin. *Patterns of Development: 1950–1970.* London: Oxford University Press, 1975.

Donaldson, Lorraine. *Economic Development: Analysis and Policy.* Mineola, N.Y.: West Publishing Co., 1984.

Fei, John C. H., and G. Ranis. *Development of the Labor Surplus Economy: Theory and Policy.* Homewood, Ill.: Irwin, 1964.

Frank, Andre Gunder. "Sociology of Development and Underdevelopment of Sociology." In *Latin America: Underdevelopment or Revolution?* New York: Monthly Review Press (1969): pp. 21–94.

Goulet, Denis. *The Cruel Choice.* New York: Atheneum, 1971.

_____. "An Ethical Model for the Study of Values." *Harvard Educational Review,* 41, 2 (May 1971): pp. 205–227.

Hirschman, Albert O. *The Strategy of Economic Development.* New Haven: Yale University Press, 1958.

Jameson, Kenneth, and Charles K. Wilber, eds. *Directions in Economic Development.* Notre Dame, Ind.: University of Notre Dame Press, 1979.

Kay, Cristobal. "Reflection on the Latin American Contribution to Development Theory." *Development and Change,* 22 (1991): 31–68.

Keyfitz, Nathan. "Population and Sustainable Development: Distinguishing Fact and Preference Concerning the Future Human Population and Environment." *Population and Environment,* 14, 5 (May 1993): 441–61.

Kuznets, Simon S. *Modern Economic Growth.* New Haven: Yale University Press, 1966.

Lipton, Michael. "A Note on Poverty and Sustainability." *IDS Bulletin* (January 1992): 12–16.

Meier, Gerald M. Do Development Economists Matter?" *IDS Bulletin,* 20, 3 (July 1989): 17–25.

Moore, Mick. "Interpreting Africa's Crisis: Political Science versus Political Economy." *IDS Bulletin,* 18, 4 (October 1987): 7–15.

Myrdal, Gunnar. *Asian Drama: An Inquiry into the Poverty of Nations.* New York: Pantheon, 1968.

———. *Economic Theory and Underdeveloped Regions.* New York: Harper & Row, 1971.

Nurkse, Ragnar. *Problems of Capital Formation in Underdeveloped Countries.* Oxford: Basil Blackwell, 1958.

Pantin, Dennis. "Long Waves and Caribbean Development." *Social and Economic Studies,* 36, 2 (June 1986): 1–20.

Peet, Richard, and Michael Watts. "Introduction: Development Theory and Environment in an Age of Market Triumphalism." *Economic Geography,* 69, 3 (July 1993): 227–53.

Pieterse, Jan. "Dilemmas of Developmentalism Discourse: The Crisis of Developmentalism and the Comparative Method." *Development and Change,* 22 (1991): 5–29.

Randall, Margaret. "When the Imagination of the Writer Is Confronted by the Imagination of the State." *Latin American Perspectives,* 16, 1 (Winter 1989): 61–115.

Ranis, Gustav, et al., eds. *Comparative Development Perspectives: Essays in Honor of Lloyd G. Reynolds.* Boulder, Col.: Westview Press, 1984.

Sen, A. K. "Development as Capability Expansion." *Journal of Development Planning,* 19 (1989): 41–58.

Wilber, Charles K., ed. "The Methodological Foundations of Development Economics." *World Development,* (Special Issue), 14, 2 (February 1986).

PART TWO / ECONOMIC DEVELOPMENT
AND UNDERDEVELOPMENT IN HISTORICAL PERSPECTIVE

Andersen, Robin. "Images of War: Photojournalism, Ideology, and Central America." *Latin American Perspectives,* 16, 1 (Winter 1989): 61–96.

Bairoch, Paul. *The Economic Development of the Third World Since 1900.* Translated from the fourth French edition by Cynthia Postan. Berkeley: University of California Press, 1975.

Baran, Paul. "On the Roots of Backwardness." In *The Political Economy of Growth.* New York: Monthly Review Press (1957): 134–62.

Barret-Brown, Michael. *The Economics of Imperialism.* Baltimore: Penguin, 1974.

Bhatt, V. V. "Economic Development: An Analytic-Historical Approach." *World Development,* 4, 7 (July 1976).

Bryceson, Deborah F. "Peasant Cash Cropping vs. Food Self-Sufficiency in Tanzania: A Historical Perspective." *IDS Bulletin,* 19, 2 (April 1988): 37–46.

Furtado, Celso. *Economic Development of Latin America: A Survey from Colonial Times to the Cuban Revolution.* Cambridge, England: Cambridge University Press, 1970.

Gerschenkron, Alexander. *Economic Backwardness in Historical Perspective.* New York: Praeger, 1965.

Gould, John D. *Economic Growth in History: Survey and Analysis.* London: Methuen, 1972.

Griffin, Keith B. *The Underdevelopment of Spanish America.* London: G. Allen, 1969.

Juneja, Monica. "The Peasant Image and Agrarian Change: Representations of Rural Society in Nineteenth Century French Painting from Millet to Van Gogh." *Journal of Peasant Studies,* 15 (1987–88): 445 ff.

Kitching, Gavin. *Development and Underdevelopment in Historical Perspective: Population, Nationalism and Industrialization.* New York: Methuen, 1982.

Logan, Bernard I. "The Reverse Transfer of Technology from Subsaharan Africa to the United States." *Journal of Modern African Studies,* 25, 4 (December 1987): 597–612.

Morawetz, David. *Twenty-Five Years of Economic Development: 1950 to 1975.* Washington, D.C.: World Bank, 1977.

Polanyi, Karl. *The Great Transformation: The Political and Economic Origins of Our Time.* Boston: Beacon Press, 1957.

Reynolds, L. G. *Economic Growth in the Third World, 1850–1980.* Economic Growth Center Series. New Haven: Yale University Press, 1985.

Rodney, Walter. *How Europe Underdeveloped Africa.* Dar es Salaam: Tanzania Publishing House, 1972.

Rostow, W. W. *Stages of Economic Growth.* 2d ed. New York: Cambridge University Press, 1971.

Rowe, William, and T. Whitfield. "Thresholds of Identity: Literature and Exile in Latin America." *Third World Quarterly,* 9, 1 (January 1987): 229–45.

Thomas, C. *Dependence and Transformation.* New York: Monthly Review Press, 1976.

PART THREE / RESTRUCTURING THE WORLD: DEMOCRACY, DEBT, AND DIFFERENTIATION

Ahmed, Masood, and Lawrence Summers. "A Tenth Anniversary Report on the Debt Crisis." *Finance and Development,* (September 1992): 2–5.

Amin, Samir. *Imperialism and Unequal Development.* New York: Monthly Review Press, 1977.

Apter, David, and Louis Goldman, eds. *The Multinational Corporation and Social Change.* New York: Praeger, 1976.

Arrighi, G. "Labor Supplies in Historical Perspective: A Study of the Proletarianization of the African Peasantry in Rhodesia." *Journal of Development Studies,* 6 (April 1970): 197–234.

Bath, G. Richard, and Dilmus James. Dependency Analysis of Latin America. *Latin American Research Review,* 11, 2 (1976).

Buelens, Frans. "The Creation of Regional Blocs in the World Economy." *Intereconomics,* (May/June 1992): 124–32.

Burg, Steven L. "Why Yugoslavia Fell Apart." *Current History* (November 1993): 357–63.

Caporaso, James A. "Dependence, Dependency, and Power in the Global System: A Structural and Behavioral Analysis." *International Organization,* 32, 1 (Winter 1978).

Cardoso, Fernando Henrique. "The Consumption of Dependency Theory in the United States." *Latin American Research Review,* 12, 3 (1977).

_____, and Enzo Faletto. *Dependency and Development in Latin America.* Berkeley: University of California Press, 1978.

Claessens, Stijn, and Ishac Diwan. "Recent Experience with Commercial Bank Debt Reduction: Has the "Menu" Outdone the Market?" *World Bank,* 22, 2 (1994): 201–13.

Cole, S. "World Bank Forecasts and Planning in the Third World." *Environment and Planning,* A, 21 (1989): 175–96.

Culpeper, Roy. "The Debt Crisis and the World Bank." *Canadian Journal of Development Studies,* 9, 2 (1988): 285–301.

Darrat, A. F. "Are Exports an Engine of Growth? Another Look at the Evidence." *Applied Economics,* 19, 2 (February 1987): 277–83.

Desta, Asayehgn. "Africa's External Debt in Perspective." *Journal of African Studies,* 15, 1 & 2 (Spring–Summer 1988): 23–32.

Dhonte, Pierre. *Clockwork Debt: Trade and the External Debt of Developing Countries.* Lexington, Mass.: Heath, 1979.

Dos Santos, Theotonio. "The Structure of Dependence." *American Economic Review,* 60, 2 (1970).

Emmanuel, Arghiri. *Unequal Exchange: A Study of the Imperialism of Trade.* New York: Monthly Review Press, 1972.

Falk, Richard. "In Search of a New World Model." *Current History,* 92, 573 (1993): 145–49.

Frank, Andre Gunder. *Capitalism and Underdevelopment in Latin America: Historical Studies of Chile and Brazil.* New York: Monthly Review Press, 1967.

Gibbon, Peter. "The World Bank and African Poverty, 1973–91." *The Journal of Modern African Studies,* 30, 2 (1992): 193–220.

Girling, Robert Henriques. *Multinational Institutions and the Third World: Management, Debt, and Trade Conflicts in the International Economic Order.* New York: Praeger, 1985.

Gotur, Padma. "Interest Rates and the Developing World: Interest Rates in the Developed World Have Pervasive and Important Effects on Debt, Growth and Commodity Exports in Developing Countries." *Finance and Development,* 20 (December 1983): 33–36.

Helleiner, G. K., ed. *A World Divided: The Less Developed Countries in the International Economy.* New York: Cambridge University Press, 1976.

Hymer, S., and S. Resnick. "International Trade and Uneven Development." In J. Bhagwati, R. Jones, R. Mundell, and L. Vanek, eds., *Trade, Balance of Payments and Growth.* Amsterdam: North Holland, 1971.

Isla, Ana. "The Debt Crisis in Latin America An Example of Unsustainable Development." *Canadian Women's Studies,* 13, 3 (1993): 65–68.

Jakobeit, Cord. "The EBRD: Redundant, or an Important Actor in the Transformation of Eastern Europe?" *Intereconomics,* (May/June 1992): 119–23.

Kamaluddin, Mohammad. "Democracy, Development, Debt and the Dispossessed in Bangladesh." *Peace Research,* 25, 4 (1993): 59–62.

Kim, Eun Mee. "Foreign Capital in Korea's Economic Development, 1960–85." *Studies in Comparative International Development,* 24, 4 (Winter 1989–90): 24–45.

Kim, Yung Myung. "Patterns of Dependency and Development: A Comparative Analysis of Radical and Conservative State Policies in Peru, Egypt, Brazil and South Korea." *Korea and World Affairs,* 8, (Winter 1984): 812–44.

Kozminski, Andrzej K. "Transition from Planned to Market Economy: Hungary and Poland Compared." *Studies in Comparative Communism,* 25, 4 (1992): 315–33.

Kwon, J. K., and Y. G. Yoo. "Welfare Inequality among Urban Households in South Korea: 1965–83." *Applied Economics,* 19, 4 (April 1987): 497–510.

Lang, Franz Peter. "Strategic Trade Policy for Eastern Europe." *Intereconomics* (July/August 1992): 182–89.

Linnemann, Hans, and Atul Sarma. "Economic Transformation in Eastern Europe: Its Genesis, Adjustment Process, and Impact on Developing Countries." *Development and Change,* 22, 1 (1991): 69–92.

Logan, Ikubolajeh Bernard, and Kidane Mengisteab. "IMF-World Bank Adjustment and Structural Transformation in Sub-Saharan Africa." *Economic Geography,* 69, 1 (1993): 1–24.

Looney, Robert E. "The Impact of Arms Production on Income Distribution and Growth in the Third World." *Economic Development and Cultural Change,* 38, 1 (October 1989): 145–54.

Magdoff, Harry. *The Age of Imperialism.* New York: Monthly Review Press, 1969.

Moss, Joanna, and J. Ravenhill. "Trade Diversification in Black Africa." *Journal of Modern African Studies,* 27, 3 (September 1989): 521.

Muller, Edward N. "Dependent Economic Development, Aid Dependence on the U.S. and Democratic Breakdown in Third World." *International Studies Quarterly,* 29 (December 1985): 445–69.

Parsons, John E. "Bubble, Bubble, How Much Trouble? Financial Markets, Capitalist Development and Capitalist Crises." *Science and Society,* 52, 3 (Fall 1988): 260–89.

Peng, Yali. "Privatization in Eastern European Countries." *East European Quarterly,* 26, 4 (1993): 471–84.

Peschel, Karin. "European Integration and Regional Development in Northern Europe." *Regional Studies,* 26, 4 (1992): 387–97.

Petras, James, and H. Brill. "Latin America's Transnational Capitalists and the Debt: A Class Analysis Perspective." *Development and Change,* 19, 2 (April 1988): 179.

Prebisch, Raoul. "The Role of Commercial Policy in Underdeveloped Countries." *American Economic Review,* 49, 2 (May 1959).

Rosenberger Leif. "Economic Transition in Eastern Europe: Paying the Price for Freedom." *East European Quarterly,* 26, 3 (1992): 261–78.

Schmitter, Philippe C., with Terry Lynn Karl. "The Conceptual Travels of Transitologists and Consolidologists: How Far to the East Should They Attempt to Go?" *Slavic Review,* 53, 1 (1994): 173–85.

Shumaker, David. "The Origins and Development of Central European Cooperation: 1989–1992." *East European Quarterly,* 27, 3 (1993): 351–73.

Singer, H. W. "The Distribution of Gains Between Investing and Borrowing Countries." *American Economic Review,* 40, 2 (May 1950).

Stein, Leslie. "Third World Poverty, Economic Growth and Income Distribution." *Canadian Journal of Development Studies,* 10, 2 (1989): 225–40.

Tsakloglou, P. "Development and Inequality Revisited." *Applied Economics,* 20, 4 (April 1988): 509–32.

Yuanchen, Dai. "Can Plan and Market Coexist in a Socialist Economy?" *Chinese Economic Studies,* 25, 4 (1992): 60–78.

Van Brabant, Jozef M. "1992, The Revolutions in Eastern Europe and East-South-North Relations." *Journal of Development Planning,* 21 (1992): 227–57.

Voszka, Eva. "Ownership Reforms or Privatization?" *Eastern European Economics,* (Fall 1991): 57–85.

PART FOUR / AGRICULTURE IN DEVELOPMENT

Adams, Dale W. "The Conundrum of Successful Credit Programs in Floundering Rural Financial Markets." *Economic Development and Cultural Change,* 36, 2 (January 1988): 355–68.

Agarwal, Bina. "Who Sows? Who Reaps? Women and Land Rights in India." *The Journal of Peasant Studies,* 15 (1987): 531.

Alier, Juan Martinez. *Haciendas, Plantations and Collective Farms.* London: Frank Cass, 1977.

Altieri, Miguel A. "Sustainability ends, Agro-ecology Begins Grassroots Field Work in Latin America." *Ceres,* 134 (March–April 1992): 33–39.

Ash, Robert F. "The Agricultural Sector in China: Performance and Policy Dilemmas during the 1990s," *The China Quarterly* (1992): 547–76.

Barkin, David. "Cuban Agriculture: A Strategy of Economic Development." *Studies in Comparative International Development,* 7, 1 (Spring 1972).

Barraclough, Solon, ed. *Agrarian Structure in Latin America.* Lexington, Mass.: Heath, 1973.

Berry, R. A., and W. Cline. *Agrarian Structure and Productivity in Developing Countries.* Baltimore: Johns Hopkins University Press, 1979.

Bowie, Katherine A. "Unraveling the Myth of the Subsistence Economy: Textile Production in Nineteenth-Century Northern Thailand." *The Journal of Asian Studies* 51, 4 (November 1992): 797–823.

Brass, Tom. "Unfree Labor and Capitalist Restructuring in the Agrarian Sector: Peru and India." *The Journal of Peasant Studies,* 14, 1 (1986): 50–77.

Chapman, Duane, and Randolph Barker. "Environmental Protection, Resource Depletion, and the Sustainability of Developing Country Agriculture." *Economic Development and Cultural Change,* 39, 4 (1991): 723–37.

Clay, E. L., and B. B. Schaffer, eds. *Room for Manoeuvre: An Exploration of Public Policy Planning in Agricultural and Rural Development.* Cranbury, N.J.: Associated Universities Press, Inc., 1984.

Dejanvry, A., et al. "Land and Labor in Latin American Agriculture from the 1950s to the 1980s." *The Journal of Peasant Studies,* 16 (1988): 396.

Fafchamps, Marcel. "Solidarity Networks in Preindustrial Societies: Rational Peasants with Moral Economy." *Economic Development and Cultural Change,* 41, 1 (1992): 147–74.

Figuera, A. "Agrarian Reformisms in Latin America: A Framework and an Instrument of Rural Development." *World Development,* 5 (1977).

Galdwin, Christina H., Kathleen A. Staudt, and Della E. McMillan. "Providing Africa's Women Farmers Access: One Solution to the Food Crisis." *Journal of African Studies,* 13, 9 (1987/88): 131–41.

Ganapathy, R. S. "The Political Economy of Rural Energy Planning in the Third World." *Review of Radical Political Economics,* 15 (Fall 1983): 83–95.

Ghai, D., et al., eds. *Agrarian Systems and Rural Development.* New York: Holmes and Meier, 1979.

Gladwin, C. H., et al. "Providing African Women Farmers Access: One Solution to the Food Crisis." *Journal of African Studies,* 13, 4 (Winter 1986–87): 131–41.

Goldsmith, Arthur. "The Private Sector and Rural Development: Can Agribusiness Help the Small Farmer?" *World Development,* 13 (October–November 1985): 1125–38.

Griffin, Keith. *The Political Economy of Agrarian Change.* London: Macmillan, 1974.

_____. *Land Concentration and Rural Poverty.* 2d ed. London: Macmillan, 1980.

Gurley, John. "Rural Development in China 1949–1972, and the Lessons to Be Learned from It." *World Development,* 3, 7–8 (July–August 1975).

Heyer, R., P. Roberts, and G. Williams, eds. *Rural Development in Tropical Africa.* London: Macmillan, 1981.

Johnston, Bruce F., and John W. Mellor. "The Role of Agriculture in Economic Development." *American Economic Review,* 51, 4 (September 1961).

_____, and P. Kilby. *Agriculture and Structural Transformation: Strategies in Late-Developing Countries.* New York: Oxford University Press, 1975.

_____, and W. C. Clark. *Redesigning Rural Development: A Strategic Perspective.* Baltimore: Johns Hopkins University Press, 1982.

Lipton, Michael. *Why Poor People Stay Poor: A Study of Urban Bias in World Development.* Cambridge, Mass.: Harvard University Press, 1977.

Longhurst, Richard. "Cash Crops, Household Food Security and Nutrition." *IDS Bulletin,* 19, 2 (April 1988): 28–36.

Morales, Edmundo. "Coca & Cocaine Economy and Social Change in the Andes of Peru." *Economic Development and Cultural Change,* 35, 1 (October 1986): 143–62.

Muralt, Jurgen Von, and L. Sajhau'. "Plantations and Basic Needs: The Changing International and National Setting." *IDS Bulletin,* 18, 2 (April 1987): 9–14.

Mutsaers, Antony. "Industrial Development: A Natural Growth if Rooted in Agricultural Demand." *Ceres,* 21, 2 (March–April 1988).

Otsuka, Keijiro, and Y. Hayami. "Theories of Share Tenancy: A Critical Survey." *Economic Development and Cultural Change,* 37, 1 (October 1988): 31–68.

Paarlberg, Robert, and Michael Lipton. "Changing Missions at the World Bank." *World Policy,* 8, 3 (Summer 91): 475–98.

Pearse, Andrew. *Seeds of Plenty, Seeds of Want: Social and Economic Implications of the Green Revolution,* New York: Oxford University Press, 1980.

Pingali, Prabhu L. and Vo-Tong Xuan. "Vietnam: Decollectivization and Rice Productivity Growth." *Economic Development and Cultural Change,* 40, 4 (1992) 697–718.

Puntasen, Apichai, Somboon Siriprachai, and Chaiyuth Punyasavatsut. "Political Economy of Eucalyptus: Business, Bureaucracy and the Thai Government." *Journal of Contemporary Asia,* 22, 2 (1992): 187–206.

Reilly, Charles A. "The Road from Rio: NGO Policy Makers and the Social Ecology of Development." *Grassroots Development,* 17 1 (1993): 25–35.

Rich, Bruce. "The Emperor's New Clothes: The World Bank and Environmental Reform." *World Policy Journal,* 7, 2 (Spring 90): 305–29.

Schejtman, Alexander. "The Peasant Economy: Internal Logic, Articulation, and Persistence." *CEPAL Review,* 11 (August 1980): 115–34.

Southgate, Douglas, and Morris Whitaker. "Promoting Resource Degradation in Latin America: Tropical Deforestation, Soil Erosion and Coastal Ecosystem Disturbance in Ecuador." *Economic Development and Cultural Change,* 40, 4 (1992): 787–807.

Spooner, Neil. "Does the World Bank Inhibit Smallholder Cash Cropping? The Case of Malawi." *IDS Bulletin,* 19, 2 (April 1988): 66–70.

Stavenhagen, Rodolfo, ed. *Agrarian Problems and Peasant Movements in Latin America.* New York: Doubleday, 1970.

Teubal, Miguel. "Internationalization of Capital and Agroindustrial Complexes: Their Impact on Latin American Agriculture." *Latin American Perspectives,* 14, 3 (Summer 1987): 316.

Yudelman, Sally W. "Women Farmers in Central America Myths, Roles, Reality." *Grassroots Development,* 17, 2 (1994): 2–13.

PART FIVE / INDUSTRY IN DEVELOPMENT

Beenstock, Michael. "International Patterns in Military Spending." *Economic Development and Cultural Change,* 41, 3 (1993): 633–49.

Brauer, Jurgen. "Military Investments and Economic Growth in Developing Nations." *Economic Development and Cultural Change,* 39, 4 (1991): 873–84.

Bullock, Brad, and Glenn Firebaugh. "Guns *and* Butter? The Effect of Militarization on Economic and Social Development in the Third World." *Journal of Political and Military Sociology,* 18 (Winter 1990): 231–66.

Chudnovsky, Daniel, and Masafumi Nagao. *Capital Goods Production in the Third World: An Economic Study of Technological Acquisition.* Dover, N.H.: Frances Pinter (Publishers) Ltd., 1983.

Cody, John, et al. *Policies for Industrial Progress in Developing Countries.* New York: Oxford University Press, 1980.

Cukor, Gyorgy. *Strategies for Industrialization in Developing Countries.* New York: St. Martin's Press, 1974.

Deyo, F. C. *Dependent Development and Industrial Order: An Asian Case Study.* New York: Praeger, 1981.

Goulet, Denis. *The Uncertain Promise: Value Conflicts in Technology Transfer.* New York: IDOC North America, 1977.

Halevi, Joseph. "Asian Capitalist Accumulation: From Sectoral to Vertical Integration." *Journal of Contemporary Asia,* 22, 4 (1992): 444–69.

Hein, Simeon. "Trade Strategy and the Dependency Hypothesis: A Comparison of Policy, Foreign Investment, and Economic Growth in Latin America and East Asia." *Economic Development and Cultural Change,* 40, 3 (1992): 495–521.

Hirschman, Albert O. "The Political Economy of Import-Substituting Industrialization in Latin America." *Quarterly Journal of Economics,* 82, 1 (February 1968).

Kim, Won-Bae. "Industrial Restructuring and Related Labour Issues in Korea." *IDS Bulletin,* 20, 4 (October 1989): 32–36.

Kirkpatrick, C. H., and F. L. Nixson, ed. *The Industrialization of Less Developed Countries.* Dover, N.H.: Manchester University Press, 1983.

Lee, E. *Export-Led Industrialization and Development.* Geneva: International Labour Office, 1981.

Leff, Nathaniel H. "Disjunction between Policy Research and Practice: Social Benefit-Cost Analysis and Investment Policy at the World Bank." *Studies in Comparative International Development,* 23, 4 (Winter 1988): 77–87.

Matthews, Ron. G. "The Development of a Local Machinery Industry in Kenya." *Journal of Modern African History,* 25, 1 (March 1987): 67–94.

Mengistu, Berhanu, and Y. Haile-Mariam. Public Enterprises and Privatization in Subsaharan Africa." *Third World Quarterly,* 10, 4 (October 1988): 1565–90.

Mortimore, Michael. "A New International Industrial Order." *CEPAL Review,* 48 (December 1992): 39–48.

Mytelka, Lynn K. "The Unfulfilled Promise of African Industrialization." *African Studies Review,* 32, 3 (December 1989): 1–76.

Nankani, Helen. "The Lessons of Privatization in Developing Countries." *Finance and Development,* 27, 1 (March 1990): 43–45.

Newham, Mark. "Power Generation." *South* (May 1988): 85–87.

Roca, Sergio G. "State Enterprises in Cuba under the New System of Planning." *Cuban Studies,* 16, 1986: 153–80.

Roemer, M. "Resource-Based Industrialization in the Developing Countries: A Survey." *Journal of Development Economics,* 6 (1976).

Subbarao, A. V. "Influence of Political Structure on Worker Participation in Developing Asian Countries." *Canadian Journal of Development Studies,* 8, 1 (1987): 97–115.

Thoumi, Francisco E. "Why the Illegal Psychoactive Drugs Industry Grew in Colombia." *Journal of Interamerican Studies and World Affairs,* 34, 3 (1992): 37–63.

PART SIX / THE HUMAN DIMENSION OF DEVELOPMENT

Adams, J. D. "The Threat to Education from Structural Adjustment: A Realistic Response." *IDS Bulletin,* 20, 1 (January 1989): 50–54.

Adelman, I., and C. T. Morris. *Economic Growth and Social Equity in Developing Countries.* Stanford, Calif.: Stanford University Press, 1973.

Ayensu, Edward S. "Beyond the Crisis in African Agriculture: Balancing Conservation and Development" *Ceres,* 20, 3 (May–June 1987): 13–24.

Barrios De Chungara, D. *Let Me Speak!: Testimony of Domitila, A Woman of the Bolivian Mines.* New York: Monthly Review Press, 1978.

Berger, Peter. *Pyramids of Sacrifice: Political Ethics and Social Change.* New York: Basic Books, 1974.

Brundenius, C., and M. Lundal. *Development Strategies and Basic Needs in Latin America: Challenges for the 1980's.* Boulder, Col.: Westview, 1982.

De Almeida-Filho, Naomar De. The Psychosocial Costs of Development: Labor, Migration, and Stress in Bahia, Brazil." *Latin American Research Review,* 17, 3 (1982).

De Jesus, Maria Carolina. *Child of the Dark.* New York: Dutton, 1962.

De Schweinitz, Karl De, Jr. "Economic Growth, Coercion, and Freedom." *World Politics,* 9, 2 (January 1957).

Elliot, Charles. *Patterns of Poverty in the Third World: A Study of Social and Economic Stratification.* New York: Praeger, 1975.

Handwerker, Penn W. "Women's Power and Fertility Transition: The Cases of Africa and the West Indies" *Population and Environment: A Journal of Interdisciplinary Studies,* 13, 1, (Fall 1991): 55–78.

Holzman, Franklyn. "Consumer Sovereignty and the Rate of Economic Development." *Economia Internazionale,* 11, 2 (1958).

Hunt, Paul. "Children's Rights in West Africa: The Case of the Gambia's Almudos." *Human Rights Quarterly,* 15 (1993): 499–532.

Johansson, Sten. "The Missing Girls of China: A New Demographic Account." *Population and Development Review,* 17, 1 (March 1991): 35–51.

Lewis, W. Arthur. "Is Economic Growth Desirable?" In *The Theory of Economic Growth.* Homewood, Ill.: Irwin, 1955.

Mengistu, Berhanu, and Y. Haile-Mariam. "The Status and Future of Privatization in Sub-Saharan Africa." *Journal of African Studies,* 15, 1 & 2 (Spring–Summer 1988): 4–9.

Mizan, Ainon Nahar. "Women's Decision-Making Power in Rural Bangladesh: A Study of Grameen Bank." In Wahid, Abu, ed. *The Grameen Bank.* Boulder, Colo: Westview, 1993: 127–53.

Nair, Kusum. *Blossoms in the Dust.* New York: Praeger, 1962.

O'Donnell, Guillermo. *Modernization and Bureaucratic Authoritarianism: Studies in South American Politics.* Berkeley: Institute for International Studies, University of California, 1973.

O'Manique, John. "Development, Human Rights and LAW." *Human Rights Quarterly,* 14 (1992): 383–408.

Rahman, Atiq. "The Informal Financial Sector in Bangladesh: An Appraisal of Its Role in Development." *Development and Change,* 23 (1992): 147–68.

Schultheis, Michael. "Refugees: A Special Issue." *African Studies Review,* 32, 1 (April 1989).

Sell, Ralph R., and S. J. Kunitz. "The Debt Crisis and the End of an Era in Mortality Decline." *Studies in Comparative International Development,* 21, 4 (Winter 1986–87): 3–30.

Thomas-Slayter, Barbara P. "Politics, Class, and Gender in African Resource Management: The Case of Rural Kenya." *Economic Development and Cultural Change,* 40, 4 (1992): 809–28.

Von Bülow, Dorthe "Bigger Than Men? Gender Relations and Their Changing Meaning in Kipsigis Society, Kenya." *Africa,* 62, 4 (1992): 523–46.

Waal, Alex De. "Is Famine Relief Irrelevant to Rural People." *IDS Bulletin,* 20, 2 (April 1989): 63–67.

_____. "A Re-assessment of Entitlement Theory in the Light of the Recent Famines in Africa." *Development and Change,* 21, 3 (July 1990): 469–90.

Wolf, Diane L. "Daughters, Decisions, and Domination: An Empirical and Conceptual Critique of Household Strategies." *Development and Change,* 21, 1 (January 1990): 43–74.

PART SEVEN / WHAT IS TO BE DONE?

Agarwala, Ramgopal. "Planning in Developing Countries: Using the Lessons of Experience to Formulate a Workable Approach." *Finance and Development,* 22 (March 1985): 13–16.

Avramic, Dragoslav. "Development Policies for Today." *Journal of World Trade,* 17 (May–June 1983): 189–206.

Bustamante, Fernando. "Ecuador: Putting an End to Ghosts of the Past?" *Journal of Interamerican Studies and World Affairs,* 34: (Winter 1992/1993): 195–224.

Frank, Andre Gunder. *Capitalist Underdevelopment or Socialist Revolution? In Latin America: Underdevelopment or Revolution?* New York: Monthly Review Press, 1969.

Freire, Paulo. *Pedagogy of the Oppressed.* New York: Herder and Herder, 1972.

Gladwin, Christina H., Kathleen A. Staudt, and Della E. McMillan. "Providing Africa's Women Farmers Access: One Solution to the Food Crisis." *Journal of African Studies,* 13, 4 (Winter 1986–87): 131–41.

Gran, Guy. *Development by People: Citizen Construction of a Just World.* New York: Praeger, 1983.

Gutierrez, Gustavo. *A Theology of Liberation.* Maryknoll, N.Y.: Orbis Books, 1972.

Hirschman, Albert. *A Bias for Hope.* New Haven: Yale University Press, 1971.

Jackson, Cecile. "Environmentalisms and Gender Interests in the Third World." *Development and Change,* 24 (1993): 649–77.

Laszlo, E. *Regional Cooperation among Developing Countries—The New Imperative of Development in the 1980s.* New York: Pergamon, 1981.

Leontief, W., Anne Carter, and Peter Petri. *The Future of the World Economy.* New York: Oxford University Press, 1977.

Mayoux, Linda. "A Development Success Story? Low Caste Entrepreneurship and Inequality: An Indian Case Study." *Development and Change,* 24 (1993): 541–68.

Meier, Gerald M. *Emerging from Poverty: The Economics that Really Matters.* Fair Lawn, N.J.: Oxford University Press, 1984.

Myrdal, Gunnar. *The Challenge of World Poverty: A World Anti-Poverty Program in Outline.* New York: Pantheon Books, 1970.

Nyerere, Julius K. *Freedom and Development.* Oxford: Oxford University Press, 1974.

O'Donnell, Guillermo. "Brazil's Failure: What Future for Debtor Cartels." *Third World Quarterly,* 9, 4 (October 1988): 1157–66.

Ravenhill, John. "Adjustment with Growth: A Fragile Consensus." *Journal of Modern African Studies,* 26, 2 (March 1988): 179–210.

Roy, Sanjit. "The Tilonia Model: A Successful Indian Grassroots Development Strategy." *Canadian Journal of Development Economics,* 8, 2 (1987): 355–74.

Ruttan, Vernon W. "Cultural Endowments and Economic Development: What Can We Learn From Anthropology?" *Economic Development and Cultural Change,* 36, 3 (April 1988 Supplement): s247.

Seidman, Ann. "Towards Ending IMF-ism in Southern Africa: An Alternative Development Strategy." *Journal of Modern African Studies,* 27, 2 (March 1989): 1–22.

Sideri, Sandro, "Restructuring the Post-Cold War World Economy: Perspectives and a Prognosis." *Development and Change,* 24 (1993): 7–27.

Singh, Yyoti Shankar. *A New International Economic Order: Towards a Fair Redistribution of the World's Resources.* New York: Praeger, 1977.

Sipos, Sandor, and H. Sitarska. "Technological and Organizational Change: A Challenge to Eastern Europe." *IDS Bulletin,* 20, 4 (October 1989): 37–43.

Woods, Dwayne. "Civil Society in Europe and Africa: Limiting State Power Through a Public Sphere." *African Studies Review,* 35, 2 (September 1992): 77–100.

Wynne, Brian. "The Toxic Waste Trade: International Regulatory Issues and Options." *Third World Quarterly,* 11, 3 (July 1989): 120–46.